Newsday

The Staff of Long Island Our Story Presents

HOME TOWN

The Raynor family
celebrates the
Fourth of July
in Rockville Centre
in about 1910.

LONG ISLAND

The history of every community
on Long Island in stories and photographs

Foreword by Billy Joel

HOMETOWN LONG ISLAND

GREENPORT:
Theodore Roosevelt addresses a crowd at a train stop in 1898, the year he was elected New York's governor.

Fullerton Collection, Suffolk County Historical Society

Billy Joel enjoys a boat ride off Shelter Island.

Newsday Photo / Don Jacobsen

My Long Island

I could live anywhere, but I am on Long Island because this is the land of my childhood. I love Italy. I love France. I love the South Pacific. I've even flirted with the idea of moving to Lake Como in Italy, and living like a baron. I've been all over the world, but I want to be here.

I have a very, very strong attachment to Long Island. Now I live on the East End, which has the small-town aspects I saw growing up in Hicksville. I always seem to be looking for that — for that sweet place that I knew when I was a child.

Actually, I was born in the Bronx, but I only remember Hicksville and Levittown. To my parents, Levittown was a miracle. They bought a house on a quarter-acre of land in the country for some ridiculously low down payment and there they started new lives. They were able to get out of the city, to jump far ahead of what their parents had. Now I look back on this. I live in this big house in East Hampton next to the ocean. But basically, I'm a guy from Hicksville.

I took my daughter back to Hicksville to see the house I grew up in. I almost got lost trying to find the house. My daughter said, "Daddy, you were poor." I said we didn't have money, but we didn't think of ourselves as poor. I was lucky to have grown up where I grew up and to have known the people I knew in Levittown.

We had all these great city games. We played stickball, Chinese handball, stoop ball, chicken fights and Johnnie on the Pony. We played ring-a-levio. We played Red Rover. And every once in a while I could hear a tractor working on a farm near our subdivision. The farmer's name was Swierupski. Farmer Swierupski, like doctor or professor. We didn't call him Mr. Swierupski. We called him Farmer Swierupski. There are no farms there anymore. I left Nassau County around the same time as the farmers did.

When we were kids, my mom used to take us exploring — to the North Shore, to Cold Spring Harbor, to Oyster Bay, to Huntington, to Matinecock and to the South Shore. She would also take us to Westbury Music Fair to see musicals. She loved Long Island. We mostly went to the North Shore because we weren't so much beach people as we were shore people. We liked being on a shore or in a cove, being able to swim out to a boat. There were so many nooks and crannies on the North Shore and those old estates were staggering. We would see them and dream.

The land of my childhood is that, too — a land of dreams. Like Jones Beach. I remember being inspired going to Jones Beach and seeing that big spire that Robert Moses commissioned, and I thought it was our Campanile, the tower in the Piazza San Marco in Venice.

When I was a kid, there were still farms in Nassau. And Hicksville was really a town — and there was a downtown. There was a movie theater, a shoe repair place, a soda fountain where kids went on dates. We would play in the sumps. We played Army and cowboys and Indians. And we'd hang out at the Village Green and smoke cigarettes and listen to New York radio stations on transistor radios. We could hear the greatest rock and roll music ever recorded. I fell in love with doo-wop and soul music, James Brown, the Drifters and the Temptations.

No matter where I grew up, I would have been doing some kind of music because I was my father's and my mother's child and they were musical. But I don't know if I'd have been a songwriter without Long Island. I don't know if I would have been as lyrical or as eclectic. I grew up not that far from where Walt Whitman spent his youth. And he wrote of America while being on Long Island. Winslow Homer painted America here on Long Island. And so did Thomas Moran.

It's my home. When I go out on a boat and I return, I feel like Adrian Block, John Cabot or Henry Hudson. I get far enough out so I can't see land and I navigate my way back. I recognize the familiar land forms and I think, there it is, my island.

I like the land and the life and the people. I like the speech pattern. And there's that — it's almost endearing — inferiority complex Long Islanders have because we're the country bumpkins compared to our big-city cousins. I thought that gave us a sense of identity that we weren't New York City people.

Long Islanders know what they aren't, who they aren't. The big city is Manhattan. We're surrounded by water and all this natural beauty. There really is no place like this anywhere else. If you look at the map, we're really an exploded archipelago. There's Manhattan Island, Staten Island, Long Island, Randalls Island, Wards Island, Roosevelt Island, Governors Island, Ellis Island, Shelter Island, Plum Island, Block Island, Gardiners Island, Robins Island. And many more, all the way out to Nantucket.

I was always proud that I was an Islander. We could go clamming when we were kids. That was our birthright. What makes us unique is this micro-ecosystem we live in — it's very fragile. That's why we have to try to preserve the open space we have and keep the waters clean. My daughter says as we drive down our street, "Daddy, it's so beautiful here." I open the window of my bedroom when I go to sleep and listen to the waves hitting the shore. And then I dream of music that comes from the sea.

The history of Long Island fascinates me. This island was built by the bones of whales. It's even shaped like a whale. You know Paumanok is really what it is. It's incredibly poetic. It's extraordinary.

I think everybody ultimately has to identify where they're from to know who they are. I have a very good sense of where I am and who I am and where I come from and maybe where I'm going. I can't imagine living anywhere else.

Long Island still feels very good to me. I want to live here for the rest of my life.

Billy Joel

The R. R. Station and Trolley, Trestle, Amityville, L. I.

Amityville Historical Society

Mause Street, Forest Hill, L. I., N. Y.   281

Collection of Joel Streich

Postcards of Amityville, postmarked 1911, and Forest Hills, postmarked 1931.

Introduction

This book is a companion volume to "Long Island: Our Story" — the chronicle of Long Island from the Ice Age to the Space Age. "Long Island: Our Story" was a broad-brush view of an area with a remarkable history, much of which had never before been told. "Hometown Long Island" offers a close-up look at that same suburbia. It tells the stories of the nearly 300 communities that make up Queens, Nassau and Suffolk — the places where we live and work, where our children go to school. They are places with their own fascinating histories.

The stories of these counties, towns, villages and hamlets belong to all of us — newcomers and natives alike. Like many of you, I've lived a part of that story. I was born in Freeport and grew up in a South Shore community that was mostly summer homes until several years after World War II. Then year-round homes sprang up among newly converted vacation cottages and the future arrived in force, without fanfare.

Over the decades that followed, Long Island was transformed into a different type of metropolitan region. But the histories of our towns and villages became part of our own identities as stores and homes and industries swirled around us. One consequence of this explosive growth was that residents developed a stronger appreciation for their communities — for the people and places and historic moments that make Long Island special.

I believe that "Long Island: Our Story" built a bridge for readers between the communities of today and yesterday. It showed how our past shaped our present. "Hometown Long Island" extends that bridge.

We hope you enjoy it.

Raymond A. Jansen,
Newsday Publisher

The Old Mill and Pond, Centreport, L. I.

The R. R. Station Sea Cliff, L. I.

Postcards From the Collection of Joel Streich

Scenes of Centerport and Sea Cliff from the early 1900s.

Contents

Town, City and County Histories

Nassau County . . . . Page 2
City of Glen Cove . . . . Page 6
Town of Hempstead . . . . Page 9
City of Long Beach . . . . Page 30
Town of North Hempstead . . . . Page 32
Town of Oyster Bay . . . . Page 46

Suffolk County . . . . Page 60
Town of Babylon . . . . Page 64
Town of Brookhaven . . . . Page 72
Town of East Hampton . . . . Page 94
Town of Huntington . . . . Page 100
Town of Islip . . . . Page 112
Town of Riverhead . . . . Page 124
Town of Shelter Island . . . . Page 128
Town of Smithtown . . . . Page 130
Town of Southampton . . . . Page 136
Town of Southold . . . . Page 146

Queens County . . . . Page 152
Communities of Queens . . . . Page 153

Growing Up on Long Island
Baby Boom Era Personalities and Scenes From Our Communities . . . . Page 180

Billy Joel, Hicksville . . . . Page 182
Patti LuPone, Northport . . . . Page 183
Jerry Seinfeld, Massapequa . . . . Page 184
Billy Crystal, Long Beach . . . . Page 185
Rosie O'Donnell, Commack . . . . Page 186
Eddie Murphy, Roosevelt . . . . Page 187
Paul Simon and Art Garfunkel, Forest Hills . . . . Page 188
Bob Costas, Commack . . . . Page 189
Howard Stern, Roosevelt, Rockville Centre . . . . Page 190
John Tesh, Garden City . . . . Page 191

More Hometown Heroes
Twenty-Five More Long Island Success Stories . . . . Page 193

Notables
Some well-known people who were born, reared or resided on Long Island . . Page 210

Your Hometown
Index to More Than 280 Community Histories . . . . Page 212

General Index . . . . Page 213
Acknowledgements and Staff . . . . Page 218

A spirit of independence and a modern suburb studded with pockets of opulence

Nassau

Nassau County, birthplace of American suburbia, celebrated its 100th anniversary in 1999, but its colonial roots reached back more than three centuries, to when almost half of it was acquired by two Englishmen in one of Long Island's most prodigious land deals.

The saga began inauspiciously in 1640 when a small band from Massachusetts landed on the North Shore, only to be driven off by the Dutch, who claimed territory as far east as Oyster Bay. The English went east to settle Southampton. But three years later, John Carman and Robert Fordham crossed Long Island Sound from Stamford, Conn.; they negotiated with the Indians for a deed to a 10-mile-wide swath from Long Island Sound to the Atlantic Ocean and founded the first English settlement on the Hempstead Plains. The colonists who followed negotiated a patent from the Dutch, who hoped more Englishmen would come to help control the Indians. The English obliged. By 1653 they were colonizing what later became Oyster Bay, Westbury, Jericho and Hicksville. In 1664 they drove out the Dutch.

The independent colonists were no more eager to pay taxes to the duke of York than they were to pay the Dutch. Their chafing brought about the colonial assembly of 1683, which created the counties of Suffolk and Queens. Queens included the Towns of Oyster Bay and Hempstead. North Hempstead split from Hempstead during the Revolution, when Patriots in the north broke from the Loyalists in the south. But in the next century they shared a growing desire to split off from Queens County.

The planting of the Queens County Courthouse on the Hempstead Plains in 1785 sowed the seeds of resentment, and secessionist talk increased after the Civil War, when western Queens became increasingly urbanized and Democratic, the eastern towns rural and Republican. Finally, in 1898, when Queens joined greater New York City, the eastern towns found themselves still part of Queens but not of the city. Community leaders met in Allen's Hotel in Mineola and resolved that the Towns of Oyster Bay, Hempstead and North Hempstead form a new county.

From Manhasset to Port Washington, L. I.

Collection of Joel Streich

A road between Manhasset and Port Washington is a bucolic scene in an old postcard, above. At left, the daughter of the William Robertson Coes, Natalie Mai Coe, poses in about 1922 at the family's Upper Brookville estate, which became the Planting Fields Arboretum.

Nassau County Museum Collection, Long Island Studies Institute

Suggested names — Matinecock, Norfolk, Bryant, Sagamore — lost out to Nassau, once the legal name for all Long Island. It honored the late 17th-Century King William III, who came from the Dutch House of Nassau. Nassau County came into being on Jan. 1, 1899. On July 13, 1900, then-New York Gov. Theodore Roosevelt of Oyster Bay laid the cornerstone for the first Nassau County Courthouse on land purchased in 1869 by Alexander T. Stewart, founder of Garden City.

The 20th Century brought rapid change, accelerated by two world wars. In the early years the Hempstead Plains became the site of pioneer aviation feats, motorcar and horse racing. On the northern Gold Coast, rich New Yorkers played polo and chased the fox. South Shore communities became popular beach resorts.

Robert Moses, New York's master builder, turned a barren shore into famed Jones Beach. After World War II, communities of subdivisions spread across Nassau at a dizzying pace, creating the tightly packed suburbia, populated by nearly 1.3 million people by the 1990s. But the sprawl still left room for pockets of opulence: According to Worth magazine, 11 of the nation's 30 most expensive communities in the late 1990s were in Nassau, all but one (Hewlett) on the North Shore.

NASSAU

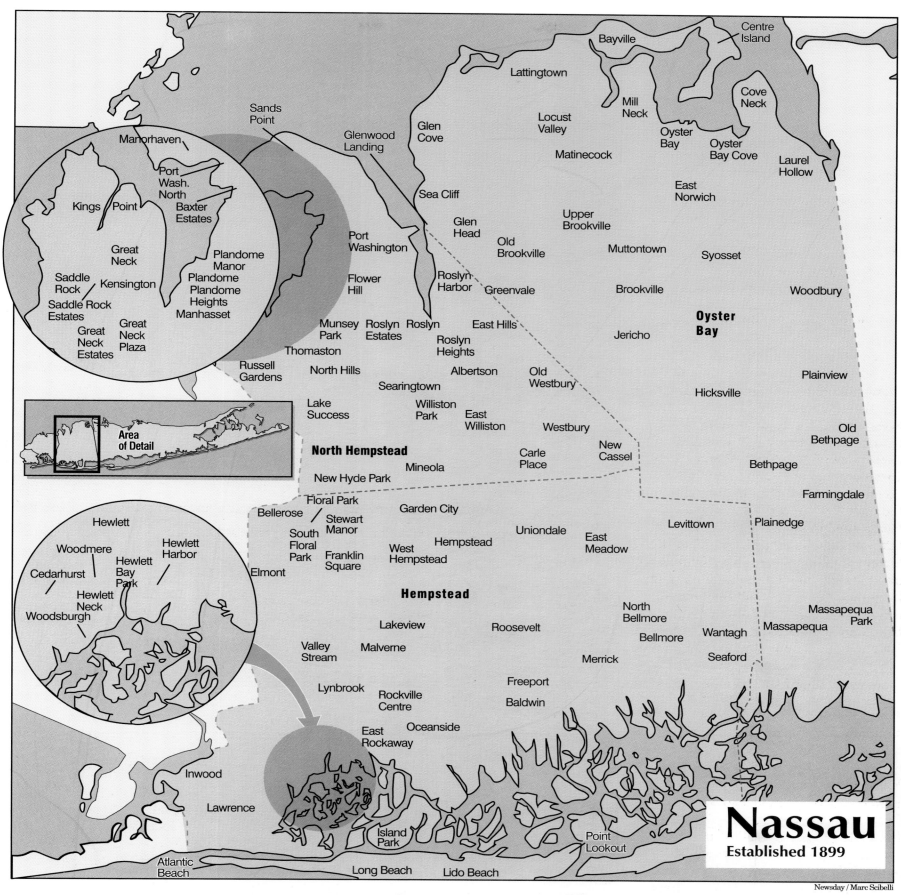

Nassau
Established 1899

Newsday / Marc Scibelli

Battle Row: Old Bethpage street was so named in the 1920s because brickyard workers lived there and on paydays tended to drink and get into brawls.
Guinea Woods Road: Old Westbury highway named either for the Guinea hens that once ran wild in the area or gold guinea coins British soldiers are reputed to have lost during the Revolution.
Old Courthouse Road: Herricks street was site of old Queens County Courthouse before 1899.
Piping Rock Road: The Matinecock road takes its name from a huge rock that served as a meeting place for Indians where they smoked a pipe. (There are several large rocks in the area but no one

Gazetteer

The stories behind some prominent roads and places in Nassau

knows which one is *the* Piping Rock.)
Shelter Rock Road: Manhasset road named after Shelter Rock, the largest known boulder carried by glaciers to the Island; Indians used it for shelter.
Skunk's Misery Road: Several possible explanations are offered for the name of this Lattingtown road.

One is that settlers misheard the Indians' name for the area; others say the area once had a lot of skunks or skunk cabbage.
Sugar Toms Lane: East Norwich road named for Thomas Cheshire, who had a still and used to walk into town to buy bags of sugar to make his brew.
Weberfield Place: Freeport street named for late 19th Century vaudeville comedy team of Joseph Weber and Lew Fields, who lived in the village.
I.U. Willets Road: Named for farmer Isaac Underhill Willets, whose Albertson property was bisected in 1850 — despite his protests that "Long Island has more roads now than it will ever need."

Collection of Ted Smith / Al Williams

SEA CLIFF: Bathers crowd into the water at the Pavillion, a public bathhouse, circa 1910.

Westbury Historical Society

WESTBURY: In full regalia, members of Hook and Ladder Co. No. 1 assemble in front their headquarters in 1910 for a group photo. The company headquarters was built in 1897.

Nassau County Museum Collection, Long Island Studies Institute

HEMPSTEAD: It's about 1921, corner of Main Street and Fulton Avenue, and Officer Gardner keeps a sharp eye out as he operates the first stop-and-go indicator.

GARDEN CITY: Onlookers gaze at the force of a fire on Sept. 7, 1899, that destroyed the Garden City Hotel.

Collection of Vincent F. Seyfried

NASSAU COUNTY: In about 1890, horses pull a buggy along Merrick Road.

Nassau County Museum Collection, Long Island Studies Institute

NASSAU

Nassau County Museum Collection, Long Island Studies Institute

A Fixture in Glen Cove

THEN &
NOW

Autos hadn't completely replaced horse buggies when postcard photographer Henry Otto Korten took this view of Glen Street, looking north, in Glen Cove, around 1912. The Tudor-style building at right is the post office, which was built in 1905 and served as the city's post office until 1933.

For six decades after the post office closed, the substantially altered building housed a furniture store. A large plate-glass window was installed on the second floor so large appliances could be viewed from the street, and a storefront "box" was built onto the first floor.

In 1995, architects James and Laura Smiros bought the building to use as offices, and returned it to its original look. A 1998 photo shows the restored building and, farther north, the intersection of Pulaski Street. (At the time of the earlier photograph, the street was named Mill Street and dead-ended at Glen Street.)

At the far left of the 1998 photo is the headquarters of software company Acclaim Entertainment Inc.

Newsday Photo / Bill Davis, 1998

City of Glen Cove

Embracing the waterfront yet again

BY BILL BLEYER
STAFF WRITER

In the 1660s, New York was undergoing a building boom and lumber was in great demand. A potential supply existed in northwestern Oyster Bay, where there was also a creek to accommodate vessels that could carry the lumber to the city.

A young Rhode Islander named Joseph Carpenter had all of this in mind when he purchased 2,000 acres along Hempstead Harbor from the Matinecock Indians on May 24, 1668.

Carpenter and his partners, brothers Robert, Daniel and Nathaniel Coles, and Nicholas Simkins, all of Oyster Bay, planned to build a sawmill. They retained the name the Matinecocks had given the area: Musketa (also spelled "musquito"), which translated roughly as "the place of rushes." Soon the owners, self-proclaimed as "The Five Proprietors of Musketa Cove Plantation," had dammed a small stream, Carpenter built the sawmill and lumber was on its way to New York.

Musketa Cove's geographical attributes prompted a family of wealthy New York City merchants, the Waltons, to invest in waterfront land and purchase several mills that were operating in the early 1700s. But milling was not the only way residents made money. In 1699, Lord Bellomont, colonial governor of New York, described Musketa Cove as one of the four biggest smuggling ports on Long Island. (Undocumented legend has it that Captain Kidd buried treasure in Glen Cove.)

During the Revolution, the British maintained their ships on the shores of Hempstead Harbor and there were several skirmishes with Patriot forces that traveled by water from Connecticut. And the waterfront continued to play a major role in the developing city after the war. Mining began in the early 1800s after physician Thomas Garvie discovered deposits of clay suitable for pottery on his property, later called Garvie's Point. It was at around this time that steamboat service to and from New York City, begun in 1829 by the Linnaeus, brought an abrupt change from an agricultural economy to one based on tourism and heavy industry.

The first major factory came in 1859 when Duryea Corn Starch Manufacturing Co. built a plant on the south side of Glen Cove Creek. By the end of the Civil War, the plant was the largest manufacturer of corn starch in the world, employing nearly 600 people. The starch works transformed Glen Cove into a company town, with employees living in company-owned (and substandard) apartments and buying their food and clothes from the company store. The starch factory closed about 1900 and burned to the ground in 1906.

Meanwhile, the steamboats turned the community into a summer resort for New York City residents. To serve this clientele, the area still known as The Landing developed with a half-dozen large hotels, boarding houses, rental cottages, oyster bars and saloons. The largest hotel was the Pavillion Hotel, which was used as a convalescent home for wounded soldiers during the Civil War.

The steamboat traffic also helped sink the name of Musketa Cove in 1834. Residents felt outsiders were confusing the Indian name with biting insects and wanted a change to boost

A postcard depicts Glen Street in Glen Cove in 1905.

Collection of Joel Streich

tourism. While many people have traditionally thought the city was renamed after Glen Coe in Scotland, city historian Dan Russell said a manuscript by Edward Coles, discovered about 1990, gives what he believes is the true story. Coles, born

Newsday Photo / Jim Nightingale
Visiting Glen Cove in 1960, Soviet Premier Nikita Khruschev kicks up his heels outside Killenworth, a residence for Soviet UN personnel.

about 1808 and a trustee of the public school and a colonel in the militia, wrote that he proposed the name Glen Cove because "it was descriptive of the village, it being situated in a glen, and it would also be retaining the name cove, which was also descriptive of the village location."

As more visitors arrived by steamboat, wealthy New Yorkers began to build permanent summer homes in the 1850s. Among the first were Charles A. Dana, editor of the New York Sun, and artist John LaFarge. By 1910, Glen Cove could boast of Gold Coast mansions owned by financier J.P. Morgan (whose summer home on East Island was once guarded by former marines after an assassination attempt in 1915); five-and-dime store magnate F.W. Woolworth and Henry Clay Folger, founder of the Folger Shakespeare Library in Washington.

But the biggest estate compound belonged to the family of Charles Pratt, a founder of Standard Oil, who came to Glen Cove about 1890 and ultimately owned more than 1,100 acres. Pratt's six sons and two daughters later built their own homes, most of them still standing in the 1990s. Among them are homes that are now the Webb Institute and Harrison House Conference Center, and Killenworth, the longtime retreat for the Soviet and then Russian delegations to the United Nations.

About half of the city's land was taken up by Gold Coast estates early in the 20th Century. It was chartered as a city in 1918 because of residents' concerns that it was giving more tax money to the Town of Oyster Bay than it was getting back in services and because residents, particularly the Gold Coast estate owners, wanted more local control.

At the approach of the millennium, the city again would see its future in the waterfront — in the form of tourism. Plans were being developed to reshape old factory sites on the north side of Glen Cove Creek into marinas, restaurants and entertainment facilities.

Where to Find More: "Glen Cove History" by city historian Daniel Russell, Box 390, Glen Cove, N.Y. 11542.

245 St. Bellerose, L.I.
May. 6, 1925

Photo Courtesy of Wayne Duprez

BELLEROSE: By 1925, homes were already well established in Bellerose, a model community that was the vision of Helen M. Marsh, a real estate developer who came from Massachusetts.

Nassau County Museum Collection, Long Island Studies Institute
BALDWIN: A clam digger in the waters off Baldwin in 1908.

Nassau County Museum Collection, Long Island Studies Institute
BALDWIN: By 1914, Baldwin was a haven for recreation, as hotels and boarding houses were built throughout the community.

Town of Hempstead

The annals of colonial Hempstead Town began when English families from Connecticut settled on a stream-fed meadow with a 1643 deed from the "Indyans of Marsapeague, Mericock and Rockakway."

That much is known. But the colonists were soon grazing cattle on the vast 70,000-acre Hempstead Plains, and here mystery comes in, according to retired town historian Myron H. Luke. "Where did the cattle come from?" he asked in a 1998 interview. "Did they ferry them in barges across the Sound?" Such details may never be known because the earliest town records were contained "in a mouse-eaten book that disappeared in the late 19th Century," Luke said.

The 50 English settlers had a patent from New Netherlands Gov. William Kieft that stipulated their colony grow to 100 settlers in five years. They had no trouble complying. Hempstead eventually grew into the nation's most populous town and the place from which the Age of Aviation took off.

Earliest known town entries, dating from May 2, 1654, tell of town meetings and land distribution. Capt. John Seaman owned most of the southeast, what eventually became Seaford, Wantagh and part of Massapequa. The southwest area later known as the Five Towns was mostly common pasture, crowded with cattle, sheep and horses owned by English settlers.

Hempstead, which was joined to Queens County in 1683, was a hotbed of Toryism during the Revolution. A town meeting called in 1775 to pledge allegiance to the king antagonized the Patriots in the north, and North Hempstead's break to become a separate town became official in 1784. At war's end, thousands of Hempstead Loyalists fled to escape reprisals.

The 1800s brought a multitude of railroads. The South Side Railroad from Valley Stream to the Rockaway peninsula, completed in 1869, spurred creation of the Five Towns of Hewlett, Woodmere, Cedarhurst, Inwood and Lawrence, though the appellation covers three hamlets and six incorporated villages. The rail lines merged into the Long Island Rail Road in 1875.

But it was the airplane that drew the spotlight to Hempstead in the early 1900s, as flyers — including, of course, Charles Lindbergh — set records from the fields around Mineola, the seat of the newly formed Nassau County.

In 1947 the Hempstead Town Board changed the building code to allow homes to be built without basements. The plains became Levittown, and Roosevelt Field, Lindbergh's famous departure point, became the site of a major shopping mall.

Nassau County Museum Collection, Long Island Studies Institute

HEMPSTEAD: A trolley passes horse-drawn competition. Hempstead was a stop on the Mineola-Hicksville run in the 1910s through 1926.

ATLANTIC BEACH
A Solid Community Was Built on Sand

Beginnings: Atlantic Beach, in some respects, was created out of nothing in a relatively short period. The village occupies the western end of the barrier island dominated by the City of Long Beach. But until about 1900, the island didn't extend that far. It existed first as a sandbar and then grew into an extension of the barrier island. Freeport developer Stephen Petit created Atlantic Beach, dredging tons of sand from the bottom of Reynolds Channel onto the sandbar during the 1920s. Petit's aim was to build a quiet ocean resort for New Yorkers. For a few years, beach clubs turned a profit, but most collapsed along with the stock market in 1929. By then, however, there was a bridge to the rest of Long Island and a handful of year-round homes.

Turning Point: A twist on the not-in-my-backyard sentiment, common across Long Island, led to Atlantic Beach's incorporation as a village in 1962. After the Depression ended, Atlantic Beach had restored itself as a quiet resort anchored by a permanent community of several hundred residents. For decades, only club members and residents used the beaches, but in the early 1960s the Town of Hempstead decided to open the beaches to all town residents. Not on my beaches, responded property owners. They incorporated the village as a way to keep outsiders off their beaches. The Atlantic Beach Club was destroyed by fire in 1984. Other well-known clubs included the Seacliff and the Catalina.

Brushes With Fame: The secluded clubs of Atlantic Beach were attractive to the rich and powerful from the start. Actress Ethel Barrymore and several Vanderbilt family members spent summers there, and the former Atlantic Beach Club was one of New York City Mayor Jimmy Walker's favorite hangouts.

Where to Find More: The Atlantic Beach file at the Long Island Studies Institute at Hofstra University in Hempstead.

BALDWIN
Piles of Clam Shells Tell of First Inhabitants

Beginnings: Merrick Indians were the first human inhabitants of the South Shore between the Rockaway peninsula and the Seaford area. Piles of clam shells found alongside Milburn Creek indicate Indians lived in the area at some time. Records of the first European settlement are unclear, but by 1660 the area was called Hick's Neck, in honor of English settler John Hicks. The community got its start in 1686, when the Town of Hempstead gave John Pine permission to build a mill. It soon became the focus of what was then called Milburn, but in 1855 the hamlet changed its name to Baldwinsville in honor of Francis P. Baldwin, a state assemblyman and Queens County treasurer. Because an upstate village was already named Baldwinsville, the post office shortened it first to Baldwins and then to Baldwin.

Turning Point: By 1830, an inn run by John Lott attracted sportsmen from New York City and was the center of port activity for the Town of Hempstead. Use of the port declined, but Baldwin was on the map for recreation, and the hamlet grew as plank roads and then the railroad made it more accessible. By 1890, the community had three hotels and several boarding houses. A real estate boom in the late 1920s rapidly expanded the hamlet.

Claims to Fame: The first American monoplane may have been invented by two Baldwin brothers, Albert and Arthur Heinrich, in 1910. Film director Jonathan Demme grew up in Baldwin.

Where to Find More: "Hick's Neck — The Story of Baldwin," published by the Writers' Program of the Works Progress Administration in 1939; the Baldwin Fire Department 110th Anniversary Yearbook, published in 1996. Both available at the Baldwin Public Library.

BELLEROSE
A Female Visionary Brings a Town to Life

Beginnings: Bellerose Village owes its development, and much of its charm, to a Massachusetts real estate developer who was years ahead of both Levittown and Betty Friedan. In the early 1900s, Helen M. Marsh had a dream of developing a model community of modestly priced houses. Moderately well-to-do and fiercely independent at a time when women were not expected to have business acumen, let alone clout, she visited Long Island and decided on the undeveloped grassy plains of western Nassau for carrying out her plan. Marsh sold her family home in Lynn, Mass., and formed the United Holding Co. in 1906 to raise the $155,000 needed to buy 77 acres of mostly gladioli fields. She had other enterprises, including a silver mine in Colorado, but during the financial panic of 1907 she sold more than $50,000 in personal securities to save the property.

Turning Points: The first house in Bellerose Village rose in 1910 and Marsh moved in. She lived in each of the first 22 houses as it was completed, sometimes staying for several weeks to make sure it was built to her standards and she could find the "right" buyer who shared her vision. She was a hands-on developer, to say the least. She laid out boulevards, streets and houses around circular flowerbeds. When drought struck, she drove through the area with a borrowed horse and wagon watering the foliage. She kept fires burning in houses under construction during the winter months. Her United Holding Co. was dissolved in 1922, and that same year a Bellerose resident, Edgar C. Ruwe, joined her to form the Marsh and Ruwe Co. The village was incorporated in 1924.

Bellerose Terrace: This unpretentious 600-home community was built in the 1920s close enough to throw a quarter over the Nassau-

Please Turn the Page

9

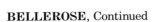

BELLEROSE, Continued

Queens border to another Bellerose. (All the Belleroses took the name of the railroad station that Helen Marsh built in 1911.) In 1939, construction of the Cross Island Parkway sliced Bellerose Terrace in two.

Where to Find More: Reference material in the Queens Borough Central Library, Long Island Collection, Jamaica.

BELLMORE, NORTH BELLMORE
The Smiths Made A Name for Themselves

Beginnings: The first settlers were Dutch from New Amsterdam and Quakers from New England. The community began to take shape in 1676 with the transfer of more than 100 acres by John Smith, an original Hempstead settler, to his son, Jeremiah. The resulting farming community was called Little Neck until 1818 when a bridge was built to allow Merrick Road to span a creek. At that point the community along Merrick Road, which was where the early residential growth took place, was named New Bridge. When the railroad arrived in 1867, it named the station Bellmore although the surrounding community retained the name New Bridge. Between 1870 and 1880, as businesses began to sprout around the station, more and more people began to call the community Bellmore. That name became official when the first post office was established with the name Bellmore in the general store near the station in 1883.

What became North Bellmore was initially called Smithville about 1850 because so many Smiths lived there. In 1867, when residents petitioned for a post office in that area, the government said no because there was a Smithville upstate. But it approved the name Smithville South. That name lasted until 1920, when the post office was renamed North Bellmore.

Turning Points: The Bellmore area experienced several spurts of growth. The first came with the arrival of the railroad. At the turn of the century, large farms in the Smithville South area were subdivided for housing. The construction of Sunrise Highway in the 1920s brought more residents, and a housing boom after World War II brought the biggest population boom of all.

Claims to Fame: Comic Lenny Bruce and former CIA director William Casey grew up in Bellmore. Actor George Kennedy, a native, acted as honorary chairman of the community's tricentennial in 1976. Metropolitan Opera star Helen Jepson had a cottage in Bellmore during the 1920s.

Where to Find More: Kenneth Foreman's "A Profile of the Bellmores," at the Bellmore Memorial Library.

CEDARHURST
A Name Game On the South Shore

Beginnings: What became Cedarhurst was inhabited at the time of the Revolution by Indians, farmers and slaves or tenants at Rock Hall, a large plantation built nearby (in modern Lawrence) in 1767. The entire Five Towns area was occupied by British troops and was a Tory stronghold.

How It Grew: The early name was Ocean Point. After the arrival of rail service in 1869, the area gained popularity, mostly via the Rockaway Hunting Club, built in Cedarhurst in 1878. At the time, the area was part of Queens, becoming part of the new Nassau County in 1899. The hunting club, which covered almost the entire community of 1.5 square miles, was noted for fox hunting,

steeplechase and polo. Boundary changes would later put it in Lawrence. In the early 1800s, the Five Towns' only school was in Cedarhurst. District 15 eventually would cover Lawrence, Cedarhurst, Inwood and part of Woodmere. The first library in the Five Towns, the private Peninsula Community Library, opened in Cedarhurst in 1930 and closed in 1950.

Turning Points: One was the construction in 1833 of the palatial Marine Pavilion spa in nearby Far Rockaway, which had 160 rooms and drew thousands of visitors to the Five Towns area. After the South Side Railroad arrived, a post office was formed in 1884, and Ocean Point was renamed Cedarhurst, partly at the request of the hunt club. The name apparently came from the grove or "hurst" of cedar trees surrounding the post office. The village was incorporated in 1910, following demands for street improvements. The first village president was Horatio P. Vandewater. Village Hall was built in 1959.

Claim to Fame: The village earned a reputation as a commercial hub of the Five Towns, with many fine shops, and its village park became the area's cultural-recreational center, offering periodic fairs, carnivals and musical programs.

Where to Find More: "Five Towns," handbook by the League of Women Voters of the Five Towns, 1977, and "The Story of the Five Towns," by the Writers Group of the federal Works Progress Administration, 1941, at Peninsula Public Library, Lawrence.

EAST MEADOW
Sheep Kept an Eye Out For Lurking Wolves

Beginnings: Although there is no meadow left in East Meadow, its name accurately describes what it once was — the portion of the Hempstead Plains east of the Meadow Brook, which ran through the plains before a parkway took its place. Surveyor Thomas Langdon reported to the 1655 Hempstead Town meeting that the east meadow was suitable for grazing, and three years later cattle took up residence there. Wolves prevented sheep-pasturing there until settlers exterminated them in the early 1700s. By the end of the century 14,000 sheep grazed on the plains, supplying much of the young nation's wool.

Turning Point: The post-World War II Baby Boom exploded East Meadow's population from 2,000 to 25,000 in just over a decade. Almost instantly it was transformed from a rural community to a modern suburb as farmers sold their land to developers.

Cedarhurst Village Hall

The Cedarhurst Firehouse, possibly decorated for a Fourth of July celebration, in an undated photo. The village has earned a reputation as a commercial center in the Five Towns.

Holidays Gone By: Parting Day, the last Monday in October, was a major celebration in 18th Century East Meadow. That was the day sheep on the meadow were driven to the public pen, identified by earmarks and sent home with individual farmers. Unclaimed sheep were auctioned. The day became a carnival with merchants, acrobats, clowns and politicians. Even non-sheep owners attended.

Claim to Fame: Horses attracted the first crowds to East Meadow. A horse track was established in the Salisbury area in 1665, and other tracks came and went while the plains were undeveloped. In later years, early cowboys rounded cattle, and the Meadow Brook Hunt Club was established for the amusement of well-heeled guests of the Garden City Hotel.

Brush With Fame: Future first lady Eleanor Roosevelt lived for a time as a child on Newbridge Avenue. The house has since been razed.

Where to Find More: "East Meadow, Its Past and Present," published in 1976 by the East Meadow Public Library; "East Meadow, Yesterday & Today," by Mary Louise Clarke, available at the East Meadow Public Library.

EAST ROCKAWAY
Victims of Shipwrecks Buried by Villagers

Beginnings: Once it was called Near Rockaway because it was the section of the Rockaway peninsula closest to Hempstead. English settlers migrating from New England in the 1640s bought the land from a tribe called Rockawanahaha, meaning "People of a Sandy Place," as it surely was.

First Bakery: In 1688, Joseph Haviland built a tidewater gristmill and a nearby bakery to supply farmers and tradesmen with bread. It was the first public oven in New York. Townspeople could bake their own for 3 cents a loaf. The Old Grist Mill, a community gathering place for two centuries, was moved in 1963 to Memorial Park. It was turned into a museum open on summer weekends.

The Revolution: Near Rockaway produced some of Long Island's staunchest Loyalists, including Col. Richard T. Hewlett, Isaac Denton and Isaac Smith. There was even a plot to kill George Washington when he came through Long Island during the war, but it was discovered and foiled by Patriots.

The Bristol and Mexico: Two of the worst shipwrecks on Long Island occurred in the winter of 1836. The Bristol from England was battered on the rocks here, and seven weeks later the Mexico, carrying Irish immigrants, suffered

the same fate. Villagers buried 193 victims of the two disasters in the Sandhole Cemetery and raised money to erect a monument on the spot called Mariner's Grave.

Turning Points: Near Rockaway was a flourishing seaport on Hog Inlet (now East Rockaway Inlet) with packets carrying oysters and farm produce to New York City, until 1869 when the Long Island Rail Road came through, drawing business to Pearsalls Corners (later Lynbrook). Trains were called Huckleberries because they were so slow and made so many stops that passengers could alight and pick huckleberries. Near Rockaway got its first post office and new name in 1869. The village was incorporated in 1900 with a population of 969 and its own police force, which merged with the county force in 1930.

Where to Find More: The Old Grist Mill Museum at Woods and Atlantic Avenues contains village artifacts and historical material.

ELMONT
Arrival of Horses Caused a Stampede

Beginnings: Elmont's vast fields were largely uninhabited until 1647. That's when brothers Christopher and Thomas Foster were granted a large tract of land in western Hempstead, stretching from modern-day Elmont all the way to the South Shore. They called it Foster's Meadow and used it to raise sheep and cattle. Before long, they sold off much of their holdings to other farmers. Unlike most citizens of Hempstead Town, a majority of Foster's Meadow residents supported the Revolution — a stance that prompted the British to rip down the community's church. After the war, the area developed slowly, with farmers moving out from Brooklyn and western Queens in search of more land.

The Name: A popular misconception is that Elmont's name derives from Belmont Race Track, which is located there. But residents decided to change the name from Foster's Meadow to Elmont in 1882, more than 20 years before the track opened. (Nor was the track named for Elmont; it was named after its developer, financier August Belmont.) There is no record of who or what Elmont is named for.

Turning Point: More than anything, the racetrack's opening in 1905 transformed Elmont. Farms were sold to make way for houses, many of which were bought by people who worked at the track. One of the first neighborhoods was developed by Jacob Wollkoff for Jewish immigrants seeking to move out of the city. "Never in the history of Greater New York [have] so many unpronounceable [street] names been suggested for any colony in the United States," the Brooklyn Daily Eagle remarked in 1907. Businesses sprouted along Hempstead Turnpike to serve workers and visitors. For a time, Belmont Park hosted air races as well as horse races. The first international air meet ever held in the United States was at Belmont, and it included a race to the Statue of Liberty and back. The combination of the racetrack and the post-World War I real estate boom made Elmont an early and prime candidate for suburbanization.

Claim to Fame: The first intercity air mail service between New York and Washington, inaugurated in 1918, used Belmont Park as the New York terminal. Famous for another sort of air mail was NFL quarterback Vinnie Testaverde, who graduated from Elmont's Sewanhaka High School.

Equine Tragedy: One of the worst accidents ever to befall horse racing happened at Belmont. In January, 1986, a barn fire destroyed 44 thoroughbreds and a work horse.

Where to Find More: "History of Elmont," published in 1971, and other material available at Elmont Public Library.

Newsday Archive

CEDARHURST: It's an image of backroom politics from an era when such meetings were common. In November, 1920, a group of Republican Party leaders gathered for a birthday party for G. Wilbur Doughty, then Nassau County GOP leader, at the Kohlers Hotel in Cedarhurst. Doughty, who made his fortune in oysters in Inwood, held a considerable amount of political clout for years. Seated at left are Steve Pettit, onetime sheriff; an unidentified man; Lt. Gov. Jeremiah Wood and Doughty. The man at the head of the table is not identified. At the right side of the table, from left, are Assemb. Thomas A. MacWhinney; contractor Andrew Weston; J. Russel Sprague, who was Doughty's uncle; Archibald Patterson and an unidentified man. The two men standing at the left are identified as Sheriff Smith and County Clerk Thomas Cheshire. The rest of the men standing are not identified.

Nassau County Museum Collection, Long Island Studies Institute

ELMONT: In 1905, Elmont was known for its horse racing, but the only place this horse raced to was the nearest tavern to deliver beer.

Newsday Photo,1998 / Bill Davis

FREEPORT: A post office mural by William Gropper entitled "Suburban Post in Winter" (1936).

Nassau County Museum Collection, Long Island Studies Institute

FLORAL PARK: Trolleys stop to take on passengers in 1910.

Nassau County Museum Collection, Long Island Studies Institute

FREEPORT: The waterfront as it looked at the end of World War II in 1945.

Nassau County Museum Collection, Long Island Studies Institute

FREEPORT: Women work on a boat at the oyster house on Freeport River, circa 1890. Oystering thrived after the Civil War.

FLORAL PARK
Planting Seeds For Its Growth

Beginnings: Before Europeans arrived, the area that would become Floral Park marked the western edge of the great Hempstead Plains. Indeed, it was initially known as Plainfield. Until the Civil War, the area consisted of widely scattered farms. The community began to develop in the early 1800s, thanks to the Long Island Rail Road and Jericho Turnpike, both of which came through what had then become known as Hinsdale and served farmers. Hinsdale boasted of more than two dozen fine flower farms in the years after the Civil War.

Turning Points: In the mid-1870s, seed seller John Lewis Childs came to Hinsdale, a growing village centered on its flower farms. With an intent to promote both his own seed company and the village, Childs urged that Hinsdale change its name to Floral Park. Using that name as a return address, Childs set up a thriving mail-order seed business. His business was so successful that the Floral Park post office was built primarily to handle the enormous volume of his mailings. Childs was a civic leader as well, urging the incorporation of the village in 1908 and helping to plan neat residential areas. Deed covenants restricted homes to no more than two stories and called for a selling price of at least $3,000, a substantial sum then. Well into the 1920s, Floral Park nurseries provided a blaze of color for riders on the Long Island Rail Road, but the real estate boom of that decade quickly converted the flower fields into residential neighborhoods. The tiny adjacent village of South Floral Park was known at 1900 as Jamaica Square, when it was one of the few racially integrated communities on Long Island. It incorporated as a village in 1925.

Where to Find More: "The Story of Floral Park," published in 1958 by the village of Floral Park, available at Hicksville Public Library.

FRANKLIN SQUARE
German Immigrants Worked the Land

Beginnings: Like much of what was to become central Nassau, Franklin Square was part of the vast, grassy Hempstead Plains. It remained undisturbed by humans for thousands of years, by virtue of its position far inland. Its earliest use was as communal sheep grazing land for Hempstead farmers. After the Revolution, crops were planted. Except for a few families, there was little in Franklin Square until 1852, when Louis Schroerer built a hotel. It attracted two things that established Franklin Square as a community — travelers on the Hempstead-Jamaica Turnpike, and many other German settlers.

Turning Point: Germans came in significant numbers in the years after 1850, particularly after 1870. Many were farmers, some growing a wide variety of produce and others raising chickens or pigs. After World War I, the real estate boom reached Franklin Square. It was one of the fastest-growing communities of the 1940s. Homes completely replaced farms by 1952.

Unsolved Mystery: No one knows exactly why Franklin Square is so named. Some suggested it was for Benjamin Franklin, but he had no connection to this area. Others believe it was named for a local person, now unknown.

Brush With Fame: Novelist Alice Hoffman grew up in Franklin Square.

Where to Find More: "The Way It Was, a Story of Old Franklin Square," by Paul van Wie of the Franklin Square Historical Society.

FREEPORT
Action on the Nautical Mile

BY BILL BLEYER
STAFF WRITER

Freeport began billing itself as the "Boating and Fishing Capital of the East" in the 1940s, but its shoreline has been attracting visitors for hundreds of years — and not always for legal purposes.

Once Freeport attracted smugglers and rumrunners. Later, visitors would flock there to fish on charter boats and eat in seafood restaurants. But everyone came after the Meroke Indians, who were attracted to the bay and streams by the abundance of food and of shells for wampum.

Edward Raynor came in 1659 from Hempstead to what was then called the Great South Woods. He cleared land and built a cabin, and the area became known as Raynor South, later Raynortown. The names stuck for nearly two centuries. In 1853, residents voted to rename the community Freeport. They adopted a variation of Free Port, the nickname used by ship captains who during colonial times landed their cargo without paying customs duties. Oystering became a thriving industry after the Civil War, though it declined at the beginning of the 20th Century because of changing salinity in the bay and because of pollution.

The South Side Railroad arrived in 1868, and within a few years the improved access resulted in a building

A 1900 view of the Sportsmen's Channel, near Woodcleft

Freeport Historical Society; Newsday Photo

boom led by developer John J. Randall, who arranged the dredging of Woodcleft Canal — site of the fabled Nautical Mile — and other canals. Residents voted to incorporate the village in 1892. Six years later the village set up its own electric utility.

For a quarter-century starting in 1902, the New York and Long Island Traction Corp. ran trolleys through Freeport to Jamaica, Hempstead and Brooklyn. The trolleys went down Main Street to a ferry dock near Woodcleft Avenue, where boats traveled to Point Lookout's ocean beach. The short-haul and short-lived Freeport Railroad joined the mix in 1913, running trains down Grove Street from Sunrise Highway to the waterfront. The train was nicknamed "the Fishermen's Delight," and cartoonist Fontaine Fox supposedly used it as inspiration for his famous "Toonerville Trolley That Meets All the Trains."

Elinor Smith, who grew up in Freeport, focused international attention on the village when fellow pilots voted her the best female pilot in America in the 1920s. Smith soloed at 15, earned her pilot's license the following year and at 17 performed the daring stunt of flying

under all the East River bridges. Merrick Road was the site of an airplane factory owned by Arthur and Albert Heinrich, who in 1910 flew the first American-made, American-powered monoplane.

Freeport was a rumrunning center during Prohibition. Freeport Point Shipyard, founded by Fred and Mirto Scopinich just after World War I, built rumrunners as well as the Coast Guard boats that chased them. From 1937 until 1945 the shipyard built small boats for the U.S. and British navies. The family moved the operation to East Quogue in the late 1960s. Another renowned Freeport family still in the boat business is the Grovers, who started with a marina and dealership operated by Al Grover in 1950. The family built fishing skiffs from the 1970s until about 1990; Al Grover and his sons took one of their 26-footers from Nova Scotia to Portugal in the first outboard-powered crossing of the Atlantic in 1985.

Other prominent maritime industries were established in the village. The Columbian Bronze Corp., founded in 1901, made the propeller for Nautilus, the world's first nuclear-powered submarine, before folding in 1988.

Freeport has a number of other claims to fame. It was the home of Long Island's first 24-hour radio station: WGBB, founded in 1924. Freeport Municipal Stadium, completed in 1931, drew crowds of up to 10,000 to "midget" auto races from the '30s until after World War II, when stock-car racing took over. In the early '30s a semipro baseball team, the Penn Red Caps, named after Pullman Car porters, played in the stadium, and the prewar years saw the Brooklyn Football Dodgers using Freeport as their mid-week training site.

Freeport's most famous resident, band leader Guy Lombardo, moved to the east shore of Woodcleft Canal in 1940. Known as Mr. Freeport, he owned the popular East Point Restaurant. Lombardo had gotten involved in hydroplane racing in 1939 and owned a succession of eight cabin cruisers and racing boats named Tempo. He was national Gold Cup champion in 1946, which allowed him to bring the hydroplane race to Jamaica Bay the next year; he dropped out because of lubrication problems with his boat.

Lombardo wasn't the first show business star to discover the village. Vaudeville actors established an artist's colony by 1910. They founded the Long Island Good Hearted Thespian Society (LIGHTS), which built a club in 1915-16 and presented shows during the summer for more than a decade. Later, actors Broderick Crawford and Susan Sullivan lived in Freeport. Other famous residents have included Branch Rickey, owner of the Brooklyn Dodgers, and Henry Slocum, inventor of the inflatable "Mae West" vest-style lifejacket. Television programmer Brandon Tartikoff, TV sports commentator Dick Schaap and gossip columnist Cindy Adams also grew up in Freeport.

Beginning in the 1960s, Freeport began to see a growing ethnic population that continues to transform the community.

Where to Find More: Freeport Historical Museum, open at the end of April.

GARDEN CITY
Stewart's Ambitious Plan for the Plains

BY ANDREW SMITH
STAFF WRITER

Thousands of years before tree-lined streets stretched past graceful, formal homes, the place that would become Garden City sat in the heart of the Hempstead Plains, the only prairie east of the Mississippi River.

It was a flat, barren meadow — as clean a sheet of paper as any developer could hope for. No hills. No forest to clear or swamps to fill. In pre-colonial times, Indians lived on the shores, using the plains only for hunting. Then, for more than a century before Garden City was developed in the mid-1800s, the plains were public land in the Town of Hempstead, used as pastures available to all. Some of Long Island's first horse-racing tracks were laid out on the plains. Every so often in the years after 1850, town officials would try to put the 7,000 acres they controlled up for sale, but voters routinely vetoed the attempts.

Finally, in 1867, the sale narrowly won voters' approval, and two years later Charles Harvey agreed to buy the plains for $42 an acre. Harvey, one of the backers of New York City's elevated railways, was secretive about his plans for the Nassau land. Rumors spread that he would make the plains into an enormous cemetery, or build a jail. Enter wealthy New York merchant Alexander T. Stewart. He offered to pay an astounding $55 an acre — and promised to invest millions of dollars to build homes, roads and neighborhoods. It would be one of the nation's first planned communities.

Harvey desperately increased his bid to $56 an acre, but on July 17, 1869, Hempstead residents voted 1,077 to 52 in favor of Stewart's offer. Harvey threatened to sue, but in September Stewart received his deed for the plains for $395,328.35 in cash. The money paid for a new town hall, a poor house and other expenses.

Stewart and his architect, John Kellum, got to work laying out their new village, which Stewart named Garden City, after Chicago's informal nickname. Stewart liked the sound of it.

Much of 1870 was spent clearing and grading land and building an occasional house. The first

Newsday Photo, 1973 / Stan Wolfson
A wrecking ball goes to work on the old Garden City Hotel, a local landmark.

one, a two-story cottage at 4 First St., was the headquarters for the enterprise. Workers erected 28 miles of white picket fence around the empty blocks, and Kellum had 6,500 sugar maple trees transplanted from Flushing. (The first house was razed in the 1960s, but the fence in front remained.)

In 1871, builder James L'Hommedieu of Great Neck won the first contract to build 20 "fine villa residences" in Garden City, priced between $2,000 and $20,000. Construction began the following year on the original Garden City Hotel. Despite the trappings of a fine village, residents were slow to arrive. They may have been put off by Stewart's insistence on retaining ownership of the entire village. He leased every house and every business to occupants. By the end of 1874, only 40 families had moved to Garden City. But Stewart persevered. He built a railroad to serve Garden City. He built a water-works and the first sewage system in what was then Queens County. He built more stately houses.

And then he died, in April, 1876. His village was still a shell, with empty roads, saplings and empty houses. Residents began referring to the picket fences around empty lots as "Stewart's ribs." Stewart's widow began work on a massive memorial to him — the magnificent Cathedral of the Incarnation. The Episcopal church was completed in 1885. Mrs. Stewart died the following year. There were no heirs.

Nassau County Museum Collection
Alexander Stewart, circa 1860

Control of the village passed to the newly formed Garden City Corp., and in the 1890s, the village came to life. The company cleared away Stewart's ribs, encouraged renters to buy their homes and hired famed New York architect Stanford White to remodel the Garden City Hotel. It was an instant success. The hotel attracted the Astors, the Vanderbilts, the Pierpont Morgans — the richest citizens of the day. A golf course was similarly successful.

At the same time, the inability to attract land buyers prompted the Garden City Corp. in 1910 to sell 40 acres on Franklin Avenue to Doubleday, Page & Co. — a rare invitation to industry from the planned community. Former President Theodore Roosevelt laid the cornerstone and the publishing plant's 700 employees soon were turning out 6,500 books a day. Doubleday dubbed it Country Life Press, a name that lives in a railroad station by that name. (The plant closed in 1988 and was converted to offices.)

The Army's use of the remaining plains as campgrounds during the Spanish-American War and World War I brought visitors to the hotel and village. And nearby Roosevelt and Curtiss airfields attracted aviators. Charles Lindbergh stayed at the hotel in the week before his flight to Paris in 1927.

In time, thanks both to the railroad and automobiles, Garden City finally began to fill up. It incorporated as a village in 1919, and its exclusive reputation led nearby communities to spring up and associate themselves with it, particularly Stewart Manor and Garden City Park. Adelphi College (later upgraded to university) moved from Brooklyn to Garden City in 1929, becoming the first four-year college in Nassau or Suffolk. And in the 1930s, hundreds of houses were built to accommodate a population boom, though Garden City used a strict zoning code to preserve Stewart's vision. Alone in central Nassau, the village retained a sense of orderly development, true to its rigorously planned roots.

Claims to Fame: The Episcopal cathedral and a more modern — but less stylish — version of the Garden City Hotel remain. (So does the headquarters building of the former Vanderbilt Parkway, now a home near Clinton Road.) Homegrown Garden City celebrities include John Tesh, Susan Lucci and Telly Savalas.

Where to Find More: "The Founding of Garden City," by Vincent F. Seyfried, and "The History of Garden City," by M.H. Smith, Garden City Public Library.

HEMPSTEAD VILLAGE

See story on Page 17.

THE HEWLETTS
A Four-Part Segment Of the Five Towns

Beginnings: The patriarch of the family after whom the four Hewlett communities are named was George Hewlett, who came to America in the late 1600s from Buckinghamshire, England, and eventually owned most of the land that became the Five Towns area of the Rockaway Peninsula.

The Revolution: Col. Richard Hewlett, a descendant of George and one of the foremost American Tories, led various units against the Patriot army and participated in a failed plot to kill Gen. George Washington. He fled to Canada, but other Hewlett descendants forged a dynasty of local leadership in education, religion, politics, the arts and business.

Turning Points: Though the area had been called Hewlett for generations, the name was changed to Fenhurst in 1892 when the Long Island Rail Road created a depot in the community, and its president at the time, Austin Corbin, decided on that name. Five years later, in 1897, family descendant Augustus J. Hewlett countered by donating land to the LIRR, on the condition that the station (and hence, the area) would be called Hewlett again. It was. The following year, the Hewlett-Woodmere school district was established. It celebrated its 100th anniversary in 1998.

The Four Hewletts: Hewlett proper became an unincorporated hamlet covering about one square mile, with a 1998 population of 6,575. Three incorporated villages were created during a 1920s building boom. Hewlett Harbor was

established in 1925 on what once was the private Seawane Club, composed of socially prominent and wealthy families. Hewlett Neck, the smallest village at three-fourths of a square mile, was set up on a portion of Woodmere in 1927. The site was a prominent polo field from 1875 to the early 1900s, when Woodmere High School leased it for a football field. Hewlett Bay Park was built by attorney Carlton Macy, also in 1927. The community once had guarded entrance gates, and, one history said, "sale covenants were not uncommon."

Big Money: According to census information, the three Hewlett villages in 1996 had the highest median family incomes on Long Island, each at $191,686 (on a par only with Kings Point).

Where to Find More: "Five Towns," a handbook by the League of Women Voters of the Five Towns, 1977, and a section on Five Towns history, South Shore Record newspaper, 1976, at the Hewlett-Woodmere Public Library.

INWOOD
Boisterous Fishermen Offended the Farmers

Beginnings: Cheek-by-jowl today with Kennedy International Airport, Inwood once was virgin forest rimmed by extensive marshes reaching west into Jamaica Bay. Tradition says Indians often gathered there because it was a cornucopia of oysters, clams and mussels, for making happy palates and wampum. The 1800s brought a few farming and fishing families descended from early Hempstead Town settlers, with names such as Cornell, Sprague, Doughty, Johnson, Rhinehart and Smith.

Name Game: The fishermen called themselves North West Pointers, reflecting their fairly isolated location on the Rockaway Peninsula.

Please Turn to Page 17

GARDEN CITY: It may have not been up to more modern motorized methods, but in 1946, a horse provided effective power to plow a path.

GARDEN CITY: Horse carts and dirt roads from about 1900.

Nassau County Museum Collection, Long Island Studies Institute

HEMPSTEAD: A cornerstone is laid at the Masonic Temple at Fulton Street, east of Main Street, on Aug. 20, 1910.

Newsday Photo

Nassau County Museum Collection, Long Island Studies Institute

HEMPSTEAD: A woman checks on her car on Main Street during a storm on Dec. 26, 1947. At right, horse-drawn wagons await the train at the Hempstead depot in about 1910.

Nassau County Museum Collection, Long Island Studies Institute

Pedestrians encounter a newfangled motorcar at the intersection of Front and Main Streets in the village in an undated photo.

HEMPSTEAD VILLAGE

Why It's Called The Hub

BY RHODA AMON
STAFF WRITER

It was called The Hub. Public transportation radiated from Hempstead Village like the spokes of a wheel. Pre-World War II homemakers would bus to Hempstead to shop. Almost everyone, in fact, shopped in Hempstead Village, the oldest community in Nassau County. While Mineola was the seat of county government, Hempstead was where you went for almost everything else.

To the English settlers in 1644, it was the place where several converging streams provided rich irrigated pasturage for cows and oxen. With a whole island to choose from, they settled in the spot where St. George's Church was built, facing Front Street. Presbyterian followers of the Rev. Richard Denton, they built a meeting house to serve for both town meetings and religious services.

Historians differ on the derivation of the name. One version holds that it comes from the town of Hemel-Hempstead, birthplace of Robert Fordham, who first scouted the area with John Carman (probably his son-in-law, though this has not been proven). Other historians trace the name to the Dutch *Heemstede,* since the Dutch were there before the English.

The Dutch were at war with the Indians, and the first English settlers found themselves in a dangerous paradise. Seven Indians charged with stealing pigs in 1644 were confined in Fordham's cellar. New Netherlands Gov. William Kieft sent 120 soldiers, who dealt savagely with the native population.

All seems to have been peaceful by 1665 when the new English governor, Richard Nicolls, who had dislodged the Dutch the year before, called a convention in Hempstead, the largest and richest of the English settlements, according to historian Bernice Schultz Marshall. Delegates from all over Long Island and Westchester came expecting to write a new code of law but found themselves asked to rubber-stamp the Duke's Laws, already formulated by the duke of York, with no colonial input. Hempstead residents were among the most vocal protesters of "taxation without representation." They were finally granted a colonial assembly in New York City in 1683, but the assembly attached the Town of Hempstead to Queens County, another cause of unrest during the next two centuries.

Though largely Tory during the Revolution — and suffering from both sides — Hempstead was visited by President George Washington on his tour of Long Island

in 1790. He describes a stopover, probably for lunch at Simmonson's inn, but says nothing of the devastation he must have seen after the seven-year British occupation.

The village, the largest community in the Town of Hempstead, was incorporated in 1853. Though it had a volunteer fire company since 1832, its bylaws required that any male resident who refused to help put out a fire would be fined $3.

In the late 1800s and early 1900s, Hempstead was the summer home of wealthy New Yorkers. The millionaire August Belmont had a country estate in the heart of the village. Journalist Arthur Brisbane's estate was just east. Elliott Roosevelt, a summer renter, brought his little daughter, Eleanor, who became first lady of the nation. William K. Vanderbilt II, founder of the Vanderbilt Cup races in 1904, drove the first motorcar into Hempstead at more than 6 mph. The village board promptly set a speed limit at 6 mph.

In later years the country estates gave way to middle-income housing and shops, and the village became increasingly urbanized. Arnold Constable, the first New York department store to move to Long Island, located in Hempstead Village in 1940. Other large stores followed. However, the tremendous building boom that followed World War II created giant shopping malls all over Long Island, and the major stores began moving out to where the money was.

But Hempstead remained a recognized name in education circles. Hofstra University, begun as a small commuter college in converted homes on Hempstead Turnpike in 1935, would later become a well-known university with an enrollment of more than 12,000 on a 238-acre campus.

With urbanization, meanwhile, the black population in the village grew rapidly in the second half of the 20th Century. The 1990 census listed more than 29,000 African-Americans, making up roughly 60 percent of the village population. About 9,000 residents were of Hispanic origin. The African American Museum, opened by Nassau County at 110 N. Franklin St., began in 1970 to tell the history and contributions of African-Americans through films, programs and children's workshops.
Where to Find More: "Colonial Hempstead," by Bernice Schultz Marshall; "Vignettes of Hempstead Town," by Myron H. Luke; "The Roots and Heritage of Hempstead Town," edited by Natalie A. Naylor, at the Hempstead Public Library and Long Island Studies Institute, Hofstra University, West Campus.

INWOOD, Continued

One history says, "They were considered a hard-living, more or less lawless lot. Boisterous and rough, their horseplay and fighting were particularly annoying to the more peaceful farmers in the neighboring settlements." Another name starting in the 1870s was Westville. Because that name existed upstate, a new name had to be chosen to get the community of 1,100 residents the post office it sought in 1888. Several names were considered at a public meeting, including Rawayton, Bayhead, Custer, Pike's Peak, Spring Haven, Elco and Rahway. Inwood won, but the origin of the name isn't clear.

Turning Point: The coming of the railroad to the Rockaways in 1869 was key. By 1885, Westville had many cottages, several substantial homes, a church, library, law office, a private school, two pharmacies and a brass band. The core of the economy was production and shipping of shellfish to world markets. Early in the 1900s, Inwood had a heavy influx of immigrants, mainly Italians and Albanians. Blacks followed, mostly after World War II, and in 1990 constituted 26.3 percent of the population of 7,767.

Where to Find More: The Long Island Studies Institute, Hofstra University, Hempstead, and "The Story of the Five Towns," by the Writers Program of the federal Works Progress Administration, 1941, at Peninsula Public Library, Lawrence.

ISLAND PARK

It Took Lots of Mud
To Make It a Home

Beginnings: Rockaway Indians raised pigs and cattle and made wampum from clam shells on the island until Europeans arrived in the mid-1600s and the Indians moved eastward.

Revolution: Patriots viewed Hog Island, as the future Island Park was known from 1665 until 1874, as a strategic stronghold for keeping the British away from Long Island's southern shoreline. After the British captured Long Island in 1776, the Patriots made repeated raids on the Tories camped at Hog Island, and on July 11, 1780, the British warship Galatea pursued a Patriot sloop through Jones Inlet and forced it ashore on Hog Island.

Turning Points: In 1870, the New York and Long Beach Railroad, later part of the Long Island Rail Road, laid tracks from Lynbrook to Long Beach across the island. At the time, the island was known as Barnum Island, for the man who owned most of it: P.T. Barnum, though not *the* P.T. Barnum, the promoter and circus owner. In 1910, two developers, Frank Lawson and William Austin, bought Barnum Island, with plans to make it the "Venice of the United States," complete with canals. World War I killed their idea, and in 1921 they sold the island to the Island Park-Long Beach Corp., and the island was renamed Island Park. The corporation brought in a giant dredge that for more than a year pumped mud five feet deep on the undeveloped island to allow development. An electric plant and waterworks were built, followed by the first 15 houses along Kildare Road. Between 1922 and 1926, so many homes were built on the southern end of the island that the railroad station was relocated from the north end of the island to the south. A business district developed along Long Beach Road. The village was incorporated in 1926, when there were fewer than 1,000 property owners. What was a summer resort for city

Please Turn to Page 21

Lindbergh, UPI Photo; Above, Newsday Archive

OVER LONG ISLAND: Just a few minutes after taking off from Roosevelt Field in 1927, the fuel-laden Spirit of St. Louis carries Charles Lindbergh, left, toward Paris, where he would arrive 33½ hours later on the first solo transatlantic flight.

Nassau County Museum Collection, Long Island Studies Institute

ROOSEVELT FIELD: A British blimp hovers after the first transatlantic airship crossing, a four-day trip from Scotland in 1919.

Newsday Archive

ROOSEVELT FIELD: Biplanes line up just before the start of an air derby on Sept. 6, 1928.

Newsday Photo / Harvey Weber

ROOSEVELT FIELD: The airport that served as a historic stage for pioneer aviators closes for good on May 31, 1951, to make way for light industry factories (construction on a shopping mall would begin in 1955). Above, Lewis Miller and police Sgt. Scotty Begg lower the field's windsock on that last day in 1951.

Newsday Photo / Bill Senft

ROCKVILLE CENTRE: Invited to speak by the Poor People's Campaign Committee for Nassau County, the Rev. Martin Luther King Jr. addresses a packed house in the auditorium of Southside High School on March 26, 1968. Just nine days later, on April 4, King was assassinated as he stood with some of his advisers on a motel balcony in Memphis.

ROCKVILLE CENTRE: Workers strain on top of wreckage and on the ground to cut away cars twisted and overturned in a Long Island Rail Road crash on Feb. 17, 1950, that killed 32 people and injured 208. The collision occurred in a "one-track gantlet," used at different times by eastbound and westbound trains. Authorities said the eastbound train ran a stop signal. Days later, under fire, the railroad installed tripping devices in the gantlet to stop trains automatically and avert head-on collisions.
In an unrelated event only nine months later, a Babylon-bound train slammed into a stalled train at Richmond Hill on Thanksgiving Eve, killing 78 commuters in the LIRR's worst crash.

Newsday Photo / Howie Edwards

Collection of Joel Streich

LIDO BEACH: A black-and-white postcard, circa 1940, sports a promotional view of Lido Estates, built on a barrier island that got its start when William Reynolds dredged a channel to create Long Beach. In 1929, he built the Moorish-style Lido Beach Hotel, but it never really became a major resort. The hotel was converted to residential condominums in the 1960s.

New York State Parks, Recreation and Historic Preservation

LAKEVIEW: Workers clear cuttings for a golf course in 1933 at what became Hempstead Lake State Park. The lake was created for the William Oliver mill, which closed in 1873.

ISLAND PARK, Continued

residents became primarily a middle-class, year-round community with a large Italian and Greek population.

Claim to Fame: In 1945, Alfonse D'Amato, at the age of 8, moved from Newark, N.J., to Island Park with his family. After three terms in the U.S. Senate, D'Amato still called Island Park home.

Where to Find More: "Short History of Island Park," available at the Island Park Public Library, 99 Radcliffe Rd.

LAKEVIEW

Making the Lake For People to View

Beginnings: At first, there was no lake to view. The area was one of the few in central Nassau that was not part of the Hempstead Plains. It was, instead, covered with swamps and streams that fed Mill River. It wasn't until the mid-19th Century, when William Oliver built Long Island's largest gristmill, that a body of water was created. The mill was removed in 1873 to build a reservoir for the city of Brooklyn

— a feat that failed, but left Hempstead Lake behind. The area first was named Skodic, for a farmer, and then more formally was called Woodfield. Later names were Norwood and Hempstead Gardens, but in 1910 the Long Island Rail Road established a Lakeview station, and, as often happened, the railroad's choice stuck.

Turning Points: The coming of the railroad made it possible for commuters to live in Lakeview. Also, the Doubleday, Page & Co. publishing plant in nearby Garden City employed many residents. In the 1960s, Lakeview became a mostly black community. In 1968, the Malverne school district, which served Lakeview, closed the Woodfield Road Elementary School — the only one in Lakeview — and forced parents to pay to get their kids to school. Ironically, the school board argued that it closed the school to ensure that all elementary schools remained racially integrated.

Brushes With Fame: Nineteenth-Century boxing champion John L. Sullivan and 1996 Olympic gold-medal hurdler Derrick Adkins lived in Lakeview.

Where to Find More: "Lakeview," published by Bruce Haldeman, chairman of the Lakeview Historical Preservation Society.

LEVITTOWN

See story on Page 22.

LIDO BEACH

A Resort Development That Didn't Develop

Beginnings: Like the rest of the barrier island on which it sits, Lido Beach existed first as an uninhabited, barren sandbar. The island got its start when William Reynolds dredged the channel that bears his name to create the resort of Long Beach. The dredging made the island accessible to pleasure boats. In 1929, after Reynolds had been defeated for re-election as Long Beach mayor, he turned his attention to the unincorporated area just east of the city and built the Moorish-style Lido Beach Hotel, naming it for the resort villa in Italy. Reynolds envisioned the hotel as an anchor for another resort community, but the stock market crash that year and the subsequent Depression halted development for almost a decade.

Turning Point: World War II revitalized the hotel: the Navy used it as a discharge station. When the war ended, developers Bernard and

Seymour Jacovitz led a building boom in the area near the hotel. Completion of the Loop Parkway in 1934 made Lido Beach more accessible — until then motorists had to wend their way through streets in Long Beach, Island Park, Oceanside and Rockville Centre — but unlike Long Beach, Lido Beach never developed into a major resort. Indeed, the hotel that gives the community its name was converted to residential condominiums in the 1960s, leaving Lido Beach almost entirely residential. Residents fought to keep it that way at various times, sometimes successfully, sometimes not. Nightclubs and bathing clubs arrived, but residents did manage to beat back an attempt in the 1960s that would have allowed multistory apartment buildings.

Hot Spots: Lido Beach was home to a Nike missile-launch control center during the early 1950s. When the center closed in the 1960s, the land was turned over to the Long Beach school district, which used it for a maintenance facility. Lido Beach was later home to the Malibu night club, a regular stop on many national rock tours; it closed in 1996.

Where to Find More: The Lido Beach file at the Long Island Studies Institute at Hofstra University in Hempstead.

LAWRENCE

Always a Bastion of Quiet Elegance

BY TOM MORRIS
STAFF WRITER

One of Long Island's showcase communities, and the most populous of the Five Towns area's six villages, Lawrence has been a bastion of quiet wealth and architectural elegance since its founding in the late 1800s.

Rock Hall, a splendid Georgian mansion built in 1767 as a plantation, was converted to a Hempstead Town museum in the heart of the village, featuring Chippendale furniture and hand-planed walls. Founded in 1878, the sprawling Rockaway Hunting Club remained a citadel of deep-rooted, deep-pocketed American families who into the 1900s carried on traditions of fox hunts, steeplechase, polo and, in later years, golf, tennis and skeet shooting.

Lawrence has been called home by the likes of Edward H. Harriman, owner of the New York Central Railroad, banking titan Russell Sage, U.S. Attorney General George W. Wickersham (under President William Howard Taft) and Secretary of War Henry L. Stimson (under President Franklin D. Roosevelt). Summer residents have ranged from the irascible Irish author Oscar Wilde to American funnyman Milton Berle.

Before the Civil War, New York City investors Alfred N. Lawrence and his brother Newbold began buying up farms that traced back to the ownership of Jacob Hicks in 1659. Right after the war, in 1869, the South Side Railroad arrived in the area. Lawrence appeared on its first timetable that June. The following year, the Lawrences donated land for a rail depot and pressed their aim of making Lawrence a summer resort for the rich.

It came almost naturally because of the huge popularity of the nearby Rockaway area among well-heeled New York City people earlier in the 1800s, and their tendency to seek new venues when masses of working immigrants discovered the same seaside delights.

Lawrence became the Five Towns' first incorporated village in 1897, at the height of its heyday as an opulent resort. The snooty Osborne House opened in 1884 in the Isle of Wight section of south Lawrence. The same year, the Rockaway Hunt Club, which had originated four miles west in Far Rockaway, had an "ing" added and was moved to Lawrence. By 1886, as the gilded age evolved, there were about 100 mansions in Lawrence, but the post-War War II building boom in Lawrence and Cedarhurst consumed many of the estates, as well as large tracts of woods, meadows and marsh.

Lawrence would be tightly run since the incorporation in 1897 by leading residents, many of whom lawyers, businessmen, engineers and other professionals. Up to the mid-1960s, only landowners could vote in village elections. The 4.5-square-mile village of 6,500 residents (1990s) became a mixture of old and new architectural influences — Georgian, Edwardian, French Provincial, Tudor and contemporary. Among famous architects who left their work were Marcel Breuer and Stanford White.

Where to Find More: "Village of Lawrence, N.Y., a Brief History of a Long Island Community," 1977, by the Village of Lawrence, at Peninsula Public Library, Lawrence.

Rock Hall Museum Photo

Rock Hall, shown in the early 1900s, was a mansion built in 1767. It later became a town museum.

Veterans of World War II and others line up in 1947 to be among the first of those who would rent the new homes planned on the Hempstead Plains by Levitt & Sons.

Photo by Ed Cortese

LEVITTOWN

A Prototype for American Suburbia

BY RHODA AMON
STAFF WRITER

Believe it. A newspaper ad in 1949 read "This is Levittown! All Yours for $58!" It went on to promise that "lucky fellow, Mr. Veteran" that "Uncle Sam and the world's largest builders have made it possible for you to live in a charming house in a delightful community . . ."

A small down payment, a Federal Housing Authority-guaranteed risk-free mortgage, and it was yours, a single-family house priced at $7,990 complete with Bendix washer, glass-walled living room and fruit trees. Thousands of house-hungry World War II veterans bought it. Some were already there, the pioneers who rented the first Cape Cods at $60 per month in 1947.

By 1951, 17,447 homes stretched across the farmlands of Island Trees, parts of Wantagh, Hicksville and Westbury. Eventually, Levittowns stretched across America. The brassy venture of a Long Island builder — backed by the postwar largesse of Uncle Sam — would transform the piecemeal American building industry into an assembly-line enterprise, churning out thousands of cookie-cutter subdivisions.

But if you were Mr. and Mrs. Veteran who bought into William J. Levitt's dream, you probably did not go wrong. You may not have loved living in look-alike housing on the Hempstead Plains — some didn't — but if you held on, you probably sold your house for double or triple its purchase price. And a half-century later, though seared by bitter controversies and flaws in the original plan, Levittown remained a mostly pleasant community.

The story of Long Island's most famous suburb — as told in books, articles, films — began with the receding glaciers that left behind a vast prairie covering most of central Nassau County. Indians lived along the coasts, getting their livelihood from the sea. But the English who settled Hempstead in the 1640s loved the plains. No forests to clear, no hills. They used the plains as common pasture for sheep and cattle.

Alexander T. Stewart, the department store tycoon, bought what was left of the plains in 1869 but developed only Garden City. Likewise, the 1920s real estate boom that developed western Nassau bypassed the plains east of Hempstead. Gradually the prairie was filled in mostly by German and Dutch immigrants, who planted large potato farms.

Three factors merged at the close of World War II to change the plains — and the way Long Islanders live. One was the golden nematode — the potato bug — eating away the farmers' profits and driving them to sell the farms. Another was the thousands of GIs returning to live in Quonset huts or their in-laws' crowded apartments. A third factor was the U.S. government, already engaged in a Cold War with communism, wanting to show that a democracy could provide decent housing for its veterans. More than $20 billion was pumped into the homebuilding industry.

When Levitt & Sons announced plans to build 2,000 homes, 4,495 applicants rushed in with $60 deposits.

Recruited by Levitt, 800 veterans and families, many pushing baby strollers, crowded Hempstead Town Hall on May 27, 1947, when the town board made a momentous decision: to allow homes to be built without basements. The crowd broke into applause.

Life in the raw new community was hectic — and fun. "It was like joining a club," recalled early settler Estelle Strichartz. "We were all young with little kids, and we helped each other. One family had the only telephone on the block — they were good about calling us to the phone."

The controversies came later. One involved Levitt's racist policy. At first there was a covenant reading: "The tenant agrees not to permit the premises to be used or occupied by any person other than members of the Caucasian race . . ." After such covenants were banned by the U.S. Supreme Court and the FHA would not back mortgages linked to segregationist rules, the covenant was dropped but the practice continued.

Levitt's forgetting to provide for schools turned the growing neighborhoods into battlegrounds as school taxes spiraled. There were battles over book-banning, traffic jams, the demise of businesses on the village greens. By the 1960s all the social problems of suburban sprawl surfaced in Levittown, along with a generation of talented men and women, including composer-singer Billy Joel.

But the house itself — the basic Cape Cod and later the ranch — proved a functional design that could be expanded to fill everyone's needs. A half century later, Levittown had become an architectural polyglot with no two houses alike.

Newsday Photo

Levitt homes being mass-produced.

22

Newsday Photo / Edna Murray

LEVITTOWN: In 1947, above, Mr. and Mrs. Theodore Bladykas and their 14-month-old twins, Patricia Ann and Betty Ann, become the first family to move into the development. What started as affordable rental homes for returning World War II veterans would, by 1951, become a complex of 17,447 homes blanketing the farms of Island Trees and spilling over into Wantagh, Hicksville and Westbury.

The growth of suburbia led to a persistent ritual: rush hour. At left, traffic builds as defense workers jam a road near Levittown in 1951.

Newsday Photo / Harvey Weber

POINT LOOKOUT: The U.S. Life Saving Station at Point Lookout in 1895. The area was occupied by shacks on wood pilings and was inhabited only in the summer.

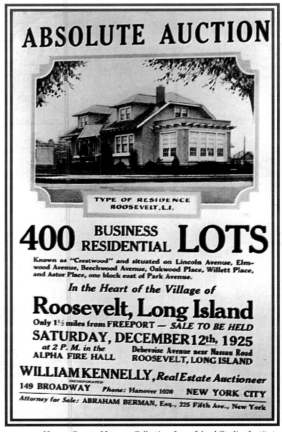

ABSOLUTE AUCTION

TYPE OF RESIDENCE
ROOSEVELT, L.I.

400 BUSINESS RESIDENTIAL LOTS

Known as "Crestwood" and situated on Lincoln Avenue, Elmwood Avenue, Beechwood Avenue, Oakwood Place, Willett Place, and Astor Place, one block east of Park Avenue.

In the Heart of the Village of

Roosevelt, Long Island

Only 1½ miles from FREEPORT — SALE TO BE HELD

SATURDAY, DECEMBER 12th, 1925

at 2 P. M. in the   Debevoise Avenue near Nassau Road
ALPHA FIRE HALL   ROOSEVELT, LONG ISLAND

WILLIAM KENNELLY, *Real Estate Auctioneer*
INCORPORATED

149 BROADWAY   Phone: Hanover 1020   NEW YORK CITY

Attorney for Sale: ABRAHAM BERMAN, Esq., 225 Fifth Ave., New York

ROOSEVELT: A place of business in 1909. At right, housing is advertised in December, 1925. In 1902, residents named the community in honor of the then-president of the United States, fellow Nassau County resident Theodore Roosevelt.

LYNBROOK

Fondness for Brooklyn Lives On in a Name

Beginnings: Lynbrook sat at the crossroads of major trading routes for hundreds of years. For most of that time, however, the routes were dirt paths used by Merrick Indians. Colonists used those trails as well, and by 1785, a small community had been established where several trails met — a spot still known as Five Corners, at the intersection of Merrick Road, Hempstead Avenue, Broadway and Atlantic Avenue. Initially it was known as Bloomfield, but it soon became better known as Pearsalls Corners, after general store owner Wright Pearsall. The community began to grow in the years after 1853, when Merrick Road was covered with planks. A toll house stood on the road where the modern Toll Gate Court was located.

Turning Point: Pearsalls Corners' position as a crossroads resulted in both Merrick Road and the South Side Railroad ending there for a time. Stagecoaches were available from there to Long Beach, Rockville Centre or Hempstead. Meanwhile, the community grew on its own, and soon supported several hotels. Bicyclists would take the train there during the bike craze of the 1880s and 1890s and use it as a base for 100-mile rides. As the area was developed and its ties to the rural past were forgotten, residents felt no affection for their community's name. Because many had moved from Brooklyn, in 1894 they reversed that city's syllables and renamed the village Lynbrook. They even adopted Brooklyn's Dutch motto as their own: *Een dracht mackt maght* (In unity there is strength). The village was incorporated in 1911.

Claims to Fame: French chef Henri Charpentier, the inventor of crepes suzettes, ran a nationally known restaurant in Lynbrook from 1915 to 1930. Henri's closed when the effects of Prohibition forced Charpentier into bankruptcy. Fruit-store owner Jimmy Costas is said to have coined the remark, "Yes, we have no bananas," which evolved into a popular pre-World War II song. Anti-Communist Whittaker Chambers grew up in Lynbrook.

Where to Find More: "Lynbrook Legacy," by Steven Willner, published in 1961, "History of Lynbrook," at Lynbrook Public Library.

MALVERNE

Subdividing Farms For New Yorkers

Beginnings: Malverne emerged from a larger area of farms known collectively as Norwood. Rockaway Indians hunted and may have lived in the area. Originally it was heavily wooded, with several streams. These streams often overflowed their banks. That and a high water table helped form Grassy Pond, a popular place to skate, near what would become the intersection of Hempstead and Franklin Avenues. Europeans arrived near the beginning of the 1800s. The same water table that made the land good for farming, however, also had a tendency to flood basements of new homes. Several companies attempted to maintain railroad service through Norwood to West Hempstead, but none succeeded until the consolidation of the Long Island Rail Road.

Turning Points: The Amsterdam Development and Land Co., managed by Alfred Wagg, began subdividing farms in 1911 to accommodate people moving out from New York. When the postal service asked Wagg to change the name of the area from Norwood — there were several others in New York State — an investor in the land company, Ernest Childs, suggested naming it after Malvern, an English village. No one knows how an "e" got tacked onto the end of the name. The village incorporated in 1921. Racial strife swirled around Malverne in the 1960s when the Malverne school board decided to close a school in predominantly black neighboring Lakeview in an attempt to integrate schools in white neighborhoods.

Claims to Fame: Celebrity residents have included actor Tony Danza, vaudevillian George Moore, sports columnist Walter (Red) Smith and former Nassau County Executive Francis Purcell, who earlier had been mayor of Malverne.

Where to Find More: "Malverne, the Story of Its Years," available at the Malverne Public Library; "Malverne's 75th Anniversary Commemorative Journal," published in 1996 by the Malverne Historical & Preservation Society.

MERRICK, NORTH MERRICK

Buccaneers Preyed Upon Merchants

Beginnings: Named after its first inhabitants, the Merrick Indians, the land changed hands in 1643 when sachem Tackapousha signed a treaty with Merrick's first colonists, English settlers who escaped the oppressive reign of King Charles I. During the colonial period, Merrick became a trading center because vessels could enter Jones Inlet and sail up deep channels to docks beside what became Merrick Road. During the War of 1812 these channels, canals and coves made Merrick a haven for buccaneers who preyed on merchants. Pirates in whaleboats once robbed prominent landowner George Hewlett and two friends while they were duck hunting, ripping the silver buttons from their coats. At one point, residents armed with muskets captured one bandit leader and shipped him to New York in irons for trial.

Merrick as Mecca: During a surge of religious activity in the 1860s, Methodists from around the state congregated in Merrick annually. In the beginning, horses and buggies were pulled into two circles around an open field for 10 days of services. The camp normally attracted about 300 worshipers, but some meetings were attended by up to 10,000. Circular streets, such as Fletcher and Asbury Avenues, lined with small cottages that developed around the campground, remained in the North Merrick neighborhood called Tiny Town by residents.

Turning Points: The construction of the South Shore Railroad, predecessor of the Long Island Rail Road, through Merrick in the late 1880s began a period of development. The boom in population and growth after World War II gradually led to Merrick and North Merrick developing distinct identities and separate school districts.

Claims to Fame: Actor Ed Begley lived in Merrick, where his actor-son, Ed Begley Jr., grew up. Years later, so did singer Deborah Gibson.

Canine Celebrity: A headstone near the railroad station honors an unusual commuter, Roxy, a yellow mongrel that spent its life traveling on the Long Island Rail Road. Roxy began by accompanying the stationmaster on trips, and it's said that the dog once traveled as far as Philadelphia before returning to Long Island. Roxy died in 1934 and was buried beside the tracks.

Where to Find More: See "Memories of the Merricks," published by the Merrick Historical Society, at the Merrick Public Library.

OCEANSIDE

Real Estate Sharpies Peddled Marshland

Beginnings: Rockaway Indians were the first residents in what was to become Oceanside. Because of diseases and cruelty of European settlers, they died out not long after the Europeans arrived in the area at the end of the 1600s. In 1682, the Town of Hempstead granted 100 acres in the area to St. George's Church so it could support itself. The property was known for many years as the Parsonage Farm, even after the church sold it in 1826. The area's religious roots were apparent in Oceanside's original name of Christian Hook. Gristmills in nearby communities soon attracted settlers, and farmers, fishermen and baymen got the community going during the 1800s. Oyster harvesting, particularly, provided a solid living for residents.

Turning Points: Oysters prodded the first significant change since colonial times, when residents decided that oysters would sell better if they came from "Oceanville" instead of Christian Hook. The new name was made official in 1864, and Oceanville oysters were known to be

of high quality. The post office forced another name change in 1890 because another Oceanville existed in New York. The community changed its name to Ocean Side, which was condensed in 1918. This same period marked Oceanside's conversion from a rural and fishing hamlet into a city suburb. The 1920s saw a real estate boom so explosive that swindlers were able to sell marshland to unsuspecting buyers. Sidewalks constructed for show sank into the ground. The 1920s also saw the construction of something more substantial — Oil City, the area of oil tanks near the water. Another building boom took place in the 1950s.

Home Brew: During Prohibition, many stores in Oceanside sold malt syrup, hops, corn sugar and yeast — the raw ingredients of beer. Many speakeasies operated there.

Brush With Fame: Actor David Paymer grew up in Oceanside.

Where to Find More: "The Story of Oceanside," at Oceanside Public Library, and "The History of Oceanside," at Baldwin Public Library.

POINT LOOKOUT

Unpaved Streets, And Proud of It

Beginnings: Point Lookout sits on the eastern tip of what was for many years little more than a jumbo-sized sandbar off the South Shore. That changed in about 1900 after William Reynolds dredged the channel that bears his name and built the city of Long Beach. The eastern end of that island was occupied by a collection of shacks on wood pilings. Inhabited only during summer, it was known as Nassau-by-the-Sea and was accessible only by ferry from Freeport. The community burned to the dune some time before World War I, but gradually snug bungalows reappeared for summer residents, this time under the community name of Point Lookout, apparently because of its location at the end of a peninsula. Streets remained unpaved into the 1940s, and residents were happy to keep it that way. In 1936, they objected, in vain, to the Town of Hempstead establishing a public park there, complaining that it would attract people from elsewhere in the area.

Turning Point: The Loop Parkway was completed in 1934, finally making it easy to get to Point Lookout, though it was not until the 1950s that summer bungalows were renovated and expanded into permanent homes in significant numbers and a tiny business district appeared. Streets were paved, and the post office arrived. In time, Point Lookout had almost 2,000 year-round residents and about 3,500 during the summer. But as in the days when it was Nassau-by-the-Sea, the main attraction of the place was ocean and the relative isolation.

Brushes With Fame: Among the celebrities who maintained unpretentious summer homes at Point Lookout were actress Marlene Dietrich and bodybuilder Charles Atlas.

Where to Find More: In the Point Lookout file at the Long Island Studies Institute at Hofstra University, Hempstead.

ROCKVILLE CENTRE

See story on Page 26.

ROOSEVELT

Developers Opened The Doors to Blacks

Beginnings: In the centuries before European settlement, Roosevelt was a part of the great forest separating the Hempstead Plains from the meadows and marshes along the South Shore. Indians used the woods for hunting, and even after Europeans arrived it was decades

Newsday Photo
From left, LIRR President Frank Aikman Jr., Lynbrook Park Commissioner William Albern and Mayor Francis X. Becker place a new sign on the train station in 1967. The sign symbolizes the village's claim of being the only community in the nation with that name.

Please Turn the Page

ROCKVILLE CENTRE
Home to Sea Captains and a Diocese

BY ANDREW SMITH
STAFF WRITER

As the winter of 1643 arrived, so did some visitors to a village established by the Rockaway Indians.

The community, at the southern end of what was then a swamp, was in the approximate area where Rockville Centre stands now. About 500 people lived there, led by the one-eyed sachem Tackapousha, and some suspect that Shellbank Avenue in the village took its name from enormous piles of shells the Rockaways had amassed to make wampum.

The visitors were John Carman and Robert Fordham, representatives of a group of Englishmen who were unhappy where they lived at the time, in Stamford, Conn. Carman and Fordham forged south from Hempstead Harbor to Tackapousha, and negotiated the purchase of the southern half of modern-day Nassau County.

Indians coexisted peacefully with the new residents, but European diseases — smallpox and measles — wiped out almost the entire population in less than 50 years. The last of the Indians moved to Barnum Island, leaving little trace behind. The area remained largely uninhabited until 1710, when Michael DeMott constructed a dam for a mill across the stream at the southern end of what was then Long Swamp.

The isolated settlers in the area wanted nothing to do with the rebellion against the British 60 years later. They became a nuisance to the rebels, and Gen. George Washington ordered them arrested. Several hid out in the swamp north of DeMott's mill, at a spot near modern-day Peninsula Boulevard. Rebel soldiers persuaded the Tories to surrender with a single shot, which injured George Smith in the shoul-

Nassau County Museum Collection, Long Island Studies Institute

It's about 1910 and members of the Raynor family of Rockville Centre are all decked out to celebrate the Fourth of July.

der. It was the first blood of the Revolution spilled on Long Island.

The area became known as Near Rockaway, and by 1849 there were enough people to warrant a post office. Residents wanted to honor the current mill owner and civic leader, Mordecai Rock Smith, but the name Smithtown was already in use in Suffolk County. So, they used his middle name and dubbed their community Rockville Centre. The mill disappeared a few years later when the Brooklyn Water Supply Co. tried to build a massive reservoir there. Its failure resulted in what would become Hempstead Lake.

The combination of water company activity and a new plank road to Jamaica spurred development in Rockville Centre and elsewhere on the South Shore. Sea captains came to favor Rockville Centre, because it was close to the sea and to the port of New York. Indeed, Maine Avenue was named for the many captains who

came from that state. (And some became eternal residents: When the winter of 1836-37 brought two horrifying shipwrecks on the South Shore, residents collected money to bury the victims in the Mariners' Lot at the Sandhole cemetery in the village.)

The 1860s marked the arrival of the Wallace brothers, men who would shape Rockville Centre's development for decades. George Wallace owned the South Side Observer, an influential Freeport newspaper, but in 1873 he moved it and himself to Rockville Centre.

Wallace, a former teacher who became a state assemblyman, soon began campaigning for the formal incorporation of Rockville Centre. Residents debated the issue for more than two decades before voting to do so in 1893. (Wallace also introduced the bill in the legislature that established Nassau County in 1898.)

Within months of Rockville Centre's incorporation, the board of trustees began to set up its electric and water supply service — utilities that remained through the 20th Century. Indeed, it was thanks to Rockville Centre's own electric utility that the village escaped the blackout that crippled the Northeast in 1965.

In 1927, the new Sunrise Highway reached Rockville Centre on its way to the Suffolk County line and beyond, and the village's population doubled during that decade. Twenty years later, during Long Island's seminal postwar boom, the Roman Catholic Church decided to split the Brooklyn Diocese in two. The eastern half, serving Nassau and Suffolk Counties, became the Diocese of Rockville Centre in 1956, and St. Agnes Church in the village became the new cathedral.

Where to Find More: "The History of Rockville Centre," by Preston Bassett and Arthur Hodges, Rockville Centre Library.

ROOSEVELT, Continued

before anyone lived in the area. After the colonists came, the stagecoach route from Hempstead to Babylon passed through the area, and in the late 1700s some entrepreneurs tried to take advantage of the potential business by building taverns. Thus, the community got its first name — Rum Point. The more genteel Greenwich Point became the community's name about 1830. In 1902, when a post office was established, residents renamed it in honor of the president of the United States, fellow Nassau County resident Theodore Roosevelt.

Turning Points: The railroad didn't serve Roosevelt, causing its development to lag behind other parts of Nassau. After 1900, however, a trolley line from Jamaica to Freeport passed through Roosevelt, and that spurred the first suburban development. Farms became neighborhoods. Neighborhoods became business districts. The post-World War II building boom affected Roosevelt in much the same way as the rest of central Nassau, but with an important difference. Unlike in Levittown and elsewhere, Roosevelt's developers did not discriminate against blacks. Indeed, they advertised in black publications and neighborhoods, and by 1957 the community was 20 percent black. After a court battle about racial segregation in Roosevelt elementary schools, many white families left in the late

1960s, tipping the racial balance.

Claims to Fame: Basketball great Julius Erving, author David Halberstam, comic Eddie Murphy and radio star Howard Stern all grew up in Roosevelt. From the 1950s, the United Cerebral Palsy Center there was recognized as the foremost treatment center for the disease in the world. Igor Sikorski, founder of the helicopter company that bore his name, built a helicopter in a house on Clinton Avenue in 1923.

Where to Find More: In the Roosevelt file at the Long Island Studies Institute at Hofstra University, Hempstead.

SEAFORD
Eastward Ho! On Sunrise Highway

Beginnings: Indians fished, hunted and lived along the coastal land that became Seaford. For a time there was a Lake Tackapausha in the northwest section of Seaford, named for (but spelled differently) the Rockaway sachem who deeded the Town of Hempstead to the English. Indians may have called the area Ruskatux; Seaford Creek was once Ruskatux Creek and the southern part of the hamlet was known as Ruskatux Neck. One of the first settlers in Hempstead was Capt. John Seaman of Seaford, England. He won a patent for the area and oversaw the start of

Jerusalem South — Seaford's first European name. Other settlers called the area as Seamans Neck. Although villages sprang to life in the 19th Century on the route of the Long Island Rail Road, Jerusalem South initially was unaffected. The hamlet, renamed Seaford in honor of Seaman's hometown in 1868, remained a farming area for more than a century, gaining a post office, a church, a one-room school and a few hundred residents by then — although city residents had discovered it as a summer retreat.

To Market, to Market: Corn and wheat were grown on farms owned by Seaman heirs, while baymen harvested Great South Bay oysters. Fishing and oystering were difficult because of clumps of land lying just beneath the water's surface. So baymen in the mid-1800s invented the Seaford Skiff, a flat-bottom sailboat that did away with the need to row in shallow water. It was used up and down the Eastern Seaboard.

Turning Point: The opening of Sunrise Highway in 1929 provided a stream of settlers that lasted for more than 40 years. From a base of about 1,200 people before the road reached Seaford, the population more than tripled in 25 years. Rural Seaford was obliterated in the postwar baby boom, when the population increased by almost six times in the 20 years after 1960.

Where to Find More: "Seaford, Long Island, N.Y., 1643-1968, 325th Anniversary," "Seaford Long Ago," at the Seaford Public Library.

STEWART MANOR
Pooling Resources To Create a Village

Beginnings: The grassy Hempstead Plains that covered much of modern-day central Nassau include what became Stewart Manor. After Europeans settled Hempstead in the 1640s, they used the plains to graze cattle. During the Revolution, British troops confiscated the cattle and used the plains to raise horses and drill troops. By the mid-1800s, the town-owned plains were seen as useless and were sold to wealthy New York merchant Alexander T. Stewart. He developed Garden City on the plains and sold off most of the rest of the land. As late as the 1920s, long after Garden City had become established, its neighbor to the west was still treeless, barren and largely unoccupied.

Turning Point: The history of Stewart Manor, as its name implies, is bound up with that of Alexander Stewart's Garden City. Realty Associates, a Brooklyn developer, hoped in the 1920s to develop a portion of Garden City, but that village's developer, the Garden City Co., would not sell land to Realty Associates. Realty decided to buy land as close to Garden City as possible, and in 1925 began building and

Please Turn to Page 29

Newsday Photo / Don Jacobsen

ROOSEVELT: Art is the object as women work on free-form sculpture during a State University Cooperative College class at Roosevelt High School in 1971.

Newsday Archive

STEWART MANOR: At first it was Sunrise Gardens, and then Stewart Manor. This 1926 aerial view shows the first housing development. Residents voted to create a village the following year.

Newsday Photo

VALLEY STREAM: A 1972 photo shows a bygone Long Island tradition, taking a date to watch a movie under the stars at the Sunrise Drive-In.

New York State Office of Parks, Recreation and Historic Preservation

WANTAGH: Cars head for Jones Beach on a sunny Fourth of July in 1936.

STEWART MANOR, Continued

selling houses on Jefferson Street and Elton Road. Realty called the new community Sunrise Gardens, and the company promised to build a country club and a pool for residents. Homes sold well, even though Sunrise Gardens had unlighted dirt roads, no stores and no police. But what apparently irritated early residents most was the community's name. They begged Realty to change it, and the company did in 1926 — to Stewart Manor. Residents voted to incorporate as a village in 1927, primarily to avoid being annexed by the adjacent village of New Hyde Park. That same year, the promised country club and pool opened.
Bleak Humor: After the stock market crash of 1929, so many village residents killed themselves that some referred to it as Suicide Manor.
Claim to Fame: Stewart Manor had the first community pool on Long Island, and one of the first in the state.
Where to Find More: "The Golden Anniversary of the Village of Stewart Manor," published in 1977, available at the Lynbrook Public Library.

UNIONDALE

Military Marches Out, Commerce Marches In

Beginnings: Uniondale was long a part of the great Hempstead Plains, the prairie that stretched across what would become central Nassau County and was used as common pasture land after the English arrived in the 1640s. But the portion that became Uniondale has a lengthy military history. It was an enlistment center during the Revolution, an infantry training center during the War of 1812 and a camp during the Civil War, the Spanish-American War and World War I. The establishment of Mitchel Field on its northern edge grew into an Army Air Corps base during World War II and an Air Force base until 1961. The community itself, however, consisted mostly of modest farms for three centuries. It was known first as Turtle Hook, because of the turtles that crawled out of nearby ponds to sun themselves on a bend — or "hook" — in the road between the plains and Roosevelt. In 1853, residents decided Turtle Hook was an "unsuitable" name and changed it to Uniondale. There is no record of why that name was chosen.
Turning Point: Mitchel Field spurred Uniondale's change from a farming community to a suburban one, particularly after World War II. Many members of the military lived in Uniondale when they were based at Mitchel Field, and so did civilians who worked there. (Unlike Levittown and many other postwar suburbs, Uniondale opened its doors to minority residents early, and as a result its population has been more diverse than that of most other Long Island communities.) Mitchel Field's closing in 1961 also contributed to Uniondale's substantial commercial development. Much of Hofstra University, Nassau Community College, the Nassau Veterans Memorial Coliseum and office buildings occupied the site by the 1970s and '80s.
Claim to Fame: In the late 1900s, Long Island's major-league sports were centered in and around Uniondale. The New York Nets played basketball at the Coliseum between 1968 and 1977, and the New York Islanders played hockey there. The New York Jets football team trained at Hofstra.
Where to Find More: The Long Island Studies Institute at Hofstra University.

VALLEY STREAM

The Bicycling Craze Rolled Into Town

Beginnings: Rockaway Indians were Valley Stream's first residents, hunting in the forests alongside the area's several streams. Europeans first used the land for farming, dating to the late 1700s, and several small communities sprang up. There was Hungry Harbor, a settlement of squatters named for the status of its residents, along with Foster's Meadow toward the north and Tigertown to the northeast. The name Valley Stream dates to 1843, when Scottish immigrant Robert Pagan lobbied for a post office. The area remained rural for decades. The planked Merrick Road offered the first easy transportation from the area in 1853.
Turning Points: Construction of the railroad to Far Rockaway in 1869 meant hundreds of passengers had to change trains in Valley Stream, often waiting for hours. Hotels sprang up to serve them, transforming Tigertown into what became known as Rum Junction. The 1890s bicycling craze prompted city residents to seek places for country excursions. Valley Stream was close enough for hundreds of cyclists to visit by train every weekend day, prompting the construction of Etlick's Oval, a cycling track on West Merrick Road. Hotels and bicyclists encouraged the development of a larger business district. In 1922, developer William Gibson began building hundreds of homes to accommodate people who wanted to move out of crowded New York City. Gibson did more than any one person to populate the village, which incorporated in 1925. Later expansion of Sunrise Highway to six lanes accommodated the last building boom in the village.
Crime Wave: In the first recorded instance of crossover crime on Long Island, gamblers facing crackdowns by the newly formed New York City took the train to Valley Stream on Jan. 18, 1898, and set up shop in several local bars.
Claims to Fame: Curtiss Aircraft in Valley Stream operated what was the largest commercial airport on Long Island from 1930 until 1933, when the Depression led to its closure. Green Acres Mall — one of Long Island's first malls — opened on the airport site in 1956. Snapple Beverages got its start in Valley Stream, as did actors-filmmakers Ed Burns and Steve Buscemi, both of whom made movies set in their hometown (Burns' "The Brothers McMullen" and Buscemi's "Trees Lounge").
Where to Find More: "History of Valley Stream," at Waldinger Memorial Library, Valley Stream.

WANTAGH

A Millionaire's Lake Sprang a Leak

Beginnings: Wantagh took its name from the Indian sachem who led two Algonquian groups, the Delawares and the Mohegans. The Indian population declined steadily after European settlers arrived. In 1650, when a boundary was established between Dutch and English territory, the English ended up with the eastern part of what became the Town of Hempstead, including Wantagh. Many Quakers lived in the area and their meetinghouse, built in 1827, remained standing next to a Quaker cemetery at Wantagh Avenue and Twin Lane. Landowners held slaves who played an important role in the development of Wantagh, and after the Revolution many of them continued to live there as freedmen.
Turning Points: In 1867 the Long Island Rail Road extended its tracks through Wantagh, and houses and shops sprouted up around the station. After Sunrise Highway was built in 1929, hotels followed and Wantagh became a resort fishing area. Once the Jones Beach Causeway opened in 1929, the community became a gateway to the popular beach.
Unforgettable Characters: Richard Nixon's dog Checkers is buried at the Bide-A-Wee animal cemetery on Beltagh Avenue. One of Wantagh's more interesting human residents, meanwhile, was developer Edward (Daddy) Browning, a self-made millionaire. In 1921 he purchased about a square mile of land between Jerusalem and Beltagh Avenues with the intention of creating an estate with several islands on a large lake. He hired laborers to clear land and dam up two streams. But the project foundered because no one bothered to seal the bottom of his man-made lake with clay and all the water disappeared. But what really gave Browning notoriety was his 1926 marriage, at the age of 51, to 15-year-old Frances (Peaches) Heenan of Hempstead. The marriage collapsed six months later amid sensationalist headlines.
Where to Find More: "A Short History of Wantagh," at the Wantagh Public Library.

WEST HEMPSTEAD

A Visit From Farmer Washington

Beginnings: West Hempstead, a four-square-mile unincorporated area in the Town of Hempstead, was once a central meeting place for Long Island Indians. Later it was a flourishing farm community when President George Washington, a knowledgeable planter, passed through the area in 1790 and commented on the agricultural techniques. Farmer Joseph Gildersleeve built a house on Hempstead Turnpike in 1794. His farm was later purchased by Hiram K. Bedell, who built a larger house about 1835. The Bedell house has been moved to Nassau County's Old Bethpage Village Restoration.
Turning Points: In the early 1800s Oliver's Eagle Flour Mill in what later became Hempstead Lake State Park was the largest gristmill on Long Island. The Long Island Rail Road built a station on Hempstead Turnpike west of Hempstead Village in 1891 and called it West Hempstead. The railroad provided service to Mineola until 1935, when West Hempstead became a terminal. During the Depression, one-quarter of West Hempstead land went on the auction block.
Brushes With Fame: Aviator Orville Wright lived in West Hempstead in the early 1900s. Winthrop-University Hospital in Mineola, Long Island's first voluntary hospital, had roots in the St. Ann's Health Resort in West Hempstead in the late 1800s.
Where to Find More: Reference material in the Hempstead Public Library and the Long Island Studies Institute, Hofstra University.

WOODMERE

Largest Community In the Five Towns

Beginnings: When the South Side Railroad arrived in the Five Towns area in 1869, Woodmere and its tiny neighbor to the south, the present-day village of Woodsburgh, were one. The depot land was donated by liquor tycoon Samuel Wood, who about this time bought most of the surrounding land in a section known in earlier times as Browers Point, after early settlers. Wood, who had grown up in Rockaway, built two hotels, one the massive Woodsburgh Pavilion, catering to wealthy people. He named his new resort compound Woodsburgh, after his own family. He sold large tracts to New York millionaires to build summer places.
Turning Points: The name Woodsburgh was changed to Woodmere in 1890 to avoid post office conflict with another Woodsburgh upstate. In 1901, 23 years after Wood's death, New York City investor Robert L. Burton bought the 400-acre Wood estate and tore down the hotels and their cottages, which had nearly 600 rooms combined. He began selling land for home lots. In 1909 the Hudson Realty Co. took over from Burton, continuing the shift from resort to wealthy residential enclave. In 1912, the southern portion of what was at that time Woodmere became the Village of Woodsburgh, and retained that name as an incorporated entity. The rest of the section remained Woodmere, an unincorporated part of Hempstead Town.
By the 1990s: Woodmere became the largest community in the Five Towns at 2.6 square miles, and consequently its most populous, with 15,388 residents in 1998. And while the Village of Woodsburgh was strictly residential, Woodmere developed a business district around Broadway.
Where to Find More: "The Story of the Five Towns," compiled by the Writers Program of the federal Works Progress Administration, 1941, and South Shore Record newspaper special section on history of Five Towns, 1976, at Hewlett-Woodmere Public Library, Hewlett.

WOODSBURGH

All Homes, and Fine Ones at That

Beginnings: Samuel Wood, a wealthy, 76-year-old liquor merchant who had grown up in Rockaway, founded this exclusive little Five Towns community that still bears his name. He came from Brooklyn in 1869 and bought several farms around Browers Point in what was then Far Rockaway, Queens. Envisioning his own duchy, Wood built two establishments: the three-story Woodsburgh Pavilion, a grand amalgam of mid-Victorian and French Riviera styling that could accommodate 500 guests, and a smaller, elegant spa called Neptune House. Visiting celebrities included Lillian Russell and Diamond Jim Brady. Wood also gave land for a depot for the new South Side Railroad branch. He named his new community for himself and his three deceased brothers, bachelors (like him) who had left Wood their fortunes.
Turning Point: When Wood died in 1878, the entire property went to Abraham Hewlett, descendant of the area's earliest white settler, George Hewlett. Abraham Hewlett continued it as a fashionable resort. In 1901, the entire community was bought again, by Robert L. Burton, who tore down the hotels and all but one dwelling, turning the land into plots for expensive year-round homes. The village, which was incorporated in 1912, became entirely residential and in the late 1990s had one of Long Island's highest median family incomes ($158,692).
The Last Rockaway: Woodsburgh is the site of a monument to Culluloo Telewana, described as the last of the Rockaway Indians, who died in 1818. The eight-foot granite stone was placed 70 years later, in 1888, by Abraham Hewlett, who as a child knew the Indian.
Where to Find More: The WPA title "The Story of the Five Towns," at the Hewlett-Woodmere Public Library.

Nassau County Museum Collection, Long Island Studies Institute
WEST HEMPSTEAD: Swimmers cool off in Hall's Pond in about 1930.

Tax Rate Will Be Slashed Under New 'Tight' Budget

Long Beach Life

D. A. TO ASK CHAIR FOR MAYOR'S ASSASSIN; WALSH HAS 'FIGHTING CHANCE' TO SURVIVE

MAYOR KEEPS PROMISE AS 20 PT. REDUCTION IS EFFECTED FOR 1940

WAIVES EXAMINATION; INDICTMENT EXPECTED BY GRAND JURY TUESDAY

A Martyr
An Editorial

Victim's House Still Stands At the Scene of a Murder

A Long Beach Police Department photograph taken Nov. 15, 1939, shows the scene at the intersection of what was then Jackson Boulevard and West Beech Street (foreground), following the assassination of Long Beach Mayor Louis F. Edwards by a disgruntled officer, Alvin Dooley.

Edwards had just walked out of his brick and stucco house on West Beech (at right in the photo above) with his driver, James Walsh, when they were accosted by Dooley, who had been stationed in the police booth appearing at left in the photo above. Dooley, a former president of the city's Patrolmen's Benevolent Association, was irked that he had been moved from motorcycle cop to foot patrol. In addition, Walsh had recently defeated Dooley for the PBA presidency, with Edwards' backing.

Pulling out his .38-cal. service revolver, Dooley shot and killed Edwards and seriously wounded Walsh. Dooley then walked over to police headquarters, where he announced that he had shot the mayor. Dooley was tried for murder — Walsh recovered sufficiently to testify — and Dooley was convicted of second-degree manslaughter. He served 15 years in prison for the crime. He was later arrested for child molestation and died in prison.

After the shooting, Jackson Boulevard was renamed Edwards Boulevard. The police booth was demolished in the 1940s, but the house remained.

IT HAPPENED HERE

Top, Long Beach Police Department Photo; Above, Newsday Photo / Bill Davis, 1998

The police photo shows the Long Beach intersection at Jackson Boulevard and West Beech Street where Long Beach Mayor Louis F. Edwards was shot in 1939 by a disgruntled police officer, Alvin Dooley. The shooting took place in front of Edwards' house — at right in the top photo, and as it appears in the photo above. Edwards died in a police car on the way to the hospital. Local newspapers trumpeted the shocking story of the assassination.

City of Long Beach

Riding the waves of a colorful history

BY BILL BLEYER
STAFF WRITER

A mayor assassinated by a cop assigned to protect him. Political scandals. Celebrity residents like Bogie and Cagney. And a boardwalk construction project hyped with a parade of elephants.

To call the history of Long Beach colorful doesn't quite do it justice.

The story starts out conventionally enough with Rockaway Indians spending summers hunting, fishing and whaling on the island. After the Indians sold the area to colonists in 1643, the barrier island was used by baymen and farmers for fishing and harvesting salt hay. But no one lived there year-round for more than two centuries — not until Congress established a lifesaving station in 1849. A dozen years before, 62 people died when the barque Mexico carrying Irish immigrants to New York ran ashore on New Year's Day.

The first attempt to develop the island as a resort was organized by Austin Corbin, builder of the shorefront Oriental Hotel in Brooklyn. He formed a partnership with the Long Island Rail Road to finance the New York and Long Beach Railroad Co.

It laid track from present-day Lynbrook to Long Beach and the first passenger train ran on May 31, 1880. By July, the company had opened the 1,100-foot-long Long Beach Hotel, at the time the largest in the world. The railroad brought 300,000 visitors the first season. By the next spring, tracks had been laid the length of the island, but after repeated winter washouts they were removed in 1894.

Corbin's development scheme ultimately failed, as did two successive efforts. In 1906, along came William Reynolds, a 39-year-old former state senator who developed four Brooklyn neighborhoods — Bedford-Stuyvesant, Borough Park, Bensonhurst and South Brownsville — as well as Coney Island's Dreamland, the world's largest amusement park. Reynolds, who also owned a theater and produced plays, gathered investors and acquired the oceanfront from its private owners and the rest of the island from the Town of Hempstead in 1907 so he could build a boardwalk, homes and hotels.

Reynolds had a herd of elephants march in from Dreamland, ostensibly to help build the boardwalk, but in reality just to publicize it. Dredges created a channel 1,000 feet wide on the north side of the island so Reynolds could bring in large steamboats and even seaplanes to carry more visitors. The new waterway was named, naturally, Reynolds Channel.

To ensure that Long Beach lived up to Reynolds' billing as The Riviera of the East, he required every building to be constructed in an "eclectic Mediterranean style" with white stucco walls and red tile roofs. And they could be occupied only by white Anglo-Saxon Protestants. After Reynolds' corporation went bankrupt in 1918, these restrictions were lifted and Long Beach became a melting pot filled by immigrants from overseas.

The new town attracted wealthy businessmen and entertainers. Before Reynolds' bankruptcy, he built a theater called Castles by the Sea with the largest dance floor in the world for dancers Vernon and

Long Beach Historical and Preservation Society

Elephants put in an appearance at the boardwalk in Long Beach in about 1907. They were marched in by the flamboyant entrepreneur William Reynolds, ostensibly to help construct the boardwalk, but in reality to generate publicity.

Irene Castle. (It burned down in the 1930s.) In the '40s, Jose Ferrer, Zero Mostel, Mae West and other famous actors performed at local theaters. And Jack Dempsey, Cab Calloway, Humphrey Bogart, James Cagney and John Barrymore lived in Long Beach decades before anyone heard of Long Beach's famous modern-day native, Billy Crystal.

Long Beach's most colorful period was the Roaring Twenties. The city became a center for rum-running, which was orchestrated by Police Commissioner Moe Grossman, according to historians. "Residents reported stories of areas on the beach being roped off when cases of illegal booze were to be landed," according to former city historian Edward Graff. "The signal as to whether it would be 'safe' to land allegedly was the light in the clock tower of the old city hall."

In 1923 the world-famous Prohibition agents known as Izzy and Moe raided the Nassau Hotel and arrested three men for bootlegging. In 1930, five city police officers were charged with offering a bribe to a Coast Guard officer to allow liquor to be landed. The police had another problem a year later: a mystery that captivated the nation in the summer of 1931. A beachcomber found the body of a beautiful young woman named Starr Faithfull. She had left behind a suicide note, but others believed she had been murdered.

By this point, official corruption had become almost a regular feature of life in Long Beach. In 1922, the state Legislature designated Long Beach a city and Reynolds was elected the first mayor. He was promptly indicted on charges of misappropriating funds. When he was found guilty, the clock in the tower at city hall was stopped in protest. When a judge released Reynolds from jail later that year on appeal, almost the entire population turned out to greet him. And the clock was turned back on.

Reynolds' problems were minor compared to those of Mayor Louis F. Edwards. As Edwards was leaving his home in 1939, patrolman Alvin Dooley, who had been assigned to the booth in front of the mayor's house, fatally shot him and seriously wounded his driver and bodyguard, patrolman James Walsh. Edwards had taken away Dooley's motorcycle and backed Walsh over Dooley in an election for PBA president. Dooley spent 15 years in prison.

Long Beach's heyday as a resort ended because of cheap air travel and the advent of air conditioning, city historian Roberta Fiore said. "With air conditioning, people didn't have to escape the city in the summertime and the airplane got them farther away faster," she said.

By the 1960s and '70s, "Long Beach got very depressed," said Alexandra Karafinas, head of the Long Beach Historical Society. "The hotels had mental patients in them and welfare recipients. The property values were way down. There were some race riots here."

Urban renewal began in the late 1970s and the city sported new housing, a new shopping center on Park Avenue and other improvements. "The renaissance took place in the early '80s," Fiore said. "For example, the Grenada Towers was closed in 1975 by court order because it was deemed uninhabitable. In 1980 it was not only reopened as a condominium but it was placed on the National Register of Historic Places."

Where to Find More: Long Beach Historical and Preservation Society.

Long Beach Historical and Preservation Society

A poster advertises the sale in 1919 of 1,031 lots, averaging about $785 apiece, and 50 bungalows. With an arrow, it points out that Long Beach is just 23 miles from Manhattan.

Town of North Hempstead

In September, 1775, almost a year before the future nation declared its independence from George III, the people of Great Neck, Cow Neck and other areas north of Old Country Road signed their own Declaration of Independence.

The signers, passionate Patriots, declared their independence from the Town of Hempstead, which, in their opinion, had the bad habit of pledging allegiance to the king. Therefore, the northern necks declared themselves "an entire separate and independent beat or district." The "beat" would officially become the Town of North Hempstead in 1784.

During the Revolution, the northern Patriots had their own militia headed by Capt. John Sands of Cow Neck (later Port Washington), which invaded South Hempstead in search of arms. The rift caused a north-south animosity that would take years to heal.

The first North Hempstead Town Board, headed by Patriot Adrian Onderdonk, had to cope with an impoverished area, devastated by an avenging British occupation. The councilmen met in Roslyn taverns and didn't get a permanent home until 1907, when the present town hall opened in Manhasset.

In the meantime, steamboat service from Manhattan began in 1836, and the Long Island Rail Road inched eastward, bringing a commuter population, including the rich and powerful whose mansions monopolized the waterfront and the inland "horse country." Determined to protect their rights and resources, they incorporated as villages with the power to set zoning restrictions. North Hempstead eventually became a town of villages — 30 of them, more than in any other town on Long Island (and only one fewer than in all of Suffolk County). "The smaller the unit of government the more you are heard," explained town historian Joan G. Kent. In 1936, a revised county charter denied zoning power to future villages.

By the late 1920s the Gold Coast era had begun to ebb; the great estates were sold to developers and the beach resorts became year-round communities. The trend was accelerated with the building boom that followed World War II.

ALBERTSON
Developments Grew On Former Farmland

Beginnings: Albertson sits just north of the great Hempstead Plains, and like the prairie itself, was first cultivated as farmland by early European settlers in the 1640s. John Seren, a member of the initial group of settlers to come from Connecticut in 1644, settled there first. His name, after a spelling change, is the source of the neighboring community of Searingtown. In the second group of settlers, this time from Virginia, was a man named Townsend Albertson. He ran a farm and a gristmill, leading it to be named Albertson Square. The community remained stubbornly rural for three centuries. Indeed, in

East Williston Village Historian
EAST WILLISTON: An artist's view of the Willis Lake Stock Farm in the 1890s

1850, when a road was cut through Isaac Underhill Willets' farm to Old Westbury, he protested that "Long Island has more roads now than it will ever need." The road, I.U. Willets Road, was named in his honor. When the Long Island Rail Road built a branch to Glen Cove in 1864, it named the local station Albertson, and that designation stuck for the community.

Turning Points: Builder William J. Levitt bought acres of Albertson farmland in 1946 and covered them with mass-produced houses — one of several communities in which he perfected the method that he would use to build Levittown the following year. Other developers quickly bought the remaining farmland and in less than two decades none was left. By the mid-1960s, Albertson was as well developed as any of the older suburbs in Nassau County.

Claims to Fame: The oldest Methodist church in Nassau-Suffolk, on the Albertson-Searington border, was built in 1788 by Jacob Searing, a descendant of John Seren. The National Center for Disability Services, a major school and source of employment for severely handicapped people, located its offices in Albertson.

Where to Find More: In the Albertson file at the Long Island Studies Institute at Hofstra University, Hempstead.

CARLE PLACE
The Prototype For Levittown

Beginnings: Carle Place, like the rest of modern-day central Nassau County, existed initially as a fragment of the Hempstead Plains. The prairie was viewed as largely worthless by the English settlers of 1644. One of those settlers was Capt. Thomas Carle, who purchased land in the area in 1656. He and his neighbors turned cattle and sheep loose on the plains to graze and thought little else of it. Not until 100 years later did farmers realize the land could be cultivated. One of Carle's descendants, Silas Carle, had become a successful pharmaceuticals merchant in New York City. Some time after 1800, he returned to Long Island to build a showy house on 220 acres for his family. Indeed, it became a local landmark, referred to by residents as "the Carle

place," a name that eventually came to be applied to the community that developed around it, replacing the name Frog Hollow.

Farm Country: For decades, the Carle place was one of the few homes in an area dominated by small farms, most of which were run by Polish, German and Irish immigrants. Although the Long Island Rail Road ran right through Carle Place since the 1830s, it wasn't until 1923 that the hamlet warranted a station. Indeed, it had gained a post office only in 1916, making the name Carle Place official.

Turning Point: In 1946, developer William J. Levitt bought 19 acres for an experiment. His crews brought precut lumber to the site and rapidly assembled 600 low-cost houses. The population swelled by five times in five years. It transformed Carle Place, and served as the prototype for the gargantuan development Levitt began the following year a few miles away: Levittown. Before long, the last potato farms in Carle Place were developed as well.

Brush With Fame: Guitar virtuosos Joe Satriani and Steve Vai grew up in Carle Place. Vai took lessons from Satriani there.

Where to Find More: In the Carle Place files at the Long Island Studies Institute at Hofstra University, Hempstead.

EAST HILLS
Leading Family Saved By Irving Berlin

Beginnings: Did George Washington visit East Hills? No one knows for sure, but the Father of Our Country is believed to have inspected the Onderdonk Paper Mill in Roslyn on his 1790 tour of Long Island, and from there he could have walked or ridden 100 yards to the future East Hills. What is known is that East Hills was part of the vast land purchase — including the Towns of Hempstead and North Hempstead — made by the Rev. Robert Fordham and John Carman after they crossed Long Island Sound from Stamford, Conn., in 1643. The first mention of an East Hills connection appears in 1661 records of "a path alongside Harbour Hill," now Harbor Hill Road.

Turning Points: In the late 1800s, East Hills became the home of a few wealthy families. Grandest was the Harbor Hill mansion of the Clarence Mackay family, designed by famed architect Stanford White and finished in 1902. Here in 1924, the Mackays entertained the prince of Wales (later, briefly, Edward VIII) and Charles A. Lindbergh after his solo flight to France in 1927. The mansion was demolished in 1947 to make way for the Country Estates development. The Mackays lost their fortune and had to be bailed out by their spurned son-in-law, songwriter Irving Berlin. The East Hills polo field became Fairfield Park.

New Beginnings: East Hills was incorporated in 1931 with a population of 269 in 65 homes. Robert H. Willets, an eighth-generation resident, was elected the first mayor of the village, which was then 98 percent farm or estate, 2 percent homes. By the '90s the percentage was reversed: 98 percent residential, less than 2 percent undeveloped land. One other statistic of note: While some 6,674 village residents lived within the borders of the Town of North Hempstead in 1998, a tiny piece of the village lies in the Town of Oyster Bay. How tiny? In '98, just 18 East Hillers were residents of Oyster Bay.

Where to Find More: Village history brochure available in Village Hall.

EAST WILLISTON
Making Windmills, Bricks, Carriages

Beginnings: The gently rolling land that became East Williston was located on the northern edge of the vast Hempstead Plains. Indeed, for about 200 years, the area was known simply as the North Side. One of the first settlers on the North Side was Englishman Henry Willis, who bought a farm in 1675 from John Seaman, himself one of the original settlers on Long Island's South Shore. The Willis family grew to substantial size over the years, and convinced relatives from England to immigrate as well. By the mid-1800s, the several hundred acres on both sides of Willis Avenue had acquired the name of Williston.

Turning Point: The building of the railroad from Mineola to Glen Cove in 1865 made Williston accessible to New York, Jamaica and Brooklyn. The railroad stimulated industrial development, particularly manufacturers of bricks, windmills and carriages. Other tradesmen followed, and a small community formed around the business district. The establishment of a post office in 1879 forced Williston to change its name, for there already was a Williston in upstate Erie County. Residents decided upon East Williston. The village was incorporated in 1926. Population grew slowly — except for a mild burst in the 1950s — and then steadily to 2,477 by 1998.

Claim to Fame: The Corvette of the horse-drawn carriage era was designed and built in East Williston by Henry M. Willis. By 1888, he was selling the two-wheeled, two-seat East Williston Runabout Road Cart. His ads said it was "acknowledged by hundreds to be a little ahead of anything in the Cart Line ever put upon the Market." It was no idle boast. The sleek road cart sported a supple suspension, allowing it to float over the rutted roads of the time. But the body also could be locked to the axle, allowing the cart to be raced on a track. More than 1,000 carts were built at the Oakley and Griffin factory in East Williston, which bought Willis' business in 1889.

Brush With Fame: Comedian Carol Leifer grew up in East Williston.

Where to Find More: "East Williston History 1663-1970," by Nicholas Meyer and Cyril Lewis, available at the East Williston Public Library.

NASSAU

Levittown? No, East Hills

After this photo of an unidentified housing development was published in Newsday as a "History Mystery" in 1998, several readers were quick to identify it as the Strathmore section of East Hills in the Town of North Hempstead. The homes were built by Levitt & Sons around 1947 and originally cost in the mid-teens.

One of the readers who recognized the development was Robert Kramer, an oral and maxillofacial surgeon who lived in the area from 1977 to 1982. "I used to run those streets all the time," he recalled. "I said: 'Hey, wait a minute, this looks familiar.'"

In the top photo, an aerial view looking toward the southeast, the road in the center that curves near the top is Village Road; at the extreme lower left is Salem Road. Below is a photo of the area in 1998.

According to Kramer, the homes originally were available in four basic models, which many owners have expanded over the years. In late 1998, homes typically fetched $450,000 to $600,000, said Emmett Laffey of Century 21 Laffey Associates, a real estate agent.

Top, Newsday Photo; Above, Newsday Photo / Ken Sawchuck, 1998

GREAT NECK: A postcard from about 1910 depicts All Saints Church.

All Saints Church, Great Neck, N. Y.

GREAT NECK: Artist Frances Flora Palmer drew this pastoral scene at the foot of Spinney Hill for Curier & Ives in 1857.

GREAT NECK

A Jewel in a Gold Coast Setting

BY ANDREW SMITH
STAFF WRITER

Great Neck was prime real estate for centuries, long before theater stars, captains of industry and well-to-do commuting suburbanites made it the western anchor of the Gold Coast.

The Great Neck peninsula was surrounded by water rich in oysters, crabs, clams and many types of fish, and the land was thick with rabbits, beavers, foxes and other animals useful both for their fur and their meat. The Matinecock Indians alternately called it Menhaden-Ock, which may be translated as "place of fish," or Wallage. When Europeans arrived in the 1640s, the name Menhaden-Ock evolved into Madnan's Neck. Some attributed the mangled name to Anne Heatherton, an English woman of uncertain sanity who tried to claim possession of the peninsula in 1640 before the Dutch chased her out. In any event, by 1670 the name Great Neck (compared to Little Neck just to the west) was in use, and during the next century it supplanted Madnan's Neck as the name for the peninsula.

Indians co-existed peacefully in the area for several decades, although the Rockaway sachem Tackapousha protested well into the 1680s that the Indians were undercompensated for Madnan's Neck and Cow Neck, the peninsula to the east that became Port Washington. English settlers appointed a committee in 1684 to settle the issue, although it is unclear whether they satisfied the Indians or merely ignored the issue until smallpox had decimated the native population.

Seventeenth Century settlers initially used Great Neck as a giant cattle pen. With water on three sides, a fence along the southern end kept cows well confined. Soon, families began acquiring land on the peninsula for farming. By 1681, there were enough farmers to form a viable political bloc, sometimes supporting different candidates in elections than the rest of what was then Hempstead Town. Halfhearted moves to secede from Hempstead flared up periodically.

Gristmills were built, furthering development. The Saddle Rock Grist Mill, run for many years by Henry Allen, dates to 1702. Sawmills and clothing mills also operated on the peninsula.

As the Revolution neared, Great Neck and Cow Neck were two of the colonies' most fervently anti-British communities. Indeed, in early 1776 they formed an association and wrote a loyalty oath — the first in America — that any newcomer had to swear to. Like the rest of Long Island, Great Neck suffered during the long British occupation.

After the war, Great Neck became part of the new Town of North Hempstead and the focus returned to agriculture. Great Neck farms supplied much of the New York area. The boat landing at the Grist Mill saw a steady stream of produce headed for the city, and an equally steady stream in return of manufactured goods — as well as manure scooped from city streets, to be used as fertilizer on Great Neck farms. As farmers prospered, businesses such as blacksmiths and carriage makers set up shop in the area.

The landing soon saw steamboat service, which became popular with commuting tycoons after wealthy industrialists started buying up farms for estates in the 1870s. William R. Grace, a wealthy trader who served as mayor of New York in the 1880s, built a 200-acre estate in Great Neck and some of the area's shopping districts. He named one of them Thomaston, after the town in Maine where his wife was born.

Grace was also somewhat responsible for the start of what became Great Neck's substantial Jewish population. He brought his tailor, Avram Wolf, to Great Neck to live. One of Wolf's sons, I.G., became a major real estate salesman in Great Neck, later making Jews feel welcome in Great Neck. Temple Beth El was the first synagogue in Great Neck, built in 1929.

As the 20th Century dawned, other well-known estate owners included oil tycoon Harry Sinclair and hotel executive Ellsworth Statler. The chairmen of two auto giants, Alfred P. Sloan of General Motors and Chrysler Motors founder Walter P. Chrysler, lived in mansions in Kings Point. William K. Vanderbilt II, who had an estate in nearby Lake Success, was a proud member of the Vigilant Fire Co., often pitching in to fight fires.

In addition, the glamor of Great Neck attracted many Broadway actors, musicians, artists and film stars of the day. The result was a society scene famously immortalized by F. Scott Fitzgerald in "The Great Gatsby," which he wrote in Great Neck Estates.

In the early part of this century, the rich and less-rich alike were protective of Great Neck's quiet character. They were leery of what they perceived as weak North Hempstead town zoning and building laws, so a succession of villages was incorporated across the peninsula. Great Neck Estates and Saddle Rock were first, in 1911. Kensington was next, in 1917. Kings Point and Great Neck followed in 1922. Lake Success formed in 1927, Great Neck Plaza in 1930 and Thomaston in 1931. Russell Gardens was the last village incorporated, in 1931.

The Depression brought much of the high times to an end. Many of the estates were subdivided. Apartments and commercial development, particularly on Middle Neck Road in Great Neck Plaza, led to persistent traffic problems. That, in turn, led to the village becoming the first on Long Island to install parking meters, in 1946. The density and ethnic diversity that characterized much of Great Neck since the early 1960s gave the area a more lively, more cosmopolitan aspect than much of the rest of Long Island.

Where to Find More: "This Is Great Neck," by Roberta Pincus; "The Book of Great Neck," by Gil and Devah Spear, published in 1936, and other material available at the Great Neck Public Library.

Nassau County Museum Collection, Long Island Studies Institute
Students at Great Neck School, about 1900

FLORAL PARK

See story on Page 13.

FLOWER HILL

From Forest to Farms, A Village of Growth

Beginnings: The village, which one day would occupy parts of Manhasset, Roslyn and Port Washington, was farms and pastures in the 1600s, thanks to hardy pioneers who cleared away forest and brush. The early settlers — Hewletts, Kissams, Loves and Motts — operated farms so large and productive that the sons of one farm family, the Hewlett brothers, had their own canning factory, the largest in the Town of North Hempstead by the late 1800s, each season shipping 200,000 cans of fruits and vegetables and 150 barrels of ketchup. Only three of the early farmhouses remain. One of them, the Sands-Willets House, later the headquarters of the Cow Neck Peninsula Historical Society, was part of the inland farm of the Sands family (who also owned Sands

Point). The farms extended to Manhasset Bay on the west and to Hempstead Harbor on the east.

The Name: Who knows? This was the conclusion of the late local historian Milton Hopkins, who discounted the theory that the name was based on the abundance of wildflowers in the meadows, since, he said, a large part of Flower Hill was not meadow but forest. "Flower Hill is an old name, appearing in the oldest documents found and we had best leave it at that," concluded Hopkins.

The Hospital: The Hewlett farm was purchased in 1900 by Carlos Munson, a Cuban-born Quaker and owner of the Munson Steamship Co. He acquired a neighboring home and 15 acres, which he donated to the Sisters of the Franciscan Missionaries of Mary in 1922, for use as a summer camp for city children. By 1936 the sisters were caring for children suffering from rheumatic fever, in the Munson carriage house converted into a sanatorium. It later was expanded to St. Francis Hospital, the second-largest cardiac center in the country in the 1990s.

Where to Find More: "Manhasset, the First 300 Years," in the Manhasset Library.

GREENVALE

Cattle Traders Stopped to Socialize

Beginnings: Beneath the quiet facade of the tiny, unincorporated community of Greenvale lies a sometimes exciting, though hazy, past. In the years before the Civil War, Greenvale went by the name Bull's Head, for the hotel-tavern that stood at the present-day Northern Boulevard and Glen Cove Road. Cattle traders on their way to New York City stopped at the tavern to socialize. Some reports tell of a dangerous crossroads described as an eastern Dodge City where shootings were common, though very little proof of Greenvale's history is available except for second-hand accounts from old-time residents. Wishing to dissociate from the tavern, residents moved to change their community's name. Beer's Map of 1873 shows the first trace of Greenvale, listing a post office a mile from where Greenvale stood years later. The Long Island Rail Road from 1885 listed Green Vale as a stop.

Turning Point: The late 1800s marked the establishment of a viable community, straddling the North Hempstead-Oyster Bay town lines and

with an economy centered around agriculture. With the 1900s came wealthy landowners who bought farms from original settlers and created extravagant rural homes. Italian and Polish laborers came in droves to build these palaces and to work the land. Many inhabitants of Greenvale today are descendants of these working-class pioneers. The first years of the new century saw Greenvale attract a small, but notable number of commercial establishments including two plant nurseries, Wheatley Gardens (1909) and Lewis & Valentine Nurseries (1914), and later, a famous landscape architectural firm, Innocenti and Webel (1931), which designed landscapes for the DuPonts, Fords, Rockefellers and Astors, among others. Greenvale roads also served as thoroughfares for the Vanderbilt Cup racers in the early 20th Century.

Claim to Claim to Fame: Greenvale is a college town — sort of. The C.W. Post Campus of Long Island University opened in 1954 on Northern Boulevard and for 40 years used a Greenvale mailing address. But because most of the campus was in neighboring Brookville, the college used that postal designation.

Where to Find More: Reference material in the Bryant Room of the Bryant Library, Roslyn.

KINGS POINT

Twenties Galas, Portrayed in 'Gatsby'

Beginnings: It was through unlucky circumstances that former New York Gov. John Alsop King first built on the land that was later called Kings Point. In the mid-1800s, after King and a relative inherited a strip of land north of Great Neck, a coin toss decided who would get the fertile farmland to the east and who would be stuck with the rocky shoreline and woods. King, who was also a congressman and a founder of the Republican Party, lost. He built a home on the craggy shore overlooking Long Island Sound — now among the most expensive real estate on Long Island. Kings Point became part of a loose group of associations that included Elm Point, Grenwolde, East Shore and Gracefield.

Turning Point: In 1924 Kings Point and the surrounding areas were incorporated as one village by residents concerned about preserving its rural charm and individuality. Some of the key people in the move to incorporate were driven by environmental conservation issues, ideals well ahead of the time. The village became a model of the Roaring Twenties on Long Island's Gold Coast, with wild jazz parties thrown by such glamorous residents as Wall Street titan Jesse Livermore, store owner Henri Bendel and car manufacturer Alfred P. Sloan, among others. Such lavish events set the stage for F. Scott Fitzgerald's novel, "The Great Gatsby," in which Kings Point was portrayed as West Egg.

The Academy: In 1942 the federal government established the U.S. Merchant Marine Academy on a Kings Point estate purchased from auto manufacturer Walter P. Chrysler. His 35-room marble mansion became the administration hall. The academy was the only military institution from which undergraduate cadets served in World War II. More than 260 cadets gave their lives.

Fame and Fortune: Besides Sloan, Chrysler and Livermore, Kings Point has been the home of mansions belonging to actor and playwright George M. Cohan, electric energy pioneer William S. Barstow and copper mogul Arthur S. Dwight.

Where to Find More: "This Is Great Neck," published by the League of Women Voters of Great Neck, at the Great Neck Public Library.

LAKE SUCCESS

A Reluctant Host To the United Nations

Beginnings: Remembered for housing the United Nations after World War II, Lake Success is part of the remnants of the last glacier of the Ice Age. One of the largest "kettle-hole" lakes on Long Island, it abounded with rumors of an underground channel to Long Island Sound, though geologists dispelled that myth in the mid-19th Century. The Matinecocks, early inhabitants, called the lake Sucut after one of their chiefs, from which Dutch settlers derived the present name.

Turning Points: The area once known as Lakeville was populated by Dutch settlers in the early 1600s and by English immigrants in 1644. In 1790 Queens County Sheriff Uriah Mitchell transported yellow perch from Lake Ronkonkoma to Lake Success in one of the first experiments to stock Long Island lakes with fish. In the late 19th Century, millionaire William K. Vanderbilt II bought $250,000 worth of land around Lake Success for his summer home. The area became a blooming summer resort, so much so that in 1926, residents incorporated as a village to create laws to discourage unwanted tourists. World War II

Please Turn to Page 39

MANHASSET

Home of Wealth and Power

BY RHODA AMON
STAFF WRITER

Neither town nor village, Manhasset is four square miles of suburbia. It contains three villages and parts of three others, and shares a peninsula with Port Washington. Once considered an ideal cow pasture, it has been home to some of the nation's richest and most powerful people.

The Matinecocks, who had a village on Manhasset Bay, made wampum from oyster shells, which they prized more than real estate because land was plentiful. Eventually, they lost it all. The Dutch West India Co. claimed it in 1623 and drove off the first English settlers in 1640. Three years later, however, the peninsula was gobbled up by English colonists in a purchase that extended all the way to Long Island's South Shore.

By 1659 there were 309 cows grazing on the peninsula known as Cow Neck. The settlers closed off the area with a five-mile fence, and each farmer could graze as many cows as the number of "gattes," or fence sections he had built. When the fence came down in 1677, the pasturage was divided among the settlers. The Manhasset area became Little Cow Neck. North of it was Upper Cow Neck, later Port Washington.

One of the largest landowners was Matthias Nicoll, who was elected mayor of New York in 1674 and speaker of the Colonial Assembly in 1683. Nicoll's son William commissioned shipwright Joseph Latham to build a gristmill on the Nicoll property, later Plandome Manor. The 1693 Plandome Mill, which remained in service until 1908, later became a private residence.

For most of the 18th Century, Dutch and English families — Onderdonks, Mitchells, Hewletts, Schencks — operated large farms. The Schencks owned all of present-day Munsey Park and a large part of Strathmore-Vanderbilt and North Hills.

Little Cow Neck, like most of the northern necks, was committed to independence during the Revolution and suffered heavy damage during a seven-year British occupation. British forces burned the 1719 Quaker Meeting House, seized the Plandome Mill, and damaged houses, barns and churches.

Manhasset, gradually recovering, adopted its present name in 1840, a derivation of the Indian term Manhansett, which means "island neighborhood." It was still dairy country but with a burgeoning oyster industry. Community life changed with the coming of the Long Island Rail Road in 1898. Wealthy New Yorkers eyed Manhasset's lush countryside for country homes close to their offices. Estate owner Mary Travers donated land for a Manhasset railroad station if the LIRR agreed to provide one train a day in both directions — or else pay for the land.

Meanwhile, commerce was developing along North Hempstead Turnpike (later Northern Boulevard), particularly in the area called Spinney Hill, where the road from Great Neck climbs steeply. The area known as

Manhasset Valley developed as a business center with five blacksmiths, wheelwrights, hotels and restaurants. The upscale Jaffe's Department Store opened in 1903. The less affluent also settled in the Manhasset Valley-Spinney Hill area, including Polish and Italian families and later black families from the South, recruited to work on the big estates.

North Hempstead Town, which had been created in 1784, opened a town hall on Plandome Road in 1907, making Manhasset the town seat. But, as in other parts of the town, village fever spread across Manhasset. Plandome Village was the first to incorporate in 1911, on 90 acres originally developed by the Plandome Land Co. and later expanded as an upscale community. Then came the Great Sewer Revolt of 1929, which followed the creation of the Manhasset Sewer District. Residents of Plandome Heights, Plandome Manor and Munsey Park voted to incorporate rather than pay taxes for sewers they didn't want. (Histories of Flower Hill and North Hills, two other villages partly in Manhasset and incorporated about the same time, are featured elsewhere in this volume.)

Plandome Heights was built on property once owned by Bloodgood Haviland Cutter, who was called the "Long Island farmer poet." He died in 1906, leaving his land to the American Bible Society. One portion became a sand-mining operation, while the "heights" was purchased in 1909 by Benjamin Duke, a founder of the American Tobacco Co., who envisioned a colony of tobacco executives rivaling Tuxedo Park. Duke died in 1929, the year Plandome Heights incorporated, his plan unrealized.

Newsday Photo

An old schoolhouse in the area known as Manhasset Valley as it looked in 1970; it has since been moved to the Old Bethpage Village Restoration.

Munsey Park's roots go back to conservative newspaper publisher Frank A. Munsey. After purchasing the Louis Sherry mansion (later the Strathmore-Vanderbilt Country Club) in 1922, Munsey amassed 663 acres that he willed in 1925 to the Metropolitan Museum of Art in Manhattan. A model community was developed on the Munsey property, with all the houses authentic American Colonial reproductions and the streets named for American artists.

Plandome Manor, a half-square-mile village, includes within its boundaries the Plandome railroad station, a post office, golf course, beaches, pond and the Science Museum of Long Island. Its history dates to the 17th-Century Nicolls who originated the name Plandome, from the Latin for "pleasant" or "peaceful home."

Among the best-known residents of the Manhasset area were industrialists Warner M. Leeds, known as the Tin-Plate King, who gave his name to Leeds Pond; socialite Payne Whitney, and Leroy Grumman, founder of the Grumman Aircraft Corp. But perhaps the most famous of all was Manhasset High School athlete Jim Brown, one of the greatest fullbacks in National Football League history.

Where to Find More: "Manhasset the First 300 Years," at the Manhasset Library.

Newsday Photo, 1974 / Stan Wolfson
KINGS POINT: Nancy Wagner is one of the Merchant Marine Academy's first female students.

Fullerton Collection, Suffolk County Historical Society
LAKE SUCCESS: In this undated photo, a well in the community provides a sunny resting spot.

Newsday Photo
NEAR LAKE SUCCESS: Builder Richard Silbert points out construction work on the Long Island Expressway to Ed McGinnes, an engineer for the State Department of Public Works, in 1958.

Nassau County Museum Collection, Long Island Studies Institute

NEW HYDE PARK: A favorite watering hole in 1946 was Rudy's Nassau Inn, owned and operated by Rudy Holst.

Nassau County Museum Collection, Long Island Studies Institute

MINEOLA: Horse-drawn dairy wagons get ready for their daily run in 1915 in a community that by 1900 had become a center of activity on Long Island.

MINEOLA

First Farmers, Then Lawyers

BY RHODA AMON
STAFF WRITER

Midway between the North and South Shore villages of western Long Island stretched a vast prairie called the Hempstead Plains. The area was populated mostly by farmers until 1787, when the opening of the Queens County Courthouse — Nassau was then part of Queens — brought a bumper crop of lawyers to what was then called Clowesville. In 1997, 1,353 lawyers listed their business address in Mineola, the seat of Nassau County government, law and politics.

But it was newfangled transportation — planes and cars in the early 20th Century — that was Mineola's greatest claim to fame.

Mineola first became a hub in the 1830s when the Long Island Rail Road built a track from Jamaica to Hicksville with stops in Brushville (later Queens Village) and at the Clowesville courthouse. In 1839 the railroad extended a line from Hempstead Village to the main branch. The little village at the junction became known as Hempstead Branch.

One train a day with a wood-burning engine called Fred ran between the Branch and Hempstead. The fare was 42 cents. Passengers, it was said, "marveled at the complete desolation of the area from the two stops on the plains," according to historian Thomas Barrick in "Mineola: Heartbeat of Nassau."

Actually, it was not that desolate. It was rich farmland where corn, potatoes, cattle, sheep and poultry produced considerable wealth. But by the mid-1800s, the percentage of farmers was dwindling. By 1844 the Branch had its own post office called Mineola. The first postmaster reportedly picked the name of an Indian chief who led an uprising in Nebraska. He liked the musical sound of it.

The name, officially adopted in 1858, became known nationwide in the early 1900s, as daring young aviators made pioneer flights from the Mineola fields, staking Long Island's claim to being "the cradle of aviation." Glenn Curtiss came in 1909 with the Golden Flyer, which he kept in a tent next to the Gold Bug Hotel on Old Country Road. Leather-helmeted fliers hung out at the Gold Bug, nicknamed Aeronautical Headquarters. Crowds watched Curtiss take off in his boxlike craft every morning. More of the curious turned out to watch a young flier named Charles Lindbergh take off on his historic flight to Paris in 1927 from the adjacent Roosevelt Field. Local aviation buffs always counted this a Mineola "first."

It was not the only first out of Mineola. The first coal used as fuel on Long Island was burned at the home of John J. Armstrong, who was county judge

until 1877. That was the year when the "Old Brig" courthouse was vacated after 90 years of housing law-breakers. The county court moved from Mineola to Long Island City. But Mineola was not court-less for long. When Queens County joined New York City in the big consolidation of 1898, Nassau seceded, and Mineola became the new county seat.

By that time, it was a bustling community. The Meadow Brook Hunt Club still chased the fox through eastern Mineola, but many of the large farms were breaking up into small building lots. The Mineola Park Co., an 1890s developer, offered 25-by-100-foot lots at $50 and up (one dollar weekly without interest), in a community described somewhat inaccurately in the company ads as "a few minutes ride by the Long Island Rail Road from 34th St., N.Y." No matter how small, nearly every house was surrounded by a white picket fence.

The village was incorporated in 1906. It already had a volunteer fire department, started in 1888, and a police force since 1899. Auto racing was a popular sport and drivers vied for a chance to compete in the Vanderbilt Cup Races, started in 1904 by William K. Vanderbilt II, with a triangular course that skirted Mineola on Jericho Turnpike, and began and ended at a point west of Jericho. "Between planes with their sputtering kerosene engines in the sky, and unwieldy cars rumbling on tracks and roads, people were asking, 'What is the world coming to?'" noted the Mineola Diamond Jubilee history in 1981.

During World War I, Camp Mills, an embarkation camp set up in Garden City, filled Mineola with soldiers, while the Army Air Force was crowded into cattle sheds on the Mineola County Fairgrounds. "Owning a store was like owning a gold mine," wrote Barrick. "On an average Sunday 50,000 people visited the Rainbow Division."

The Hempstead Plains Aviation Field, renamed Hazelhurst Field during World War I, became the site of daredevil air shows after the war. On the ground, a building boom was going on. The Mineola Theatre opened in 1927, a showplace of its time.

Two years later the Depression hit. In the '30s, unemployed Mineola men got jobs with the Works Progress Administration, painting and repairing the fairgrounds, which had opened in 1866. But in 1937 the county took over the northeastern section of the fairgrounds to erect courthouse buildings, and in 1952, the county requested the rest of the grounds. The fair was gone, but Mineola, with its rows of stone government buildings, was still the heart of Nassau.

Where to Find More: "Mineola: Heartbeat of Nassau," by Thomas Barrick; "Mineola: Diamond Jubilee, 1906-1981," in the Bryant Library, Roslyn.

A crowd gathered as a post office was dedicated in Mineola about 1936.

Nassau County Museum Collection, Long Island Studies Institute

LAKE SUCCESS, Continued

proved a major turning point with the construction of the $40-million Sperry Gyroscope plant in 1941. The plant, employing 20,000 at its peak, became headquarters for the fledgling United Nations in 1946. Lake Success, a reluctant host, was called the "World's Capital." After the UN moved to Manhattan in 1951, the 1.5-million-square-foot facility had a series of defense industry owners.

Where to Find More: "History of the Village of Lake Success," by Kate Van Bloem in Great Neck Public Library.

NEW CASSEL

Freed Slaves Worked Their Own Land

Beginnings: In the century after Europeans turned the vast Hempstead Plains into a common pasture land, two groups helped settle the area that became New Cassel. The first was former slaves, freed in the mid-1700s by Westbury-area Quakers who came to reject ownership of fellow humans as a matter of conscience. These blacks established a small farming community called Grantsville, near the northern edge of what became New Cassel. The other group was Hessian mercenaries who fought for the British during the Revolution. When the war was over, they decided they liked the area and set up their own farming community. They named it New Cassel, after a town in Germany that many of them came from. Despite the presence of the Long Island Rail Road from the 1840s, descendants of the original blacks and Germans lived quietly for decades with little to do with the rest of the world. Poor immigrants from other parts of Europe — the Ukraine, Poland and Ireland — settled in New Cassel to farm in the early 1900s.

Turning Point: With the explosive development of Nassau County after World War II, farmland quickly gave way to housing. New Cassel's always significant black population made it one of the few places on Long Island to welcome minorities during the 1950s and 1960s. Meanwhile, New Cassel's proximity to the railroad and Old Country Road made it attractive to manufacturers. Governmental neglect — primarily poorly enforced building codes and a lack of maintenance of the few public facilities there — by the Town of North Hempstead and Nassau County in the 1970s and 1980s resulted in some deterioration, which the community fought to overcome.

Claim to Fame: Thanks to the establishment of Grantsville before the Revolution, New Cassel was one of the first communities of free blacks on Long Island, and one of the oldest in the state.

Where to Find More: Historical Society of the Westburys.

NEW HYDE PARK

Babe Ruth Threw Out The First Ball

Beginnings: Irish Thomas Dongan, appointed New York's royal governor by King James II in 1682, was so popular a change from his predecessors that the Towns of Hempstead and Flushing decided to give him 900 acres for a summer home in what later became the North New Hyde Park area. In 1688, Dongan built a mansion on what later became Lakeville Road, but he didn't have long to enjoy it. James was toppled by anti-Catholic forces, and Dongan fled to New England and then to Ireland in 1691.

The Name: In 1715, Dongan Manor was sold

Please Turn the Page

NEW HYDE PARK, Continued

to New York Lt. Gov. George Clark, who renamed it Hyde Hall after his wife, Ann Hyde. The name Hyde Park was applied to an area described as "ye estate, North of Hempstead Plain — one-half mile southe of Lake Success." The estate was subdivided into farms in the 1800s. The mansion burned in 1819, was replaced in 1826 and survived into the 1940s. Because there was a Hyde Park upstate, the area was named New Hyde Park when a post office opened in 1871.

Turning Points: It was cattle country until the mid-1800s when competition from the western plains squeezed out cattlemen, who turned to farming. Brothers Emanuel and John C. Christ and Philip S. Miller were young German immigrants who arrived after the Civil War and transformed the community. The Christs ran an inn, general store, sawmill and blacksmith shop; Miller built a meeting hall and planted hundreds of trees. John's son, Philip, became chairman of the Nassau County Board of Supervisors, 1907-16, and his son, Marcus, became a leading judge. A mile-square area was incorporated as the village of New Hyde Park in 1927. The population grew rapidly as farms were subdivided into housing developments starting in the 1920s.

Neighbors: North New Hyde Park remained an unincorporated section of the Town of North Hempstead, and nearby Herricks was developed mostly as part of the post-World War II building boom that covered much of Nassau County with houses. Herricks apparently took its name from Herricks Path, which existed as early as 1659 (though for whom the path was named is lost to history). The Herricks school district, drawing students from several communities in North Hempstead, was established in 1813, making it one of the oldest in Nassau County.

Babe Ruth Was Here: Showman Jim Barton and his wife, Kay, a Ziegfield Follies veteran, organized Barton's Night Hawks, a semi-pro team, and built Barton's baseball field in 1938. Babe Ruth threw out the first ball on opening day, and Roy Campanella played there. The property was sold for stores in 1957.

Where to Find More: "The Early History of New Hyde Park," by George E. Christ, grandson of Emanuel, at New Hyde Park Library.

NORTH HILLS
Between a Rock And This Place, Much History

Beginnings: There really is a Shelter Rock, an 1,800-ton boulder, the largest known one on Long Island, deposited by a mighty glacier more than 11,000 years ago near what became Shelter Rock Road in the village of North Hills. The Matinecocks, who had a village on the site, used its 30-foot overhang for shelter and weaved many legends around it, as did the European colonists who arrived in the 1600s. The stories range from runaway lovers riddled with arrows before they could reach the shelter to buried treasure (never found). The giant boulder is on the private estate of the late John Hay Whitney, publisher and ambassador to England. It's not visible from the road.

Turning Points: The English settlers built a fence in 1658 along what became Northern Boulevard. The north side was cow pasture; the south, including the North Hills area, became a farming community. One of the largest farms in 1848 belonged to Isaac Underhill Willets, namesake of I.U. Willets Road (which bisected his property, to his displeasure). The farm was later converted to a golf club. By the early 1900s about a dozen families owned huge estates, including railroad magnate Nicholas F. Brady, who built Inisfada, the fourth-largest residence in the country. It later became the St. Ignatius Retreat House. To protect their way of life, North Hills landowners organized a village in 1929 with two-acre zoning. Decades later, a 10-year battle raged over a zoning ordinance, passed in 1970, which, among other provisions, allowed for multifamily housing at 10 units to an acre, cluster housing and commercial development. A new building code in 1980 resulted in relative quiet.

Fame and Fortune: New York Yankees co-owner Daniel Reid Topping, CBS executive William S. Paley, industrialist Joseph Peter Grace and financier-publisher John Hay Whitney were among the rich and powerful who lived in North Hills.

Where to Find More: "Manhasset, the First 300 Years," in the Manhasset Library.

PORT WASHINGTON

A Suburb United in Diversity

BY RHODA AMON
STAFF WRITER

Port Washington was named for a president who never slept there or even visited. More than most places, Port Washington would provide a study in contrasts. Though a model of modern suburbia, its Main Street became an antiques row. Its average income in the late 1990s ranged from $50,000 in its blue-collar neighborhoods to more than $185,000 on its Gold Coast.

And though an amalgam of four villages, parts of two others and an unincorporated area — linked only by a ZIP code and a school district — Port Washington has seen its residents unite to fight for a common pasture, for independence, for putting a stop to sand mining or incinerator construction, for converting the 1909 Main Street School into a center for all ages.

In 1998, Port Washington marked two centennials. The first train arrived with great flourish in 1898, the same year the Mill Pond Model Yacht Club was established, one of this seagoing community's enduring hobbies.

The first battles were waged in the 1670s, when the British Crown granted land on the peninsula then known as Cow Neck to "deserving subjects" — much to the consternation of those already there. "The early colonists had enclosed the whole peninsula for cattle grazing and they felt the land was theirs," said George L. Williams, historian of the Village of Port Washington North. The first homesteader, John Cornwall (variously spelled Cornwall, Cornhill or Cornell in history books) built the first house about 1676 near Manhasset Bay. The house was torn down by angry cattle owners, but Cornwall persevered. More settlers arrived and the fence came down.

Port Washington continued to be called Cow Neck until 1857. Wanting a more dignified name, residents decided to commemorate Washington's 1790 visit — to Roslyn, which was close enough.

Had Washington detoured to Cow Neck on his whirlwind postwar tour of Long Island, he would have encountered some of his most ardent supporters. Carried by ship or horseback, news of the battles of Lexington and Concord in 1775 fired up this small, isolated community. Local militia set up beacons on Sutton's Hill, later called Beacon Hill, to signal the approach of British warships, and conducted a spy operation known as the Secret Road during the British occupation beginning in 1776.

After peace and order were restored and the Town of North Hempstead severed from the Town of Hempstead, North Shore transportation improved. The North Hempstead Turnpike, later called Northern Boulevard, opened in 1801, though travelers had to pay 2 cents to use it from Roslyn to Spinney Hill in Manhasset. By 1830 Port residents had stagecoach service to the city, and in 1836, steamboats to Lower Manhattan.

But another New York City connection was to have the greatest impact on Port Washington's landscape and population. A fine-grained sand was found on the shores of the peninsula, and a massive sand-mining operation began in 1865. Whole hills were leveled to produce concrete for city sidewalks and skyscrapers. For decades city paving contracts specified "Cow Bay Sand." Workers recruited from European communities — particularly Polish and Italian — later brought their families and settled in ethnic pockets. Some workers were buried in sand avalanches. There was widespread protesting of what was called "the rape of Long Island," but mining continued into the mid-1900s.

Meanwhile, the arrival of the railroad in 1898 ushered in the commuter age, and Port Washington's population swelled. The easy commute brought the rich, who converted farms into large estates. Artists and writers came, first as summer people. Sinclair Lewis wrote his first novel on the train to Manhattan; poet William Rose Benet composed his ballads of the West on the eastbound train, and cartoonist Fontaine Fox created his "Toonerville Trolley" in the early 1900s, when a trolley ran to Mineola.

A seaplane factory opened in 1929 on Port Washington's Manhasset Isle, on the west shore of the peninsula, from which, a decade later, the famous Pan-American Clippers took off across the Atlantic. As industries replaced summer colonies, home developers saw the need for housing more people on smaller plots and felt constrained by North Hempstead Town's zoning regulations, said Larry Rose, trustee-historian of Manorhaven, one of nine villages that incorporated on the Port Washington-Manhasset peninsula in the early 20th Century.

First to incorporate in the Port Washington area was Sands Point, in 1910. After Manorhaven formed in 1930, the village of Baxter Estates, smallest on the peninsula, was incorporated in 1931, led by resident Carolyn B. Dissoway, the first woman admitted to the bar in Nassau County. The village contained one of the area's oldest houses, the 17th Century Baxter house, once the home of the village's namesake, Oliver Baxter. Port Washington North incorporated the following year with only 250 residents, many centered around the historic Mill Pond. Change accelerated in the 1950s when the old Treadwell farm became the Soundview Village complex, and, with it, Soundview Shopping Center, the first and largest in Port Washington.

Where to Find More: "Port Recalled," by Virginia Marshall; "The Mill Pond," "Lower Main Street," "Port Washington in the 20th Century," by George L. Williams, at Port Washington Library and Cow Neck Peninsula Historical Society.

Around the Millpond, Down Neck, Port Washington, L. I.
Collection of Joel Streich
Cow Neck in an old postcard photograph

Nassau County Museum Collection, Long Island Studies Institute

BAXTER ESTATES: The estates along Shore Road in 1914 set a tone of elegance. The center home belonged to Police Chief Fred Snow.

Nassau County Museum Collection, Long Island Studies Institute

PORT WASHINGTON: A view from Manhasset Bay in 1946; the old Warwick Hotel, later the Diwan Restaurant on Shore Road, is among structures visible in the photo.

ROSLYN: Admiral Aaron Ward and his wife, Anne, at the gardens at the Willowmere Estate in an undated photograph.

OLD WESTBURY: In 1890, the best place to play on a farm was in the barn. While farming was a mainstay of life at the time, by the 1920s much farmland had been replaced by estates.

ROSLYN

Making History, and Preserving It

BY RHODA AMON
STAFF WRITER

In the rich drama of Roslyn history, two strong-willed men who lived 200 years apart played seminal roles.

Hendrick Onderdonk came to Roslyn in 1752, operated a gristmill and two paper mills, and also ran the community like a benevolent baron, making it a commercial center for rural Long Island.

Roger Gerry came to Roslyn in 1950, recognized it as an endangered historic gem and restored it.

A third player was George Washington, who made a cameo appearance as president in 1790, when he visited Onderdonk and praised him for operating his mills "with spirit and to profit." The general, who had held a ragtag army together for seven years to finally win independence, received a warm reception in Roslyn, where revolutionary spirit had run high.

The Roslyn that Onderdonk found in 1752 was a Dutch-English settlement called Head of the Harbor, and later, Hempstead Harbor. It is believed to have been the spot where the first English colonists from Connecticut landed in 1643 and then pushed south to Hempstead on an old Indian trail, later called Roslyn Road. Early settlers also found an east-west path leading to Flushing; it became North Hempstead Turnpike in 1801, and later, Northern Boulevard.

In 1701 the settlers built the gristmill that Onderdonk took over in 1759 and ran for 43 years. Inland farmers brought their grain to be ground into flour and shipped directly to New York and New England ports. In 1773 Onderdonk built what was possibly the nation's first paper mill on a dam over Roslyn Creek. Onderdonk also ran a store and a bakery, and in 1769 was elected supervisor of the Town of Hempstead. (Both the Town of North Hempstead and Nassau County were yet to be established.)

After the Revolution, the Roslyn businessman, who had ties to both sides but favored independence, was a Queens County representative to the State Assembly that created the Town of North Hempstead in 1784. The house where he lived until 1801 later became the Washington Manor restaurant. The gristmill became a tea room in 1916, with a guest list that included actors Gloria Swanson, Norma Shearer and Leslie Howard. The Roslyn Mill, which closed in the 1960s, languished empty until Nassau County began restoration plans on the urging of Roslyn Mayor Janet Galante and a restoration committee.

The Valentine family acquired the two paper mills in 1801 and ran them for almost a century. William M. Valentine, Roslyn's leading merchant in the late 1800s, was the victim of a historic mugging. He was assaulted by "cowardly ruffians" in 1882 and never recovered, according to the Roslyn News. The 1870 Valentine home became the Roslyn Village Hall in 1962.

Roslyn, which got its name in 1844 reportedly because it reminded some of the Roslin Castle area in Scotland, became a colony of artists and writers, attracted by the scenic harbor and William Cullen Bryant, a leading poet and publisher who settled there in 1843. Bryant donated a library-meeting house to the people of Roslyn for their "intellectual and social improvement," in time for the nation's 1876 centennial. The Bryant Library moved to the Roslyn War Memorial building on Paper Mill Road in 1952.

Roslyn acquired its Clock Tower in 1895, a gift from the children of philanthropist Ellen Ward. The tower serves as a gateway to the old Roslyn valley — the 18th and 19th Century houses and businesses along Main Street and East Broadway.

But time was taking its toll. The Roslyn that Roger Gerry found in the 1950s was showing its age. Bypassed by a Northern Boulevard viaduct, historic houses were deteriorating. Some were derelict. And plans to widen Main Street into a major north-south thoroughfare by Nassau County threatened to further demolish old Roslyn. Gerry, an oral surgeon with a penchant for historic preservation, came to the rescue. He organized Roslyn Preservation Inc., which bought threatened historic structures and resold them to buyers who would restore them. He also established the Roslyn Landmark Society, which began annual tours, and the pristinely preserved area was protected as a national historic district. Gerry died in 1995, but a colony of historic-minded citizens continued his work.

Earlier, Roslyn residents sought to control their own zoning destiny by incorporating as villages. Roslyn Harbor and Roslyn Estates incorporated in 1931; Roslyn followed in 1932. (Roslyn Heights, an unincorporated area of upscale homes, and parts of East Hills and Flower Hill complete the Greater Roslyn area.)

Roslyn Estates began as a large-scale home development by the Dean Alvord Co. in 1906. Residents formed the Association of Roslyn Estates in 1911, the oldest existing residents' association in Nassau County. The association later opened a tea room, which in 1949 became the Wee Tappee Inn. The village's winding roads, with names such as The Intervale and Diana's Trail, and ponds called The Loch Little Turf Pond and the Black Ink Pond, were glorified by author Christopher Morley.

Morley, whose name was given to a county park, was one of the well-known writers who came to Roslyn in the 1920s, first as a summer resident. He was buried in the Roslyn Cemetery, along with the Bryant family. Another author, Michael Crichton, grew up in Roslyn Heights and was a graduate of Roslyn High School Class of 1960.

Where to Find More: "Roslyn — Then and Now," by Roy W. Moger; "Old Roslyn," by Peggy and Roger Gerry; other reference material in the Bryant Library, Roslyn.

Collection of Joel Streich

The Roslyn Memorial Clock Tower, which the village acquired in 1895, depicted in an old postcard photograph

OLD WESTBURY

Even They Couldn't Stop the LIE

Beginnings: Old Westbury's roots are far from the Gatsby-era Gold Coast mansions for which it became famous. Such displays of extravagance would have been unfathomable to the humble English Quakers who settled this portion of the Hempstead Plains. Edmond Titus and Henry Willis were the first European settlers there, establishing farms in the 1670s. Willis named the area Westbury after a town in his home county of Wiltshire, England. The Religious Society of Friends was established early in what was to become Old Westbury. William Willis, Henry's son, donated land south of what became Jericho Turnpike for a Quaker meeting house in 1700. Farmers were attracted because of its combination of plains, useful for farming, and forests, which supplied firewood. Indeed, it was known alternately as Plainedge or Woodedge. As the village of Westbury developed, the area to the north was known first as Westbury Station and then, since 1912, as Old Westbury.

Turning Point: The isolated farmland on the gently rolling hills of Old Westbury held great attraction for the industrialists of 100 years ago. From the 1880s to the 1920s, numerous grand estates replaced the farms. Millionaire landowners included Thomas Hitchcock Sr., Harry Payne Whitney and John Phipps, whose grounds have served since 1958 as Old Westbury Gardens, a museum and arboretum open to the public. The village also became home to the New York Institute of Technology, created in 1963 from the former estate of Cornelius Vanderbilt Whitney.

Tally Ho: Horse breeding was a byproduct of the new wealth of Old Westbury. The nearby Meadow Brook Club offered members fox hunts and, more famously, polo. Tommy Hitchcock Jr., perhaps the world's greatest polo player, lived and rode in Old Westbury. His celebrity in the 1920s rivaled that of Babe Ruth.

No Through Road: The influential estate owners of Old Westbury were among the few who forced roadbuilder Robert Moses to alter his plans, making him move the route of the Northern State Parkway five miles south to avoid the village. And even though they were unable to resist the Long Island Expressway, they ensured that no exits were built and that no streetlights would shine on it in the village.

Where to Find More: "History of Long Island — Old Westbury," by Esther Hicks Emory, and other materials available at Historical Society of the Westburys.

Nassau County Museum Collection, Long Island Studies Institute

WESTBURY: An 1890 photo of the Hicks-Seaman homestead built in about 1695.

SANDS POINT
'Elegantly Rustic Way of Life'

Beginnings: The Sands brothers, James, Samuel and John, came in 1695 and bought 500 acres at the tip of a peninsula called Cow Neck from the Cornwalls, who had been there 20 years. The Sands and Cornwalls surely knew they had valuable real estate, though they never knew how valuable. By the 1900s, Sands Point was divided among 50 of the nation's wealthiest families. It was F. Scott Fitzgerald's East Egg, described in 1927's "Great Gatsby" as a place of "white palaces glittering on the water."

The Name: It came from the Sands family, not from the beaches. Prosperous farmers and sea captains, the family owned vast farms on Sands Point and an inland farm in Flower Hill, later the Sands-Willets House, headquarters of the Cow Neck Peninsula Historical Society. On a voyage to Virginia, Capt. John Sands brought back young locust trees; their descendants flourished even at the end of the 20th Century.

The Revolution: Another John Sands was a colonel in the Continental Army and his wife also became a heroine of the Revolution. During the British occupation, she was asked to deliver gunpowder, hidden on their farm, to a whaleboat waiting at the Point. Disguised as an old woman, she delivered the powder, but was fired on by Hessians. She leaped into the whaleboat and escaped. Seven Sands brothers served in Washington's Army.

Turning Point: In 1910, Sands Point land-holders sought incorporation to control zoning and preserve what historian Joan G. Kent called "their elegantly rustic way of life." The original scheme for three villages was consolidated into one, the first of four on the peninsula. The larger estates eventually gave way, and the once all-residential village would contain a church, synagogue, county park and preserve.

Claims to Fame: Former New York Gov. Averill Harriman, publishers William Randolph Hearst, Conde Nast, John Hay Whitney, along with Newsday founders Alicia Patterson and Harry Guggenheim all called Sands Point home.

Where to Find More: "Long Island, a History of Two Great Counties, Nassau and Suffolk," edited by Paul Bailey; "Port Remembered," Ernie Simon, at the Port Washington Library.

SEARINGTOWN
Oldest Methodist Church in Nassau-Suffolk

Beginnings: In the mid-1600s, John Seren was one of the first landholders in this area on the northern edge of the Hempstead Plains. The spelling of his family's name evolved to Searing, leading to what became known as Searingtown. The family name also graced the Searing Memorial Methodist Church, which was built on the somewhat indistinct border between Albertson and Searingtown. The church was founded in 1785, after itinerant preacher Philip Cox visited widow Hannah Searing and preached for her neighbors. The core of the current building was built in 1788 on land donated by Jacob Searing, Hannah's grandson.

Turning Point: Searingtown remained a rural community for three centuries, trading crops for services and manufactured goods until the housing boom after World War II transformed it and the rest of central Nassau County. In 1946, builder William J. Levitt developed much of neighboring Albertson. Other developers swooped in after him and in two decades covered the farms with suburban subdivisions.

Claims to Fame: The first meeting of the North Hempstead Town Board, on April 14, 1784, took place in the home of Samuel Searing in Searingtown. The Searing Memorial Methodist Church, begun in 1788 and renovated many times since, was the first Methodist church built in Nassau or Suffolk Counties.

Where to Find More: In the Searingtown and Albertson files of the Long Island Studies Institute at Hofstra University, Hempstead.

WESTBURY
Harness Racing, And Now Shopping

Beginnings: Westbury was settled on a small portion of the Hempstead Plains. Indians did not live there, but they traveled through the area on paths approximately where Old Country Road and Jericho Turnpike were later built. English Quakers Edmond Titus and, a few years later, Henry Willis were the first to live in Westbury, using it for farming in the 1650s. Willis named it Westbury for a town in his home county of Wiltshire. Westbury soon became a center of Quaker life. Meetings of the Religious Society of Friends there in 1671 were among the first in the United States. Westbury Quakers also were among the first New Yorkers to free slaves, doing so for reasons of conscience in 1776.

Turning Points: After 1880, the extravagantly rich began building lavish estates in what later became Old Westbury. The estates required maintenance, and as a result a business district developed on Post Avenue. One subdivision, Breezy Hills, was developed in 1914 specifically for Italian gardeners. Merchants depended almost entirely on the estates for business until World War I, when the Army's Camp Mills — later known as Mitchel Field — provided another source of income. The village incorporated in 1932. Six years later, the Northern State Parkway came through, sparking the beginnings of a housing and population boom that continued through the post-World War II period. The year before William Levitt started work on the suburb that bore his name, he built 220 homes in Westbury for returning servicemen. By 1954, almost all of the village's available land was developed.

Off to the Races: For almost five decades, Westbury's Roosevelt Raceway was a center of American harness racing. George Morton Levy came up with enough innovations — including night racing and an all-weather track — to attract horsemen and bettors from 1940 to 1988, when the track closed. By the 1990s, the area was part of a burgeoning commercial center.

Where to Find More: "The History of Westbury in the Twentieth Century," by Sheila Lesnick, published in 1981; "Your Westbury," published in 1965, and other material at Westbury Memorial Public Library.

WILLISTON PARK
Nearly Destroyed By the Depression

Beginnings: The area that became Williston Park sat where the northern edge of the vast Hempstead Plains met woods used by Matinecock Indians to hunt and camp. Henry Willis, in 1675, was the first European to settle in the immediate area, and because of what became his large family, locals began calling the area Williston. It remained rural for more than 200 years, until the Long Island Rail Road forged north toward Glen Cove from Mineola. Williston initially warranted only a freight station, but soon industry — such as brick and carriage works — attracted enough residents to justify both a passenger train station and a post office.

Turning Point: After World War I, as a real estate boom spread east from the city, the community east of the railroad tracks formed the incorporated village of East Williston in 1926. Those on the west side followed suit a few months later, forming the village of Williston Park. That year, New York developer William Chatlos bought 195 acres in the village and announced his plans to build 1,000 homes. By the following summer, model homes were being eagerly inspected by city dwellers and many purchased what became known as Happiness Homes. Many of those houses remain, albeit significantly expanded and updated. In the village's first four years, the population exploded from 495 people to almost 4,500. The Depression almost destroyed the infant village, but a sense of charity and the federal Works Progress Administration provided work for the unemployed, contributing to the construction of the original Williston Park Public Library.

Where to Find More: "50th Anniversary of the Incorporation of the Village of Williston Park," published in 1976, available at the Williston Park Public Library.

WESTBURY: Rachel Hicks of the noted Hicks family took this photo of children on Post Road around 1890.

WESTBURY: Members of the Society of Friends congregate at the Quaker Meetinghouse around 1900.

BETHPAGE: A fire truck and the company's men about 1920 in Central Park, which changed its name to Bethpage in 1936 as citizens sought to avoid confusion with a park in Manhattan

BAYVILLE: A chauffeur drives his car at Rouse Estate in about 1910. By 1900, farming had given way to estates and cottages as the community became a summer resort.

Town of Oyster Bay

There's only been one president from Long Island, and he lived in the Town of Oyster Bay. Theodore Roosevelt built his only house, Sagamore Hill, in Cove Neck in 1885, and during his presidency, 1901-1909, the Victorian mansion served as the summer White House.

Long before any Roosevelts arrived, Matinecock Indians inhabited the area. The first English settlers joined them in 1640: brothers Edward and Timothy Tomlins and others from Lynn, Mass. The Dutch, who had jurisdiction over the area, kicked them out, but four years later another group of Englishmen arrived. Then, in 1653, colonists Peter Wright, Samuel Mayo and the Rev. William Leverich came from Cape Cod and settled near Oyster Bay Harbor, purchasing a large part of what would become the town from the Indians. This came five years after Robert Williams of Hempstead had bought a tract comprising what later became Hicksville and adjoining areas.

The first recorded town meeting was held Dec. 13, 1660. Oyster Bay, which had been under nominal Dutch jurisdiction, was officially brought under English control seven years later, through a patent issued by Gov. Edmund Andros. A 1683 representative assembly called by Gov. Thomas Dongan created county boundaries, and Oyster Bay became part of Queens. Additional land purchases came later in the 17th Century. Thomas Powell made the Bethpage Purchase from the Massapequa Indians in 1695. Thomas Jones became the first white man to settle in Massapequa, then known as Fort Neck, in 1696.

In the Revolution most residents were Loyalists, and British troops occupied Oyster Bay hamlet, with headquarters at Raynham Hall, later converted to a museum owned by the town.

In the late 19th Century, the Long Island Rail Road, steamboats and improved roads brought new residents. Farmland was developed for housing, and communities such as Sea Cliff became resorts. Wealthy city residents began to buy large tracts to establish estates on the emerging Gold Coast, a few of which remain, if in different form.

Arguably, one of the most important aspects of town history was an event that never happened: In the early 1970s, Robert Moses wanted to build a bridge through Oyster Bay to Westchester. The span would have vastly changed life in that part of town, but the idea was defeated by political and environmental opposition on the North Shore.

West Main Street, Showing Post Office, Oyster Bay, L. I.

Collection of Joel Streich

OYSTER BAY: The clip-clop sound of a horse pulling a wagon can be imagined in a quiet scene on a postcard dated Sept. 8, 1907.

BAYVILLE

Moses' Bridge Idea Met Troubled Waters

Beginnings: In 1658 Daniel Whitehead of Oyster Bay purchased land from the Matinecock Indians. At the time, the eastern section of the peninsula was known as the Pines and the western section as Oak Neck. In 1674 the land was divided among 23 men who used it for pasture. Initial development centered near the western end of the village, the area later known as Friendly Corner.

Bridge to the Future: In 1859 the name was changed to Bayville. Because of its isolated location, some people traveled by water taxi from Oyster Bay or a ferry that ran from Stamford, Conn., until 1937. To improve access, a bridge across Mill Neck Creek was completed in 1898 with donated funds. Another bridge, the fourth on the site, was built in 1938.

Turning Points: The earliest businesses were farming, converting oyster and clam shells left by the Indians into lime, and harvesting salt hay. By the late 1800s, much of the land in the village was used for growing asparagus. Farming died out after the turn of the century as the community became a summer resort with small cottages, several estates and an entertainment complex called the Bayville Casino, built in 1913. The biggest estate was owned by stock market speculator Harrison Williams, who later donated his stables to the village for use as a village hall and library, and an adjacent 28-acre wooded tract as a preserve. Bayville became an incorporated village in 1919.

Clam to Fame: Besides its popular beaches, Bayville could boast about the firm of Frank M. Flower & Sons, founded in 1887. By the late 1990s, the company was the last one on Long Island dredging for both oysters and clams. It also cultivated oysters at its hatchery built in the early 1960s and seeded sections of Oyster Bay.

Run-in With The Master Builder: A large chunk of the business district and many homes would have disappeared if Robert Moses' 1965 proposal to build a bridge across Long Island Sound to Rye had not been killed in the early 1970s after wetlands were donated to the federal government for a wildlife preserve.

Where to Find More: "The Times and Tides of Bayville, Long Island, N.Y.," Bayville Library.

BETHPAGE

Biblical Name and Fish Put It on the Map

Beginnings: Unlike much of the vast Hempstead Plains, this area was used by Indians because a stream, the Massatayun, flowed through it, providing fish. When Englishman Thomas Powell purchased the area from the Massapequa Indians, he noted the nearby hamlets of Jericho and Jerusalem (now Wantagh) and turned to the Gospel of Matthew in naming his purchase: ". . . as they departed from Jericho, a great multitude followed him, and when they drew night unto Jerusalem and were come to Bethphage . . . then sent Jesus two disciples." Powell changed the spelling, however, supposedly because he didn't like words with too many h's in them. When Powell died in 1721, the Bethpage purchase was divided among his 14 children. Quakers settled in the area, establishing

Nassau County Museum Collection, Long Island Studies Institute

BAYVILLE: Arriving by automobile or horse carriage, beachgoers enjoy the pebbled shore around 1910.

Please Turn the Page

Continued

a school in 1741.

Not *That* Central Park: Around the time of the Civil War, locals adopted the name Central Park for their community. In time, taverns, hotels and a business district grew around it. But by the 1930s, residents had tired of having their community confused with a park in Manhattan. It was not unusual for mail intended for Long Island's Central Park to be misdirected to Manhattan. In 1931, the state park commission purchased the Benjamin Yoakum estate and nearby farms, and gave the new state park the historic name of Bethpage. Residents petitioned the postal service to change the name of Central Park to Bethpage in 1936.

Turning Point: That year, the Grumman Aircraft Engineering Corp. picked the open spaces of Bethpage for its airport and factory. Grumman evolved into Long Island's largest employer and one of the most famous names in aviation. Among other aircraft, the lunar module that landed on the moon in 1969, was built in Bethpage. Grumman transformed Bethpage into a modern suburb. The company was taken over by Northrop in 1994, which began selling off buildings and land. In 1998, Cablevision Systems Corp. moved into the old Grumman headquarters.

Brush With Fame: The Beau Sejour hotel, founded in 1908 by Frenchman Bernard Pouchan, sat off the Vanderbilt Parkway. Celebrities including opera star Enrico Caruso, filmmaker D.W. Griffith, Gen. George Marshall, President Harry Truman, actor Charlie Chaplin and, of course, the Vanderbilts, flocked to its restaurant. Roald Amundsen stayed there while preparing for his expedition to the North Pole. The hotel was razed in 1974.

Where to Find More: "The Bethpage Purchase," a series of 1961 articles from the Long Island Forum in book form, and other material available at the Bethpage Public Library.

BROOKVILLE
Yesterday's Woodland, Today's College Town

Beginnings: When Oyster Bay Town purchased what would become Brookville from the Matinecocks in the mid-1600s, the area was known to some as Suco's Wigwam. Most pioneers were English, many of them Quakers. They were soon joined by Dutch settlers from western Long Island, who called the surrounding area Wolver Hollow, apparently because wolves gathered at spring-fed Shoo Brook to drink. For most of the 19th Century, the village was called Tappentown after a prominent family. Brookville became the preferred name after the Civil War and was used on 1873 maps.

Turning Points: Brookville's two centuries as a farm and woodland backwater changed quickly in the early 1900s as wealthy New Yorkers built lavish mansions. By the mid-1920s, there were 22 estates, part of the emergence of Nassau's North Shore Gold Coast. One was Broadhollow, the 108-acre spread of attorney-banker-diplomat Winthrop W. Aldrich, which had a 40-room manor house. The second owner of Broadhollow was Alfred Gwynn Vanderbilt II, who was owner of the Belmont and Pimlico racetracks. In 1931, estate owners banded together to win village incorporation to head off what they saw as undesirable residential and commercial development in other parts of Nassau County.

Reluctant College Town: Brookville became the home of the C.W. Post Campus of Long Island University, but it didn't want to be for fear a college would draw troublesome traffic and other activity. Long Island University in 1947 bought the 178-acre Marjorie Merriweather Post estate just outside the village. Brookville battled six years in court to stop creation of the college, and lost. The village in 1954 was al-

lowed to annex the campus land so it could have some control over its development. Relations between the two improved, and the campus won attention as the home of the Tilles Center for the Performing Arts. The DeSeversky Conference Center of the New York Institute of Technology also gained note. The center was formerly Templeton, mansion of socialite and businessman Winston Guest.

Strange Interlude: The federal government in 1958 built a Nike guided missile installation in Brookville for use in case the nation was attacked. The site later became a nature preserve.

Where to Find More: "Early History of the Village of Brookville," by Harry Macy, "Village of Brookville Reference Guide," a village publication, at Jericho Public Library.

CENTRE ISLAND
A Center of Life Among the Very Rich

Beginnings: Formed by glaciers 25,000 years ago, Centre Island, actually a claw-shaped peninsula, hosted its first summer residents a mere 10,000 years ago, when the Matinecocks came in their dugout canoes to fish, hunt and gather shellfish. Apparently they were rewarded. The first Dutch explorer in Oyster Bay Harbor in 1639 reported "oysters a foot long and broad in proportion." By the end of the 1900s, the island's sand dunes and wetlands were relatively unchanged, but its oysters were smaller.

Island for Sale: The earl of Sterling, who had a patent from Charles I for most of Long Island, sold Centre Island plus Lloyd Neck to a sailor named Mathew Sinderland for 10 shillings in 1639 — unknown to the Matinecocks, who sold it to the Dutch in 1650. Thus there was hot contention until 1666, when the Town of Oyster Bay bought Centre Island, though it's not clear from whom. The island was then sold to Joseph Ludlam, who later sold the lower half to Thomas Smith. The families were leading farmers for generations. The island was then known as Hog Island (for a cartographer, not an animal).

The Revolution: George Washington ordered a whaleboat raid on Hog Island, where Thomas Smith, King's Justice for Oyster Bay, lived. Smith, a Loyalist harassed by Patriots throughout the war, was respected enough to remain in office after the Revolution.

Turning Points: Hog Island became Centre Island, probably because of its position in the center of Oyster Bay Harbor, about

1844. The island blossomed as a summer colony in the late 1800s. The opening of the Seawanhaka Corinthian Yacht Club in 1871 brought leading yachtsmen to the island. After World War I, the proliferation of beach bungalows caused concern among residents, who incorporated as a village in 1926. Seventy years later, the village continued to be an enclave of the rich on large estates. Residents have included William T. Moore, president of Moore-McCormack steamship lines; Roosevelts, Pells, and other prominent and wealthy families.

Where to Find More: "A History of Centre Island," by Malcolm MacKay and Charles G. Meyer Jr., at the Oyster Bay-East Norwich Library.

COVE NECK
Teddy Roosevelt's Summer White House

Beginnings: Theodore Roosevelt lived here. George Washington slept here. And in the late 1990s, computer executive Charles B. Wang owned more than an eighth of this tiny, elite peninsula village jutting into Long Island Sound. It was settled by English farmers in the 1650s, and by 1682, the Cooper family, for whom Cooper's Bluff on its east end was named, farmed a large part of it. Mary Cooper, colonial farm wife, kept a diary from 1768-73, and hers was no limousine life. In all weather she walked the three miles to Oyster Bay, fording the Cove Brook which crossed the road. The brook was later piped underground. The Cooper house remained a private residence.

The Revolution: Capt. Daniel Youngs, a descendant of early settler Thomas Youngs, spent the war harassing Hessian soldiers who tried to steal from his cider press. After the war he hosted Washington in his 1651 house. A marker noted that "George Washington rested here on April 23/24, 1790." The house was sold in 1954 to P. James Roosevelt, a cousin of President Theodore Roosevelt. Wang bought it in June, 1997.

Turning Points: Cornelius Van Schaack Roosevelt, grandfather of Theodore, was the first Roosevelt to discover Cove Neck as a vacation site in 1871, and induced family members to join him. Theodore Roosevelt built a Queen Anne Revival home on 70 acres called Sagamore Hill. It was the Summer White House between 1901-09 and later became a National Historic Site.

A Village Small: In 1927, 24 voters of the newly created village arrived in limousines at the Howard C. Smith estate and elected him first village president. The one-square-mile

village was made up of 12 estates with 40 voters. After that, not much happened in the idyllic village until the crash of Avianca Flight 52 in 1990 broke the peace. Seventy-three people aboard died, and 85 survived. The aircraft had run out of fuel.

Brushes With Fame: Besides Roosevelt, celebrated residents have included tennis star John McEnroe and Wang, chairman of Computer Associates International.

Where to Find More: "The Diary of Mary Cooper," available from Oyster Bay Historical Society; Theodore Roosevelt biographies at Sagamore Hill National Historic Site.

EAST NORWICH
Highways Ran Over Many Older Homes

Beginnings: The Matinecock Indians were the first on the scene, about 8,000 or 9,000 years ago. The first white settlers to remain in the Oyster Bay area arrived in 1644. After the land in Oyster Bay hamlet was all taken, later arrivals moved south, congregating around the intersection of two roads that later became Routes 106 and 25A. As early as 1680, James and George Townsend owned land in what became known as Norwich after the family's ancestral home in England.

Revolution: Oyster Bay was held by the British but Patriots held meetings in Norwich. In December, 1778, Hessian mercenaries marched into Norwich and remained for two years. After the war, Norwich grew slowly, not getting its own post office until 1846. Because of the confusion with another Norwich upstate, postal authorities changed the name to East Norwich in 1862. By 1900, many of the old family farms were bought up and converted into estates.

Turning Point: The highways that led to the creation of East Norwich eventually began to eat away at it. In 1928, Nassau County proposed widening Route 25A from two tree-lined lanes to four. Community opposition killed the plan but only after the trees had been cut down. But it failed to block a 1961 plan to widen both Routes 25A and 106. Work began in 1963, sparing only a few old houses along Route 25A. The John Layton store was relocated to Old Bethpage Village Restoration.

Triumph and Tragedy: William K. Vanderbilt II put East Norwich on the map when he routed his second Vanderbilt Cup Race through the hamlet in 1905. During the 1906 race, a car

Please Turn to Page 51

EAST NORWICH: A view of the East Norwich Hotel from an old postcard

Collection of Joel Streich

48

NASSAU

BETHPAGE: The World War II effort was on in 1944 as Grumman produced some 20 F-6 Hellcats a day to be used in the Pacific. By May, 1944, Grumman had produced 12,275 Hellcat aircraft.

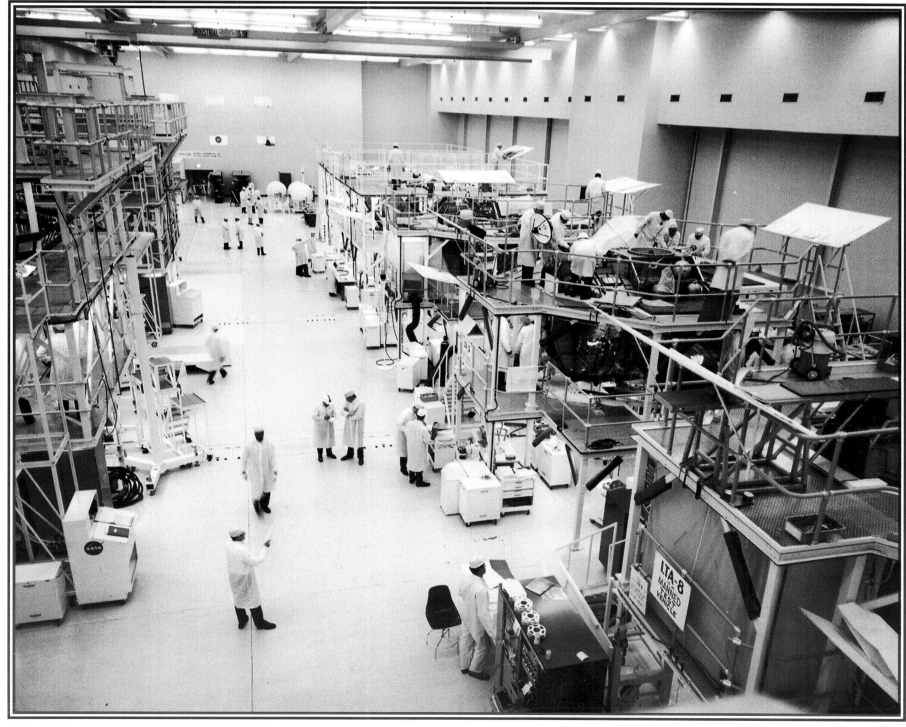

BETHPAGE: By the late 1960s, Grumman was active in another pursuit — designing and assembling lunar landing modules for America's astronauts.

Newsday Photo / Howard Edwards

HICKSVILLE: In 1952, Dwight Eisenhower campaigned for president from an open car. Former Gov. Thomas Dewey and Nassau GOP boss J. Russel Sprague accompanied him.

HICKSVILLE: Singer Billy Joel autographed this photo for his seventh-grade American history teacher, Richard Evers. The photo, showing Joel and his first combo in August, 1965, was published in the Aug. 12, 1965, issue of the Mid-Island Herald. Evers later became the Hicksville historian and archivist.

Gregory Museum Collection, Hicksville Public Library

EAST NORWICH, Continued

failed to negotiate the 90-degree turn, killing two spectators and injuring a third.

Famous Sons: The most famous East Norwich family name is Pynchon. William Pynchon, a surveyor and civil engineer who came to Long Island to find work in the late 1800s, surveyed the site of what would become Jones Beach. His son, Thomas R., served as Oyster Bay Town supervisor and his grandson, Thomas R. Jr., became a novelist who wrote "Vineland" and "Mason and Dixon."

Where to Find More: "Crossroads — A History of East Norwich," by John E. Hammond, available at local libraries.

FARMINGDALE

Hardscrabble Start, Then It Took Wing

Beginnings: Farmingdale sits near the eastern end of what was the Hempstead Plains, the vast, treeless prairie that covered central Nassau County. Englishman Thomas Powell purchased about 15 square miles, including the area that became Farmingdale, from the Massapequa Indians for 140 pounds in 1695. He and his children divided the land into lots and began more than a dozen decades of agriculture in the area.

Over time, a gristmill, a tavern and a few other businesses were established. The community that formed called itself Hardscrabble. Whose idea that was remains unknown.

Turning Point: Real estate speculator Ambrose George opened a general store in Hardscrabble in 1841 and bought several acres. He changed the name of the hamlet to Farmingdale by 1845, subdivided his land and laid out streets. Within a few decades, industry began to locate in Farmingdale, including a lumberyard, a brickworks and at least six pickle factories. The bricks were used for buildings as near as Garden City and as far as Chicago.

The village incorporated in 1904. The farms provided an impetus for the state to establish the Agricultural and Technical College in 1914. Many of the remaining farms were bought out in the years after World War I, when aircraft companies — particularly Liberty — looked for manufacturing space. The industrialization resulted in the village's population doubling by the mid-1930s. The last open spaces were gobbled up by the post-World War II building boom. The village's population in 1998 was 8,214.

Claim to Fame: Charles Murphy's famous Mile-A-Minute bicycle ride — a publicity stunt in which Murphy tried to keep up with a Long Island Rail Road train and wound up setting a bicycle speed record — took place in Farmingdale on June 30, 1899.

Where to Find More: "Farmingdale: A Short History From the Ice Age to the Present," by Dorothy Vining, published in 1983, and other material available at the Farmingdale Public Library.

GLEN HEAD

Did the Hessians Make a Yule Tree?

Beginnings: Glen Head was once part of the large Cedar Swamp area east of Hempstead Harbor — but not the part 17th-Century Dutch and English pioneers cared about. They bypassed its 200-foot, hilly terrain for the more easily farmed land a few miles east, around the Brookvilles. What is now Glen Head waited about 100 years before farmhouses appeared in any number.

The Revolution: British troops and their Hessian (German) supporters harried families, looting their food and animals and forcing men into such work as hauling ammunition. Throughout the seven-year war, Hessians maintained a camp in what later became Glen Head, adjacent to the Old Brookville line. Some histories suggest that the Hessians may have "built" one of America's first Christmas trees in Glen Head in 1776 by cutting off branches of pines and fashioning them into symmetrical holiday ornaments about 3 feet high. (Small yule trees were not a part of English or Dutch traditions at the time, but were part of Hessian culture in Europe; the only major Hessian encampments in the colonies were in Glen Head and Newark, N.J.)

Turning Point: About 1850, the Duryea starch factory, said to be one of the country's largest industrial plants, opened nearby in Glen Cove. It attracted hundreds of workers, many of whom settled in Glen Head. The hamlet also had an early brick factory, boat-building and other blue-collar crafts. Early in the 1900s, Glen Head, a 1.6-square-mile unincorporated part of the town, attracted many Norwegian and Polish immigrants, but after World War II the influx was largely Italian.

Memories: Old-timers chuckled at the memory of the long-gone four-room school on Cedar Swamp Road called Frog College, because there were so many frogs on the school grounds, which served Glen Head in the 1920s. The first aerial delivery of newspapers in the nation took place between Glen Head and New Rochelle Oct. 12, 1912 — a nine-mile over-water hop at 50 mph, nine years after the world's first airplane flight. Identical rail depots with gingerbread trim were built in 1888 in Glen Head and Sea Cliff, but Glen Head's was torn down in 1961.

Where to Find More: Local history collection of Glen Cove Public Library and Cedar Swamp Historical Society.

GLENWOOD LANDING

Hamlet Delivers Great Memories but No Mail

Beginnings: When George LaTourette moved to Glenwood Landing in 1894, the 1-square-mile hamlet had one store and about a dozen homes linked by dirt roads. "You would walk to the banks of the bay and if you called out your name it would echo and re-echo," LaTourette recalled in 1964.

Memories: Jeanne LaTourette, George's granddaughter, fondly recalled how Harry Houdini, the famous magician, a summer resident of Glenwood Landing who knew her father, bought her $10 worth of Fourth of July firecrackers when she was 7. Other old-timers recalled the Karotsony Hotel beach resort that catered to busloads and boatloads of New York tourists and never seemed to run out of beer and whiskey, even during Prohibition. Next door was Fyfe's Shipyard, where the customers included North Shore millionaires such as banker J.P. Morgan, who had a chauffeur-driven touring car and an enormous yacht. The yard, no longer in existence, made high-speed, torpedo-carrying PT boats for the Navy during World War II. In the 1920s, Smallwood's Restaurant at Mott's Cove on the harbor catered to many New Yorkers. Joe Smallwood, a former English boxing champ, ran such a fine establishment, one account said, that one bounder who overdid his affections for a lady got special treatment: Smallwood "threw him out right through a window, glass and all."

Landmark: In 1905, a small electric power plant was built on the Glenwood Landing shore. It later grew into the Long Island Lighting Co.'s 15.7-acre generating station. Its stacks, visible for miles around, rose 246 feet.

Unusual Stamp: The Glenwood Landing post office was established on Dec. 1, 1891, but even a century later had never delivered mail. It remained one of the few on Long Island where residents were required to go to pick up their mail from boxes. Whether to start delivery service was a perennial debate, with traditionalists winning every time.

Where to Find More: Long Island Studies Institute, Hofstra University, Hempstead.

Nassau County Museum Collection, Long Island Studies Institute

GLENWOOD LANDING: A photo taken around 1910 shows the post office at a distance on Glenwood Road, and a bridge at School House Road. The pond was later filled in.

HICKSVILLE

Bound Together By Railroad Ties

Beginnings: For centuries, miles of prairie grass gently waving in the breeze spread across the spot that would become Hicksville. The community — and the rest of central Nassau County — was founded on the Hempstead Plains. That made it unattractive to Long Island's Indians, who preferred to live in the forests near the seashore or by streams, where hunting and fishing were easy. Legend says that when Welsh settler Robert Williams proposed in 1648 to buy a large portion of the eastern plains, including Hicksville, the Matinecock Indians didn't think they were giving up much. And most British settlers were just as uninterested in this part of the prairie, because it was so remote from Hempstead and other settlements. The land lay vacant for almost two centuries, until Jericho businessman Valentine Hicks — son-in-law of the nationally famous Quaker preacher Elias Hicks — turned his attention to the prairie land he had acquired.

LIRR to the Rescue: In 1834, Hicks formed a land association with some others with the idea of creating a town on the plains. But there was no easy way to get to this planned town until the Long Island Rail Road started building east from Jamaica. Perhaps because Hicks was a member of the railroad's board of directors — and later its second president — the railroad got to Hicksville by 1837. Initially, no one saw the attraction of this station in the middle of nowhere, but by 1849 German and Irish refugees began farming nearby and drilling wells for water, and Hicksville turned out to be a convenient depot for produce. A community grew up around the station. The German population was so strong that Hicksville's first newspaper, in 1873, the Long Island Central Zeitung, was printed in German.

Turning Point: Thanks in part to the significant German population, several pickle works were built in Hicksville in the 1890s. One, owned by the Heinz Co., also produced ketchup, vinegar and sauerkraut. The pickle plants died when a blight hit the cucumbers before World War I and Hicksville farmers turned instead to potatoes. In the 1940s, that crop, too, was blighted, but the post-World War II building boom bailed out farmers and by 1959 had transformed Hicksville into a bustling suburb. And its train station is the most heavily used east of Jamaica.

Claim to Fame: Music star Billy Joel grew up in Hicksville.

Where to Find More: "The Story of Hicksville, Yesterday and Today," by Richard Evers, 1961; "Hicksville's Story: 300 Years of History, 1648-1948," 1948, by the Hicksville Tercentennial Committee, at the Hicksville Public Library.

JERICHO

Quakers Spread Faith Far and Wide

Beginnings: The rolling hills on which Jericho lies served as a sort of gateway between the Hempstead Plains and the forests of the North Shore before European settlers arrived. Although it once had an Indian name (Lusum, which may have meant "the farms"), it was farther from the shore than most Indian settlements. Though it remains unclear if Indians lived there, the area was part of the large land purchase that Welsh settler Robert Williams made in 1648 from the Matinecock sachem Pugnipan. It was attractive to both Indians and Europeans because of a spring pond that supplied fresh water. Williams himself moved from Hempstead to Lusum in the 1670s. The small farming community became a center of the Quaker religion and by 1692 the Quakers had named the community Jericho. Jericho and Westbury Quakers were among the first New Yorkers to free their slaves as a matter of conscience in the 1770s.

Claims to Fame: Jericho was known nationwide as the home of Quaker preacher Elias Hicks. Born of a Quaker father, he met his future wife, a Jericho woman named Jemima Seaman, at a Quaker meeting. They married in 1771. He was physically imposing and a powerful speaker, and he traveled thousands of miles across the new country preaching the faith. His son-in-law, Valentine Hicks, was the second president of the Long Island Rail Road and the founder of Hicksville. Jericho Turnpike, once an Indian trail and later the main artery for farmers traveling from Jamaica, was named for the community where it ended in the early 1800s.

Turning Point: Despite its location on the turnpike that bears its name, Jericho avoided suburbanization far longer than most of Nassau County — as late as 1940 it had fewer than 600 people. But in 1952, Phoebe Underhill Seaman

Please Turn the Page

Nassau County Museum Collection, Long Island Studies Institute

FARMINGDALE: The rail station about 1910, not long after Farmingdale had incorporated.

Collection of Joel Streich

LOCUST VALLEY: An old postcard depicts the Piping Rock Club.

Nassau County Museum Collection, Long Island Studies Institute

MASSAPEQUA: The Old Mill on Carman Road in 1911.

JERICHO, Continued

— a great-great-granddaughter of Elias Hicks — subdivided her property and Jericho was never the same. No longer did Quaker farmers dominate a pastoral hamlet. Instead, Jericho became a busy suburb with bustling office parks near the expressway. 1998's population was listed as 13,717.

Where to Find More: "Old Jericho and Its Quakers," by Marion Jackson; "Jericho Friends Meeting House, 1788-1988," published in 1988 by Jericho Friends Meeting; "The History of Jericho," by Ted Kaplan, at the Jericho Public Library.

LATTINGTOWN
Once a Simple Marsh, Now a Posh Preserve

Beginnings: Later known for its stately estates and aura of manicured grandeur, Lattingtown was at first just a marsh, largely ignored by Matinecock Indians who chose to live in more accommodating spots nearby. Even though fish spawned in the tidal marsh, the Matinecocks apparently drove no hard bargain when they sold much of the area to Robert Latting and his son, Josiah, in 1660. For a while, Josiah Latting had a successful business selling the reeds from the marsh for thatched-roof houses. (His 20-acre site later became a wildlife preserve owned by Nassau County, though without public access.) For 2½ centuries, a few farmers settled in the area, but with no train station or main road, the tiny community remained isolated and quiet.

Turning Point: Those very qualities led to the end of the farms. After 1900, wealthy industrialists transformed the farms into estates. In the early years of this period, much of Lattingtown was owned by two attorneys, Paul Craveth and William Guthrie, the village's first mayor after it incorporated in 1931. Guthrie's main client was the banker J.P. Morgan, who had an estate next door in Glen Cove. Guthrie's 300-acre estate, Meaudon, required so much of its staff to live on the grounds that a school bus stopped there just for children of the staff. Guthrie and Craveth sealed the village's high-brow image in the 1930s when they bought out and razed the small commercial district to ensure that Lattingtown was strictly residential.

Denial Amid Indulgence: In Lattingtown, one of the wealthiest communities in the country (with a median family income of $134,000 in the mid 1990s), an 118-acre estate existed where residents took vows of poverty — St. Josephat's Monastery. The Basilian monks who lived there since 1944 used the 74-room mansion as a place of quiet prayer. The mansion was once owned by industrialist J.E. Aldred until he went bankrupt in 1942. A bank seized it and found no buyers until the order snapped it up for $75,000, a bargain even then.

Where to Find More: In the Lattingtown file of the Long Island Studies Institute at Hofstra University, Hempstead.

LAUREL HOLLOW
The Nurturing Of Nobel Prize Winners

Beginnings: The craggy terrain on the west side of Cold Spring Harbor in Nassau County wasn't too attractive to farmers after English settlers bought it in 1653 from the Matinecock Indians. Sawmills and gristmills were an early industry, but the pace of life quickened with the start in 1836 of a whaling center on the Suffolk side of the harbor: Cold Spring Harbor. Most whaling-support operations and the homes of employees were located on the west side, in Bungtown,

named after the bungs, or plugs, used to seal the opening of barrels.

St. John's Episcopal Church was also erected in 1836, three years after the state had opened its second permanent fish hatchery, on present-day Route 25A. Both landmarks are in Laurel Hollow.

Turning Point: By the start of the 1900s, well-to-do New Yorkers including Louis Comfort Tiffany, a world-famous stained-glass artisan and son of the founder of Tiffany & Co., and Henry W. de Forest, a lawyer and financier, established large estates. Oyster Bay Town fought, and finally won, bitter court battles with them over public access to the waterfront. De Forest's Nethermuir, which was razed in 1960, was noted for exquisite gardens created by Frederick Law Olmsted, the designer of Central Park. Tiffany's Laurelton Hall, completed in 1905, was destroyed by fire in 1957.

The Name: The village incorporated in 1926 as Laurelton. Because of confusion with a Queens County community of the same name, the village changed it to Laurel Hollow in 1935.

Claim to Fame: Laurel Hollow (1997 population 1,766, in 2.9 square miles), gained attention as the home of the 107-acre Cold Spring Harbor Laboratory, an internationally recognized genetic and cancer research center that was placed on the National Register of Historic Places. The experimental stations from which it grew were established in 1893, predating the village. (See more information on Page 103.)

Where to Find More: "History of the Incorporated Village of Laurel Hollow," 1951, and local history collection at Cold Spring Harbor Public Library.

LOCUST VALLEY
Lavish Estates In the Woods

Beginnings: Oyster Bay Town's hamlet of Locust Valley originally was part of a larger region called Matinecock, settled in 1667, that covered what became northern Nassau County. The mostly English farmers in 1730 changed the local name to Buckram, probably after Buckenham, a town in Norfolk County, England, from which some of the pioneers had come. At a public meeting in 1856, the name became Locust Valley because of the many locust trees in the area.

Turning Point: Rail service reached Locust Valley by 1870, and by the start of the 1900s the community and its environs were attracting rich people who built lavish woodland estates. One was publishing tycoon Frank Doubleday of Mill Neck. The horse farms, polo fields and private clubs soon followed.

Pride of the Valley: The area is steeped in Quaker tradition. The Matinecock Friends Meeting House at Piping Rock and Duck Pond Roads, later located in Glen Cove but historically part of Locust Valley, was built in 1725. It was destroyed by fire in 1985 and rebuilt the next year. It was placed on the National Register of Historic Places. Two privately owned dwellings built about 1698 became town landmarks: the Joseph Weeks Jr. and William Hawxhurst houses on Oyster Bay Road. Two private schools in Locust Valley, Friends Academy and the Portledge School, each on more than 60 acres, earned national reputations.

Wider Identity: The one-square-mile, unincorporated hamlet of 3,930 people (1998 population) was off the beaten path for most Long Islanders. Though the village itself was largely middle class, Locust Valley always had a wider identity: People generally agreed that

the surrounding wealthier incorporated villages of Lattingtown, Matinecock and Mill Neck, at least, were also part of what was called Locust Valley. Several communities were under the postal and school umbrella of Locust Valley.

Where to Find More: Local history collection of the Locust Valley Library.

MASSAPEQUA
After Jones Came, The Beach Got a Name

Beginnings: "Great Water Land" was what the first inhabitants, the Massapequa Indians, called the place. When white settlers arrived, conflict ensued. In 1653, Capt. John Underhill, an Englishman working for the Dutch, led troops in an attack on a peaceful community of Indians at a site believed to be near the intersection of what later became Merrick and Cedar Shore Roads. Underhill's troops killed 120 Indians in the only Indian "battle" on Long Island.

Famous Family: Soon after the massacre, a Quaker family from Connecticut, the Townsends, who had been prevented from settling in New Netherlands because of their religion, bought land from the Massapequa sachem, Tackapousha. John Townsend gave the land to his daughter, Freelove, and her husband, Thomas Jones, who were the first white settlers in the area in 1696. Jones and his wife owned 6,000 acres, including, he decided, the sandbar that is now named after him: Jones Beach. Jones had seven children, including David, who in 1770, when he was 71, built Massapequa's first mansion, Tyron Hall, later called Fort Neck House, on what is now Merrick Road between Cartwright Boulevard and Beverly Street. It burned down in the 1930s. Thomas Jones died in 1713 and is buried in the Floyd-Jones Cemetery behind the Old Grace Church on Merrick Road.

Turning Points: Massapequa served as a resort in the middle years of its history, particularly after the Long Island Rail Road reached the hamlet in 1867. The Vanderwater Hotel, at the corner of Hicksville and Merrick Roads, was built in 1796 and played host to notables including future President Chester A. Arthur and Civil War Gen. Joseph (Fighting Joe) Hooker. In the 1920s, entertainers Will Rogers and Annie Oakley rented houses in Massapequa, around the time that vacant land began to be bought up by developers who turned the area into a suburban residential community.

Monkey Business: In 1934, Frank Buck, who collected animals for zoos and circuses,

opened Frank Buck's Jungle Camp on land that was later occupied by the Sunrise Mall. It featured lions, elephants, antelopes and a 75-foot-high "monkey mountain" inhabited by 500 rhesus monkeys. The zoo got a lot of publicity when someone left a plank across the moat that surrounded the monkey mountain and 150 of them escaped.

Claims to Fame: Presidents Ronald Reagan and George Bush referred to Massapequa as quintessential suburban America. It probably had something to do with the fact that their speech writer, Peggy Noonan, was from Massapequa. Others who grew up there: Alec Baldwin and his actor brothers, as well as comedian Jerry Seinfeld, and Ron Kovic, the Vietnam War veteran and peace activist who wrote "Born on the Fourth of July."

Where to Find More: "Illustrated History of Massapequa," published by the Massapequa Post, at the Massapequa Library.

MASSAPEQUA PARK
Planes Once Landed In the Village

Beginnings: The incorporated village shares the early Indian history of Massapequa. Then, in the 19th Century, families of German descent relocated from Brooklyn to what is now Massapequa Park, and the resulting community was known as Wurtenberg or Stadtwurtemburg. The main attraction and center of activity was the Woodcastle Hotel, a rooming house built in 1868 on Front Street next to the fire department as a summer resort. It was destroyed by fire in 1952 and replaced by houses.

Turning Point: In 1928 readers of The New York Times saw ads for Massapequa Park, a development built by a real estate firm owned by Michael J. Brady, Frank Cryan and Peter Colleran. The three Irish-Americans described their project as having "a bit of Old Erin" and gave the area many Irish street names. In 1931, Massapequa Park was incorporated as a village to ensure control of land use and other issues.

Claims to Fame: The village once had its own airport, the Fitzmaurice Flying Field, named in 1929 for James Fitzmaurice, the first man to fly a plane from Europe to the United States. It is said that more than 100,000 people came to the dedication of the field on Roosevelt Avenue. The field was used by private planes and eventually an insecticide-spraying business. Later, two schools were built on the site.

Where to Find More: "Illustrated History of Massapequa," published by the Massapequa Post and available at the Massapequa Library.

Nassau County Museum Collection, Long Island Studies Institute

LOCUST VALLEY: Commuters wait at the train station on Birch Hill Road in the early 1900s.

MATINECOCK
The Most Expensive Place in America?

Beginnings: The Village of Matinecock was once just a wooded wedge of northern Oyster Bay Town where in the mid-1600s English and Dutch farmers began displacing the Matinecock Indians. In those days, Matinecock referred to a large area extending from Flushing to Huntington and south almost midway through Long Island. Matinecock meant "hill country" or "land that overlooks," because the gently rolling hills overlook Long Island Sound. As European settlement advanced, the region became notable for acceptance of the then-controversial Quaker religion. The historic 1725 Society of Friends Matinecock Meeting House, though in Glen Cove, stood only a few feet from the modern village that took the name Matinecock.

Turning Point: Near 1900, well-heeled New York City residents began buying land in northern Nassau for Gold Coast estates. By the late 1920s, about a dozen little incorporated villages were being established to gain local control of development. Matinecock became a village April 2, 1928.

Claims to Fame: The all-residential village (1998 population: 891) hit the limelight in 1997 when Worth magazine said it might be America's most expensive community. Matinecock ranked No.1 nationally in home prices, based on home sales in 1995 and 1996. The survey put Matinecock's median home price at $1,472,500, meaning half the houses sold for more than that. The village's census-based median family income in 1996 was $153,147.

Famous Landmark: The village's legendary Piping Rock Club was founded in 1912. Because of the enormous wealth of surrounding neighborhoods, the club up to World War II hosted events attended by heads of state, world royalty and entertainment and sports figures. They included Presidents Woodrow Wilson and Warren Harding, the duke of Windsor, Will Rogers and Bing Crosby. By the 1990s, the clientele were still rich, but not as attuned to opulence and royalty.

Where to Find More: Assorted articles in the local history collection, Locust Valley Library.

MILL NECK
The Picture Of Refinement

Beginnings: In about the 1630s, the Mohenes sold this prized real estate to English settlers for assorted coats, utensils and wampum. Then the Indians watched as the English drove out the Dutch in the battle for ownership in 1663. The name comes from the mill Henry Townsend built in 1661 with a grant from his fellow freeholders.

Quaker Sanctuary: Townsend and his brother John were signers of the Flushing Remonstrance of 1657, the nation's first declaration of religious freedom. The daughters of early settler Peter Wright also were zealous Quakers, as well as early feminists. Mary and Hannah Wright journeyed to Boston in 1660 to protest the execution of Quaker Mary Dyer. In 1661, Hannah, then 16, and her other sister, Lydia, protested the treatment of Quakers in Massachusetts and Rhode Island.

Gold Coast: The Vanderbilts, Whitneys, Rockefellers and Levitts have all called Mill Neck home. William Robertson Coe purchased 409 acres starting in 1913 for his Planting Fields estate with its 75-room mansion, which he gave to the state in 1949 as a horticultural showplace. The village incorporated in 1924 and became the site of many mansions, including Oakley Court, built in 1936 (formerly owned by Alfred Vanderbilt and Cornelius Vanderbilt Whitney), and the 1923 English Tudor mansion of Lillian Dodge, which in 1951 became the Mill

GLEN COVE: People gather at a rebuilt Matinecock Meeting House in 1986, about seven months after the original building had burned to the stone foundation. The first building had stood since 1725. Though in Glen Cove, the Quaker house of worship was built only a few feet from the modern village that took the name Matinecock.

Neck Manor School for Deaf Children. The 1906 estate, once owned by Abby Rockefeller, became the home of William Catacosinos, who was president of the Long Island Lighting Co. in the 1990s.

Ironic Development: La Colline, the 1964 estate of developer William J. Levitt, was later subdivided.

Brushes With Fame: Movie-makers found perfect settings in Mill Neck. "Trading Places" (1983) and Charles Bronson's "The Death Wish" (1974) were shot at Mill Neck Manor, while "Hair" (1979), among other movies and commercials, was filmed in Oakley Court.

Where to Find More: "The Mansions of Long Island's Gold Coast," by Monica Randall, in many libraries.

MUTTONTOWN
Town of Majestic Hills, Estates and Incomes

Beginnings: This upscale village in northern Oyster Bay Town traces its name to the early English and Dutch settlers of the mid-1600s who found the rolling hills ideal for the thousands of sheep that grazed there, providing mutton and wool. First mention of Muttontown in town records occurred just after 1750, identifying it as a "former great sheep district" between Wolver Hollow (later called Brookville) and Syosset.

Turning Points: Around 1900, wealthy families from New York City established large homes in Muttontown as part of Gold Coast fever. A majestic example was Knollwood, a 60-room mansion erected by Wall Street tycoon Charles I. Hudson in 1906-1907. It had elements of Greek Revival, Italian Renaissance and Spanish styling, with towering Ionic front columns. Two other estates became the Woodcrest Club and the Muttontown Golf and Country Club, the village's major private sanctuaries. Another seminal change for Muttontown was its post-World War II growth, from 382 people in 1950 to 3,121 in 1997 in a village of 6.1 square miles, and where the median family income in 1996 was one of Long Island's highest: $160,378.

The Albanian Connection: The 550-acre, Nassau County-owned Muttontown Preserve, open to the public, was located in the village. Part of it was once Hudson's Knollwood estate, sold in 1951 to King Zog I of Albania. Zog never lived there, and sold it in 1955 to Lansdell K. Chris-

tie, who had made a fortune mining iron ore in Liberia. The 60-room mansion was razed by Christie in 1959 after extensive vandalism. But the county at various times purchased a total of about 430 acres from Christie for the preserve.

Church Site: Because of the way village boundaries were drawn when Muttontown was incorporated in 1931, the landmark Brookville Reformed Church, completed in 1734 and historically linked with Brookville, found itself situated a short way into Muttontown, at Brookville and Wheatley Roads, where Brookville, Upper Brookville and Muttontown converged.

Where to Find More: "Long Island Country Houses and Their Architects, 1860-1940," and local history collection, including newspaper and Long Island Forum files, at Syosset Public Library.

OLD BETHPAGE
Bethpage Became 'Old' Thanks to 'Central Park'

Beginnings: The hills surrounding Old Bethpage mark the far eastern edge of the vast Hempstead Plains. Despite the nearby forest, Indians used this land sparingly, because it had no nearby streams. Indeed, after Englishman Thomas Powell acquired it as part of his 15-square-mile purchase in 1695, it was sparsely populated for the same reason. Powell named his purchase from the Massapequa Indians after Bethphage, a place described in the Bible's gospel of Matthew as between Jericho and Jerusalem. Powell dropped one of the h's, but his purchase was between Long Island's Jericho and Jerusalem, later known as Wantagh. Powell's 14 children split up his purchase and it evolved into several farming communities. Old Bethpage, then known as Bethpage, was one of the smaller, quieter ones. It wasn't until the 1870s, after Alexander T. Stewart purchased the plains, that industry came to Bethpage in the form of a large brickworks located on the road to Farmingdale. The works supplied bricks for Stewart's Garden City and beyond until it closed in 1981.

Turning Point: Bethpage, still a tiny farming community, became Old Bethpage against its will in 1936, when the adjacent — and larger — community of Central Park decided that it would call itself Bethpage. The 1940s saw a potato blight wipe out most of the crops. That and the post-World War II housing shortage transformed Old Bethpage from farmland to

suburb. By 1966, its population had ballooned from a few dozen in 1936 to about 5,000 people; 1998's population was 5,435.

Claim to Fame: Old Bethpage Restoration became a recreation of a 19th Century Long Island community, and some of the buildings were built by members of the Powell family. It opened in 1970.

Where to Find More: "Our Town: Life in Plainview-Old Bethpage 1600 Through Tomorrow," by Richard Koubek, published in 1987, available at the Plainview-Old Bethpage Library.

OLD BROOKVILLE
From Farmers To Captains of Industry

Beginnings: Like the rest of the Brookville area, what became the Village of Old Brookville was part of mid-17th Century land purchases from the Matinecock Indians by Oyster Bay Town and early settlers in the Cedar Swamp territory east of Hempstead Harbor. English and Dutch farmers were the first white inhabitants. By the mid-1800s, their descendants were selling much of their corn to a starch factory in nearby Glen Cove, where the manufacturing residue was excellent cattle fodder coveted by farmers from miles around. Another occupation was the breeding of trolley car, brewery and delivery horses for New York City. The Rushmore house on Glen Cove Highway, the oldest house in the village, was built in part in 1690 and retained its original handmade shingles and nails.

Turning Points: The heavily wooded Brookvilles, only about 25 miles from the city, were attractive to wealthy New Yorkers eager to build Gold Coast mansions. An elegant example was Rynwood, the 60-room mansion built in 1927 on 127 acres for Sir Samuel Salvage, a titan of the rayon industry who was knighted in 1942 for service years earlier to Great Britain. The second owner was Margaret Emerson, widow of socialite Alfred Gwynne Vanderbilt and daughter of Isaac E. Emerson, who invented the headache remedy Bromo Seltzer. The restored mansion was called Villa Banfi, and the grounds were part of Banfi Vintners. Old Brookville became a village in 1929, when it had 278 residents, 29 of whom voted on the incorporation issue.

Village Notes: Old Brookville in 1997 had 1,931 residents and a 1996 median family income of $159,738, among Long Island's (and the country's) highest. The 4-square-mile village coordinated a police force that protected Old Brookville and several surrounding estate villages.

Where to Find More: "History of the Incorporated Village of Old Brookville," edited by Silas Anthony Reed, 1985, and local history collection, Jericho Public Library.

OYSTER BAY COVE
Final Resting Place Of a President

Beginnings: Tucked in between Oyster Bay and the Cove Neck peninsula, this village of 2,270 people (1998 population) spread over 2,654 acres of winding country roads and colonial homes was settled in the early 1600s by English families who farmed the land for generations. The Fleet and Youngs families were the principal landholders in the area for many years. The Fleets farmed in the area of Cove Road and Yellow Cote Road, while the Youngs were located on the edge of Cove Neck.

Gold Coast: "The Cove," as it was originally called, was discovered in the late 1800s by wealthy New Yorkers seeking country homes.

Please Turn to Page 57

Nassau County Museum Collection, Long Island Studies Institute

MILL NECK: A more classic image of a train than later electric versions, the Long Island Rail Road's G-5 locomotive No. 27 steams through Mill Neck in 1953.

Nassau County Museum Collection, Long Island Studies Institute

OYSTER BAY: A steam-powered sand dredge operates on the shoreline in 1946.

Storied Copper Beeches

Coe Hall Photo

The copper beeches arrive in 1915 at the port of Oyster Bay, where they were transported by a team of 72 horses to the Planting Fields estate.

I t stands in majesty over the great lawn at Planting Fields Arboretum in Oyster Bay, 80 feet tall with arms that reach out 100 feet.

In its youth, the copper beech was one of two that grew outside the home of young Mai Rogers in Fairhaven, Mass. When she became the wife of an industrialist named William Robertson Coe and they built and estate in Oyster Bay called Planting Fields, she longed for the trees from her childhood.

When her father died, Mai Coe asked if the trees could be transplanted to her new home. Each weighed 29 tons. This was in 1915, and it cost $4,000 and took 2½ days to ship the beeches 300 miles by barge. Then it took 12 days for a team of 72 horses to carry them through the streets of Oyster Bay. Electrical wires along the way had to be taken down. One tree didn't survive, but the other thrived.

Newsday Photo / Bill Davis, 1998

The survivor of the pair of copper beeches, right, transported from Mai Coe's childhood home in Massachusetts, has grown up and out over the years. Coe Hall is in the background.

OYSTER BAY HAMLET
The Place a President Made Famous

BY BILL BLEYER
STAFF WRITER

It was Dutch explorer Adrian Block who named Oyster Bay in 1615 for its abundance of shellfish. The well-protected, productive bay provided food for the Matinecock Indians and then became a magnet for traders, fishermen, shipbuilders and sailors. But it was a president who made Oyster Bay famous.

Theodore Roosevelt, who built Sagamore Hill in Cove Neck in 1885, was part of the flock of influential city people who came to Oyster Bay in those years. As New York City police commissioner from 1895 to 1897, he commuted to Manhattan from the Oyster Bay train station. When he moved on to become governor, there was no phone at Sagamore Hill so Roosevelt's calls came into Snouder's drug store in Oyster Bay. Young Arthur Snouder carried messages by bicycle to Roosevelt's home. Roosevelt had a phone installed by the time Sagamore Hill served as the summer White House during his two-term presidency, which began in 1901. He housed his staff initially in the Oyster Bay Bank building on Audrey Avenue, and when he needed more space in 1903 he moved them into the Moore Building, which still stands on the corner of South and East Main Streets. Roosevelt attended Christ Church, and his pew is marked by a plaque.

Centuries before T.R. made Oyster Bay famous, English colonists Peter Wright, Samuel Mayo and the Rev. William Leverich came from Cape Cod and settled near Oyster Bay Harbor in 1653, purchasing land from the Indians that extended down into what later became Hicksville.

During the colonial era, Oyster Bay had a reputation as a hotbed of smuggling. Ships would bring in regular trade goods but evade paying custom duties on them. "It was so heavy that John Townsend, the customs collector, was threatened with bodily injury and petitioned the town fathers to quit his job," said local historian

John Hammond. He noted that Oyster Bay was Captain Kidd's last port of call before sailing to Boston, where he was arrested, transported to London and hanged.

Loyalist sentiment prevailed during the American Revolution. British troops occupied the hamlet and fortified a hill overlooking it. The Redcoats' headquarters were Raynham Hall, home of Patriot Samuel Townsend, whose son Robert was a spy for Gen. George Washington. The house later became a museum owned by the town.

Shipbuilding predated the Revolution, and

Nassau County Museum Collection, Long Island Studies Institute
Theodore Roosevelt addresses a political rally in Oyster Bay about 1910. After becoming president in 1901, he housed his staff in the hamlet during summer stays.

continued well past it. Perhaps the earliest shipyard was at the end of Ships Point Lane before the war. The last one was Jakobson Shipyard in the southwest corner of the harbor. It was founded in 1938 and during World War II employed 600 workers to build minesweepers, tugboats and even mini-submarines for the Navy. It became the largest tugboat construction facility east of the Mississippi before ceasing operations in 1993. The town later acquired the property to

establish a maritime history center.

As in other North Shore communities, transportation in Oyster Bay became much easier with the launching of steamboat service to New York in 1840. The dock was located at Steamboat Landing Road in the southeast corner of the harbor until another dock to the west at the foot of Ships Point Lane supplanted it in 1880. The New York service ended about 1870. When the Oystermen's Dock was built near the business district in 1888, ferries ran from there to Stamford, Conn., until the 1930s.

The Long Island Rail Road began service to Oyster Bay on June 24, 1889, after extending the branch from Locust Valley. The LIRR briefly used Oyster Bay as a transfer point for its train-and-steamboat service to Boston. In the spring of 1892, LIRR cars packed with passengers were loaded from a 1,000-foot wharf onto a steamboat that ferried them to Norwalk, Conn., where they were pulled to Boston by the Housatonic Railroad.

Shellfishing on a commercial scale began in the late 1880s, when the town began issuing leases for sections of bay bottom. One of the original baymen to stake out a claim in 1876 was William Flower. His business was expanded by his sons and became Frank M. Flower and Sons Inc., an oyster and clam company that survives as Long Island's only shellfish cultivation and harvesting company.

Unlike surrounding waterfront communities, Oyster Bay never developed into a resort town. But in the late 1800s, several boarding houses and hotels were erected near the water, including the Trout Pond Inn. It had a basement trout pond, which was also used by the management to keep beer kegs cool. Theodore Roosevelt loved to tell the story of how one of the kegs leaked, getting the trout drunk.

T.R. wasn't the only Oyster Bay resident generating national headlines early in the 20th Century. Mary Mallon got lots of publicity after being dubbed Typhoid Mary by the press in 1906. Mallon, a cook, was identified as the first person to carry the disease without contracting it herself.
Where to Find More: The Oyster Bay Historical Society.

OYSTER BAY COVE, Continued

Banker Mortimer Schiff, the son of railroad financier Jacob Henry Schiff, assembled 1,000 acres for his estate in 1900. Northwood, his Tudor-style showplace designed by famed architect Charles P.H. Gilbert, was completed in 1906. Other mansions followed. Threatened by the building boom of the 1920s, Oyster Bay Cove incorporated as a village in 1931 and has two-acre zoning. The Schiff estate was subdivided after the death of Mortimer's son, John, in 1987.
Brushes With Fame: Theodore Roosevelt, the 26th president, was buried in the Youngs Memorial Cemetery, created by the pioneer Youngs family in 1658. Roosevelt's cousin, Emlen, bought the remaining plots plus 12 acres when T.R. died in 1919. The surrounding land became one of the nation's first National Audubon bird sanctuaries. The late Dorothy Schiff, daughter of Mortimer, and owner and publisher of the New York Post, was another famous resident.

Where to Find More: "Long Island Country Houses and Their Architects, 1860-1940," edited by Robert B. MacKay, Anthony Baker and Carol A. Traynor.

PLAINEDGE
Potatoes Replaced By Subdivisions

Beginnings: As its name implies, Plainedge is located at the edge of the former Hempstead Plains, the vast prairie left behind in central Nassau County after the glaciers retreated. The area was purchased in several sections from 1688 to 1699 from the Massapequa Indians by English settlers Thomas Powell and William Frost. The land was used mostly as pasture for cattle at first, and later, by 1800, as hay farms. In the mid-1800s, as poultry-raising became profitable, thousands of turkeys covered the fields. The end of the century saw farmers planting cabbage for sauerkraut and cucum-

bers for pickles, but those crops were abandoned in the early 1900s because of blight. A similar fate awaited the replacement crop, potatoes, in the 1940s.
Turning Point: The failure of the potato crop was less traumatic for farmers in the Plainedge area, because the real estate boom caused by servicemen returning from World War II made their land valuable for something else — houses and shopping centers. By 1960, there were more than 6,000 homes in Plainedge, where previously there had been only a handful.
Is It a Place? Even by the 1990s, Plainedge was one of the few communities on Long Island that did not exist as far as the postal service was concerned. Although its school district dated to the early 1800s and it had a library for more than three decades, Plainedge still did not rate a post office (or a fire department, for that matter). Plainedge was split into the ZIP Codes that covered Bethpage, Massapequa, Seaford and Farmingdale.
Where to Find More: The local history file at the Plainedge Public Library.

PLAINVIEW
A Holy Place For LI's Indians

Beginnings: A small kettle pond fed by a freshwater spring at the edge of the Hempstead Plains was the basis of Plainview's origins. It was an indentation in the ground left behind by retreating glaciers. The pond — just northeast of the modern-day intersection of Old Country and Manetto Hill Roads — became a holy site for Indians across Long Island, who valued rare sources of fresh water. They named the pond Moscopas, meaning "hole of dirt and water," and the hill Manetto, a word for "god." Indians hunted in the area, often after praying at the foot of Manetto Hill. Hempstead settler Robert Williams, originally of Wales, purchased land west of Moscopas from the Matinecocks in 1648. The major European land purchase, however, was in 1695, when Thomas Powell's

Please Turn the Page

SEA CLIFF: A 1906 postcard shows youths lined up for a race.

Collection of Joel Streich

PLAINVIEW, Continued

Bethpage Purchase extended north to Moscopas. A tiny farming community formed near the pond, taking the name Manetto Hill. It remained isolated and insignificant for more than a century.

Turning Point: The railroad's arrival at nearby Hicksville in 1837 opened the vast markets of Brooklyn, western Queens and New York City to Manetto Hill farmers. The opening of the brickworks in nearby Old Bethpage in the 1860s attracted more people to the area. In 1885, Manetto Hill asked for a post office but was turned down because another community upstate had a similar name. The following year, residents decided to call their community Plainview, because of the prairie vistas from the top of the hill. The early 20th Century saw blights attack the two major crops of cucumbers and potatoes. By the time the post-World War II housing boom arrived, farmers were ready to sell. Plainview's population exploded from 1,155 in 1950 to more than 35,000 a decade later.

Claim to Fame: Before blight wiped out Plainview's lucrative cucumber crop in the early 1900s, it was a major source of America's pickles, supplying works in Farmingdale and the big Heinz plant in Hicksville.

Where to Find More: "Our Town: Life in Plainview-Old Bethpage 1600 Through Tomorrow," by Richard Koubek, published in 1987, and other material at the Plainview-Old Bethpage Public Library.

SEA CLIFF
Victorian Homes Escaped Demolition

Beginnings: Matinecock Indians lived for centuries at the spot where Sea Cliff was settled. Dome-shaped wigwams spread along the bluff above Hempstead Harbor, where Matinecock Indians would fish in the harbor and raise crops on the field behind the bluff. The obviously productive farmland attracted British settlers, and in 1668 Joseph Carpenter bought the area from the Matinecocks. Isolated from main roads, the community, then named Carpenterville, remained quiet for more than two centuries — except during the Revolution, when the British established a camp there.

Turning Point: Things changed in 1871, when the Metropolitan Camp Ground Associ-

ation of the Methodist Church bought 240 acres from the Carpenter family and converted it into a huge camp-meeting site, covering virtually the entire village. The association built a 5,000-seat church, a boardwalk, a steamboat pier and hundreds of tent sites, all with the idea of attracting the faithful. Come they did, by steamboat and train. Families would stay for one or two weeks, living in tents and cooking meals outside. After a while, some Methodists decided the place was nice enough to live in year-round, so tents were gradually replaced with buildings. In 1883, the village was incorporated with the new name of Sea Cliff. By the 1890s, the fervor of camp meetings had been replaced by the relaxation of resorts. Excursion steamers traveled to the village from New York, and the 300-room Sea Cliff Hotel became one of the largest resorts on the Atlantic coast. That era ended when automobiles made other areas accessible in the 1920s. In the 1930s, a wave of immigrants from Russia seeking to escape communism settled in Sea Cliff, leaving it with a significant Russian population.

Claim to Fame: The real estate booms before and after World War II passed Sea Cliff by because it was not easily accessible by car or train, so many of the old Victorian homes — later the village's most distinct feature — escaped being ripped down and replaced with newer ones or with strip shopping centers. Many buildings were put on the National Register of Historic Places. In 1969, Jim Aiello took steps to attract fellow artists to the declining village with shows and markets, and those spurred a rejuvenation.

Where to Find More: Historical files at the Sea Cliff Public Library, the Syosset Public Library and the Long Island Studies Institute at Hofstra University, Hempstead.

SYOSSET
For Centuries, A Land of Plenty

Beginnings: The heavily forested hills south of Oyster Bay were among the lands used for hunting by Matinecock Indians during the thousands of years before European settlers arrived. It was too far from the shore to serve as a settlement for Indians, but occasional discoveries of arrowheads were indications that Indians used the woods. Indeed, the name Syosset may come from the Indian word *suwasset*, which means "place in the

pines." Syosset was included in Robert Williams' 1648 land purchase from the Matinecocks, but the Quaker farmers who settled nearby Jericho didn't venture that far north, and early Dutch settlers in Oyster Bay didn't climb into the hills for some time. Eventually, some Dutch families did clear land in the mid-1700s, and a small, isolated farming community was established. By 1824, a few businesses, including a small hotel, made up Syosset's core.

Turning Point: Syosset was connected to the rest of the world in 1854, when the Long Island Rail Road built a spur north from Hicksville. The access to New York agriculture markets attracted more farmers to the area, and a commercial district formed around the train station. A post office was established in 1855. Farming remained the dominant trade until shortly before World War II, when the community's larger population triggered an expansion of the business district on Jackson Avenue. After the war, the housing shortage made it profitable for farmers to sell out to developers.

Giving the Slip: On those rare occasions when Theodore Roosevelt wanted to give well-wishers the slip when he returned to Sagamore Hill in Cove Neck, he would take the train to Syosset instead of Oyster Bay, and ride his horse home through the woods.

Alfred E. Newman Slept Here: Mad magazine cartoonist Mort Drucker lived in Syosset.

Where to Find More: "Looking Back on Syosset," by Patricia Tunison, published in 1975, at Syosset Public Library.

UPPER BROOKVILLE
So Rich, the Butlers Had Their Own Country Club

Beginnings: As the official village history says, "It might have been Lower Brookville." The new village founded in 1932 was, after all, downstream in the area's little valley. When Hope Goddard Iselin, the doyenne of the millionaires and socialites who were behind the incorporation, heard the name Lower Brookville proposed, she is said to have haughtily replied: "I refuse to live in lower anything. If you must call it something, and I suppose you must, call it Upper Brookville." They did. And in a way, she set the tone for a village long known to protest anything that would threaten its sylvan solitude.

Gatsby Days: Upper Brookville was the kind of place master builder Robert Moses had in mind

when he lamented all the villages that were incorporating on Nassau's North Shore between 1929 and 1932. Together, he asserted, they were "the wealthiest, most snobbish and most reactionary community in the United States." Perhaps Moses was right. The official village history described its first 20 years as its "baronial" period — even the butlers had their own country club, set up by J.P. Morgan's man. Opposed to Moses' brand of encroaching development, Upper Brookville annexed hundreds more acres the same year it incorporated, notably what became the state's Planting Fields Arboretum. In 1950, the village fought creation of C.W. Post College, part of Long Island University, in nearby Brookville. In 1952, it battled to keep members of the Russian United Nations mission from living tax-free in the village, but lost that one, too. But there were victories: against sandmining in the 1950s and the bridge that was never built across Long Island Sound between Oyster Bay and Rye in the 1960s. And in a case that went to the U.S. Supreme Court, the village's five-acre zoning was upheld in 1981.

How to Run a Meeting: The second mayor, Morris W. Kellogg (1936-1940), held village board meetings in his home. They would start promptly at 5 p.m., and Kellogg instructed his butler to serve a tray of martinis exactly a half hour later. At other times, meetings were held at officials' private clubs in Manhattan. Arthur H. Dean, the fifth mayor of Upper Brookville (1952-1958), missed a lot of meetings: He was U.S. ambassador to South Korea during the Korean War — the same time he was mayor of Upper Brookville.

Where to Find More: "History of Upper Brookville, 1932-1982," by village historian John L. Rawlinson, Jericho Public Library.

WOODBURY
Corporate Giants Roam the Land

Beginnings: Woodbury was part of the large land purchase that Welsh settler Robert Williams made in 1648 from the Matinecock Indians. Woodbury and Syosset were an area known generally as East Woods, used initially the way the Indians did, for hunting. By the mid-1700s a small number of farmers began to cultivate land in the area. The center of the community was a tiny schoolhouse, notable mainly because poet Walt Whitman taught there for the 1837-38 school year. The tiny community remained isolated, connected only by old Indian paths to Cold Spring Harbor and Jericho, until the railroad arrived in nearby Syosset in 1854. In time, that attracted more farmers to the area, who saw that the Syosset train station opened up the large markets of western Queens, Brooklyn and New York.

Turning Point: Some of the farms were converted to estates a century ago, when wealthy New Yorkers built grand mansions across the North Shore. In Woodbury, Andrew Mellon owned Woodlands on South Woods Road. He gave the estate to his daughter as a wedding gift. It later became the Town of Oyster Bay's public golf course. Other farms were eaten up during the real estate boom after World War II. Although Woodbury was less densely developed than the rest of Nassau, most of the farms became either residential neighborhoods, office parks near Jericho Turnpike or the Long Island Expressway, or shopping centers. As of 1999, Meyer's Farm, at nine acres, was the last in Woodbury.

Claims to Fame: Woodbury's corporate residents have included dieting company Weight Watchers, and until it moved to Bethpage in 1998, Cablevision Systems Corp.

Where to Find More: In the Woodbury files at the Syosset Public Library and the Long Island Studies Institute at Hofstra University.

View from the Dock, Sea Cliff, L. I.

SEA CLIFF: A scene from an old postcard. The Metropolitan Camp Ground Association of the Methodist Church built a boardwalk and a steamboat pier in 1871 to attract tourists.

LOOKING NORTH ON MAIN STREET, SYOSSET, LONG ISLAND, N.Y.

SYOSSET: An undated postcard depicts Main Street. Farming was a way of life in Syosset until after World War II, when landowners started to sell to housing developers.

Suffolk

From an English colony nourished by soil and sea to suburbia knitted together by rails

By the time Suffolk County was formed in 1683, English settlers already had been living on the East End for more than 40 years. The pioneers of Southampton and Southold Towns stepped ashore in 1640, only a year after the arrival of the first English settler, Lion Gardiner, at the historic island just off the East Hampton shore that still bears his name. Separated by miles of wilderness from the Dutch pioneers who came to the west end of Long Island in the 1620s, the English colonists were mostly Puritans from New England, strongly influenced in social, political and religious matters by life in Massachusetts. They farmed and fished, and later would develop their own whaling and shipping fleets. They held annual town meetings that ruled on everything from pig control to who would be allowed into the community.

Their flinty independence had much to do with their dismay at becoming part of the Province of New York after the British took New Amsterdam in 1664 and James, duke of York and brother of King Charles II, became their immediate ruler. The region was then known as the East Riding of Yorkshire. Among other things, the duke abolished their town meetings, having no intention of allowing representative government. Only after years of protest and resistance from Long Island and elsewhere did he agree to changes, finally deciding that citizens would be more agreeable to paying taxes if they had representation.

Those changes came from a New York General Assembly session in New York City in October, 1683. It divided New York into 12 counties, including Kings (Brooklyn), Queens (including what became Nassau) and Suffolk. The Assembly passed a charter of liberties guaranteeing the political and civil rights of the people of New York, and established a new court system at the town and county level. Many problems lay ahead, but it was a start for the new Suffolk County, named for a county of the same name northeast of London.

Suffolk in the 18th Century prospered from farming, fishing, lumbering, shipping and other trades, and continued closer ties with New England than with the rest of New York. Many New Yorkers cast their lot with the British during the Revolution, but most people from Suffolk were Patriots eager for an independent America. A famous anti-British spy ring operated out of Setauket, and after the war George Washington himself dropped in to say thanks.

After the Revolution, Suffolk became prominent in whaling, peaking with Sag Harbor's heyday in the 1840s, and

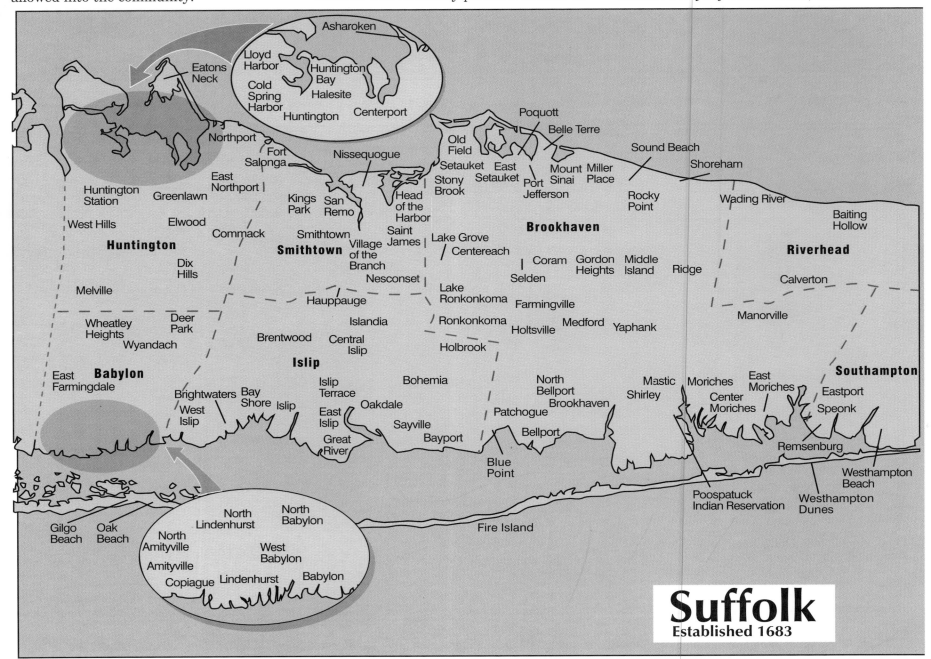

Suffolk
Established 1683

shipbuilding proliferated in places such as Port Jefferson, Greenport and Northport. Over the decades, the growth of New York City spurred demand for Suffolk's farm crops as well as shellfish, firewood, and sand and gravel.

A major turning point occurred with the completion of the Long Island Rail Road to Greenport in 1844, and subsequent migration of thousands of city residents seeking summer fun on the Island, many of whom stayed. The years after the Civil War were marked by the start of many industries that attracted immigrants who contributed to the area's economic and cultural life. By the late 1800s, huge estates were built on both shores even as developers were starting to cut up large blocks of land for those of lesser means.

By the time World War II began, Suffolk, no longer able to depend on traditional farming and fishing, turned increasingly to manufacturing, especially for defense purposes. As the 1950s dawned, huge population gains drove development. In 1960, Suffolk switched to a county executive and charter form of government, a sure sign that the years of rural life were over and the suburban revolution was in full force.

Gazetteer

The people behind the names of some prominent roads and places in Suffolk

Bread and Cheese Hollow Road: A popular myth about this road, which divides the Towns of Huntington and Smithtown, says Richard (Bull) Smith stopped here in 1663 to munch bread and cheese during a day-long ride to determine the perimeter of the land the Indians would give him to establish Smithtown. But you'd have to be named Smith to believe it: Historians say Smith probably bought his land from Lion Gardiner of Gardiners Island.

Caleb Smith State Park: Caleb Smith was the great-grandson of Smithtown's founder. In 1751, he built his farmhouse in what is now the 543-acre state preserve between Jericho Turnpike and Veterans Memorial Highway in Smithtown. Part of his house exists within the park museum.

Gin Lane: Though it's in a posh part of Southampton Village, the name has nothing to do with cocktail hour. "Gin" was an English word for cattle enclosures in colonial times.

Granny Road: This Farmingville-to-Coram road is named for Granny Penny, a beloved samaritan of the late 18th Century who doctored the area's sick as far east as Yaphank.

Mott's Hollow Road: A Thoreau-like character called Uncle Mott in 1861 built himself a cabin in the woods in what now is Belle Terre. He avoided townfolk in favor of blissful solitude, but caught the eye of W.M. Davis, Port Jefferson's foremost artist, who left paintings of Uncle Mott's house.

Mount Misery Road: One yarn has it that a young couple in 1851 built a house on a hilly road in Huntington and the place burned down. They rebuilt, and it burned down a second time. That's misery. Another account says the road was named 300 years ago by settlers who dreaded driving a horse and wagon up nearby Hartman hill. The road now cuts through West Hills County Park in Huntington.

Rogues Path: Part of what used to be a longer east-west road in Huntington still bears the name. It came from the unsavory reputation the highway received at the end of the Revolution, when travelers were robbed and farmhouses looted.

Whiskey Road: This old road was laid out in 1753 from Ridge to Middle Island, and legend has it a young swain seeking to get more quickly through woods to his beloved's farm several miles away offered jugs of whiskey to motivate the workers, who were allowed to sip as they went. The road turned out so crooked it had to be straightened by the town three years later.

William Floyd Parkway: This county parkway extending from Shirley to East Shoreham was named for William Floyd (1734-1821), a signer of the Declaration of Independence and member of Congress whose Mastic estate is now part of Fire Island National Seashore. **— Tom Morris**

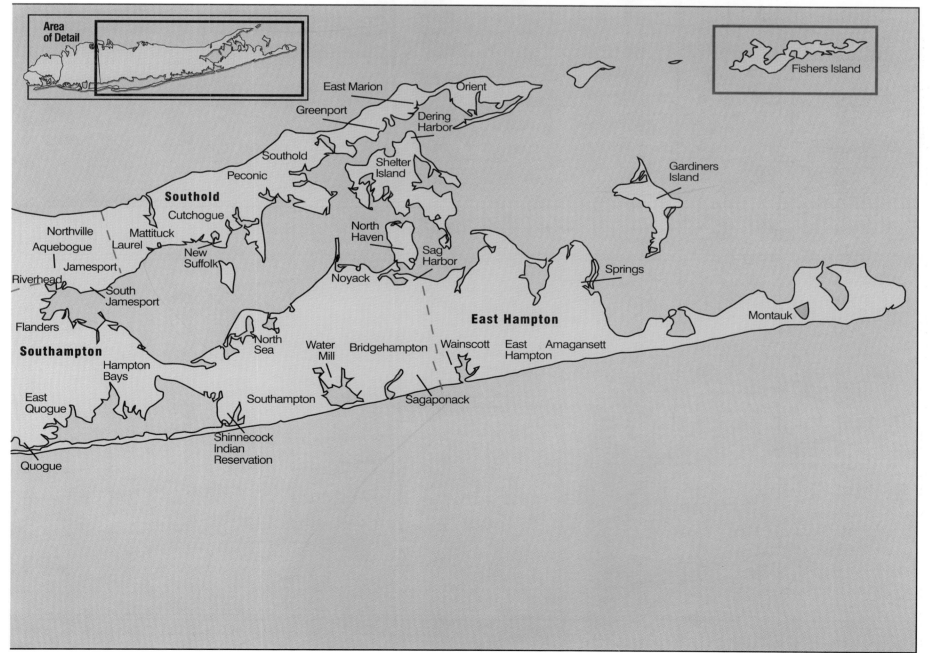

Area of Detail

Fishers Island

East Marion
Orient
Greenport
Dering Harbor
Southold
Shelter Island
Peconic
Gardiners Island
Southold
Cutchogue
Northville
Mattituck
North Haven
Aquebogue
Laurel
New Suffolk
Sag Harbor
Jamesport
Springs
Riverhead
South Jamesport
Noyack
Flanders
East Hampton
Southampton
North Sea
Montauk
Hampton Bays
Water Mill
Bridgehampton
Wainscott
East Hampton
Amagansett
East Quogue
Southampton
Sagaponack
Shinnecock Indian Reservation
Quogue

Fullerton Collection, Suffolk County Historical Society

MEDFORD: Cheers sound and flags wave as the first connecting train through the East River tunnel passes through the community in 1910.

Nassau County Museum Collection, Long Island Studies Institute

WEST SAYVILLE: Oyster sheds await a day's harvest in about 1910. It was in 1912 that Dutch oystermen led by John Ockers established the Bluepoint Co.

Newsday Archive

MONTAUK: Sheriff's deputies pose with a casino wheel seized in a 1929 raid.

Southold Historical Society / Reginald Donahue

SOUTHOLD: Albert Einstein strolls with a local resident, David Rothman, at Nassau Point in 1939. In the summers of 1938 and 1939, the physicist rented a cottage on the point and sailed often on Peconic Bay. On Aug. 2, 1939, Einstein signed a letter that alerted the White House of scientific discoveries that could lead to powerful nuclear weapons.

63

4th GRADE   1908-09

Fourth-Graders 90 Years Apart

Sneakers and blue jeans
weren't the style in 1908-09
when fourth-grade students
at the Park Avenue School in
Amityville posed for a class picture on
the front steps of the school building in a
photo, top, from the collection of the
Amityville Historical Society.

But they certainly were in style in
1998, when a contingent of fourth-grad-
ers from the Park Avenue School sat
on the same steps of the building — used
as the district's Administration Building, known as
Park Avenue
North — for a
group shot of
their own.

THEN & NOW

The school
building, at Park Avenue and Ireland
Place, was built in 1894 and replaced a
small one-room schoolhouse on
Merrick Road and a school for black
students in North Amityville. Black
and white students went to the new
school together in grades one through
12. The Park Avenue Elementary School
of 1998 was built in the 1930s and had
about 780 students in grades three
through five.

Apart from clothing styles, fourth-
graders changed a great deal during the
20th Century, Park Avenue Principal
Kathleen Kelly said in 1998. "Now
they're learning through TVs and
computers," Kelly said, but "in many
ways, they're less self-sufficient."

Town of Babylon

The last of Suffolk County's 10 towns to be formed, Babylon was born the way many political entities are born: out of resentment. Until the late 1800s, the southwestern corner of Suffolk was part of the Town of Huntington, and people referred to it as Huntington South. It was a designation that perturbed its residents, who felt neglected in town affairs. Finally in 1872, the residents of Amityville, Babylon and Breslau (later called Lindenhurst) asked the State Legislature to separate Huntington into two townships. Their secessionist plea may have been helped by the weather. Of the 713 people who braved the cold on a particularly frigid day in January, 1872, 445 were from what then became Babylon. The town was officially formed on Jan. 3, 1873.

AMITYVILLE

Al Capone Was In the Lineup

Beginnings: When the Carmans family built a mill at Carmans Lane around 1700, the area was known as Huntington West Neck South. Salt hay sprouting from the region's marshy wetlands and harvested for animal feed was the big draw for settlers who carved up the one-time Indian land into small farms. From its beginnings, Amityville was a commercial center. The earliest mills, such as Ireland's mill, which operated until 1915, soon expanded into other ventures. The Irelands, another founding family, opted for a tavern and bakery. Carman's was a general store and post office for a time. Even as late as the turn of the century, neighbors from Massapequa and Copiague came to Amityville to do their shopping.

Turning Point: Like other South Shore communities in the early 1900s, Amityville evolved into a summer playground, where the rich and famous built homes, rented cottages or relaxed in several seaside hotels. Annie Oakley of Buffalo Bill's Wild West Show often visited the homes of Fred Stone, a popular vaudevillian, on Clocks Boulevard and comedian and satirist Will Rogers, who rented across the street. There was also the infamous gangster Al Capone, whose tenure in Amityville was marked by nothing more sensational than an occasional vacation baseball game on his lawn.

Washington Ate Here: On his historic postrevolutionary trip across Long Island in 1790, the first president dined at the East Amityville home of Zebulon Ketcham, whose home had recently been an inn and a tavern. In his diary Washington recalled Capt. Ketcham's home as being a "very neat and decent one."

How It Got Its Name: Tired of the cumbersome name of Huntington West Neck South, residents met in 1846 to decide on a name for the post office. According to one version, the meeting soon turned into bedlam, causing one participant to exclaim, "What this meeting needs is some amity." Another version has Samuel Ireland, the prominent mill owner and largest landowner in town, standing up and declaring that they should name the village after his boat. Its name was Amity.

Where to Find More: "Amityville History Revisited," by William T. Lauder, at the Amityville Historical Society.

BABYLON

A Rowdy Tavern Inspired a Name

BY MOLLY MCCARTHY
STAFF WRITER

At first, it was little more than a stagecoach stop. Gradually over two centuries, it evolved from farming village to summer resort to suburban bedroom community.

But like many Long Island villages, Babylon's diverse history is hard to encapsulate. Home to master planner Robert Moses, Babylon also was where wireless communications and black professional baseball got their starts. "There were many eras of Babylon," said Alice Zaruka, president of the Babylon Village Historical Society. "It was a stagecoach stop, then the trolley came, then the hotels. There were 11 hotels in the village during its summer resort heyday. Then it turned into a commuter community."

Before the hotels and the trolley and the railroad, there wasn't much but salt hay. No dwellings existed in Babylon before 1700. And, even by the time the Revolution came, there were only a few settlers in the region.

When Nathaniel Conklin built his home at the corner of Main Street and Deer Park Avenue in 1803, Babylon was still known as Huntington South and a rowdy tavern called the American Hotel stood next door. Conklin's mother wasn't thrilled about the hotel's proximity, characterizing the place as "another Babylon." However, the younger Conklin prevailed, built the house and carved a retort to his mother on the chimney. The stone tablet reads: "New Babylon. This House Built By Nat. Conklin 1803." Minus the "New," the name stuck.

Conklin, in that day the area's largest landowner, soon built a tannery that would spearhead Babylon's rise as a commercial center. Some entrepreneurs invested in grist, saw and flour mills, while others capitalized on the bluefish and eels pulled from the bay and shipped to Brooklyn markets.

By the 1890s, Babylon was described as a "thriving country town," in the words of one observer at the time, a "spick-and-span array of cottages embowered in trees, flowers and shrubbery, and resting on the shore, of a great, blue-bosomed, green-edged tranquil bay." Two miles north of the shore, millionaire August Belmont maintained a sprawling estate with its own private racetrack that would later be transformed into Belmont Lake State Park. Closer to the village, the 350-room Argyle Hotel enticed wealthy New Yorkers to spend their summer leisure by Babylon's bay.

Frank Thompson, an African-American, managed a huge service staff as a head waiter at the Argyle Hotel. When they weren't waiting tables in the lavish dining areas of the hotel, Thompson and his cohorts were on the baseball field. Thompson formed a team he called the Athletics, which in 1885 was christened by a promoter as the Cuban Giants to make the black team more acceptable to white American fans. Thompson and his mates didn't know it at the time, but they would later be designated the first all-black professional team in America.

And it wasn't long after that that Babylon collected another first. In 1901, shortly after returning from Newfoundland, where he received the first wireless transmission — or three short clicks signaling the Morse code letter S — from across the Atlantic, physicist Guglielmo Marconi came to Babylon. Having found a suitable spot near the shore, he set up shop in a 12-foot-square wooden shack at Fire Island Avenue and Virginia Road. Though it looked more like a tool shed, Marconi's shack became the first shore-to-ship wireless relay station. From there, Marconi could communicate with ships offshore using the wireless communications system that was the forerunner of commercial radio.

Moses, a Connecticut native, first saw Babylon in the early 1920s when friends invited him and his wife, Mary, out for summer weekends. Moses fell in love with Babylon and the entire South Shore, renting a bungalow in the summer of 1922 and eventually buying a home on Thompson Avenue. Many of Moses' grand ideas, like Jones Beach, were hatched on drives or boat rides around his new hometown. Because Moses had no drivers' license, a driver chauffeured him around Long Island. In fact, Babylon residents in the

Babylon Historical and Preservation Society

The Argyle Hotel, open 1882-1904, provided the first black pro baseball team. At left, a souvenir recalls Guglielmo Marconi, whose transmitter was in Babylon.

1930s often spotted the state parks commissioner's limousine speeding through the streets of the village on the way to the dock, where he'd board a state-owned yacht to explore area waterways.

Despite his hectic schedule, Moses always found time for a swim, sometimes twice a day, either at Jones Beach, in the bay or in the creek behind his home. More than any other feature, it was the water that first attracted Moses and kept him there.

In 1996, Alice Zaruka's group interviewed several old-timers about growing up in Babylon, and water was foremost in their recollections. "They were fishermen, clammers or captains for wealthy people who had boats," Zaruka said. "Their love of the water was the main thing. It's a central part of Babylon's heritage."

Claim to Fame: Besides Moses, Marconi, Belmont and baseball, there was Bob Keeshan — Babylon was the home of the man known as TV's first Captain Kangaroo.

Where to Find More: "Huntington-Babylon Town History," by the Huntington Historical Society, 1935, Babylon Village Historical and Preservation Society.

Newsday Archive

A Highway S-Curve

An undated photograph from Newsday's files, believed to be from the early 1940s, shows the S-curve on Montauk Highway just east of Cooper Street in Babylon. The curve was part of a two-lane section of Montauk Highway completed in 1912, according to Christopher Cotter, senior landscape architect at the State Department of Transportation's regional office in Hauppauge.

In a 1998 photograph, the area is the southern terminus of a portion of state Route 231, built from 1966 to 1970, between the Southern State Parkway and Montauk Highway.

As part of the project, the S-curve was eliminated and Montauk Highway was reconstructed as a four-lane, separated roadway.

Newsday Photo / Bill Davis, 1998

COPIAGUE

It Could've Been Marconiville

Beginnings: Like neighboring Amityville, Copiague's main reason for being in the early days was its harbor. The water drew settlers such as Zebulon Ketcham, Nehemiah Heartte and Abraham Wanzer, who built mills to grind corn or saw wood along the region's waterways.

Washington Ate Here, Too: Both Amityville and Copiague claim the historic moment when America's first president sat down to dinner at Zebulon Ketcham's Inn during Washington's 1790 tour of Long Island. The inn was located where Deauville Boulevard meets Montauk Highway. (A plaque marks the spot.) Though the plot later clearly existed in Copiague, the region was, at one time, known as East Amityville.

Turning Point: Besides East Amityville, Copiague also was referred to as Huntington South and Great Neck at various points in its history. But the hamlet finally got its own identity in 1895. The residents chose Copiague, an Indian word meaning "sheltered harbor." Five years later, the railroad came. And, in 1903, the hamlet got a post office.

It Could Have Been Marconiville: In 1906, a young Italian engineer named John Campagnoli purchased a large tract along Great Neck Road north of the railroad tracks. A close friend of inventor Gugliemo Marconi, Campagnoli renamed the area Marconiville and built a hotel of the same name facing the railroad station. Even though Marconi was a frequent house guest of Campagnoli's, the name didn't flatter the physicist into settling permanently in Copiague. The hotel didn't stay long either. The Marconiville Hotel burned to the ground in 1925. Only Marconi Boulevard remained.

Where to Find More: "Copiague: Your Town & Mine," by Elizabeth Eide, at the Copiague Public Library.

DEER PARK

Once a Retreat For John Quincy Adams

Beginnings: Jacob Conklin was one of the first settlers in the region that in the late 1600s was still thick with scrub oak, pine and carpets of vine. When Conklin went north to visit Huntington village, he'd tell people about his farm located "south toward the Great Bay before you get to the swamp. My farm is in the deer park." Apparently Conklin and his few neighbors shared their new home with the deer that thrived in the thick underbrush. The name stayed even when the deer did not.

Ye Olde Spring: A fighting Irishman by the name of Casey rose to the rank of general during the war. When the fighting was over, Casey retired to West Deer Park, where he opened a resort at the Deer Park spring. He called it Colonial Spring and operated it until his death in 1808. The spring was still there in the 1990s, said Bill Frohlich, a member of the Babylon Town Historical Commission who had seen it burbling in a wooded area owned by the Usdan Center for Creative and Performing Arts on Colonial Springs Road.

Pickles and Plants: In the early 1900s, Hymie Golden ran a pickle works on a strip of land he leased from a local woman for $5 a year and a carload of pickles. When the factory caught fire in 1932, residents complained that the town smelled like sauerkraut for a week. And at one time, Deer Park was the leading dahlia-growing community in the state. Thousands of dahlias were shipped to New York City up to the 1950s. No fewer than 200,000 dahlias were grown in one spectacular season in 1952.

Turning Point: As late as 1870, Deer Park had only a blacksmith shop, railroad station and a dozen houses. It wasn't until after World War II that the place boomed like so many others on Long Island. By the 1970s, the population hit 30,000; in 1998 it was listed as 28,650.

Brushes With Fame: Although a native of Quincy, Mass., ex-President John Quincy Adams bought a summer home in Deer Park in 1835 and spent many summers there until his death in 1848. The boundaries of the Adams place were forgotten but it was somewhere in the vicinity of Adams Street, a half-mile west of Deer Park Avenue. On Nov. 22, 1921, comedian Rodney Dangerfield was born at 44 Railroad Ave. (later Acorn Street) to vaudevillian Phil Roy and his wife. Although Dangerfield left Deer Park early in his childhood, he returned in 1970 for Rodney Dangerfield Day. A week later, Dangerfield brought the plaque he received to an appearance on Johnny Carson's "Tonight" show.

Where to Find More: "Deer Park Thru the Years," by Anthony F. Cesare, and "Recollections: Deer Park, 1900-1950," by the creative writing-illustrative design class of Deer Park High School.

EAST FARMINGDALE

Rural Area Soars Into The Wild Blue Yonder

Beginnings: This agricultural area was largely untouched until it evolved as the outer reaches of Farmingdale Village in the mid-19th Century. Indeed, there was no need to distinguish it from Farmingdale until that village incorporated in 1904. Some time after that, the portion of the community over the Suffolk County line became known as East Farmingdale. It retained its rural aspect for some time, known most for its several pickle works on Broadhollow Road.

Turning Point: In 1917, Lawrence Sperry set up an aircraft company on the flat land of East Farmingdale, the first of several that would be located there. The site was taken over in 1926 by the Fairchild Airplane Manufacturing Co. In 1931, Russian aviator Alexander de Seversky opened another aircraft company there, building planes in which he set a world speed record of 177.79 mph on Oct. 8, 1933. In 1938, his company was reorganized and became Republic Aviation Corp., a pioneering aircraft company. It began to fade after its takeover in 1965 by Fairchild Hiller Corp. of Maryland, and it was closed in 1987. But its legacy was the industrialization of East Farmingdale, forever erasing its agricultural roots.

Claim to Fame: Republic and, later Fairchild Republic, produced the P-47 Thunderbolt fighter during World War II, the F-84 Thunderjet of the Korean War, the F-105 Thunderchief fighter during the Vietnam War era, and the A-10 Warthog tank killer of the 1970s and 1980s.

Where to Find More: "Picture History of Aviation on Long Island," by George C. Dade and Frank Strnad (Dover Publications, 1989).

LINDENHURST

Babe Ruth Left Town That Day as a Winner

Beginnings: Not until the early 1800s did a few farmhouses sprout up along dirt roads that would later form the main thoroughfares of Lindenhurst. Life passed quietly for the first generation of settlers, until Thomas Welwood arrived in the 1860s. A Brooklyn real estate agent, Welwood saw great potential in the pine brush clearings near the tracks of the new South Side Railroad, which first rolled through the area in 1867. By 1869, Welwood had acquired so much land in the region that the new railroad station was christened Wellwood, a misspelling that persisted through the 1990s.

Turning Point: Welwood found a business partner in Charles Schleier, a German immigrant and wallpaper hanger from Brooklyn. Schleier soon became Welwood's agent and started selling 25-by-100-foot lots to fellow Germans in Manhattan, Brooklyn and even his native homeland. As part of the pair's marketing scheme, Wellwood was renamed the City of Breslau in 1870 after Schleier's hometown in Germany.

Many Germans bought the pitch and some land, transforming the seaside village into a little Germantown. It wasn't long before church services were delivered exclusively in German, and German was taught in the local school.

Turning Point II: Just as the Breslau plan was taking off, Welwood's and Schleier's partnership soured, culminating in a long court battle. The litigation caused many people to lose their homes and bred much resentment among the new inhabitants. It was this bitterness, some contend, that led residents to vote for yet another name change in 1891. This time, they opted for Lindenhurst, inspired by the lovely linden trees that lined Wellwood Avenue.

Brush With Fame: It was a cold, windy October day at the Meridale Baseball Park at West Montauk Highway and South Second Street. But nothing could keep the crowds away on that brisk fall day of 1930. That was the day Babe Ruth came to Lindenhurst.

Accompanied by other big-leaguers such as Lou Gehrig, Ruth played an exhibition game against Addie Klein's Lindenhurst Nine, an amateur baseball club. Bundled up in blankets and overcoats, none of the 4,000 fans seemed to mind that the local team got beat by Ruth and his cohorts by a score of 10-4.

Where to Find More: "The Growth of Our Village From Wellwood to Lindenhurst," edited by Louis Hirsch; also see a collection of local newspaper columns entitled "Historically Yours," written by Lindenhurst Village Historian Evelyn Ellis, compiled and indexed in the Lindenhurst Memorial Library.

NORTH AMITYVILLE

See story on Page 69.

NORTH BABYLON

Belmont's Huge Estate Attracts a President

Beginnings: Only scattered farms in "Huntington South" existed in the first half of the 19th Century in what later became North Babylon. The Town of Babylon was created in 1872, and about that time large, lavish estates were being carved out of the dense woods.

Turning Points: Financier and diplomat August Belmont in 1868 completed his 1,100-acre country mansion, nursery and stud farm for the breeding of thoroughbred stallions whose names were to become internationally famous. Among them were Kingfisher, The Ill-Used, Matador and Fiddlesticks. The estate was one of the most complete in the country for breeding and racing horses, with 500 acres under cultivation for feeding horses and other livestock, 150 more acres in grass and another 50

Please Turn to Page 69

Lindenhurst Village Museum Photo

LINDENHURST: An early-1900s photo looks south on Wellwood Avenue, near Gates Avenue. The photographer was atop the Liberty Hose Co. tower.

Newsday Photo / Cliff De Bear

NORTH AMITYVILLE: In 1963, hobbyists gathered their aircraft at Zahn's Airport, which opened in 1945. In 1980, the airport was closed to make room for an industrial park.

Amityville Historical Society

NORTH AMITYVILLE: The Von Nessen family farm as it appeared in about 1944. Portions of the land were later divided for the Ronek Park housing development.

NORTH AMITYVILLE

Where Freed Slaves Could Make a Home

BY MOLLY McCARTHY
STAFF WRITER

When Irwin Quintyne went shopping for a new home in Levittown after World War II, the real estate agents told him bluntly that blacks weren't wanted. So Quintyne turned to the only community he knew of that would welcome his family — North Amityville.

"I saw an ad in The Amsterdam News for homes in Amityville. I got a GI loan and bought a house on Bayview Avenue," Quintyne recalled in 1997. "It seemed we were almost guided here by the racism on Long Island. After Levittown, North Amityville was it."

Actually, there were several communities on Long Island where blacks settled in the postwar housing boom. Besides North Amityville, there were Wyandanch, Roosevelt, Hempstead and West Hempstead. Quintyne wasn't aware of those places at the time; he picked North Amityville because he had a friend who lived there.

As political scientist Andrew Wiese argued in a paper on racial segregation on Long Island presented at a Hofstra University conference in 1993, black suburbs like North Amityville grew out of historic black enclaves in unincorporated areas that were out of reach of municipal restrictions designed to exclude blacks. In North Amityville's case, the hamlet was excluded when the predominantly white Village of Amityville incorporated in 1894.

"In these places, race acted as a double-edged sword, carving small spaces for black families adjacent to older communities largely because developers for whites would not risk building there and no concentrated white elite was in place to organize against them," Wiese wrote. "Developers ceded these places to the African-American market." This is in contrast with a place such as Gordon Heights, a community in Brookhaven Town that was deliberately marketed to blacks starting in the early 1900s.

The history of North Amityville as a black enclave actually goes back to the 1700s, when the first blacks came to Amityville as slaves, freed slaves or indentured servants. While some may have worked their own land, others were employed by the wealthy white farmers who settled along the shore. They were founding black families: Fowlers, Millers, Squires and Devines. By 1815, they were meeting in one another's homes for religious services. With help from Montaukett Indians who first settled in the area, the Bethel African Methodist Church was founded. It became one of the Island's oldest black congregations.

As slaves were gradually emancipated across New York, many in communities like Amityville continued to work the land as tenant farmers or as laborers. Some moved into commercial or retail industries, providing services for the burgeoning black enclave. They opened barber shops, liveries, groceries and delicatessens. And when Amityville became a premier summer destination for vacationers, many blacks were hired to work in the hotels and resorts built by the sea.

Lillian Miller, in a 1997 interview, recalled stories her late husband, Norman, told about his earliest ancestors. "His grandmother was born on the Shinnecock reservation, and his grandfather used to go to the bay every day to fish. He kept cows and chickens," said Miller, who still lived in the house her husband built on Columbus Boulevard in 1932. "And Norman's mother used to work as a servant for old Dr. Luce in the village." Lillian's own parents, John and Lillie Kenney, moved to North Amityville in 1923, when Lillian was 9 years old. Originally from Charleston, S.C., the couple spent the early part of their marriage in upper Manhattan until they could afford a move to the country. When they had enough money, Lillie opened a deli on Albany Avenue near Smith Street and John had a barber shop nearby.

These three families, the Millers, the Kenneys and the Quintynes, neatly illustrate the dominant patterns of black migration on Long Island. First, there were the freed slaves who farmed the land just as the early white settlers did. Then there were families like the Kenneys, who came in the early

part of this century to work as servants in the large summer hotels or open businesses catering to the growing summer populations. And, finally, middle-class families like the Quintynes were driven to these same communities where earlier black families provided an anchor.

In a 20-year span ending in 1960, the African-American population on Long Island grew by 50,000. But the bulk of that growth didn't come until the 1950s when new suburban developments such as North Amityville's Ronek Park were sprouting up to cater to the black middle class.

Many streets that would make up Ronek Park, like Bayview Avenue and Emerald Lane, were carved out of a farm the Von Nessen family ran for more than 30 years. Bought by Thomas Romano, the land that once produced fruits and vegetables sprouted ranch homes that sold in 1951 for $8,400 apiece. Romano eventually built more than 1,000 three-bedroom homes in Ronek Park, according to Wiese.

"When we built our house, there were a few others," remembered Lillian Miller. "Now, they're all around. As they years went by, it all filled in. I guess people just kept coming."

Where to Find More: "A History of North Amityville," by Walter G. Clerk, in the Amityville Public Library; "Racial Cleansing in the Suburbs: Suburban Government, Urban Renewal, and Segregation on Long Island, New York, 1945-1960," by Andrew Wiese; "Contested Terrain: Power, Politics, and Participation in Suburbia," edited by Marc L. Silver and Martin Melkonian.

A women's group poses at a North Amityville church in the 1920s or '30s.

NORTH BABYLON, Continued

acres in paddocks. The estate had more than 30 buildings, including the 24-room mansion.

Chester Arthur, president from 1881-85, fished there often. A large part of the estate became the Army Air Corps' Camp Dam in World War I. The Long Island State Park Commission later created Belmont Lake State Park on part of the site, and the agency set up headquarters there upon its creation in 1924 under

master planner Robert Moses. Several other wealthy men, including Austin Corbin, banker and president of the Long Island Rail Road, and industrialist Col. M. Robert Guggenheim (brother of Newsday founder Harry) had estates nearby.

Turning Points: LIRR service reached Deer Park in 1842, turning what was called Babylon Lane (later Deer Park Avenue) through "South Deer Park" (North Babylon) into a busy, rutted, stagecoach route. It also was used for "horse

racing and trotting, foot racing, greased-pig chasing and sack racing," a history said. The first school, in 1810, was a one-room log cabin on Phelps Lane. The 1932 grade school on Deer Park Avenue became a town landmark. Soon after World War II, housing developments began popping up on what had been estates, farms and woods.

Landmark: Two English ship cannons from the Battle of Lake Erie, Sept. 10, 1813, won by Commodore Oliver Hazard Perry, were resur-

rected from a Pittsburgh junkyard and placed in front of the Belmont mansion in the late 19th Century to adorn the front of park commission headquarters. August Belmont's wife was Perry's niece and daughter of Commodore Matthew Perry, who in 1853 opened Japan to the West.

Where to Find More: "From Paddock to Park, the Story of Belmont Lake State Park," May, 1941, Long Island Forum, and assorted historical papers, North Babylon Public Library.

NORTH LINDENHURST
From the Boondocks To the Center of Town

Beginnings: So remote was Babylon's town seat before World War II that when 82 two-story houses were being built on small lots in the woods two miles north of Lindenhurst Village in the early 1930s, it was the talk of the town. What would become North Lindenhurst had been part of the privately owned City of Breslau property in 1870. Breslau's bounds were shrunk when it became the Village of Lindenhurst in 1923, and the scrub-oak belt to the north was strictly boondocks, said Evelyn Ellis, president of the Lindenhurst Historical Society. For several years during the Depression, no one bought the houses in the woods, and many were left unfinished, though they were selling for $2,500, said Frieda Brion, whose family bought one in 1936 and who owned one after getting married. When the war began, so did North Lindenhurst, as defense production lured thousands to the area.

Turning Points: By 1950, housing was fast replacing the woods. One builder donated land and a building as part of his development, and the structure was later used by the North Lindenhurst Civic Association. In 1957, 12 men met there to form a fire department. Zahn's Airport, a private field on the North Amityville-North Lindenhurst line, opened in 1945. It was bought by the town in 1980 and turned into an industrial park. North Lindenhurst, with 11,000 residents in 1998, became heavily residential, with scattered industry and commerce along its main routes, Straight Path and North Wellwood Avenue. The first school, William Rall Elementary, was built in the 1950s.

Landmark: Babylon Town Hall was moved from Babylon Village to Sunrise Highway, North Lindenhurst, about the center of the town, in October, 1958.

Where to Find More: "Town of Babylon, 125th Anniversary Commemorative Photo Album," 1997, and papers dealing with local history, Lindenhurst Memorial Library.

OAK BEACH, GILGO BEACH
Robert Moses' Outing A Beach Love Affair

Beginnings: Crusty old baymen would refer to the 18-mile barrier island that stretched from Jones Beach to Captree as "the strand." And centuries before there was an Ocean Parkway, it was simply a collection of empty beaches and swampy marshland. In 1695, a Welsh privateer named Maj. Thomas Jones bought thousands of acres from the Indians and used the land as a whaling outpost. Long after Jones' death, people continued to call it Jones Beach. Besides a few hunting shacks, there were no dwellings on the main beach or adjacent islands until 1879, when Henry Livingston built a cottage on Oak Island. Before that, mainland farmers used to drop off cattle at the island to graze the pastures until they were picked up in late fall. But by 1900, the Oak Island steamer was ferrying summer vacationers back and forth to cottages and boarding houses that sprang up at the bustling beach resort.

To Market, to Market: Even before the Revolutionary War, entrepreneurs harvested the salt hay, sedge and black grass along the island's shores to ship to New York City. The hay was valuable livestock bedding, and early settlers used it to thatch roofs, fill mattresses and mulch crops. While the rest of the country celebrated Labor Day, Long Islanders ushered in the Ma'shin' Seas'n (a contraction of Marshing

Newsday Photo

OAK BEACH: A 1982 view. Water enthusiasts come to a place where mainland farmers used to drop off cattle to graze.

Season), when crews of cutters staked their claims and spent days loading the Island's bounty onto hay boats. By 1764, Huntington Town officials, who then controlled the barrier island, tried to regulate salt-hay harvest by granting leases to cut hay. Although modified, those agreements prevailed more than 200 years later, requiring all residents to lease their land from Babylon Town.

Turning Point: Robert Moses, a Connecticut native, became enchanted with the barrier beaches after friends invited him to Babylon in 1922. He rented a cottage in Oak Beach for many years, later moving to Gilgo. Besides turning half of "the strand" by the 1930s into a summer refuge for city dwellers known as Jones Beach State Park, Moses — and his parkways — opened up the summer-only communities of Oak Beach, Gilgo Beach, Captree and others to year-round residents.

Where to Find More: "By-gone Days at Oak Beach," by Ulla S. Kimball in Long Island Forum, October, 1968, and "The Old Time Ma'shin' Season" by Julian Denton Smith in Long Island Forum, July, 1956. Also see scrapbook and postcard collections kept by the Babylon Village Historical and Preservation Society.

WEST BABYLON
The Community With The Biggest Population

Beginnings: Until World War II, West Babylon was a slimly populated checkerboard of woods and farms north of the established villages of Babylon and Lindenhurst. Walt Whitman, at 17, taught school there in the winter of 1836-37, presiding in a tiny schoolhouse (long gone) said to have been on the north side of modern Montauk Highway just east of Great East Neck Road. His parents, Walter and Louisa Van Velsor Whitman, had a farm a few yards away; the Great South Bay Shopping Center was later built there.

Turning Point: The area was the southern end of Huntington Town until Babylon Town's creation in 1872. The first West Babylon school in the new town was built in 1880 on the south side of Montauk Highway, where the Bulk's Nurseries windmill, now gone, was a landmark. By 1887, West Babylon had developed a small community around the farms where Great Neck Road, Arnold Avenue and Farmingdale Road met.

Now and Then: During the 1920s, the West Babylon Athletic Club was a force in countywide community sports, especially baseball and basketball. During the Depression, the West Babylon Cardinals took on that mantle, but the small-town farming and sports way of life fell apart with the coming of World War II. Bulb farms like Bulk's and VanBourgondien's faded (the latter became a park and site of Our Lady of Grace Catholic Church). The brick Main School, built in 1930, became apartments for the elderly. The old Haab farm on Route 109 became West Babylon High School in 1960. Bergen Point County Golf Course and the Southwest Sewer District plant were built on former wetlands near Great South Bay. Montauk Highway, in the late 19th Century a dirt road flanked by modest-sized estates, became a teeming commercial strip. Thanks to the postwar housing boom, the community became the town's most populous with 42,903 residents in 1998.

Where to Find More: Historic papers at West Babylon Public Library.

WYANDANCH, WHEATLEY HEIGHTS
Cutting Through Brush To Find a New Life

Beginnings: To its earliest settlers, the area was known as West Deer Park. But in the 1880s, the

area was renamed Wyandance after a local brickyard, the Wyandance Brick and Terra Cotta Corp. It soon reverted to West Deer Park when the yard burned down in 1894. However, residents adopted Wyandanch, one of many spellings of the great Indian sachem's name, in 1903 to avoid confusion with neighboring Deer Park. Meanwhile, Wheatley Heights got its name from a 1913 housing development promoted by Bellerose businessman William Geiger.

Turning Point: Misled by the carefully worded ad copy describing "valuable land" in the "pure healthy air of Long Island's Pine Woods," working-class Irish immigrants moved to Wyandanch in the 1920s and '30s, often without viewing the lots first. When John Douglas Jr. arrived at the Wyandanch railroad station in 1923, it took him days to get to his property. First, he had to whack through 1,200 feet of scrub oak. Douglas' land was in the middle of pine barrens that would, in time, be wiped out by development. The area was also rife with forest fires, often sparked by debris spitting from the coal-burning steam engines as they chugged through the bleak terrain. The roots of Wyandanch's black community also dated back to the late 1920s. A white real estate agent from Rockland County, Charles E. Hagedorn, sold the first lots to pioneering black families in a section of Wyandanch called Little Farms, between Little East Neck Road and Straight Path south of Patton Avenue. The black community grew in the 1950s and '60s, after middle- and working-class blacks, turned away from white suburbs, found acceptance in the already established black enclave.

Brushes With Fame: William K. Vanderbilt II, great-grandson of railroad magnate Cornelius Vanderbilt, erected an estate off Conklin Road in Wheatley Heights; locals dubbed it the "Castle." Later sold to the brother of presidential adviser Bernard Baruch, the Castle went on to house the Sisters of the Good Shepherd, who would run the Madonna Heights girls school. Part of Vanderbilt's Long Island Motor Parkway, built between 1906-1908, ran through Wyandanch, with narrow bridges running over Little East Neck Road and Colonial Springs Road. The bridges were demolished in the early 1960s. Looking for a quiet escape from the White House, President Ulysses S. Grant in the 1870s found tranquillity in West Deer Park in the 1870s during visits to the home of his brother-in-law, James J. Casey, the Suffolk County sheriff.

Where to Find More: "Deer Park-Wyandanch History," by Verne Dyson, 1957; a series of articles entitled "Pine Barren Pioneers" in the October, November and December, 1980, Long Island Forum.

West Babylon Public Library

WEST BABYLON: Purchased in 1944, this is the first fire truck owned by the local fire department.

WEST BABYLON: Holland native Jack Bulk built a windmill at his nursery business in 1929 from Dutch blueprints. A hurricane in 1972 blew off the vanes and the mill was demolished in 1983.

WEST BABYLON: In 1982, the main school building was torn down. From 1930 until 1952, it was the only school in the community, but by the 1940s, it had started to become inadequate.

Suffolk County Historical Society Photo

PATCHOGUE: A battery-powered Suffolk Traction Co. car in April, 1911. The car operated between Patchogue and Blue Point.

Courtesy of Lake Grove Postmaster Antonio Vattiato

CENTEREACH: An undated photo shows what was once the post office for New Village, when the community was known by that name.

Town of Brookhaven

The largest town in Suffolk County at 368 square miles, Brookhaven is also among the oldest. In 1655, the first pioneers landed at Setauket, where the early town business was conducted. Officially, Brookhaven was not recognized as a town until 1788. And by then, its boundaries had spread. Its territory had reached the South Shore, compelling the town fathers to move meetings to a more convenient midpoint. They chose Coram, where town meetings were held for the next century. (From the 1950s through 1986, meetings were held at town hall in Patchogue, and then were moved to the decidedly unhistorical sounding Building 4 in Medford.)

BELLPORT

See story on Page 74.

BELLE TERRE
Developer's Dream Hit a Hard Road

Beginnings: This upscale village on the east side of Port Jefferson Harbor traces its roots to a deed obtained in 1660 from the Setauket Indians by a British adventurer named John Scott and a second deed of 1687 to Richard Woodhull, William Smith and Richard Floyd Jr. Early names were Mount Misery Neck and Oakwood.

Great Expectations: Belle Terre evolved from the short-lived dream of Dean Alvord, a rich New York City real estate man who began development in 1912 of what he intended to be a bastion of wealth and privilege to rival Newport, R.I. Alvord's dream turned into a nightmare with the economic tumult of World War I. He went bankrupt before making much progress. But Alvord, who built Roslyn Estates and completed Brooklyn's South Prospect Park, was a big thinker. He named his exclusive development Belle Terre ("Beautiful Earth") Estates, reflecting the hilly, treed seaside location. He built a magnificent private club (destroyed by fire in 1934), a golf course, a beach club, miles of bridle paths, and insisted that the roads follow the contours of the land in natural curves. Alvord hired the famous architect Stanford White to design the gatehouse (now village hall), erected some luxurious Tudor-style homes (he took the first one) for sale to club members only, and erected two large, open-topped arbor trellises with fluted Grecian columns facing Long Island Sound (destroyed by a hurricane in 1938). The dream was barely emerging when the bubble burst.

The Dream Recast. Some of the land fell into the hands of sand and gravel companies, which in the absence of zoning laws began mining and dredging operations that lasted for years during the 1920s and resulted in litigation that extended into the 1930s. The 596-acre, all-residential village was incorporated in 1930, and tight control put on development. The village had about 850 residents in 1998.

Where to Find More: "The Seven Hills of Port Jefferson," by Patricia and Robert Sisler, and papers by village historian Nancy Orth, Port Jefferson Free Library.

BLUE POINT
For Mae West, Village Was Her Oyster

Beginnings: The Indians knew it as Manowtassquot or, roughly, "land of the basket rush," after years of harvesting the rush from the area's marshes to make baskets and mats. Deeded to English colonists in 1664, the area was controlled by the Winthrop family until the 1750s, when it was sold to Humphrey Avery. In desperate need of cash to settle his debts, Avery later devised a lottery, dividing up the land and hawking tickets to aspiring landowners. He sold 8,000 tickets for 30 shillings each — and raised enough money to buy back Blue Point and part of East Patchogue.

The Revolution: Blue Point was a strategic seaport held by the British during the Revolutionary War, a fact well known to the rebels who frequently raided British ships docked in the harbor.

Turning Point: Blue Point became a summer resort area in the 1880s after the Stillman family, members of the Baptist Church, began performing baptisms at their bayside home. So many people began showing up to be baptized, the Stillmans built additional changing rooms outside their home. These evolved into bathhouses, where people could rent bathing suits for 25 cents apiece. Eventually, Stillman's bathing beach grew to 600 bathhouses and other resort hotels followed.

Claim to Fame: The Blue Point oyster, pulled by baymen from the hamlet's rich oyster beds since its beginnings. The Blue Point oyster became synonymous with the best oysters money could buy. Even Queen Victoria preferred them above any other variety. She only insisted that the rough shells be sanded before they were served in Buckingham Palace.

The Name: No one's really sure where it came from, but one leading theory is that baymen coined it after noticing "a blue haze" over the point as they returned to shore.

Men shuck oysters in Blue Point's bygone days. The local oyster was prized by England's Queen Victoria.

Why Not a Duck: In the late 1890s, Capt. Billy Graham built a 20-foot-high replica of the great Egyptian sphinx on the lawn of his roadside inn in hopes of attracting famous politicians, movie starlets and sportsmen. His plan worked. It wasn't long before notables such as Teddy Roosevelt and Mae West came to check it out. Mae West even offered to buy it. The sphinx outlived the inn and was moved to Bayport, keeping watch out front of Fontana Concrete Products.

Where to Find More: "Blue Point Remembered," by Gene Horton, at the Bayport-Blue Point Library, 203 Blue Point Ave.

BROOKHAVEN
From Whales to Trout, Treasures Attract

Beginnings: The seaside hamlet's natural treasures of salt hay and shellfish were attractive to the English colonists who settled in Setauket in 1655. So much so that many decided to make the place their home, negotiating a deal with the native Unkechaugs in 1664 for land encompassing Brookhaven and neighboring Bellport. As if that weren't enough, the settlers three years later finagled from Tobaccus, sachem of the Unkechaugs, the rights to every whale pulled from the surrounding waters. The price: 5 pounds of wampum or colored shards of seashell the Indians used as currency.

Turning Points: Brookhaven was originally known simply as Fireplace, for the fires lit along the western edge of Carmans River to guide whaling ships safely ashore. In 1871, a group — "modernizers," in the words of former town historian Osborn Shaw — gathered in Fireplace and decided the hamlet's name needed changing. With apparently little concern for the confusion a new name might cause, they picked Brookhaven, the moniker used since 1666 for the entire township. The new name stuck.

Brush With Fame: In the late 1820s, American statesman Daniel Webster, then a U.S. senator from Massachusetts, rented land bordering the Carmans River and secured fishing rights for himself and a few of his friends, including future President Martin Van Buren. Webster's fishing prowess is immortalized in a Currier & Ives lithograph that depicts him pulling a 14-pound trout out of what locals believe is the Carmans mill stream.

Where to Find More: Bellport-Brookhaven Historical Society, 31 Bellport Lane, Bellport.

CENTEREACH
Legendary Gold Solidified a Family

Beginnings: Until 1927, Middle Country Road in Centereach was a two-lane dirt road where teenagers played baseball every Sunday afternoon. It took longer for middle Island communities such as Centereach to evolve. The earliest settlers congregated in the more populous seaside communities on the North and South Shores. Still, founding families — all farmers — such as the Hawkins clan saw opportunity in the undeveloped land originally known as West Middle Island. Born in 1750, Eleazer Hawkins was a prosperous sea captain and farmer. According to family tradition, Hawkins discovered an abandoned ship full of gold on one of his voyages, a booty that would allow him to purchase large farms for each of his nine sons. In the 1860 census, six of the 75 heads of household still bore the Hawkins name. For much of the 19th Century, Centereach was known as New Village. In 1916, residents were forced to choose a new name as New Village was already taken by another town upstate. Centereach seemed a logical choice, considering the hamlet was smack dab in the middle of the Island.

Turning Point: By the 1950s, the real estate market was ripe for low-cost homes. Entrepreneurs filled the bill in Centereach with developments such as Cedarwood Park and Dawn Estates. In 1967, Bernard Kaplan, whose firm built Dawn Estates, looked back to consider why they had such success.

Please Turn the Page

The corner of Main Street and Bellport Lane as it appeared in 1970; many homes on Bellport Lane were built by sea captains. In fact, the village was named for a pair of sea captains.

Newsday Photo

BELLPORT

Yachts and Poetry by the Bay

BY MOLLY McCARTHY
STAFF WRITER

E.B. White spent a summer there and later wrote a poem about it. Artist William Glackens immortalized its beaches in his impressionistic paintings. And Elmer Sperry, inventor of the gyroscope, loved it so much he retired there.

No, not Newport. Bellport.

The unassuming fishing village was, for a time, among the most popular summer spots on Long Island, attracting great statesmen, financiers, actors, writers, journalists and artists. By the 1880s, they streamed into the welcoming village, bringing their families, their bathing suits and their yachts. They rented cottages or built their own or stayed in one of the many hotels and rooming houses that were springing up: The Wyandotte, The Homestead, The Bay House, The Goldthwaite. Most were on or near the waters of Great South Bay.

"It was a wonderful way to grow up," recalled Nancy Ljungqvist, who spent time as a child in her grandfather's Bellport Lane home, where she whiled away the summers of the 1930s and '40s sailing and playing tennis. "We had a huge group of friends who came every summer."

E.B. White's biographer recounted the summer of 1918 when White's sister hoped her teenage brother would overcome his shyness with girls and learn how to dance. A portion of White's poem "Zoo Revisited," was inspired by his vacations at Bellport. White wrote of the moment "summer takes complete command belly to sun and back to sand," and "how well I know . . . the bay and the way the wind blows the tide ebbs and the tide flows."

Bellport began as a modest outpost of farmers and seafaring folk. Most of the homes that still line Bellport Lane were built by sea captains. In fact, the village was named for a pair of sea captains. The Bell brothers, Thomas and John, came to the region in the early 1800s, enticed by the opportunities of the young seaport.

By 1829, the brothers had built a dock into the bay and a shipyard, carving out cross streets and main thoroughfares into the surrounding terrain. When the post office was established in 1834, the Bells hoped to name their new home Bellville, but the name was already taken by an upstate village. They settled on Bell Port, which was later joined into one word.

As early as the Civil War, dignitaries such as Christian Godfrey Gunther, one of several New York City mayors who vacationed in Bellport, sailed their yachts along the southern shore of Long Island and docked off Bellport. Many of these luminaries were drawn by the region's simple pleasures.

"There was a family orientation to the place that people liked," said Rita Sanders, curator of the Bellport Museum Complex. "People wanted to know that they could bring their families out here to a safe, clean and wholesome environment."

Birdsall Otis Edey, an early organizer and president of the Girl Scouts of America, summered in Bellport with her two sisters, her mother and her father, a state senator. Edey, affectionately nicknamed Bird, made up lyrics that she and her buddies sang to the tunes of Gilbert and Sullivan while sailing aboard a neighbor's boat they coined The Walloping Window-Blind. At 25, Edey wrote and produced an operetta entitled "The Pirate of the Great South Bay" that she and her friends performed in the summer of 1897 in one of a half-dozen Bellport theaters called The Nearthebay Playhouse.

It was William Glackens who recorded these summer holiday scenes in soft pastels on canvas. Glackens spent at least five summers in Bellport before the polio epidemic of 1916. A member of the Ashcan School, a label bestowed by critics who ridiculed the artists' realistic style and subject matter, Glackens was said to have planned the Armory Show of 1913 in a rented cottage in Bellport.

The seasonal frivolity was somewhat dampened by the Great Depression, which led to the closure of the great summer hotels. But many of the traditions continued, ushering in the famous through World War II. During their parents' divorce, a young Jacqueline Bouvier vacationed in a summer cottage on Maple Street with her sister, Lee.

Ljungqvist recalled starting out early on a summer day and running down to the Bellport dock to catch one of the ferries, the Ruth or the Mildred A, to the barrier beach owned by the village. Once there, Ljungqvist handed over the change she pulled from the pocket of her jeans in exchange for a cup of clam chowder, some gingerbread and a soda sold from a little wooden shack on the beach.

Claim to Fame: Working in his woodshop one day in 1866, Bellport carpenter Oliver Perry Robinson accidentally discovered that tiny steel balls of buckshot made a board move easily across a flat surface. He patented the idea, later known as ball bearings.

Where to Find More: "Bellport and Brookhaven: A Saga of the Sibling Hamlets at Old Purchase South," compiled by Stephanie S. Bigelow and available at the Bellport Museum Complex.

CENTEREACH, Continued

"Land prices were low, speculation hadn't yet taken place, and we could sell them a home for $7,000, a price they could pay," Kaplan said. In three decades, Centereach's population exploded, from 628 residents in 1940, to nearly 20,000 in 1970, and 26,856 in 1998.

Claim to Fame: Forest fires were a constant concern for Centereach residents. With a single fire truck and a modest wooden firehouse, the Centereach Fire Department was founded in 1933. In 1977, a 43,000-square-foot firehouse was erected, dwarfing the puny fire station of yesteryear. By 1999, the community had three fire stations, 17 fire trucks and three ambulances.

Where to Find More: "The Chronicle of Centereach," by Luise Weiss and Doris Halowitch, Middle Country Public Library, 1989.

CORAM

A Longtime Spot For Town Meetings

Beginnings: There wasn't much at Coram before 1750. For the earliest white settlers, it was a stop along the route from Setauket to Mastic. In fact, its name is derived from the Indian word Wincoram, meaning "a passage between hills or a valley."

The Revolution: On returning from a successful raid on Fort St. George in Mastic in the fall of 1780, Patriot Maj. Benjamin Tallmadge and 12 men rode into Coram on horseback, setting fire to 100 tons of hay. The stacks belonged to the British, who hoped to keep their horses fed through the winter. A decade later, President George Washington, who as the Revolutionary general had ordered the hay-burning, stopped in Coram for lunch on his way to East Setauket.

Turning Point: By 1790, Brookhaven Town officials were looking for a more convenient polling place than Setauket, still an arduous journey for landowners in Mastic. Coram clinched the honor, serving as Brookhaven's town seat for nearly 100 years. Though it might sound grand, the designation meant simply that farmers in horse-drawn wagons met every April at Lester H. Davis' house. They swapped horses, gossiped and voted in the annual election. In 1884, the town was divided into election districts, ending the town meeting days in Coram.

Brush With Fame: Clarence Mulford, author of the popular series "Hopalong Cassidy," summered in Coram from 1908 to 1912.

Where to Find More: Brookhaven Town Historian's Office, Patchogue.

EASTPORT

See story on Page 137.

FARMINGVILLE

An Obelisk Honors Vietnam Veterans

Beginnings: After its initial settlement in the late 18th Century by farmers, this quiet, hilly enclave in central Brookhaven was called Bald Hills and Mooney Ponds, but Farmingville finally stuck. The hamlet between Lake Ronkonkoma and Coram was probably part of the original purchase of Brookhaven land from the Setauket (Seatalcott) Indians in 1655, which extended roughly from Long Island Sound to the middle of the Island, according to town historian David Overton. The first farmhouses appeared in the 1770s, but the community's name proved ironic:

Please Turn to Page 77

Bellport Public Library

A copy of a Currier & Ives print showing Daniel Webster hooking a 14-pound trout out of a creek in the Bellport and Brookhaven area.

Suffolk County Historical Society

CORAM: Until 1884, farmers would travel to the home of Lester Davis for the annual meeting to elect officials. More important, they would swap horses and gossip. This is the 1880 meeting.

HOLTSVILLE: Workers clear wreckage of a collision on Dec. 21, 1880. The locomotive Springfield, while clearing snowdrifts, had struck the back of a passenger train near what is now Holtsville.

LAKE GROVE: Jimmy Campbell carried mail from Lake Grove to what is now Centereach around 1900. Above, the U.S. Post Office in Lake Grove as it looked in 1910.

FARMINGVILLE, Continued

The sandy pine barrens soil and hilly terrain were not ideal for agriculture, as President George Washington observed on his tour of Long Island in 1790.

School days: Education is serious history in Farmingville. The first school was built in 1817 after residents of Bald Hills asked to be a school district. The second school was erected in 1850 to replace the first one. Classes were conducted there until 1929, after which the building was bought by a private group, the Farmingville Reunion Association, mostly families of people who attended the school. Starting in 1883, the group held an annual picnic at the school. The school was preserved and the home of Elijah Terry, the first teacher, was moved next to it. Terry's house on Horseblock Road, built in 1823, was placed on the National Register of Historic Places.

Turning Points: Farmingville received mail via Holtsville for years, but in 1950 became a separate post office. It wasn't recognized as a community by the federal census until 1980. In the 1970s, the community began to see the emergence of a Portuguese community.

Landmark: On Nov. 11, 1991, the 40-member Suffolk County Veterans Memorial Commission dedicated a soaring obelisk-shaped Vietnam War memorial at the Bald Hill site.

Where to Find More: "Bald Hills-Mooney Ponds-Farmingville, A History of the Community," by Marilyn S. Rosenzweig, 1986, Sachem Public Library, Holbrook; also, the Farmingville Historical Society.

GORDON HEIGHTS

See story on Page 78.

HOLBROOK

See story on Page 118.

HOLTSVILLE
The Taxman Sets Up A Regional Shop

Beginnings: A few farmhouses apparently existed in the huge tracts of woods and fields around the Brookhaven-Islip Town boundary in the late 1700s, but historians say that the first maps showing homes in Holtsville — known as Waverly in the early years — are dated 1838 to 1844. Historian Virginia Terry Meyer said one of her forebears, Daniel Terry, was known to be the first owner in what would become Holtsville, buying 1,000 acres from the town in 1749. The establishment of Waverly Station by the Long Island Rail Road in 1843 gave the place identity, connecting the trains to the stagecoach line then in use along the present north-south Waverly Avenue and making shipments of lumber and farm products easier.

Turning Points: A year after rail service began, a real estate man named Smith P. Gamage was selling lots south of the tracks. One of the first buyers was Robert Farmer, who set up a stage stop and store and was the first postmaster. Because there was another Waverly upstate, the name was changed to Holtsville in 1860, according to LIRR records. The change honored the then U.S. postmaster general, Joseph Holt. Historian Richard M. Bayles in 1874 reported 15 houses in Holtsville, a general store and a school. The first school was built in 1870 and existed until 1907.

Claim to Fame: In 1972, Holtsville became famous (or maybe infamous) to millions in the Northeast when an Internal Revenue Service center for processing federal income tax forms was opened on a 67-acre site on Waverly Avenue.

Skyviews Photo

HOLTSVILLE: A 1971 view shows development, with Sunrise Highway cutting diagonally.

It Might Have Been: In 1974, the private Regional Plan Association proposed Holtsville as a "downtown center" of Suffolk, at a time when grandiose plans were afoot to make Long Island MacArthur Airport into a major air-railbus transit hub. When local opposition mounted, planners said it was "just a concept."

Where to Find More: "Historical Sketches of Suffolk County," by Richard M. Bayles, 1874, Holtsville historical summary by Civic Council of Sachem and Ronkonkoma, 1963, and newspaper clippings, Sachem Public Library, Holbrook.

LAKE GROVE
Ever Heard Of West Middle Island?

Beginnings: By the early 1700s, an old Indian footpath from Brooklyn and Queens reached into Suffolk as part of the King's Highway — later Middle Country Road. It bisected what later was called Lake Grove, but there wasn't exactly a rush into the woods. Local historians say the first farmhouses didn't appear for nearly a century. The first church group, Methodist Episcopal, was formed in 1796 and built a church in 1852-53. The Methodist Episcopal group was part of a countywide circuit of itinerant preachers after 1820. Later, it became part of the Smithtown circuit. Meetings were held in a

schoolhouse until the church was built. The community's first church building, built in 1818, was the First Congregational Church of New Village. That building was preserved and was depicted on the village seal. Lake Grove was long entangled in identity problems, surrounded by Stony Brook, Lake Ronkonkoma and Centereach. In the early 19th Century, the area was variously called Lakeland, Lakeville, New Village, Ronkonkoma or West Middle Island because there was lots of space, unclear boundaries and few people. The community was named in the mid-1800s for the groves of trees near Lake Ronkonkoma.

Turning Points: Early in the 1900s, cottages on small lots, many of which later became year-round houses, appeared. The advent of a housing project called Stony Brook Lawns, combined with changes in the bounds of the postal and school districts, brought concern that Lake Grove's identity was being threatened. In 1954, the county built Nesconset Highway (State Route 347), which intersected Middle Country Road adjacent to Lake Grove, creating a commercial crossroad that attracted sprawling Smith Haven Mall in early 1968. Town approval of the mall zoning rekindled the desire for more local control and led to incorporation of the three-square-mile village in 1968.

Where to Find More: "Sketch of Lake Grove," by Addie M. Overton, 1970, Middle Country Library.

LAKE RONKONKOMA, RONKONKOMA
A Special Lake And a Tourist Magnet

Beginnings: Smithtown founder Richard Smith's original holdings included the headwaters of the Nissequogue River east to a "freshwater pond called Raconkamuck," which translates as "the boundary fishing place" in the Algonquian language. What became known as Lake Ronkonkoma once served as a boundary between lands occupied by four Indian communities: Nissequogues, Setaukets, Secatogues and Unkechaugs. It was eventually owned by the Town of Islip under the terms of the Nicolls Patent, while land around it would be controlled by three governments — Smithtown, Islip and Brookhaven. That's because different Indian communities gave separate deeds to the land under their control.

The Lake: Long Island's largest freshwater lake was created by a retreating glacier. Over the years it became the subject of many legends. One had it that the lake was bottomless, another that there were secret underwater connections to Long Island Sound or Great South Bay.

Turning Points: The Smithtown side of the lake was settled by the 1740s, but it was not until the late 1890s that the area gained widespread public attention. That's when boarding houses and hotels were erected to accommodate a growing number of tourists drawn by claims that the lake's waters had special healing powers. By the 1920s, beach pavilions had sprung up. The Long Island Rail Road, which was completed to nearby Lakeland in 1842 (the depot was moved to Ronkonkoma in 1883), helped transform what had been a sleepy farming hamlet.

Claim to Fame: From 1908 to 1910, auto races on William K. Vanderbilt II's 48-mile Long Island Motor Parkway drew international attention. The two-lane concrete speedway stretched from Queens to Vanderbilt's Petit Trianon Hotel on the Islip side of the lake. The hotel was fashioned after an 18th-Century building at the Palace of Versailles in France. It was the site of swank parties enjoyed by Long Island's elite after their drive through the countryside.

And Then There Was Maude: Many theater people were attracted by the beauty of the lake. One of the most prominent was Broadway actress Maude Adams, famous for her portrayal of Peter Pan during the Victorian era. In 1898 she bought a farm called Sandy Garth and additional property totaling 700 acres which later became known as The Cenacle, one of the Island's most prominent farms. Sachem High School and Samoset Junior High School were built on part of the land, which was sold to the school district after her death in 1953.

Burning Crosses: The Ku Klux Klan held meetings in Lake Ronkonkoma in the 1920s. Local Klan members focused more on Catholics and Jews than blacks, and burned crosses on the lawns of enemies. The Klan faded out by the mid-1930s in that area.

Where to Find More: "Smithtown, New York 1660-1929," by Noel J. Gish; "Three Waves, the Story of Lake Ronkonkoma," by Ann Farnum Curtis, 1976, all at Sachem Public Library, Holbrook.

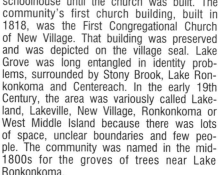

Courtesy of Lake Grove Postmaster Antonio Vattiato

A photo published in the Lake Ronkonkoma Mirror in 1932 shows the dogged determination of mail carriers. When Charles Benson went on his appointed rounds, his pet Pete rode on the hood or running boards of the mail truck.

MANORVILLE
A Patriot Haven And Cranberry Heaven

Beginnings: Although early land patents made it difficult to determine precise boundaries, historians are certain Manorville lay within the huge tract known in the 1700s as the Manor of St. George, granted to William (Tangier) Smith in a royal patent of 1693. The Smith family did not own Manorville long. In 1721, it was sold to a group of colonists from Southold.
The Revolution: A natural depression in the landscape left by a glacier and known as a kettle hole proved a good hiding place for a band of Patriots during the war. The hole was named for a Captain Punk, who hid there with his men to avoid detection by the British. Some early residents referred to Manorville as Punk's Hole. The hole still exists about 1,000 feet south of Hot Water Road, just east of its intersection with Halsey Manor Road.
Turning Point: When the railroad reached the hamlet in 1844, the station was named St. George's Manor. But the first station agent, Seth Raynor, was an ardent Patriot during the Revolution and detested the label St. George because of its association with the British king. Raynor brought paint, brush and ladder from his home one day, erasing "St. George's" and leaving "Manor." The next year, a post office was opened, and the hamlet was designated Manorville.

Natural Bounty: Manorville, mostly forest, was a prime target for harvesters of cordwood. In fact, it was a fuel stop for the railroad's early wood-burning locomotives. As passengers dined at hotels such as the Little Delmonico and The Maples, laborers, equipped with bucksaws, sawed wood and stacked it on the train.

By the late 1870s, a Massachusetts entrepreneur by the name of George W. Davis had converted a portion of North Manorville into cranberry bogs. More than 25,000 bushels of cranberries were shipped annually by railroad to New York City. Among the most popular and best-tasting cranberries on the market, they were sold under the name Blue Diamond. The bogs no longer exist.
Where to Find More: Manorville Historical Society.

MASTIC
Upstart Colonists Challenged the King

Beginnings: The Algonquians inhabited its shores for thousands of years, farming, fishing and hunting. But it took the English barely two generations after landing on Long Island in 1640 to make Mastic their own. By the early 1700s, the Floyds, the Nicolls, the Woodhulls and the Smiths had carved huge estates out of the ragged-edged peninsula jutting into Moriches Bay. One of the principal landowners, William (Tangier) Smith, died in 1705 and left his property to his descendants. Four years later they began construction on a house at the Manor of St. George.
The Revolution: When the British took control of Long Island, the Smith manor house became Fort St. George, a key military outpost for the British. And, for that reason, the rebel Patriots, led by Maj. Benjamin Tallmadge, raided the fort in November, 1780, capturing more than 50 men and destroying the strategic stronghold. Smith's neighbor, William Floyd, who signed the Declaration of Independence, fled his estate, as did most non-Loyalists during the British occupation. Floyd's family waited out the war in Middletown, Conn., returning when peace resumed. Both the Smith and Floyd manor houses later became museums open to the public. Another Mastic landowner, Nathaniel Woodhull, died at the hands of the British and was buried in a family plot in Mastic Beach.
Brush With Fame: Mastic was almost home to a first lady. William Floyd's daughter, Kitty, was briefly engaged to James Madison, who met Kitty while she was staying with her statesman father in a Philadelphia rooming house. Kitty dumped Madison in 1783 for a young medical student.
Where to Find More: "A Portrait of William Floyd," by William Q. Maxwell; "The History of Mastic Beach," a pamphlet produced by the Mastic Beach Property Owners Association, available at the Mastic-Moriches-Shirley Library, Shirley.

MEDFORD
Teddy Roosevelt's 'Flying Leap'

Beginnings: When the Long Island Rail Road reached the community in 1843, it was a flat wilderness of scrub oak and pine, but a good connection for the stagecoach line that ran between Patchogue and Port Jefferson along what was Stage Road (later called Route 112). People started coming from miles around to get their mail. The soil was poor for farming, but the woods offered copious lumbering, and there were miles of land to be sold. The railroad held an auction in New York City in 1850 to peddle lots. The O.L. Schwenke Land & Investment Co. bought four square miles, and sold 25-by-100-foot lots for $10 to $75.
Kooky Caper: Tradition says businessmen anxious to lure land buyers to Medford once resorted to building near the tracks a dummy factory front, with a phony roof and stack that seemed to puff smoke when tar paper was burned at its base as trains neared. Agents spread the word on trains that Medford was a great place to buy property, hoping some riders would look around. No word on how many got snookered.
Landmarks: A long-standing house, believed to be Medford's oldest in the 1990s, was built

Please Turn to Page 81

GORDON HEIGHTS
Built by Blacks, From the Ground Up

BY MOLLY MCCARTHY
STAFF WRITER

In 1927, Louis Fife bought a parcel of land, sandwiched between Coram and Middle Island in the wilderness of Suffolk County, from "Pop" Gordon, who ran Gordon's Hotel. Fife then knocked on doors in Harlem, Brooklyn and the Bronx, offering farmland to working-class black families for as little as $10 down and $10 a month. Borrowing Gordon's name, Fife called his company the Gordon Heights Development and Building Corp. It was one of Long Island — and the nation's — earliest housing developments marketed to blacks.

Two decades before Levittown, Gordon Heights was distinct from the postwar subdivisions that would rise to shelter returning veterans and their families. Fife's earliest advertisements characterized Gordon Heights more as a farming than a bedroom community. The homeowners in Gordon Heights weren't expected to commute daily to their city jobs. In fact, it took hours to get from Gordon Heights to the city by car in the early days. Less interested in the commuter, Fife, a white man who saw an untapped market in working-class blacks, targeted southern blacks or West Indian immigrants who had migrated to the city but longed to return to the land.

The families came, if somewhat slowly. Many bought land, waiting years to build their homes and move into them. For some, the delay resulted from their inability to get bank loans. Jobs tied others to the city, so they could get out to Gordon Heights only on weekends. "My mother tended to be adventurous, and I think she began to tire of the city," said Ronald Armstrong, whose father commuted into the city when the family, originally from Barbados, moved to Gordon Heights in 1937. "It was sort of a new frontier."

The fact that most homes were built piecemeal contributed to the sense of community in Gordon Heights. Long before Yvonne Rivers and her family moved into their home in 1947, her father trekked out on weekends to clear the land, burn tree stumps and gather the ash for their garden. "Most put up homes one room at a time," Rivers recalled in 1997. At 18, she bought a one-acre plot behind the family homestead for $1,000.

Even though black families rejoiced at being able to build their own homes, the early years in Gordon Heights were hard. Parents sent children out to collect wood to heat their homes, and kerosene provided the only light. It would be the late 1940s before the homes got running water and electricity. Street lights would not arrive until 1969. Because they could not rely on neighboring communities for fire protection, Gordon Heights created its own volunteer fire department in 1947. It purchased two used fire trucks, and residents mixed sand, pumped water and carried bricks to help build the firehouse. In 1959, a credit union was founded so residents could get loans. Both enterprises continue to operate.

Armstrong recalled one snowy day in the early years when he and a few other kids missed the school bus. Instead of heading home, they walked several miles in knee-deep snow to Port Jefferson High School. They arrived three hours later and were scolded for their tardiness.

Still, Gordon Heights was a dream come true for many blacks. Yvonne Rivers was 6 years old when her mother left her with friends in Gordon Heights for a week-long visit in the summer of 1943. When Rivers got home to her family's Bronx apartment, she asked her mother, "Can we move to the country?" And Rivers kept asking until, in 1947, her parents scraped together $96 for the one-acre plot on which they erected a house sold as a kit at Gimbels.

"You're six years old, living in New York and can't get off your stoop and don't really know why," remembered Rivers. "I found it so enchanting to be able to open the door, get off the stoop, run across the street and never have to worry about cars or anything. It was such freedom." But she marveled at the sacrifices the early homeowners made. "Who would leave running water, transportation, electricity . . . Who would do this besides people who have a deep commitment to something?" she said. "They all came out for one reason. They wanted to build a community."
Brush With Fame: Locked out of upstate resorts like the Catskills, black entertainers of the 1940s and '50s such as Ethel Waters and members of The Ink Spots vacationed in Gordon Heights. Prominent black leader Adam Clayton Powell Jr., who was first elected to the House of Representatives in 1945, and Hazel Scott spent their honeymoon at a friend's home in Gordon Heights.

The cover of the Gordon Heights Bulletin, summer 1952, celebrates an anniversary.

The
GORDON HEIGHTS BULLETIN
Published by the Gordon Heights Development and Building Corporation
489 Fifth Avenue, New York City   Tel. MUrray Hill 7-5058
SUMMER, 1952
SILVER ANNIVERSARY
1927 – 1952
Courtesy of Robert G. Wilson

MEDFORD: Hal Fullerton, a publicist for the Long Island Rail Road, and his wife, Edith, set up Prosperity Farm in 1907 to spread the word that Brookhaven's scrubby land could be farmed. At top, Edith, left, with children Eleanor, Loring and Hope. Below, Edith tends flowers with Loring. Former President Theodore Roosevelt visited the Medford farm in 1910.

MILLER PLACE: Workers load cordwood on a ship in an undated photo.

MANORVILLE: A man stands at a cranberry bog.

EAST MORICHES: An illustration of the local fire department from more than a century ago.

MEDFORD, Continued

near the tracks at Stage Road and occupied by Jacob Beck, a Schwenke employee. The first school was built in 1903 and taken down in 1997, to the dismay of local preservationists. The White House Hotel, Medford's first, was built in the early 1900s. It became the Landmark Cafe in the late 1900s.

Brush With Fame: Theodore Roosevelt, just out of the White House, in 1910 visited Medford's Prosperity Farm, an 80-acre experimental agricultural station established in 1907 by the LIRR to show that crops could be grown successfully on pine barrens soil. An article in the Brooklyn Daily Eagle of Aug. 10, 1910, reported that Roosevelt was being driven by car over a sandy, soggy trail between Medford and Wading River. When the auto began to sink in a mire, the item related, "Col. Roosevelt made a flying leap and landed in a clump of bushes."

Where to Find More: "Pictorial History of Medford, N.Y., 1844-1994," by Mary Gubitosi, Patchogue-Medford Public Library; "Medford, L.I., 1776-1976," by Ida Medeck, Suffolk County Historical Society, Riverhead.

MIDDLE ISLAND

A Crossroads For Long Island

Beginnings: Before the Long Island Expressway came along, the main passage east on Long Island was Middle Country Road, bisecting the communities later known as Coram, Ridge and Middle Island. In the 1700s, passengers traveled by stagecoach along Middle Country Road on their way to Greenport from New York City, often stopping at Brewster's tavern in what was first known as Middletown.

Turning Point: With increased traffic, people began to build homes along this main thoroughfare, and in 1811 the community's postmaster, Benjamin Hutchinson, made a decision to change the name to Middle Island.

Brush With Fame: Ralph Johnstone took off from Belmont Park on Oct. 27, 1910, in a single-engine biplane in hopes of winning an air show competition. Instead, he flew into history. Ushered by a strong wind, Johnstone was carried east, all the way out to Middle Island. On the way, he set a new world altitude record of nearly 9,000 feet. Barely having a chance to savor the glory, Johnstone died in a crash two weeks later during another air show.

Notable Resident: After the death of his wife in 1869, artist Alonzo Chappel, a Brooklyn native, chose to spend the last years of his life near Corwins Pond in Middle Island. Chappel built his reputation painting battle scenes from the Revolutionary and Civil Wars such as "The Battle of Long Island" and "Battle of Cedar Mountain." Corwin's Pond was later renamed Artist's Lake, perhaps in deference to Chappel. Chappel died in 1887 and was buried in Union Cemetery in Middle Island.

Natural History: Cathedral Pines County Park held the legacy of "Uncle Billy" Dayton, who in 1812 planted some white pine trees on his land on the road to Yaphank. By the end of the 20th Century, the "Pine Cathedral" was the largest white pine forest on Long Island.

Where to Find More: The Thomas R. Bayles local history collection at Longwood Public Library, located at 800 Middle Country Rd., Middle Island, including books such as ("Longwood Long Ago," by Suzanne Johnson), pamphlet files, photos, old postcards and maps.

Newsday Photo

MILLER PLACE: A 1972 photo of the Miller Place Country Store on Main Street, site of many houses from the 18th and 19th Centuries.

MILLER PLACE

Legacy of a Family Divided by Revolution

Beginnings: This beautiful and historic community on Long Island Sound was named after the prolific family of Andrew Miller, a barrel maker-turned-farmer. He arrived from Setauket about 1679, buying land from John Thomas, who apparently was the first settler. Miller died Dec. 24, 1717, and was buried in Mount Sinai's Sea View Cemetery.

The Revolution: Miller's Place, as it was known, was primarily on the Patriot side, but the Miller family was divided. Avowed Tories were Richard Miller, son of Andrew, and Capt. Solomon Davis. Richard Miller was shot dead in May, 1776, by militia near Selden while recruiting for the British. In August, 1781, in midnight raids on houses of two Patriot Miller families, the British mutilated a Miller family man, who survived, but shot dead 16-year-old William Miller when he looked out a window to see what the commotion was about. Davis, who became very rich as a privateer serving the British, was murdered in Jamaica after the war.

Turning Points: Miller's Place became Miller Place in 1894, about the time the tourist trade began and the same year the railroad came (though it discontinued service in 1938 for lack of business). After World War II, development was steady, and many old houses of the 18th and 19th Centuries remained along Main Street (North Country Road), and the community was listed on the National Register of Historic Places.

Where to Find More: "History of Miller's Place," by Margaret Davis Gass, at Port Jefferson Public Library and Comsewogue Public Libraries in Port Jefferson Station, and "Miller Place," by the Miller Place Historical Society, including list of 28 historic houses.

THE MORICHES

Jefferson and Madison Stopped for a Visit

Beginnings: Believed to be named for an Indian who once lived there, the area encompassing Moriches, Center Moriches and East Moriches went through a dozen spellings after the first Europeans arrived. Take your pick: Meritche, Merquices, Maritches, Marigies, Meritces, Moritches, Muriches, Moricha and Meriches all have been spotted in historical records. William (Tangier) Smith, who already owned hundreds of acres in Brookhaven known as the Manor of St. George, snagged some land in the Moriches area in patents of 1691 and 1697. But he retained little of those purchases due to competing claims from earlier settlers who had deeds with the Indians.

Turning Point: The railroad arrived in 1881, opening the Moriches to vacationing New Yorkers. Among them was 16-year-old Julia Hand of Brooklyn, whose family operated the Hand rooming house on the banks of Senix Creek. Julia kept a diary of her 16th summer in the Moriches in 1886, offering a slice of life in the 19th-Century seaside town. When she wasn't doing chores at the boarding house, Julia rowed along the creeks, sailed on the bay and picnicked at the beach. On Aug. 12, she wrote: "Had a regular Jones breeze all day. We went to the beach in the morning & Mrs. J. took some trimming along which she unearthed for the occasion & insisted on my showing her every stitch, she talked so much that Sandy commenced to hunt for a cork — with a bottle on the end of it, & we laughed every minute."

Claim to Fame: The old Ketcham Inn or Terry's Hotel, as it was known from 1783 to 1852, was built on the stagecoach route from Brooklyn to Sag Harbor (later Main Street in Center Moriches) and was a popular rest stop for many years. By far the inn's most famous guests, Thomas Jefferson and James Madison, sojourned there in 1791 during their historic visit to Long Island. In the 1990s, the Ketcham Inn Foundation Inc. spearheaded efforts to restore the building, a portion of which dated from 1693.

Radio Days: The golden age of radio, circa the 1920s, brought an early radio station to the east end of Smith Street in East Moriches. Run by the Independent Wireless Co., the station housed a spark transmitter used to communicate with ships off shore. Only problem was the transmissions wiped out popular radio programs like "Amos 'n' Andy," prompting residents to form a protest group called the Suffolk County Radio Protective League. A compromise was struck. The company agreed to keep the station silent during the prime-time shows, unless there was an SOS call. Later, nothing remained of the station, but the area still carried the name Radio Point. In July, 1996, East Moriches was the site of one of the most urgent emergency calls in Long Island history: the explosion of TWA Flight 800.

Where to Find More: "The Illustrated History of the Moriches Bay Area," by Van and Mary Field; "Teen-Age Diary of '86," Long Island Forum, November, 1960; the complete Julia Hand diary in "Nettie's Diary: The 1880s Diary of Nettie Ketcham," edited by Van and Mary Field.

MOUNT SINAI

'Old Man's' Out, Biblical Name's In

Beginnings: On June 10, 1664, agents of the new plantation at Setauket, that then was pioneering Brookhaven Town, bought all the Indian land east of Port Jefferson Harbor as far as Wading River. That included what was to become Mount Sinai. At the start, much of this purchase was known by the peculiar name "Old Man's." Most historians trace the name to a Capt. John Scott, a known scoundrel who in the mid-18th Century apparently had duped an elderly retired English Army officer, Maj. Daniel Gotherson, into giving him a large amount of money to buy land near Long Island Sound. The buy was not officially recognized, Scott fled and people would allude to the property Gotherson thought he owned as "the old man's."

The Revolution: Patriot Col. Benjamin Tallmadge landed at Old Man's Harbor the night of Nov. 21, 1780, with troops in eight boats before their surprise predawn attack Nov. 23 on British-held Fort St. George in Mastic.

Milestones: A road called the Upper Cartway in 1716 was made part of a town route later known as North Country Road. The oldest house was believed to be a salt-box type on Rocky Hill Road built about 1705 for Benjamin Davis. It was altered in appearance in the 1930s. A meetinghouse existed in Old Man's as early as 1720, but the first permanent church, the First Congregational Church of Brookhaven, wasn't organized until Dec. 23, 1789. Boat building began at the harbor as early as 1808, but industry did not flourish because of harbor depth and access, and most business gravitated to Port Jefferson.

The Name: On April 29, 1840, after postal officials refused to accept "Old Man's," the first local post office was established. According to tradition, the wife of postmaster Charles Phillips opened her Bible at random and laid down her knitting needle on the name Mount Sinai.

Where to Find More: "Historical Sketches of Northern Brookhaven Town," by former town historian Osborn Shaw, and "Suffolk County Historical Society Register," September, 1982, at the county historical society, Riverhead.

NORTH BELLPORT

Modest Beginnings, A Hopeful Alliance

Beginnings: What became an 800-acre community north of the affluent Village of Bellport was used as farmland until the mid-1950s, when Pace Developers built about 300 small houses between Montauk and Sunrise Highways. The buyers were mostly moderate-income people, but within a decade, defense plant layoffs, alleged "blockbusting" techniques by real estate operators, and placement of welfare families set the community on a decades-long battle with blight, crime and unemployment.

Turning Point: In the late 1990s, the state declared part of North Bellport an economic development zone, eligible for tax abatement and other benefits. Brookhaven Town increased financial aid and code enforcement. The Long Island Housing Partnership in 1994 built 13 one-family houses that sold at below-market prices. The Concerned Citizens for a Better Community and the Boys and Girls Club were active. The Bellport-Hagerman-East Patchogue Alliance, a nonprofit community improvement agency, rented 36 rehabilitated homes. "We have not had an easy history," Helen Martin, a longtime resident and director of the alliance, said in 1997. "But I'd say the community in the last two years has become better off than in more than 20 years. You see it in appearance and in attitude. More white and Hispanic families are moving in. People are coming together."

Where to Find More: Newspaper files and various papers in the South Country Library, Bellport.

Collection of Joel Streich

BROOKHAVEN: A 1940 postcard of a local store and post office. The area was originally called Fireplace, for the fires lighted along the edge of Carmans River to guide whaling ships.

Collection of Joel Streich

BLUE POINT: A postcard of the bathing beach, circa 1920. The oyster brought fame to the area, whose name stood for the best money could buy.

SETAUKET: A shipbuilding center of the 19th Century because of its low lying and protected harbors, the area was a favorite wintering spot for vessels, such as these in Scott's Cove, circa 1890.

RONKONKOMA: Iceboats skim the lake, Long Island's largest freshwater body, in about 1930.

OLD FIELD

Wealthy Industrialists Found a Playground

Beginnings: Fearing attack from Indians crossing the Sound from Connecticut, early white settlers built their homes farther inland at first and left their animals to graze on the common pastureland where Old Field was later founded. The first evidence of a house built on the grassy neck north of Setauket dates to 1725. The name Old Field may have come from Indians who referred to the "old field" after they began tilling new soil on neighboring Strongs Neck. A lighthouse was built on Old Field Point in 1823 and later replaced with an updated version in 1868. That version which was eventually used for village hall.

Pre-Revolution: As proof of just how remote Old Field was in its earlier days, Dr. George Muirson was ordered by Brookhaven officials in 1770 to move his medical practice from Setauket to Old Field. Muirson's primary occupation at the time was stemming the spread of a smallpox epidemic. Old Field was considered the place "most Safe and Least Dangres to ye inhabitants of this Town of Brookhaven."

Turning Point: Having been mostly a farming and fishing community for much of the 19th Century, the character of the settlement was transformed around 1900 by the arrival of wealthy industrialists. They turned Old Field into their leisure village, building summer estates where they could sail, canoe and ride horseback. To ease their commute from New York City, Quaker Path was extended in 1903 to the Stony Brook railroad station, an event celebrated by a parade of carriages along the new thoroughfare.

Marine Center: Owned by the state Department of Environmental Conservation, Flax Pond, along the Old Field shoreline, became the site of a marine biology laboratory operated by the State University at Stony Brook.

Where to Find More: The Richard H. Handley Long Island History Room in the Smithtown Library.

POOSPATUCK RESERVATION

Looking for an Upturn After Years of Turmoil

Beginnings: The Unkechaug tribe, of which the Poospatucks were part, occupied the land from Patchogue to Westhampton when English and Dutch settlers arrived on Long Island in the 17th Century. The tribe was noted on the East Coast for its high-grade wampum made from seashells. Poospatuck means "where a little river flows into tidewater."

Turning Points: On July 2, 1700, as Indian dominance faded, William (Tangier) Smith, lord of the Manor of St. George in Mastic, gave the Poospatucks 175 acres "to be lived upon and planted forever." But in colonial times, Poospatuck men were sold in the slave trade, women were taken as concubines and eventually there was intermarriage, first with runaway or freed slaves who came to Long Island to find work, later with the general population, according to Poospatuck historians. Over the centuries, the reservation on the west bank of the Forge River in Mastic was reduced to about 53 acres with 136 residents in 1998, compared to about 200 residents in 1700. Much of the land was lost when the Smith family took back 100 acres in 1730 and other parcels were lost in questionable transactions, according to historian John Strong.

Good Signs: The reservation, the smallest in the state and owned by the tribe, endured a history of poverty and internal divisions. However, it saw some economic improvement in the 1990s. In 1994 a new tribal chief, Harry B. Wallace, and a council were elected under county

Please Turn to Page 87

PATCHOGUE

Still Banking on the River

BY RHODA AMON
STAFF WRITER

It was nicknamed Milltown because of the many mills — gristmills, sawmills, paper, wool, cotton mills — that operated on Patchogue waterways from as early as 1750. The village's permanent name may have derived from Pochaug or Paushag, which were the early settlers' interpretation of the name of Indians who lived in the vicinity.

It's a good thing the village's ultimate name was "steered in the proper direction over the years, or the community might have become known as 'Poached Egg,'" mused Frank J. Mooney in "The Patchogue Story," a folksy 1987 account of 250 years of what he decided is "Suffolk County's most enterprising village."

At one time, villagers set their clocks by the noon whistle from the giant Patchogue-Plymouth Lace Mill, which closed in 1954. Most of the mills succumbed in the 1940s and '50s, outpaced by foreign competition and by the industry movement to the South and overseas for cheaper labor.

The lace works was once known as "the Patchogue College because so many Patchogue kids went there when they finished high school," Marjorie Roe, president of the Greater Patchogue Historical Society, said in 1997. Workers also came by stagecoach from Sayville and other South Shore communities. The mill employed as many as 1,200 during World War II, when it manufactured camouflage netting and other war products.

Paradoxically, it may have been curtains for the lace mill because its products were too good for this modern, disposable world. "They lasted forever and never had to be replaced — I still use a lace tablecloth my mother bought in the '30s," said Roe, a sixth-generation descendant of Capt. Austin Roe, a chief spy for Gen. George Washington during the Revolutionary War.

Austin Roe's son, Justus, erected Patchogue's first hotel in 1808, and the family continued building ever-larger hotels for the rest of the 19th Century. Patchogue was then a thriving seaport with oyster, fishing and boat-building industries as well as mills on the Patchogue River and Great South Bay.

Its recorded history dates from 1664, when Connecticut Gov. John Winthrop purchased "nine necks of land" extending from Great South Bay to the middle of the Island. Some were sold to Humphrey Avery of Boston, who, in need of cash, disposed of them by lottery. The "lot" that was to become Patchogue was won by Leoffer d'Leofferda in 1759. It proved a good investment. Attracted by waterpower, settlers and shipping entrepreneurs soon flooded the area. Schooners set out from Patchogue to do commerce up and down the East Coast and even to the Mediterranean. The Army Corps of Engineers dredged the Patchogue River in 1890, making it the only deep-water port on Long Island's South Shore. Until 1922, Patchogue was a U.S. port of entry with a customs house on South Ocean Avenue.

It also proved a handy port for bootleggers during the Prohibition era of the 1920s. The notorious New York City gangster Dutch Schultz set up a headquarters in Patchogue, giving lucrative employment to farm boys who helped unload and hide the illegal kegs. But that's getting ahead of the Patchogue story.

The Long Island Rail Road arrived in 1869, and for a while Patchogue was the end of the South Shore line. It brought thousands of summer visitors from the city, seeking the cool southwest breezes. The village, which incorporated in 1893, became a summer colony, with hotels accommodating as many as 1,600 guests. It was also the starting point for great bicycle races, in which Roe family members starred. The last of the family's hotels, the elegant Eagle Hotel, burned down in 1934.

Tourism gradually declined after 1920 as the affordable motor car took tourists to farther destinations, according to village co-historian Hans Henke's pictorial history of Patchogue in its boom years from 1840 to 1915. In the late 1990s, efforts were underway to bring back the tourist industry, if not the mills. The 1858 one-room schoolhouse was restored, and the village began doing the same to the elegant Patchogue moviehouse of the 1920s to serve as a community theater. The lace mill was demolished in 1999 and construction was begun on a 60,000-square-foot Swezey's department store. In addition, plans were underway in 1999 to open the Suffolk Sports Hall of Fame in the 1912 Union Savings Bank building at South Ocean Avenue and Church Street, according to village co-historian Anne Swezey. A featured exhibit would be an 1892 catboat built by Gil Smith, Patchogue's best-known boat builder.

Plans were also afoot to bring new life to the Patchogue River. The village, working with the Fire Island National Seashore, which had headquarters and a ferry terminal on the river, also expressed hopes to develop a year-round commercial recreation area and visitors center.

Where to Find More: "Images of America: Patchogue," by Hans Henke, "The Patchogue Story," by Frank J. Mooney.

Shands Family Photo

Inside Shands General Store on West Main Street, about 1915

Nassau County Museum Collection, Long Island Studies Institute

PATCHOGUE: East Main Street before trolley rails were laid in 1907. Buildings on the right include town offices, Roe's Hotel, and in the distance with an ornate tower, the Fishel building.

Nassau County Museum Collection, Long Island Studies Institute

PATCHOGUE: The Clifton Hotel near Grove Avenue on the Great South Bay. The hotel opened in 1883 and was expanded several times before being torn down about 1940.

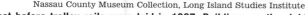

Suffolk County Historical Society

OFF PATCHOGUE: Several hardy souls pose in a postcard showing a 28-foot high iceberg. The photo is dated March 21, 1907.

PORT JEFFERSON: The First National Bank of Port Jefferson in Hotel Square about 1890. The location in the heart of the village later became East Main Street.

PORT JEFFERSON: The harbor circa 1906. Once, it was a shipbuilding center, but by the 1870s, the industry had gone to steamships and iron-hulled vessels, which needed larger yards.

PORT JEFFERSON

Ships Were King in 'Drowned Meadow'

BY BILL BLEYER
STAFF WRITER

It would have been difficult to find an adult male in mid-19th Century Port Jefferson who wasn't employed in building wooden vessels. It was a time when Long Island was a major ship producer, and Port Jefferson was the local industry's capital. The village turned out 327 wooden vessels between the late 1700s and 1884, and during the peak years of construction in the 1850s, when the village's population was about 300, there were 12 shipyards.

Shipbuilding in Drowned Meadow, as the community was initially named, was launched by John Willse, a farmhand who began building vessels in 1796 in what would become Poquott. The next year he purchased land on the southeast corner of the harbor, where he built six ships. By 1809, Willse had taken on Richard Mather as an apprentice and within five years Mather had married Willse's daughter and constructed five sloops to become the community's largest shipbuilder. The family would dominate local shipbuilding for decades.

The boom ended in the 1870s when steamships and iron-hulled vessels, which required larger yards and more machinery than was available in Port Jefferson, were replacing sailing craft. By 1900, only three major shipyards remained. One of the last gasps of the industry came in 1901, when the schooner Martha Wallace, at more than 200 feet the largest sailing ship ever built on Long Island, was launched.

World War I provided a temporary revival when the government financed renovation of the shipyards for construction of steel-hulled war vessels. Between 1917 and 1919, the number of shipyard workers mushroomed from 250 to more than 1,100, but when the war ended, shipbuilding was gone for good.

Long before anyone thought of building ships, the Setauket Indians controlled the area they called Suwassett, meaning "land of small pines." Between 1655 and 1687 the Indians sold land to settlers, who called the area Drowned Meadow because much of it, including the latter-day business district, was a marsh.

William Simson was the first recorded property owner in 1661. John Roe, a shoemaker from Queens, was the first person of European descent to actually live in the area. He moved into a new house in Drowned Meadow in 1682 and his descendants dominated the area into the 19th Century.

Filled with Patriots during the American Revolution, Drowned Meadow, like many Long Island communities, suffered at the hands of the occupying British forces. But it was during the War of 1812 that the village experienced its most dramatic wartime moment. One night in 1813, two British warships sailed into the harbor and captured seven merchant ships lying at anchor. The only American fortification, Fort Nonsense in Poquott, so

Port Jefferson Historical Society

A Port Jefferson shipbuilding crew sits with the schooner J.H. Parker, launched in 1884. Among them were John R. Mather and cousin William H. Mather, both in the second generation of the Mather shipbuilding family.

named because of its seeming insignificance, opened fire with its single cannon, managing to bring one warship aground. It was Fort Nonsense's finest (and only) hour.

A major turning point came in 1840, when William L. Jones began building a 500-foot dock that signaled the end of the marsh and the beginning of today's Port Jefferson. Land along the dock was filled in and built up during the subsequent years, eventually becoming Main Street. On Aug. 31, 1852, the village was designated an American port of entry, and a federal customs house was constructed on East Main Street. The building was relocated to High Street. In 1875, the peak year for shipping, 239 ships cleared customs.

As the village expanded, residents decided Drowned Meadow was not a proper name for a prospering seaport. So residents gathered at the schoolhouse March 7, 1836, and adopted Democrats' suggestion to name the port after Thomas Jefferson.

There was regular ferry service to Bridgeport, Conn., beginning in 1872. The need for expanded service led to the formation of the Port Jefferson Steamboat Co. (later named the Bridgeport and Port Jefferson Steamboat Co.) in 1883 by Capt. Charles Tooker and his brother-in-law Edward Davis. Entrepreneur P.T. Barnum, a Bridgeport resident, was one of the original stockholders. Barnum bought property in Port Jefferson's Brick Hill neighborhood with the idea of using it as the base for his traveling circus. When residents quashed that idea, Barnum subdivided the tract for housing. One of the streets running through his former land is still named Barnum Avenue.

After the demise of shipbuilding, Port Jefferson reinvented itself as a vacation spot. Bridgeport and Port Jefferson Steamboat Co. ferries brought visitors. Beaches with bathhouses opened around the harbor. After 1900, Port Jefferson became a center for auto touring and racing. The Port Jefferson Automobile Club sponsored hill climb races on East Broadway, and one of the contestants was Henry Ford.

By 1910, Port Jefferson Harbor was the site of sandmining. The excavation continued until after World War II, drastically altering the harbor's configuration, eliminating wetlands and killing the shellfish industry.

During the Roaring Twenties, powerboats unloaded cases of illegal liquor and gaming parlors did a brisk business. About the same time, the Ku Klux Klan became active. A 1923 carnival featured a "Klan Night" that attracted 2,500 people.

After World War II, community leaders tried to reverse a decline with an urban renewal project and, in 1963, by incorporating as a village. And in 1999, officials were considering creating a seaport museum at the former Mobil oil terminal, itself a former shipyard.

Where to Find More: Port Jefferson village historian.

POOSPATUCK, Continued

monitoring. A major cleanup of trash and dumped material was undertaken and new state-financed education programs emphasizing Indian culture and language were started. Wallace also led efforts to replace trailer homes with permanent houses. And he set a goal to expand the reservation, and to provide living space for tribal members living elsewhere, by regaining several hundred acres that he said were lost in improper deals over four centuries.
Where to Find More: "We Are Still Here: The Algonquian Peoples of Long Island Today," by John Strong, Mastic-Moriches-Shirley Library in Shirley.

POQUOTT
A Pleasant Place, But Not Well Fortified

Beginnings: There wasn't much there at the start but a man apparently could at least get a drink. What became Poquott 268 years later began as George's Neck on July 23, 1662, named after George Wood, a "newcomer" to the 7-year-old Setauket colony when he was authorized to keep the "ordinary" — or tavern — at the wooded neck on the west side of Port Jefferson Harbor. The first mention of George's Neck in town records is Jan. 6, 1668. Eleven years later the neck was divided into 15-acre lots. Former Brookhaven Town historian Osborn Shaw wrote in 1955 that the notorious Capt. John Scott, a rogue real estate man who had three houses in the area, may have been the first white settler.
War of 1812: A small fort was established at the north end of the neck on lands of the Van Brunts, early settlers, that later became Tinker's Point, the site of expensive modern homes. Because it had only one cannon to defend Setauket and Port Jefferson, the installation was known locally as Fort Nonsense.
Turning Point: After World War I, landed families on the neck, concerned by development pressure on the harbor, pushed to form an incorporated village to control zoning. A "population boom" from 1928 to 1930 keyed more to gerrymandering than migration boosted the number of residents from 132 to 250, clearing the way for a court to drop its view that there were too few people to form a village. The vote to create 420-acre Poquott, an Indian name meaning "cleared land," carried 47-18 on Dec. 20, 1930.
Two Sections: Poquott, a residential nook north of Route 25A, was divided into two sections with no direct road link between them. The east side along Washington Street was older, with many modest homes on relatively small lots. The west side, on Van Brunt Manor Road, would see very expensive places, including the newer Tinker Bluff section.
Where to Find More: "Historical Sketches of Northern Brookhaven Town," by Osborn Shaw, Port Jefferson Free Library.

PORT JEFFERSON STATION
Rapid Growth Rode On Nesconset Hwy.

Beginnings: The area was first known as Comsewogue, which in the language of the Setauket Indians means a place where several paths come together. The first white resident was William Tooker, who by 1750 was living in a house on Sheep Pasture Road at Reeves Road. (The house remained standing through the 1990s.)

Turning Points: Port Jefferson Station remained primarily a farming community until the 1950s. But there was a spurt of development in 1873, when the Long Island Rail Road extended service to Port Jefferson. The depot was designed by Stanford White. The construction of Nesconset Highway in the mid-1950s opened the area for rapid development. The area known as Comsewogue has drifted south over the years.

Claim to Fame: Maurice Richard in 1909 erected a factory south of the tracks and west of Route 112. It housed his Only Car Co., the name referring to the fact that the car's engine had only one cylinder. Richard produced only a few cars before the company failed. In 1921, the Port Jefferson Lace Co. opened in the warehouse and eventually expanded and became the Thomas Wilson & Co., employing 300 people. The lace factory produced mosquito netting, camouflage nets and parachutes in World War II and surgical leotards that helped prevent vascular problems for the first astronauts. The lace operations continued into the 1980s.

Where to Find More: Port Jefferson village historian and Brookhaven town historian.

RIDGE
Minutemen Organized To Defend a Family

Beginnings: Long before droves of senior citizens were drawn to the huge Leisure Village retirement community starting in 1970, the Randalls took up residence on Whiskey Road. In 1728, Stephen Randall staked out a farm in the mid-Island terrain that was once the hunting ground for the region's Indians. So many Randalls followed that Ridge was first called Randallville. Early maps also identified it as Ridgeville or Ridgefield, inspired by the geographical feature on its north side. Some would refer to the area as "the Ridge," as the Smith family once did.

The Revolution: Stephen Randall, like landowners in Bridgehampton, East Hampton and Southampton, organized a company of Minutemen to defend his homesteads.

Turning Point: The Manor of St. George, a vast land patent granted William (Tangier) Smith in 1693, extended from Mastic to Middle Country Road and included a portion of Ridge. The colonel's grandson, William Smith, built a manor house called Longwood in 1790. The Smith family summered at Longwood, spending winters at the manor house in Mastic. Years later, the last Smith to live at Longwood gave 50 acres to the Longwood School District for the junior and senior high schools. The Longwood manor house would later be owned by the Town of Brookhaven.

Natural Bounty: Through the 1800s, firewood was cut at Ridge's farms and hauled to Long Island Sound, where it was piled along the bluffs for transport to New York City. It then sailed up the Hudson on barges to Haverstraw and was burned at the brickyards. Years later, the old landing roads leading to the Sound were all that remained of the once-thriving lumber industry at places such as Ridge and Middle Island.

Where to Find More: The Thomas R. Bayles local history collection at Longwood Public Library, Middle Island, including "Longwood Long Ago," by Suzanne Johnson.

Skyviews Photo

ROCKY POINT: An aerial view in 1970. The closing of the Wading River rail line in 1938 and the Depression crimped the land boom of the 1920s.

ROCKY POINT
Radio History Made In a Wildlife Area

Beginnings: The rocky terrain of this hilly hamlet was acknowledged at the start: The first mention of the place in Brookhaven Town records was Rocky Hollow in November, 1714. An entry in 1755 called it "Rocky poynt hollow." Noah Hallock, from Southold, is said to have been the first white settler, in 1721. He built a house that year near what is now called Hallock Landing, and it's still there, with the family cemetery. A large boulder, one of Long Island's biggest, once stood in full splendor behind the Hallock house, but was later surrounded by houses.

The Way It Was: The early main industry was shipment of cordwood across Long Island Sound to Connecticut. The first one-room schoolhouse was built in 1862. The post office was established in 1872, when the population was about 300. The Long Island Rail Road began serving Rocky Point in the spring of 1895, but that Wading River line was discontinued Sept. 1, 1938, for lack of business. That and the Great Depression crimped the land boom of the 1920s, when the New York Daily Mirror sponsored lot sales in Rocky Point. The newspaper built a fancy clubhouse, which was given to the new North Shore Beach Property Owners Association in 1929.

Claim to Fame: On Nov. 5, 1921, President Warren G. Harding, from his White House desk, broadcast an international message to inaugurate the world's first commercial wireless service, via the huge Radio Corp. of America station at Rocky Point. It had a field of towers 412 feet high and covered 6,200 acres. With changes in technology, most of the RCA land was given to the state in 1972 and became a pine barrens wildlife management area. Wireless inventor Gugliemo Marconi sent the first wireless message to a ship at sea from Babylon Village in 1901. The historic shack he broadcast from in Babylon was moved to the front of the Rocky Point School complex on Rocky Point Road.

Where to Find More: "Historical Sketches of Northern Brookhaven Town," by Osborn Shaw, "Rocky Point, A Historical Perspective," by Dagmar Von Bernewitz, Shoreham-Wading River Public Library, Shoreham.

SELDEN
Whaleboats Ferried Rebels From Danger

Beginnings: The founding farmers of the mid-1700s called it Westfield and spent many early winters hacking wood from their newly acquired lots. The extra income earned from selling the cordwood came in handy for families such as the Roes, Nortons and Longbothams, trying to eke out a living in the sparsely settled region. Built about 1752, the Norton family home was the oldest remaining in Selden but was gutted by fire in the fall of 1996. Local preservationists are still unsure of the landmark's future.

The Revolution: Honing his combat skills in the French and Indian War, Daniel Roe served as a captain in the Revolutionary War. Besides winning battles against the British, Roe kept busy evacuating rebel families from Long Island following the British occupation. In swift-moving whaleboats, Roe piloted the families and their belongings across Long Island Sound to Connecticut. It would be seven years before Roe, his wife Deborah, and their 12 children returned to Westfield.

The Name Game: Like many other Long Island communities, Westfield residents were too late. By the time a post office was established there in 1852, the name Westfield was already taken. Residents substituted Selden, in honor of Henry Selden, a prominent New York judge and lieutenant governor from 1857 to 1858, a curious choice because Selden had no apparent connection to the community. Perhaps they were persuaded by Selden's promise to do "something handsome" for the hamlet. No one knows whether Judge Selden ever did.

Turning Point: Small vegetable and fruit farms still lined Middle Country Road in the early 1930s when real estate agents began selling housing lots to buyers from New York City for as little as $19 for a quarter-acre lot. Buyers came by the busload, enticed by advertisements that boasted paradise garden plots, vacation camps or retreats set in "beautiful high-wooded or open-level sections." Called Nature's Gardens, the development was the first of many that would gradually transform Selden into a 20,000-strong suburban community by the late 1990s.

Where to Find More: "The Hamlet of Selden: An Historic Chronicle," by Luise Weiss, available at the Middle Country Public Library.

SETAUKET

See story on Page 91.

SHIRLEY
A Name Change Sinks Due to Lack of Harbor

Beginnings: Brooklyn native Walter Shirley caught his first glimpse of the Suffolk County woodlands that would later bear his name during World War I. Shirley was an Army private and bugler at Camp Upton. One night he snuck out of camp to explore but got lost in the wilderness. While stationed at Upton, Shirley, who sang as well as bugled, met composer Irving Berlin. After the war, Shirley and his piano player helped promote Berlin's songs at movie houses. But Shirley soon bored of show biz, opting instead to shift to real estate. He began selling land around Rockville Centre and Oceanside, later moving his sights to the lands he first saw as a private at Camp Upton. For $8,000, Shirley bought a small tract of land from William K. Vanderbilt II near Lake Ronkonkoma during World War II.

Turning Point: It didn't take long for Shirley to turn his initial $8,000 investment into a multimillion-dollar company. The tiny bungalows were marketed as summer or retirement homes and offered for as little as $20 a month. So many were enticed by Shirley's installment plans that 5,000 homes soon dotted the new landscape. In 1952, Shirley offered the post office a parcel of land, on one condition: The new post office had to bear his name. Shirley's "Town of Flowers," as early advertisements called it, did not hold up well. In later years, critics pointed to Shirley's quarter-acre plots and minimal infrastructure as examples of shoddy planning.

A New Revolution: In the mid-1980s, barely three decades after Shirley came to be, a faction of residents began a movement to replace the name. Some wanted a name more steeped in history. The leading alternative was Floyd Harbor. But as the Shirley faithfuls pointed out, Shirley had no harbor. In fact, the Keep Shirley Shirley slogan was "Where's Da Harbor?" Residents voted for a name change in 1987, but because the traditionalists boycotted the vote, the U.S. Board of Geographic Names wasn't persuaded that enough of the community supported the swap.

Where to Find More: Mastic-Moriches-Shirley Library, 425 William Floyd Pkwy., Shirley.

Fullerton Collection, Suffolk County Historical Society

ROCKY POINT: From left, Alanson E. Dickinson, Sarah Angeline Dickinson and Irene Hallock Dickinson at their home, built around 1830. The house was unoccupied after 1887, but Alanson Dickinson was sentimental about it and would not allow it to be touched. On the day he died, March 1, 1917, a heavy snow fell and collapsed the home, a family member said.

Fullerton Collection, Suffolk County Historical Society

ROCKY POINT: A view of Route 25A in November, 1938; the area's land boom was still suffering from the Depression, and the LIRR had just stopped service on the Wading River branch.

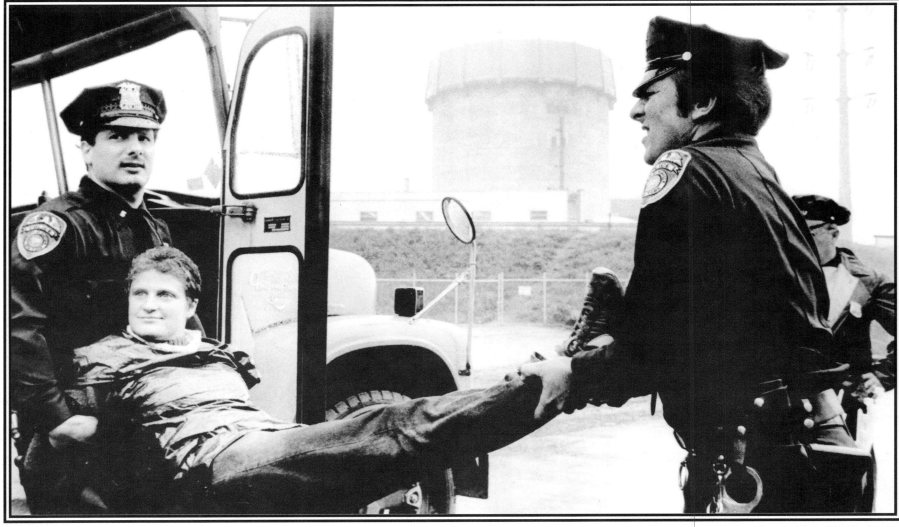

Newsday Photo, 1979 / Jim Peppler

SHOREHAM: Construction of a nuclear power plant by the Long Island Lighting Co. drew protesters in June, 1979. The plant was finished but, because of safety concerns, was eventually shut down.

Three Village Historical Society

SETAUKET: The village green in rural Setauket in about 1885.

Three Village Historical Society

SETAUKET: In about 1930, an automobile passes over a bridge at Setauket Bay.

Main Street in East Setauket, circa 1900. Throughout the 19th Century and up to World War II, Setauket and East Setauket showed strong interest in the raising, trading and racing of horses.

Three Village Historical Society Photo

SETAUKET

Spy Ring Foils the British

BY TOM MORRIS
STAFF WRITER

Setauket: cradle of Brookhaven Town, seat of its government for well over a century, crucible of divided loyalties during the Revolution and home of George Washington's gallant Patriot spy ring.

Setauket: shipbuilding center of the mid-19th Century, onetime producer of pianos and rubber products, briefly a lively tourist center, and a hamlet where natural beauty and colonial roots tastefully blend the past and present.

In a deed dated April 14, 1655, five men from New England and one from Southold bought about 30 square miles bordering Long Island Sound, reaching from Smithtown to Port Jefferson Harbor, from the Setauket Indians in return for European-made metal and cloth goods. Settlement began soon after, along both sides of what would become the landmark Mill Pond off Main Street, though no more than 20 families lived there in the first few years. The founders briefly called the place Ashford, after a town in Kent, England, but Setauket, the Indian name for "land at the mouth of the creek," prevailed.

The Nicolls Patent of March 7, 1666, established the town boundaries and designated the name Brookhaven instead of Setauket. But Setauket was the only place of any size or importance in Brookhaven until after the Revolution and was the seat of town government until 1789.

The British controlled Long Island throughout the war after defeating Gen. George Washington in Brooklyn in August, 1776, and Setauket became a hot spot of Patriot guerrilla warfare. The Redcoats turned it into a garrison town by seizing the Presbyterian Church and making it a fort. Local families' loyalties were split between the rebel and Tory causes for most of the war.

The Battle of Setauket occurred Aug. 22, 1777, when 500 Patriot troops, led by Col. Abraham Parsons, came ashore from Fairfield, Conn. In a four-hour skirmish, they unsuccessfully tried to force the British out of Setauket, retreating across the Sound when word came that English ships were about to close off their escape route.

Maj. Benjamin Tallmadge, a 24-year-old Setauket native who had an illustrious record in the Revolution, led an assault in November, 1780, in which he captured the British Fort St. George in Mastic and burned a large quantity of hay that had been stockpiled in Coram. The exploit was applauded by Washington, who by then knew of Tallmadge's valor in heading a Patriot spy ring. The super-secret ring, Setauket's most dramatic war role, was created in 1778 to gather information about British troop movements and other military activity on

Long Island, in New York and as far off as Pennsylvania.

Here's how it worked: Robert Townsend of Oyster Bay, the only member not of Setauket, posed as a Tory merchant in New York City to gather information. Austin Roe, a Setauket tavern and innkeeper, also played a merchant and carried Townsend's messages by horse from the city to Setauket, 55 miles through enemy lines a couple of times a week. He delivered them to Abraham Woodhull, a young farmer on Conscience Bay in Setauket who passed them to Caleb Brewster, who commanded a fleet of whaleboats that harassed Tory and British shipping on the Sound. Brewster carried the espionage information to Tallmadge, who was headquartered in Connecticut and forwarded it directly to Gen. Washington.

One ring member, Ann Smith Strong (known as Nancy in the spy records) used her clothesline to let Woodhull, whose farm was across Conscience Bay, know Caleb Brewster's whereabouts. If the whaleboat captain was in town, Nancy would hang a black petticoat among the usual red or white ones worn by women of the day. The number of handkerchiefs on her line told Woodhull at which of six landing spots Brewster and his boat could be found. The spy ring operated for five years without being unmasked. After the war, Washington visited Setauket to meet the spies, staying the night of April 22, 1790, at Roe's inn, which he wrote in his diary was "tolerably decent with obliging people in it." The house was moved in 1936 to a spot just north of Old Post Road and was privately owned.

Setauket in the 1800s became a thriving shipbuilding center. By 1840, shipyards dotted the harbor. Setauket had a brush with manufacturing in the mid-to-late 19th Century, including the R. Nunns Clark & Co. piano factory, and the Long Island Rubber Co., a maker of such things as shoes and boots. The village also had a brush with art. A Setauket native, William Sidney Mount, became one of America's best-known painters. He was born in 1807, though his family moved seven years later to Stony Brook, where he lived the rest of his life.

Throughout the 19th Century and up to World War II, Setauket and East Setauket showed strong interest in the raising, trading and racing of horses. And early in this century, Setauket was a tourist center, though there was aversion to some related commerce and industry and the trend faded. Since World War II, the hamlet, with its colonial village green and historic homes and buildings, remained almost entirely residential. Greater Setauket would eventually include East and South Setauket and Strongs Neck.

Where to Find More: "Setauket, The First Three Hundred Years, 1655-1955," by Edwin P. Adkins; "Three Village Guidebook," by Howard Klein; "Discover Setauket, Brookhaven's Oldest Settlement," by Three Village Historical Society and Steven B. Schwartzman, all at Emma S. Clark Memorial Library, Setauket.

SHOREHAM
A Nuclear Power Plant Produces Controversy

Beginnings: Before it became Shoreham in 1906, the community had a succession of names, all of them inspired by notable residents or local industry. There was Woodville Landing and Woodville, stemming from the abundance of cordwood harvested from its forests in the mid-1800s. It was also known for a brief time as Swezey's Landing after Daniel Swezey built his general store there in 1885. And, when entrepreneur James Warden came along in 1895, parceling the land into two-acre plots, he preferred Wardenclyffe.

Brush With Fame: With backing from financier J. P. Morgan, radio pioneer Nikola Tesla, Guglielmo Marconi's arch rival, came to Shoreham in 1901 to build his World Telegraphy Center. Designed by McKim, Mead and White, the power plant housed a laboratory, wireless transmitter and production facilities for Tesla's vacuum tubes. But financial problems plagued the project from the start and doomed it to failure. The 180-foot tower and unfinished complex were demolished in 1917.

Turning Point: Fifty years later, another kind of power plant came to Shoreham, generating only controversy. The Shoreham nuclear power plant was nearing completion in 1975 when 15,000 protesters gathered outside the complex, bringing the project to a halt. The plant, which was supposed to be built for $65 million and ended up costing $5.5 billion, remained closed on the 419-acre site on the west bank of Wading River.

Where to Find More: "Shoreham: A Historical Perspective," by Dagmar Von Bernewitz; "The Life and Times of Nikola Tesla: Biography of a Genius," by Marc J. Seifer; "Tesla: Man Out of Time," by Margaret Cheney.

SOUND BEACH
Read All About It! Lots for Sale for $89.50

Beginnings: In contrast to the deep colonial roots of neighboring Miller Place, Sound Beach emerged at the end of the Roaring Twenties as a result of a New York City newspaper circulation war. The Daily Mirror bought more than 1,000 acres in 1928 — a decade before rail service in the area was discontinued for lack of business — and the next year began advertising 20-by-100-foot lots for $89.50. Other city sheets did similarly in San Remo, Mastic Beach and part of Rocky Point. Buyers showed up in Sound Beach lugging their groceries and other necessities because there were almost no services, only "unspoiled desolation," as one local historian put it. Some pitched tents until they could build summer cottages. Life in the country was primitive — kerosene lamps, outhouses, no electricity or running water at first.

Coming of Age: Most of the original cottages were converted to year-round houses after World War II. Legal battles played out over public access to the narrow beaches at the foot of the cliffs on Long Island Sound. Sound Beach was long known for reasonably priced housing and an off-the-beaten-path character. It had about 9,300 residents in 1998, and no schools of its own; school district lines ran down the middle of the community, meaning that half of the children attended classes in Miller Place, half in Rocky Point. St. Louis De Montfort Roman Catholic Church, completed in 1978, became one of the most imposing buildings in the area.

Kooky Landmark: In the 1990s, the quiet business section was marked by a red, 6-foot-tall, smiling plaster tomato atop Rubino's Restaurant. However, it was taken down in 1997 when the landlord said it was a target of vandals.

Where to Find More: "Miller Place and Sound Beach, A Historical Perspective," by Dagmar Von Bernewitz, Shoreham-Wading River library.

STONY BROOK

One Man Leaves Many Footprints

BY TOM MORRIS
STAFF WRITER

The colonial ambience that marked late-20th Century Stony Brook owed less to the American Revolution than to the Ward Melville revolution.

Melville, a 20th-Century shoe tycoon with a lifelong love of Stony Brook, radically rebuilt its downtown center just before World War II, transforming it from a down-at-the-heels fishing village into a quaint rendition of an early-19th Century American town that became one of Long Island's esthetic delights.

The Melville revolution went even further: In 1956, he donated 480 acres of land just south of Route 25A for a state university campus he thought would look like William and Mary, the Virginia colonial college, to complement what he dubbed his "living Williamsburg." The positive impact of the State University at Stony Brook would, of course, be enormous. But Melville, who died in 1977 at 90, lived to resent the often-panned brick-and-block look of what became the 1,100-acre campus.

Newsday Photo, 1966
Benefactor Ward Melville

Melville also funded the Museums at Stony Brook, saved historic homes and provided other community assets, leaving a legacy in a period of about 25 years that seemingly altered forever the community's fairly unremarkable background.

Stony Brook, in contrast to neighboring Setauket, played no special role in the American Revolution. It had peaked economically by 1855 as part of the local shipbuilding industry. It enjoyed just a brief fling as a resort town from about 1890 to World War I, with six hotels at the turn of the century.

Stony Brook is believed to have been settled in 1660, second to Setauket (1655) in Brookhaven Town history. The Setauket Indians called the place Wopowog, for "land at the narrows," characterizing the narrow inlet from Long Island Sound into Stony Brook Harbor that divided the Towns of Brookhaven and Smithtown. The first road approved — Main Street — was mentioned in town records on May 25, 1685.

In 1699, Adam Smith, a son of Smithtown founder Richard (Bull) Smith, built the first gristmill. It was destroyed in a storm in 1751, rebuilt nearby and was still standing — and working — through the 1990s. It was listed on the National Register of Historic Places. The first school, no longer in existence, was built about 1750 on what became Christian Avenue. Beneath a large oak tree in the front yard on April 23, 1790, the whole school stood to wave to President George Washington as he rode through after an overnight stay in Setauket.

On March 24, 1807, a post office was established at Stoney Brook, the spelling of which was changed to Stony Brook in 1884. Among Stony Brook's most famous adopted sons were William Sidney Mount, the 19th Century genre painter, and Micah Hawkins, a part-time composer whose operetta, "The Saw Mill," ran successfully in New York City in 1824 and is said to be the first American light opera.

Three Village Historical Society Photo
Two views of Stony Brook's Main Street: in about 1900, above, and in 1962, showing the post office building on the two-acre village green

Newsday Photo

Dramatic change came after a free dinner given by Melville, founder of the Thom McAn shoe chain, at the Three Village Inn (built in 1751) in Stony Brook Jan. 19, 1940. For about 80 people he outlined a plan considered earlier but not pursued by his father, Frank Melville, also a shoe manufacturer, to rebuild the business section, which was in visible decline during the Great Depression.

Melville lived in Manhattan and Old Field, but his family had summered in Stony Brook since 1900 and he loved the place. He quickly persuaded about 35 merchants to sell him their properties and become renters. Among the selling points were low rents, the prospect of national acclaim (which they later got in spades from architectural groups) and the attraction of customers from outside the area (which also occurred, according to a survey after one year in the new setup that showed profits up by about 30 percent).

Town clearances were obtained swiftly — nobody had yet heard of "environmental impact statements" — and Melville spent $500,000 in 1940-41 for the rebuilding of Main Street into a crescent-shaped business district of attached stores centered around the Federal-Greek Revival-style post office on a two-acre village green. Melville gave permanent control of the project to the nonprofit Stony Brook Community Fund, which in 1997 was renamed the Ward Melville Heritage Organization.

The group also managed other Melville contributions to the community, notably the internationally known, three-building museum complex, which housed a large collection of Melville's treasures, including Mount paintings and horse-drawn carriages, and other items of local history. On land given by Melville, the state opened the university in 1963, bringing major assets and opportunities to the area, along with thousands more homes, traffic and commercial buildup on surrounding major roads.

Where to Find More: "Historical Sketches of Northern Brookhaven Town," by Osborn Shaw; "Stony Brook, A Historical Perspective," by Dagmar Von Bernewitz, at Emma S. Clark Memorial Library, Setauket; "Three Village Guidebook," by Howard Klein, Three Village Historical Society, East Setauket.

YAPHANK

Community Took Off With Railroad's Arrival

Beginnings: John Homan built two mills on the Carmans River in the mid-18th Century, inspiring Yaphank's first name — Millville. When the post office opened in 1846, residents had planned on using Millville. That is, until they learned there were 13 other Millvilles in New York State. So Yaphank was substituted, taken from the Indian word "Yamphanke," meaning "bank of a river."

Turning Point: The arrival of the Long Island Rail Road in 1843 transformed the sleepy mill town into a bustling commercial center.

In three years in the 1850s, three churches were built in addition to an octagon-shaped schoolhouse encouraged by William J. Weeks, an early president of the LIRR and prominent citizen of Yaphank. Weeks was fascinated with octagonal architecture and even built his own Yaphank home with eight sides. It's gone now. By 1875, Yaphank had two grist mills, two lumber mills, two blacksmith shops, a printing office, an upholstery shop, a stagecoach line, two doctors, a shoe shop, two wheelwright shops, a meat market, a dressmaking shop and general store.

World War I: The Yaphank railroad station was the first glimpse thousands of troops had of Army life as they stepped off the train headed for boot camp at nearby Camp Upton in the fall of 1917. More than 30,000 men would pass through before the war ended, including songwriter Irving Berlin. It was there he wrote "Yip Yip Yaphank," a musical comedy that had a brief run on Broadway.

World War II: As Hitler's Nazi regime prepared to conquer Eastern Europe, German-American supporters in 1937 gathered along Upper Lake in Yaphank, holding rallies, carrying Nazi pennants and listening to the speeches of Fritz Kuhn, an aspiring American führer. The 42-acre campground started out innocently in 1936 as a gathering place for members of the German-American Settlement League, which was later co-opted by Kuhn and other Hitler followers. With Kuhn at the helm, footpaths were renamed Hitler, Goering and Goebbels Streets, and the camp hosted summer weekends for hundreds dressed in Nazi garb and hailing allegiance to Hitler. The outings ended and the campground returned to its bucolic beginnings in the summer of 1938 after league directors were arrested and indicted on civil rights charges.

Brush With Fame: Mary Louise Booth, the first editor of Harper's magazine, lived in Yaphank in a home that dated to 1795.

Where to Find More: "The Early Years in Middle Island, Coram, Yaphank and Ridge," by Thomas S. Bayles, available at the Longwood Public Library, Middle Island, and Yaphank Historical Society.

STONY BROOK: A ship enters the harbor at Shipman's Point in an undated photo.

Three Village Historical Society

Suffolk County Historical Society

YAPHANK: A horse and sleigh provide passage on snowy Yaphank Avenue in a photo taken before 1900.

Suffolk County Historical Society

YAPHANK: Resident William Jones Weeks (1821-79), once head of the LIRR, could write the Lord's Prayer skating on ice.

Newsday Photo / Bill Davis, 1997

The beach at Amagansett as it appeared in 1997. In 1942, a discarded pack of cigarettes and a trail in the sand helped U.S. agents find expolsives buried by Germans for later bombings of U.S. sites.

Newsday Photo

State troopers stop a car in Suffolk County during a search for German spies in 1942. At left, items recovered from boxes buried in the sand at Amagansett included a shovel, an explosive disguised as a piece of coal, an army cap and a fountain pen that would detonate explosives. Below, Coast Guardsman John Cullen, left, and German George Dasch.

Photo by Ira Schwarz, 1992

Newsday Photo

AP Photo, 1948

Nazi Saboteurs At Amagansett

They came to bomb America.

It was June 13, 1942, just six months since America had entered World War II. In foggy darkness, four men got off on a German U-boat in rafts, landed on the beach in Amagansett and began burying boxes of explosives intended to blow up U.S. power and industrial plants.

Suddenly, through the fog, the leader of the four, George Dasch, saw a light approaching. It was just after midnight and Coast Goardsman John Cullen, holding a flashlight, was on beach patrol. Dasch approached Cullen and said he and his friends were fishermen. Cullen knew night fishing was prohibited in war-time, and he grew suspicious when another man spoke in German. Dasch dismissed his comrade and thrust $260 in cash at Cullen. "Take it," he said. "Forget about this. Forget you ever saw us."

IT HAPPENED HERE

Cullen backed away and ran to his Coast Guard station to alert superiors. Meanwhile, the four men rode a Long Island Rail Road train from Amagansett to New York City.

In Manhattan, where the four had checked into hotels, Dasch told a fellow German, Ernest Burger, that he opposed their plan and would reveal it to U.S. officials. He persuaded Burger to back out.

Dasch took a train to Washington and called the FBI from a hotel, asking to see chief J. Edgar Hoover. Agents quickly picked him up. Dasch showed them $84,000 in cash that was to be used to help carry out the bombings and to bribe Americans for help.

Dasch also startled agents by revealing that another team of four Germans had traveled to Florida in a U-boat and landed at Ponte Vedra Beach. They also intended to commit sabotage.

Within two weeks, all eight had been arrested in New York and the Midwest. At a military trial July 2, the suspects expressed opposition to Germany's Nazi regime, but all were convicted of spying and conspiracy charges. Six were electrocuted. Dasch had expected to be hailed for preventing the bombings, but he and Burger were imprisoned. Paroled after the war, Dasch returned home but was ostracized when German newspapers reported his wartime story.

— Lawrence Striegel

Town of East Hampton

EAST HAMPTON VILLAGE
The First Resort of the Wealthy

BY TOM MORRIS
STAFF WRITER

Exuding the charm of a tranquil American colonial place, East Hampton Village nevertheless developed much of its modern grace during its emergence as an affluent resort community in the 1870s. The evolution from pioneer beginnings of a 1600s Puritan enclave to the quiet elegance of a renowned village three centuries years later provides one of Long Island's richest histories.

After East Hampton Town's founding in 1648 by a handful of English immigrants, most from Lynn, Mass., the first settlers built their huts and cottages on both sides of Main Street.

The 17th-Century inhabitants were almost all strongly independent Puritans, who named the community Maidstone for the first 14 years, after their home area in Kent, England. By 1651, the new Maidstone had 37 families, most from Connecticut and Southampton, which had been formed a few years earlier.

What became an area of large Victorian homes near the ocean around Lily Pond Lane in the village was once the best grazing land. The village played a key role in the huge cattle drives to Montauk that occurred annually for most of three centuries.

Perhaps nothing better evokes the village's early history than the South End Cemetery just off Main Street, where the oldest stone, that of the first minister, Thomas James, dates to 1696. James was a friend and business associate of Lion Gardiner, who also was interred in the cemetery.

Gardiner lived for many years in the village and was the guiding force in the entire town's early development. He was known for his amicable dealings with the Montauketts, which resulted in much of the land on the East End being ceded to the settlers without feud or bloodshed. Gardiner was generally a calming influence, though in 1657, his daughter Elizabeth, then 15, set the fledgling community on its ear by accusing a woman, Elizabeth Garlick, of witchcraft. She was acquitted at a trial in Hartford, Conn.

The village preserved some historic places, including two of its most venerable houses, on Main Street. Home Sweet Home, built in 1650, was the boyhood home of actor-playwright John Howard Payne, who penned the famous song the house was named after. Adjacent is the Mulford house, circa 1680, also one of Long Island's oldest. There is also Huntting Inn, which encloses a 1699 house built for the community's second minister, and Clinton Academy, the first college prep school in the state, established in 1784. The venerable Hedges Inn, family owned from 1652 to 1923, was perhaps most famous as an inn between 1954 and 1964 under the late Henri Soule.

It was in the 1870s that the major turning point occurred: the start of the summer colony that would transform East Hampton and give it a stamp of sedate prosperity. Well-to-do New York vacationers began to pour in from the nearest rail station six miles away in Bridgehampton and via steam packet. Scribner's Magazine in 1877 commissioned a group of writers and artists — known as the Tile Club — to depict the best

Collection of Joel Streich
An old postcard shows the village in horse-and-buggy days.

of Long Island, and they quickly discovered the ambience of East Hampton. The Tile Club lingered for two decades, attracting more visitors, and by the 1880s the village had become a thriving resort for well-heeled New Yorkers.

In 1891, the Maidstone Club was organized — dominated, as one history book put it, by "genteel, Episcopalian and rich" summer visitors. One of its founders was Thomas Moran, an artist and Tile Clubber who first came to national attention with large canvases of Yellowstone and Yosemite that helped create the national park system. Moran's former home on Main Street was placed on the National Register of Historic Places. It adjoins the summer White House used in the 1840s by President John Tyler, whose wife, "the rose of Long Island," was the former Julia Gardiner of East Hampton. The first couple turned heads as they strolled down Main Street.

Another president's wife, Jacqueline Kennedy, spent many childhood days at Rowdy Hall, a social hall that served as the center of an artists' colony in the 1890s and was later turned into a rambling house that remains on Main Street. Jackie's parents, Jack and Janet Bouvier, rented the house after their 1928 marriage, and held her second birthday party there.

After the railroad was extended to East Hampton in 1895, the gates opened wide to summer visitors. Some arrived with 10 or more servants at their shingled mansions near the shore. The village incorporated in 1920.

The resort reputation was longstanding. Officers of the crown once came to East Hampton for the "waters." In 1869, a society writer for a New York newspaper declared East Hampton to be "innate with good breeding and good family," excluding "rabble . . . the vulgar parvenus that so often make life wretched" in other places.

A local celebrity was actor John Drew, who could be seen driving on Main Street in his carriage with his niece, Ethel Barrymore. (Actress Drew Barrymore was named for John Drew.)

Where to Find More: "East Hampton, a History and Guide," by Jason Epstein and Elizabeth Barlow, 1985, Random House; "East Hampton on Long Island," Suffolk County Tercentenary pamphlet, 1983; "The Land of Home Sweet Home," by Marjorie A. Denton, Paxson Press 1962; Long Island Forum collection; at East Hampton Public Library.

Newsday Photo / Bill Davis
Home Sweet Home was the home of John Howard Payne, who penned the famous song.

From the Montauk Lighthouse to the Victorian mansions of Sag Harbor, from the hoary byways of East Hampton Village to the enduring beauty of Gardiners Island, East Hampton Town presents a rich cross section of Long Island history.

The town was founded April 29, 1648, with the purchase from the Montaukett Indians of about 31,000 acres of land reaching from the eastern boundary of Southampton to Hither Hills. Most of the small colony of first settlers were from Lynn, Mass., who had tight ties to their fellow English pioneers in Connecticut.

In fact, it was two Connecticut colony governors who swung the deal with the Indians for the land. Nine years earlier, in 1639, Lion Gardiner had bought the island that would bear his name, located three miles north of East Hampton, and it was owned ever since by the Gardiner family.

Between 1658 and 1686, about 10,000 more acres were bought at Montauk to be held in common by the freeholders of East Hampton for use as summer pasture for their herds of cattle and sheep.

Town settlement began along what became Main Street in East Hampton Village. But soon the community branched out, building roads to Northwest, a section of town where the first port was created (decades before Sag Harbor's founding in 1730), and to the meadows of Accabonac (Springs) and the grazing lands of Wainscott.

A gristmill was built at Northwest in 1653, eliminating the initial dependence on Southampton for grinding grain. Carpenters, blacksmiths and the like had to be invited in from other communities at first, but self-sufficiency came quickly.

Early government ties to Connecticut were broken in 1664 when the Dutch surrendered New Netherlands to the British, and Long Island — reluctantly on the East End — became part of the colony of New York.

By the time Sag Harbor was established, the town was exporting hides, beef, tallow, pork, hoops, staves, cattle, horses, shoes, grain and fish to the West Indies and elsewhere. When the Revolution ended, Sag Harbor became the state's leading customs port.

The town, with about 16,900 people in 1998, would be best known as a summer resort and playground of the rich and famous, and for its picturesque farms and open space, including a world-class fishing center at Montauk.

AMAGANSETT
A Fishing Community, Site of a Nazi Landing

Beginnings: Jacobus Schellinger brought more to early Long Island than his business ambitions when he moved from New Amsterdam to East Hampton after the English took over the Dutch colony in 1664 and renamed it New York. Three of his children — Abraham, Jacob and Catherine — wanted land to farm, so in 1680 they moved three miles east and founded Amagan-

Please Turn the Page

MONTAUK

A Light at the End of the Island

BY TOM MORRIS
STAFF WRITER

'**M**ontauk — The End,'' proclaimed a bumper sticker, a sentiment to capture the delight people find in the ocean-kissed shores and rolling green hills of Long Island's most way-out community. Years after Dutch explorer Adrian Block landed there in 1614, Montauk as it was survived more or less intact. Though a magnet for tourism and a world-class fishing mecca, better than half its 10,000 acres remained as public lands through the 1990s.

Yet looking back at the vagaries of history, Montauk could have been a transatlantic seaport, a military center, "the Miami of the North," a rich man's enclave or a place of Dutch rather than English heritage — all things that once loomed but never happened.

"It's certainly true that the best of old Montauk has survived. The Indians were squeezed out, but it's amazing to think more than half the land at Montauk is public after almost 400 years," John Strong, a history professor at the Southampton Campus of Long Island University, said in 1997.

The Dutch might have moved in quickly after Block found Montauk in 1614, drastically changing early Suffolk history, but they became preoccupied at the other end of Long Island before being kicked out of New York by the British 50 years later. The first settlers, most of British stock, snapped up Montauk's entire 10-by-2-mile mass of hills and boulder-strewn valleys from the Montaukett Indians for about 100 pounds in 1687.

As a British crown possession before the Revolution, Montauk could have been overrun by Redcoats for strategic purposes during the war, but it wasn't. Since they controlled the region for seven years after winning the Battle of Long Island in August, 1776, the British settled for frequent harassment of people on the East End. (In April, 1776, 12 British ships with 650 men showed up in Fort Pond Bay, seemingly intent on plunder and occupation. According to tradition, Capt. John Hulbert of the militia boldly marched his much smaller force of 100 men along a hill in front of the ships, had them reverse their coats in back of the hill and march out into full view again, giving the impression of a far bigger force than it was. The British didn't land and soon left.)

Montauk's most recognized symbol, the lighthouse, went into operation in 1796, six years after President George Washington signed the congressional order to build it. (Originally about 300 feet from the shore, erosion later left the beacon near the edge of a cliff.)

Though the original "proprietors," as the British settlers were dubbed, had turned Montauk into a huge summer pasture for sheep and cattle, there was no end of squabbling over land rights. Their heirs in 1879 sold the whole 10,000 acres of land, reaching from the Montauk Lighthouse to Napeague, for $151,000 to Arthur Benson, a wealthy wheeler-dealer. The developer of Brooklyn's Bensonhurst said he

Collection of Wayne Duprez

A view of Montauk, looking west, taken around 1930 by photographer Charles Duprez. At right is the seven-story office tower built by developer Carl Fisher.

wanted to turn Montauk into a hunting and fishing resort for tycoons. Benson did erect eight splendid "cottages," designed by famed architect Stanford White, at the foot of Ditch Plains Road but he died soon after. Call it fate, call it a break for Montauk or call it economic opportunity lost, but he never overwhelmed the area with his dreams.

In 1895, Benson's estate sold 5,500 acres to promoters led by Austin Corbin Jr., president of the Long Island Rail Road, who had extended the line to Montauk that year in hope that Fort Pond Bay would become a port of entry for transatlantic shipping as his friend Benson had anticipated. Corbin figured the setup would save passengers a day at sea and pump new money into railroad coffers, but the idea never flew.

Meanwhile, in the summer of 1898, the pastures east of Lake Montauk were dotted not with cattle

but with the white tents of the U.S. Army. After the Spanish-American War, almost 30,000 American soldiers, including many of Col. Theodore Roosevelt's Rough Riders, quarantined at Montauk. Many of them were suffering from tropical diseases and died at Montauk, but the Army pulled out the same year and cattle retook the range.

In 1926, Carl Graham Fisher, a dynamic entrepreneur, arrived in Montauk and left lasting monuments. Fisher thought big, achieved big and just once — at Montauk — failed big. He created Miami out of mangrove swamps and woods in the early 1920s, and now he bought 9,000 acres of Montauk for $2.5 million, vowing to create the "Miami of the North" around Lake Montauk and drowsy little Montauk Village.

He soon built Montauk Manor, a 178-room luxury hotel on a bluff overlooking Fort Pond Bay and erected an incongruous seven-story office tower at the traffic circle. Both still stand. From the penthouse on top of the tower he liked to regale visitors (and investors) with his dreams for massive development that probably would have made the great sachem Wyandanch collapse on the spot.

Fisher became excited about the prospects for the deepwater port that had eluded his predecessors. But the stock market crash of 1929 did him in and and he went bankrupt in 1932. Again, Montauk had avoided what seemed at the time inevitable big-time development.

During World War II, Montauk was turned into a busy military town by the Army and Navy. Houses were moved, docks and hangars built, and major artillery emplacements installed around Camp Hero on the south side of the point, as they were around other strategic locations nationally. After the war, most of the Camp Hero land eventually became part of Montauk State Park.

In the 1940s, summer cottages sprouted around Montauk, and in the 1960s motels proliferated to serve the summer throngs who wanted to escape more crowded places. But the year-round population hardly grew. "With all the changes over all that time, we survived as a beautiful open place," Peggy Joyce, president of the Montauk Historical Society, said in 1997. "It could have been a lot worse."

Where to Find More: "A Pictorial History of Montauk," by Albert R. Holden, Holden's Publication, 1983; "East Hampton: A History and Guide," by Jason Epstein and Elizabeth Barlow, 1985; both in East Hampton Public Library.

AMAGANSETT, Continued

sett ("place of good water" in Indian language).
Seaside: Amagansett was a major home base for whaling captains, including the legendary "Capt. Josh" Edwards. The last whale was taken off Amagansett in 1907. Menhaden, or mossbunker, fishing — first with shore nets and later with huge purse seines dropped from boats — was important for Amagansett until recent years.
Landmarks: A boulder with a plaque commemorating a well spring of the Montauketts was placed on Indian Wells Highway near the ocean. A 1725 building, was turned into a museum at Main Street and Windmill Lane, on land settled by the Schellinger brothers.
Claim to Fame: Or infamy? In the wee hours of June 13, 1942, four German saboteurs in a rubber boat launched by a Nazi submarine landed at Amagansett, bent on committing mayhem

in this country. They encountered a Coast Guardsman who reported them, touching off a 15-day manhunt. Two of the four were executed in 1942, and two given long prison terms after cooperating with the FBI.
Where to Find More: "East Hampton, A History & Guide," by Jason Epstein and Elizabeth Barlow; "Amagansett," by Carleton Kelsey and Lucinda Mayo, in the East Hampton Public Library.

GARDINERS ISLAND

A 1639 Settlement Still in One Family

Beginnings: It's hard to say whether Lion Gardiner realized how deep his roots would reach when he bought the magnificent island in Napeague Bay on March 10, 1639, from Wyandanch, sachem of the Montauketts. The cost is

said to have been "a large black dog, a gun, some powder & shot, and a few Dutch blankets . . ." He won perpetual rights to the island from Charles I of England.
Isle Profile: Even in the 1990s, the 6-by-3-mile island between Long Island's forks remained in almost pristine condition, with woods of white oak, swamp maple, wild cherry and birch, and fields where pheasant, wild turkey and woodcock roam near the quiet beaches, cliffs and ponds. "It was a real oldtime plantation," M.A.E. Cooper wrote in 1935, recalling arriving on the island as a child in 1874. Her father was an overseer and her mother a housekeeper. "I spent those happy childhood years in what seemed like a little paradise."
Strange Doings: Gardiner's youngest offspring, Elizabeth, born on the island Sept. 14, 1641, was the first child of English parentage born within what became New York

State. It wasn't a good omen — she died at 15, apparently as a result of giving birth, but not before accusing Elizabeth Garlick, a local woman, of witchcraft. Decades later, in 1699, Capt. William Kidd, a privateer in trouble with the English government for alleged piracy, buried a treasure of gold and gems on the island. John Gardiner, Lion's grandson, cooperated with the British in surrendering the booty, which some accounts place at 20,000 pounds sterling, which would be worth millions of dollars in the late 20th Century.
The Revolution: The Gardiners supported East Hampton's resistance to British oppression, and during the war the island was plundered of crops and animals and left in ruins.
Where to Find More: "Gardiners Island: A Collection of Historical Highlights of the Island," 1958, and "The Manor of Gardiners Island" by Martha J. Lamb, 1885, in the Suffolk County Historical Society, Riverhead.

MONTAUK POINT LIGHT HOUSE, L. I.

Left, Courtesy of the Water Mill Museum; Above, Courtesy of Wayne Duprez

A "penny postcard," above, from about 1900. At right, another angle of the Montauk Lighthouse.

Montauk Point Lighthouse Museum

A bird's-eye view from about 1950.

Lighting the Way

Greeting voyagers at sea and on travelers land for two centuries, the Montauk Lighthouse always was a favorite subject for postcards.

Here are a few vintage cards, as well as other old images of the proud, weather-beaten tower.

Commissioned in 1792 by George Washington, the lighthouse drew 111,000 visitors in 1998, said Tom Ambrosio, executive director of the lighthouse's museum. In 1999, the museum offered some 20 different Montauk lighthouse postcards for sale. Milt Price of the Tomlin Art Co. started making Long Island postcards in 1936 and by 1999 had produced 40 of the Montauk lighthouse. They remained his top sellers.

The lighthouse's first major restoration was completed in 1999 and offered a reason to update those cards. Off and on for about a year, a chimney company from Buffalo inspected and repaired stonework, decking and windows. The finishing touch was two new coats of paint, with black at the cap, a brilliant white body and a new reddish brown stripe that Ambrosio said replaced another shade of brown that was incorrect.

Left and Center, Montauk Point Lighthouse Museum; Above, National Archives

A romantic drawing of the lighthouse appeared with a story in Harper's magazine in September, 1871.

The lighthouse was depicted in a card that was one of 50 in Hassan Tobacco's "Light House Series." At right, a photo of the all-white tower taken in 1871. Tom Ambrosio of the lighthouse museum said the tower's "day mark" navigational stripe was added in 1899.

Pollock-Krasner House and Study Center, East Hampton; Right, Newsday Photo / David L. Pokress
Jackson Pollock paints "Autumn Rhythm" in 1950 at his studio in Springs. At right is a postage stamp issued in his honor in 1999.

SPRINGS

The Bonackers And the Artists

Beginnings: The first crude houses in Springs — a gem of woods, sparkling water and verdant salt meadows around Accabonac Harbor — are believed to have been built in 1649, a year after the founding of the Town of East Hampton. Tradition has it that the first families were workers from nearby Gardiners Island and squatters from New England who found the soil terrible for farming but the fishing profitable.

What It Is: The "Springs" refers to the freshwater springs at the head of Accabonac Creek, which was named for the area's profusion of nuts. "Bonacker" originally meant a person who lived on Accabonac Harbor and was something of a hick. In the 1990s, East Hampton natives were proud to be called Bonackers. Modern Springs covered more than 5,400 acres in the school district, including Gardiners Island. Since 1960, Springs' population soared from 437 to about 4,560 in 1998.

Turning Point: When the arrival of the railroad sparked the East Hampton summer colony in the 1890s, many Springs folks turned to serving resort needs. They became the plumbers, carpenters and electricians who kept the lavish Hampton "cottages" going.

Landmarks: Among more than 60 buildings were preserved, including the community center with historic Ashawagh Hall, the Anderson Library, the Charles Parsons Blacksmith Building, Presbyterian Church, Springs General Store, Pussy's Pond Park and several old houses on Fireplace Road.

Claim to Fame: Springs became the artistic heart of the Hamptons. The exodus of New York City artists to Springs began in the 1940s. It included Jackson Pollock, the most noted American painter of his time and a giant of the school of modern art. He died in 1956 and was the first "outsider" buried at Springs' ancient Green River Cemetery. World-renowned painter Willem de Kooning died in 1997 in the Springs studio where he'd lived much of his life.

Where to Find More: "Springs, A Celebration," published in 1984 by the Springs Improvement Society, "The Springs in the Old Days," by Ferris G. Talmage, in the East Hampton Public Library.

WAINSCOTT

One-Room Schoolhouse Is One of Only Two

Beginnings: Four years after East Hampton Town was founded in 1648, the first mention of the rich soil of Wainscott occurs in official records, citing an order that "a cartway shall be laid out to Wainscott where it may be most convenient." It wasn't exactly the LIE, but by 1688 John Osborn arrived, shortly joined by other settlers. Osborns had been farming Wainscott land for more than 10 generations through the 1990s. It was named after a village north of Maidstone, England, an area immortalized in Charles Dickens' "Great Expectations."

Survival: Wainscott, in the town's southwest corner, held on to its rural charm, despite new, expensive housing that had eaten away some of the potato fields next to the ocean. The "boom" of the 1980s and '90s increased the year-round population by nearly a third, from 421 to about 560 in 1998.

"Wainscott has kept a lot of the character of hundreds of years ago, even if there's been huge change along Montauk Highway," Lisa Liquori, East Hampton Town planning director, said in 1997. The one-room schoolhouse (19 students, grades 1-3) on Main Street remained one of two in use on Long Island in the late 1990s. The other was in adjacent Sagaponack.

Turning Point: The Georgica Association, a private group of the well-to-do who built handsome places on large lots at Georgica Pond, established Wainscott's reputation for style and privacy in the 1890s. The association forced changes in the road patterns to preserve that privacy. During World War II, the association acquired the landmark windmill off Beach Lane. It had been built in Southampton in 1813, brought to Wainscott in 1852 and then moved to Montauk in 1922 by private interests.

Where to Find More: "East Hampton, a History & Guide," by Jason Epstein and Elizabeth Barlow, and "Sketches From Local History," by William D. Halsey.

AMAGANSETT: Gabriel Edwards, member of a long line of seafaring Edwards on the East End, with a whaling crew.

East Hampton Town Marine Museum

WAINSCOTT: Fish caught in nets are hauled ashore in about 1880.

East Hampton Historical Society

Town of Huntington

As Long Island's fifth oldest town, Huntington has evolved since the 1600s with many faces: tiny pioneer outpost, guerrilla stronghold in the American Revolution, home of Walt Whitman, whaling center, mother of Babylon Town, Gold Coast enclave and thriving suburban township.

On April 2, 1653, three Oyster Bay men — Richard Houldbrock, Robert Williams and Daniel Whitehead — made a deal with Asharoken, a Matinecock chief, to buy the land between Cold Spring and Northport Harbors, reaching from Long Island Sound almost as far as what became the Northern State Parkway. By 1656, the rest of the north side of town had been bought east to the Nissequogue River at Smithtown, and eventually the town was extended south to Great South Bay. In 1872, Babylon Town was formed from southern Huntington.

The origin of the town's name has never been clear, but historians believe it stemmed from the fact that it was formed during the brief rule in England of Oliver Cromwell, whose birthplace was Huntingdon, England. Early town meetings were held for two centuries in taverns or at the "town spotte," later known as the village green.

Despite British control of Long Island during the Revolution, Huntington's role was notable. Town landowners in mid-1774 signed a declaration of rights challenging British authority. A year later, the town meeting ordered 80 men to be drilled in preparation for hostilities. The signing of the Declaration of Independence in 1776 set off wild celebration in Huntington.

The British made the town a major garrison to harass Long Island. Guerrilla attacks by Patriots and those invading by boat from Connecticut stung the Redcoats. They answered with such desecrations as destruction of the Presbyterian Church and construction of a fort on the town cemetery. Capt. Nathan Hale, a spy for Gen. George Washington, landed at present-day Huntington Bay. Nearby Halesite was named for the famed Patriot, who is believed to have been caught and executed in New York on Sept. 22, 1776.

Northport became the major shipbuilding area. Cold Spring Harbor was Suffolk County's second largest whaling port (behind Sag Harbor) from 1838 to 1860. Poet Walt Whitman was born at West Hills in 1819 and died in Camden, N.J., at age 73.

The 1890s and early 1900s saw Gold Coast development, with estates including those of Marshall Field III, William K. Vanderbilt II, Walter B. Jennings and Otto Kahn. After World War II, the suburban boom drove the town's population from 47,506 in 1950 to about 191,300 in 1998.

CENTERPORT: An easy summer Sunday in 1895 at Camp Alvernia, the nation's first Catholic summer camp

Franciscan Brothers Photo

ASHAROKEN

See story on Page 104.

CENTERPORT
Midway Point Became A Vanderbilt Home

Beginnings: Matinecocks resided on the Little Neck Peninsula before the arrival of European settlers in the 1600s. The first of these was an English Quaker, Thomas Fleet, who in 1660 built a home by a small cove that later bore his name. White residents gave the community a succession of names: Stony Brook, then Little Cow Harbor about 1700, Centreport in 1836 and Centerport after 1895. The name Centerport reflected the community's position midway between the east and west boundaries of the Town of Huntington. It soon had more mills along the waterfront than any other Long Island community. The hamlet was strongly anti-British during the American Revolution, in part because farmers' crops and animals were often plundered. After the war, it was a quiet place with baymen working the waters and sailing vessels carrying grain to mills and leaving with barrels of flour.

Turning Point: The economic pace quickened in the beginning of the 19th Century when Centreport became a summer resort. After the Civil War, the Long Island Rail Road was extended to the area in 1868, and the number of summer visitors mushroomed. In 1888, the Order of Franciscan Brothers set up a summer retreat along the eastern shore of Centerport Harbor north of the mill dam. Mount Alvernia, later Camp Alvernia, was the first Catholic summer camp in the nation. The first major year-round housing development did not come until 1927, when Huntington Beach was constructed with 750 lots along streets named for presidents.

Claim to Fame: Centerport's most famous resident, William K. Vanderbilt II, arrived in 1907 and built his 43-acre Eagle's Nest estate near the northern tip of the peninsula. After his death, the property, with its 24-room Spanish-Moroccan house, was donated to Suffolk County, which opened it as a museum in 1950. Located on the grounds were six marble columns from Carthage and two iron eagles New York's old Grand Central Station. A planetarium, with a 60-foot dome, was one of the nation's largest.

Brush With Fame: Russian-born composer Sergei Rachmaninoff spent the summers of 1940 and 1941 living on the former Honeyman estate on Little Neck Road and worked on his final composition, "Symphonic Dances."

Where to Find More: The book "Centerport," by Harvey Weber.

COLD SPRING HARBOR

See stories on Pages 102 and 103.

COMMACK

See story on Page 130.

DIX HILLS
Roads Led to Growth In Dick's Hills

Beginnings: The community took its name from Richard, or Dick, Pechagan, a Secatogue who controlled the hilly area in colonial times. Settlers began building cabins and setting up farms in the 1680s. And on May 2, 1700, Pechagan sold what was known locally as Dick's Hills to the trustees of the Town of Huntington for a few bottles of rum and some coats and axes. Over the years, the spelling was changed from Dick's to Dix.

The Revolution: Most residents were Patriots with many local men enlisted in militia units. The Gilbert Carll Inn on Jericho Turnpike was a training center for local soldiers until the English occupied the area in September, 1776. After that, the soldiers resorted to guerrilla warfare, ambushing English and Hessian troops marching on the turnpike.

Turning Points: As transportation improved over the years, the population jumped. In 1817, Jericho Turnpike was completed through the area as an old east-west coach road was widened, straightened and improved; tolls were charged every five miles. In 1842, the Long Island Rail Road reached the area and the nearby Deer Park station was built. In 1950, the Northern State Parkway came through, triggering a postwar housing boom and erasing many farms and nurseries. The Long Island Expressway

Please Turn to Page 103

The Old Mill and Pond, Centreport, L. I.

CENTERPORT: A postcard dated about 1910 depicts the Old Mill and Pond.

Collection of Joel Streich

DIX HILLS: The firehouse as it stood in June, 1951. It was about this time that the Northern State Parkway was built, triggering a housing boom in the area.

Newsday Photo

SUFFOLK

In Cold Spring Harbor, two views of Route 25A.

A Timeless Road Still Wends

The top photograph, taken by professional photographer Charles Duprez sometime in the late 1920s or early '30s, depicts Route 25A in Cold Spring Harbor, looking west from Harbor Road.

The two white buildings to the left of the road in the photograph are on the grounds of the Cold Spring Harbor Fish Hatchery, first opened by the state in 1883 and, since 1982, an independent nonprofit educational facility. The smaller structure, erected in 1927, was a storage building at the time and was later used for exhibits, according to Normal Soule, the facility's director. The larger building is the original hatchery and manager's residence, which was built in 1887 and razed in 1959, and replaced by another aquarium building.

THEN & NOW

At the time the photograph was taken, Route 25A was known as County Road 545, but it also might have been called Cold Spring Harbor-Syosset Road, or North Hempstead Turnpike — names that appear on a 1950 Hagstrom road map, according to Christopher Cotter, senior landscape architect for the New York State Department of Transportation's regional office in Hauppauge.

A 1998 photo at right shows asphalt resurfacing, more utility poles, and additional road markings and road signs. After lengthy wrangling between the state and local residents over the scope of changes to Route 25A in this area, a compromise was reached. Plans called for the roadway to be resurfaced and for intersection improvements at the entrance to the Cold Spring Harbor Laboratory, just west of the hatchery on the north side of the roadway.

Top, Collection of Wayne Duprez; Above, Newsday Photo / Bill Davis, 1998

DIX HILLS, Continued

followed seven years later with similar results.

Claims to Fame: In 1908, William K. Vanderbilt II and other investors completed the 35-mile-long Vanderbilt Motor Parkway, America's first limited-access and concrete highway. The section running through Dix Hills is still in use, flanked by large landscaped homes. These weren't the first large houses constructed in Dix Hills. During the Gold Coast era, the Goulds, Vanderbilts and Baruchs set up large estates and hunting lodges in Dix Hills. Development of Pilgrim State Hospital, the world's largest mental hospital, began in 1928. Its first units opened in 1931 and by 1935 it housed nearly 9,000 patients.

Where to Find More: Huntington Town historian and the Huntington Historical Society.

EAST NORTHPORT

'East' Was Added When the Trains Came

Beginnings: This community — at eight square miles the largest and most populous in the Town of Huntington — began as a farming area in the 1700s. The first tract of land was purchased in 1653 by Richard Houldbrock, Robert Williams and Daniel Whitehead from Chief Asharoken of the Matinecocks, who had maintained hunting camps in the area. Part of the area was known as Clay Pitts for the clay that was first used by the Indians for cooking vessels and then by white settlers for making bricks.

The Revolution: The area was occupied by British troops from 1776 until the end of the war in 1783. The British plundered farms for provisions while Patriots maintained a camp in Bread and Cheese Hollow, and under the direction of Maj. Jesse Brush until he was captured in 1780. There were frequent raids by Patriot soldiers who came from Connecticut in whaleboats. When the war ended, more settlers arrived and cleared land for farms.

Fields of Plenty: The major agricultural products in the early days were potatoes, cabbages and cucumbers, which were used to make pickles. The first pickle works was established by William Soper in 1892. Several others followed, including Rothman's Pickle Works, which remained in business until 1961 and could have 15,000 barrels of sauerkraut in production at the same time.

Turning Points: The community was composed of various small hamlets, such as Clay Pitts, until the late 1800s, when the Long Island Rail Road was extended to Port Jefferson and a second station was opened for Northport. Because there already was a station in the village, people began to call the area around the new station East Northport, even though the community itself was south of Northport. The new station attracted merchants who formed the area's first business district on Larkfield Road and Laurel Road. A stagecoach ran between the East Northport trains and Northport from 1868 to 1902, when it was replaced by an electric trolley. East Northport's biggest transformation came after World War II when farm fields were replaced by new housing developments. Its estimated population in 1998 was 20,565.

Claim to Fame: The Northport VA Medical Center was founded in 1928 as the 1,000-bed Veterans Hospital in Northport. It put the community on the map and became a major employer.

Where to find more: "East Northport — An Incomplete History," by Molly Schoen, published by the Rotary Club of East Northport.

COLD SPRING HARBOR

Tourists Replaced the Whales

Cold Spring Harbor developed as a company town. And the company was run by the Jones family.

The descendants of Maj. Thomas Jones, a prominent Massapequa landowner for whom Jones Beach was named, not only established Long Island's largest whaling company, they also built mills and launched other ventures, including an attempt at railroading.

Before the Joneses arrived, Matinecocks lived in the area they called Wawapex, meaning "place of good water." An Indian village was on the stream on the east side of the harbor in an area white settlers called Wigwam Swamp. On April 1 and 2, 1653, the Matinecocks sold land around the harbor to three Englishmen from Oyster Bay. Because of the freshwater springs, the English called the area Cold Spring.

In 1682, John Adams erected the community's first mills, a sawmill and gristmill, after damming the stream running north into the harbor. Eventually, two more dams were built across the stream to power additional mills. Benjamin Hawxhurst in 1700 built the first of several woolen mills. Another industry developed by 1713 when Jonas Wood began making bricks near Wigwam Swamp. Eventually, the Crossman family bought out several brickyards, and by the 1880s it would employ up to 400 men before closing down just before the 1900s because the locally available firewood was depleted.

On April 23, 1790, residents gathered to build their first schoolhouse when a coach carrying President George Washington arrived. He contributed a silver dollar before departing for Oyster Bay. It was an apt symbol. Because of its growing commerce, Congress in 1799 declared Cold Spring a port of entry with its own surveyor of customs, a designation maintained until 1913. Cold Spring was also the site of some shipbuilding. John Jones operated a shipyard about 1812 and many schooners and sloops were built there and at two other shipyards.

Cold Spring's first post office was established in 1825, and that July the post office and the community were renamed Cold Spring Harbor. The first church, St. John's Episcopal, became a Long Island landmark. It was erected in 1836 in what became the Village of Laurel Hollow, across the county line in Nassau.

John Jones was the first member of the Jones family to come to the Cold Spring Harbor area in the early 1800s. He married into the prominent Hewlett family that had built a gristmill in 1791. His sons, John H. and Walter R., were ambitious businessmen who created Cold Spring Harbor's industrial boom. They started out running a gristmill south of the harbor, adding woolen mills later. The younger John built a general store on the east side of the harbor.

With foreign competition undercutting their woolen mills, the Jones brothers decided to branch out into whaling. In 1836, they invested $20,000 to buy the old bark Monmouth. The next year they purchased the Tuscarora. The two ships did so well that in 1839 the brothers and their partners formed the Cold Spring Harbor Whaling Co., built docks and enlarged the fleet. Most whaling-support operations and the homes of employees were located on the west side of the harbor in Bungtown, named after the bungs, or plugs, used to seal the openings of barrels. By 1852, the whaling company owned nine vessels, including the Sheffield, the largest whaler to sail from Long Island.

Walter Jones died in 1855, followed by John four years later, leaving the local industry without a leader. When the last of the ships returned in 1862, the hamlet's whaling era was over after 37 voyages. The demise of whaling led to an economic slump that persisted for more than two decades. The Cold Spring Harbor Whaling Museum was opened in 1942 to tell the history of the industry.

Because the nearest Long Island Rail Road station was in Hicksville, the Jones brothers had shipped their mill products to New York by schooner. Now they pursued a rail connection. The Long Island Rail Road did not have the funds to develop branch lines, so the brothers organized the Hicksville & Cold Spring Branch Rail Road to build a 9-mile line. Work began in 1854 and tracks were laid from Hicksville to Syosset. A right-of-way was graded most of the way to Cold Spring Harbor, but because of logistical problems, tracks did not reach town until 1867 and were routed farther south than the Joneses had planned.

Cold Spring Harbor developed into a resort in the 1880s, ending the slump. Tourists came by rail or on excursion boats to stay at large hotels such as the Glenada on the eastern shore of the harbor. When the hotel closed, the property was purchased by millionaire Walter Jennings, who razed the building but retained its annex for use by residents. Later it became the Cold Spring Harbor Beach Club.

The economic revival was also buoyed by the

Cold Spring Harbor Whaling Museum
A painting of the harbor by Edward Lange, circa 1880

opening in 1883 of the state's second permanent fish hatchery in one of the old whaling buildings and the founding of the Brooklyn Institute of Arts and Sciences Biological Laboratory in 1890 at the hatchery. In 1904, the Carnegie Institute of Washington established a Station for Experimental Evolution adjacent to the lab. This became Cold Spring Harbor Laboratory, a leading molecular biology research and conference center actually located in the village of Laurel Hollow, which incorporated in 1926. Seven researchers associated with the 107-acre center have won Nobel prizes for their work in genetics: laboratory president James Watson, and Barbara McClintock, Alfred Hershey, Richard Roberts, Phillip Sharp, Salvador Luria and Max Delbruck.

Where to Find More: The Cold Spring Harbor Whaling Museum.

ELWOOD

Plains Area Attracted Farmers and an Artist

Beginnings: About 1725, the Town of Huntington decided to promote settlement in the Eastern Plains area, including a community called North Dix Hills. A tract almost 2 square miles was surveyed, and farmers moved in to take advantage of the flat land and fertile soil.

Turning Points: A general store was founded between 1850 and 1870 by one of the earliest residents, Jacob Soper, in his house at 462 Elwood Rd. It remained a private residence in the 20th Century. One of Soper's sons, Henry Edgar Soper, who lived next door to his father and helped out in the store, decided the community should have its own post office. In 1873, he got the job as first postmaster, working out of the general store. It was at that point that North Dix Hills became Elwood. No one knows how the name Elwood was chosen. The initial 2-square-mile settlement eventually grew to 5½ square miles with Elwood school district boundaries. Major growth did not come to Elwood until well after World War II. In 1950, the census put the population at 300, and five years later the hamlet still had many dairy farms. Housing began to boom in the late '50s. The 1998 population was estimated at 10,817.

Claim to Fame: Edward Lange, a renowned Long Island artist, resided in the Elwood area. Born in Germany in 1846, Lange in 1872 took title to three tracts near the Commack border and started to farm. He painted scenes of homes, towns and farms near his homestead in his spare time. In 1880, Lange launched into a full-time career as a commercial artist. He developed a thriving business documenting Long Islanders' homes, farms and communities on canvas and also doing promotional scenes for hotels and tourist-related businesses until he moved to Washington State in 1889. (In this book, see Pages 103, 109, 131 and 133 for four of his works.)

Where to Learn More: Barbara Brand, Elwood's unofficial historian.

FORT SALONGA

See story on Page 130.

GREENLAWN

With a Gardiner's Help, Pickles Thrived

Beginnings: The community, originally called Old Fields, was included in the First Purchase of Huntington by Richard Houldbrock, Robert Williams and Daniel Whitehead from the Matinecocks in 1653. The land was initially used as pasture by settlers in Huntington, but by 1780, farm families with prominent names like Brush, Wick, Jarvis, Kissam and Whitman had settled in the area. The first commercial building was the general store built in the 1860s and owned and operated by Hezekiah Howarth. The structure still stands on Broadway.

Turning Points: The Long Island Rail Road arrived in 1868 and transformed the hamlet. The first post office was established with Howarth as postmaster. Hotels were erected, and a stagecoach ran from the station north to Centerport. And the railroad brought a name change. The station initially was called Centerport but the railroad changed it — over the objections of residents — to Greenlawn-Centerport in 1870 and eventually just Greenlawn.

Please Turn the Page

EATONS NECK, ASHAROKEN

Shining a Light on a Perilous Sea

BY BILL BLEYER
STAFF WRITER

Eatons Neck had the distinction of being one of six royal manors on Long Island during the colonial era, but it was to gain wider notoriety for the submerged rocks running a mile out from shore into Long Island Sound. The reef off Eatons Neck Point presented the most treacherous location for mariners on Long Island's North Shore, becoming the site of more than 200 wrecks.

In 1798, the owner of Eatons Neck, John Gardiner, already was maintaining an oil lamp on a pole to guide passing ships when the new federal government paid him $500 for 10 acres that it planned to use as the site of the Island's second lighthouse, after Montauk. The same year, John Sloss Hobart, former owner of Eatons Neck, became a U.S. senator and helped get a lighthouse bill passed and signed by President John Adams. The light was lit the following spring with Gardiner's 19-year-old son, John Jr., as the first keeper.

The lighthouse did not preclude further shipwrecks, so in 1848 the Life Saving Benevolent Association of New York raised money for rescue stations on Long Island. The one on Eatons Neck was completed in March, 1849, and was manned by volunteers. Two shipwrecks on the same day in 1873 prompted a campaign for a full-time professional lifesaving crew. Two years later, Congress set up the U.S. Life Saving Service, which established a station at Eatons Neck in 1876. With a reduction in shipping, the government closed the station in 1921, but with ships continuing to run aground it was reopened as a Coast Guard station in 1935.

Before there were shipwrecks or even ships, the area was controlled by the Matinecocks. In 1646, they sold the peninsula to Theophilus Eaton, governor of New Haven. The first settlers probably came from Connecticut about 1653, when the first deeds were recorded. The Manor of Eatons Neck had several owners, including Hobart, who inherited the peninsula in 1754 and was a Patriot leader during the Revolution and later a justice of the first Supreme Court of New York State. John Gardiner, a member of the family that owned Gardiners Island, bought Eatons Neck in 1792 — the last time it was held by a single owner — and for a time Eatons Neck was called Gardiners Neck.

By the second half of the 19th Century, the peninsula had been carved into a half dozen estates. It also became home to an industry: sand minding, which moved into high gear in 1884 when Nicholas Godfrey leased West Beach from the Jones family and began mining the sand spit extending into Huntington Bay. Godfrey named the area Port Eaton and used machinery he had patented the year before — the first steam-driven digging machine in the United States. Later the Steers Sand and Gravel Co. leased the site and renamed it Sand City; the name stuck, though mining ceased in 1964.

Eatons Neck became a tourist destination when Benjamin Mitchell opened a picnic area called Locust Grove in 1895. It had a dock to accommodate steamers from New York. Business thrived until June 15, 1904, when the General Slocum caught fire on its way to Locust Grove; 1,021 passengers and crew died and the publicity killed Locust Grove. Undeterred, Mitchell opened the even bigger Valley Grove nearby the next year and it lasted until 1919.

While most of Eatons Neck was estates, more modest development began about 1900 along the beach in what became Asharoken. William Codling, a Northport lawyer and one of the largest landowners in the county, began to market a development he called Asharoken Beach. Codling lived in the model house, which was razed last year. By 1915, Asharoken Beach had developed into a summer resort for upper-class families. In 1925, the property owners established an incorporated village to increase control over beaches and roads.

One of the peninsula's more prominent residents was Henry Sturgis Morgan, founder of Morgan Stanley and grandson of J.P. Morgan. Between 1936 and 1939, Morgan purchased 448 acres to become the largest landowner on Eatons Neck. During World War II, the government used the estate to train Army Signal Corps troops. Several private owners became residents there.

The two communities have had many prominent residents and guests. Theodore Roosevelt sailed to Eatons Neck for outings. Maj. Alexander deSeversky, founder of Seversky Aircraft, which later became Republic Aircraft and then Fairchild-Republic, moved to Asharoken Beach in the 1930s. In the same decade, New York Mayor Fiorello LaGuardia and playwright Eugene O'Neill rented houses, and O'Neill finished ''Mourning Becomes Electra'' there.

Antoine deSaint-Exupery, the French aviator and writer, spent half of 1942 on the peninsula, where he wrote and illustrated the classic children's book ''The Little Prince.'' Movie star Marlene Dietrich and Jackie Gleason were frequent visitors in the 1950s. Cartoonist and sculptor Rube Goldberg was an Asharoken resident and in 1953 designed what became the village seal with a portrait of the Chief Asharoken.

Where to Find More: ''Faded Laurels — The History of Eatons Neck and Asharoken,'' by Edward A.T. Carr, Heart of the Lakes Publishing, 1994.

Eaton's Neck Lighthouse, L. I.

Huntington Historical Society

The lighthouse, in about 1910, warns of the reef that claimed about 200 ships.

Huntington Historical Society

EATONS NECK: A man peers through a telescope as he and others pass time at the Eatons Neck Life-Saving Station in a photo taken between 1885 and 1890.

Greenlawn-Centerport Historical Association

GREENLAWN: In the 1930s, workers at Golden's Pickle Works prepare cabbage for sauerkraut. Golden's operated along the railroad tracks in Greenlawn.

GREENLAWN, Continued

A new station was built in 1910.

Claim to Fame: Pickles made Greenlawn famous. One of the first farmers to see the benefit of growing small cucumbers was Alexander Gardiner, a descendent of the famous East End family. Gardiner, who had a 600-acre estate west of the hamlet, encouraged other farmers to grow cucumbers and built a pickle works adjacent to the railroad in the 1880s. Samuel Ballton, a former slave from Virginia who escaped to Union lines during the Civil War and fought in two regiments, came to Greenlawn in 1873 and entered the pickle business. He was said to have produced a million and a half cucumbers for pickles in one season and was dubbed the Pickle King of Greenlawn. The industry was killed off by "white pickle blight" in the 1920s, though the plants continued to convert cabbage into sauerkraut into the 1930s.

Brush With Disaster: The Columbia Hook and Ladder Co. was organized in 1902 and built a firehouse in 1905 near the railroad. In 1908 the fire department raised enough money to build an opera house next to the firehouse on Gaines Street so vaudeville performers who lived in the hamlet could perform with local amateurs. Only a few performances had been held before Oct. 31, 1909, when a fire started in the firehouse and quickly spread to the adjoining opera house and hotel. The entire west side of the block was destroyed along with all the firefighting equipment.

Where to Find More: "The History of Centerport and Greenlawn — A Brief Outline," by the Greenlawn-Centerport Historical Association; the Harborfields Public Library.

HALESITE

A Revolutionary Hero Gives His Name

Beginnings: Before the Long Island Rail Road came to Huntington in 1868, the community then known as Huntington Harbor was the town's center of transportation and commerce. Because it took days to travel overland to New York City, most produce and people were carried by schooners making regular trips from docks in Halesite. The trips — bearing cordwood and agricultural products to the city and manure from city horses back to Huntington farms for fertilizer — took five to six hours when conditions were favorable. By the 1860s, steamboats were taking an increasing part of the traffic. There was ferry service to Connecticut between 1765 and 1916, and boatyards built sloops, barges and, during World War II, subchasers for the Navy. The harbor was also the site of a gristmill that was built in 1752 and lasted until 1930. A dam that served that mill later became Mill Dam Road.

Turning Point: Halesite didn't get its current name until George Taylor, who owned a large estate that was mostly in neighboring Huntington Bay, lobbied for a local post office. Taylor had named his property Halesite in honor of Revolutionary War spy Nathan Hale, who had landed in Huntington Bay. So when postal officials told him that Huntington Harbor was too long to fit on signs, Taylor suggested Halesite. On July 3, 1899, the name became official.

Brushes With Fame: Among Halesite's residents in the 20th Century were entertainer Fanny Brice and her husband, gambler Nicky Arnstein, who ran an illegal crap game at the fire department's annual fund-raising carnival. William Randolph Hearst set up mistress Marion Davies in a hideaway. Actresses Dorothy and Lillian Gish rode bicycles around the hamlet. Albert Einstein spent several summers living along the harbor and sailed to Halesite to pick up mail and groceries. Henry Fonda docked his yacht there.

Where to Find More: The Huntington town historian and the Huntington Historical Society.

The circus is in town! This photo shows a circus parade on Huntington's main street around 1903.

Huntington Historical Society Photo / Ben Conklin

HUNTINGTON

It Struggled but Endured

BY TOM MORRIS
STAFF WRITER

'The Town Endures."

That motto, inscribed inside the historic 556-pound bell on display at the Old First Presbyterian Church on Main Street in Huntington, symbolized the hamlet's early struggle to survive.

That struggle began with the town's initial settlement in 1653, when crude dwellings began to go up around the "town spotte," later known as the village green. Life was simple and often difficult. The early arrivals had few possessions. They fashioned simple tools and furniture. They planted basic crops such as grain, peas, beans and corn, and raised cattle, sheep, horses, pigs, ducks and geese. Public stocks were constructed, and flogging was another method of punishment.

At first, through town meetings, Huntington was virtually self-governing. For three decades after 1664, as part of the new New York colony, it squirmed under the Duke's Laws, which were unpopular because they took away local control. The struggle to endure became even more intense with the Revolution.

Huntington was the Suffolk County headquarters of foraging British cavalry parties that seized and shipped provisions for their army and navy. Redcoats plundered farms, forced fearful residents to work for them, and beat or killed dissidents. Perhaps the worst outrage of the war was the British desecration of the Burying Hill, or cemetery, which was located behind the present town historian's office off Main Street. To build an encampment called Fort Golgotha, the Redcoats destroyed more than 100 headstones, decimated fruit trees, stripped boards from barns and homes and wrecked two churches. Legend has it that the British baked bread in ovens made from the monuments and some loaves bore the reversed inscriptions of these early tombstones.

Many residents were Tory sympathizers, but most backed the cause of American freedom. In the spring of 1775, gunpowder sent by the New York Provincial Congress was stored for use by Suffolk Patriots in a later-preserved building owned by Job Sammis, known as The Armory, in the heart of Huntington. There were numerous guerrilla raids by Patriots, prompting oppressive martial law against the townspeople.

In November, 1777, there were more than 300 British soldiers in the hamlet, with barracks and storehouses erected around the Presbyterian / Congregational Church, which had been built in 1715 opposite the present town hall. In the church's belfry was a prized bell cast in London and bearing the name of the town. Town trustees, as a precaution, hid the bell at the house of John Wickes, but a British armed detail wrested it from him, threatening him with death. The bell was put aboard an armed brig, then transferred to New York City for use on British ships. At the end of the war, word made its way to Huntington that the bell was aboard a brig called the Rhinoceros in the East River. Town leaders successfully petitioned the British admiralty for its return. The words "THE TOWN ENDURES" were cast inside by town leaders, and the bell was returned to the belfry, where it served as a working church bell for another two centuries, until 1967. After that, the bell was put on display in the church.

When President George Washington visited Huntington in 1790, the town had 2,000 residents. Most lived in Huntington hamlet, with farmhouses scattered in the rest of the town. By 1810, the town population was 4,424. A turning point came in 1867, when the Long Island Rail Road reached Huntington, bringing summer visitors, mostly to Cold Spring Harbor, but boosting the economy in Huntington hamlet as boarding houses and stores multiplied.

The 20th Century began with a mammoth three-day celebration of the town's 250th anniversary, on July 4, 1903, with President Theodore Roosevelt as the key speaker. Among the hamlet's major achievers this century was Joseph T. Cantrell, a Main Street carriage maker who moved a few blocks to Wall Street in 1908. There, he fitted a wooden wagon body to a Model-T Ford frame, inventing the station wagon. He won contracts with General Motors, Dodge and Studebaker, and his special customers included Marshall Field and the Duke of Windsor. Another inventor was Fred Waller, a Brooklyn native who came up with the first water skis in 1925 and marketed them from his Huntington factory. He became most famous as the inventor of Cinerama, a three-dimensional movie technique introduced to the public in 1952.

The hamlet has had at least one brush with infamy. In 1873, a Huntington poet and schoolteacher, Charles G. Kelsey, was tarred, feathered and murdered in a famous love-triangle case, bringing the sobriquet "Tar Town" upon Huntington. Charges were brought against prominent citizens but no convictions were obtained. In the midst of the investigation, the Brooklyn Eagle called Huntington a town "of abominable women, fiendish men and imbecile officers."

Still, the town endures.

Where to Find More: "A Brief History of the Town of Huntington," by Matthew B. Bessell, "The Irony of Submission, the British Occupation of Huntington and Long Island," 1992, Huntington Historian's Office, "Huntington in Our Time, 1900-1975," by Christopher R. Vagts, Huntington Historical Society.

Main Street Showing Central Church, Huntington, L. I.

HUNTINGTON: A postcard of Central Church on Main Street, circa 1910.

Collection of Joel Streich

HUNTINGTON: Boat traffic is heavy at Steamboat Landing in this postcard from about 1915.

Collection of Joel Streich

SUFFOLK

LLOYD NECK: The Lloyd Neck Lighthouse in June, 1906, as seen on a postcard.

MELVILLE: Even in 1972, commuters had to be creative to find a parking space on Route 110 near the Long Island Expressway.

LLOYD HARBOR

From 'Place by Sharp Rock' to Gold Coast

BY BILL BLEYER
STAFF WRITER

They weren't the first residents, or even the first white residents, but the Lloyd family of farmers and traders gave its name to the harbor that almost bisects the community. And when the community incorporated in 1926, joining the Lloyd Neck and West Neck areas, the name of the resulting village became Lloyd Harbor as well.

The Lloyds were preceded initially by the Matinecock Indians, who in 1654 sold 3,000 acres on what became Lloyd Neck to three English settlers from Oyster Bay. The Indians called the neck Caumsett, meaning "place by sharp rock." The property changed hands several times during the next two decades, with the peninsula acquiring the name Horse Neck because Huntington farmers grazed horses there.

Boston merchant James Lloyd acquired the neck in 1676. A decade later Thomas Dongan, lieutenant governor of New York, issued a grant to Lloyd so his land became the Lordship and Manor of Queens Village. But Lloyd remained in Boston, leasing the land until his 24-year-old son Henry in 1711 gave up a shipping business in Newport, R.I., to farm the Lloyd Neck tract. His home, the Henry Lloyd Manor House, survives in Caumsett State Park. One of his slaves, Jupiter Hammon, was America's first black poet.

After Henry's death in 1763, his son Joseph built the Joseph Lloyd Manor House. A Patriot, he fled to Connecticut during the Revolution and the

British built Fort Franklin, named for Benjamin Franklin's Tory son, William, on Lloyd's land in 1778. Another fortification was built on the east side of the neck, near a large rock called Target Rock because British warships were said to have used it for target practice.

The last Lloyd to own the estate was Henry IV, who acquired it in 1841 and built a dock in 1852 as a stop for Oyster Bay-to-New York steamboats. In the

An 1881 artwork by Edward Lange shows how Long Island Sound steamships brought New Yorkers to Lloyd Neck to enjoy days of picnicking and swimming in the late 1800s.

Newsday Archive

early 1880s, steamboats brought tourists to a recreation complex called Columbia Grove. A chemical company director, William Matheson, bought the waterfront property in 1900 and built a mansion. Singer Billy Joel once lived in the gatehouse. Matheson's daughter, Anne Wood, leased the Joseph Lloyd Manor House to Charles Lindbergh in

1940-41 and in 1968 donated it to the Society for the Preservation of Long Island Antiquities.

In 1921 publisher Marshall Field III bought almost three square miles of Lloyd Neck and created an estate called Caumsett. Field's widow in 1961 sold 1,426 acres for the creation of Caumsett State Park. Robert Moses' plan to extend Bethpage State Parkway to Caumsett and construct two golf courses and a beach was killed by public outcry.

Other Gold Coast properties also were adapted for new uses. The Roland Conklin estate was acquired in 1924 by the Roman Catholic Diocese of Rockville Centre, which established the Seminary of the Immaculate Conception. The 80-acre estate of financier Ferdinand Eberstadt was donated to the U.S. Fish and Wildlife Service and became Target Rock National Wildlife Refuge in 1970 to block a proposed Long Island Lighting Co. nuclear plant. The George McKesson Brown estate became a private school, Coindre Hall, and later a county park.

The West Neck area is not lacking in history. The Van Wyck-Lefferts Tidal Mill, built about 1794 on the west side of Huntington Harbor, was later acquired by the Nature Conservancy. In 1955 the Army acquired more than 20 acres on West Neck Road and built a Nike missile base that was phased out in 1963. Three years later, 93 acres including the Nike site was sold to Friends World Institute to create Friends World College. The college was chartered by the state on Dec. 22, 1966, and closed in June, 1991.

Where to Find More: Village historian at village hall.

HUNTINGTON BAY
Prominent Citizens Enjoyed a Chateau

Beginnings: Originally known as East Neck, the area was settled in the early 1670s when a trail — later Cove Road — connected Huntington Harbor with Fleets Cove to the east. Several large farms occupied the area, including those operated by the Conklin and Chichester families.

Revolution: American spy Nathan Hale is believed to have come ashore from Connecticut somewhere in the community before being captured by the British, probably in Manhattan or western Long Island, and hanged. His famous last words were said to be: "I only regret I have but one life to lose for my country."

Turning Point: In the second half of the 19th Century, East Neck was discovered by wealthy city residents who converted farmland into small summer estates. Among the most prominent was philanthropist August Heckscher, who made his fortune in steel, coal and real estate. His estate was named Wincoma, and some of the outbuildings remained. Farquahar Ferguson, founder of Armour Meat Co., built a castle overlooking Huntington Harbor; it has since been demolished, though the estate wall and some smaller buildings remained. Another prominent summer resident was George Taylor, who named his estate Halesite in honor of

Revolutionary War spy Nathan Hale. It was Taylor who suggested the name Halesite for the adjacent hamlet.

Casino Royale: The most interesting architectural creation in this era was the Chateau des Beaux Arts, a hotel and dining casino constructed in 1906 on a site overlooking Northport Bay. Famed French restaurateurs Louis, Andre and Jacques Bustanoby hired the New York architect Stanford White to design their casino, modeled after one in Monte Carlo. It had a lounge that could accommodate more than 1,000 guests and a golf course. The casino was maintained by the Huntington Bay Club until it was demolished in 1957 after tides undermined its foundation. Only after World War II, when many of the estates began to be broken up for the development of smaller homes, did Huntington Bay gain a sizable year-round population. The name of the community gradually shifted from East Neck to Huntington Bay, so that name was used when the Village of Huntington Bay was incorporated in 1924.

Claims to Fame: Singer Harry Chapin was a resident and his family continued to live in the village after his death in 1981. George Cortelyou, postmaster general and treasury secretary during President Theodore Roosevelt's administration, had a summer house in the village.

Where to Find More: Village historian at Village Hall.

HUNTINGTON STATION
A Downtown Grew Up Around a Station

Beginnings: There wouldn't be a Huntington Station if the Long Island Rail Road hadn't built a Huntington station. In 1867, the railroad extended its tracks to the hills south of Huntington and built a depot surrounded by farmland. After 1900, a thriving downtown evolved. The hamlet was originally called Fairground — the name came from a racetrack a mile from the station. So when a post office was established in the railroad station on July 24, 1890, it was called Fairground. But in 1912 the name of the post office and the community was changed to Huntington Station. In 1909-10, the railroad created the current underpass on New York Avenue and a new station was built on the east side of New York Avenue north of the tracks.

Designated Driver: The first street transit system in Huntington was a horse-drawn stage that operated between the train station and Halesite starting in 1867. "Uncle Jesse" Conklin drove the route for 56 years, missing only one train and that occurred only because it was the first time he decided to carry a watch. He never carried the watch again.

Turning Point: Much of the business district was demolished and replaced by parking lots in a mid-1960s urban renewal project that also included a public-housing project to the

west of the train station. In 1970, the 260-unit Whitman Village was built there as a private cooperative.

Vanished Landmark: Most of the original businesses and homes were modest, but there was one Gold Coast mansion, the home of H. Bellas Hess, owner of one of the country's largest mail-order catalog businesses. The Italian-style stucco mansion burned down in 1958. The 150-acre property was later occupied by the Big H shopping center and Huntington High School. Plans to bring a K mart to the largely vacant Big H shopping center were discussed in 1999.

Where to Find More: "Portrait of a Small Town," by Alfred V. Sforza, 1996.

MELVILLE
Corporate Offices Raised on Farmland

Beginnings: Melville developed at the intersection of two Indian paths that became major roads. One was first known as Neguntalogue Road and later South Path. It was traveled by Indians and then settlers bringing salt hay from the South Shore to Huntington, and later became Route 110. This was crossed by an east-west road later known as Old Country Road. Indians originally called the area Sunsquams. After settlement by whites, it was first known in the 17th Century as Samuel Ketcham's Valley after one of the earliest residents. Later it

Please Turn the Page

MELVILLE, Continued

was called Sweet Hollow, perhaps because early settlers found wild honey in the trees growing there.

Turning Points: In 1817, Jericho Turnpike was laid out by town officials so wagon traffic could avoid a steep hill on Old Country Road in West Hills. Old Country Road lost its significance as the main east-west artery, depressing Sweet Hollow's prospects. The name Sweet Hollow was replaced by Melville in school records in 1854 although Sweet Hollow was still used by some people. No one knows how the Melville name was chosen. In 1909 a trolley began trips along Route 110 to Huntington but was shut down a decade later after farmers complained that its whistle frightened their animals.

Suburbia Arrives: In the early years of the 20th Century, many of the farms were sold for development. The rapid changes worried long-time residents who pushed for creation of an incorporated village to control land use and services. In a 1950 vote, incorporation was defeated, leaving control in the hands of Huntington town officials. Melville became known for office buildings housing such companies as Swissair, Arrow Electronics, Chyron and Newsday.

Where to Find More: The Huntington town historian and the Huntington Historical Society.

WEST HILLS

Whitman's Birthplace Built by His Father

Beginnings: Before the official founding of the Town of Huntington in 1653, this area attracted hunters who built a stone fort on what later became Chichester Road as protection from nearby Indians. On the same road was the Peace and Plenty Inn, built in the 1600s and the focus of social life for centuries. It remained as a private home in the latter 20th Century. President Theodore Roosevelt rode there on horseback from Sagamore Hill. There were about 28 families in West Hills by the end of the Revolution, and the community was known for one of those families, the Whitmans. They emigrated from England to New England and then to Long Island and became landowners from 1668 until 1835. The first Whitman in the Huntington area was Joseph, who had extensive holdings. Walter Whitman, a carpenter, in 1810 built the house where, on May 31, 1819, his second child was born — the future poet Walt Whitman. His birthplace was made a state historic site. Whitman lived here for his first four years before moving with his parents to Brooklyn. He returned often, including when he founded The Long Islander newspaper in 1838. Much of the Whitman property became part of Suffolk's West Hills Park.

Turning Point: To protect the Whitman birthplace from being sold to another owner, 50 famous New York literary figures founded the Walt Whitman Birthplace Association in 1949. With more than 7,000 people contributing, the purchase was secured for $20,000. The property was donated to the state in 1957.

Claims to Fame: West Hills County Park is the site of Jayne's Hill, the highest spot on Long Island, at 400.4 feet. The area was also once known for its spring water. Mountain Mist Springs, located on the west side of Sweet Hollow Road north of Chichester Road, produced water that reportedly had "medicinal qualities." A bottling plant once occupied the site. During the Spanish-American War, water from the springs was reportedly shipped to Montauk for troops returning from Cuba.

Other Than Whitman: Henry L. Stimson, who served in the cabinets of four presidents, in 1903 developed an estate called High Hold near Sweet Hollow Road. His house is gone but the caretaker's cottage remained.

Where to Find More: Huntington town historian and the Huntington Historical Society.

NORTHPORT

A Harbor of Transformations

BY BILL BLEYER
STAFF WRITER

The first Europeans known to have seen Northport were Dutch sailors exploring the Long Island coast in 1650. The harbor continued to play a pivotal role in local history ever since.

When the explorers came, the area was already the home of Matinecocks who camped along streams and called the area Opcathontyche, meaning Wading Place Creek. In 1656, Asharoken, head of the Matinecocks, sold land in the area to settlers from Huntington who cleared it for farms. The area at that point was called Great Cow Harbor, presumably because of the unusual proximity of cattle pastures to the harbor mouth.

By the Revolution there were 31 families, including Bryant Skidmore, whose house remained at 529 Main St. Although British troops occupied the area, the only bloodshed came in 1781 when Joseph Buffet was killed when he and his slaves tried to recover livestock taken by a raiding party. Meanwhile, what later became Crab Meadow Beach was the site of an important Revolutionary moment. In 1781, 100 American raiders in whaleboats from Connecticut landed at the beach and burned the British Fort Slongo. (For more details about this battle, see the history of Fort Salonga on Page 130.)

After the war, Great Cow Harbor began to grow rapidly. A new settlement grew at Red Hook, where Main Street and Route 25A intersect. Sailing vessels carried cordwood to New York and returned with horse manure for fertilizer.

After Woodbine Avenue was fashioned out of a dirt trail, the business district, including the post office, shifted from Red Hook to the harbor. The name Northport first appears in town records of 1837, though there is no record of how it was selected.

The harbor took on one of its most important roles — and began to take its present-day shape — during the War of 1812, when shipyards began to appear along Bayview Avenue. By 1840 shipbuilding had become the community's first major industry.

Its most successful shipbuilder was Jesse Carll, who in 1855 set up shop at Bayview Avenue and Main Street, later the site of the village park. Carll remained the leading shipbuilder in Northport until 1890; his son Jesse continued to run the yard until 1918.

Ultimately, Northport turned out more than 200 sailing vessels by the time the industry waned in the late 1800s, when steel hulls, for which the local yards were unsuited, began to replace wood, and improved roads diminished the need for coastal trading vessels.

The late 19th Century brought ferries from New York City and an increase in visitors that filled boarding houses built earlier in the century. But it was another maritime trade that came to dominate the harbor. Shellfishing developed in 1848 when oyster beds were discovered in Northport Bay. The catch was processed on docks along Bayview Avenue. By about 1900, oystermen had banded together to form Long Island Oyster Farms Inc., which survived until 1990. Shellfishing continued, however, as 2000 approached.

In 1881, Edward Thompson, who had been a successful oysterman, and James Cockcroft established the Edward Thompson Law Book Co., which eventually was housed in a large brick building at the corner of Woodbine and Scudder Avenues. The Thompson firm published the country's first legal encyclopedia and its law books were shipped around the world. The company moved to Brooklyn in the 1930s, but not before its staff of lawyers had a major impact on the village's development into a modern community. In 1894, the law-book people led the drive that made Northport the first incorporated village in the Town of Huntington; they also developed its fire department, the public library — an original Andrew Carnegie library, in 1914 — and a debating society.

In 1895, the Thompson principals brought electricity to the community. They started the Northport Electric Light Co., which built a steam-powered plant where Cow Harbor Park was later located. In 1911, the Northport utility along with ones in Islip, Amityville and Sayville merged to form Long Island Lighting Co.

One industry tied to the harbor that wore out its

Woodbine Avenue in Northport around 1900. The buildings on the left were replaced by a harborside parking lot and park. The Thompson Law Book Co. occupied the brick building on the corner at right.

Newsday Archive

welcome was sand mining. In the 1950s residents battled the Steers Sand and Gravel Co., which had been operating in the village since 1923, about the company's removal of the sand and gravel from the foot of Steers Avenue. The sand pit was halted just short of Ocean Avenue, and "the pit," as locals referred to it, became a housing development.

In 1867, when the Long Island Rail Road was extended from Syosset to Northport, a station was established in the village, near the latter-day Route 25A and Church Street. It lasted only six years, however: In 1873 the station was moved to East Northport. An electric trolley ran from the business district to the train station from 1902 to 1924, and some of the tracks remained. A horse-drawn trolley operated in the 1970s and '80s as a weekend tourist attraction.

By 1920, the waterfront, which had played such a critical role in Northport's history, had fallen into decay after a century of heavy commercial use. The village purchased land along the harbor and created Northport Memorial Park in 1932. By 1998, the village's population was estimated at 7,530.

Where to Find More: Village historian, the Northport-East Northport Public Library and the Northport Historical Society Museum.

Nassau County Museum Collection, Long Island Studies Institute

NORTHPORT: An illustration depicting the Northport Yacht Club in 1905. By the late 19th Century, well-to-do visitors from New York City were spending summers at nearby boarding houses.

Northport Historical Society / F. Yamaki

NORTHPORT: The historic harbor, as seen about 1900, was a major center for shipbuilding and shellfishing. It also was a terminal for ferries from New York City.

Town of Islip

BRENTWOOD

A Place Built on Dreams

BY TOM MORRIS
STAFF WRITER

Josiah Warren and Stephen Pearl Andrews were brilliant and idealistic men, social reformers whose dream was to create a utopia where everyone would live in harmony, where profit would be a dirty word and absolute personal freedom — including "free love" — would be the ultimate goal.

So it was in 1851 that Warren and Andrews founded Modern Times, a social experiment that occupied, for a volatile 13 years, the land that later would be part of Brentwood. Short-lived though it was, Modern Times left its mark as a place whose time had not yet come: Its maverick residents, who never numbered more than 150, were free to cohabit with or without marriage. To be sure, this was what gave the place its reputation as a "Sodom of the pine barrens," but it was only part of what Modern Times was about. The village operated harmoniously for several years without police, courts or crime. All residents were allowed total personal freedom as long as their actions hurt no one else. Food, clothing, land and housing — all the necessities — were sold at cost.

The experiment, like several others that surfaced in mid-19th-Century America, was aimed at revolutionizing human society. Warren provided the impetus. A low-key inventor and social philosopher, he had served at New Harmony, a radical experiment in communism established in Indiana in 1824 that turned out to be quite disharmonious after a couple of years. Warren put his central credo this way: "Man seeks freedom as the magnet seeks the pole or water its level, and society can have no peace until every member is really free." At 59, he wanted to set up a model village near an eastern city, and the sparsely settled woods of western Suffolk County were just right.

Modern Times was hacked out of Islip Town's pine barrens in 1851 by Warren and Andrews, an unconventional radical lawyer and ardent women's rights advocate. It was Andrews who, in 1853, drew the backing of radical free-love advocates Thomas Low Nichols and his wife, Mary Gove. Gove and Nichols, New Yorkers who lived for a time at Modern Times, were nationally known for their strident demands for total sexual freedom in or out of marriage — including a woman's right to choose the fathers of her children.

Roger Wunderlich, editor and founder of the Long Island Historical Journal and the author of a 1992 book, "Low Living and High Thinking at Modern Times, New York," said Modern Times' sexual-marital experiment overshadowed its other goals and exposed the young village to public censure it could never live down. "The translation of free love to free lust . . . was the heaviest cross that the village bore," Wunderlich wrote. As to its legacy: "The hot light of marital reform seared Modern Times' reputation but pointed the way to the future."

Modern Times was one of the last of about 50 experimental American communities in the mid-1800s. In a 1945 magazine article, Helen Beal Woodward wrote, "Those towns stood for everything eccentric — for abolition, short skirts, whole-wheat bread, hypnotism, phonetic spelling, phrenology, free love and the common ownership of property." The others were in decline

when Modern Times started, and on Sept. 7, 1864, faced with national scandal, the Civil War and internal dissension over the ban on profit-making, villagers ended the experiment. They renamed the place Brentwood, after a more decorous place in Essex, England. Eventually, the town changed "from a bastion of radicalism into a sleepy village with a shady past," wrote historian John C. Spurlock.

Soon after the name change, modern Brentwood began to emerge. The school district was expanded, churches, farmers' clubs and a cemetery association formed. And the face of early Brentwood continued to change as the 1900s dawned. The magnificent old home of capitalist Robert W. Pearsall became the 125-room Austral Hotel, which failed, its 350 acres bought in 1896 by the Sisters of St. Joseph for a motherhouse, novitiate and academy. It became a landmark local institution. The state in the 1930s built Pilgrim State Hospital (in West Brentwood), which was to become the world's largest mental institution. Meanwhile, the famous Long Island Motor Parkway was built through Brentwood, en

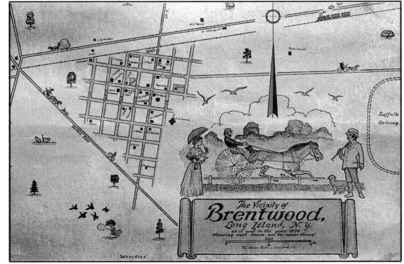

Brentwood Public Library
A map shows the community's modest size in the 1870s, after Modern Times failed.

route to Lake Ronkonkoma, in 1908.

Brentwood's population exploded with the postwar building boom, from 5,000 in 1950 to about 45,500 in 1998, making Brentwood Islip Town's most populous place, and in the late 1900s, it became a gateway to Long Island for waves of people of Hispanic heritage, most recently from Central America and the Caribbean. They followed the tide of Italian, Irish and Puerto Ricans who flocked to Brentwood from the 1940s to the 1960s. In the late 1990s, about 48 percent of the school district's students were of Hispanic descent.

"It was primarily cheap land that brought Modern Times to Long Island, and in a way has been the economic motivator for bringing so many people to modern Brentwood," according to Islip Town historian Carl A. Starace. He said the social radicals who founded Modern Times would be pleased to know that the land in which they incubated their utopian dreams would offer opportunity and promise to so diverse a population more than a century later.

Where to Find More: "Low Living and High Thinking at Modern Times, New York," by Roger Wunderlich, 1992; "A Century of Brentwood," by Verne Dyson, 1950, at Brentwood Public Library.

In the early years of its existence, Islip Town was owned entirely by a handful of wealthy men who ran it like feudal lords and didn't even bother to call a town meeting for a decade after the town was established.

William Nicoll, a wealthy and well connected New Yorker, became the father of Islip Town on Nov. 29, 1683, when he bought the tract that would become East Islip from the Secatogue Indians. Nicoll (not to be confused with Richard Nicolls, the first deputy governor of New York) made four other purchases in the next four years and in 1687 received a royal patent for all his buys: 51,000 acres covering the eastern half of present Islip Town. He did not get what became Islip hamlet, which went to his friend, fellow politician and business partner Andrew Gibb.

Meanwhile, the land that later became historic Sagtikos Manor in West Bay Shore was granted to Stephan Van Courtlandt in 1693, West Islip was patented to brothers Richard and Thomas Willett, friends of Nicoll, in 1695, and Bay Shore to John Mowbray in 1708, after a friend of Nicoll passed up the opportunity.

The colonial legislature in 1710 created Islip Town, in roughly its present-day configuration, but Nicoll was in no hurry to get Islip rolling. He was a veteran politician whose career included service as the New York colony's attorney general, and one who was the legislature's speaker at the time that body created Islip. "The patentees, led by Nicoll . . . knew that establishing a town would mean electing an assessor and paying taxes, so the law was not carried out," historian Patrick J. Curran wrote in "A Brief History of the Town of Islip" in 1983.

When Nicoll retired as speaker in 1718, the legislature ordered the town to begin functions. The first meeting was finally held in April, 1720. Its records fail to say where it was held, but historians say it probably was at Nicoll's farm estate on Great South Bay at what eventually became Heckscher State Park. Benjamin Nicoll, son of the owner, was elected first town supervisor at that meeting.

Because of its manorial nature, Islip developed slowly. One reason cited by Curran was its "almost complete lack of identity. Most of the other towns on Long Island were established by one family or a group with a common background and a church that became the center of community life. This was not true of Islip.

Early concerns in the record included pig control and prohibiting fishing in town waters "to any forrienor" — a harbinger of what would become a searing issue through generations in the town: bay rights, which only began to fade as an issue after World War II. It was almost a century before Nicoll family control started to crack. In 1786, the state legislature opened the Nicoll holdings in the eastern half of the town for sale to the public to pay off the family's creditors for debts incurred in the Revolution.

Nassau County Museum Collection, Long Island Studies Institute

BAYPORT: The impressive 50-acre estate of Charles F. Stoppani dominated the waterfront on the Great South Bay in about 1900.

"Onetah" Dr. Ross' Health Resort, Brentwood, L. I.

Collection of Joel Streich

BRENTWOOD: A postcard showing Onetah, a health resort, in about 1910. Brentwood, built among the pines in the mid-1800s, was orginally a utopian community called Modern Times.

Slow Change In Bay Shore

Back in the 1940s, when the photograph above of Bay Shore's Main Street was taken, looking southwest at Fourth and Maple Avenues, the downtown area was a bustling shopping area for South Shore residents. And it continued that way into the 1950s.

"You would just take a walk down Main Street, meet some people, say hello and have a soda," said Frank Manhardt, president of the Bay Shore Historical Society, who moved to the community in 1956. "It was thriving, where everyone went to shop."

Bay Shore's downtown began to decline in the 1960s, as the construction of shopping malls sapped the vitality of downtown stores. By the late 1980s, empty stores and loiterers were a fixture of downtown, keeping shoppers away.

A 1998 photo of the same intersection, right, shows little new construction over a half-century, though sidewalks were spruced up and storefronts renovated in an ongoing effort to revitalize the downtown area. In the 1990s, the area added housing, businesses, cultural facilities and the Touro College of Health and Science.

"The economy's gotten better in the past five years or so," Manhardt said in 1998. "It's making a dramatic change."

Top, Newsday File Photo; Above, Newsday Photo / Bill Davis, 1998

BAYPORT

The Railroad's Arrival Woke Up a Hamlet

Beginnings: The land that would become Bayport, in the southeast corner of Islip Town, was part of Brookhaven Town between 1666 and 1697. That year, William Nicoll, the Islip Town founder, who had made his first land purchases from the Secatogue Indians four years earlier, added the future Bayport to his holdings. After the Revolution, William Nicoll IV, seeking money to pay debts, sold off what would be about two-thirds of southern Bayport to Jeremiah Terry and Gersham Hawkins. The Bayport Heritage Association recognizes Dec. 16, 1786, the date of the Terry deed, as the hamlet's founding date.

Name That Place: In 1834, Middle Road, south of and parallel to Montauk Highway, was built to connect the farms between Sayville and Blue Point. Bayport was first dubbed Middle Road, later Southport. Because there was another Southport upstate, the name was changed to Bayport when a post office was established in 1858.

Turning Points: The first school — one room — was built about 1819. According to historian Charles P. Dickerson, a young British naval officer named Lt. Burrill jumped ship in Gardiners Bay, East Hampton, and became the first teacher. He stayed in town 30 years. The first store, on Middle Road, was opened by Warren Hawkins in 1860, when the federal census showed there were 79 families. Some of their houses remained along Middle Road into the late 1990s. The railroad arrived in 1869, swiftly altering the sleepy farming, fishing and wood-cutting hamlet. Handsome summer estates emerged near the bay and the Sans Souci Lakes, at the head of Brown's River, which once were commercial cranberry beds. The fire department was organized Aug. 15, 1891. "They bought a hook and ladder truck so heavy that there were not enough members to pull it to the fire," Dickerson wrote. Meanwhile, there was trolley service along Middle Road between 1910 and 1919, and flower growing was a big business in the first half of the 1900s. 1998's population was about 8,160.

Where to Find More: "Bayport, Fading Views," by Donald H. Weinhardt, Bayport Heritage Association, 1986; "A History of the Sayville Community," including Bayport, by Charles P. Dickerson, 1975; both at Bayport-Blue Point Public Library.

BAY SHORE

Its Boats Delivered Trouble to the British

Beginnings: In October, 1708, Queen Anne of England confirmed John Mowbray's purchase of land that was to become Bay Shore and Brightwaters. Mowbray, a tailor and teacher from Southampton, was said to have paid the fish-dependent Secatogue Indians "several eel spears" for the Bay Shore-Brightwaters land. Sagtikos Manor to the west of the hamlet was traditionally considered part of Bay Shore, but its original patent in 1693 went to Stephen Van Courtlandt, a Dutch merchant related by marriage to William Nicoll, a wealthy New York politician who received the earliest royal grants for land that would become Islip Town.

The Revolution: Artisans produced excellent small boats that, according to an 1849 account, "gave the British a large amount of trouble." That account says that on Aug. 27, 1776, as the Battle of Long Island raged to the west in Brooklyn, "The din of the cannonballing could be heard" in Bay Shore.

The Name Game: The Indians called Bay Shore Panothicut or Penataquit, which experts believe meant "crooked creek." The primitive early colony had no particular name, but some accounts say — without elaboration — that it was called Sodom in the early 19th Century. It was known as Mechanicsville by 1842, probably, historians say, for the men who worked in mills and boatyards there. The name was changed back to Penataquit in 1849, but the Indian name proved unpopular because it was too difficult to spell. "Bay Shore" arrived in 1868 to reflect the community's location on the shore of the bay just as the era of summer tourism was starting.

Turning Points: In the mid-19th Century, hotels began to spring up, and by the 1880s, rail service and summer visitors expedited change. This was a gentle time of gaslight and horse-drawn carriages, summer estates and bicycle riding, sailboats and steam trains. Southside Hospital, begun in Babylon in 1913, was moved to Bay Shore in 1923. The hamlet had a brief fling as a movie production center in 1915 and 1916, but one thing that did stick was the regular Bay Shore-Fire Island ferry service, which began in 1862. Bay Shore remained a vibrant business and residential center through the 1950s, fading in the 1960s with the rise of major shopping centers, a decline the community was still trying to reverse in the late 1990s.

Where to Find More: "A Brief History of Bay Shore," by Etta Anderson Tuttle; "When Bay Shore Was Penataquit," by Nathaniel R. Howell; "Descriptive Sketch of Bay Shore," at Bay Shore-Brightwaters Public Library, and publications of Bay Shore Historical Society, 22 Maple Ave., Bay Shore.

BOHEMIA

A Settlement Born Of Search for Freedom

Beginnings: Three young couples seeking freedom from the Hapsburg rule in Austria and Hungary arrived in the heavy woods of mid-Suffolk on March 5, 1855, and became the founders of what was to become the Islip Town community of Bohemia. They were John Vavra, John Kratchovil, Joseph Koula and their wives. Koula, a cabinet maker, built a house for each pair, and part of one home still existed in the late 1990s. The men soon chanced upon the William Ludlow estate in Oakdale, took laborers' jobs, and encouraged friends and relatives in Europe to come over. In 1859, the growing Czech settlement was christened New Village of Tabor. Tabor meant "camp."

Settlement: Many of the newcomers came from the central European area known since the Middle Ages as Bohemia. They bought plots for about $10 an acre, and in 1869, a one-room schoolhouse was built for $600. The first industry was cigar making, at which the Bohemians were expert. Families began the trade at home, and soon there were about eight cigar factories in the area. This continued until about 1930, when machine-made cigars in New York City quickly replaced most made by hand.

The Name Game: Residents voted in 1894 to rename the place Bohemia, but several attempts were made to change it again. In 1942, the New York Post suggested in an editorial that the name be changed to Lidice, to keep alive the name of a Czech town where executions by the Nazis occurred. Local opposition scuttled the idea.

Key Landmark: On Sept. 26, 1893, the community dedicated a statue to Jan Hus. According to the Bohemia Historical Society, it was the first monument to honor the fearless Czech priest who was burned at the stake July 6, 1415, for preaching religious freedom a hundred years before Martin Luther's reformation. It was erected in the Union Cemetery on the south side of Church Street.

Where to Find More: "A History of Bohemia, Long Island," by the Centennial History Book Committee, 1955, printed by the Bohemia Historical Society, and "A History of the Sayville Community," including Bohemia, by Charles P. Dickerson, 1975; both at Connetquot Public Library, 760 Ocean Ave., Bohemia.

BOHEMIA: The community's first fire truck, 1893. From left, firefighters Anton Bartick, Joseph Novotny, Joseph Fisher, Anton Fisher and Rudolph Voska.

Bohemia Historical Society

Newsday Photo / Cliff DeBear

CENTRAL ISLIP: An aerial view of the campus of the state psychiatric center in 1981. The facility had 10,000 patients and more than 1,000 employees by 1955. It was closed in 1997.

Main Street, looking East   Islip, Long Island, N. Y.

Collection of Joel Streich

ISLIP: A view of Main Street in about 1930. After the railroad arrived in the 1860s, the hamlet became the seat of town government.

BRIGHTWATERS
4,000-Foot Canal Led To a Community

Beginnings: For two centuries after John Mowbray was given a royal patent in 1708 for the tract that included Brightwaters, nothing much disturbed the bucolic section of saltwater swamps, freshwater lakes and woods adjacent to Bay Shore. Real estate developer Thomas Benton Ackerson changed all that. He bought the Charles E. Phelps estate of several hundred acres to start a planned community.

Turning Point: From 1908 to 1918, Ackerson and his three brothers filled the swamps, dug a 4,000-foot boat canal from Great South Bay to Montauk Highway, created a model community of 100 homes priced from $3,500 bungalows to $20,000 mini-mansions — then went broke. The Ackersons' financial woes worried the new homeowners, who banded together and won incorporation as a village in 1916. The first president — mayors came later — was none other than Thomas Benton Ackerson. To solve his financial problems, he made an outright gift of the boat canal, lakes and park area to the new village, which thrived as a quiet residential enclave with only a small business district. By 1998, the population was about 3,300.

Whence the Name: It was taken from the Indian name Wohseepee, which roughly meant "sunlit ponds" or "bright waters," alluding to the five lakes north of Montauk Highway. Ackerson named one of the lakes in his development Nosrekca — Ackerson spelled backward.

Brush With Fame: For about a year, even as the Ackerson firm fought to survive, Brightwaters earned some celebrity as a hangout for stars of silent movies. Vitagraph Studio of Brooklyn opened a branch in Bay Shore in 1915, and gawkers on the streets of Bay Shore and Brightwaters could spot such entertainers as Marie Dressler, Fatty Arbuckle and Norma Talmadge. The stargazing lasted about a year before Vitagraph moved to Hollywood.

Where to Find More: "A Local History of Brightwaters From Colonial Times to the Present," by Fred M. Monner, research paper, 1964; "Brightwaters — A Profile," by Gene Gleason, New York Herald Tribune article, 1964; at Bay Shore-Brightwaters Public Library.

CENTRAL ISLIP
A City Facility Arose in Pine Barrens

Beginnings: In the summer of 1841, Edgar Fenn Peck, a wealthy New York doctor who had just moved to Smithtown, began the first serious exploration of the virtual wilderness of what would become Central Islip. He was convinced the pine barrens was an area suitable for development, though many disagreed. A year later, the Long Island Rail Road arrived at what was called Suffolk Station, and the adjacent Central Islip was effectively born. In 1848, a close friend of Peck, George Kasson Hubbs, bought 939 acres, much of northern Central Islip, from William Nicoll VII, a descendant of the original patentee of Islip Town, for $4,225.50. Hubbs (a friend of Walt Whitman) married Ruth Wheeler, for whom he named Wheeler Road. For three decades, Suffolk Station depot was a rail and stagecoach center, and most of the early arrivals were of English descent or birth.

Turning Point: Central Islip was transformed from a country crossroads into a widely known mental hospital complex starting in 1887, when New York City purchased 1,000 acres one mile south of the rail tracks, for $25 an acre, for a farm colony. It formally opened May 6, 1889, with 49 male patients from the city's Wards Island mental facility, followed by 40 women the next year. Only six years later there were 1,000 patients at Central Islip. Jobs were created and houses

Nassau County Museum Collection, Long Island Studies Institute

CENTRAL ISLIP: A crew in the community railroad station keeps the trains running on time in 1928. From left, station master Eugene Costello, block operator Norman Mason and agent George Ayling.

built nearby. The State Legislature in 1896 put all New York City asylums under the Manhattan State Hospital of Central Islip. There were 122 buildings by 1914, and 10,000 patients and more than 1,000 employees by 1955. At that point it declined steadily as tight state budgets and changing therapies combined to accelerate transfers of patients to other facilities or into local communities. In 1997, the facility was closed and the remaining patients transferred to Pilgrim Psychiatric Center in West Brentwood. 1998's population was about 28,300.

Where to Find More: "Central Islip, My Home Town," by Anne Frances Pulling, 1976, Jo-Lar Lithographing Co., Central Islip; "The History of Central Islip," by Verne Dyson, 1954, the Brentwood Village Press, at Central Islip Public Library.

EAST ISLIP
An Eccentric's Estate Becomes a State Park

Beginnings: For decades before Jan. 16, 1890, this small community was part of what was known as "east of Islip." The citizens obviously didn't want much change: The official name bestowed on that date was East Islip. The area was part of the original 51,000-acre purchase from the Secatogues by Islip founder William Nicoll.

Slow growth: The community, which covered a territory reaching east to Bayport and north to Lake Ronkonkoma, was long sparsely settled, with farming, fishing, boat building, lumbering and some shipping the

mainstays of the economy. Residents used churches in surrounding communities for years. Rail service, available since 1842 via Brentwood, reached East Islip in 1868. Its hotels — the Pavillion, the Somerset and the Lake House — often were the site of the town meetings held each April. A one-room schoolhouse was replaced by one with two rooms in 1857. The original Hewlett School for privileged young women, begun in Hewlett in 1915, was moved to an estate site on Suffolk Lane, East Islip, in 1941. By 1998, the population was estimated at 14,250.

Claim to Fame: East Islip became the home of Heckscher State Park, which would have been named Deer Range State Park if not for philanthropist August Heckscher's donation of $262,000 toward the purchase of the Great South Bay estate of George C. Taylor, a wealthy eccentric who died in 1908. The estate was unoccupied for 16 years until 1924, when Robert Moses, president of the new Long Island State Park Commission, moved to take it for a state park. That triggered a five-year court battle against wealthy local opponents led by W. Kingsland Macy, a powerful Republican who later went to Congress. At a hearing during the long legal fight, Gov. Al Smith heard a millionaire express fear the park would be "overrun with rabble from the city." Smith retorted, "Why, that's me," and promptly signed some key papers.

Where to Find More: "East of Islip," a short history by the Friends of the East Islip Library, 1959, and "History of the Long Island State Parks," by Chester R. Blakelock, executive secretary, Long Island State Park Commission, published by the Long Island Forum, 1959.

Islip Bathing Beach   Long Island, N. Y.

Collection of Joel Streich

ISLIP: A postcard from about 1930.

FIRE ISLAND

From Pirates to Slavery to Fun in the Sun

BY TOM MORRIS
STAFF WRITER

Since the 1600s, the famed Fire Island barrier beach has been the setting for Indians, settlers, whalers, pirates, buried treasure, shipwrecks, slaves, murdering thieves, valiant life-savers, developers, gay people and the pursuit of seashore fun for everybody.

Once, in the late 17th Century, the entire sandspit was owned by an ambitious and well-connected Englishman, William (Tangier) Smith. Later it became a fabled resort of 18 private communities interwoven with a series of public parks. Connecting those two points in history is a Babylon entrepreneur named David S.S. Sammis, who bought 120 acres just east of the Fire Island Lighthouse in 1855 and built a huge hotel that marked the end of the barrier's reputation as a somewhat scary, even dangerous place.

The origin of the name Fire Island has never been clear to historians. Some say it resulted from errors by 17th Century mapmakers who confused the word "fire" with "five," for the five small islands around what was then known as Huntington East Gut, later Fire Island Inlet. Others say it came from fires set on the beach by Indians signaling the mainland or by settlers calling for help when a whale was landed on the shore. And another suggestion is the Dutch word *vier* (four), easily confused with the word fire. In earlier times, when seals were prevalent, the Secatogue Indians had called the barrier Seal Island. One thing seems certain: Fire Island wasn't always an island. In earlier times, it was a peninsula attached to the shore around Quogue.

Smith, the original settler-owner, had grown up in the court of Charles II in England. He came to America at 20, became a friend of New York colonial Gov. Thomas Dongan and set about collecting a real estate empire in Brookhaven. In 1693 Smith received a royal grant that included the entire barrier beach from the inlet to about the Southampton Town line, about 24 miles. He called the estate the Manor of St. George, and its remnants — the manor house and surrounding grounds — were

opened to the public as part of the Fire Island National Seashore in Shirley.

Brookhaven had about 100 slaves by 1800, and boats called slaverunners sailed through Fire Island Inlet to supply estates. Local historians have written that stockades were built on the beach to hold slaves for sale.

Pirate activities on the Fire Island coast are well documented, and legends are legion. As early as 1795, ship "wreckers" appeared. Jeremiah Smith, considered the first inhabitant of Fire Island, built

Ocean Beach Historical Society and Art Museum

In Ocean Beach a crowd gathers at the dock in about 1920. Fire Island's reputation began to improve when David S.S. Sammis arrived in 1855 to begin making it into a resort area.

a hut — later a sizeable house as business prospered — at what became Cherry Grove. Smith was said to have lured ships ashore with lights and murdered the crews to get the booty. There were yarns about "two brutal women" who in 1816 were said to have murdered 10 crewmen from a ship they waylaid.

Between 1640 and 1915, more than 600 ships were reported in distress off Fire Island, prompting the first lighthouse on Fire Island in 1825. Its successor was built in 1858 at what then was the inlet. Unmanned rescue huts had been put up by volunteer groups as early as 1805. Starting in 1887, the new U.S. Life-Saving Service created 23 manned stations in Suffolk — 11 on Fire Island, where many heroic rescues

occurred.

As the 19th Century waned, so did Fire Island's dubious reputation. Smelly fish-oil factories were eliminated. Far fewer ships foundered as the steam vessel era arrived. Mainland groups began to come to Fire Island for picnics. The key turning point had been the arrival in 1855 of David S.S. Sammis, the man who first made Fire Island a resort. His huge Surf Hotel drew large, monied crowds for three decades, until 1892, when the state, in an emergency move, took it over and turned it into a quarantine station for ship passengers after a cholera scare in Europe. In 1908, the hotel site, in Kismet, became the first state park location on Long Island.

As the 1900s unfolded, Fire Island grew, with Ocean Beach established in 1908, Saltaire in 1910 and Cherry Grove — dubbed "the summer capital of the gay world" by one author — emerging in the 1920s and '30s, burgeoning after World War II. Homosexuals found a base at Cherry Grove when Ocean Beach and Seaview began making them unwelcome. Their numbers increased slowly through the Depression, but in 1939 the opening of Duffy's Hotel brought a new surge of popularity. In the late 1900s, according to historians, about 90 percent of Cherry Grove's residents have been gay, and they dominate also at nearby Fire Island Pines.

By 1927, Robert Moses was head of the new Long Island State Park Commission and pressing for a highway to Fire Island. World War II put his plans on hold but by 1954 Moses had built the Captree Causeway across the bay to the inlet and the road seemed inevitable. But opponents who believed a road would ruin the barrier organized and stopped the plans, enticing the federal government to back creation of a public park. In September, 1964, President Lyndon B. Johnson signed the bill creating the Fire Island National Seashore. At the end of the 1900s, that seashore extended about five miles to the west of where it ended in the mid-1800s, the result of natural sand-shifting forces. The "new" land became the site of Robert Moses State Park.

Where to Find More: "Fire Island, 1650s-1980s," by Madeleine C. Johnson, at Bay Shore-Brightwaters Public Library, and other area libraries.

GREAT RIVER

Arboretum Grows With Tycoon's Care

Beginnings: This small residential community developed roots in the 1840s, when Erastus Youngs and his family began building and repairing boats on the west shore of the Connetquot River near Great South Bay. With hardly anyone else around, the place was called Youngsport for 30 years. Alva Vanderbilt, the Oakdale socialite, bought the Youngs property later and gave it to a Brooklyn church, which used it as a summer camp for city children.

Turning Point: With the arrival of the railroad in 1868 at adjacent Oakdale, and the start of the Oakdale estate era, the name was changed to Great River. Most of the tycoons

who built nearby in the late 19th Century belonged to the Southside Sportsmen's Club, which had a private rail stop called "The Club" at Great River. The first Great River rail depot went up in 1897.

Claims to Fame: In 1886, William Bayard Cutting, financier, lawyer and railroad baron, built a huge Tudor-style mansion he called Westbrook on what later became Montauk Highway. His tycoon pal William K. Vanderbilt had built the Idle Hour mansion on the east side of the river only four years earlier. The Cutting estate totaled 931 acres, including a golf course, and the mansion had 22 fireplaces, rich dark paneling brought from England, some of it 400 years old, and exquisite stained-glass windows by famed jeweler Louis C. Tiffany, another member of the Southside club. More important, perhaps, Cutting brought trees and shrubs from

around the world to create a magnificent arboretum. He died in 1912. His family left the mansion and arboretum to the state and they were opened to the public in 1954. At the mouth of the river is a large tract called Timber Point, once a farm of Islip Town founder William Nicoll in the 17th Century. Timber Point later became an estate and then a county-owned golf course. Great River's population was about 1,400 in 1998.

Where to Find More: "Bayard Cutting Arboretum History," published by Long Island State Park and Recreation Commission, 1984; Long Island Forum articles and "East of Islip," by the Friends of the East Islip Library, 1969, at East Islip Library.

HAUPPAUGE

See story on Page 133.

HOLBROOK

Divided by Railroad, Then by Expressway

Beginnings: The land was part of a royal patent obtained by William Nicoll, a wealthy New York City politician, in 1697, certifying his purchases from the Secatogue Indians. But there was almost no colonial settlement for a century and a half, until 1848, when Alexander McCotter bought about 5,000 acres and offered small tracts for sale. In 1860 the first school was built about 1,000 feet south of the railroad, and the first church, Presbyterian, was built in 1863. The building became St. John's Lutheran Church near 1900 and was designated by the town as a historic structure. Holbrook's late

Newsday Photo / Cliff DeBear

FIRE ISLAND: Looking west from Point O'Woods, the aftermath of a devastating nor'easter that hit in mid-March, 1962.

Collection of Bob Doxsee Jr.

ISLIP HAMLET: The Doxsee Co. factory around 1900. At the turn of the century the hamlet had started to grow along with the clam canning business, which shipped products worldwide.

Above, Newsday Photo / Jim Cavanagh; Right, Newsday Photo / George Rubei

OAKDALE: Adelphi Suffolk College, the first liberal arts college in the county, opened at the former William K. Vanderbilt Idle Hour estate in 1962. Above, its first commencement, June 13, 1963. In 1968, the school became Dowling College, named after benefactor Robert W. Dowling. At right, tuxedoed guests take cocktails at a Dowling dinner-dance on June 2, 1971.

HOLBROOK, Continued

development is illustrated by this remarkable fact unearthed by Agnes Rysdyk, who spent years examining the hamlet's history: The first white person born in Holbrook, Maria Davidson, died in 1950. She was 94.

Splitsville: Holbrook lies mostly in the northeast corner of Islip Town, but partly in Brookhaven. It was divided by the Long Island Rail Road in 1844 when the land was almost completely pine barrens, and again by the Long Island Expressway in the 1960s as the postwar population boomed. Holbrook had 320 people, mostly on farms, in 1930; in 1998, there were about 22,000 people in the Islip Town section of the community and 5,100 in the Brookhaven Town portion.

The Name: The origins are obscure, according to Rysdyk, who said some old-timers contended the name emerged because the place was called Old Brook in the 1800s, after a brook or stream of uncertain location.

Showman: One of the most popular men in the hamlet's history was Henry Heine, a golden-voiced tenor soloist who ran minstrel shows around Long Island for 35 years. He was immersed in community affairs and was known as Holbrook's honorary mayor.

Where to Find More: "Holbrook's Past Shows the Loss of Rural Flavor," by Agnes Rysdyk, Suffolk County News supplement, March 1, 1973; "Memories From Holbrook," by Gurtha H. Strand, 1985, and "Sketches of Suffolk County," by Richard Bayles, 1874, all at Sachem Public Library, Holbrook.

ISLANDIA
A Late Arrival
Born in Controversy

Beginnings: Amid sharp controversy, this 2¼-square-mile incorporated village was carved out of northeast Central Islip and south Hauppauge in April, 1985, next to the busy interchange where Exit 57 of the Long Island Expressway crossed Veterans Memorial Parkway. Islandia became Long Island's first new village since Lake Grove was established in 1968. Islip Town and Suffolk County planners charged before the 505-178 approval vote that the incorporation bid was a transparent effort to gain zoning control to lure new industry and make the village a tax haven for residents. They warned that too much industrial buildup would further aggravate traffic problems around Exit 57, and later criticized the new village's willingness to give concessions to businesses seeking zoning changes.

The Founder's View: Warren Raymond, who dominated the incorporation effort and became the first mayor, said in 1997 that taxes paid by industry had a minor effect on village property taxes, most of it going to school districts, the county and town. "The village has been very successful. Most of the growth has been what we had hoped to see — upscale homes," Raymond said.

Who's There: The village listed 162 businesses in 1997. The big ones that moved in since 1985 include Computer Associates and the Radisson Hotel on the LIE, the large, glass-walled Pavilion office complex at the interchange, and nearby Islandia Center, a shopping mall on Veterans Highway. The 1998 population was estimated at 2,900.

Identity Confusion: In the late 1990s, the village was served by three post offices (Central Islip, Ronkonkoma and Hauppauge), three school districts (Central Islip, Connetquot and Hauppauge) and three fire districts (Central Islip, Lakeland and Hauppauge).

OAKDALE
On the Gold Coast South

BY TOM MORRIS
STAFF WRITER

Oakdale was a scion of America's gilded age of the late 1800s, where powerful men of incredible wealth built South Shore gold coast mansions and dwelt in manorial splendor.

It may seem peculiar, but it all began because a good old boy of the time named Eliphalet (Liff) Snecedor ran a terrific tavern in the woods, in what later became Connetquot River State Park. Soon after its founding in 1820, Snedecor's Tavern began drawing New York bluebloods and business barons who wined and dined in remote joy when they weren't fishing and hunting nearby. "Liff's food is as good as his creek," a magazine writer declared in 1839, referring to the Connetquot River, "and the two are only second to his mint juleps and Champagne punch; whoever gainsays either fact deserves hanging without benefit of clergy." In 1866, as the railroad reached the area, Liff's wealthy patrons formed the Southside Sportsmen's Club, and soon the race was on to see who could create the most superb spread in the thick forests adjoining Great South Bay.

The most prominent were William K. Vanderbilt, grandson of railroad magnate Cornelius Vanderbilt; Frederick G. Bourne, president of the Singer Sewing Machine Co., and Christopher Robert II, an eccentric heir to a sugar fortune. Meanwhile, William Bayard Cutting, a lawyer, financier and railroad man, built his estate next door in Great River, which had once been west Oakdale.

Oakdale was part of the royal land grant given to William Nicoll, who founded Islip Town in 1697. Local historian Charles P. Dickerson, writing in 1975, said Oakdale's name apparently came from a Nicoll descendant in the mid-1800s. The community has other claims to historical distinction: St. John's Episcopal Church, built in 1765, became the third oldest church on Long Island. In 1912, Jacob Ockers of Oakdale organized the Bluepoint Oyster Co., which became the largest oyster producer and shipper in the country.

But the mansions dominated Oakdale's past. In 1882, Vanderbilt built the most noted one, Idle Hour, his 900-acre estate on the Connetquot River. The lavish, wooden

110-room home was destroyed by fire April 15, 1899, while his son, Willie K. II, was honeymooning there. Willie and his new wife escaped. It was promptly rebuilt of red brick and gray stone, with exquisite furnishings, for a princely $3 million. Probably *the* social event there was the 1895 wedding reception of Vanderbilt's daughter, Consuela, to the duke of Marlborough. After Vanderbilt's death in 1920, the mansion went through several phases and visitors, including a brief stay during Prohibition by gangster Dutch Schultz. Around that time, cow stalls, pig pens and corn cribs on the farm portion of Idle Hour were converted to a short-lived bohemian artists' colony that included figures such as George Elmer Browne and Roman Bonet-Sintas. In 1962 the estate became home of Aldephi Suffolk College. In 1968 the school became Dowling College.

By 1888, Christopher Robert II built a spectacular castle just east of Idle Hour called Pepperidge Hall, magnificently furnished in the French style for his young wife. But the pair didn't get along. On Jan. 2, 1898, she told police she found Robert shot to death in his Manhattan apartment. It was ruled suicide and she moved to Paris. The mansion fell into disrepair and was razed in 1940.

In 1897, Frederick G. Bourne, who began with 438 acres but later owned several thousand acres reaching to West Sayville, completed his mansion, Indian Neck Hall, on the east side of Oakdale. Bourne was active locally, as commodore of the Sayville Yacht Club, and was generous to the local fire department. The eastern part of his estate was later comprised of the West Sayville County Golf Course and the Suffolk County Marine Museum, while much of the middle portion was covered with homes. Bourne died in 1920. Six years later the mansion, on the western end, became the site of LaSalle Military Academy, operated by the Christian Brothers, a Catholic order. In 1993, the brothers converted the academy into a kindergarten-through-high school "global learning community."

Where to Find More: "The Old Oakdale History," William K. Vanderbilt Historical Society of Dowling College, 1983; Oakdale chapter of "A History of the Sayville Community," by Charles P. Dickerson, 1975, and Long Island Forum articles, all at Connetquot Public Library, Bohemia.

Frederic G. Bourne, president of the Singer Sewing Machine Co., completed Indian Neck Hall in 1897. In 1926 the mansion became the site of LaSalle Military Academy.

Nassau County Museum Collection, Long Island Studies Institute / Henry Otto Korten

ISLIP HAMLET
America's Cup Sailors
Trained on the Bay

Beginnings: On March 26, 1692, Andrew Gibb, a friend and business partner of William Nicoll, Islip Town's founder, received a royal patent that made him owner of what was to become the pivotal community in Islip Town — the hamlet of Islip. The land Gibb obtained came to only about 3,500 acres but was the center of town commerce and social life in early times and the seat of town government.

The Revolution: The Gibb tract, still intact, was owned by Capt. Benijah Strong, captain of the Islip Militia Company and a volunteer in Maj. Benjamin Tallmadge's daring 1780 raid on Fort St. George in Mastic.

Turning Points: By 1808, there was only one store and no houses on the south side of South Country Road (later Montauk Highway). That all changed after the railroad arrived in the late 1860s. The hamlet soon became the town's largest community and the seat of government. By 1900, it had 1,727 residents, a school, four churches, boatyards and the Doxsee clam canning factory that shipped worldwide. But two major fires hurt the prosperity. The worst, in February, 1905, destroyed 17 businesses and five apartment houses on the north side of Main

Street. After the fires, most commercial growth gravitated to Bay Shore and Patchogue.

Claims to Fame: In about 1900, Islip hamlet was noted for its sailors, trained on the bay, who defended the nation in America's Cup competitions. Most notable was Capt. Hank Haff, who in 1895 skippered the 123-foot Defender to victory over England, using an all-American crew for the first time.

Legend Has It: That when Schuyler Livingston Parsons built a sumptuous estate in Islip in about 1900, he had to settle for his second choice of name. Both he and William K. Vanderbilt reportedly wanted to call their estates

Please Turn the Page

SAYVILLE

The World Was Its Oyster

BY TOM MORRIS
STAFF WRITER

I n 1836, 50 years after its official settlement, Sayville finally got a name. But it wasn't easy.

Tired of being called simply "over south," the area's residents met in the old Bedell Tavern on Main Street to pick a name. The result was a tie between Edwardsville and Greenville, which referred to community founders. Then someone suggested Seaville. This was adopted but, local histories assert, the clerk misspelled it "Sayville."

Things haven't always been so wonky. Over time, Sayville has been a major source of wood for New York City, the oyster capital of the United States, a center of Long Island theater and a bustling resort town after the railroad arrived in 1868.

Sayville was part of the huge royal grant given to William Nicoll, a wealthy New York City politician, in 1697 — and the root of Islip Town. After the Revolution, mainly because of British ravaging of the land, William Nicoll IV was in debt and successfully petitioned the new state legislature — a requirement at the time — for the right to sell off some land to pay bills.

As a result, in 1786, in the first sale of the original Nicoll holdings, John Edwards, 48, of East Hampton, who had already settled in the area in 1761, bought what became the eastern part of Sayville for about $3 an acre. It stretched from Great South Bay to about a mile north of modern Montauk Highway. Edwards' son Matthew built a house that is believed to be contained within the circa-1830 structure that later housed the Sayville Historical Society.

The section called West Sayville was acquired by John Greene, a member of a Huntington family, in 1767. One of Greene's sons built a house on what became the corner of Montauk Highway and Cherry Avenue. It was mentioned in the diary of President George Washington as a stopover, on April 22, 1790, during his tour of Long Island.

The first settlers were Congregationalists, but were without a church of their own. In 1845, a prominent Brooklyn cleric, Nathaniel Prime, decried that there were only two churches in all of Islip Town. "The greater part of the population must be living in utter sin without means of salvation . . .," Prime declared. "The state of morals in Islip Town presents the most undesirable residence of any area on Long Island." Two years later, a Methodist church was built in Sayville. It remained the community's oldest church.

By 1830, New York City's growth had created a market for wood and the cutting and shipping of locally abundant pine soon became a very important part of Sayville's economy. Its economic history was tied to that of West Sayville, notable as a stronghold of Dutch settlers who came to dominate the regional fishing industry. By 1912, Dutch oystermen led by Jacob Ockers established the famed Bluepoint Co. at the foot of Atlantic Avenue in West Sayville, which long reigned as the world's largest producer and shipper of oysters.

Meanwhile, the South Side Railroad had reached Sayville in 1868, and summer tourism opened wide the

Iceboaters at Sayville in a postcard from 1912
Collection of Joel Streich

gates of change. In the succeeding five decades, 30 hotels were built in the area. One of the lures for visitors was Fire Island across Great South Bay. The period between 1880 and 1930 is also remememberd as the era of Sayville's greatest beauty, with its grand Victorian homes, wide, tree-canopied streets and vibrant shopping.

Among the finest houses of the period were those of Frank S. Jones, president of the Jewel Tea Co., and Meadow Croft, owned by John Ellis Roosevelt, a cousin of President Theodore Roosevelt, who visited. It became part of the Suffolk County Sans Souci Lakes Nature Preserve. The Florence Bourne Hard estate, reaching from Montauk Highway to the bay in West Sayville, was purchased by Suffolk County in 1967 and became the West Sayville County Golf Course.

Henry C. Bohack, a grocery chain founder, lived on Main Street in Sayville for many years and built a store there in 1925.

One other notable resident was an itinerant preacher named George Baker. The son of a Georgia slave, he moved to a house on Macon Street in Sayville in the 1920s and said he had a vision that he was God and that his name was Father Divine. His Sayville home, called Heaven, drew busloads of followers on weekends. After a few bouts with the law, Father Divine moved his mission to Harlem.

The community's long history as a theater center was perhaps best symbolized by the 1,500-seat Sayville Opera House, which opened Aug 7, 1901, and operated for almost a half-century before movies and radio ended its run. The building burned down in 1961. The opera house attracted top performers including Lillian Russell and Fred Stone and was used to warm up several Broadway shows.

During World War I, Sayville was the site of the German-owned Telefunken wireless radio station that was suspected of informing Germany of the whereabouts of American and other allied ships. All Germans were ordered out of the station in February, 1917, after President Woodrow Wilson sent Marines to the site.

Where to Find More: "A History of the Sayville Comunity, Including Bayport, Bohemia, West Sayville, Oakdale and Fire Island," by Charles P. Dickerson, 1975; "A History of Early Sayville," by Clarissa Edwards, Sayville Historical Society, 1935; both at Sayville Public Library.

---

ses in this residential community were located. Local sources said the name came from the fact that the community was north of, or above, East Islip, and because a terrace connotes a strip of land planted with trees and shrubs. 1998's estimated population was 5,500.

Memories: About the time the Wolperts were building homes, the Petrom Circus began giving shows in an old hunting lodge that attracted patrons for miles around. According to a local history, "Hearsay has it that people brought their own oil lamps to help illuminate the evening shows," featuring monkeys, dogs, horses and acrobats.

Where to Find More: "'East of Islip, An Early History," by the Friends of the East Islip Library, 1969, at East Islip Library.

RONKONKOMA

See story on Page 77.

WEST ISLIP

An Inn for Coaches, And Automobiles

Beginnings: Twelve years after Islip Town founder William Nicoll received his first royal patents on the east side of town in 1683, most of the land that would make up West Islip was granted to friends of his, brothers Thomas and Richard Willett, confirming their purchase of it from the Indians. The land stayed in the family for decades. In 1750, Nathaniel Conklin, a pioneer of "Huntington South," which was to become Babylon Town, built a mill on Sumpawams Creek separating West Islip and Babylon, an early landmark that stood until 1910. Because it is adjacent to Babylon, West Islip once was referred to as East Babylon.

Indian Echoes: Historians say West Islip probably was the home of the sachem of the Secatogue Indians, who lived between Babylon and Yaphank. On June 6, 1960, 13 Indian skeletons were discovered in the excavation of a winter fire pit near the bay and estimated to be more than 5,000 years old. A plaque was placed on a large boulder, both donated by shoe tycoon Ward Melville to mark the find.

Islip's First Church: Historians say it was the Presbyterian Church of Islip and Huntington South built about 1730 — 20 years after the town was established — on what would become Montauk Highway near Sequams Lane. The British destroyed the church in 1778 and took the wood to Hempstead to build barracks.

Leading Landmark: LaGrange Inn on Montauk Highway, one of the oldest on Long Island, was opened just after the Revolutionary War by the Higbie family and became a key stop on the Brooklyn-to-Patchogue stagecoach line. It was named after the home in France of the Marquis de Lafayette, who helped the Patriot cause in the Revolution. Tradition says he visited the inn in 1824.

Turning Points: During the late 1800s, the community was a haven for wealthy estate owners, many of them New York City business leaders with names such as Sutton, Arnold and Magoun. Early in the 1900s, many Ukrainian people settled in West Islip, seeking refuge from political and economic hardship. A major figure was William Dzus, inventor of an industrial fastener used widely by the military in World War II and a founder of the West Islip Public Library in 1957. Good Samaritan Hospital opened in 1959, and the Captree Causeway across the bay in 1954. West Islip's population was estimated at 28,650 in 1998.

Where to Find More: "First History of West Islip," by Gerald and Judith Wilcox, 1976, and oral history cassette tape collection, West Islip Public Library.

ISLIP, Continued

Idle Hour and agreed to decide the matter with a flip of a coin. Parsons lost and chose the name Whileaway.

Where to Find More: "A Brief History of Islip Hamlet," by Carl A. Starace, and "Origins of the Gibb Patent: The Story Behind Islip's Founding," by Robert H.D. Finnegan, 1994, both via The Historical Society of Islip Hamlet.

ISLIP TERRACE

Real Estate Agent Added a German Flavor

Beginnings: There were only a few farmhouses in the area north of East Islip as the 19th Century ended. In 1914, as World War I began, Andrew Wolpert Sr., a Bavarian native who had been a real estate agent in New York City, and his three sons began building houses in the

woods between East Islip and Central Islip State Hospital. The Wolperts wanted to attract people of German origin, according to historians. The place was known as Germantown, but the war brought pressures to change the name of the community. Many people who moved there worked in the state hospital.

Turning Point: The name was changed to Islip Terrace in December, 1922, when the post office was established in the former Wagner Hotel on Carleton Avenue, where the handful of busines-

SAYVILLE: In an undated photograph, proud firefighters march through the village during a firefighters' tournament.

WEST SAYVILLE: Oyster sheds at the harbor in about 1910. Like many communities on the South Shore, West Sayville found economic sustenance from the ocean.

Suffolk County Historical Society

BAITING HOLLOW: The Edward E. Prince farmhouse in an undated photo. Local farmers grew corn, potatoes, caulifower, mulberry trees and even daffodils.

Suffolk County Historical Society

JAMESPORT: Ships are tied up at South Jamesport Cove on a winter day in this undated photograph.

124

Town of Riverhead

The seat of Suffolk County government since the colonial assembly decreed it in 1727 didn't become a township for another 65 years.

When it did, in 1792, it was created out of the west end of Southold Town, which had been established in 1640. People in the western part of Southold, including the larger settlements of Wading River and Old Aquebogue (Jamesport), grew weary of traveling up to 25 miles over crude dirt paths through wilderness to attend the important annual town meetings in Southold hamlet.

Riverhead Town was divided from Southold on March 13, 1792, at the end of the American Revolution, becoming the ninth of 10 Suffolk towns. But the area's roots go deeper. In 1659, John Tucker and Joseph Horton, both of Southold, won the right to set up a sawmill there, and they are considered the first white settlers. In 1690, grist and fulling (cloth finishing) mills were set up to take advantage of water power along the Peconic River.

During the 18th Century, the town spawned several industries, including cordwood, textiles, shipbuilding, ship anchor production for the Navy, button, chocolate and cigar factories, and cranberry growing. Potatoes became the major crop in the 1880s, but the transformation of the town into a commercial agricultural giant did not start until early in the 1900s. Commercial duck farms, important early in the 20th Century, faded with post-World War II development.

Riverhead, with an estimated population of just 24,500 in 1998, had more than half of all of Long Island's remaining farms — about 11,000 of Suffolk's 32,000 agricultural acres. The Riverhead Town Agricultural Society, formed in 1863 as the Farmer's Club, was the nation's oldest cooperative when it was disbanded in the 1950s.

In the 1990s, Riverhead tried to encourage tourism via an aquarium, the Tanger Outlet Center and Splish Splash water park. Though many county offices and facilities were relocated to Hauppauge and elsewhere, Riverhead remained the county seat.

AQUEBOGUE
Of 'Witch's Hat,' Farm Stands, Wineries

Beginnings: When white settlers first bought the land that would form most of the Town of Riverhead in the late 1600s, they referred to the entire region as Aquebogue, an Indian word meaning "head of the bay" or "cove place." Eventually, individual communities took on their own names such as Baiting Hollow and Jamesport. The hamlet eventually known as Aquebogue was settled about 1758.

Turning Point: Frustrated at having to travel so far to annual town meetings held in Southold village, the early settlers of the Aquebogue area lobbied to split from Southold to create their own town. On March 13, 1792, Southold was divided into two towns — Southold and River-

AQUEBOGUE: Main Street as it appeared in 1966

Newsday Photo

head — and the first town meeting was held in John Griffing's home on April 3. By 1998, the population was about 2,200.

To Market, to Market: In the 1990s, Aquebogue gained renown for its wineries and farm stands. But, in the 1840s, Aquebogue was known for its general store and its eagle-eyed proprietor. When he wasn't tending to his store or lumberyard, Benjamin Franklin Wells was probably on the roof peering through a telescope. Wells liked to watch for schooners coming up the bay carrying lumber that needed to be brought to his dock on Meetinghouse Creek.

Kooky Landmark: Since the late 1920s, an unusual roadside market stood on the south side of Route 25 in Aquebogue. Built as a vegetable stand, the wood-shingled structure resembled a miniature lighthouse and was often referred to as the "witch's hat." The property changed hands several times and a number of items were peddled there, from plants to Girl Scout cookies. Though somewhat run down, the stand remained, signaling to motorists headed east that they were entering North Fork turf.

Where to Find More: "The Story of Riverhead," by Evelyn Rowley Meier, at the Riverhead Free Library.

BAITING HOLLOW
You Name It, And Farmers Tried to Grow It

Beginnings: Though this section of the original Aquebogue purchase was divvied into 60 lots as early as 1660, there was not much activity there until the late 18th Century. That is, except for the building of a cart path through the "Great Woods" in 1702, easing travel from Southold to Brookhaven Town. The latter-day Sound Avenue mirrored the course of the old path. Early travelers actually inspired the name Baiting Hollow, referring to a pond where they "baited" or watered their horses. The 1825 census listed just 261 inhabitants, compared with 1998's population of about 1,200.

Turning Point: Corn, potatoes, cauliflower, mulberry trees, even daffodils — you name it and Baiting Hollow farmers tried growing it. So much so that Baiting Hollow developed a reputation for experimental farming and drew agricultural specialists interested in

studying plant diseases and pesky insects. In 1923, New York State bought the old Homan farm on Sound Avenue and established a research farm.

Brush With Fame: After visiting the Baiting Hollow mansion of Wall Street tycoon J.G. Robin in 1907, Theodore Dreiser, author of "An American Tragedy" and "Sister Carrie," used the Long Island setting in a short story titled "Vanity, Vanity." Calling Robin's home "unpretentiously pretentious," Dreiser later talked about what struck him: "It was . . . so really grand in a limited and yet poetic way." The manor, on the north side of Sound Avenue just east of Fresh Pond Avenue, was torn down in the 1980s and the property became part of Wildwood State Park. The only remnants were the manor's carriage house and a concrete boundary wall running along a portion of Sound Avenue.

Where to Find More: "Dreiser and Driftwood Manor," Long Island Forum, December, 1961. "The Story of Riverhead," by Evelyn Rowley Meier, at the Riverhead Free Library.

CALVERTON
Cranberries, Pickles And Jets Took Off

Beginnings: Named in 1868 for Bernard J. Calvert, the hamlet's first postmaster, Calverton was essentially a farming community carved out of marshland. Before that, it had been called Baiting Hollow Station after the railroad came in 1844 and, alternately, as Hulse's Turnout, indicating the point travelers turned north to the Hulses' place in Wading River. The Indians called it Conungum or Kanungum, meaning a "fixed line" or "boundary."

The Cranberries: Like areas in neighboring Manorville and Riverhead, Calverton's wetlands made it ideal for cranberry bogs. At its peak in the early 1900s, the cranberry business employed hundreds of women and children who picked berries by hand and earned about $2 a day. The last of the cranberry farms, Davis Marsh off Swan Pond Road in Calverton, closed in the 1970s and later became the site of the Swan Lake Golf Course.

Pickle Works Wreck: As the Shelter Island Express sped toward its next stop after pulling

out of Manorville on Aug. 13, 1926, the train hit a faulty switch and plunged into Golden's Pickle Works. Six people died, including the engineer, who drowned in the vat. The incident was known as the Great Pickle Works Wreck.

Turning Point: In 1953, the U.S. Navy acquired 4,000 acres in Calverton and leased it to Grumman Aircraft Engineering Co. The aviation giant spent several decades assembling planes there for the Navy, including the Tomcat and E-2C Hawkeye. In a reduction of its Long Island operations, Grumman in 1995 shut down its Calverton plant, which once employed 3,000. The last Grumman plane took off from Calverton in June, 1995. The Navy then returned the facility to the Town of Riverhead, which planned to sell it. In 1996, a hangar on the grounds was used by federal agencies to rebuild the wreckage recovered from the 1996 crash of TWA Flight 800. In 1978, Calverton became the home of a 1,052-acre national cemetery as the Long Island National Cemetery in Pinelawn became filled. More than 133,000 veterans and relatives had been buried in Calverton by the late 1990s. Calverton's live population in 1998 was about 5,200.

Where to Find More: "The Story of Riverhead," "Echoes From the Past" and other materials at the Riverhead Free Library.

JAMESPORT, SOUTH JAMESPORT
Little Deep Thinking Went Into Port Dream

Beginnings: Sorting out the early years of these old Riverhead hamlets is rather tricky. Consider this passage, taken from a history published in the 1960s: "The name Aquebogue was first applied to the entire area of the Aquebogue purchase. Later, it was attached to the ancient village now called Jamesport. After the development of another settlement a few miles to the west, the new community was called Upper Aquebogue, and the older one was called Lower, or Old, Aquebogue. The original Jamesport was not laid out until 1833 on the Bay. By a curious shift of names, Jamesport became South Jamesport, Lower Aquebogue became Jamesport, and Upper Aquebogue acquired for all time thereafter the ancient name of Aquebogue." For simplicity's sake, consider that South Jamesport was founded as Jamesport in the early 1800s by James Tuthill, who had dreams of turning the tiny Peconic Bay community into a major shipping port. In 1833, Tuthill named his town James' Port, laid out streets and built a dock. What Tuthill didn't consider was that the waters off Jamesport were much too shallow at low tide to accommodate cargo ships. Tuthill's dream did come true — but for Greenport, a neighboring hamlet on the North Fork more accessible to larger ships. The latter-day Jamesport began around 1690, when the first settlers built homesteads and attracted tradesmen to their midst, establishing a modest 18th-Century commercial outpost.

Fish Story: Bunker fish oil was a boom product for many years. Crews of fishermen would head to Peconic Bay in season and weave a seine sometimes a half-mile long to harvest the bunkers, also called menhaden. The small fish were then processed for crop fertilizer or oil used in lamps and for paint. About 15,000 bunkers were used to fertilize an acre of land, so it was not unusual to see catches in the hundreds of thousands. In the 1790s, the bunker business was considered fairly lucrative, with the price ranging from 50 to 75 cents per 1,000 fish.

Please Turn the Page

JAMESPORT, Continued

Camping Ground: Methodists discovered the rural serenity of Jamesport in 1835 and set up camp in a grove of magnificent oak trees. They returned summer after summer for their annual Methodist assembly. They erected tents at first, later replacing them with attractive Victorian cottages. Perhaps the biggest change on the Jamesport landscape by the end of the 20th Century was the introduction of wineries. 1998's population was estimated at 1,756.

Where to Find More: "The Story of Riverhead" by Evelyn Rowley Meier, at the Riverhead Free Library, and "Hawkins Brothers of Jamesport," Long Island Forum, May, 1953.

NORTHVILLE

Farm Museum Shows Hallocks' Deep Roots

Beginnings: Northville, formerly known as Sound Avenue and Success Post Office, was once a productive farm community north of Riverhead hamlet. The first white landowner was William Wells, a Southolder who purchased the land from the Indians in the late 1600s. Though Wells never lived on the land, his grandson did set up a homestead along Sound Avenue as early as 1724. Other farmers followed.

Turning Point: In the 1920s, Northville was briefly the only incorporated village in Riverhead Town. On Dec. 3, 1921, Sound Avenue, as Northville was then known, held its first village election. The experiment in self-governance did not last long, especially when the founding fathers discovered how expensive the distinction was. The village was dissolved in 1930, but not before voters elected to change the community's name in 1927 to Northville. 1998's population was about 690.

A Farming Legacy: The Hallocks go back for generations in the Northville area, first settling in the 1680s along what would become the Riverhead-Southold border. Born in 1749, Capt. Zachariah Hallock was a farmer and shoemaker, cobbling more than 1,700 pairs of shoes from 1771 to 1820. Most of what was later referred to as Hallockville was owned by Zachariah in the early 1800s. At least 15 of the Hallock homes and outbuildings are preserved along Sound Avenue as part of the Hallockville Farm and Folklife Museum.

Claim to Fame: With fertile fields and plenty of produce, Northville farmers of the 1890s itched for ways to get their goods to New York markets more cheaply than by rail. They dreamed of a deep-water pier where large ships could dock and carry away the hefty cargo. The Iron Pier, jutting 350 feet into the Sound, debuted in 1900. It lasted only four years, succumbing to shifting ice floes in the harsh winter of 1904. Pier Avenue, the road that once connected the dock to Sound Avenue, was the iron hulk's only legacy.

Where to Find More: "A Brief History of Hallockville," Long Island Forum, February, 1978; "The Story of Riverhead," by Evelyn Rowley Meier, and "A History of Riverhead Town," by Elisabeth S. Lapham, both at Riverhead Free Library.

WADING RIVER

Washington Was Here, Before He Was Famous

Beginnings: In 1671, the town fathers in Brookhaven declared that "there shall be a settlement of eight families or eight men at the Wading River." Joined by others from Southold in the next few years, the early settlers attempted to rename the community Westholde, but it never stuck. Wading River was likely the closest English equivalent to the Indian word Pau-

RIVERHEAD HAMLET
At the Center of Power

BY TOM MORRIS
STAFF WRITER

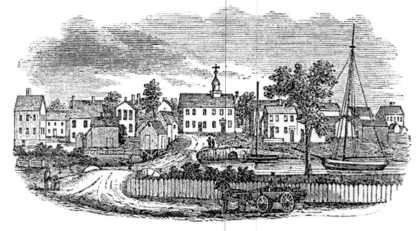
From "Historical Collections of the State of New York"
An early engraving of the central part of Riverhead, Suffolk's county seat

Riverhead's "downtown" was nothing to write home about in 1804 when Timothy Dwight, visiting president of Yale College, described it succinctly and unsympathetically in his diary: "The courthouse, a poor decayed building, and a miserable hamlet containing about ten or twelve houses stand near the efflux of this river."

At the time, of course, all of Long Island was still trying to recover from its long subjugation by the British during the Revolution, and Riverhead Town was only 12 years old. Before the Revolution, the hamlet had been known as Suffolk County Court House because one had been built, with a jail, in 1727, when the spot was designated Suffolk's county seat. It had been a long time coming: When Suffolk was established in 1683, the colonial government ordered a court and jail be built to serve both Southold and Southampton. The two towns fought over the location for decades; finally the courthouse went up in the part of Southold that in 1792 split off to become Riverhead, named for its location at the mouth of the Peconic River.

In addition to the courthouse, there were then two mills, the handful of houses and John Griffing's home-and-tavern in which the early annual town meetings were held. (By contrast, Wading River, at the west end of the town, had been settled since 1671 and was a thriving seaport town.)

Life was primitive. River water power was important, and several more mills, for cutting logs, grinding grain and finishing cloth, were built in the hamlet. Most unusual was the Riverhead Water Works Tower Mill, which provided water to the community for many years. It was copied after a European castle, and though made of wood was cleverly designed to look as if made of stone. (It was razed just before World War II.) Farming was the core family occupation, but Riverhead also produced shoes, harnesses, cigars and coffins. Some Riverheaders were carpenters and later, some became shipbuilders.

During the Revolution, residents suffered from British plundering of food and livestock. After the war, the new State Legislature confiscated the property of 59 New York residents and banished them as British Loyalists. One was Parker Wickham, a wealthy ex-Southold Town supervisor. Part of his land was an 800-acre tract that later formed most of Riverhead hamlet. Wickham fled to New London, Conn., and died there in 1785.

The first meeting house in the area that became Riverhead was the Old Aquebogue Presbyterian, built in 1731; later it was the Jamesport Congregational Church. The first common school mentioned in town records is 1810, but as early as 1790 there was a teacher who "kept" school in what was later Jamesport.

On May 30, 1814, during the War of 1812, the British warship HMS Dispatch captured the Eagle, a small American armed boat, after a fierce fight at Roanoke Point directly north of Riverhead. In another clash, the British captured the sloop Nancy near Northville, but only after Americans firing from the bluffs ran out of ammunition.

The first county clerk's office was built in Riverhead hamlet in 1846, about the time the Long Island Rail Road arrived and significantly spurred the farm economy. The old courthouse panned by the Yale president in 1804 was replaced in 1856 by one on Griffing Avenue. That one was damaged by fire and replaced by the present courthouse at the Griffing Avenue complex in 1929. With Suffolk's growth, a new county center was built in 1958 adjacent to Riverhead hamlet. In a piece of historical irony, it's on the Southampton Town side of the Peconic River, where the county jail, built in 1967, also is located. Though Riverhead remained the county seat, many county offices were located in Hauppauge in the 1960s. The Riverhead community's population was about 8,730 in 1998.

Bar Associations: Early in the 1900s, as towns voted annually to be "dry" or "wet," and often disagreed, one tavern-keeper with a place on the Riverhead-Brookhaven town line simply moved the bar from one end of the building to the other when necessary. Meanwhile, the original Griffing tavern where the first town meeting had been held became the Long Island House in 1863 and was run for three decades by temperance man John P. Terry without a drop of liquor served. The Griffing family ran its own place after 1862, and one proprietor, Hud Griffing, advertised, "location unsurpassed, nearest hotel to the brewery, right across from the jail, convenient to all cemeteries."

Where to Find More: "A History of Riverhead Town," by Elisabeth S. Lapham; "200 Candles for Riverhead," a bicentennial history of early Riverhead Town, by Justine Warner Wells, and "The Riverhead Story," by Evelyn Rowley Meier; all at Riverhead Free Library.

quaconsuk or "the river where we wade for thick, round-shelled clams." It evolved into a commercial center for nearby North Shore hamlets in the 1700s.

Young Washington Slept Here: Long before he took the oath of office in 1789, George Washington and his horse spent a night at the Horn Tavern on the Old Post Road (later Middle Country Road). It was February, 1756, and Washington was a 24-year-old colonel in the Virginia regiment traveling a common route through Long Island on his way to Boston for official business. Only years later, after Washington's rise to power, did the proprietor tell his children he wished he'd paid the future president more mind.

Turning Point: Looking to ensure it had future freight business, the Long Island Rail Road embarked on an unusual sideline starting in 1906. In hopes of luring settlers (i.e. potential customers) to eastern Long Island, railroad executives devised a scheme to prove how fertile the sandy soil could be in communities like Wading River. They called in special agent Hal B. Fullerton to clear 10 acres of the worst land he could find and see what he could raise. The farm was so lush with beets, onions, melons, carrots, corn and squash that former President Theodore Roosevelt came to Wading River in the summer of 1910 to inspect what was coined Peace and Plenty farm. By 1998, Wading River had about 5,890 residents.

Spies Among Them: During World War II, the FBI ran a secret counter-intelligence operation out of a house on Northside Avenue. It used a high-powered radio station to send bogus information to Germany, ostensibly from a U.S.-based Nazi spy ring, eliciting useful responses.

Where to Find More: "Echoes From the Past," by Elisabeth S. Lapham, "The Story of Riverhead," by Evelyn Rowley Meier, both in the Riverhead Free Library.

Suffolk County Historical Society

RIVERHEAD: On the Fourth of July, 1903, President Theodore Roosevelt delivers a speech from the stage at the Suffolk County Fair.

Suffolk County Historical Society

NORTHVILLE: The Iron Pier stood from 1900 to 1904.

Collection of Ruth R. Meyer

RIVERHEAD: Benjamin T. Davis, right, and a hired hand at his Livery Stable in 1916.

127

Town of Shelter Island

BY TOM MORRIS
STAFF WRITER

When Nathaniel Sylvester, a young sugar merchant, married 16-year-old Grissell Brinley in England in early 1652 and sailed for America, neither could know the adventures ahead. Their marriage would start with a shipwreck, see them open their wilderness home to cruelly persecuted Quakers, and end with their legacy as the founders of the Town of Shelter Island.

As early eastern Suffolk pioneers, the Sylvesters prospered on their remote island, had 11 children, and succored New England Quakers at a time when it was dangerous to do so. Their brave defense of religious freedom won the reverence of later generations in this country and in Great Britain.

The Sylvesters were shipwrecked off Connecticut on their honeymoon trip, where they stopped first to visit family in Barbados, then headed for Newport, R.I., to prepare to move to Shelter Island before their boat accident. They survived and became the first white settlers of what was to be named Shelter Island. After their arrival in March, 1652, they used the island's white oak to make sugar barrels used in trade with Barbados. Nathaniel's brother Constant, and two other sugar merchants, Thomas Middleton and Thomas Rouse, were co-founders but didn't live on the island, and in 1673 Nathaniel became sole owner.

Historians are unclear whether the Sylvesters themselves were Quakers, but they recognized and detested the religious intolerance of the time. James Bowden, in his "History of the Society of Friends," said Shelter Island and the colony of Rhode Island were the only places in the North American colonies a Quaker could go without risking severe suffering in the 1650s. Among those martyred for their beliefs who found asylum with the Sylvesters were Lawrence and Cassandra Southwick and Mary Dyer, major figures of early Quakerism.

According to most historians, however, it wasn't shelter for Quakers that gave the island its name. In papers confirming the deed of Dec. 27, 1652, by which the Manhanset Indians conveyed the island, it was called "Ahaquatawamok," or "Island sheltered-by-islands." Sylvester died in 1680, leaving the island equally to his five sons. But no headstones mark graves of anyone who died on the island prior to 1729. In 1884, his family placed a monument at the head of Gardiner's Creek.

An unspoiled island sheltered by islands

Newsday Photo, 1965
A beach on the island, much of which has been preserved

In 1695 the family sold one-quarter of the island to William Nicoll, who controlled 90,000 acres of Islip via royal patent. Five years later, in 1700, 1,000 acres of the 8,000-acre island were sold to George Havens of Newport, whose family was to become deeply entwined in the government and civic affairs of the island for more than two centuries. Shelter Island became a town in 1730, when there were 20 men, mostly heads of farm families, living there. William Nicoll II was the first supervisor.

The major turning point for Shelter Island came in 1871 with the sale of land that became Shelter Island Heights to a group of men from Brooklyn who opened an era of development. By the summer of 1872 visitors were pouring into the new Prospect House hotel, and that fall a Massachusetts group bought 200 acres across from Dering Harbor. In 1874 they opened the Manhanset House hotel, a huge and wildly successful resort that entertained some 15,000 guests in the next decade. The hotel was destroyed by fire in 1910, effectively marking the end of the period of rambling summer hotels. In their place came cottages in what became the Village of Dering Harbor and in unincorporated areas with names such as The Heights, West Neck, Montclair Colony, Westmoreland Farms, Silver Beach, South Ferry Hills, Ram Island and Hay Beach.

How sheltered should Shelter Island be? The question was pondered by many islanders throughout the 20th Century. In the 1930s, there was serious talk about building bridges to Shelter Island from Greenport and North Sea, setting off furious debate. The bridges didn't materialize, and the major move to protect the island came in 1980, when the Mashomack Peninsula, 2,039 acres covering 30 percent of the island, was purchased as open space by the Nature Conservancy. The peninsula remained undeveloped. Though Shelter Island's population doubled in the second half of the 20th Century, to about 2,330 in 1998, it shook off major efforts to make it a watering hole for visitors. Twentieth Century Shelter Islanders worried about the population increase, the limited fresh water supply and proposals to allow rental apartments and bed-and-breakfasts. Nathaniel and Grissell Sylvester surely would have been astonished to see Shelter Island what became, but they probably would have recognized it as about the closest Long Island could offer to a shorefront Shangri-La.

The house the couple built in 1652 was torn down and replaced a few feet away in 1733. Asked about the future of the replacement house, Alice Fiske, widow of the last direct Sylvester descendant, Andrew Fiske, said in 1997, "I don't discuss that, but rest assured it will be left in good hands."

Where to Find More: "History of Shelter Island: 1652-1932"; ; "The Smallest Village: The Story of Dering Harbor, Shelter Island, N.Y., 1874-1974," Shelter Island Public Library and other libraries.

Shelter Island Historical Society
The Prospect House hotel, one of several summer resorts, opened in 1872 and burned down in 1942.

DERING HARBOR

State's Tiniest Village Rose From Hotel's Ashes

Beginnings: The state's tiniest incorporated village — 200 acres — lies on the north side of Shelter Island facing Greenport. It rose phoenix-like in 1916 on the site where the legendary Manhanset House hotel had stood from 1874 to 1910. The sprawling, 300-room resort, one of two on Shelter Island that emerged in the 1870s and changed it from a backwater to a booming resort, was destroyed by fire May 14, 1910. Wealthy "cottagers" who lived around the hotel became alarmed that key services it provided, including fresh water, fuel, street maintenance and sewage disposal, would be lost. They bought the hotel site for about $85,000 and formed the village in 1916.

Ladies First: Ten male voters were needed to pass the incorporation but couldn't be mustered. It was prior to women's suffrage but a loophole allowed women to vote on municipal incorporations. Three did, though they were unable to vote in the election of village officials.

Turning Point: The dominant figures among the wealthy cottagers, Charles Lane Poor and Benjamin Altha, had contending visions. Altha favored opening the site to development. Poor demanded it be kept a quiet summer residential enclave. He became the second mayor, in 1919, and his views prevailed.

Namesake: The village and the picturesque harbor that separates it from Shelter Island Heights were named after Thomas Dering, a prominent Boston merchant who married Mary Sylvester of Shelter Island's founding family on March 9, 1756. Dering became the town's second supervisor and a prominent member of the new nation's Congress, a supporter of the Declaration of Independence and member of the convention that forged New York's first state constitution.

Where to Find More: "The Smallest Village: The Story of Dering Harbor, Shelter Island, N.Y., 1874-1974," by Stewart W. Herman, at the Shelter Island Historical Society.

128

Nassau County Museum Collection, Long Island Studies Institute / Henry Otto Korten

SHELTER ISLAND: A peaceful day along Clinton Avenue around 1900. The Shelter Island Yacht Club, on Chequit Point, appears in the distance.

Nassau County Museum Collection, Long Island Studies Institute

SHELTER ISLAND: The Menatic, a side-wheel steamer ferry, docks in a photo taken from White Hill. The ferry was retired in 1920. A bathing beach with a diving platform is in the foreground.

Town of Smithtown

SMITHTOWN

Smith's Saga, Minus the Bull

BY BILL BLEYER
STAFF WRITER

Richard Smith dominates the history of Smithtown just as the statue of his bull Whisper dominates the western approach to the town named after him.

The legend of "Bull" Smith goes like this: Indians made an agreement with the English settler allowing him to keep all the land he could travel around in one day on his bull. No dope, Smith made his trip on June 21, the longest day of the year, in about 1665.

It's a nice story — if only it were true. In fact, according to historians, the headstrong Smith settled in Southampton about 1643 and befriended the influential Lion Gardiner, only to be banished in 1656 for his "irreverent carriage towards the magistrates." Smith and his family settled in Setauket and obtained from Gardiner the land that would become Smithtown in 1663. The Town of Smithtown was created two years later after Smith confirmed his ownership with a patent from Gov. Richard Nicolls and met the legal requirement that he settle the area with 10 families. "It wasn't hard to do when he and his wife had nine children," according to Louise Hall, director of the Smithtown Historical Society.

Before Smith arrived, about 500 members of the Nesequakes Indians had occupied the area. The first deed recorded was in 1650 — and not by Richard Smith. Speculators from Connecticut signed an agreement with Nasseconseke (Nesconset), sachem of the Nesequakes, to exchange land for trade goods. But they never recorded their deeds, creating the opening for Smith. He spent a dozen years in English and Dutch courts defending his titles against men with competing land claims. It was not until 1677 that the last pieces of land were declared his by the Andros Patent.

During the Revolution, patriotic fervor remained high in the face of British military rule. Wealthy resident Caleb Smith, a fourth-generation descendant of Bull, refused to take an oath of allegiance to King George III and was whipped and shot at by the Redcoats.

The major military action in the town during the war came at Fort Slongo, a British fortification erected near Long Island Sound in what became Fort Salonga. On Oct. 3, 1781, 100 American troops who had crossed from Connecticut in whaleboats captured 20 Redcoats and burned the fort.

Waterways continued to play an important part in the town's development. The Nissequogue River was the site of a series of mills starting before 1680. The river was also a natural home for development of a shipbuilding industry. Among the vessels built in the 19th Century was the 35-foot oyster sloop Nellie A. Ryle, constructed in 1818 by Slope and Scudder and more than a century later was put on display at Mystic Seaport in Connecticut. Some relatively large ships were built

Smithtown Historical Society / A.R. Pardington
A scene in 1911 at Riverside Garage, across Jericho Turnpike from where the bull statue was placed

along the river as well, including the 129-foot brig Tanner, launched in 1855.

Commercial use of the river dried up after the Long Island Rail Road arrived in 1872. Smithtown leaders' interest in a rail link to carry agricultural products to the city led to a plan for the Smithtown-Port Jefferson Railroad, later part of the Long Island Rail Road. The arrival of the railroad coincided with a back-to-nature movement that attracted tourists and sportsmen. The Brooklyn Gun Club was organized in 1872 to purchase Caleb Smith's home and the undeveloped land near the head of the Nissequogue, one of the state's most productive brook trout streams. The club was renamed the Wyandanch Club in 1893 in honor of the Montaukett sachem before becoming the centerpiece of Caleb Smith State Park in 1963.

Fishing wasn't the only pastime to bring attention to Smithtown. Lady Suffolk, a filly foaled in 1833 on a farm on the west side of the Nissequogue, became the most famous horse in America. David Bryant saw racing potential in her and bought her for $112.50. In her first race in 1838, Lady Suffolk won $11. Owner and horse continued racing for 16 years. In 1845, when the horse was 12, she trotted a mile in less than two minutes and 30 seconds, setting a record for trotters. Lady Suffolk, the subject of numerous Currier & Ives lithographs, continued to win races at the age of 20.

A runaway slave from Maryland who spent time in Smithtown also made history. Around 1830 Epenetus Smith II, a fifth-generation descent of Bull, found a young boy named Garnet in New York City. Smith took him home as his ward. Smith sent Garnet to college and he became a Presbyterian minister. The Rev. Hervey Highland Garnet became a celebrated abolitionist in England and then in Washington on the eve of the Civil War. He became a confidant of President Abraham Lincoln and urged him to issue the Emancipation Proclamation in 1863. When Garnet was chosen by the president as the orator for the celebration of the first anniversary of the proclamation in 1864, he became the first black man to address the House of Representatives.

Although blacks were not its main target, the Ku Klux Klan was active in Smithtown in the 1920s. The area's Klan members, who did not hide their identities, focused more on Catholics and Jews. They still burned crosses on the lawns of enemies. The Klan faded out by the mid-1930s.

Before World War II, what Smithtown remained rural. The earliest businesses and the first post office had sprung up near the headwaters of the Nissequogue on the western edge of the current business district. Establishment of the LIRR station pulled commercial development east until it met up with the businesses in the Village of the Branch. The Town of Smithtown's population was estimated at 114,180 by 1998.

Where to Find More: "Smithtown, New York 1660-1929," by Noel J. Gish, at Smithtown Public Library branches.

COMMACK

Vanderbilt Parkway Brought It Up to Speed

Beginnings: Indian inhabitants called the area Winnecomac — Algonquian for "pleasant land." This was later shortened to Comac and pronounced, some historians insist, as Com-mack, not Co-mack. Because the community was split between Huntington and Smithtown and because of conflicting deeds resulting from purchases from different Indian sachems, there were many boundary disputes. They were not resolved until 1675 when Smithtown founder Richard (Bull) Smith was successful in claims made in Dutch and English courts. The resulting dividing line between the two towns also divided the properties of prominent early families with names such as Burr, Wicks, Harned and Whitman, the ancestors of the poet.

Turning Points: Commack's landscape changed dramatically in 1911 with the construction of William K. Vanderbilt II's Long Island Motor Parkway, America's first limited-access highway. Portions still existed as the year 2,000 approached. After World War II, the population grew and was estimated at 36,000 by 1998.

Claims to Fame: Commack was once renowned for raising and training race horses. The Burr family track off Burr Road was one of the nation's most famous trotting racetracks in the 19th Century, and Commack was where the celebrated racehorse Lady Suffolk won an impressive string of victories. In 1918-1919, the aviation section of the U.S. Army Signal Corps ran a training facility named Brindley Field on a 90-acre tract on the east side of Larkfield Road from Jericho Turnpike to Burr Road. At the height of activity, more than 50 planes were based at the field, which also had 16 wooden barracks and five steel hangars.

Famous Natives: Comedian Rosie O'Donnell (Commack High School South Class of 1980) and sportscaster Bob Costas (Class of 1970).

Where to Find More: "Smithtown, New York 1660-1929," by Noel J. Gish, at Smithtown Public Library branches.

FORT SALONGA

While Redcoats Slept It Off, an Attack

Beginnings: In 1695 Sarah Smith, wife of Smithtown founder Richard (Bull) Smith, deeded to her son Daniel 100 acres at Bread and Cheese Hollow, also known as Fresh Pond. There were clay deposits in the area which are believed to have been used by the Indians for making pottery. In 1684, the Long Island Brick Co. was established and for more than 200 years bricks from the area were shipped all over Long Island and to New England. Pirate captain William Kidd's ship, the Adventure Galley, was anchored off Treadwells Neck in the 1690s, according to reports at the time. Some old maps indicate a point marked as Kidd's Money Hole. But rumors that some of Kidd's treasure remains buried on the beach at Fort Salonga have never been substantiated.

The Revolution: The British built Fort Slongo, a minor redoubt on a hilltop near Long Island Sound, as part of their coastal defenses after taking control of the Island in 1776.

Please Turn to Page 133

Nassau County Museum Collection, Long Island Studies Institute

SMITHTOWN: Town Supervisor John N. Brennan speaks at the unveiling of the Richard (Bull) Smith Monument on May 1, 1941.

Smithtown Historical Society

SMITHTOWN: A watercolor by Elwood artist Edward Lange depicts the residence of Thomas R. Smith in 1880, as seen on a color postcard.

The Boulevard, Kings Park, N. Y.

KINGS PARK: The Boulevard, a stately avenue that led to the community's state-run psychiatric center in 1910.

Scholl's Pond, Hauppauge, L. I. N. Y.

HAUPPAUGE: Scholl's Pond, as depicted in a postcard from 1910.

KINGS PARK

A Beacon For Those In Need

BY **BILL BLEYER**
STAFF WRITER

Smithtown Historical Society

A painting by Edward Lange depicts the Society of St. Johnland, an Episcopal priest's institution for the needy.

Kings Park was a quiet farming community known as Indian Head until Episcopal priest William Augustus Muhlenberg came to town in 1869.

Muhlenberg, who had founded St. Luke's Hospital in New York City to help the underprivileged and handicapped, was about to realize his dream of an orphanage and home for the disabled and mentally ill in a rural setting.

After purchasing the 400-acre Smith Farm in northwestern Smithtown and later an adjacent 200 acres, he created the Society of St. Johnland to carry out his plans. The result was a self-sufficient community with a church, cottages, and homes for the disabled and elderly and for boys. Much of the acreage was farmed to supply food, and a typesetting facility was created to help residents generate additional income. This was augmented by gifts from benefactors including Cornelius Vanderbilt and his wife, who provided $20,000 plus $2,000 a year in maintenance for a home for orphaned girls. The community that developed around the complex initially shared the name St. Johnland.

Muhlenberg's complex was just the first of several major institutional and social experiments to find a home in the hamlet. In 1872 — the year the Long Island Rail Road arrived — officials in Brooklyn decided to purchase 870 acres adjoining Muhlenberg's tract. Over local objections, in 1885 they established the Kings County Farm to care for the poor and the mentally ill. By 1892, there were four large buildings and 30 cottages, and there were cafeterias and heating and electric plants and a dairy to make the facility self-supporting.

In 1891, the railroad changed the name of its station from St. Johnland to Kings Park because of the Brooklyn connection. And in 1895 Dr. Oliver Dewing waged a successful campaign to have the Kings County farm converted into a state hospital for the mentally ill — the first such facility on Long Island. Five years later there were 2,697 patients attended by a staff of 454. This gave the hospital a larger population than the rest of the Town of

Smithtown. At various times, nine of 10 residents worked at the hospital. By 1998, all but a few hundred residential clients had been transferred to Pilgrim Psychiatric Center in Brentwood, and the Kings Park complex was up for sale by the state. Kings Park at about 16,220 residents that year.

Other nonprofit groups followed Muhlenberg and the Kings County farm to the area. The Jewish Agricultural and Industrial Society bought two Smith family farms in 1905 to set up Indian Head Farm, a 500-acre tract where immigrant Romanian and Russian Jews would be taught farming skills. Kings Park was selected because of its flourishing Jewish community — it had one of the earliest synagogues on Long Island, built in 1908 by a congregation called Jewish Brotherhood of Kings Park. (The synagogue was destroyed by fire in 1962.) In the end, the immigrants were not interested in farming, so the experiment was abandoned.

In 1906, the Howard Colored Orphan Asylum,

Newsday Archive

A livery stable in the hamlet, about 1900

which had been founded in Brooklyn in 1866, purchased property in Saint James in an attempt to teach farming skills to blacks. In 1910, the group left Saint James and bought Indian Head Farm and changed the name to the Howard Orphanage and Industrial School. It closed in 1918 because of a lack of funds.

"That seems to be the story of Kings Park," Smithtown Historical Society Director Louise Hall said of Kings Park's institutions and social experiments. "The community grew up around the institutions and the employees settled there."

Beginnings: Before white settlers arrived, Indians inhabited the area, probably using it as a wintering site. Remains of a 1,000-year-old Late Woodlands Period Indian long house were discovered in 1994 in the area of Indian Head Road. The first settlers were descendants of Smithtown founder Richard (Bull) Smith. Obediah Smith's home on St. Johnland Road — built around 1700 — is the oldest surviving house in the hamlet. The area remained open land and farms until the 1860s.

Claim to Fame: Besides the state hospital, the unincorporated hamlet became known for 1,266-acre Sunken Meadow State Park.

Brush With Disaster: On May 15, 1917, the "Flats Fire" broke out in the business district on the south side of Main Street in an area known as The Flats. Pushed by a strong breeze, the fire moved north and jumped Broadway. By the time it was extinguished, eight buildings were destroyed at a loss of more than $100,000. The result was the shifting of the business district farther to the west.

Where to Find More: "Smithtown, New York 1660-1929," by Noel J. Gish, at Smithtown Public Library branches.

FT. SALONGA, Continued

The fort was named after the British engineer who designed it and served as the Redcoats' easternmost fortification on the North Shore. In October, 1781, the British were preparing a fleet in New York City to relieve the trapped command of Gen. Charles Cornwallis at Yorktown, Va. Gen. George Washington wanted to keep the British troops in New York and arranged an attack on Fort Slongo as a diversion. The night of Oct. 2, 1781, 100 American raiders set out in whaleboats from Connecticut. Landing at what was later called Crab Meadow Beach, they were in position by early the next morning while most British officers were still celebrating the weekend at a local inn and their soldiers were sleeping off their extra Saturday night rum rations. The Americans achieved complete surprise and chased the British off into the woods. The raiders burned the fort, and

the British fleet never left New York in time to save Cornwallis. All that remains of the original fort is a fenced-in mound of earth in the backyard of a private home on Brookfield Road.

Turning Point: Fort Slongo became Fort Salonga when a post office was established after the turn of the century. "How the name was changed from Fort Slongo to Salonga is known only to the U.S. Postal Service," Noel J. Gish wrote in a history of the Town of Smithtown. By 1998, there were about 9,460 residents in Fort Salonga.

Brush With Fame: In 1911, black educator and author Booker T. Washington bought a house in the community and spent several summers there. White neighbors organized to try to buy him out when rumors spread he wanted to buy additional land to create a school for black students.

Where to Find More: "Smithtown, New York 1660-1929," by Noel J. Gish, at Smithtown Public Library branches.

HAUPPAUGE

An Industrial Park Where Farmland Was

Beginnings: The area around the headwaters of the Nissequogue River was dubbed Hauppauge by the Indians; it means "overflowed land" in English. With the arrival of European settlers, ownership of the area was divided between the Towns of Smithtown and Islip. On the Smithtown side, the land was owned by founding father Richard Smith and then handed down to other family members. But the first settler was Thomas Wheeler, who built a small house at the intersection of Hauppauge (Route 111) and Townline Roads before 1740. The area became known by the Revolution as The Wheelers. That name stuck until 1843, when it reverted to Hauppauge. The earliest development was near Wheeler's farm. He was followed by other settlers with still prominent local names such as

Blydenburgh. These settlers farmed the land and cut trees for cordwood.

Turning Points: In the 20th Century, the early farmsteads began to be developed. In 1907 Joseph Blydenburgh's home at Hauppauge and Townline Roads was purchased by the Brooklyn Industrial School Association, which sent 257 children to spend their summers there. Renamed Locustdale, the facility operated for 47 years. Other farms gave way to county and state office buildings and commercial structures. Though Riverhead remained the Suffolk county seat, Hauppauge, because of its location, became the practical center of Suffolk County government beginning in the 1960s. In the 1990s, it also became the home of the largest industrial park on Long Island and the second largest in the country, with more than 1,350 companies. Hauppauge had an estimated 19,800 residents in 1998.

Where to Find More: "Smithtown, New York 1660-1929," by Noel J. Gish, at the Smithtown Public Library.

NISSEQUOGUE: Village hall in 1975; it once was a schoolhouse.

Newsday Photo / Bob Luckey

LAKE RONKONKOMA

See story on Page 77.

NESCONSET

Creating a Street To Reach Their Land

Beginnings: Nesconset was one of the last parts of Smithtown to be developed because it was heavily wooded. Even by 1900, only three roads — Lake Avenue, Gibbs Pond Road and Browns Road — crossed the area named for the sachem of the Nissequogue Indians. So when Louis and Clementine Vion, French immigrants who had come to New York City in the 1890s, moved to Nesconset in 1900 , they had to fell trees to create Midwood Avenue to reach their property.

Turning Points: It was not until early in the 20th Century that enough roads were built to spur settlement by a significant number of residents. Nesconset didn't get its own post office until 1910, and then the community's population was only 50. The first postmaster was Henry Whittaker, who was also pastor of the Lake Ronkonkoma Episcopal Church and operator of the Nesconset General Store. There was little other commercial activity in the early years. Louis Vion and Charles Nicosia opened a small concrete block factory, and later the Kutil family opened a pearl button factory. By 1920 the commercial construction pace had picked up and a lumberyard opened on Jericho Turnpike. New housing and commercial development boomed when Smithtown Bypass opened in the 1950s. By 1998, Nesconset had about 12,090 residents.

Where to Find More: "Smithtown, New York 1660-1929" by Noel J. Gish, at the Smithtown Public Library.

SAINT JAMES, HEAD OF THE HARBOR, NISSEQUOGUE

Keeping in Touch With the 19th Century

Beginnings: These three communities have shared their histories for more than three centuries. European activity in the area dates to 1677, when Smithtown founder Richard Smith began deeding land on Stony Brook Neck — in what later became Head of the Harbor — to one of his sons, Adam. Adam Smith constructed the first house on the east side of Three Sisters Harbor, which became Stony Brook Harbor. Starting in the 1690s, Richard Smith deeded land to his other children and they established farms; the area would become Nissequogue.

Turning Points: There were only a few homes in the area by the 1850s. They were centered around the intersection of North Country and Moriches Roads. In 1856 the area around the intersection developed its own identity as Saint James. This occurred because Episcopalians, who had been worshiping in Setauket or Islip, decided they needed their own church closer to home. The U.S. Postal Service established a post office and named it Saint James after the church that had been completed in 1854. The new hamlet experienced a development boom through 1900, giving the area south of North Country Road the nickname Boomertown. Saint James grew even faster after the Long Island Rail Road arrived in 1872, bringing tourists to occupy newly built hotels. Nissequogue and Head of the Harbor residents were appalled by the uncontrolled sprawl and sought to distance and protect themselves from it. This was accomplished when Nissequogue incorporated as a village in 1926, followed two years later by Head of the Harbor. The new villages passed zoning regulations to maintain their historical appearance.

Claims to Fame: The most prominent resident of the area was architect Stanford White, who with his wife, Bessie Smith, purchased the Carman Farm in Head of the Harbor in 1884. They remodeled it and renamed it Box Hill. White was buried in the Saint James Episcopal Church cemetery. The Saint James-Head of the Harbor area established a large historic district that included the Saint James Long Island Rail Road Station, Saint James General Store and Deepwells, an 1845 Victorian estate that in about 1900 was the home of state Supreme Court justice and later New York City mayor William Gaynor. Early in the 1900s, prominent theatrical actor Willie Collier built two homes in Saint James, and an actors colony evolved, attracting John, Lionel and Ethel Barrymore.

Noble Experiment: In 1906 the Howard Colored Orphan Asylum, which had been founded in Brooklyn in 1866, purchased property in Saint James in an attempt to teach farming skills to blacks. In 1910 the group shifted its activities to Kings Park.

The Beast: Easily its most bizarre episode was recorded in 1918. Residents spent a good part of the summer hunting or trying to avoid "The Wild Ape." Witnesses reported encounters with a large beast that threw stones with great accuracy and killed stray dogs and attacked humans. Finally, William Clark shot and killed the creature in the Long Beach area of Nissequogue. It weighed 90 pounds and was believed to have been a chimpanzee or an orangutan that likely escaped from a ship docked in Port Jefferson. Clark was paid $16.90 by the town as a bounty.

Where to Find More: "Smithtown, New York 1660-1929" by Noel J. Gish, at the Smithtown Public Library branches.

SAN REMO

Italian-Americans' Place in the Sun

Beginnings: The west side of the Nissequogue River was owned by the family of Smithtown founder Richard Smith beginning in the 17th Century. In 1793, three entrepreneurs built a dock near the mouth of the river on land owned by Aaron Smith. Schooners carrying cordwood left what became known as Aaron's Landing for New York and New England. By 1900 the Long Island Rail Road had killed off most of the river commerce, and the dock and neighboring beach evolved into recreational uses. In 1918, state officials banned shellfishing in the river because of pollution from the psychiatric hospital in Kings Park, a decision that wiped out the last of the commercial uses of the river.

Turning Points: In 1922, the publisher of the Italian-language newspaper Il Progresso purchased 194 acres along the west bank of the Nissequogue. To boost circulation, the paper offered 20-by-100-foot plots for $50 to anyone taking a subscription. It named the resulting community San Remo after a town on the Italian Riviera. Italian-Americans from New York built cottages and even tent dwellings on their tiny lots to escape the summer heat in the city, and the newspaper publishers built a clubhouse for residents as a center of community life.

Where to Find More: "Smithtown, New York 1660-1929," by Noel J. Gish, at the Smithtown Public Library.

VILLAGE OF THE BRANCH

Tavern Owner Listed What the British Took

Beginnings: An early Smithtown community developed where the northeast branch of the Nissequogue River crossed Hauppauge Road (Route 111). The community was called simply The Branch. It was settled around 1700 by Joseph Blydenburgh, who in 1692 married Deborah Smith, a granddaughter of Smithtown founder Richard Smith. About that time, a tavern was built, probably by Amos Dickinson; later it was called the Epenetus smith Tavern. "By 1750 there were so many houses going up that they decided to move the Presbyterian church from Nissequogue to what was now becoming the center of the town," said Louise Hall, director of the Smithtown Historical Society.

Turning Point: The arrival of the railroad in 1872 spurred commercial development on Main Street, filling in the gap between The Branch and the area known as Head of the River to form downtown Smithtown. As town leaders debated the need for municipal services after World War I, residents of The Branch voted to form an incorporated village in 1927 to ensure control of land use and services. The village was less than a mile square and had only 162 residents. 1998's population was about 1,600.

Claims to Fame: President George Washington stopped at the widow Blydenburgh's boarding house during his tour of Long Island in 1790. Earlier, during the British occupation of Smithtown, the widow was reported to have told Redcoats seeking to seize provisions that she was "only a poor widow." She directed them to Epenetus Smith's tavern. He kept a list of everything they took, and that document still existed in the 20th Century. Villagers preserved many homes from the colonial era. In the 1960s, village officials created a historic district listed on the National Register of Historic Places. It included important buildings such as the Epenetus Smith Tavern and the old library.

Where to Learn More: "Smithtown, New York 1660-1929," by Noel J. Gish, at the Smithtown Public Library branches.

SAINT JAMES: The Everett Smith General Store, built in 1856 and seen here in earlier times, later operated as the Saint James General Store, the oldest continuously run shop of its kind in the country.

Smithtown Historical Society

Smithtown Historical Society

SAINT JAMES: A postcard illustrates the railroad station. It was built in a Victorian style in 1872-73. Later it was listed on the National Register of Historic Places.

Smithtown Historical Society

VILLAGE OF THE BRANCH: Main Street (Route 25A) in the village in an undated photograph. The village incorporated in 1927.

BRIDGEHAMPTON: A July 20, 1877, newspaper shows the wreck of the ship Circassian and "the escape of the four sole survivors." The square-rigger sailing from England to New York City ran aground on Dec. 11, 1876. Passengers and crew of 47 were rescued, but a salvage company put 20 crew members and 12 local workers, including 10 Shinnecock Indians, back aboard to try to save the ship. Another storm hit Dec. 29, breaking up the ship and killing 28, including all the Shinnecocks.

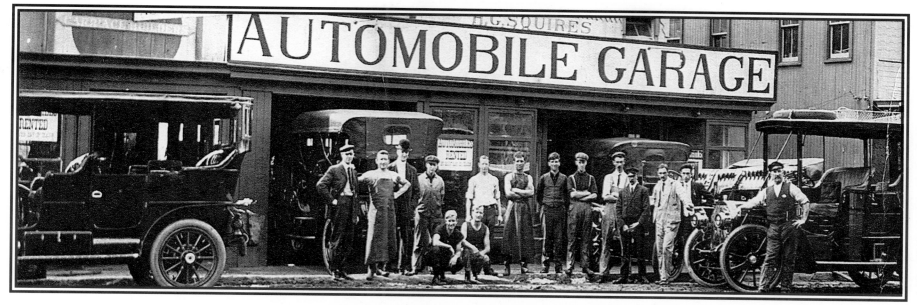

SOUTHAMPTON: In the early 1900s, chauffeurs often gathered to talk shop at the H.G. Squires carriage and auto garage. The road was still dirt, but the cars were top of the line.

Collection of Robert Keene

Town of Southampton

Southampton was arguably the first English settlement in what would become New York State — with the exception of Gardiners Island — though the "first town" distinction also is claimed by Southold.

Southampton began with a small group of families from Lynn, Mass., who landed in June, 1640, at Conscience Point in what later became North Sea. Southold says its pioneers came a little earlier that year, but concrete proof eluded historians. Although many think the town was named for the English port of Southampton, it was actually named for the earl of Southampton, a benefactor of American settlements. Gardiners Island, in East Hampton Town, was settled in 1639.

The first boatload of Southampton settlers, said to be eight men, a woman and a boy, landed at North Sea on Little Peconic Bay. With help of friendly Indians, the Puritan band migrated about five miles south near the ocean to establish crude housing; the area would become Southampton Village.

They soon built a meetinghouse, used for church services, town meetings, court matters and other purposes. Historians think the building was built in about 1641, on the small hill where Southampton Hospital was built.

The town's trailblazers learned from the Indians how to plant corn and fertilize it with fish, how to grow crops, dig clams, trap game and make "samp," a nourishing porridge. The original land acquisition from the Indians covered the eastern portion of the town; the area west of Shinnecock Canal was acquired in 1666. The town was first patented in 1676. It wasn't recognized as a town until after the Revolution, on March 7, 1788, but had kept records since its founding days.

In those early times, residents in the town meetings made laws, elected officials, levied taxes, tried cases — and built a jail as well as the church. Robert Keene, town historian from 1979 through 1998, said the population included 40 families by late 1640, and

had grown to 738 whites, 80 blacks, 152 Indians "and two merchants" by 1689. But Southampton grew slowly during the next two centuries. Farming and fishing predominated. After 1850, the town saw rapid change. Well-to-do New York City people came to vacation. The advent of the railroad in the 1870s accelerated the process, and by 1890 the first tourist boom had begun.

BRIDGEHAMPTON, SAGAPONACK
Woodrow Wilson Led Parade of Notables

Beginnings: Bridgehampton records its start in 1656 when Josiah Stanborough, an original settler of Southampton, built a house in Sagg, later known as Sagaponack. Soon after the first settlers moved in, a bridge was erected over Sagg Pond, joining Sagg and Mecox to its west. They named the lane that crossed the small causeway Bridge Street, which likely inspired the hamlet's future name: Bridge Hampton (later bridged itself to form one word). Most of the founding families were in some way connected to the whaling industry, the East End's most profitable pursuit in colonial times. Once Sag Harbor was settled about 1730, whaling fell off. But the soil in Bridgehampton was rich enough for farming to take over.

The Revolution: Most Bridgehampton families rallied to the Patriot cause. Capt. John Hulbert of Bridgehampton raised a company of volunteer militia in 1775 and marched his men to Montauk to prevent a foray by a British fleet. Later the company was ordered to upstate Ticonderoga to take charge of British prisoners. The community suffered under the British occupation starting in 1776, and many fled to Connecticut.

Turning Point: Bridgehampton was known as the summer place to be and be seen as early as the late 1800s. Woodrow Wilson was there in 1898, vacationing with his family at the old Topping boarding house on Main Street in Sagaponack. In 1916, Mary Pickford filmed a movie, "Huldah of Holland," in a mock Dutch village with the Hayground windmill used as a backdrop. In the 1990s, TV newsman Peter Jennings and other celebrities had homes in Bridge-

hampton. By 1998, Bridgehampton had about 2,285 residents; Sagaponack had about 400.

Hometown Hero: He once described himself as "just a potato farmer from Long Island who had some ability." But to baseball fans, Bridgehampton's Carl Yastrzemski was much more than that. With 452 career home runs for the Boston Red Sox before his retirement in 1983, he was inducted into baseball's Hall of Fame in 1989.

Where to Find More: "Bridgehampton's Three Hundred Years," edited by Paul H. Curtis, at the Riverhead Free Library.

EASTPORT
Ducks Fit the Bill To Pay the Bills

Beginnings: Hard to imagine — it's barely 1½ square miles — but Eastport started out as two communities, Seatuck and Waterville. The two hamlets joined in the 1850s and hoped to be christened Seatuck, but the U.S. Post Office said no. Seatuck was too close to Setauket. The runner-up was Eastport. Gristmills were built by local creeks, one as early as the 1730s, and farming was the mainstay of the community.

The Ducks: Eastport was the unofficial capital of Long Island duck farming. A few years after the Pekin duck was introduced to the United States from China in 1873 (not to be confused with *Peking* duck, an American dish developed in the 1950s), the first commercial farms sprouted along the creeks leading to Seatuck Cove and Moriches Bay. By 1900, 29 farms dotted the Eastport landscape, whittled to 15 by the late 1940s when Long Island produced 6.5 million of the ducks going to market. Penny postcards and early photographs depict men "picking" the ducks, and women plucking the birds before they were shipped. Mervin Tillinghast, who worked summers on a duck farm and freezing plant as a teenager, recalled: "We packed them in the freezer, six to a box. Waited 24 hours and took them out. Then they were packaged for Swanson and other companies. I made sure I wore a lot of extra clothing. It was about 20 degrees below zero in those freezers." Though there were other farms in East Moriches and Speonk, many farmers brought their ducks to Eastport for processing.

Turning Point: Pollution pressures of the late 1960s and early '70s put most of the duck farms

out of business. The farmers were forced to build pollution pits to divert the duck waste from waterways. In the late 1990s, Chet Massey, whose family has operated a duck farm in Eastport since 1944, was the only duck farmer left. By then, antiques reigned where ducks once roamed. In 1997, 15 antique shops lined Eastport's main street, drawing crowds of weekend shoppers and tourists headed to the Hamptons. By 1998, Eastport had about 1,515 residents.

Where to Find More: "History of Eastport, L.I., N.Y., 1775-1975," by LeRoy Wilcox, available at the Mastic-Moriches-Shirley Library.

FLANDERS
Where the Big Duck Rules the Roost

Beginnings: This heavily wooded hamlet in northwest Southampton Town was virtually uninhabited by whites in colonial times. Among its early settlers were Dutch who settled in the area about the end of the 18th Century. They gave the location its name because it reminded them of Flanders, a region of Holland. In the 1800s, families from New York City and western Long Island summered here. The community also produced cordwood, and loggers used it as a rest stop on their way to the South Fork.

Turning Point: Before World War II, the few residents were mostly blue-collar people who had more in common with adjoining Riverhead than with most of their resort town. In the 1950s and 1960s, small suburban ranch-style homes on small lots popped up along Flanders Road (Route 24). Many were summer places, but later became year-round homes. In the 1980s and '90s, Flanders saw the addition of many costlier homes, especially along Pleasure Drive in the thick pine barrens between Route 24 and Sunrise Highway. By 1998, there were about 3,360 Flanders residents.

Claim to Fame: In 1988, Route 24 in Flanders became the home of the famous Big Duck, a 20-foot-high concrete version of the white Pekin duck and a symbol of Long Island, though the duck industry faded after World War II. Donated to Suffolk County in 1987, it was placed on the National Register of Historic Places. It was built in 1931 and originally was a store on West Main Street, Riverhead.

Where to Find More: Riverhead Free Library.

Collection of Wayne Duprez

The wooden Bays movie theater was a popular spot for entertainment in the hamlet of Hampton Bays when this photo of Montauk Highway was taken around 1930.

Hampton Bays: Good Ground

The hamlet of Good Ground had only recently changed its name to Hampton Bays to capitalize on the growing popularity of the Hamptons as a summer resort when this photo of Montauk Highway, looking east, was taken by photographer Charles Duprez sometime about 1930.

At the time, movies at the Bays theater cost only 35 cents — 25 cents at matinees.

"It was an old wooden theater, everything creaked," recalled Sandy Sullivan, president of the Hampton Bays Historical Society, who watched films at the theater as a youngster before it was torn down in the early 1950s. The site became a vacant lot; a new multiscreen theater opened in the late 1990s.

Just behind the theater marquee is the sign for Schultz's meat store, which became an antique shop. And across the street was the brick building housing the Hampton Bays National Bank, which was replaced by a newer building housing a branch of the Bank of New York.

Newsday Photo / Bill Davis, 1999

The movie theater, the brick bank and the hanging street lamps were gone, but the Hampton Bays streetscape otherwise seemed to change little.

HAMPTON BAYS

Giving Good Ground For Hamptons Cachet

Beginnings: In the 1990s, some oldtimers still referred to Hampton Bays as Good Ground, as it was called until 1922. Among the first buildings in the area was the Canoe Place Inn, built as a home in the early 1700s and named for the spot where the Indians used to leave their canoes when fishing or hunting.

The Revolution: Before the British took Long Island, colonists built a fort on the high ground along what would become the west bank of the Shinnecock Canal. From there, they had a good view of approaches from the Peconic and Shinnecock Bays. They called it Fort Lookout. After the Battle of Long Island in 1776, the British took control of the strategic outpost and garrisoned 200 troops there.

Turning Point: The rumblings began in the late 19th Century. A faction of the community just didn't think Good Ground a good enough name. The battle culminated in 1922 when the revisionists finally won out over tradition and changed the name to Hampton Bays. Apparently, they hoped to capitalize on the popularity and emerging cachet of the Hamptons in order to beef up summer tourism. 1998's population was listed at 8,271 by the Long Island Power Authority.

Claim to Fame: By about 1900, the Canoe Place Inn had graduated from modest coach inn to luxury getaway for celebrities, politicians and wealthy industrialists. Coined "The Tammany Hall of the East," it was particularly popular among such New York pols as New York Gov. Alfred E. Smith, who spent 30 summers fishing along the Shinnecock Canal. Other notables included Cary Grant, Helen Hayes and boxing champ John L. Sullivan, who trained there.

Kooky Landmark: For nearly 70 years, a larger-than-life wooden statue of Hercules — once the figurehead of the USS Ohio — stood across the road from the Canoe Place Inn, drawing attention from visitors and residents alike and sparking the piece of folklore that held that girls who kissed the statue's brow would be married within the year. Eventually the property — and Hercules — were sold. Later, Hercules watched over Stony Brook from a small pavilion near the harbor.

Where to Find More: "Good Ground Remembered," by Helen M. Wetterau, available at Riverhead Free Library.

NORTH HAVEN

From Hog Farmers To Actors' Colony

Beginnings: The earliest recorded reference to Hog Neck, as the area was first called by white settlers, was in 1641 when it shows up in Southampton town records. That reference records an order to residents on the east side of Hog Neck to fence in their property to guard against the danger of "cattle and hogs astray." The peninsula was inhabited by Manhasset Indians for hundreds of years before whites arrived. On Oct. 3, 1665, the Indians sold Hog Neck to Southampton officials known as freeholders, "forever reserving liberty of hunting and fishing and fowling." By 1680 Hog Neck had been laid out into 47 lots, which were distributed by a lottery. The next year roads were laid out and permanent English settlement began. In earlier years, Hog Neck had been used primarily as pasture. While the first two and a half centuries of habitation by whites was marked mostly by agricultural uses, there also were several industries, including fishing and production of salt through evaporation, a process that continued to the Civil War.

Turning Point: Hog Neck was renamed North Haven in 1842 because its residents thought

Please Turn the Page

SAG HARBOR

A Port Bigger Than New York

BY BILL BLEYER
STAFF WRITER

In the 1830s and 1840s, Sag Harbor was a cosmopolitan boomtown. The boom was the result of a single industry: whaling.

Sag Harbor was Long Island's whaling capital, with more than 60 whaleships and more than 800 men working on them or in related industries. The first whaleships sailed from the harbor in 1760 on short cruises along the coast, but it wasn't until 1817 that local whaleships embarked on extended cruises.

The industry's best year was 1847, when 32 ships returned with more than 67,000 barrels of whale oil. The business then declined rapidly as ships and crews were lured by the 1849 California gold rush and oil was discovered in Pennsylvania. The last Sag Harbor whaler was the Myra, which sailed in 1871 and wrecked three years later.

Before the whalers or any other whites, Algonquian Indians lived in the area they called *Weg-wag-onuch*, meaning "the land or place at the end of the hill." White settlers arrived in the late 1600s and called the area Great Meadows because much of it was tidal marsh. Residents of Sagaponack used the harbor, which became known as Sagaponack Harbor or the Harbor of Sagg. It was shortened to Sag Harbor by 1707, the first time the name is found in Southampton town records. After the marshy land was filled in, about 1730, the first small dwellings were erected by fishermen. Mills were erected and a wharf was constructed in 1761. It was extended twice by 1821 to a length of 1,000 feet. The first bridge to North Haven was built in 1799 by James Mitchell so he could construct a mill there.

During the Revolutionary War, there were 32 homes; 14 Patriot families fled to avoid plunder by the Redcoats based in a fort on Meeting House Hill. Meanwhile, the Royal Navy blockaded the port. The biggest excitement during the war came on May 23, 1777, when American Lt. Col. Return Jonathan Meigs and 130 men rowed from Connecticut in whaleboats and raided the village, killing six British soldiers and capturing 53 others. They also set fire to 12 British vessels and captured 90 enemy sailors. Capt. David Hand became a local hero for having been captured and escaping five times during the war.

Almost from the time the village was settled, ships carried passengers and freight to and from New York, Connecticut and other destinations. In 1772, a stage wagon began running between Sag Harbor and Brooklyn. After the war — when Sag Harbor was the home of more oceangoing vessels than New York City — Congress declared the village a "port of entry" and set up a customs house. Sag Harbor was also home to Long Island's first newspaper, Frothingham's Long Island Herald, founded in 1791 and published for seven years.

During the War of 1812, a fort with more than 3,000 soldiers was established on Turkey Hill, overlooking the harbor. The British attacked on July 11, 1813; the Americans returned fire and the British retreated, leaving behind many weapons. But the war devastated the village's commercial fleet. Of the more than 20 coastal trading vessels, only three or four remained useful by 1814. After hostilities ended, it took two years for the harbor to return to its prewar level of activity.

While Sag Harbor tried to recover from the war, a fire — the first of four devastating blazes to hit the village — broke out in 1817, destroying 20 houses and stores. In response, the village in 1819 formed the Otter Hose Co., the state's first volunteer fire company.

Revival proceeded slowly, but in 1827 there was another milestone: Nathan Tinker offered the first milk delivery on Long Island. Whaling was not the only industry in Sag Harbor. There were foundries and factories making oilcloth, cigars, brooms, clocks, stockings, flour and other products. A steam cotton mill built in 1850 took up an entire block and employed 175 operators, making it the village's largest employer. By 1880 the cotton mill had failed and Joseph Fahys was persuaded to relocate his watchcase factory from New Jersey. Production began in 1882 with a work force of 350. In 1891 the E.W. Bliss Co. began to conduct experiments with naval torpedoes in Noyack Bay. The company received a $2 million order from the government during World War I and tested and manufactured torpedoes for another 30 years.

John Jermain Memorial Library
The village in 1895, when the whaling era had gone and tourist-laden steamboats were docking

One of Sag Harbor's most famous buildings, the First Presbyterian, or Old Whaler's, Church was erected in 1843-1844. The steeple was destroyed by the hurricane of 1938.

Sag Harbor's biggest benefactor was Margaret Olivia Slocum Sage. In the 19th Century she purchased and restored the Benjamin Huntting Estate as her summer cottage; it later became the Sag Harbor Whaling Museum. She also financed construction of Pierson High School, John Jermain Memorial Library and Mashashimuet Park.

In the 1870s, steamboats began docking in the village, helping to turn the East End into a resort. (A Long Island Rail Road spur was extended to the village in 1870, though it was abandoned in 1939.) By 1998, Sag Harbor had about 2,170 residents.

Brushes With Fame: The village also has a history of attracting writers. James Fenimore Cooper spent more than three years in Sag Harbor as part owner of the whaleship Union before publishing his first successful novel, "The Spy," in 1821. John Steinbeck left from the village for his "Travels With Charley," and more recently Lanford Wilson and E.L. Doctorow were residents.

Where to Find More: "Sag Harbor — An American Beauty," by Dorothy Ingersoll Zaykowski, at the Jermain Library.

SHINNECOCK RESERVATION
A Painful Story of an Enduring People

BY TOM MORRIS
STAFF WRITER

Though what became Southampton was inhabited by Shinnecocks at the time of the first white settlement in the mid-17th Century, the Indians lost ground steadily after that. By 1859, they were relegated to approximately 800 acres at the Shinnecock Indian Reservation.

There were between 400 and 500 Shinnecocks when English settlers arrived in Southampton in 1640, but the figures are general because Algonquians were nomadic and there was no census then, according to John A. Strong, a history professor at the Southampton Campus of Long Island University. The Shinnecocks sold some of their land around modern Southampton Village to pioneers, but disputes over use and ownership were common despite the general peace between the two cultures.

In 1703, the Indians won exclusive control of about 3,600 acres between Southampton Village and Shinnecock Canal — the Shinnecock Hills area — in a lease that was supposed to run "for one thousand years." Following decades of conflict and confrontation, Southampton Town persuaded the community in 1792 to establish trustees to oversee the sale of planting and grazing leases to outsiders. Gradual encroachment, petty harassment and legal action by

white residents undermined Shinnecock opposition to altering the lease.

For example, whites allowed their cattle and sheep to graze unattended in the hills, and they often destroyed Indian crops. In a pivotal case in 1853, Strong said, two desperate Shinnecock men, Luther and James Bunn, impounded a herd of goats owned by a wealthy white man named Austin Rose. The two Indians were sued and forced to pay damages when the court ruled that they had been negligent in maintaining their fences.

The key turning point came in 1859. With land-acquisition pressure mounting because of plans to extend the Long Island Rail Road through Shinnecock Hills, town and business interests cut a deal in which the Indians forsook their leased domain and received full title to the reservation, located south of Montauk Highway just west of Southampton Village.

Many Shinnecocks bitterly opposed the deal that confined them to the reservation — a situation being repeated with Indians in other parts of the country at the time — and protested to the state. But the state legislature approved it. Congress at the time had no jurisdiction. The Shinnecock-owned reservation, with about 375 residents in 1998, was recognized by the state and federal governments, which provided some services.

Vigilance was still required even in 1952: That year, a real estate firm began building houses on the north edge of the reservation in a title flap, but the courts upheld tribal ownership.

Women were not permitted to take part in Shinnecock council meetings until 1993. Most of the community's members were Presbyterians — the result of work by missionaries in the 18th Century.

One of the most revered by Shinnecocks was the Rev. Paul Cuffee (1757-1812), a preacher whose gravestone is close to Montauk Highway near the canal.

After World War II the community held an annual powwow on the Labor Day weekend that in the 1990s drew about 30,000 visitors. **Where to Find More:** "The Shinnecock Indians: A Culture History," edited by Gaynell Stone, 1983; Shinnecock history sketch, by Harriet Crippen Brown Gumbs, Encyclopedia of North American Indians, 1990, and "We Are Still Here," by John A. Strong.

Nassau County Museum Collection, Long Island Studies Institute Photo / Henry Otto Korten
Shinnecocks gather on a formal occasion in 1884.

NORTH HAVEN, Continued

the old name sounded derogatory. By the end of the 19th Century, North Haven had become a vacation destination, and by 1900, many actors and actresses had built homes on the former Lewis Corwin farm, which eventually became known as Actors' Colony. Among those residents was the owner of the Algonquin Hotel in New York, Frank Case, who regularly entertained prominent actors such as John Drew, Ethel Barrymore, Douglas Fairbanks Jr. and Mary Pickford. Composer Irving Berlin was also a summer resident. In the 1990s, celebrity residents included singer Jimmy Buffett and "60 Minutes" correspondent Steve Kroft. 1998's population was listed at 765.
Where to Find More: North Haven Village historian Joseph Zaykowski Jr.

NORTH SEA
First Setting Foot In Southampton Town

Beginnings: This rustic little hamlet on Little Peconic Bay is the birthplace of Southampton Town, which claims to be the state's first English colony. In June, 1640, the first 10 town founders, who came from Lynn, Mass., landed at or close to what was from that time known as Conscience Point. ("For conscience sake, we are on dry land," the one woman among the founders, Eleanor Howell, was reputed to have said upon landing.) They quickly

migrated south about six miles to a spot near the ocean to make the town's first settlement. But by 1650, according to town records, 321 acres of were given to six families. They first called it Feversham, and later Northampton, after places in England, before it became North Sea.
Why Here: Some histories say that a year before the founders arrived, Gov. John Winthrop of Massachusetts scouted the Long Island north shore by ship for likely settlement spots and liked North Sea because it had a small natural harbor surrounded by accessible meadows and woods. And it didn't hurt that a nearby encampment of Shinnecock Indians was said to be friendly.
Landmarks: Conscience Point National Wildlife Refuge dominates the harbor's west side. A 20-ton boulder at the point itself bears a plaque commemorating the 1640 landing. A one-room schoolhouse, later enlarged, eventually served as the home of the North Sea Community Association, formed in 1931, and the nearby fire department. By 1998, North Sea had an estimated 2,585 residents.
Where to Find More: Southampton Public Library, Southampton, and Southampton Historical Museum, Southampton.

NOYACK
'The Most Picturesque' Wildlife Refuge

Beginnings: Noyack's name is of Indian origin, meaning "a point or corner of land," which

referred to the hairpin-shaped peninsula that juts from the shore. The hamlet was a settlement of the small Noyack and Weecatuck tribes before the English arrived. After colonization, the odd-shaped neck in early records was called Farrington's Point or Jessup Neck, after early settler-owners in the mid-1600s. It was deeded to John Jessup in 1679. But the area around it continued to be called Noyack after the small Indian tribe that lived there.
What They Did: From the start, Noyack was a source of lumber, fish for food and fertilizer, hay, corn and grain, the location of agricultural mills that used tidal water power, and for the grazing of sheep and cattle. Extensive shell beds and mounds were found there through the decades, along with many stone implements.
What They Do: As the year 2000 approached, Noyack (1998 population, about 2,220) had no post office, no fire department, no library, no real Main Street, just a handful of small businesses. Rental of summer houses was a long-standing practice, but the 1980s and '90s brought many expensive residences, mainly south of Noyack Road, parallel to the shore of Noyack Bay. "Noyack has not lost its small-town atmosphere, but I fear it's going fast," John Bechtel, treasurer of the 500-member Noyack Civic Council, said in 1997.
Attractions: In 1954, the 187-acre Morton National Wildlife refuge was donated by Elizabeth Morton, a descendant of the Jessup family. The U.S. Fish and Wildlife Service called its holdings in Noyack "the most picturesque of the Long Island refuges," with

steep, eroding bluffs nearly 50 feet high, numerous endangered and threatened bird species, forest with numerous species of small animals, kettle holes, tidal flats, fresh- and salt-water marsh and old fields.
Where to Find More: "'Sketches From Local History," 1926, by William D. Halsey, Southampton Public Library, and U.S. Fish and Wildlife Service, Long Island National Wildlife Complex, Shirley, N.Y., 11967.

QUOGUE, EAST QUOGUE
Edison's Dream Was a Washout

Beginnings: Even before John Ogden purchased lands in the Quogue area from the Indian sachem Wyandanch in 1659, settlers from Southampton traveled there to harvest hay from its broad meadows. They loaded the hay onto barges or rafts and poled them back to their farms in Southampton. By the 1790 census, there were only 12 families said to be living in Quogue, a shortened version of Quaquanantuck, an Indian word denoting a cove or estuary.
Turning Point: Once railroad service reached Riverhead in 1844, summer boarders began pouring into oceanside communities such as Quogue. Locals referred to it as the "boarding house era," when wealthy New Yorkers came east once the weather warmed and rented rooms at hotels and rooming houses. That era lasted well into the early 1900s and also

Please Turn to Page 143

Suffolk County Historical Society

SOUTHAMPTON: The ladies of the Shinnecock Hills Golf Club, in an undated photograph, pose in front of the nation's first golf clubhouse. It was designed by architect Stanford White in 1892.

Nassau County Museum Collection, Long Island Studies Institute

QUOGUE: A three-horse stage makes its way into the village in 1910. Summer boarders created a building boom that helped the community grow in about 1910.

Collection of Wayne Duprez

SOUTHAMPTON: St. Andrews Church, constructed in 1880, dominated the landscape near Lake Agawam.

Collection of Wayne Duprez

SOUTHAMPTON: The Southampton Beach Club was a favorite destination for high society. This photo was taken in about 1930.

QUOGUE, Continued

ushered in a boom of sorts when the regular summer boarders began building homes of their own. 1998's population was about 940.

Black Gold: In the late 1800s, the ocean beaches in Quogue gleamed a shiny black. The sand was rich with iron ore deposits, which drew the attention of Thomas Alva Edison. He planned to try to extract the valuable ore from the dunes, but his efforts were dashed by happenstance. Here is Edison's account of what happened: "Some years ago I heard one day that down in Quogue, Long Island, there were immense deposits of black magnetic sand . . . My first thought was that it would be a very easy matter to concentrate this, and I found I could sell the stuff at a good price. I put up a small plant, but just as I got it started a tremendous storm came up, and every bit of that black sand went out to sea. During the twenty-eight years that have intervened, it has never come back."

Roots in the Community: A very large oak tree, partly hollow, stood for decades along Old Country Road in East Quogue and was a virtual post office for Quogue's early settlers. They called it the "old box tree" and placed their mail in the tree's hollow center to be picked up and exchanged by post riders. In 1894, the tree was damaged by fire and removed to the Quogue Post Office. Later that portion of the tree was put on display at the Old Schoolhouse Museum on Quogue Street.

Where to Find More: "Notes on Quogue, 1659-1959," by Richard Post; "Quogue as We Remember It," compiled by the Quogue Historical Society; "East Quogue Remembered," by Anita T.S. Appel; all available in the Riverhead Free Library.

REMSENBURG, SPEONK

An Enchanting Name Or a Frog's Call?

Beginnings: Before white men arrived, they sent their cows. As early as 1712, the meadows along the South Shore in what was then Speonk were leased to cattle owners from Southampton. Eventually, cattlemen found it easier to build small houses near the meadows to tend herds. Most early residents came from Southampton and Bridgehampton in the 1740s, built farms and cleared the forests. In the 1880s, duck farms thrived in Speonk, but few lasted past 1900.

Turning Point: Supposedly inspired by Indian words meaning "a high place," the name Speonk enchanted some residents and disgusted others. A Long Island Rail Road catalog in 1897 listed Speonk, calling it a "place that certainly sounds like the call of a frog." So it follows that a faction of the community in 1895 jumped at the chance to change the name to Remsenburg, in recognition of Charles Remsen, a prominent resident who donated a new Presbyterian church. The dispute got nasty when Remsenburgers removed the Speonk sign at the station and replaced it with Remsenburg. The Speonk sign was restored and the hard feelings eased with time. By 1998, the Remsenburg-Speonk population was about 1,965.

Brush With Fame: British-born humorist P. G. Wodehouse wrote many of the escapades of Bertie Wooster and his man, Jeeves, from a home on Basket Neck Lane in Remsenburg. Other local celebs included songwriter Frank Loesser, who contributed to Broadway hits such as "Guys and Dolls"; playwright Guy Bolton, who collaborated with Wodehouse on "Anything Goes," and Dave Garroway, the first host of NBC's "Today" show. The hamlets also attracted prominent visitors. One snapshot caught Alfred Hitchcock, still looking rather sinister, his wife and Mrs. Guy Bolton posing in front of a South Country Road home in the 1940s.

Where to Find More: "A History of Remsenburg," by Charles J. McDermott, at the Westhampton Free Library.

SOUTHAMPTON VILLAGE
Glamor Amid the Dunes

BY TOM MORRIS
STAFF WRITER

Within a few days of their epic landing on the north shore of Southampton on June 12, 1640, a small band of pioneers moved several miles south to the ocean and began carving out a village from the meager beginnings of a few makeshift dwellings.

Though historians have never been able to resolve the ancient squabble over whether Southampton or Southold was the state's first English settlement, the details of the Southampton landing have survived the centuries. The first arrivals at North Sea on Little Peconic Bay consisted of eight men, including their leader, Edward Howell, and his wife, Eleanor, and their 8-year-old son, Arthur. They were the first of 20 families from Lynn, Mass., who agreed to settle on then-desolate Long Island, and by that fall 40 families had arrived.

They found the Shinnecocks friendly, and it was the hospitable natives, according to local historians, who recommended the initial settlement spot the newcomers selected close to the ocean along what became Old Town Pond. The first lodgings were huts or holes in the ground about 7 feet deep with bark and sod ceilings, bark and timber walls and log-plank floors.

Southampton's settlers, almost all in their 20s, promptly built a church (First Presbyterian) and meeting hall in 1640-41 on the small hill where Southampton Hospital was built. But by 1648 the Puritan pioneers completed their move of the town center about a mile west to what became South Main Street — the heart of which evolved into one of America's premier summer resort villages.

The evolution was concentrated in the 20th Century. "From the settlement of Southampton in 1640 until 1850, or 210 years, Southampton hardly changed at all," said Robert Keene, town historian from 1979 until his death in 1998. They were two centuries of farming, fishing and whaling, tolerating the British occupation of Long Island during the Revolution, then quietly expanding with the new state and nation. The village oozes history. The earliest stone in the Old Southampton Burial Ground on Little Plains Road dates to 1649, and a newer rose marble monument marks the resting place of Edward Howell (1584-1655), who led the founders in 1640.

According to the Society for the Preservation of Long Island Antiquities, "Southampton's claim to fame" was the handsome white house on Windmill Lane occupied in the 1800s by whaling Capt. Mercator Cooper. His amazing voyage to Japan in 1845, eight years before Commodore Matthew Perry arrived there, earned him an honored place among explorers of the two nations. Another of the village's most honored citizens was Pyrrhus Concer, who was born the son of a slave in Southampton on March 17, 1814. Although he was not a slave, he was an indentured servant. When Concer was freed from his indenture at age 18, he began going to sea on whaling ships. Concer became one of the 30 crewmen on Cooper's visit to Japan, and a respected resident of the village until his death there in 1897.

From 1850 to 1870, well-heeled professional and business people were discovering the enchanting beauty of the East End. There were no places to accommodate visitors, but families, mostly on South Main Street, began to take in roomers and boarders.

Then on April 17, 1870, the Long Island Rail Road line to Bridgehampton began daily operations, triggering the first tourist boom from Westhampton to Montauk.

What is called Southampton's first summer house was built in 1879 by Gaillard Thomas, a New York City physician, atop a dune. That year an estimated 200 people were regular summer visitors, and most bought or built cottages. In the next 35 years — during which, in 1894, Southamptom became an incorporated village — the cottages gave way to large estates with sumptuous grounds presided over by the second generation of wealthy summer dwellers. The rambling new houses surfaced mostly in the Agawam Lake-Gin Lane section, later known as the estate area. Their owners became known as "rusticators" because of their zest for bucolic living. There also was a frenzy of public and private construction: The town's first club, the Meadow Club, was built in 1887, followed by the Shinnecock Hills Golf Club (the nation's first private 18-hole golf course, 1891), the Southampton Club and the Fresh Air Home for Crippled Children.

The dignified prosperity that stamped the summer colony reached its zenith in the first 15 years of the 1900s: the "golden years" of the summer colony, exemplified by the opening of the National Golf Club in 1912. "The library had been built and the Parrish Art Museum came into being," said Keene. "The streets were being paved and New York stores began to open branches in Southampton. The Village Improvement Association that had begun in the 1880s had been instrumental in making Southampton the classy place it had become."

The growth subsided with the introduction of the federal income tax in 1914 — a blow to the rich — and the onset of World War I. But the Roaring Twenties were something else, with renewed prosperity, women's suffrage, Prohibition, speakeasies and snazzy new cars creating an air of razzmatazz to which not even the staid Hamptons were immune.

The Great Depression dampened but didn't stop growth in tony Southampton Village, and the wicked 1938 hurricane staggered the seaside summer colony, but it was the end of World War II that marked the village's major turning point. The arrival of motels, condominiums and the well-off from New York City who bought old estates or built new ones brought what Keene called "the biggest social change in Southampton in 300 years." In the 1900s, writers including John Steinbeck and Truman Capote were seen around town. Later, dozens of other notables from the arts and entertainment worlds joined the colorful scene.

Where to Find More: "Village of Southampton," booklet by Centennial Committee, and other materials at Southampton Public Library.

International News Service Photo
In 1920, Southampton villagers dressed in their Sunday finery take a traditional stroll after church.

WATER MILL: Owners of the Best & Co. department store of New York built these prominent houses in the late 1800s.

Nassau County Museum Collection, Long Island Studies Institute Photo / Henry Otto Korten

WATER MILL

Boasting a Water Mill And a Windmill

Beginnings: In 1640, a group of investors from Lynn, Mass., purchased 64 square miles on the South Fork of Long Island from England's King Charles I. They complained that Lynn was becoming too crowded. Four years later, Edward Howell, a former mill owner from Lynn, struck a deal to build a water mill on the southeastern shore of Mill Pond — not two miles from the fledgling settlement of Southampton — to provide the residents with an efficient means of grinding their grain into meal. In exchange, the town gave Howell 40 acres on which to build his gristmill, plus labor to lay the millstone and build the dam. It was only a matter of time before the water mill, one of the earliest landmarks on Long Island, became a community of its own.

Turning Point: After the arrival of the Long Island Rail Road in 1875, great summer homes were built along Mill Creek, Mill Pond and Mecox Bay by the well-to-do from New York City and elsewhere. While these visitors transformed a sleepy farming and fishing community into a playground for the wealthy, their presence also provided farmers, craftsmen and other tradesmen with a steady stream of customers. Some of the summer homeowners also proved to be valuable benefactors who played a significant role in preserving the community's historical artifacts such as the old water mill. Although historians are unsure when people began referring to the hamlet as Water Mill, an early town census did refer to residents living "east of the water mill" and "west of the water mill." By the 1800s, the area also was known as Water Mills (the hamlet now had two mills, though the second was a windmill, not a water mill).

Claim to Fame: As the year 2000 approached, Water Mill residents (1998 population, about 2,140) could boast of living in the only community in the United States with a working water mill and windmill. Although the windmill was put to use only on special occasions, the water mill operated daily during the summer months. It was moved and partially reconstructed in 1726, and became one of Long Island's oldest remaining landmarks.

Where to Find More: "Water Mill, Celebrating Community: The History of a Long Island Hamlet, 1644-1994," edited by Marlene Haresign and Marsha Kranes, or The Water Mill Museum, 1 Mill Rd..

WESTHAMPTON BEACH

The Hurricane Struck With Deadly Power

Beginnings: It didn't take the English colonizers of Southampton long after their settlement in the eastern part of the town to figure out that the west end was valuable real estate, too. Their first deeds were to the part east of the Shinnecock Canal (Canoe Place) in 1640. The five or six miles west of Canoe Place were apparently explored by the settlers early but controlled by Shinnecocks. It became involved in conflicting settlers' ownership claims before being awarded to Southampton Town by the governor in 1666. That deal was known as the Quogue Purchase. The Indians were paid 70 pounds in British money plus a few trinkets, historians say. Indians called the purchased area Catchaponack, or "place where large roots grow." It covered land that later included Westhampton Beach Village and surrounding parts of the town including unincorporated Westhampton.

Turning Points: The first Westhampton church was built in 1742 and the first school in 1795, but the area remained a backwater of farming, fishing and crafts for nearly 150 years, until the 1870s, when the railroad arrived, bringing a tide of summer visitors who would change the economics and the face of Westhampton. Money got off the trains. The first hotel, the Howell House, was built in 1868 with the financial backing of colorful entrepreneur P.T. Barnum. The Oneck House and the Ketchabonack House followed, as did crude bathhouses on the oceanfront at the foot of Beach Lane, later the site of Rogers Beach and Pavilion. The community's population was about 1,600 by 1998.

Historic Event: Westhampton Beach took the worst battering of any Long Island community during the hurricane of Sept. 21, 1938. The storm came without warning and lasted from 3 to 5:30 p.m. on a Wednesday, killing 28 people in Westhampton Beach alone. Four others were still missing a month later. More than 150 houses were destroyed, Main Street was flooded and Montauk Highway inundated at one point. The storm caused more than $2 million damage.

Where to Find More: "Historical Sketch of the Incorporated Village of Westhampton Beach," by Beatrice G. Rogers, and "The Hurricane of 1938 on Eastern Long Island," by Ernest S. Clowes, both at the Westhampton Beach Public Library.

Collection of Joel Streich

WESTHAMPTON: The hurricane of 1938 came without warning and lasted from 3 to 5:30 p.m. on Sept. 21. In Westhampton Beach, 28 people died and some 150 homes were destroyed.

Collection of Joel Streich

WESTHAMPTON: Downtown was flooded in the 1938 storm.

Westhampton Historical Society

WESTHAMPTON: After the hurricane, Dune Road disappeared into the floodwaters.

Shopping Center looking East   Cutchogue, Long Island, N. Y.

Collection of Joel Streich

CUTCHOGUE: A postcard shows a scene in the community from about 1930.

Shady Side of Mansion House, Fisher's Island, N. Y.

Collection of Joel Streich

FISHERS ISLAND: A mansion porch provides a place to relax, circa 1920. Despite its proximity to Connecticut, Fishers Island was given to New York in 1879.

Town of Southold

Southold, along with Southampton, claims the title of being the oldest English town in New York State. It was founded in 1640 by Puritans from the New Haven Colony.

As the year 2000 approached, the town remained primarily an agricultural. A century and a half earlier, the advent of steamships and then the coming of the Long Island Rail Road in 1844 brought significant changes. The rail link to the city boosted farmers' sales and property values and brought tourists to new hotels and boarding houses. There was already a long history of horse racing when Southold attracted large breeding farms in the 19th Century.

World War I brought prosperity with orders for Greenport shipyards and the ensuing peace brought economic doldrums. The Ku Klux Klan became active in the era, targeting Catholics. Prohibition made the town a center of rumrunning. But it took World War II and more shipyard orders to get the economy going again. After the war, the town began to attract buyers of second homes, who continued to share the area with farmers. The town had about 20,700 residents by 1998.

CUTCHOGUE
The New Pioneers Are Growing Grapes

Beginnings: Most of the settlers who put down roots in Cutchogue after its founding about 1667 were second-generation immigrants. Newly cleared lands outside the original settlement of Southold were tax-exempt for at least three years, and homesteaders figured it might take the tax man longer than that to catch up on the backlog. So a new generation of farmers settled in to what became Cutchogue, fencing in the lands that in some cases would remain in the same family for generations. Like other North Fork communities, Cutchogue became known for its potatoes, brussels sprouts and cauliflower. The name is thought to be derived from the Indian place name Corchaug, loosely translated as "the principal place."

Turning Point: While potatoes were still a Cutchogue staple in the 1990s, a new bumper crop emerged in the 1970s when a few brave entrepreneurs planted rows of grapevines. Only two decades later, Cutchogue claimed some of the pioneers of a maturing wine industry whose Long Island vintages won a variety of awards. Cutchogue had about 2,780 residents by 1998.

Claim to Fame: Shortly before the first European settlers arrived, the Indians living in Cutchogue built a log fort as protection from invading tribes in about the 1630s. The remains of the fort, known as Fort Corchaug, were found in a densely wooded plot alongside Downs Creek. In 1997, the nonprofit Peconic Land Trust made a deal to preserve the fort, believed to be the only one of its kind left in the Northeast.

This Old House: Affectionately referred to as The Old House, the 17th-Century home of Benjamin Horton was preserved on Cutchogue's village green. Built in Southold in 1640 and later moved to Cutchogue, the house remained among the oldest in the country, and locals designated it the oldest English-type frame house in New York State (a distinction disputed by backers of the Old Halsey House in Southampton).

Where to Find More: "Southold Town 350th Anniversary Celebration Journal" and "Cutchogue: Southold's First Colony" by Wayland Jefferson, at the Riverhead Free Library.

EAST MARION

See story on Page 150.

FISHERS ISLAND: The island's fish market in 1962.

Newsday Photo

FISHERS ISLAND
Two States Wrestle Over a Tiny Spot

Beginnings: While sailing to the island that was later named for him, Dutch explorer Adrian Block discovered Fishers Island in 1614. Block may have named the island for one of his navigators, a man by the name of Vischers. The future governor of Connecticut, John Winthrop Jr., purchased the tiny island two miles off the Connecticut shore from the Indians in 1644. When Winthrop became governor of Connecticut in 1657, he ensured that Fishers Island was included in the state's royal charter. But the ownership of the island was soon confused by another royal charter in 1664, granting Fishers Island to the duke of York in addition to Long Island. It was the beginning of a 200-year battle for ownership.

The Revolution: After invading Long Island, the British blockaded the Sound and, throughout the occupation, raided Long Island's adjacent islands such as Fishers in search of food and forage. The king's soldiers stole nearly 100 sheep and some cattle from farmers before its residents removed their herds later in 1776 to the safety of the Connecticut shore. On a particularly merciless foraging expedition in 1779, the British burned homes on Fishers Island before leaving with what booty they could find.

Turning Point: In 1879, a committee of officials from New York and Connecticut awarded Fishers Island to New York. Despite the declaration, residents of Fishers Island even in the 1990s identified more readily with Connecticut, just two miles away and connected by regular ferry service, than New York, about 10 miles to the southwest. With fewer than 370 year-round residents in the late 1990s, Fishers Island remained primarily a remote summer getaway for the extremely rich with names such as Whitney, du Pont and Firestone.

Brush With Fame: The seaside scenes in the 1982 movie "The World According to Garp," starring Robin Williams and Glenn Close, were shot on Fishers Island. (Town scenes, meanwhile, were shot in Roslyn.)

Where to Find More: "Southold Town 350th Anniversary Celebration Journal"; "Fishers Island: A Book of Memories" by James and Joanne Wall; "Fishers Island, N.Y., 1614-1925," by Henry Ferguson, all at the Riverhead Free Library.

CUTCHOGUE: In an undated photo, a grocer uses horsepower to deliver essentials.

Suffolk County Historical Society / Fullerton Collection

East End Seaport Museum and Marine Foundation

A walk on the dock at the end of Main Street in 1910

GREENPORT

A Village's Sea Changes

BY BILL BLEYER
STAFF WRITER

Greenport residents, it seemed, always found ways to make money from their waterfront, but perhaps never more creatively than during Prohibition.

There was so much rumrunning of illegal booze going on that the Coast Guard felt compelled to set up a base there in 1924. Not that it made much difference. "There were several rumrunner boats tied up at the railroad dock and the Coast Guard boats would be tied up on the other side of the dock and the crews would talk to each other," village historian Jerome McCarthy recalled in 1997. Authorities did make some attempts to uphold the law: "They did have a few gun battles out on Long Island Sound before Prohibition was phased out."

Since smuggling liquor wasn't always an option, the economy has been dominated at other times by commercial fishing, whaling and shipbuilding, along with farming. By the late 1990s, the village was trying to establish itself as a center of nautical tourism. "Greenport wouldn't be here without the water," McCarthy said. "It got its start from the harbor, from trading and fishing."

There were Indians living in the area when white settlers arrived from New Haven shortly after 1640. The first real payoff from the water came in the colonial era of the next century, when Greenport became a commercial shipping center. At first, small vessels carried produce to Connecticut. Later, larger ships traveled to New York City, New England and some ultimately to Africa to engage in the slave trade.

Commercial fishing began about 1790 when the settlers followed the lead of the Indians and began catching menhaden for fertilizer. By 1881, more than 350 vessels were supplying menhaden to 97 fish factories in an industry that employed more than 2,800 men.

Whaling began in 1785 when brothers Nathaniel and Hudson Corwin equipped several small vessels. The first large whaling ship was the Petosi, which embarked in 1830. Ultimately 15 whalers operated out of the harbor.

Three of those ships were owned by the village's most prominent resident, David Gelston Floyd, grandson of William Floyd of Mastic, a signer of the Declaration of Independence. In 1857, he built one of the finest homes on Long Island, Brecknock Hall, a fieldstone house on the North Road. It was vacant in the 1990s.

Discovery of oil in Pennsylvania killed the whaling industry by the 1860s. The loss of revenue was partially offset by the growth of tourism. Several large hotels opened in the 1820s and '30s. The void was also filled by several factories built to process menhaden for paint oil.

Oysters had been a staple for the Indians, but it was not until after the beginning of the 1900s that shellfishing evolved into a major industry. By 1907, 30 processing companies were operating in Greenport. Oystering hit its peak in 1936 when 2.5 million bushels were shipped. But the industry faltered after the 1938 hurricane covered beds with sand and pollution and rising costs took their toll.

As Greenport's population swelled in the 19th Century, shipbuilding became a primary industry. The first vessel built was the sloop Van Buren in 1834. Eventually there would be six shipyards; by 1999, all but one had been replaced by development or turned into parkland. Most vessels constructed were coastal schooners. The largest was the 165-foot, three-masted Wandering Jew. When it was launched in 1880, schoolchildren were given half a day off to witness the event.

The most widely known product of the village's shipbuilding industry was the Beebe-McLellan lifesaving boat. Between 1879 and 1918, hundreds of these 25-foot self-bailing and self-righting surfboats were built for the United States Life-Saving Service and foreign agencies.

The most prominent shipyard was Greenport Basin and Construction Co. — still functioning under the name Greenport Yacht and Ship. During World War I, it built wooden submarine chasers for the Russian navy and 50-foot torpedo boats for the U.S. Navy. During World War II, more than a thousand men and women fabricated sub chasers, minesweepers and landing craft.

The village played a second role in the war. The Coast Guard used it as the base for a "picket fleet" of sailboats with volunteer crews who kept an eye out for German submarines.

The Name Game: Before the Revolution, the area was known as Winter Harbor and then Stirling in honor of Lord Stirling, one of the most prominent landowners on Long Island. The area that became the community's downtown was once known as Greenhill. In 1831 citizens voted to change Green Hill to Green Port, which a few years later was combined into one word. The community was incorporated in 1838.

Turning Point: The Long Island Rail Road began providing service to Greenport in 1844 as part of a rail and ship link to Boston. The LIRR brought prosperity, but it was short-lived. Six years later, a rail line was built along the Connecticut shore and Greenport reverted back to being a sleepy village.

Brush With Fame: In the mid-19th Century, many local men owned trotting horses that they raced on Main Street. The world's fastest trotting horse of the era, Rarus, born in 1867, was raised on the village's Conklin farm.

Where to Find More: "Greenport Yesterday and Today," by Elsie Knapp Corwin and Frederick Langton Corwin, published by Amereon House in Mattituck.

LAUREL

The First Lady, And First Grandmother

Beginnings: Because it was situated midway between Aquebogue and Mattituck on the North Fork, Laurel was known for many years as Middle District. When Riverhead Town split from Southold in 1792, the new border ran through the little farming community, dividing in half. Middle District later became Franklinville some time before residents formed their own Presbyterian church in 1831, and finally Franklinville became Laurel in 1890. The substitution may have been inspired by the area's abundance of laurel trees and bushes. In winter, many homesteaders gathered seaweed along Long Island Sound and piled it around the foundations of their homes for insulation.

Non-turning point: In 1890, Laurel had about 128 residents. That grew to 200 by 1900, at which time it was described in a survey of Long Island communities as "a pretty village at peace with all the world." Though the population in 1998 stood naar 1,200, it could still be described as a tranquil and charming backwater.

Claim to Fame: Founded in 1832, the Franklinville Academy educated area youngsters from as far away as Patchogue. Pastors of local churches generally served as teachers at the very popular academy, which in the days before public education was financed by a stock company. The academy closed in 1889 after losing many of its tuition-paying pupils to the emerging public schools.

The First Lady of Laurel: Even though some contend Anna Symmes was actually a New Jersey native, Laurel loyalists like to claim her as their own. In 1795, Symmes married William Henry Harrison, who became the country's ninth president in 1841. Symmes was first lady for a month before her husband died. Though her tenure in the White House was short-lived, she did have the added distinction of being the grandmother of another president, Benjamin Harrison. Debunking the New Jersey claim, Laurelites insist Symmes was born in Laurel and moved as an infant to New Jersey with her parents, John Cleeves Symmes and Anne Tuthill.

Where to Find More: "Southold Town 350th Anniversary Celebration Journal" and "Around the Forks: A Collection of Published Articles by Edna Howell Yeager," available in the Riverhead Free Library.

MATTITUCK

Whaleboat Raids To Attack the Tories

Beginnings: Corchaug Indians, who were the first residents of the area, sold land, including what would become Mattituck, to Theophilus Eaton, governor of New Haven in Connecticut. The meadowlands at Mattituck — believed to mean "the great creek" in the Indian language — were held in common by the residents of Southold from its founding in 1640 and were used to grow salt hay. The woodlands were also held in common until 1661 when that land was divided among individual proprietors. A year later, settlement began.

The Revolution: British troops encamped in Mattituck with officers quartered in homes and farm products confiscated to supply the troops. Many of the younger residents joined the Patriot army while their families escaped to Connecticut. From there, whaleboat raids were made against Tory farms in Mattituck. The British withdrew from eastern Long Island in 1780 and the refugees returned home.

Please Turn the Page

148

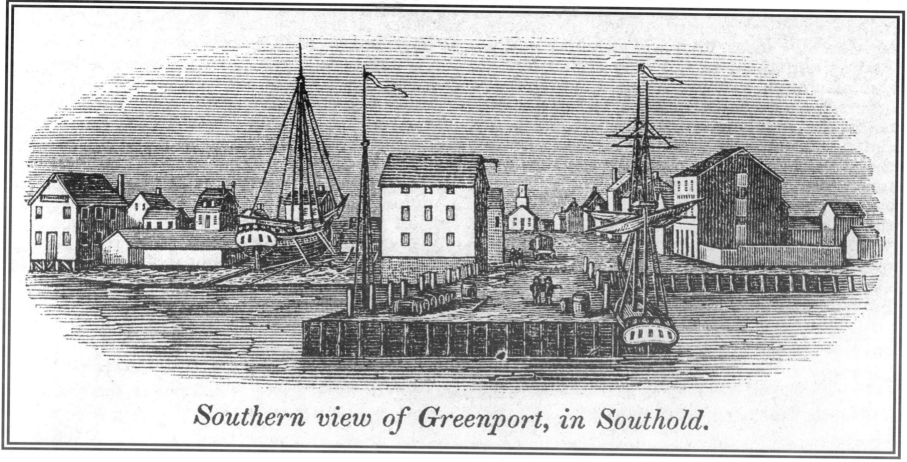

Southern view of Greenport, in Southold.

GREENPORT: An engraving from the book "Historical Collections of the State of New York" shows a shipbuilding community of old.

Huntington Historical Society

East End Seaport Maritime Museum

GREENPORT: The Booth House served as picket patrol headquarters for the Coast Guard Temporary Reserve, which organized to watch for German U-boats during World War II.

149

MATTITUCK, Continued

Turning Points: Mattituck remained virtually unchanged until 1844, when the Long Island Rail Road laid tracks through the hamlet to Greenport. The placement of the station resulted in a shift in development toward the western part of the community. The availability of quick and reliable transportation also resulted in farmers changing what they planted to focus more on vegetables that now could be sold to residents as far away as New York and Brooklyn. By 1998, the population had grown to about 4,120.
Claims to Fame: Salem Wines, member of a local seafaring family, became a boatbuilder in New York City in the early 18th Century and invented the retractable centerboard for small sailboats; it replaced the clumsy leeboards that had been attached to the sides of sailing vessels to keep them upright in earlier years. Oysters from Mattituck Creek were renowned for their quality and flavor through 1900 and were in great demand at New York City restaurants.
Where to Find More: "A History of Mattituck, Long Island, New York," by the Rev. Charles E. Craven, published by Amereon House, Mattituck, at the Mattituck-Laurel Library.

NEW SUFFOLK

What's That Out There in the Bay?

Beginnings: New Suffolk originally was part of Cutchogue. When Southold officials divided Cutchogue into lots in 1661, they held on to 180 acres on Peconic Bay that eventually became New Suffolk. John Booth was the first owner of much of this land, which was then called Booths Neck. In the 18th Century, the name was changed to Robins Island Neck. Raising livestock was the primary activity; in about 1759 James Webb was one of the first to build a home near the shore.
Turning Points: In 1836, the Rev. Ezra Young and brothers Abiel, Isaac and Ira Tuthill bought 80 acres from Josiah Albertson for $6,000 and laid out the hamlet in a grid pattern. In 1838, Ira Tuthill bought out his partners and renamed the community after Suffolk County — not the county in which it was located, but the one in England. Tuthill was a farmer, fisherman, merchant, surveyor, developer, hotel operator, blacksmith, brickyard owner, shipbuilder, deacon and the first postmaster. He promoted New Suffolk as a summer resort. Early visitors came by boat and stage and then by train after the Long Island Rail Road was constructed to Greenport in 1844. The community had about 360 residents by 1998.
Claim to Fame: From early times, New Suffolk was a busy port and shipbuilding site. By 1820, boats ran to New York on a regular basis. As late as the 1920s, potatoes were shipped to New England by boat. New Suffolk also boasted 13 scallop processing companies operating along First Street. For a time, cultivation and harvesting of oysters was also a major industry.
Fire One, Fire Two . . . : The most unusual maritime venture was the John P. Holland Torpedo Boat Co., which established a base for trials of the Holland, the first submarine commissioned by the U.S. Navy. Holland built his 53-foot vessel in New Jersey in 1898 and shipped it to New Suffolk the following year. Later sister ships, the Adder, Moccasin, Porpoise, Fulton and Columbia, also were tested on a 3-mile course in Little Peconic Bay. Ships from the Spanish-American war fleet were used as targets. Clara Barton, founder of the American Red Cross, was a passenger on one run. On another, the crew and guests were overcome by exhaust fumes and the Holland ran into the dock. Trials continued for six years until the base was moved to Groton, Conn., in 1905.
Where to Find More: "The New Suffolk Story" by Marjorie Moore Butterworth, available at the Cutchogue Free Library on Main Road.

ORIENT, EAST MARION

An Inn Plays Host To A President and a Poet

Beginnings: The first inhabitants were the Orient Focus People, Indians who lived about 1000 BC. They vanished long before the arrival in about 900 AD of the Corchaugs, who called the area Poquatuc. The Corchaugs were still present when six English families settled in 1661. The new residents called the area Oysterponds because of the abundant shellfish that they began to gather and sell to nearby communities. While farming remained the principle occupation, trading vessels began operating out of the sheltered harbor during the colonial period.
The Revolution: British troops landed in 1776. Many families fled to Connecticut, and the Redcoats periodically plundered the farms they left behind. After Benedict Arnold switched sides, he organized raids on Connecticut from Oysterponds. The British returned during the War of 1812, setting up what turned out to be a porous blockade against American ships sailing to New York City. In 1814 Commodore Stephen Decatur anchored his American squadron off Trumans Beach but never engaged the British. After the war, renewed farming and fishing brought prosperity to Oysterponds. By 1840 more than 30 schooners were operating out of the harbor, carrying fish and produce.
Turning Point: Orient and East Marion originally were called Oysterponds Lower Neck and Oysterponds Upper Neck, respectively. In 1836, the two communities went their separate ways with new names. Orient was chosen to reflect the area's easternmost position on the North Fork. East Marion was named for Gen. Francis Marion, the Swamp Fox of the Revolutionary War. "East" was tacked on because of an existing Marion upstate.
Brushes With Fame: By 1870 the tip of the North Fork had become a resort. And the Orient Point Inn, which opened in 1796, played host to President Grover Cleveland, Walt Whitman, orator Daniel Webster, actress Sarah Bernhardt and James Fenimore Cooper, who wrote "Sea Lions," set in Orient. (The inn closed in the 1960s and was demolished.) Meanwhile, members of one prominent Orient family did what they could to stave off public attention. They were the Tuthills, generally referred to in those less-sensitive days as the "Tuthill Dwarfs" or "Tiny Tuthills." Three Tuthill sisters, Cynthia, Lucretia and Asenath, were midgets and accomplished seamstresses. In the mid-1800s, their brother Rufus built them a house with reduced dimensions; it remained standing on Village Lane. Their diminutive and shy nephew, Addison, declined P.T. Barnum's invitation to join his circus.
Claims to Fame: Regularly scheduled ferry service to New London, Conn., began in the 1930s. Orient Beach State Park was created when the community deeded the bulk of the four-mile-long beach peninsula to the state in 1929.
Where to Find More: Oysterponds Historical Society.

PECONIC

Applying Grease To Wheels of Progress

Beginnings: Once called Hermitage for an elderly recluse who lived there in a shanty, Peconic was where early Southold residents came when the founding settlement became too crowded. It wasn't until the late 1860s that people began referring to the region as Peconic, thought to be derived fom the Indian word for "nut trees." Located just west of Southold, Peconic's soil was as rich and fertile as any on the North Fork. When the Irish came in the 1850s, they sharecropped in Peconic until they could afford to buy their own farms. Polish immigrants did the same 50 years later.
Turning Point: In 1844, the railroad made it to Greenport, opening up another route to New York City markets besides the Sound. The only problem was the train did not stop in Peconic, which deeply disturbed the farmers there. Their petitions for a stop were of no use. So the farmers decided to take matters into their own hands. They took goose grease and skunk oil and applied it to the rails for about a mile west of the village. When the steam-powered engine reached the slippery rails, its wheels spun furiously until it came to a halt just about where the residents hoped to put a station. Soon after that, Peconic became a regular stop, ensuring that the farmers could ship their produce to market.
Artists Colony: By about 1900, fledgling artists, some of whom studied at the Art Students League in New York City, found their way to the North Fork. Among them was Irving Wiles, who founded the Peconic school. Wiles and other artists such as Edward August Bell incorporated the summer and winter landscapes of the North Fork into their impressionist paintings. And they won awards at exhibitions such as the Paris Exhibition of 1889. Bell's cottage, known as Bell Buoy, still stood in 1998, when the community population had reached 1,150.
Momentous Visit: Albert Einstein summered in the area in 1938 and 1939. In '39, he wrote his famous letter to President Franklin Roosevelt urging FDR to investigate nuclear fission and its uses.
Where to Find More: "A Rose for the Nineties," by Rosalind Case Newell, and "Southold Town 350th Anniversary Celebration Journal," at the Riverhead Free Library.

SOUTHOLD

Suffering Under The British Rule

Beginnings: Puritans from the New Haven colony founded the hamlet of Southold in 1640 after acquiring title to the land from Orient Point to Wading River from the Corchaug Indians, who called the area Yennecott. The Rev. John Youngs left New Haven with his followers in October, 1640. Eventually, the Indians, who were not hostile, were forced out of the area or enslaved. Because almost every commodity had to come in or out by boat, shipping developed into a large industry by the 1670s. Two decades later, it had become so big, Thomas Dongan, the governor of New York, began requiring every boat sailing out of Southold to first report to New York to clear customs. Dongan dispatched a ship to the hamlet to enforce the regulation, but his captain proved amenable to accepting bribes. Shipping remained an important industry until the railroad arrived nearly two centuries later.
The Revolution: Many Southolders remained loyal to the crown, but almost half fled to Connecticut. From 1776 until the war ended in 1783, the British occupied the town, transferring the seat of government to Mattituck to better control the population. The Redcoats closed churches, plundered grain and horses, and chopped down trees for firewood. In 1777, Lt. Col. Jonathan Meigs led 170 Continental soldiers across Long Island Sound and through Southold in his successful raid on the British garrison at Sag Harbor. Jared Landon, later the first surrogate of Suffolk County, was imprisoned by the British after a Tory alleged he had guided the raiders. The Tory, Parker Wickham, who was also the town supervisor, was later declared a traitor and banished from the state. After the British left, many of the refugees returned. But the economy remained in ruins even as a second war with Britain broke out in 1812. The British sent foraging parties ashore and established a blockade of the East End, but it was so porous, most ships were able to sail to and from New York unmolested.
Turning Points: After Greenport was incorporated in 1838, it became a prosperous whaling center and attracted much of the shipping and shipbuilding industry that had been centered in the hamlet of Southold. More changes came with the arrival of the Long Island Rail Road in 1844. Trains now carried farm products to market in the city and returned with tourists for new hotels and boarding houses. But the community remained primarily agricultural. There was already a long history of horse racing when Southold became the home of large breeding farms in the 19th Century. By 1998, Southold had about 5,380 residents.
Where to Find More: "A Brief Account of Southold's History," by Antonia Booth, and "Pagans, Puritans and Patriots of Yesterday's Southold" by Warren Hall, available at the Southold Historical Society, Main Road.

Whitaker Historical Collection / Southold Free Library

SOUTHOLD: Main Road a day after the hurricane of Sept. 21, 1938, which blew down trees and buildings. In Southold, one man was killed and damage was estimated at $1 million.

PECONIC: A mainstay of life and income on Long Island's East End — the harvesting of potatoes in October of 1903.

Fullerton Collection, Suffolk County Historical Society

EAST MARION: The St. Thomas Home about 1910. By 1870, the area on the North Fork had become a major tourist spot, attracting the likes of President Grover Cleveland and Walt Whitman.

Collection of Joel Streich

NYC's most expansive borough mixes urban and ethnic style with backyard gardens

Queens

Queens Historical Society

JACKSON HEIGHTS: A 1934 photo shows the west side of 82nd Street, between Roosevelt and 37th Avenues.

Grown from a Belgian sprig and planted behind the Kingsland Homestead in Flushing in the 1840s, a tree that once grew in Queens was the first of its kind in America and the mother of all weeping beech trees in the country.

Although the great tree fell victim to old age and was cut down in December, 1998, its memory was kept alive by eight offspring that sprouted from the beech's roots and grew up in a ring around it. As living memorials to their matriarch, the offshoots not only would pay homage to the first of their species to cross the Atlantic but symbolize Queens' gift to the young nation. The largest borough in New York City, with the richest soil on Long Island — the Island gets increasingly sandy as you go east — Queens from the beginning was a garden of innovative gardens.

The early Algonquian inhabitants — Matinecocks, Jamecos, Rockaways — had an agricultural lifestyle, raising corn and squash, and also getting sustenance from the sea around them. The Dutch, who planted the first small colony in Flushing in 1637, would have starved that first winter were it not for the Matinecocks who fed them. Unfortunately the Dutch governors, with no apparent skill at dealing with Indians, were soon at war with them. The English, who had migrated to eastern Long Island to escape political and religious oppression in the Massachusetts colony,

began drifting into the fertile plains of Queens in the 1640s. Granted patents by the Dutch who wanted to keep the Indians off the land, they soon established flourishing farm communities.

In 1683, 19 years after the capture of New Netherland, England divided the New York crown colony into 12 counties.

Queens emerged as a vast territory, which included present-day Nassau. Its three colonial towns were Flushing, Jamaica and Newtown (which extended from Long Island City to Elmhurst).

The origin of the borough's name is disputed, but the leading theory holds that its namesake was Queen Catherine, the 17th-Century Portuguese princess who married England's Charles II. In any case, the burgeoning populations of Manhattan and Brooklyn were soon being fed by Queens farm produce rolling over the old Indian trail to the Brooklyn ferries.

Though Queens was absorbed into the New York City metropolis in the great consolidation of 1898 — and was rapidly urbanized after the opening of the Queensboro Bridge in 1909 and the coming of the nickel-fare subway in 1915 — it was still the borough of backyard gardens even as the year 2000 neared.

From the beginning, and since the liberalized immigration law of the 1960s, Queens also was a harbor of cultures, some say the nation's most ethnically diverse county. The newcomers cluster in Queens neighborhoods: Greeks in Astoria; Asians in Flushing and Elmhurst; Latinos in Rego Park, Jackson Heights and Woodside; Caribbeans in Springfield Gardens; Russians and Israelis in Forest Hills. The beauty of Queens, said Byron Saunders, executive director of the Queens Historical Society, is "its openness to everyone."

Gazetteer

The people behind the names of some prominent roads and places in Queens

Ditmars Boulevard: Abram Ditmars, the first mayor of Long Island City in 1870, was a descendant of Jan Jansen Ditmarsen, who emigrated from Germany and settled in Dutch Kills about 1647. ("Kill" is Dutch for "creek.")

Fort Totten: Begun in 1862 as Camp Morgan (for the New York governor at the time), the Bayside fort was renamed in 1898 after Civil War Gen. Joseph Totten (1788-1864).

Howard Beach: Named in 1916 after William J. Howard, a Brooklyn glove manufacturer who built a hotel resort in southwestern Queens in the 1890s.

Francis Lewis Boulevard: Commemorates Francis Lewis, a Whitestone Patriot during the American Revolution who was a member of the Continental Congress and a signer of the Declaration of Independence.

Poppenhusen Avenue: Conrad Poppenhu-

Poppenhusen Institute
Conrad Poppenhusen

sen, a German immigrant who started a hard-rubber plant in College Point in the 1850s, built a model community for his workers. He also was the first president of the Long Island Rail Road.

Jacob A. Riis Park: A Danish immigrant who lived in Richmond Hill in the 1870s, Riis was a social reformer, photographer and newspaper reporter who wrote "How the Other Half Lives," about poverty and squalor on the Lower East Side.

Rikers Island: Abraham Riker, a German-Dutch immigrant who arrived in 1638, was deeded this East River island (adjacent to what became LaGuardia Airport) by New Netherland Gov. Peter Stuyvesant in 1664. In 1884 the city purchased it for a penal colony.

Steinway Avenue: The main thoroughfare of a company town that was developed in 1870 by the Steinway family for employees of its piano factory in Astoria.

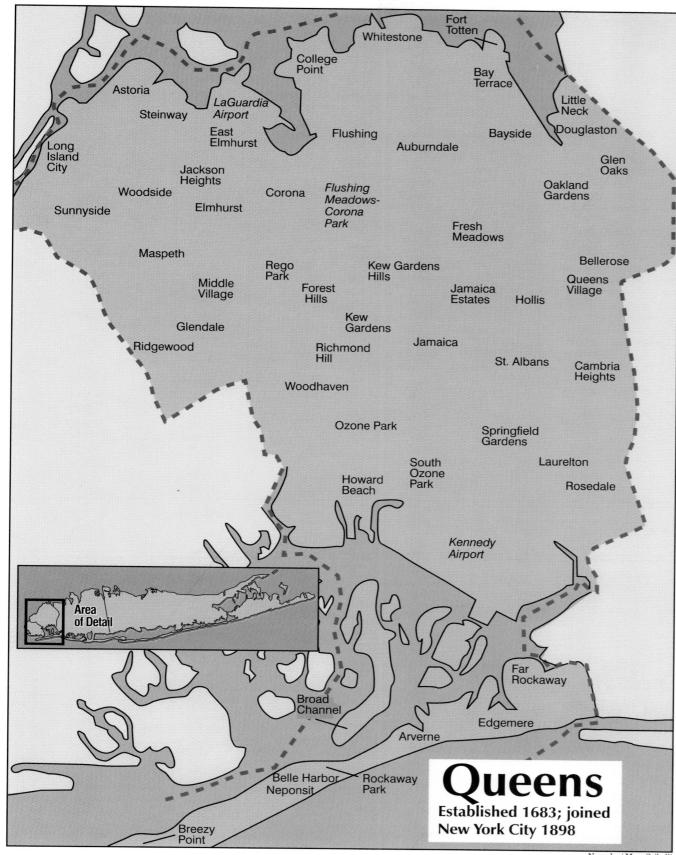

Queens

Established 1683; joined
New York City 1898

Newsday/ Marc Scibelli

ASTORIA
Filmmaking, Beer, Pianos and an Airport

Beginnings: Astoria was unofficially founded in 1652 when an adventurous Englishman, William Hallet, bought 1,500 acres along the East River from the Dutch governor, Peter Stuyvesant. Indians, not convinced the land was Stuyvesant's to sell, were appeased with beads, seven coats, four kettles and a blanket. The community became known as Hallets Cove.
The Name: Stephen A. Halsey, a fur trader, and several associates founded Astoria village in 1839. Old settlers wanted to give it the Indian name Sunswick. Halsey wanted to name it after John Jacob Astor, in hopes the millionaire

would bankroll the young community. Mysteriously, the names of the people who petitioned for Sunswick became attached to petitions for Astoria. The effort was in vain. The only money Astor invested in his namesake was a $500 endowment to a Young Women's Seminary.
Turning Point: In the 1870s, the waterfront community expanded inland as developers bought farmland. William Steinway, the son of a German immigrant piano maker, bought 400 acres and built a spacious factory and a community called Steinway with a church, library, kindergarten and trolley line. The circa-1865 Steinway mansion, a city landmark, became the last surviving example of the grand homes that lined the Queens shore, according to the Greater Astoria Historical Society. In 1886, Steinway and brewer George Ehret founded a beach resort on Bowery Bay.

The North Beach Amusement Park ended with Prohibition in 1919 and is now LaGuardia Airport. Of the beer gardens and picnic groves that flourished amid the European immigrant population, only the Bohemia Hall and Park remained.
Claim to Fame: Astoria can claim to be the birthplace of the American film industry. The Famous Players Film Co. opened in 1919, followed by Paramount Studios. After the industry moved to California, the Astoria studios turned out U.S. Army instructional films for 30 years. Restoration began in 1976, and films were once more produced at the Kaufman-Astoria Studios. The American Museum of the Moving Image opened in 1988.
Where to Find More: "A History of Long Island City to 1930," in the Queens Borough Central Library, Long Island Collection, Jamaica.

BAYSIDE
See story on Page 157.

BELLEROSE
The City's Only Working Farm Museum

Beginnings: Bellerose is an eastern Queens community not to be confused with the planned village of Bellerose and Bellerose Terrace just across the Nassau County border. The Belleroses were first settled by English colonists in 1656, part of the huge Jamaica land grant from New Netherlands Gov. Peter Stuyvesant. After the British defeated the Dutch in 1664, the area became an English colony, joined to Queens County in 1683. Until the 1900s it was largely farmland known as "the little plains."
The Name: Helen Marsh, an entrepreneur from Lynn, Mass., built a model community and a railroad station in western Nassau in 1911 and called it Belle Rose. Queens Bellerose, developed during the building boom of the 1920s, adopted the name.
Home on the Range: The Creedmoor Rifle Range was a star attraction in the 1890s, before financial problems plus a few stray bullets forced it to close in 1907. It was turned over to the Creedmoor State Psychiatric Center, which opened in 1912.
The Queens Farm. Community volunteers formed the Colonial Farmhouse Restoration Society of Bellerose in 1975 to preserve the 1697 farm property which New York State had declared surplus from its land purchase for the psychiatric center. The Queens County Farm Museum, which became the only remaining historical working farm museum in New York City, was designated a city landmark in 1976, and in 1979 it was listed in the National Register of Historic Places.
New Arrivals: In the 1990s, rising real estate prices forced the children of old residents to move away, and many of the original Irish and Northern European families were replaced by newcomers from Asiatic countries.
Where to Find More: Reference material in the Bellerose Branch Library, 250-06 Hillside Ave., and Queens Borough Central Library, Long Island Collection, Jamaica; Queens County Farm Museum, 73-50 Little Neck Pkwy., Floral Park.

BROAD CHANNEL
Islands of Jamaica Bay Linked to Mainland

Beginnings: It has been called the Venice of New York and Gateway to the Rockaways. It also has been called the Forgotten Islands of Jamaica Bay. Broad Channel, a tranquil island neighborhood, one mile long and four blocks wide, gives no hint of its stormy past. Explorer Henry Hudson and his crew were probably the first white men to see it in 1609 when they were seeking a route to China. In the 1640s, the Mohawks sold it, along with most of southeastern Queens and the Rockaway Peninsula, to the Dutch. Dutch Gov. Peter Stuyvesant opened it to English settlers in 1656, but few were inclined to homestead on the remote islands, a haven for pirates and marauders.
Turning Points: Skip a couple centuries, during which the Canarsie and Jameco tribes and a few Europeans hunted and fished on what was then a group of tiny islands. Change came in the 1880s when the New York, Woodhaven and Rockaway Railroad built a wood trestle across Jamaica Bay. The route was sold to the Long Island Rail Road, which was soon carrying more than 3 million fun seekers a year to the Rockaway beaches and Broad Channel hotels. The newly incorporated New York City took title in 1902 and leased the island to the Broad

Please Turn to Page 157

WOODSIDE: A Flushing & North Side train pulls into the Woodside station during the winter of 1872.

3033-A
Village of College Point in 1876

COLLEGE POINT: A view of the village in 1876. In the 1850s, Conrad Poppenhusen arrived, and his rubber factory changed the community forever.

Newsday Archive

FLUSHING: A view of the 1939 World's Fair in what eventually became Flushing Meadows-Corona Park. The names Ford and Firestone are visible on two pavilions.

Newsday Archive

FLUSHING: A postcard shows the Unisphere, with the Court of Peace in the foreground, at the 1964-65 World's Fair. The sphere remained a centerpiece of the park.

Newsday Photo / Alan Raia

FLUSHING: On opening day of the World's Fair's second year, in April, 1965, Dinoland proved to be one of the big attractions.

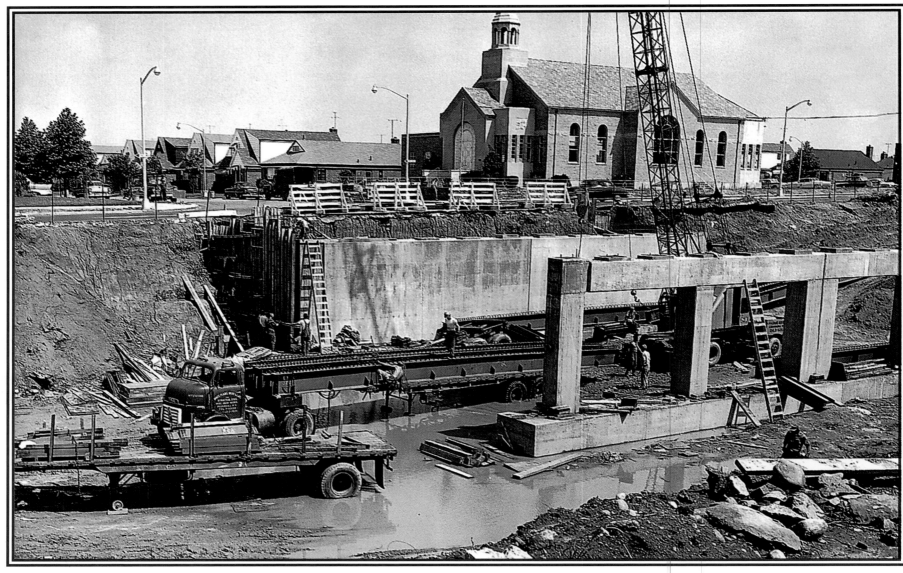

Newsday Photo / B. Sullivan

BAYSIDE: Workers dredge through the mud on July 29, 1958, to construct the Long Island Expressway.

TURN HALL,
13TH STREET AND 3RD AVE.
COLLEGE POINT, N.Y.

Collection of Joel Streich

COLLEGE POINT: Turn Hall, at the corner of 13th Street and Third Avenue, about 1910.

BAYSIDE

A City Arises in the City

BY RHODA AMON
STAFF WRITER

For a thousand years, Matinecocks gathered shells from the western shore of Little Neck Bay to make an excellent grade of wampum. In the 1950s, it was another kind of wampum — construction money — that transformed Bayside from a small, idyllic community into a virtual city within a city.

Bay Terrace, the first of the massive apartment complexes, was built on 200 acres in 1952, a self-sufficient entity with its own country club, shopping center, restaurants and library. Next came the Bay Club, with 1,037 luxury condos with their own private club, swimming pool, even a hair salon. But these gigantic centers of urban comfort rose in stark contrast with Bayside's history.

The first English settlement on Alley Creek — later Alley Pond Park — was part of a 16,000-acre land grant to English colonists from New Netherlands Gov. William Kieft in the mid-17th Century. But it wasn't until 1798 that the name Bay Side first appeared on a deed. The one-word spelling was suggested in the 1850s by Judge Effingham Lawrence, a descendant of the Lawrence family, original Flushing patentees.

For 300 years the family produced governors, mayors, judges, statesmen and at least one naval hero, Capt. James Lawrence, famed for his battle cry of "Don't give up the ship!" in the War of 1812. Family members were buried from 1832 to 1939 in the Lawrence Graveyard in Bayside. An earlier Lawrence family cemetery in Astoria dates to 1732. Both sites became city landmarks.

The Lawrences were among about a dozen land-owning families who shared most of Bayside until after the Civil War. With the arrival of the Flushing and North Shore Rail Road (later part of the Long Island Rail Road) in 1866, a building boom began. The Bayside Land Co. began promoting the area's park-like surroundings to city dwellers eager for the country life. By the 1920s, home building had reached a fever pitch and almost all the large estates succumbed.

There were rumors that the infant film industry, then ensconced in Astoria, was considering a move to Bayside because of its bucolic scenery, elegant homes and open spaces. The studios never came, but many entertainers and sports celebrities — Gloria Swanson, Norma Talmadge, W.C. Fields and John Barrymore, among others — turned Bayside into an actors' colony. Corbett Road became known as Actors' Row, and a lucky delivery boy might catch a glimpse of heavyweight boxer "Gentleman Jim" Corbett, or, later, actor Paul Newman and all-star pitcher Tom Seaver.

The Bayside Yacht Club, founded in 1902, was threatened in the 1930s by master builder Robert Moses' plans for the Cross Island Parkway along the west shore of Little Neck Bay. The problem was solved when the city agreed to provide access to the club via a bridge over the parkway.

But one controversy in the late 1990s aroused and unified Baysiders: the future of Fort Totten. As far back as the French and Indian War in the 1750s, fortifications were built on Willets Point at the tip of Bayside. During the Civil War, the fort was designed to protect New York Harbor from a Confederate sea attack. No longer needed to safeguard the city in the 1900s, the fort retained some of the city's most desirable real estate. Historians wanted to preserve it as an historic 19th-Century fort. (The 1862 Gothic-style Officer's Club already is a national landmark.)

In the 1990s, Matinecock descendants wanted to protect the bones of ancestors they said were buried there. Developers coveted the waterfront site for more luxury condos. Residents who wanted to preserve the fort as a public park for their children hoped that the emphasis on protecting the environment would carry the day.

Where to Find More: "A History of Bayside" by James A. Flux, reference volume in Queens Borough Central Library, Long Island Collection, Jamaica, and the Central Flushing and Fresh Meadows branch libraries.

Queens Historical Society

A wing of the 19th-Century home of Judge Effingham Lawrence, a member of the prominent family of Bayside. The home was built in 1672 east of 221st Street on Little Neck Bay, and torn down in 1936.

BROAD CHANNEL, Continued

Channel Corp., which filled in marshes, built streets and rented parcels at $116 a year to anyone building a summer home. Cross Bay Boulevard opened in 1925, linking motorists to the mainland, and the resort flourished. But in 1939, the Broad Channel Corp. went bankrupt. Then followed a 40-year fight by tenants to buy their land from the city and secure permanent residence.

Eminent Domain: Channelites take pride in the defeat of famous politicians who tried to evict them. Master builder Robert Moses wanted to make the whole island a wildlife refuge. The plan got nowhere until 1950 when the Metropolitan Transportation Authority built a subway to the Rockaways, filling in the waters between the islands and agreeing to create two fresh-water ponds. The northern end of the island is now the Jamaica Bay Wildlife Refuge, part of the Gateway National Recreation Area.

Where to Find More: See "The Other Islands of New York City," by Sharon Seitz and Stuart Miller (Countryman Press); other reference material in Broad Channel Branch Library, 16-26 Cross Bay Blvd.

CAMBRIA HEIGHTS

The View From Kerosene Hill

Beginnings: Cambria Heights began life as part of the St. Albans area, which in turn was part of the Jamaica Town land grant from New Netherlands Gov. Peter Stuyvesant to English settlers in 1656. For most of its history Cambria Heights was a place of bountiful farms and forests.

The Name: Some historians say Cambria was the name of a local family; others, that the name was based on a coal company from Cambria County, Pa. In either case, there's no doubt about where the "Heights" came from. The area is one of the highest elevations on Long Island, rising roughly 50 feet above sea level. At one time it was called Kerosene Hill, because the community did not have piped-in gas.

Turning Point: In the early 1920s a Brooklyn real estate and insurance dealer named Oliver B. LaFreniere began developing a 163-acre site assembled from three large farms. This started the development of Cambria Heights as a community of one- and two-family homes. Home-building grew rapidly in the 1940s after the Cross Island Parkway opened at the eastern edge of the community.

Where to Find More: Reference material in the Cambria Heights Branch Library, and the Queens Borough Central Library, Long Island Collection, Jamaica.

COLLEGE POINT

Plastics Dethrone The Rubber King

Beginnings: The Matinecocks sold 17,000 wooded acres to New Netherland Gov. William Kieft, who parceled them out among Dutch and English families in 1645. William Lawrence, a descendant of English nobility, got 900 acres in an area called Tues Neck and became College Point's first English settler. Later, Eliphalet Stratton acquired 320 acres and Lawrence Neck became Strattonport. In 1838, the Rev. William Augustus Muhlenberg, rector of St. George Episcopal Church in Flushing, founded St. Paul's College. It lasted less than a decade, long enough to permanently stamp the name College Point on the entire community.

The Poppenhusen Era: A German immigrant, Conrad Poppenhusen, arrived in College Point in the 1850s and changed it forever. Vulcanization — the process of treating rubber to give it strength and stability — had just been discovered, and Poppenhusen saw the potential of using hard rubber to replace whalebone in everything from corset stays to telescopes. Poppenhusen not only built a large factory — which attracted hundreds of immigrant workers — he created a model community with schools, a library, water and sewage systems, a railroad and a cobblestone road to Flushing. More rubber factories followed, and the small rural community became the rubber capital of the Northeast. But just as hard rubber had replaced whalebone, plastics eventually replaced hard rubber in the manufacture of small products. Poppenhusen, who also invested heavily in the development of the Long Island Rail Road, went bankrupt in 1877. His rubber company moved to Butler, N.J., in the 1930s, and the last of the College Point rubber factories closed in the 1970s.

Claims to Fame: The first free kindergarten in the nation was established in 1870 in the Poppenhusen Institute, founded by the paternalistic rubber manufacturer to provide educational opportunities for immigrant families. It continued as a cultural community center and a national and city landmark.

Where to Find More: "A History of College Point, N.Y.," by Robert A. Hecht, $5 at the Poppenhusen Institute, 114-04 14th Rd.

CORONA

Louis Armstrong Finds Harmony

Beginnings: Long before Robert Moses spotted it as the site of the 1939 World's Fair or '20s novelist F. Scott Fitzgerald scorned it as a "Valley of Ashes," central Queens was occupied by the Matinecocks. In the 17th Century, Dutch and English settlers divided it into large family farms, enjoying a bountiful harvest from lush orchards. By the mid-19th Century Corona, then called West Flushing, was an early bedroom suburb, home of well-to-do businessmen who commuted to Manhattan by ferry.

Turning Points: The Fashion Race Track, a joint venture of the National Racing Association and the Fashion Association, made the community a chic, racy place in 1854. The property for the track was purchased from Samuel Willets, a devout Quaker who tried in vain to buy it back when he learned it was to be used for racing and gambling. The track speeded the development of Northern Boulevard and a railroad link with Flushing. After the track died, developer Benjamin W. Hitchcock acquired the Smith brothers farm in the 1870s and promoted West Flushing as a working man's paradise, largely among Italian immigrants. He named it Corona, "Crown of the Hill." Thousands of immigrants from Manhattan's crowded Lower East Side were attracted by Corona's tranquility and houses with handkerchief-sized backyards. The Queensboro subway in 1905 added an easy commute. In 1939, a neighboring ash dump became the site of a World's Fair. The fair returned in 1964; it later became Flushing Meadows-Corona Park.

Claims to Fame: Louis (Satchmo) Armstrong, perhaps the greatest name in jazz, could have lived anywhere in the world, but he chose a modest frame house in Corona as his permanent residence in 1943. The house, later designated a national and city historic landmark, was converted into a museum. Louis Comfort Tiffany, the famed glass artist, chose Corona for his glassmaking factory-studio from 1893 through 1938.

Where to Find More: "The Story of Corona," by Vincent F. Seyfried, at the Queens Historical Society, Flushing; "Our Neighborhood," by Louis Armstrong, available at the Louis Armstrong Archives in the Queens College Library, 65-30 Kissena Blvd., Flushing.

DOUGLASTON

Residents Keeping The Past Present

Beginnings: This narrow peninsula on Little Neck Bay became a designated historic district, the third one in Queens. It was home to the Matinecocks until 1637, when an Englishman, Thomas Foster, received a royal grant for 600 acres on Alley Creek near modern-day Douglaston Parkway. Entrepreneur Wynant Van Zandt built a mansion in 1819 near the site of the Foster land grant.

The Name: It derived from William P. Douglas, a Scotsman who bought the peninsula from Van Zandt in 1835. The area was developed as Douglas Manor and the mansion became the Douglaston Club.

Turning Point: In 1906, the Rickert-Finlay Co. began the development of Douglaston, laying out streets and erecting spacious homes. Architectural styles included Tudor, colonial and Victorian. Eight of the homes were designed by Josephine Wright Chapman, one of America's earliest women architects. In the 1990s, the community was wholly residential and one of the most affluent in Queens.

Preservation: In 1989, the Little Neck-Douglaston Historical Society, led by Kevin Wolfe, began a drive for a historical district to preserve the community's distinctive architecture and ambiance. History-minded residents also sought to preserve the Douglaston Estate Windmill, which was built in 1870 to pump water to the then-farming community. When the windmill was destroyed by arson, residents built a water-pumping replica; it went into use at the Alley Pond Environmental Center.

Claims to Fame: Notable residents have included tennis star John McEnroe, actress Ginger Rogers and writer Ring Lardner Jr.

Where to Find More: "Through the Years in Little Neck and Douglaston," by George C. and Ernestine H. Fowler; "The Chronicle of Little Neck and Douglaston, Long Island," both at the Queens Borough Central Library, Long Island Collection, Jamaica.

ELMHURST, EAST ELMHURST

A Bastion for Loyalists, Then for the Famous

Beginnings: Elmhurst can claim to be one of the oldest English settlements on Long Island. It dates to 1643 and the ill-fated Maspat colony, which was razed in an Indian uprising, probably in retaliation for the Dutch massacre of Indians in Connecticut. Nine years later the English colonists moved inland and called the settlement by the Dutch name Middelburgh or Middleburg. It emerged as New Towne in 1664, when the British replaced the Dutch governor.

The Revolution: The vast expanse of western and central Queens had a population of only 99, and most of them were Loyalists. (With so much land, they had little to complain about.) British Gen. Sir William Howe stayed at the Samuel Renne House on what became Queens Boulevard, while the nearby 1671 First Presbyterian Church became a British prison.

Turning Points: In 1896, millionaire Cord Meyer Jr. bought land on the edge of Newtown and divided it into 1,700 building lots. He lobbied to change the name to Elmhurst to highlight the surrounding trees and disassociate the area from the odors from Newtown Creek. Meyer helped finance the New York and Queens trolley, which linked the area to the Manhattan 34th Street ferry. He also started a water company to supply the growing area. East Elmhurst remained largely rural, best known for the Gala Amusement Park near Flushing Bay until it was torn down in the 1930s to make room for LaGuardia Airport. Development followed.

Brushes With Fame: Once noted for apple orchards, Elmhurst also has been home to the famous, among them dry goods merchant Samuel Lord, who founded Lord & Taylor, and Clement Clarke Moore, who wrote "A Visit From St. Nicholas." East Elmhurst was home to jazz singer Ella Fitzgerald, Broadway dancer Charles (Honi) Coles, and black nationalist leader Malcolm X.

Landmark: The Lent Homestead, a Dutch Colonial farmhouse built in 1729 for Abraham Lent, is a reminder of East Elmhurst the way it was.

Where to Find More: "Annals of Newtown," by James R. Riker Jr. in Queensboro Central Library, Jamaica; other Newtown historical data are in the Vander Ende-Onderdonk House library at 18-20 Flushing Ave., Ridgewood.

FLUSHING and FOREST HILLS

See stories on Pages 160-162.

FRESH MEADOWS

Benedict Arnold Made Friends, and Enemies

Beginnings: Dutch sailors exploring Flushing Bay in 1628 saw a vast area of marsh and meadow. They called it Vlissingen after a town in Holland. The name means "salt meadow valley." The colony, established in the 1640s and called Flushing by the English settlers, must have seemed a little cramped after a while to farmers who needed land. They began moving to the southern "suburb" of Flushing, then called Black Stump. The name seems to have derived from rows of blackened stumps used to separate large plantations. In colonial days only two roads led out of the meadows: Black Stump Road, which ran northeast to Bayside, and Fresh Meadow Lane, which headed south toward Jamaica. The community later took the name of the more bucolic-sounding road.

The Revolution: British troops led by Benedict Arnold, a traitor to the Patriots, tramped through the meadows, making themselves at home at farms along the way, finding many sympathizers among the wealthy plantation owners but doubtlessly making enemies, too.

Turning Points: In 1868 Flushing entrepreneur Samuel Parsons opened Parsons Nurseries, one of the earliest commercial gardens, at the edge of Fresh Meadows. It later became Kissena Park. In about 1923, a Brooklyn sportsman, Benjamin C. Ribman, opened the Fresh Meadows Country Club, site of major golf tournaments. Thirty years later the 141-acre club was sold to New York Life Insurance Co. The company created a model community with a mix of row houses and high-rise buildings, a shopping center, a theater and schools. It opened in 1949 and helped Fresh Meadows become a prestigious address.

Where to Find More: "Encyclopedia of the City of New York" for a capsule history, also Fresh Meadows reference folder in Queens Borough Central Library, Jamaica.

GLEN OAKS

Towers, Two-Stories Alter the Landscape

Beginnings: East of Jamaica, west of the Hempstead Plains, neither wood nor marsh, Glen Oaks was a slice of flat terrain eagerly sought by farmers in the 1640s. It was a rural, unnamed section of Flushing, part of a 20,000-acre land grant to Massachusetts settlers. And it stayed rural and unnamed until 1923, when a golf club was built. More than anything else, however, Glen Oaks became a product of World War II, a community that emerged in time to serve thousands of returning GIs and their families looking for a home.

The Name: Reportedly the wife of the new golf club manager George Spear looked at the panoramic sweep of the land and said "Glen Oaks."

Turning Points: The Glen Oaks Golf Club, created on 167 acres purchased from William K. Vanderbilt II's country estate, was the first break in the rural landscape. By 1944, however, the Gross-Morton Co., Queens developers, had its eye on the sweep of land that inspired its name. Backed by $24 million in federal housing funds, a huge complex of two-story brick apartment buildings was completed in 1948. The rentals were snapped up by returning World War II veterans. By 1971 the golf course was gone and in its place rose North Shore Towers, three 32-story apartment buildings. Glen Oaks and New Hyde Park residents, mostly single-home dwellers, protested the project in vain.

Claim to Fame: The Queens County Farm Museum on a 52-acre rural setting shared with Floral Park and Bellerose, became a living reminder of Glen Oaks' rural past. The historic Cornell farmhouse, built in 1772 by Samuel Cornell of the pioneer Cornell family, was put on the National Register of Historic Places in 1976.

Where to Find More: Glen Oaks Branch Library, 256-04 Union Tpke., The Queens County Farm Museum, 73-50 Little Neck Pkwy.

Queens College Photo

ELMHURST: A 1920 view of Elmhurst Avenue, diagonally across top; Hampton Street is in foreground. Top left is the Flushing elevated line.

Queens Museum of Art

CORONA: Employees at work around 1900 at the glass-making factory and studio run by Louis Comfort Tiffany. The artist created stained-glass treasures there from 1893 to 1938.

Collection of Joel Streich

ELMHURST: Newtown High School circa 1925. The community remained mostly rural until the 1930s with the construction of LaGuardia Airport.

Queens Borough President's Office

A Changing Scene in Flushing

Newsday Photo / Ken Sawchuk, 1998

A creek runs through it. Flushing Creek, that is. These images were both taken from the eastern side of the Flushing Creek Bridge, with the photographers facing Northern Boulevard. After that, similarities fade.

The older photo, according to James Driscoll of the Queens Historical Society, apparently was taken around 1910. The building on the left was the American Ice Co. The fenced property in the distant left was home to the Prince family, which opened America's first commercial nursery in Flushing in 1737. The tracks embedded in the block roadbed were for a trolley that ran from Long Island City through Flushing and south to Jamaica. Another trolley ran north to College Point.

Driscoll said a new Flushing Creek Bridge was built for the 1939 World's Fair, and another later replaced it. And Northern Boulevard grew ever busier.

GLENDALE

Closing Picnic Groves To Open a Parkway

Beginnings: Once a remote swampy area with freshwater pools, Glendale was first known as Fresh Ponds. It was part of the 74,000 acres chartered to the Rev. Francis Doughty by the Dutch West India Co. in 1642. Like its neighbor, Ridgewood, it became in the 1800s a community of mostly German farmers, tilling 35- to 250-acre farms. One, the Evan Farm, was famed for its peacocks. The Jacobus Kolyer Farm became today's Liberty Park.

The Name: In 1860, a large slice of Fresh Ponds was acquired by George S. Schott. He renamed it Glendale after his Ohio hometown. Nine years later developer John C. Schooley adopted the name for his 469-lot development.

Turning Points: Starting in 1852 when a law banned future cemeteries in Manhattan, Glendale became surrounded by cemeteries in what is known as the Cemetery Belt. By the late 1800s farms were rapidly losing ground to developers. An 1870 advertising flier exhorted "the humblest mechanic" to buy lots in Glendale at $2.50 a week. The ad urged the city dweller to "look upon your poor sickly children with sadness, and wonder what is the matter with them. You see them dying by inches for the want of Fresh Air." Those who couldn't buy could rent "nice little cottages, 5 miles from Long Island City" for $75 a year.

Let the Good Times Roll: In the late 1800s a trolley led to huge picnic grounds offering athletic contests, a dance hall and bar. German-style taverns flourished. At Frank Honigman's tavern lunch was with a 10-cent glass of Jacob Rupert beer, and hot meals were free on Friday and Saturday night. By World War I, suspicions about the German community caused many of the meeting places to close. By the 1930s almost all the picnic groves were torn down to make way for the Interboro Parkway, renamed the Jackie Robinson Parkway in 1997.

Where to Find More: "Our Community, Its History and People: Ridgewood, Glendale, Maspeth, Middle Village, Liberty Park," by Walter J. Hutter and others, at the Queens Borough Central Library, Jamaica, and the Greater Ridgewood Historical Society in the Vander Ende-Onderdonk House, 1820 Flushing Ave., Ridgewood.

HOLLIS

New Kid on the Block Got Back on Tract

Beginnings: Hollis is a comparative newcomer in Queens, although the area in east-central Queens was part of the Jamaica land purchase in 1656. The Dutch encouraged colonists from Hempstead to homestead in the Beaver Pond area. And for a century, the section now called Hollis was known as East Jamaica, a farm hamlet between Jamaica and Queens Village. The area consisted of about 20 farms, and there was little development until the American Revolution.

The Revolution: Brig. Gen. Nathaniel Woodhull, commander of the Queens and Suffolk militia, was trapped by the British at Carpenter's Tavern in the future Hollis in 1776. Woodhull was fatally wounded by the British, and although he was from Mastic in Suffolk, Hollis claimed him as a hero and placed a Woodhull memorial on a granite block at PS 35, two blocks from the site of the original tavern.

Turning Point: East Jamaica remained rural until 1885 when Frederick W. Dunton, Jamaica town supervisor, and associates purchased 136 acres and sold them as home lots. He named the development Hollis after a town in his native New Hampshire. Dunton was said to dabble in astrology, and liked things "round." Hence every street in his "Hollis Woods" section had to curve

Please Turn the Page

FLUSHING

From Quakers to Asians: Welcome

BY RHODA AMON
STAFF WRITER

The welcoming Matinecocks not only sold Flushing to the Dutch at the rate of one ax for 50 acres, they also fed the colonists who would have otherwise starved in the winter of 1637. Their reward was all-out war unleashed by the tyrannical New Netherland Gov. William Kieft, with reprisals on both sides. Peace was finally restored after the arrival of English settlers in 1645.

It's not clear why Kieft invited the English from New England. It may have been because the Dutch were having trouble colonizing, Dutch farmers apparently seeing no reason to leave Holland. English rulers were better at driving people to seek refuge in the colonies, while the New England Puritans gave any nonconformist reason to flee to Long Island.

Kieft might have also wanted to repay Capt. John Underhill, an English mercenary whom he had called upon to rout the Indians in Connecticut. Underhill, a merciless Indian fighter and later a devout Quaker, remained the most controversial Flushing-ite.

In 1997, historian Myron Luke, retired editor of the Nassau County Historical Society Journal, cautioned against assessing Underhill by modern standards. "Never take a man out of his generation," Luke said. "There was a strong Indian uprising . . . They could have massacred the whites out of existence."

With peace restored, however, English settlers spread out over an area from Flushing Creek to Little Neck Bay, including what became College Point, Whitestone, Bayside, Douglaston and Little Neck. The English called the town Flushing, an anglicizing of the Dutch city Vlissingen, which harbored English refugees before they embarked for the New World.

The name Flushing was to become forever associated with the first declaration of religious tolerance in American history. The Society of Friends, the Quaker group founded in England in the early 1600s, sent its first missionaries to the colonies in 1656. Peter Stuyvesant, who had succeeded Kieft as governor of New Netherlands, did not look favorably on religious dissenters. He ordered that colonists were not to let the Quakers into their homes.

The Flushing citizens replied with the Flushing Remonstrance of 1657, asking that every man be "let to stand and fall to his own Master." Stuyvesant replied by jailing the leading signers, including the sheriff. John Bowne, a young farmer who defied the law by holding Quaker meetings in his home, was exiled to Holland. He returned with orders from the Dutch West India Co. to cease the persecution.

Stuyvesant accepted the order, and the Quakers soon became a major force in the North Shore communities. The Flushing Friends' Meeting House, built in 1694, emerged as the oldest church building in continuous use on Long Island. (Even after three centuries, the Bowne house, the oldest house in Flushing, looked much as it did in 1661.)

After the British drove out the Dutch in 1664, Flushing farmers faced another menace: the duke of York's tax collectors. The "Duke's Laws" sowed the seeds for the Revolution, which sharply divided Flushing families

a century later. Although Queens was largely Tory territory, Flushing produced a number of ardent Patriots. One Flushing-Whitestone landowner, Francis Lewis, was a member of the Continental Congress and a signer of the Declaration of Independence. The Quakers, meanwhile, remained neutral and suffered from both sides. The British used the Friends' meetinghouse as a prison, a hospital and a hay warehouse.

British troops also played havoc with the Prince Nursery, established by William Prince in 1737 as the country's first commercial nursery. The Redcoats chopped down 3,000 young cherry trees to make poles for hop vines, preferring beer to fruit.

The orchards had recovered enough by 1789, however, to welcome the new president, who came on his barge from Manhattan to buy fruit. George Washington did not chop down any of Flushing's cherry trees, but he was reportedly casing the place as a possible site for the nation's capital. He may have been discouraged by the lack of convenient transportation across the East River.

That same year, meanwhile, all of Flushing's town records were destroyed in a fire started in the home of Town Clerk Jeremiah Vanderbilt by a 17-year-old slave angered because Vanderbilt would not let her get married. In a famous case prosecuted by Aaron Burr, she was convicted and hanged.

Flushing grew slowly in the next century. A steamboat ran twice a day to Manhattan; stages ran to Brook-

Queens Historical Society Photo

A salute to Decoration Day, 1886, at Monument Square in Flushing. Eight years later, the town voted against consolidating with New York City, but eventually bowed to the inevitable.

lyn. The Long Island Rail Road opened a station in 1902 on what was then the Willets farm, and the Auburndale community grew up around it. The country homes were billed as less than 10 miles from the East 34th Street ferry landing in Long Island City.

In 1894, Flushing voted against consolidating with New York City, but eventually bowed to the inevitable. The most important events since were the opening of the Queensboro Bridge in 1909, which touched off a real estate boom, and the two World's Fairs in 1939 and 1964, leaving in their wake Flushing Meadows-Corona Park and Shea Stadium.

A major demographic change began in 1965 when the immigration law that had favored Northern Europeans was changed to permit more immigration from other areas. Asians began filling the downtown Flushing apartments once occupied by Jewish, Italian and German immigrants.

The Asian-American population swelled from 18,000 in the 1980 census to more than 49,000 in 1990, and they became a significant voting force and a source of vitality in the old village.

Where to Find More: Long Island collection, Queens Borough Central Library, Jamaica, and branch libraries.

FOREST HILLS
Tudor Style, Anyone?

BY RHODA AMON
STAFF WRITER

Before it was a model garden development or the site of a world-famous tennis club, Forest Hills in 1652 apparently looked like a dry riverbed left behind by the glaciers that formed Long Island. The Dutch called the area Whiteput, meaning pit. The British translated Whiteput to Whitepot, which gave rise to the legend that Forest Hills was bought from the Indians for three white pots.

Whitepot in Central Queens was part of the original Middleburg settlement that the English in 1664 renamed New Towne, later Newtown. The whole town was a British encampment during the Revolution, and British Gen. William Howe's regiments bedded down at what later became Union Turnpike and Queens Boulevard.

For the next century, Whitepot was farmland owned by six wealthy families. Then along came Cord Meyer Jr., heir to his father's sugar-refining fortune and the Donald Trump of the late 1800s. Meyer bought 600 acres along Queens Boulevard, visualizing a community he would call Forest Hills.

Starting in 1906, Meyer laid out streets and built a few houses, but, competing against 50 other Queens developers, he began to lose his nerve and sold 142 acres to the Sage Foundation Home Co. for $2 million in 1909. This brought in Margaret Olivia Slocum Sage, who founded the Russell Sage Foundation in 1907 with $10 million inherited from her financier husband. Given the foundation's purpose of improving the living conditions of the poor, Sage was expected to build low-income housing. Instead she set out to build a "model garden city" for urbanites of moderate means. However, because she wanted to realize a profit from the project — and because it was so well designed and proved to be so costly — it became available to only the well-to-do. The foundation, however, was changing its emphasis to research, and the profits would be turned into grants for study of urban social problems and the causes of poverty.

Forest Hills Gardens was described in a sales brochure as "the most comprehensive accomplishment in garden city or model town planning yet undertaken in America." The sales pitch went on to "confute any opinion that it has been developed with certain charitable or philanthropic objects in view . . ." Sage wanted to make it clear that Forest Hills Gardens was, as the brochure declared, "a high-class suburban residential community conducted upon strictly business principles."

Sage hired architect Grosvenor Atterbury to design English Tudor-style homes with red tile roofs and decorative masonry touches. Landscape architect Frederick Law Olmsted, designer of Central Park, was commissioned to lay out narrow, circular streets to discourage heavy traffic. Mortgages were granted only to those who could afford a $25 monthly payment, a goodly sum in those days, ensuring a community of "moderate income and good taste." Industry was banned.

In 1910, the Long Island Rail Road built an electrified link through Forest Hills, and Sage and Cord Meyer helped build an elegant $50,000 station with two staircases, arches and cobblestones. Former President Theodore Roosevelt made a famous speech from its stone steps in 1917.

After building a third of the homes, the Sage Foundation in 1922 sold its interest to the Forest Hills Gardens Corp., a property-owner group that continued to create homes in the Sage fashion. The association remained a watchdog over the architecture and maintenance of the neighborhood, although its biggest fight in the 1990s was against "unauthorized parking" generated by the shops and apartment buildings that proliferated along Queens Boulevard and Austin Street.

Attracted by the community's English ambiance and 14-minute commute, Manhattan's West Side Tennis Club relocated to Forest Hills

Collection of Joel Streich
A mostly treeless and flat block in Forest Hills, about 1931

in 1914, purchasing 10 acres for $77,000 and later building a 13,500-seat stadium. The club hosted the international Davis Cup competition for the first time in 1914 and successively after 1921. The U.S. Open, played there since the 1920s, was popularly known as Forest Hills. The Open moved to the National Tennis Center at Flushing Meadows-Corona Park in 1978.

Over the years, many famous entertainers and other celebrities lived in Forest Hills, including former vice presidential candidate Geraldine Ferraro; Horace I. Willson, founder of the Columbia Phonograph Co. that became Columbia Records; actor Carroll O'Connor; comedian Lou Costello; singers Rudy Vallee and Carol Channing; orchestra leader Hal Kemp; author and lecturer Helen Keller; and author-entrepreneur Dale Carnegie of "How to Win Friends and Influence People" fame.

Where to Find More: "An Illustrated History of Forest Hills," by Robert Minton, at the Queens Borough Central Library, Long Island Collection, Jamaica; "Forest Hills Gardens" by William C. Coleman, in North Forest Park Branch Library, 98-27 Metropolitan Ave., Forest Hills.

---

came a swanky bathing and boating resort in the 1890s. It ended when Hotel Howard and neighboring cottages were destroyed by fire in 1907. After that, sand was pumped over the meadows, Hawtree Creek was dug out and a housing boom began, lasting into the '60s. The community was further affected by the opening of Idlewild Airport in 1948 (expanded to Kennedy Airport in 1963) and the extension of the subway in 1956.

The Name: William J. Howard, a Brooklyn glove manufacturer, built a resort complex on Jamaica Bay in 1897. Undaunted when it was destroyed by fire, Howard filled in a marshland west of Hawtree Creek and created a development called Howard Estates. Today the name covers several smaller developments, such as West Hamilton Beach, Lindenwood and Rockwood Park.

Claims to the Famous: Stars such as the English actress Lili Langtry came to Howard Beach when it was a fashionable resort. Howard Beach was also the scene of an infamous racial attack in 1986. As the year 2000 approached, it was a harmonious amalgam of close-knit working-class communities.

Where to Find More: See "Old Queens, N.Y., in Early Photographs," by Vincent F. Seyfried and William Asadorian.

JACKSON HEIGHTS, JAMAICA

See stories on Pages 166 and 169.

JAMAICA ESTATES
A Wealthy Enclave
Carved in Woods

Beginnings: By the close of the 19th Century, Queens already was running out of land, villages were expanding into each other, and Jamaica was becoming the shopping center of central Queens. But there were still 503 acres of undeveloped forest, owned by the City of New York and filled with maple, elm and chestnut trees. Meanwhile, wealthy city dwellers were looking for a place in the country not too far from their connections on Wall Street and at City Hall. The answer came with the opening of the Queensboro Bridge in 1909, followed by construction of Queens Boulevard from the bridge to Jamaica. A group of wealthy New Yorkers formed the Jamaica Estates Co. in 1910, bought the Jamaica woods and began an enclave of large Tudor-style homes for people of means.

Turning Point: When the developers went bankrupt in the 1920s and auctioned their remaining lots, the property owners (275 at the time) formed the Jamaica Estates Association in 1928. They were determined to hold to the original building restrictions: only detached two-story houses with attics, no flat roofs and no house costing less than $6,000, a goodly sum at the time. In 1934, when the city assessed local property owners for the building of the Grand Central Parkway, the association joined a coalition that succeeded in having Grand Central declared an arterial highway, paid for by the state and city.

Claims to Fame: While other wealthy city neighborhoods have declined with changing times, Jamaica Estates remained an elegant place where judges, civic leaders and doctors have made their homes, among them Rep. Gary Ackerman and developer Fred Trump, father of Donald. One mansion was converted into a spiritual retreat called the Bishop Molloy House and the Immaculate Conception Monastery.

Where to Find More: See "The History of the Jamaica Estates, 1929-1969," by Thomas J. Lovely, in the Long Island Collection, Queens Borough Central Library, 89-11 Merrick Blvd., Jamaica.

HOLLIS, Continued

and have an "o" in its name. Hollis Park Gardens was developed in 1906 as a community of high-class houses.

Boom Times: From 1922 until World War II, hundreds of tract houses were built; many were later replaced by apartment houses and shops. Hollis began an economic decline in the 1960s, and community leaders worked to revitalize the area.

Claims to Fame: Notable Hollis residents have included former UN Ambassador Andrew Young, former Gov. Mario Cuomo, former chairman of the Joint Chiefs of Staff Colin Powell, and rappers Joseph Simmons, Darryl McDaniels and Jason Mizell of Run-DMC.

Where to Find More: "Old Queens, N.Y. in Early Photographs," by Vincent F. Seyfried and William Asadorian, available in the Queens Borough Central Library, Jamaica, and in stores.

HOWARD BEACH
A Fishing Colony's
Wealthy Catch

Beginnings: Sea bass, snappers, bluefish and shellfish lured Canarsie and Rockaway Indians and later settlers, to Hawtree Creek and Jamaica Bay. Indian campsites at the edge of the creek were replaced by English fishermen forming an isolated community of houses built on stilts. The area was variously nicknamed Ramblersville, The Venice of Long Island and, in the 1770s, Remsen's Landing, after its largest landowner, Col. Jaramus Remsen.

The Revolution: Remsen and his Patriots are credited with driving out the Tory guerrillas, who hid weaponry in the marshland in preparation for the British invasion. The Patriots hid their cattle and moved women and children out of harm's way. Hailed as a hero, Remsen rated a monument in Rego Park.

Turning Points: The small fishing colony be-

JAMAICA: A postcard illustrates the entrance to Jamaica Estates on Hillside Avenue, circa 1910.

HOWARD BEACH: Hawtree Avenue around 1930, as depicted on a postcard.

OZONE PARK: A postcard from about 1920 shows the railroad crossing on Jerome Avenue.

Bird's eye View of Corona, N. Y. Looking North.

CORONA: A postcard, circa 1910, looks across the community.

Jamaica Avenue, Business Section, Richmond Hill, L. I.

Collection of Joel Streich

RICHMOND HILL: This view, on a postcard from about 1910, shows a portion of Jamaica Avenue.

Collection of Joel Streich

FOREST HILLS: Austin Street, always busy, in about 1940.

JACKSON HEIGHTS

Pioneering in New Types of Housing

BY RHODA AMON
STAFF WRITER

Jackson Heights was the nation's first garden apartment community. In fact, the phrase "garden apartments" was coined in 1917 by the Queensboro Corp., which created Jackson Heights, now a New York City historic district. More than anything else, Jackson Heights was the brainchild of one single-minded entrepreneur, Edward Archibald MacDougall.

You won't find Jackson Heights on any map of Queens before 1900. What does appear is a section of the Town of Newtown called Trains Meadow after Trains Meadow Road, a colonial roadway that no longer exists. Trains Meadow was farmland, much of it owned by two old families: the descendants of the Rev. William Leveriche, who settled there in 1662, and the Barclays, for whom Barclay Street in Lower Manhattan is named. (The Barclays specialized in trotting horses and built a racetrack on Northern Boulevard.)

The Queensboro Corp. began buying up land along Trains Meadow Road in 1909 and continued through 1918, while costs rose from $6,500 to $18,500 an acre. Construction of one- and two-family brick houses began in 1910. The Queensboro Bridge had just opened and the elevated train was on its way. An advertisement in the Newtown Register proclaimed that home buyers would no longer be kept away because it was so hard to get to Queens: "Now you can reach your home here (a real home, too) by dustless electric trains quicker than you can get to a Harlem flat."

After World War I, MacDougall, head of the Queensboro Corp., could realize his dream of creating "a completely planned and self-contained garden community, filled with amenities," according to Daniel Karatzas, author of "Jackson Heights: A Garden in the City."

Jackson Heights differed from earlier planned developments such as Garden City and Forest Hills Gardens because it was based on the apartment house rather than the single-family home. MacDougall donated land for churches, built playgrounds, tennis courts and a golf course, and published a community newspaper, the Jackson Heights News. A Community Clubhouse provided leisure activities — dancing, bowling, club meetings, a drama school started by theatrical producer Oliver Mor-

osco, a resident at the time. Tenants were screened for social compatibility as well as financial soundness. Racial and religious restrictions were quietly accepted; one old resident recalled: "It was solidly white, of course, and there were whispers that one man was Jewish, but his name had been changed."

In the 1920s, Queensboro introduced cooperative ownership to its apartment tenants. During the Depression, however, a number of the co-op complexes failed. One tenant, Mildred Hughes, said her family moved from a $125-a-month apartment to a top-floor $75-per-month apartment. "A short time later the rent fell to just $55 per month, and then Queensboro offered to sell us the apartment for $500," she recalled in 1997. "But times were so difficult that we could not afford to buy it."

The tide turned in the mid-1930s, and by WWII residents raised enough in bond drives to christen a B-24 bomber, "The Spirit of Jackson Heights."

The postwar building boom brought in outside developers, some of whom did not share MacDougall's vision of a garden community. Playgrounds, tennis courts and golf course all succumbed to massive buildings. Old residents, mostly of northern European stock, began to move east to the Nassau County suburbs in the 1970s and '80s to be replaced by immigrants from other lands. Of the 11,400 newcomers who settled in Jackson Heights in the 1980s, Colombians made up the largest group, followed by large contingents of Chinese, Dominicans, Asian Indians, Ecuadoreans, Koreans, Guyanese, Peruvians, Cubans and Pakistanis.

In 1988, amid the chatter of many languages, one resident, Mike Crowley, sought to revive the spirit of Jackson Heights by founding the Jackson Heights Beautification Group. A symbol of their success came in 1993 when Jackson Heights became the borough's second historic district named by the City Landmark Preservation Commission. The idea was to accept changing times, but to draw what was best from the past — a sense of community.

Where to Find More: "Jackson Heights: A Garden in the City," by Daniel Karatzas, and "Jackson Heights: Biography of an Urban Community," by Alan F. Kornstein, at the Jackson Heights Branch Library, 35-51 81st St.

Queens Historical Society
A Jackson Heights golf course in 1934, later the site of the Dunnolly garden apartments on 79th Street, built in 1939

KEW GARDENS

Courts, Politicos And Will Rogers

Beginnings: In the 1600s most of central Queens from Jamaica Township to Long Island City was the Town of Newtown, a forest-and-farm area that during the American Revolution had a sparse, widely scattered population. However, development came rapidly in the 19th Century. In 1869, developers Albon P. Man and Edward Richmond carved out a section south of what later became Flushing Meadows-Corona Park and called it Richmond Hill. In the early 1900s, Man's sons, Arthur and Alrick, developed a community of their own at the site of the Richmond Hill Golf Club, which closed in 1909. They called it Kew after the London botanical gardens at Kew.

Turning Point: At first, Kew Gardens was an enclave of large homes offered to "acceptable purchasers only" by the Kew Gardens Corp. However, in the 1920s large apartment houses were built on the sections close to Queens Boulevard and Union Turnpike.

Claims to Fame: Kew Gardens, home of both the Queens Borough Hall and the Queens criminal courts, was also the home of jurist Richard S. Newcombe (for whom

Newcombe Plaza was named), humorist Will Rogers and UN Secretary-General Ralph Bunche, until he died in 1971. His Tudor Revival home, at 115-25 Grosvenor Rd., was named a national landmark.

Where to Find More: Back issues of Kew-Forest Life and The Reporter magazines available in the Queens Borough Central Library, Long Island Collection, 89-11 Merrick Blvd., Jamaica.

KEW GARDENS HILLS

Israelis: the Latest Wave of Immigrants

Beginnings: Kew Gardens Hills is tucked into Flushing's southwest corner, east of the Flushing Meadow, which in colonial days was an impassable swamp. Flushing farmers brought their produce to the Brooklyn markets on Vleigh Road, which ran along the eastern perimeter of the swamp. The road was later named Vleigh Place. The community was then called Head of the Vleigh.

The Name Change: Kew Gardens Hills is related to Kew Gardens in name only. "The Hills" also have been called East Forest Hills and Queens Valley. Legend has it that Abraham Wolosoff, who developed a community of small homes and apartments in southwest

Flushing in the 1930s, stayed in a Kew Gardens hotel and was so impressed with the classy neighborhood, he incorporated the name into his development.

Horses and Golf: During the 1700s the area was owned by William Furman, who called his farm Willow Glen. In 1820 it was sold to Timothy Jackson, who bred fine trotting horses. The area was still farmland in the late 1800s, but improved transportation was bringing developers. Eager to attract affluent city businessmen, developers opened the Queens Valley Golf Club in 1933, followed by the Arrowbrook and Pomonok golf courses.

The Later Community: IND subway service and the completion of Grand Central Parkway in the 1930s brought hundreds of new residents, attracted by "20 minutes from Manhattan" ads. German, Irish and Italian-Americans settled there in the '30s. In the late 20th Century, Kew Gardens Hills had become a tightly packed community of garden apartments, co-ops and private homes. The area attracted a large Israeli population, as evidenced by the immigrant-owned businesses and kosher food stores and restaurants along Main Street.

Where to Find More: Community folder in the Long Island Collection, Queens Borough Central Library, Jamaica.

LAURELTON

A Fight to Stem White Flight

Beginnings: Picture a pristine landscape of freshwater ponds, streams and fields shaped by glaciers. This is what the first English settlers saw in the 1640s when they arrived in southeast Queens from Hempstead, lured by meadows that needed no clearing and plenty of water for irrigation. English farmers lived quietly alongside the Matinecocks for almost a decade without benefit of a grant from the Dutch, who controlled the area. They were issued a patent in 1656 from Dutch Gov. William Kieft for a large area that included present-day Laurelton.

Turning Points: The community grew slowly until the late 1800s, when improved transportation opened the isolated southeast Queens villages to a building boom. In 1905, the Laurelton Land Co. designed a neighborhood of single-family homes and a few multiple dwellings. The company named the community Laurelton, presumably for the laurel bushes, but possibly the name was picked for its classy sound.

Boom Times: From the 1920s to the 1930s, Laurelton's population expanded tenfold, from 3,000 to 30,000, fueled by Jewish, Irish, Italian

Please Turn to Page 169

KEW GARDENS: Abingdon Road, circa 1930, as seen on a postcard. By the 1920s, huge apartment complexes were being built close to Queens Boulevard and Union Turnpike.

MOST ELABORATE IMPROVEMENTS OF ANY LONG ISLAND SUBURB

ONE OF THE BEAUTIFUL HOMES AT LAURELTON

LAURELTON: A 1910 postcard illustrates "One of the beautiful homes." In 1905, the Laurelton Land Co. had designed a neighborhood of single-family homes.

JAMAICA: A far cry from the bigger terminal that would follow, this station was built for the Long Island Rail Road in 1878.

JAMAICA: The blizzard of March, 1888, halted railroad traffic everywhere on Long Island. This train was stuck at Rockaway Junction.

JAMAICA

Glory Days, From the British to the El

BY RHODA AMON
STAFF WRITER

Jamaica had its glory days in the early 1700s, when it was the capital of the British colony of New York, the seat of the British royal governor. It also was the cow capital of the colony, with 600 head of cattle supplying a large portion of New York City's meat.

Along with Flushing and Newtown (later called Elmhurst), it was one of the three colonial towns in Queens before Queens became a county, before there was a United States. The Dutch came first, in 1655, negotiating with the Canarsie and Rockaway Indians, who both claimed the area around Jamaica Bay. The Indians settled for guns, blankets, kettles and "8 bottles of licker" — a hard bargain. The Dutch called the settlement Rustdorp, meaning "peaceful village."

The English came from Hempstead in 1656, negotiating with New Netherland Gov. Peter Stuyvesant for the land around the long-vanished Beaver Pond. The settlers, Daniel Denton, Rodger Linas, Robert Jackson and others, petitioned Stuyvesant for the "place called Conorasset," which "lies from a river which divideth it from Conarie see to the bounds of heemstead and may contain about twentie families." The name Jamaica came in the 1700s, probably derived from the Jameco Indians who lived at the head of the bay.

After the British forcefully displaced the Dutch, they created Queens County in 1683 and chartered the land to Gov. Thomas Dongan. Fishing, farming and cattle-raising flourished until 1776, when British troops routed Gen. George Washington's army in the Battle of Long Island and occupied the area for seven years. Though Queens was a hotbed of Toryism before the Revolution, Jamaica also produced its Patriot heroes. A company of minutemen was formed with 56 enlistees.

Rufus King, who had his country home in Jamaica, was a major in the Patriot army, later a delegate to the Constitutional Convention, where he helped forge the Constitution. Still later, as a U.S. senator and presidential candidate, he was a powerful foe of slavery. By 1814 local landowners had begun emancipating those slaves who were "less than forty-five years of age and capable of providing for themselves." A Sabbath school was set up in the Presbyterian church for "colored people growing up in

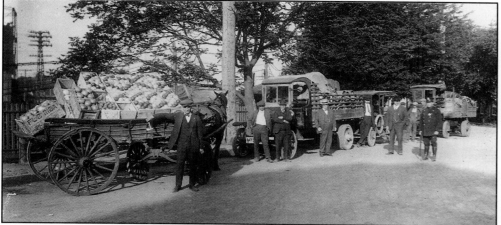
Queens Historical Society
Farmers with wagons and motorized trucks gather with produce at the Jamaica Market in the early 1900s.

ignorance of the Bible," according to the Long Island Farmer of 1822. There wasn't much education for poor whites either until 1812, when the first common school system was established. King became school commissioner. His son, John Alsop King, became governor of New York in 1857.

Transportation in Rufus King's day was over the old Indian trail to Brooklyn. Starting in 1809, the Jamaica and Brooklyn Road Co. created the Jamaica Plank Road, a toll road of planks laid crosswise. It eventually connected with the Williamsburgh & Jamaica Turnpike, later Metropolitan Avenue, creating a speedy route to the Brooklyn ferries and Manhattan. But the Jamaica area remained mainly cattle country until after the Civil War, when side streets were laid out and the shops that were to make Jamaica the shopping mecca of central Queens began to appear.

Life was not all work for 19th Century Jamaicans. The Union Course, built just south of Jamaica Avenue in 1823, became one of the best known racetracks in the young country. By the end of the century the Metropolitan Jockey Club (later Jamaica Race Track) and the Queens County Jockey Club (later Aqueduct) were providing convenient outlets for Jamaica sportsmen and their money.

The Sutphin Boulevard railroad station opened in 1913 and the "El" arrived in 1918, triggering enormous commercial growth. By 1925 the section of Jamaica Avenue from 160th to 168th Street had the highest assessed valuation in the county. In 1937 the faster underground subway, along with increased automobile traffic, doomed the El. The Transit Authority began dismantling it in 1977. Many people mourned the passing of the El, which, along with the great moviehouses, gave a certain

urban drama to Jamaica.

After World War II, Jamaica's shopping area began to lose its pre-eminence to the giant suburban malls. The ethnic makeup of Jamaica also changed. Descendants of the large numbers of Irish who had come in the 1830s to build the Long Island Rail Road moved eastward to the post-World War II suburbs, as did the German, Italian and Jewish populations that had arrived in Jamaica after the Civil War. African-Americans moved into the South Jamaica area after World War II, and were joined in the 1970s and '80s by immigrant Guyanese, Colombians, Salvadorans, Haitians and Chinese.

Over the years Jamaica attracted some of the nation's leading architects. Dudley Field designed the Grace Episcopal Church in 1862, a citadel of Gothic Revival architecture at 155-03 Jamaica Ave. and site of the original 1734 church. First Presbyterian Church of Jamaica, established in 1662, was rebuilt on Jamaica Avenue in 1813, and moved by mules around the corner to 164th Street.

Great moviehouses gave a lift to people's lives in the Depression era but declined in the age of TV. Some are lifting spirits again: They later became churches. The Valencia Theatre, designed in 1929 by John Eberson as a Spanish-style palace seating 3,500, became the Tabernacle of Prayer for All People at 165-11 Jamaica Ave.

King Manor in the 11-acre King Park on Jamaica Avenue, once part of Rufus King's working farm, remained a beautiful remnant of Jamaica's past. The oldest house in southeast Queens, it was built in the 1750s and was bought by New York City. Operated as a museum by the King Manor Association since 1900, the 29-room landmark mansion remained pretty much as it was in Rufus King's day, although the area around it vastly changed. Tours in English and Spanish attracted multicultural audiences. And, said education director Carlos Pomares, as the Long Island Rail Road, the subway and the traffic rumble by, "people find it hard to believe that this was once a farm."

Where to Find More: "Jamaica, Long Island, 1656-1776: A Study of the Roots of American Urbanism," by Jean Peyer; "Jamaica Trolleys: The Story of the Jamaica Turnpike and Trolley Line," and "Queens: A Pictorial History," by Vincent F. Seyfried, all at the Queens Borough Central Library.

LAURELTON, Continued

and German immigrants seeking homes with backyards for their children. African-Americans with the same objective began arriving in the 1940s, and at first there was little racial tension. In the mid-1960s real-estate agents triggered white flight by urging homeowners to sell before the neighborhood's racial balance tipped. Hoping to stop the blockbusting, Rabbi Harold Singer, leader of a synagogue, began a free real-estate service, employing volunteers to encourage white as well as black families to buy into the community. The experiment gained nationwide attention. By the 1990s, Laurelton's population was predominately black with some Hispanic and Asian-American residents in middle-class neighborhoods.
Where to Find More: The Queens Borough Central Library, Long Island Collection, Jamaica.

LITTLE NECK
Commuters Replace The Fishermen

Beginnings: As English and Dutch settlers put down roots on Little Neck Bay in the 1630s, the Matinecocks, who had thrived for centuries on the bay's wealth of wampum shells and seafood, found they had bartered away all but a small settlement on what was then Madnan's Neck. In 1656, a band of armed white men led by Thomas Hicks drove the Matinecocks from their last settlement. The battle was fought on what became the site of the Douglaston-Little Neck Library at Marathon Parkway and Northern Boulevard.
The Name: The Matinecocks called it Menhaden-Ock, meaning "place of fish." This was shortened to Madnan's Neck, but some say the neck of land was named for Ann Heatherton, a

squatter in 1643 known as Mad Nan. Eventually, the area was divided into two "necks" — Little Neck and Great Neck.
The Revolution: As in other places, the war separated Little Neck families into Loyalists and Patriots. The story goes that 86-year-old Thomas Foster, a descendant of an original settler, resisted the Hessian invaders and was hanged from his apple tree, but survived.
Turning Points: In the 1860s, clam and oyster fishing was a big industry, employing thousands. Pollution, however, killed the industry in the early 1900s. The Little Neck train station opened in 1866 and the rail line was extended to Port Washington in 1898. That year, Queens County was annexed to New York City and Nassau County broke away, with the boundary set on Glenwood Street in Little Neck. As bridges and tunnels opened in the early 1900s, home developers promoted Little Neck with the not-

quite-accurate slogan, "Only 26 minutes from Manhattan." Little Neck went from an agricultural community to a city suburb.
Claims to fame: William K. Vanderbilt II, whose estate straddled Little Neck and Lake Success, sponsored Vanderbilt Cup motor races starting in 1904. Bloodgood H. Cutter, the 19th Century "Long Island farmer poet," also called Little Neck home. The most poignant landmark, the Indian burial site and a split boulder inscribed, "Here rest the last of the Matinecoc," was moved from Northern Boulevard to the Zion Churchyard in Douglaston.
Where to Find More: See "Little Neck Then and Now," by Loys Gubernick, at the Douglaston-Little Neck Library, 249-01 Northern Blvd., Little Neck; "Through the Years in Little Neck and Douglaston," by George C. and Ernestine H. Fowler, at the Queens Borough Central Library, Long Island Collection, Jamaica.

LONG ISLAND CITY

A Blend of Industry and Art

BY RHODA AMON
STAFF WRITER

For one brief moment in history — 1870 to 1898 — Long Island City was a city. It had its own mayor, a territory one-third the size of Manhattan, an East River port, industries, parks and cemeteries. When New York City consolidated in 1898, Long Island City, along with the cities of Brooklyn and Williamsburgh, gave up its sovereignty.

But not its individuality. Long Island City in 1870 encompassed the communities of Astoria, Hunters Point, Blissville, Ravenswood, Dutch Kills and Bowery Bay. Dutch Kills was the first Dutch settlement on Newtown Creek in the 1640s — a small beginning for what was to become the largest entity in Queens and the most heavily industrialized with railroad yards, a tunnel, bridges and rows of factories. At the close of the 20th Century, it became an art colony with many of the factories and lofts converted to studios and art galleries.

Long Island City, which took its name from a local newspaper, the Long Island City Daily Star, had colorful mayors. The first, in 1870, Abram D. Ditmars, descended from early settlers whose name now marks a park and a boulevard. Feistiest was Irish immigrant Patrick J. Gleason, known as "Battle Axe Gleason" after he chopped down the supporting posts of a Long Island Rail Road shed he wanted moved.

Meanwhile, the area blossomed with Romanesque Revival architecture and gardens, both of the flower and beer variety. In the mid-1800s, two developers, Charles and Peter Roach, acquired the Long Island City shoreline and developed Ravenswood, Long Island's first Gold Coast, a neighborhood of riverside mansions. The 19th-Century mansions were overwhelmed by industry as 1900 approached. Hunters Point, developed in the late 1800s with Romanesque Revival architecture, became the first Queens neighborhood to be designated a New York City landmark, in 1968.

As far back as 1796 a ferry from Astoria enabled Long Island City greenhouses to supply flowers and produce to Manhattan hotels. After 1850, when burials were banned in Manhattan, cemeteries were founded in Queens and families would ferry across the East River to picnic at relatives' graves. Long Island City was becoming an important East River industrial port. It was from there that Theodore Roosevelt and his Rough Riders set out for Cuba and the Spanish-American War in 1898.

Rapid changes came at the start of the 20th Century. The Long Island Rail Road built a large plant to electrify its suburban routes and laid out the yards in Sunnyside.

Queens Historical Society

S. Liebmann's Sons was a watering hole in Astoria, which Long Island City encompassed in 1870. The city lost its sovereignty in 1898.

The Queensboro Bridge opened in 1909, sparking a building boom. The Mathews Model Flats, built in 1915-17, were mostly rows of attached six-family apartment houses, done in decorative brick and unusually light and airy for their time. The apartments stood the test of time. Deborah Van Cura, president of the Greater Astoria Historical Society in the late 1990s, made her home in the Mathews apartment once occupied by her great-grandmother in the 1920s. Sunnyside Gardens, a planned community, rose in 1924-28. Then came the giant housing complexes starting with the Queensbridge Houses in 1940 and the Ravenswood Houses for middle-income families in 1951.

Many artists found hospitable lofts in Long Island City after being driven out of Manhattan by high rents. A large Romanesque Revival building, site of an early schoolhouse, is now an artists' co-op. The International Design Center, converted from vacant factory buildings in 1986, is a showcase for the city's interior design industry. The Noguchi Museum and the Socrates Sculpture Park also became hallmarks of the art community. LaGuardia Community College took over the unused factories of the White Motor Co. and the Equitable Bag Co. But Long Island City remained the most industrialized area in Queens County at the dawn of the year 2000.

Leading Citizens: Singers Tony Bennett and Ethel Merman, the Dead End Kids and Bobby Jordan all lived in Long Island City neighborhoods. In permanent residence in the old cemeteries are Scott Joplin and Lola Montez, a famous 19th-Century courtesan.

Where to Find More: "300 Years of Long Island City," by Vincent F. Seyfried, in the Queensbridge, Ravenswood, Steinway and Sunnyside Branch Libraries, all in Long Island City.

inland settlement attempted by English colonists who nine years earlier had been driven off by the Indian wars.

Turning Points: The Williamsburgh and Jamaica Turnpike in 1816 turned the farm community into a one-street town with houses and lodgings strung along the turnpike and a toll gate at either end. It remained largely a farmer's refreshment stop until the 1850s when Manhattan closed its churchyards, and Middle Village, along with neighboring Ridgewood and Glendale, became part of the Queens "cemetery belt." The Rev. Frederick W. Geissenhainer was first to purchase land south of Metropolitan Avenue for several Manhattan churches. It became Lutheran Cemetery in 1852. More cemeteries sprouted in the farmland, and so did florists, hotels and saloons to meet the varied needs of cemetery visitors.

Local Landmarks: Niederstein's Restaurant-Hotel, built about 1865, became a favorite stopping-off place for the largely German population of the greater Ridgewood area, first for funeral parties, and later for weddings and banquets. It was preserved as a restaurant, but no longer used as a hotel. Lutheran Cemetery became the city's most important Protestant burial grounds. Its permanent residents include victims of the General Slocum, an excursion boat that burned and sank during a Sunday School outing in 1904.

Where to Find More: See "Our Community, Its History and People: Maspeth, Middle Village, Liberty Park, Ridgewood, Glendale," by Walter J. Hutter and others; "History of Queens County, 1683-1882," by W.W. Munsell; reference library of Greater Ridgewood Historical Society, 18-20 Flushing Ave.

OAKLAND GARDENS

From Indian Trail To Nature Center

Beginnings: The Matinecocks hunted and fished in the "alley," a strip of marshes and fields south of Little Neck Bay. The first European colonists chose the area in the 1640s for its rich supply of game, water and timber. From the mid-1700s to the early 1800s, the area flourished because of an Indian trail — the ancestor of the Long Island Expressway — which cut an east-west route through the alley, making it an important trading and stopping-off area.

The Name: John Hicks, a Flushing patentee, owned a farm called The Oaks that spread from what is now 46th Avenue to the Long Island Expressway. In 1859, after generations of owners, John Taylor, a Manhattan restaurant-hotel owner, and his partner, John Henderson, turned The Oaks into a horticultural farm. After Taylor died in 1886, his son, John H., and associates opened the 110-acre Oakland Golf Club. The second-oldest golf club in the East, it had a long waiting list of applicants.

Turning Point: Starting in the late 1800s, as the Long Island Rail Road pushed east, Oakland Gardens experienced a building boom. Construction of large apartment complexes and single-family developments accelerated after World War II. The Oakland Golf Club was purchased by New York City in 1960 and used for a housing development and several schools: Queensborough Community College, Benjamin Cardozo High School and PS 203.

Claims to Fame: George Washington is believed to have stopped there for a mid-morning break on his 1790 tour of Long Island, although his diary doesn't specify where. Former New York Gov. Alfred E. Smith and Sen. Robert Wagner were members of the Oakland Golf Club. The city bought Alley Pond Park on Oakland Gardens' eastern border in 1929. It became an environmental center in 1976.

Where to Find More: "A History of Bayside," by James A. Flux, Queens Borough Central Library, Long Island Collection, Jamaica, and the Central Flushing and Fresh Meadows libraries.

MASPETH

Where De Witt Clinton Planned His Canal

Beginnings: Maspeth was the site of the first English colony in Queens County. In 1642 the Rev. Francis Doughty, an unlucky pioneer from the Massachusetts colony, was granted a patent for a settlement at the head of Newtown Creek, the camping grounds of the Mespat Indians. But in 1643, in reprisal for the massacre of Indians in Connecticut, the Mohicans and Matinecocks fell upon Doughty's settlement and burned it. Nine years later the settlers established a new colony farther inland at what became Elmhurst. Maspeth was eventually settled by migrants from Brooklyn and Long Island City.

The Name: It comes from the Mespats, but has gone through a variety of spellings.

The Revolution: Like most of Long Island, Maspeth was occupied by the British after the disastrous Battle of Long Island in 1776. Sir Henry Clinton, the British commander, had his headquarters in the Clinton Mansion on Old Town Dock Road, which gave him a good view of the British fleet wintering in Newtown Creek.

Turning Points: In 1852 developers cut up two large farms into streets and building lots, opening a community from 59th Place to 69th Street, and from 55th Drive to a plank road that became Grand Avenue. Manufacturing came at about the same time. Cord Meyer, Newtown's master developer, established a carbon factory that brought many workers to the area. The residue was used to paint New York City carriages black. After the Civil War, German immigrants arrived, changing the community that was once largely English Quakers.

Brushes With Fame: Maspeth's most prominent resident was De Witt Clinton, who was both mayor of New York City (1803-15) and governor of New York State (1817-23) and lived in the 1790s in the circa-1725 Clinton Mansion. He also headed the Erie Canal Commission and planned the famous waterway from his home in Maspeth. The house burned down in 1933.

Where to Find More: "Our Community, Its History and People: Ridgewood, Glendale, Maspeth, Middle Village, Liberty Park," by the Greater Ridgewood Historical Society; "A History of Queens County, New York, New York," William Munsell, editor, at many libraries.

MIDDLE VILLAGE

A Pause to Refresh En Route to the Ferry

Beginnings: Middle Village, as its name implies, was the halfway point between Jamaica and the Williamsburgh (then spelled with an "h") ferry, a place where Queens farmers on their way to and from the Brooklyn or Manhattan markets on the Williamsburgh and Jamaica Turnpike (later Metropolitan Avenue) could park their wagons and enjoy a rest and refreshment. In 1652, before there was a turnpike, Middle Village was part of a new

MASPETH: A 1912 photo of the Down and Out Club, a social, political and business group that aimed to build the community. Members met at a tavern on Maspeth Avenue, near Clinton Hall. The name of the club was a play on the group's economic status. Although no members were wealthy, neither were they Down and Out.

MIDDLE VILLAGE: The Hirsch Bros. Saloon, at the corner of Metropolitan Avenue and 80th Street, across from St. John's Cemetery, was in operation in the late 1800s. Saloons met the needs of visitors when Middle Village, along with Ridgewood and Glendale, became part of the borough's "cemetery belt" in the second half of the 19th Century.

New York Racing Association

OZONE PARK: The old Aqueduct Raceway in an undated photograph. The track opened Sept. 27, 1894.

Jamaica and Myrtle Avenues, Richmond Hill, L.I.

Collection of Joel Streich

RICHMOND HILL: The trolley rolls through an intersection around 1910.

OZONE PARK

They Were 'Yearning To Breathe Free'

Beginnings: Ozone Park was created out of Queens farmland south of Woodhaven by two developers, Benjamin W. Hitchcock and Charles C. Denton, in 1882. Hitchcock, a Manhattan music publisher, was an experienced land speculator, having started Woodside in 1867, South Flushing in 1872 and Garden City Park in 1874. Though they carved their purchase into 316 small segments, they used the same sales pitch that grand estate planners had used: Come to the country, enjoy the fresh, invigorating country air.

The Name: In the 1990s, the word "ozone" came to connote an environmental catastrophe. In the 1880s, ozone suggested clean, fresh air from ocean and bay to crowded city tenement dwellers "yearning to breathe free."

Turning Point: The real turning point for Ozone Park came before the first house was sold. The new community lay directly in the path of the New York, Woodhaven and Rockaway Railroad's new line from Long Island City to Howard Beach and then across five miles of open water to Rockaway Beach. It was the engineering marvel of the early 1900s, drawing crowds of pleasure seekers for the thrill of riding a train for miles over open water as well as a day at the beach. Arrival of the Fulton Street El in 1915 sparked another building boom. In the late 1900s, like most of Queens, Ozone Park saw demographic changes, including arrivals by Guyanese, Haitians, Trinidadians and Colombians.

Claim to Fame: Ozone Park boasted one of the largest thoroughbred racing tracks in the nation: the 80,000-capacity Aqueduct Racetrack, where Man 'o War and Seabiscuit ran to glory. The original track opened in 1894; it reopened Sept. 14, 1959.

Brushes With Fame: The Clark Homestead at Cross Bay and Rockaway Boulevards hosted George Washington for at least one night during the Revolution. Others who stayed longer included actress-singer Bernadette Peters, Olympic skating champion Carol Heiss, rock singer Cyndi Lauper, and Gerald M. Edelman, who won the Nobel Prize in 1972 for research on antibodies. Among the more notorious, John Gotti ran the Gambino crime family from the Bergin Hunt and Fish Club on 101st Avenue.

Where to Find More: "The Story of Woodhaven and Ozone Park," by Vincent F. Seyfried, in the Woodhaven Branch Library, 85-41 Forest Pkwy.

QUEENS VILLAGE

Did Annie Oakley Get Her Gun Here?

Beginnings: Though settled by colonists in the 1640s, Little Plains, as it was then called, was mostly used as "commons," public lands for grazing cattle. In the 1700s it became a village on the edge of the Hempstead Plains, with a few narrow roads and large farms.

The Names: In 1824 Thomas Brush established a blacksmith shop, prospered and expanded to other shops, a factory, more land. The village became known as Brushville and might still be Brushville were it not for the coming of the railroad in 1834. Since this was the first station in Queens, it became the Queens station. Another entrepreneur, Civil War Col. Alfred M. Wood, former mayor of Brooklyn, bought land north of Brush's estate and built another railroad station called Queens Village. The name stuck to the entire area.

Turning Points: Development started south of Jericho Turnpike in the 1870s and the first subdivisions sprouted in 1906. But Queens Village remained largely rural until the arrival of the Roaring Twenties, when the big Queens housing boom spread east, and hundreds of row houses with small backyards offered city folk

an opportunity to escape to the country.

Shooting Stars: Legend has it that Annie Oakley got her gun here, on the Creedmoor Rifle Range built in 1873 by the newly organized National Rifle Association and used by the country's top competitors for national and international meets. The range was abandoned in 1910 and became the site for the Creedmoor State Psychiatric Center. Other local stars included the Callisters, who started a carriage business in 1853 which became a leading auto dealership in 1914. Writer-editor Christopher Morley and landscape artist Henry Miller also made their homes here.

Where to Find More: "History of Queens Village," by Vincent F. Seyfried.

REGO PARK

A 'REal GOod' Place to Live

Beginnings: In 1665, it was part of the vast central Queens area that the English settlers called New Towne (or Newtown). Later it was known as a place of rich farms where horse-drawn carriages picked up fruits and vegetables for delivery to the Manhattan markets, but it still didn't have a name until 1925, when an enterprising pre-Levittown developer of 45 acres of farmland advertised the area as a "REal GOod" place to live. Thus Rego Park got a name.

Turning Point: Home developments sprouted on the farmland in the early 20th Century, but prospective home buyers from Manhattan's crowded neighborhoods could only reach the area by taking the Jamaica trolley from the Queensboro Bridge. That changed in 1928 when the Long Island Rail Road station opened, and the population swelled. By 1939 Rego Park had the city's first Howard Johnson's. The restaurant was torn down in 1969 to make way for the 11-story Queens Tower.

Claims to the Famous: A host of 20th Century show-biz personalities found Rego Park a REal GOod place to live, including comedians Sid Caesar and Eddie Bracken, burlesque queen Gypsy Rose Lee, actresses June Havoc and Alice Faye, Miss America and city Cultural Affairs Commissioner Bess Myerson, TV producer Fred Silverman and Knicks star Willis Reed.

Where to Find More: "Pictorial History of Queens," by Vincent F. Seyfried, material in Rego Park Branch Library, 91-41 63rd Dr.

RICHMOND HILL

Home to Jacob Riis And the Marx Brothers

Beginnings: For a bit of wampum and rum, the Rockaway Indians sold a big part of central Queens to the Dutch in the early 1600s. When the English took over from the Dutch after 1664, the area became part of the Town of Newtown, which swept from Jamaica to Long Island City. The area south of what later became Flushing Meadows-Corona Park went by the strange name of Whitepot. It would be a couple more centuries before Richmond Hill would be carved out as a bit of London transported to the New World.

The Revolution: One of the bloodiest skirmishes of the Battle of Long Island in 1776 was fought along the ridge in Forest Park by what would become the golf course clubhouse.

Turning Point: In 1869, Albon P. Man, a Manhattan lawyer, and Edward Richmond, a landscape architect, laid out a community with a post office and railroad station on a tract north of the Jamaica Plank Road as far as Union Turnpike. They either named it after a famous area near London or, more likely, after Edward Richmond. In 1895, the communities of Richmond Hill, Morris Park and Clarenceville were consolidated into the village of Richmond Hill.

Claims to Fame: Danish immigrant Jacob Riis, journalist, author, fighter for the urban underdog and namesake for a bathing beach, lived at 84-14 120th St. Though the house was torn down in 1968, the Native New Yorkers Historical Society nonetheless placed a marker on the site and marked the house at 87-48 134th St. where the Marx Brothers lived. Richmond Hill was the birthplace of Jahn's old-fashioned ice cream parlor established in the 1940s by native Frank Jahn. It became a model for nostalgic ice cream parlors across the country.

Where to Find More: See "A Peek at Richmond Hill Through the Keyhole of Time," by William Krooss, and "Victorian Richmond Hill," by the Richmond Hill Chapter of the Queens Historical Society, both at the Richmond Hill Branch Library, 118-14 Hillside Ave.

RIDGEWOOD

Multiple Listings Of Historic Places

Beginnings: The thick wooded ridge abutting the Brooklyn flatlands was for centuries the hunting ground of the Mespat and Canarsie Indians — until the 1600s when Dutch and English settlers began homesteading The Ridge, as it was then called. Over the years it was called by other names — Germanian, St. James, East Williamsburgh — but the name Ridgewood was firmly established in 1910.

The Revolution: British and Hessian troops were quartered in Ridgewood after the Battle of Long Island in 1776. They cut down fences and forests for firewood during the cold winters and destroyed livestock. After the British evacuation in 1783, much of Ridgewood was in ruins.

Turning Points: The making of beer brewed change for Ridgewood in the mid-1800s. German farmers who grew grains, tobacco and fruit brought in trained brewers, and breweries and beer gardens sprouted all over Ridgewood and the surrounding area. Meanwhile, old plantations began to give way to new developments, ranging from single-family homes to large row tenements. Ridgewood and Brooklyn breweries closed their doors during the Prohibition years 1919-33.

Claim to Fame: As the year 2000 approached, parts of Ridgewood, combined with sections of Middle Village, Maspeth and Glendale, made up the largest listing on the National Register of Historic Places, with 2,980 buildings. Most of the historic area consists of rows of Renaissance and Romanesque Revival tenements and rowhouses, built in the late 19th and early 20th Centuries. Landmarks included the 1709 Vander Ende-Onderdonk House, built by Paulus Vander Ende, a Dutch farmer, and then the home of the Greater Ridgewood Historical Society.

Where to Find More: "Our Community, Its History and People," "A History of Greater Ridgewood" and other material at Greater Ridgewood Historical Society, 18-20 Flushing Ave.

Queens Historical Society Photo

A trolley, possibly on Metropolitan Avenue, runs by a sign advertising real estate for sale in Richmond Hill and Kew Gardens in the early 1900s.

ROSEDALE

Wild Roses Grew
Along the Avenue

Beginnings: The Rosedale area was the hunting ground of the Rockaway Indians until the last half of the 17th Century, when Dutch and English wheat farmers discovered the Indians had a good thing. Rosedale was part of a larger area known to the 17th-Century English settlers as Spring Field, and was fed by numerous streams, springs and creeks. The salt marshes of Jamaica Bay provided cattle fodder.

Turning Points: In the latter part of the 19th Century, the rural communities of southeastern Queens beckoned city dwellers fleeing the noise and congestion of Manhattan and Brooklyn neighborhoods. In 1871, the Long Island Rail Road opened a station called Foster's Meadow, named for an early English settler named Christopher Foster. In 1890, the Standard Land Co. of Long Island, a development agency, renamed the community Rosedale and the main thoroughfare Rosedale Avenue, probably based on the wild roses bordering both sides of the avenue. (It later became Francis Lewis Boulevard.) In 1892, the LIRR officially changed the name of its station to Rosedale.

More Turning Points: The area was rapidly growing by the early 1900s. A trolley line connected the community to western Queens. In 1926, Sunrise Highway was built, speeding Rosedale's development as a residential suburb convenient to Long Island's South Shore beaches. The Rosedale Taxpayers Association was organized in 1932 to protect local homeowners. In the 1950s and '60s, black families moved in increasing numbers into the rows of single-family homes; many white families moved to the nearby Nassau suburbs, and racial incidents thrust Rosedale into an unwelcome spotlight. In the 1980s and '90s, with the streets quiet again, new immigrants arrived, almost half of them from the island of Jamaica, followed by Haitians and Guyanese.

Where to Find More: "A History of Rosedale," by Louis Polovsky, in the Queens Borough Central Library, Long Island Collection, Jamaica.

SOUTH OZONE PARK

'The Sport of Kings'
In Their Backyard

Beginnings: Land where the Rockaway and Jameco Indians roamed by foot or canoe eventually became a close neighbor of John F. Kennedy International Airport. (An ancient burial ground of the Rockaways was found at the north end of a JFK runway.)

English and Dutch farmers took possession of the area in the 1660s, and their descendants and others continued farming almost into the 20th Century. Music publisher Benjamin Hitchcock, who developed Ozone Park in the 1880s, also marketed the area to the south for its "invigorating and healthful" breezes sweeping in from Jamaica Bay and the Atlantic Ocean.

Turning Point: In 1907, David P. Leahy from St. Louis, the Levitt of his day, built small homes in the fields south of Ozone Park. He lured less affluent home buyers with the promise that "$9 down, $6 per month" could buy a four-room cottage in the country. "Some days from now the Pennsylvania Railroad will begin operating between Manhattan and Jamaica . . . and Jamaica Bay will soon be the largest harbor in the world," his ads boasted. "South Ozone Park is ideally located between these two new improvements." Train service in Jamaica in 1908 brought a rush of buyers. In 1929 Rockaway Boulevard, the area's main commercial strip, was widened and the new Van Wyck Expressway gave residents clear sailing by motor car.

Bets and Debts: Though South Ozone Park was

Please Turn to Page 177

THE ROCKAWAYS
A Paradise for Everyone

BY RHODA AMON
STAFF WRITER

The oceanfront land that was to become one of the country's most popular playgrounds was for thousands of years a barren strip of sand, scrub growth and marshes used by the Canarsie Indians as their main shell-collecting site. The Indians called the peninsula "Rechouwacky," meaning "the place of our people." White settlers changed it to Rockaway — a peninsula described in one history book as an "elongated toeless human foot pointing west."

The area was relatively peaceful until the mid-1600s, when Dutch settlers set restrictions against the Indians, which led to a powwow and then a settlement between the Dutch government and the chiefs. After the English vanquished the Dutch in 1664, Rockaway's "neck" — later known as the communities of Rockaway Beach, Arverne, Edgemere and Far Rockaway — was ceded to the English Gov. Thomas Dongan, who granted it to settler John Palmer in 1685. Palmer held it only two years before selling his grant to Richard Cornell, a wealthy ironmaster who already had a domain stretching from Flushing and Cow Neck (later known as Port Washington) on the North Shore to the Five Towns on the South Shore.

Cornell made it his retirement home and died in Far Rockaway in 1694, leaving the area to his 10 children. Cornell descendants held the "neck" until 1808. It remained sparsely populated and was a haven for Loyalists during the American Revolution.

In 1832, a cholera outbreak in Manhattan sent hundreds of families fleeing to Rockaway's healthful ocean beaches. The first hotel, the Marine Pavilion, was built in 1833. It catered to such notables as Henry Wadsworth Longfellow and Washington Irving before being destroyed by fire in 1864.

Accessible only by private yacht, Rockaway became a playground for the rich. By the late 1800s, however, with steamer ferries bringing thousands of pleasure seekers from Manhattan and Brooklyn and a rail connection from Jamaica bringing thousands more for 50 cents round-trip, Rockaway Beach became an everyman's paradise. "With the exception of Saratoga Springs, Rockaway was the most famous watering place in America," reported William W. Munsell in his 1882 "History of Queens County." He marveled over "the largest hotel in the world . . . the colossal structure the Rockaway Beach Hotel," four city blocks long with space for 8,000 guests. The ambitious project never fully opened its doors. The Rockaway Beach Improvement Co. foreclosed on the $1.5-million project in 1882.

But the Rockaway boom continued. Leading the way was Jamaica hotel keeper James S. Remsen, who with a partner bought five miles of barren oceanfront for $525 in 1853. "When Mr. Remsen became a part purchaser of the beach, many of his friends believed him to be deranged, but after long years of earnest work and the success of his enterprise they have changed their minds," Munsell wrote. By 1881 Remsen owned "twenty hotels, the museum building, the drug store, and other property."

Rockaway Beach now rivaled Brooklyn's Coney Island

as New York's favorite summer resort. Bathers rented space in the bath houses and even their suits — women's bathing suits consisting of heavy wool bloomers, baggy skirt and blouse.

Two great fires leveled the seaside resort in 1892 and 1899, leaving the large hotels in ashes. But new permanent residents, mostly German, Jewish and Russian immigrants, were arriving. They rented summer bungalows and ran boardwalk concessions. Entrepreneur William Wainwright built Rockaway Playland in 1901, adding a roller coaster and fun house in 1925.

Meanwhile, small residential communities were developing, starting on the eastern end. In 1882 Remington Vernam purchased land between Far Rockaway and Rockaway Beach, intending to create a resort to rival Rockaway Beach. His wife, Florence, who helped design the project, noticed that her husband was signing his checks "R. Vernam" and named the new project "Arverne." The development opened with a grand hotel, the Arverne, in 1888 and in 1895 incorporated as a village called "Arverne-by-the-Sea."

The peninsula was growing longer as ocean tides car-

Newsday Photo
A 1983 aerial view of Rockaway Beach shows Playland, left of center, which closed in 1987.

ried sand westward. Real estate developers were also moving west. Belle Harbor and Neponsit were marketed as upscale communities in 1908. Houses in Belle Harbor sold for $6,000 all the way up to an extravagant $36,000. The two communities have remained upper-middle-class havens of private homes. But Cross Bay Boulevard in 1925 brought easy access to the Rockaways and hastened their demise as exclusive resorts. Grand estates became boarding houses, and large apartment complexes were built. The trend was accelerated after World War II. With the suburban exodus of the middle class in the 1950s, many housing projects were foreclosed or abandoned.

Concerned about urban decay in the 1960s, the city under Mayor John Lindsay bulldozed a large part of Arverne for urban renewal. But when the city ran into financial straits, the project was tabled.

Rockaway Beach was also changing. Playland, the last surviving amusement park in the Rockaways, began attracting a rowdier crowd. Problems with crime and injuries and skyrocketing insurance premiums finally doomed it. A bulldozer in 1987 marked the end of an era.

Where to Find More: "The History of the Rockaways," by Alfred Henry Bellot, 1918, available in the Queens Borough Central Library, Jamaica, and the Seaside (Rockaway Park), Peninsula (Rockaway Beach) and Arverne branch libraries.

EAST ROCKAWAY: Horse-drawn carriages provided public transportation before buses and cars.

Nassau County Museum Collection, Long Island Studies Institute

ROCKAWAY: A view of the Long Island Rail Road trestle over Jamaica Bay on the Rockaway Line, about 1900.

Queensborough Public Library, Long Island Division

Queens Boulevard, looking north onto Greenpoint Avenue in 1913. Below is a view of the same intersection in 1998.

New-York Historical Society Photo

Bucolic to Busy in Sunnyside

The pastoral scene above is part of the Sunnyside community in 1913. Only one building can be seen on Queens Boulevard, looking north onto Greenpoint Avenue. The building was called J.W. Burrows Central Hotel in 1872, but its use in 1913 is not known.

At a time when other parts of the borough were developing rapidly, "Farms held out to the end here. This certainly was one of the last areas to be developed in western Queens," said James Driscoll of the Queens Historical Society.

But the opening of the Queensboro Bridge in 1909 led to a trolley, whose tracks appear in the foreground, that ran from the bridge to Jamaica. In 1917 came the elevated tracks along the boulevard, and commuting to Manhattan became easier. The first major housing complex was Sunnyside Gardens, a 77-acre utopian community begun in 1924 to provide affordable working-class housing. Other complexes followed, sealing the fate of another farming community.

Newsday Photo / Patrick Andrade

Sunnyside Gardens Foundation Photo

Ice-skating in the late 1920s or early 1930s in the development, whose object was to provide affordable, healthful housing

SUNNYSIDE

Their Place in the Sun

BY RHODA AMON
STAFF WRITER

In the mid 1980s, Nancy Mastopietro returned to live in the house where she was born in 1928, in a Queens community that had stayed pretty much the way it was 70 years before.

Mastopietro came back to Sunnyside Gardens, one of Long Island's earliest Utopian communities and the jewel of the larger Sunnyside area. The project began in 1924 on 77 acres excessed from the construction of the Long Island Rail Road's Sunnyside Trainyards. The object at the time was to provide affordable housing — with open space, light and sunshine — for working families who were crowded into cold-water flats in congested city neighborhoods.

Mastopietro's parents, James and Elsie Stewart, were the kind of people philanthropist Alexander M. Bing probably had in mind when he founded the City Housing Corp., the private social-policy housing development group that built Sunnyside Gardens, which is a portion of the Sunnyside community in northeast Queens. James Stewart was a chauffeur who had immigrated to New York City from Scotland and Elsie had been a nursemaid in England. The Stewarts were living among other immigrants in a railroad flat in Manhattan when they learned through a newspaper ad about Sunnyside Gardens.

They bought an attached two-story single-family brick house for $9,500 in 1927 and settled into Lincoln Court. (Each court was named for a president.) Terms were easy: A $1,000 or $2,000 down payment bought into this new lifestyle. Mortgage payments averaged $10 a month per room. Clarence Stein and Henry Wright, famed architects of their day, modeled the neighborhood after Welwyn Gardens, one of England's garden cities. One-, two- and three-family homes were built around communal courtyards while a three-acre park was shared by all. For Nancy, an only child, it provided an idyllic childhood. "I had my own small playground; I always felt safe here. I still feel safe walking around these familiar places," she said in 1997.

Sunnyside was originally the name of the hilltop farm of Richard Bragaw, an American Patriot who was imprisoned by the British. When a railroad station was built in 1875, it was given that name. During the next two decades, many of the farms in the vicinity were subdivided into building lots. The area, then known as

Blissville, was part of Long Island City when it became a city in 1870 and joined New York City in 1898. Another nearby section was known as Celtic Park because of its large Irish population.

In 1907 the Pennsylvania Railroad, which then owned the LIRR, purchased a large hilly section for its trainyard. Workers leveled the hill to an elevation of 50 feet above the tide, and filled in 250 acres of swamp. The excess land was later acquired by the City Housing Corp. for construction of a model community. Sunnyside Gardens, begun in an age of Utopian idealism, survived largely intact, thanks to solid brick construction and the vigilance of residents.

Still, the neighborhood had its ups and downs. The first shock waves came with the Depression. More than 200 homes were foreclosed, and the City Housing Corp. went bankrupt in 1934. Sunnyside Gardens recovered in the 1940s and continued growing, with young families replacing the original homesteaders. But in the 1960s, when the 40-year deed restrictions expired, bitter disputes arose over residents' plans to cut away curbs and build driveways and private fences. To protect the development's original characteristics, the city declared it a Planned Community Preservation District in 1974.

Residents formed their own preservation group, the Sunnyside Foundation for Community Planning and Preservation, headed in 1998 by Dorothy Morehead. In 1984, after a long campaign, she said, the area (including the neighboring Phipps Garden Apartments) was designated a national historic district.

Other innovative housing projects bloomed in Sunnyside and nearby Woodside over the years, including the Metropolitan Life Houses, later called Cosmopolitan. Originally peopled by German, Irish, Jewish and Italian immigrants, Sunnyside later attracted Latin Americans and Asian-Americans. The old Knickerbocker Laundry, a relic of Sunnyside's industrial past, was purchased by the New York Presbyterian Church, with boasted a large Korean congregation.

Over the years Sunnyside produced a wealth of talent, including entertainers Ethel Merman, Perry Como, Nancy Walker, Judy Holliday, James Caan and Rudy Vallee; artist Raphael Soyer, and writers and social activists such as Lewis Mumford, Mark Starr and A.H. Raskin.

Where to Find More: "Small Town in the Big City: A History of Sunnyside and Woodside," by Pam Byers, in the Sunnyside and Woodside branch libraries and the Queens Borough Central Library, Jamaica.

SOUTH OZONE PARK, Continued

planned for the less affluent, residents had the "sport of kings" in their backyard with Aqueduct Racetrack in Ozone Park. The millions spent on the races, however, did not bring prosperity to South Ozone Park. Many homes were foreclosed in the 1970s. The New York City Housing and Development Association tackled the problem with an "urban homesteading" program which sold abandoned houses for as little as $1 to buyers who would agree to make the necessary repairs.

Where to Find More: Reference material in the South Ozone Park Branch Library, 128-16 Rockaway Blvd., and the Queens Borough Central Library, Long Island Collection, Jamaica.

SPRINGFIELD GARDENS

Brooklynites Arrived, Seeking Suburbia

Beginnings: The glaciers that receded from Long Island more than 15,000 years ago left behind ideal farming conditions — and not bad fishing, either — in southeast Queens. Ponds, creeks and springs lured English farmers from the Hempstead Plains as early as 1644. The area, known as Spring Field, was part of the Jamaica land grant to English settlers from Dutch Gov. Peter Stuyvesant in 1656. Homesteaders continued to push southward to the grassy meadows which required no clearing.

Turning Points: The Long Island Rail Road opened a station in Spring Field in the early 1900s, but the area remained largely rural until the World War I era, when developers snapped up farmland at $1,000 to $2,000 per acre. The area filled with 2½-story frame houses. From 1920 to 1930 the population ballooned, mostly with people from Brooklyn seeking a suburban home. Another population boom followed World War II.

The Name: A housing development begun in 1906 was called Springfield Gardens. This may have inspired the Long Island Rail Road to add "Gardens" to the name of its Spring Field station in 1927.

Landmarks: The old Springfield Cemetery contains the remains of the area's first settlers. The oldest surviving stone is from 1761.

Where to Find More: See "Encyclopedia of New York City," edited by Kenneth T. Jackson; "Old Queens, N.Y. in Early Photographs," by Vincent F. Seyfried and William Asadorian.

ST. ALBANS

Where Babe Ruth Honed His Golf Game

Beginnings: Part of a land grant to Dutch settlers from New Netherlands Gov. Peter Stuyvesant in 1655, St. Albans, like much of Queens, remained farmland and forest for most of the next couple of centuries. By the 1800s, the plantations of four families — the Remsens, Everitts, Ludlums and Hendricksons — formed the nucleus of this sprawling farm community in the eastern portion of Jamaica Township.

The Name: In 1899, a year after Queens became part of New York City, 100 residents officially named their community after the English village that was named after England's first Christian martyr.

Turning Points: In the 1890s, St. Albans began to emerge from a sleepy farm community. The first street lights illuminated Lazy Lane, which became Central Road and then Linden Boulevard, and Freeman's Path, which became Farmers Boulevard. New shops clustered around August Everitt's lone

Please Turn the Page

Collection of Vincent F. Seyfried

WHITESTONE: A boiler exploded on the locomotive engine Newtown at Whitestone Street on Sept. 25, 1872.

Queensborough Public Library, Long Island Division

WOODSIDE: Construction of a railroad bridge at Queens Boulevard around 1916.

ST. ALBANS, Continued

store. The St. Albans Golf Course, which was built in 1915, brought rich and famous golfers, including baseball star Babe Ruth. The Depression forced the owners of the golf course to sell to the government, and it became the St. Albans Naval Hospital, serving thousands of World War II veterans. The hospital was turned over to the Veterans Administration in 1974 and evolved into the St. Albans Extended Care Facility.

Claims to Fame: Musicians Count Basie and Fats Waller and singer Ella Fitzgerald lived here, as did baseball stars Jackie Robinson and Roy Campanella.

Where to Find More: Reference material in the St. Albans Branch Library at 191-05 Linden Blvd., and the Queens Borough Central Library, Long Island Collection, at 89-11 Merrick Blvd., Jamaica.

WHITESTONE
Making Connections By Bridge and Rail

Beginnings: One of the oldest settlements on Long Island, Whitestone was purchased in the early 1640s from Chief Tackapousha, sachem of Matinecock. In colonial days the settlement was part of the Town of Flushing.

The Names: Legend has it that the name Whitestone came from a big white rock at the point where the tides from the East River met the Long Island Sound. Other historians say the name came from a chapel erected by Samuel Legget in 1837 and called the White Stone Chapel. The community's name was later changed to Clintonville to honor New York City Mayor (and later Governor) De Witt Clinton, but reverted to Whitestone in 1854.

The Revolution: Though Queens was rife with Tories, one staunch Patriot, Francis Lewis, now best known for the boulevard named in his honor, was a member of the Continental Congress and a signer of the Declaration of Independence. After the war he returned to his Whitestone farm. After seven years of British occupation, residents showed no mercy for the Tories, many of whom fled to Canada.

Turning Points: When John D. Locke, a tinware manufacturer, built a stamping mill in 1854, his workers from Brooklyn followed, and Whitestone boomed like a Gold Rush town with hotels, stores and saloons. Another event in the 1850s was the bubbling up on Whitestone Avenue of the ''iron spring,'' which failed to produce the health-giving qualities it was hyped to possess. Whitestone was incorporated as a village in 1869, and that same year the railroad arrived, bringing millionaires who built waterfront mansions. An upscale waterfront section was developed about 1905 and was called Beechhurst for the fine beech trees growing there. Another upscale waterfront community was called Malba. The next momentous event was the opening of the Bronx-Whitestone Bridge in time for the 1939 New York World's Fair. The Throgs Neck Bridge was completed in 1961 to relieve the heavy traffic on the Bronx-Whitestone.

Brush With Fame: Poet Walt Whitman taught at the Whitestone Chapel in the 1800s.

Where to Find More: ''The Scene From Powell's Hill, From Francis Lewis to Capt. Merritt: A Story of Whitestone,'' by Harry J. Lucas, available in the Queens Borough Central Library, Long Island Collection, Jamaica; Flushing histories in the Whitestone Branch Library, 151-10 14th Rd., Whitestone.

Newsday Archive

Opening day for the Bronx-Whitestone Bridge in 1939; by 1961 the Throgs Neck Bridge was completed to handle the new traffic demands.

WOODHAVEN
Horse-Racing Got Off To a Fast Start

Beginnings: The Indians who occupied this area of southeast Queens traced a footpath that the first English and Dutch settlers, including the Ditmars, the Lotts and the Suydams, used in the late 1600s. They settled large farms east of what would become Woodhaven Boulevard.

The Race Was On: Woodhaven really took off after 1821 with the establishment of the Union Course, which became famous throughout the country. The track area extended from Jamaica Avenue south to Atlantic Avenue, more than a mile in circuit. A famous race in 1822 pitted a top horse from the South against the best of the North for a $20,000 stake, and a record $200,000 changed hands. Although denounced by the preachers of the day, horse racing continued to attract crowds to the Woodhaven area throughout the 1830s and 1840s, and inns, hotels and taverns sprang up to serve the racing public. The Centerville Race Track was founded in 1825 east of Woodhaven Boulevard, and all the famous horses of the day raced there.

Turning Point: John R. Pitkin, a wealthy trader from Connecticut, arrived in the area in 1835 with a dream of creating a major city between Brooklyn and Jamaica. He bought up the Dutch farms in New Lots, which he named East New York, and continued east to found Woodville, which became Woodhaven in 1853.

The Factory: Two French immigrants, Florian Grosjean and Charles Lalance, established a

tinware factory in 1863 and turned Woodhaven into a manufacturing community. Lalance & Grosjean, which became the largest stamping plant in the world, existed for almost a century, but sales diminished after World War II and the factory closed in 1955. In 1984, the old plant facing Atlantic Avenue became the centerpiece of a Woodhaven shopping mall.

Brush With Fame: Actress Mae West is said to have launched her career as an entertainer at age 10 in the 1838 Neirs Tavern, oldest establishment in Woodhaven.

Where to Find More: ''The Story of Woodhaven and Ozone Park,'' by Vincent F. Seyfried, and ''Old Woodhaven: A Victorian Village,'' edited by Barbara W. Stankowski, both in the Woodhaven Branch Library, 85-41 Forest Pkwy.

WOODSIDE
A Woodsy View From His Window

Beginnings: They called it ''Suicide's Paradise'' because legend held that many desperate colonials ended their lives in this isolated area of snake-infested swamps and wolf-inhabited woods. Though it was one of the earliest European settlements in western Queens, with a 1642 patent to Massachusetts settlers, the area later called Woodside grew slowly before the 1800s.

Letters From Woodside: John A.F. Kelly, part owner of the Independent Press of Williamsburg, whose father had moved to the Woodside area in 1826, would send dispatches to his paper entitled ''Letters From Woodside,'' based on the woodsy view from

his window. When developer Benjamin Hitchcock bought into the Kelly farm in 1867, he adopted the name Woodside for his proposed village.

Turning Points: The 115-acre Kelly farm was broken into building lots that sold for $100 to $300 each in 1869, triggering the first building boom. Other big estates went on the auction block; the Long Island Rail Road and the Flushing Rail Road merged and opened the Woodside Station; Northern Boulevard was constructed and in 1917 the elevated arrived. After the Queensboro Bridge opened in 1909, the population of Woodside quadrupled, reaching 6,000 in 1910. In 1924 the new City Housing Corp. began building private homes in Woodside. But the Cosmopolitan apartments at 49th Street, a complex of 16 five-story houses built in 1923 by Metropolitan Life Insurance, gave Woodside a more urban ambience. In the 1960s the Big Six Towers, a seven-building Mitchell-Lama cooperative at 47th Avenue, replaced tenements with modern, affordable housing.

Claims to Fame: Tower Square on Northern Boulevard at 51st Street, built as a railway station in 1885, was preserved as a landmark. The Jackson Social and Field Club, one of the oldest sports clubs in Queens, formed in 1902, still met in the 1990s. Elton C. Fax, author of ''Black Artists of a New Generation,'' and playwright Elyce Nass, who wrote ''Three One-Act Plays About the Elderly,'' called Woodside home.

Where to Find More: ''Woodside: A Historical Perspective,'' by Catherine Gregory,'' at Woodside Branch Library, 54-22 Skillman Ave., ''Old Queens, N.Y., in Early Photographs,'' by Vincent F. Seyfried and William Asadorian, at many libraries and book stores.

179

Newsday Photo / Walter DelToro

HUNTINGTON: Children from the Village Green School line the corridors for a duck-and-cover civil defense drill on April 6, 1958, during the early days of the Cold War.

Growing Up On Long Island

Celebrities of the postwar Baby Boom reminisce about the neighborhoods of Nassau, Suffolk and Queens that shaped their lives

Cradle of Aviation Museum Photo, Circa 1955

BALDWIN: Children ride the carousel at Nunley's, a kiddie amusement park open from 1939 through 1995 on Sunrise Highway. The carousel was eventually saved for restoration so it could be enjoyed by generations of children.

Billy Joel

Hicksville: 'I think I was the only kid in the neighborhood living in a single-parent home.'

BY STEVE WICK
STAFF WRITER

Behind his family's new house in Hicksville was a potato farm, and laying in bed on fall mornings the little boy could hear the diesel chug of a tractor tilling the soil.

It was a lovely sound, but it was not to last. Soon, the farm was sold and the tractor sounds were replaced by construction noise. First foundations, then frames, and soon another house was done. And another family with young kids was pulling up to the curb.

"I can vividly see that farm," recalls Billy Joel, who was 1 year old when his family relocated from the Bronx to a new subdivision stretched across old potato farms in Hicksville. "Years after it was gone, we'd still find potatoes in the ground."

It was 1950, on post-World War II Long Island. Joel's father was a veteran, drawn like a pilgrim to a land of promise, when he and his family moved into their new Levitt home. Everyone in the neighborhood was a newcomer, and for the boy, it was a time and a place that would deeply affect his life and the music he would write when he grew up.

Peering back through the mists of his past, Joel can smell the topsoil behind his house before it was paved over; he can see himself as a teenager hanging out at a strip mall — other boys in their new English clothes, listening to their radios; he can remember singing with a band in the basement of a Catholic church near his subdivision; he can remember driving to the North Shore, where life was so different from his own.

"Soon after we moved in, everything changed in the wink of an eye," he said. "What was there when we first moved in — it was like it just evaporated. There used to be big trees along the road near our subdivision. Huge trees. Then one day the bulldozers came in and they were gone."

Joel became one of the most popular singer-songwriters in American history and by 1998 ranked as the second biggest-selling solo artist of all time behind Garth Brooks. In 1999 he was inducted into the Rock and Roll Hall of Fame.

Like many of his generation, he was swept up by the Beatles' musical revolution in the mid-1960s, which inspired him to want to play in a rock-and-roll band. Still in his teens, he was an unknown singer in a long-haired band, one of a thousand long-haired bands trying to make it across the suburbs. He was not an overnight sensation, his journey from church basement to stadiums anything but a smooth road. But

talent won out, and Joel became a rock star.

On Long Island, where his music resonates deeply, capturing the uniqueness of the postwar suburbs, his fans seem to have a boundless interest in him and his music. Joel is, it could be said, the voice of Long Island. His tiny Levitt house and the farm 15 miles east where Walt Whitman was born in 1819 are worlds apart, but similar in many respects. Each produced a poet deeply grounded in the place of his youth.

Joel's memory of growing up on Meeting Lane in Hicksville is never far from his mind. His years there; his relationships with friends, some of whom he still has; Saturday nights at hangouts listening to a favorite disc jockey; awkward dates at a nearby Italian restaurant — the total of a million experiences, good and bad, have informed his work and his life.

"I wrote about what I knew," he said. In his 40s he made his home near the ocean in East Hampton. "I love Long Island. I grew up here, left and came back. It means a great deal to me."

On one occasion he drove his daughter, Alexa, to the house on Meeting Lane to show her where he grew up. Her reaction was, "Wow, it's so tiny." They knocked on the door, but no one answered.

"My old man got a GI loan, just like so many men. My grandfather, Karl Joel, had a factory in Nuremberg, Germany. The Nazis came in and made him an offer to buy it that was ridiculously low. 'You'll take it and like it.' The family went to Cuba. My father was 16 or 17. Then they came here. He met my mother, and they lived in a Jewish neighborhood in the Bronx." Billy was born in the Bronx on May 9, 1949.

Not long after, Joel said, "They saw an ad in one of the papers about new houses being built and they

Child, VH1 Video Image; Newsday Photo / J. Michael Dombroski, 1997
Billy Joel's music reflects his roots. He grew up in a postwar Levitt home in Hicksville.

moved to Hicksville."

Meeting Lane was lined with small houses, with patches of grass in the front, and spindly trees along the curb that would take years to grow out. If there wasn't a curve in the street, you could stand in front of your house and see every other other house up and down the street. It was a community built overnight, like a movie set. Joel's best friend then — and years later — was Billy Zampino, who lived on Terrill Lane. They spent hours each week in each other's homes, eating their mothers' cooking, listening to music, trying to figure out how to be teenagers in Hicksville.

'**E**verybody was there," Joel remembered. "Irish kids, Italian kids, Jewish kids. We played all the city games, which was what kids knew — stickball, stoop ball, kick the can. City games on suburban streets. The houses had carports and no driveways. There was a split level near us, but we thought only rich people lived in split levels."

Joel was not raised in a Jewish household, nor did he know many other Jews in the neighborhood. Looking back, he saw an awkward boy trying to fit in, who went to mass with his Catholic friends because that

was what people did.

But he learned as a young boy about recent history. Once he was going through some books in the house and found one on the Holocaust. His father's 8th Army unit, the 48th Engineers, had helped liberate death camps in Germany in 1945. Joel would later learn about his family's flight to Cuba. His grandfather's story — the fleeing to safety, the search for a new life — added a poignancy to his own life in the frontier of the Long Island suburbs.

His parents divorced when Joel was 8, a traumatic memory. "I think I was the only kid in the neighborhood living in a single-parent home," he said.

As a teenager, he played in a number of bands, none of which went anywhere. He struggled with his music, and thought it would never work out, an impossible dream not meant for him. But he never gave up, either. All the while, great change swept across Nassau County as more and more homes were built, then strip malls and multilane highways. He saw it, ingested it and wrote about it.

In his early 20s he moved to Los Angeles, but he was a fish out of water. He returned to New York, continued to write and record. And got big. Really, really big. And never forgot where he came from.

Patti LuPone

Northport: 'Come hell or high water, we were going into show business.'

Left, Newsday Archive; Newsday Photo / Bruce Gilbert, 1998
For some of the LuPones, the show-biz urge showed up early; in inset, she's front-row center of the Margette School of Dancing, with her brother Robert behind her.

BY BLAKE GREEN
STAFF WRITER

Theater review sight-bites festooned the walls of Broadway's Booth Theater, Newsday critic Linda Winer's comments among them. "She is back where she belongs ... she is wonderful," Winer observed, zeroing in on Patti LuPone's performance in David Mamet's "The Old Neighborhood" in 1998.

Early that year, over dinner with her husband, Matthew Johnson, in a restaurant down the street from the theater, the actress recalled the place where she and her older brother Robert — also a Broadway actor — grew up.

"It was a rural, fisherman's village, maybe three thousand people," she said of Northport, where the LuPone home stood surrounded by an orchard. "We all had to pick up apples; I hated those trees; what did I know?!

"The smell of the salt air, the water and the humidity, those things have never left my body," LuPone said. "I think my favorite smell in the whole world is [of] low tide."

There are three LuPone offspring, two of whom knew from childhood that "come hell or high water, we were going into show business," she said. (Patti and her twin, William, were born April 21, 1949. William became a librarian, although as children

all three siblings danced together as The Three LuPones, once winning an audition on "Ted Mack's Original Amateur Hour" on TV.)

First, however, they had to circumvent their father, Orlando, then the administrator at the village's Ocean Avenue Elementary School, who may have introduced an arts curriculum to his pupils, but envisioned teaching as the proper career path for his children.

Remembering her first recital as a tot swaying in a hula skirt, LuPone said, "I fell in love with the audience."

Before she left Northport for Juilliard, the New York stage (the title role in the musical "Evita," was among her starring roles) and television (the series "Life Goes On" and guest spots on "Frasier" and "Law & Order"), she would perform before local eyes in everything from madrigal singing groups to the marching band (she played the tuba). "The most well-known person in school," according to 1967's "Tiger Tales," the Northport High School yearbook.

Orlando and Angela LuPone were divorced when Patti was 12, but their daughter recalled what she considered the positive side: "We were free to do what we wanted to do. I had no aptitude for teaching and now the person who wanted to prevent us [from per-

forming] was out of the house. Life became a round of lessons; we were always going into New York."

Growing up in Northport meant other things, too. "I distinctly remember summers; that was what we all lived for, especially the clamming," LuPone said. "It was spectacular. My dad was in the Kiwanis Club and they'd hold these clam bakes down by Crab Meadow.

"You'd be able to dig the shoreline

and come up with little necks, then a little farther out would be the cherrystones and, of course, they'd go way out for the quahogs, the chowders.

"I remember being on the beach with a knife and cutting them open and eating them raw. We'd have these feasts. And we'd get buckets of them, for Mom to make clam sauce.

"We live in the countryside now, in Litchfield County [Connecticut], and I'm always telling Matthew I miss the water. My dad had a little 14-foot boat called Seascape. It was really a flat-bottomed lake boat, but we'd take it out on the bay. Every summer, the most fantastic yachts would pull into the pier and we'd go down and ogle."

On their Connecticut property, the Johnsons raise chickens as well as their son, Joshua. The chicks are a bit reminiscent of the LuPones' Northport neighbors "who had chickens and ducks. We'd collect the eggs in the hen house," she recalled. "They never cleaned it out. I can remember *that* smell, too.

"And the dump! It was like 'Terminator.' You'd be driving down this regular road and then, there'd be mountains of garbage! Flocks of seagulls! Sinks! Old cars! What an adventure.

'On sultry summer nights we'd sneak out and steal signs, then on the way home, swing by the store and grab some milk bottles. It was almost a ritual."

The juvenile pranks also included "plotting to peek in the windows of Chanticleer," a local mansion. "We'd be chased away by a German shepherd and shot at with a BB gun by the caretaker. Then, years later, I was called to be a babysitter at that exact house. I never looked at the baby once; I went from the cellar to the attic, it was the most spectacular house I'd ever seen.

"Long Island and Northport have changed," she observed, noting that this started when she was still living there. "LILCO put up those hideous towers while the town fathers slept. On property where we used to roam, they put up these no-trespassing signs and barbed wire fences.

"It was very traumatic. I'm a very territorial person" — one, she admitted, who gets upset when people joke about "the *Lawn-Guyland* accent. There was no accent — until everyone moved out there from Brooklyn and Queens."

183

Jerry Seinfeld

Massapequa: 'I led the swinging Sting-Ray life.'

Seth Poppel Yearbook Archives; Above, Los Angeles Times Photo / Robert Gauthier, 1995
Preoccupied with bikes and sneakers as a boy, Jerry Seinfeld didn't try comedy until college.

BY ANDY EDELSTEIN
STAFF WRITER

As an adult he grew up to prefer Porsches, but as a boy Jerry Seinfeld's vehicle of choice was the Schwinn Sting-Ray bicycle, which was just about the coolest mode of transportation a guy could have.

Especially if that guy was 11 years old and lived in Massapequa. The domain that young Jerry was the master of was the patch of town called Harbor Green.

"I led the swinging Sting-Ray life," the comedian said during a telephone interview on a brief break from filming an episode of his NBC sitcom in 1997. "And the older I get the fonder my memories are of that life."

Seinfeld said he was — and who's to dispute him? — the owner of the very first Schwinn Sting-Ray in Massapequa, which he bought at the cycle shop on Unqua Road. It was a groovy metallic-blue model with the banana seat that may or may not have made an impression on the girls in the 'hood.

"You could ride them on the handlebars or share the banana seat with them," he recalled. "Mainly you were on patrol at all times. I really didn't get the girls at 11, but I was always around the neighborhood."

Alas, Seinfeld doesn't know what happened to the bike. "I had so many different Sting-Rays — I had every one made — the three-speed, the five-speed, you name it. They would get stolen pretty regularly. The chains were like necklaces. If a crook just stared at it, it would open."

Seinfeld was born in Brooklyn on

April 29, 1954, moving shortly thereafter to Massapequa with his family — older sister Carolyn, mother Betty and dad Kal, who ran a commercial sign business, and whose sense of humor was a major influence on his son. They settled into a house at 311 Riviera Dr. S., near the water.

If Seinfeld had the classic neurotic childhood that became the raw basis of many comedians' material, he doesn't talk about it. He had what he describes as a fairly happy childhood. "I had a lot of fun," the former Cub Scout recalled. He watched his favorite TV shows ("Rocky & Bullwinkle," "Jonny Quest," "Batman," "Flipper") and soaked up his favorite comedians (Red Skelton, Jonathan Winters, the Smothers Brothers and especially Bill Cosby, whose entire LP output he owned).

His first comic routine, he told Larry King in 1991, took place when he was 8 in 1962. It was a bit about a fat girl in class that made a friend spit up his milk and cookies. "I felt the milk and I saw it all coming at me and I said, 'I would like to do this professionally.' "

Indeed, through his years at Parkside Junior High and Massapequa High School (Class of '72), his comedic skills were shared with only a few classmates. He didn't try comedy for real until 1976 in his senior year at Queens College, when he appeared at an amateur night

at Manhattan's Catch a Rising Star.

One reason he grew more fond for the Massapequa of his youth was because of the freedom of being able to come and go. "You can't do that as much nowadays," he recalled. "I'd get on my bike in the morning and take off for parts unknown like Tackapausha Preserve [in Seaford] or Bethpage State Park. Now, that was an exciting adventure."

In addition to exploring the world beyond Massapequa, he put the bike to the pursuit of commerce. Like many boys of that time, Seinfeld had a Newsday paper route for a few years. "The bike was also a superior paper-boy vehicle because of the way bags stood on handlebars."

So did anything exciting ever happen? "There was a rumor that there was a lady on my route who would answer her door in a robe. It never happened to me, but it kept me going for many a delivery."

He earned perhaps $8 to $12 a week.

"I couldn't believe I made that much," said the man whose "Seinfeld" salary was $1 million per episode.

And as young Jerry furiously pedaled his bike, no doubt on his feet — as with the mature model — would invariably be a pair of sneakers.

"I've always liked sneakers — that was something I responded to even at 6 years old," he told an interviewer. "I drove my mother crazy about getting me sneakers. She wouldn't let me wear them in the winter. She would set a day when I was allowed to start wearing sneakers again."

His favorite was Keds. "The dark blue kind that you could get only in the city," he pointed out. "On Long Island, they only had black. I've got a picture of me wearing them in my first-grade class. Every other kid in the picture has regular shoes on. I'm in high tops."

And when young Jerry got tired of riding his bike, he could cruise the waters near his home in his 8-foot Boston Whaler boat.

"I really had it all," he marveled. "A Sting-Ray and an 8-foot boat. I was like Sly Stallone there."

But as with most other red-blooded suburban boys, Seinfeld's transportation lust veered to the four-wheeled kind as he entered his teens. At Massapequa High, he even took auto mechanics, even though "everybody tried to discourage me because I was in 'college prep.'

"At about 13 I realized I wanted a Porsche," he said, "and I was unhappy until I got it. Now I have it and I'm happy."

Still, the happiest the day of his life was when he got his driver's license. "The greatest moment of my life," he recalled, especially when his mom handed him the keys to her '65 red Rambler. "I had it repainted blue for $19. The job was not nearly as good as Earl Scheib's . . . Snowflakes would actually chip the paint."

And though more than 20 years had passed since Seinfeld last regularly cruised Sunrise Highway, Massapequa — which, he has said, is Indian for "by the mall" — was mentioned in his show before the sitcom ended in 1998 after nine seasons.

The most memorable instance was a 1994 episode in which Jerry and George's ninth-grade gym teacher, Mr. Bevilacqua (portrayed by an actor), returned to officiate a rerun of a disputed race that Jerry had with a classmate.

In real life, Albert Bevilacqua was Seinfeld's phys ed and driver's ed teacher at Massapequa High. "We'd have a lecture class in driver ed," Bevilacqua told Newsday in 1994. "I'd try to animate it and be funny. After class, Jerry would say, 'You're terrific on stage, Mr. Bevilacqua. You should go to Hollywood.' " He recalled the teenage Jerry as "one of those great personality kids you never forget."

There's certainly nothing wrong with that.

Billy Crystal

Long Beach: 'You felt safe and when you feel safe, you can do anything.'

BY ANDY EDELSTEIN
STAFF WRITER

On a visit back home to Long Beach, Billy Crystal and his older brother Joel (a city councilman) were walking on the boardwalk when they stumbled across a piece of their past: the remains of a marker at the site of the long-gone municipal pool. The comedian-actor couldn't contain his excitement.

"I said we should take it," Crystal said. "It was like a piece of rubble, with a Roman ruin feel to it.

"But we didn't take it," he said, the remorse obvious in his voice.

Oh, well. But there surely will be other souvenir-hunting opportunities. Even though Crystal left in 1976, he still seems like a one-man chamber of commerce for the town where he lived for more than a quarter-century.

"It has the best beaches in the world — besides the Bahamas," Crystal said during an interview in late 1997. "I was on the beach this past summer and it felt right."

Crystal recalled his growing-up years in that South Shore city with a genuine fondness, remembering best its sense of community. "Everybody knew each other," he said. "No one seemed more special than anyone else. We're talking about 1952 or '53 when Long Beach was a small, wonderful community. No matter where you were, you fell asleep hearing the waves. It was just a great place to develop. You felt safe and when you feel safe, you can do anything.

"You always felt like there were so many places to go," he said. "We had different hangouts — swimming at the pool, seeing movies at the Laurel Theater, noshing at Beach Burger, getting a slice and a Coke for a quarter at Gino's pizzeria . . . And of course, you'd hang out on the boardwalk, or *under* the boardwalk if you were lucky."

Crystal had other kinds of luck on the boardwalk. "I was really was good at Skee-ball. I still have the tickets (which were given out according to how high your score was) at Faber's and Seidel's. I always wanted to win my mother a set of dishes . . . and never did."

Helen and Jack Crystal (who managed the family business, Commodore Records, a store and record label specializing in jazz), moved from the Bronx to Long Beach in 1950 with their three sons — Billy, 2 (born

March 14, 1947); Richie (nicknamed Rip), 4, and Joel, 8. By the mid-1950s, when the family had moved to a two-family house on Park Avenue, the Crystal boys were famous in the family for their living-room routines.

Laughter kept Crystal and his brothers close. "You had three very energetic children in a very little place," Crystal told Newsday in 1990. "It must have been unbelievable. Dinnertime was pretty wild. We loved making each other laugh. It was good stuff. There was the occasional mashed potatoes and peas in the nose, but that was too easy."

And of course there was the influence of that new medium, television, where young Billy soaked up the humor of "The Honeymooners, "Your Show of Shows" and such performers as Red Skelton, Ernie Kovacs and Jonathan Winters.

Crystal's brushes with show biz luminaries weren't limited to the tube. When he was 8, he was having dinner with his family at Russo's restaurant on Park Avenue in Long Beach, when Alan King and his wife entered the room. "He looked like a huge star, he just floated in," Crystal recalled. "I was in awe of King — after all he was a regular on Ed Sullivan." That regal entrance burned in young Billy's brain for 35 years and finally was used in his 1992 film, "Mr. Saturday Night," in which Crystal played a stand-up comic. A few years later, as a teenaged busboy at the Lido Beach Hotel, he met Sammy Davis Jr., who later became a friend as well as one of his favorite entertainers to parody.

The mature Billy Crystal became almost as well-known for his passion for baseball as for his comedy. That passion, not surprisingly, began early.

"I can remember all the times I spent in the backyard being Mickey Mantle, walking like him, thinking my knees hurt," he said. "I was a little Jewish kid with an Oklahoma accent . . . We didn't have Little League, but we played rec-center softball in the summer." He and his brothers and father would play ball on the grassy malls in the middle of Park Avenue, watching for errant cars.

"People would actually stop and

Crystal Family Photo; Newsday Photo / Ken Spencer, 1991
As a boy and as a man, Billy Crystal felt at home in Long Beach.

watch our games. I figured If I could field a ball there, I could field one anywhere."

The skills carried over to Long Beach High, where he played second base and was varsity captain his senior year. (He was also a self-styled clarinet-playing "band geek" who was voted Best Personality of the Class of '65.)

A hero closer to home was Long Beach High basketball star Larry Brown, who would go on to a successful playing and coaching career in college, and the American and National Basketball Associations.

"The Friday night basketball games were raucous and great," Crystal recalled. "Larry Brown was someone I wanted to be when I grew up. I wanted to walk like him, talk like him, even move five times [going to the hoop] like him. Brown's success meant that if you were under 5 foot 10, you could be good."

Crystal actually spent 26 years in Long Beach, staying until he was 28, married with a child and at a point in his career when Hollywood took him from his last home there, a second-floor apartment a block from the beach.

"I didn't leave Long Beach until August 2, 1976," he said. "It was hard leaving, very emotional. I was cleaning out my closets, and I found my four-letter sweater. To earn four letters was a big deal. You got the blue sweater with the white trim, while the plain letter sweater was the white with the blue trim. I got it, and I really wanted it bad. So we're moving, and [wife] Janice says, 'Get rid of this stuff. C'mon, it's a new beginning.' I said, 'But it's my sweater.' She says, 'It's a high school thing. Where are you going to wear it?' So as we're driving away, I see this guy picking through garbage, and he's wearing my sweater. This guy on Shore Road, it's got 'Billy' on the side, the 'LB,' and he's looking for more stuff. That still bothers me. I want my sweater."

Richard C. Firstman contributed to this article.

185

Rosie O'Donnell

Commack: 'I'd tell all the ushers at the theaters that I was going to be a star.'

Seth Poppel Yearbook Archives; AP Photo
Rosie O'Donnell, at left in her senior photo, loves to talk about Commack.

BY DIANE WERTS
STAFF WRITER

What could anybody possibly learn about Rosie O'Donnell's Commack childhood that she hasn't announced to the world already?

She talks about her Rhonda Lane youth constantly on her daily talk show, in her stand-up act, in all her interviews, detailing her teenybopper obsessions, her mom's death from cancer, her distant dad, her siblings, her pals, her hangouts, her showbiz dreams.

That childhood not only comes in handy on TV — when she sings vintage commercial jingles, recites old "Mary Tyler Moore" plot lines, or breaks into show tunes — but it directly shaped her, more obviously than most people, into the person she would become.

The first musical she attended — "George M!" at Westbury Music Fair when she was 6 — turned her stagestruck.

While a student at Rolling Hills Elementary School, she was already entertaining her classmates with jokes and impressions. "In first grade show-and-tell, I would do Bazooka Joe jokes from the comics," she once told an interviewer.

She'd run home to see celebrities on the Mike Douglas, Merv Griffin and Dinah Shore daytime talk shows. "I started watching them when I was 8 with my grandma," she was saying in her 30 Rockefeller Center office in June, 1995, back when her hit syndicated show was just launching. "My mom and my grandmother used to love it, that we would watch Liza Minnelli together."

Little Roseann — born March 21, 1962, the third of five children in an Irish-Catholic family, and the oldest girl — was painfully close to her mother, after whom she had been named. That influence lives on in every joke she makes. She remembered her mom "made all the teachers laugh" at PTA meetings. "I knew she had this thing that people wanted, that people would go to her because of this comedy thing." When her mother died of cancer in 1973, the week Rosie turned 11, the little girl took refuge in the same TV set that had once brought them so joyously together.

"In my house, it took the place of parenting," she said. "My mother had died and my father was bereft, and there was really a lack of interaction with all the children." Every Sunday the tube-tied O'Donnell kids ran for "the Newsday [TV] supplement that was sort of wiggly [the old horizontal format magazine], and we would memorize the entire schedule of what was on and when." She was especially fond of "My Three Sons," the Fred MacMurray sitcom about a household run by a single father.

Media-mad Rosie wrote fan letter after fan letter, said goodnight to David Cassidy posters on her bedroom walls, and rode the LIRR (sometimes cutting school to attend Wednesday matinees) to Broadway shows such as "Pippin." "I'd tell all the ushers at the theaters I was going to be a star," she told Newsday during her own Broadway run in "Grease."

It was in high school at Commack South that her show biz lust turned serious. She'd always been in school plays (such as "Witness for the Prosecution"), but now she took up a friend's challenge to turn her smart mouth into stand-up in local clubs.

Roseann O'Donnell made her debut in 1988 one open-mike night at Mineola's Ground Round when she was 16. "I looked like I was 12, with this cute little haircut and big sweatshirt and sweatpants, and I was this little tough girl, and the audience — grown-ups like my parents' age — were like, 'Look at this little kid with chutzpah.' "

It extended offstage, where Rosie hung with a clique of other Catholic girls. They'd go to Tiffany's Wine and Cheese Cafe on Jericho Turnpike "with fake IDs and drink sangria. It was right across from the Commack Motor Inn, where they had mirrored ceilings over the beds and where everyone wanted to go to have sex for the first time. I don't think anyone did, but it was always, 'Hey, we're going to CMI.' "

More often, Rosie was going to Long Island comedy clubs, especially Richie Minervini's East Side on Jericho Turnpike in Huntington. While earning a living after high school by working in places such as the catalog department at Sears, she was honing her stand-up act, watching other local jokesters such as Jerry Seinfeld, and learning how to mine humor in her own Irish-Catholic family life and her Long Island youth. Eventually the outspoken funny lady would hit the road, win several rounds on "Star Search" in 1984, and make her way to L.A., where TV shows such as VH1's "Stand-Up Spotlight" and movies such as "A League of Their Own" were waiting.

In the 1990s she moved into Helen Hayes' former estate in Nyack, but was close enough to home to keep tabs on old friends; for one 1997 installment of her daytime talk show, she filled the audience with her Commack classmates and teachers, who reminisced about the old days.

And she never forgot the women in her neighborhood who, like her mother, had developed cancer. She worked benefits for cancer research. O'Donnell proved a powerfully moving witness about that Commack cluster in Lifetime's "Say It, Fight It, Cure It" special in 1997, talking about the battle with tears streaming down her face.

Turned out we could learn something new about Rosie O'Donnell after all.

Eddie Murphy

Roosevelt: 'I'd spend hours in my basement making up routines.'

Newsday Photo / William J. Senft Jr., 1987; Right, Newsday Archive

The comedian in Mineola in 1987, and in a school portrait.

BY GENE SEYMOUR
STAFF WRITER

The novelist Gustave Flaubert believed that wild, original artists could best be cultivated in safe, bourgeois surroundings. It's hard to know what the author of "Madame Bovary" would make of Eddie Murphy's life (except that it might make a great novel on its own terms), but he would have found easy proof of his thesis in the comedian's pre-adolescence in Roosevelt.

Born in Brooklyn on April 3, 1961, Murphy moved to the predominantly African-American, middle-class suburban community in 1970 when he was 9. The preceding years were unsettled ones. His parents had divorced when he was 3, and his father, Charles, a New York City transit policeman, died five years later. His mother, Lillian, married Vernon Lynch, a foreman at a Breyers ice cream plant shortly before they moved to a two-story ranch house in Roosevelt.

It is not enough to say that, by the time his family moved east, Murphy had watched a lot of television. To read all the available accounts of Murphy's life is to determine that

Eddie *inhaled* television, its sitcoms, movies, talk shows and cartoons. School was just something that filled time before he came home to carry out his real studies in front of the set.

By his teens, Murphy had gone well beyond being able to imitate cartoon characters and comedians. "I'd spend hours in my basement making up routines," he told a reporter years ago. He was already writing comedy bits, practicing karate kicks and working out some of the impressions of Al Green, Elvis Presley and other entertainment icons. "I'd say his three main influences were 'West Side Story' [the movie], Elvis Presley and Bruce Lee," Lillian Lynch recalled in a 1983 interview with Rolling Stone.

Still it wasn't until July 9, 1976, when Murphy hosted a talent show at the Roosevelt Youth Center, that he knew for certain that he wanted to dedicate his life to show business. His ambition was fed by a self-confidence that was uncanny for someone so young.

"He would tell us both, 'I'm going to be a millionaire by the time I'm 22," Vernon Lynch recalled. "He was."

"You got the feeling he had things

worked out for himself and he was just putting in time until he could go do them," recalled David Better, a social-studies teacher at Roosevelt Junior-Senior High School, to whom Eddie once proclaimed his intention to one day be "bigger than Bob Hope."

Roosevelt Junior-Senior High School, the alma mater of basketball legend Julius Erving, was regarded by Murphy as "a never-ending party, just a place to get laughs," he said in an early 1980s interview. Given the fact that he spent most of his high school years working at Long Island comedy clubs all night and sleeping at the home of his friend Clinton Smith during the day, it was somewhat remarkable he maintained a low-C average through graduation. In fact, he was forced to repeat the 10th grade. But after doubling up on classes and attending summer school, he managed to catch up.

Murphy's comedy resume, in contrast, was expanding. He cut his performing teeth at such Island spots as the Blue Dolphin in Uniondale and the White House Inn in Massapequa, whose proprietor, Richard M. Dixon,

made his name imitating the 37th president of the United States. Murphy didn't start collecting real money for his routines until he moved up to Huntington's East Side Comedy Club. Manhattan clubs including the Improvisation and the Comic Strip soon followed.

In those years, Murphy's routines were heavily influenced by his two heroes, Bill Cosby and Richard Pryor, especially the latter in his heavy use of expletives. "Back then," he told Newsday in 1981, "profanity was my hook."

When Murphy graduated from high school in 1979, he was voted the "most popular boy" in class and declared his artistic intentions in the class yearbook with this quote: "In reality, all men are sculptors, constantly chipping away the unwanted parts of their lives trying to create a masterpiece."

He enrolled at Nassau Community College that fall, ostensibly to study theater. But his comedy career had moved him beyond the need for academic credentials. He formed a group, the Identical Triplets, with two young white comics named Rob Bartlett and Bob Nelson. The New York Times covered a comedy workshop at the Garden City school's cafeteria, and while the story's focus was on Nelson and Bartlett, it described the moment in the act when "Irish Eddie Murphy" was introduced by Nelson. "I'm not Irish, I'm black," Murphy deadpanned to the startled and tickled audience.

A year after Murphy entered Nassau, a radically revised version of "Saturday Night Live" went on the air. Its producers were looking for a black cast member and Murphy, after six auditions, was brought on as a "featured player," which, in the "SNL" hierarchy, is beneath the rank of cast member. It didn't take very much — or very long — for Murphy's magnetism and confidence to raise him above the rest of the cast of what many regard as the worst of "SNL's" 23 seasons.

Murphy literally exploded into America's consciousness from that year and onward through the 1980s in such movies as "48 HRS," "Beverly Hills Cop" and "Trading Places." The precise impersonations, knowing pop-culture references and personal observations Murphy accumulated while growing up in the comfort of Roosevelt became the foundation of his worldwide success as a movie star.

Simon and Garfunkel

Forest Hills: They met at a rehearsal for a sixth-grade production of 'Alice in Wonderland'

BY JAMES KINDALL

The basement of a rather unremarkable Forest Hills home once served as the training ground for a remarkable twosome formerly known as Tom and Jerry. It was there that Paul Simon and Art Garfunkel, face to face before a microphone, developed a symbiosis that would make them musical legends.

"We'd be sitting nose to nose, looking right into each other's mouths to copy diction," Art Garfunkel explained in "Simon & Garfunkel: The Biography," a book by Victoria Kingston about the duo's early days. "I'd want to know exactly where his tongue would hit the top of his palate when he'd say a T, to know exactly how to get that T right. And I could see that you could be almost right, or even better than almost right. And that all of that really was the difference between whether or not it sounded professional."

Years later, it would be hard to find someone who hadn't been exposed to Simon's evocative lyrics and Garfunkel's haunting voice. Their "Bridge Over Troubled Water" became recognized internationally as one of the most affecting tunes ever written, while the sound track from the 1967 movie "The Graduate" defined the dazed alienation of an American generation. Both artists have been inducted into the Rock and Roll Hall of Fame.

Throughout their careers, the two produced emotionally revealing tunes that hit home. That, according to Simon, was the point.

"At its best, songwriting for me means peeling back layers," he wrote in Musician magazine. "It's discovery."

Exactly how much their growing up in Queens contributed to this success is hard to say.

Both singers are known as private people who rarely grant interviews. Neither was available for this story. But their childhood environment certainly was pivotal. They were born just weeks apart in 1941, Simon on Oct. 13, and Garfunkel on Nov. 5. If Simon's parents hadn't moved from Newark, N.J., to Forest Hills, his career might have been dramatically different. Because it was here, after all, that he met Garfunkel.

Their first encounter took place at a rehearsal for a sixth-grade production of "Alice in Wonderland."

Paul was the White Rabbit, Art the Cheshire Cat.

Simon knew of the other boy. He had heard him sing in the third grade when the willowy youngster shocked an auditorium into silence with his rendition of Nat (King) Cole's hit, "Too Young."

Despite differences, they were drawn to one another immediately. Simon was short and athletic. (He used to hustle kids at stickball, losing the first game on purpose.) "I had a great childhood," he

Newsday Photo / Daniel Sheehan; Top, AP Photo, 1957

Art Garfunkel and Paul Simon reunite for a concert at The Paramount theater at Madison Square Garden in 1993. At top, the duo in their late teens as Tom and Jerry.

once said. "It was all about ball playing on the streets, in the playgrounds." His sense of humor tickled the blond, blue-eyed Garfunkel, a man once described as looking like a huge dandelion.

Neither was "part of the crowd" at school. Soon they were walking home together, talking sports and music, listening to the new sounds of rock and roll being broadcast on programs such as Alan Freed's "Rock and Roll Party" or Dick Clark's "American Bandstand."

Both have credited their stable, middle-class upbringing (the houses on Simon's block looked so much alike his father was constantly parking in the wrong driveway) with contributing to their musical growth. Simon was proud that the elder Simon was a bass player in a radio band and later a City College education teacher. Simon's mother was an elementary school teacher. His parents approved of his musical aspirations, but encouraged it as a hobby.

Garfunkel's father was a businessman, his mother a secretary. Despite having no show business background, they inspired him to improve his voice by buying him tape recorders. Later, he said his parents were the ones who taught him self-discipline and values.

After honing their style at home, the boys began playing to enthusiastic audiences at sock hops and private parties in the mid-1950s and eventually were signed as Tom and Jerry by Big Records. One of their singles, "Hey! Schoolgirl!," reached No. 54 on Billboard's top 100 in 1958. The duo appeared on "American Bandstand."

Subsequent releases weren't as pop-

ular. The record company folded and the two broke up.

Simon became a studio musician, learning how to play several instruments and record in different harmonizing voices. (One of the people he worked with was Carole King). He also earned a bachelor's in English literature from Queens College, entered Brooklyn Law School, then dropped out to take up music again.

During this time, he ran into Garfunkel, who was studying architecture at Columbia University. Both had become enamored of the folk-rock sounds of people such as Bob Dylan and Joan Baez. They began singing together again, sometimes jamming in Washington Square Park and playing at local clubs, where they developed a following. By this time, Simon, tired of teen lyrics, had switched to more serious themes determined to be a "proud failure" as a songwriter.

Things looked bright again when they were signed by Columbia Records, but critics mostly ignored their album. Then fate knocked down the door. A Florida disc jockey noticed a surge of requests for one of the album songs, "The Sounds of Silence." Without the musicians' knowledge, Columbia added a rock accompaniment and re-released it as a single. It hit the charts in 1965 and, to the surprise of the two singers, went gold.

From that point on they began sending song after song up the charts. Cre-

ative differences and other pressures began pulling them apart later in their career. Simon was doing the lion's share of arranging and composing; Garfunkel was drawn away by movie appearances in 1970's "Catch-22" and 1971's "Carnal Knowledge."

They split in 1971, but reunited on special occasions, most notably a packed 1982 performance in Central Park. Simon, who kept a home in Montauk, staged annual "Back to the Ranch" concerts at Deep Hollow Ranch there to raise funds for the Nature Conservancy.

Both continued to record. Simon's emphasis shifted to poly-cultural world music, resulting in several hit albums. He resurfaced for a tour with Bob Dylan after his failed 1998 Broadway musical, "The Capeman." Garfunkel also turned out successful albums, but concentrated on concerts.

For many people, however, they would remain forever linked as the flawless duo, part of which can be attributed to Simon's father.

In the Simon and Garfunkel biography, Paul tells about how as a kid he never really considered himself anything special vocally. But one evening his father passed by his room while he was practicing songs from a record.

"That's nice, Paul," his dad said. "You have a nice voice."

For an insecure boy, it was just the right shot of confidence at just the right time.

"That was it," Simon said. "From that moment on, I thought of myself as someone who could sing."

Bob Costas

Commack: 'To tell you the truth, I was a bit of a goof-off just bobbin' around in high school.'

Photos Courtesy of Bob Costas

Bob Costas grew up listening to the great sports announcers and reading the sports pages.

BY BOB HERZOG
STAFF WRITER

If you compare Bob Costas' odyssey to that of a major-league baseball star, you'd have to call his "Commack Years" the equivalent of a low-level minor-league experience.

Commack was the place where the sports-loving Costas made plenty of "rookie" mistakes, sometimes lost his focus and didn't leave too many clues to his future greatness. But he did pick up enough life experience and sports knowledge to help him advance to the next level. For a promising player, that would be Triple-A, one step below the majors; for Costas, it was Syracuse University, where he thrived in the classroom and the broadcast booth.

By the time he graduated and entered "The Show" — doing radio play-by-play for the American Basketball Association's Spirits of St. Louis — he was considered a hot prospect in the major leagues of sportscasting. Unlike other flashy rookies, Costas did not burn out, but soared to the top of his profession, where he became NBC's most prominent sports voice.

It's a baby boomer's tale that had roots in an exploding suburban town. Commack was sort of a Levittown East in the 1960s — housing developments sprang up so fast that one seventh-grade Long Island history textbook referred to the community as "Boom Town USA." Born March 22, 1952, Robert Quinlan Costas and his family (father John, mother Jayne and sister Valerie) moved to Commack in 1964, onto a street named New Highway. Their ranch house was a short walk from Woodpark Elementary School — with its asphalt basketball court and grassy field of dreams.

"We'd play football after school — tackle football with no equipment in all kinds of weather," Costas recalled. "It's a wonder we didn't get killed. We shoveled snow off the basketball courts. And of course it was our baseball field in the summer."

Costas attended Green Meadows Junior High, where he befriended music teacher Andy Blackett. "He was the first black teacher in my school. I met him in the eighth grade and was tremendously impressed," Costas said. "He carried himself with humanity and dignity and reached so many kids. I had him for general mu-

sic, but we became friends outside the classroom. I stayed in touch with him until he died in 1992 of ALS [amyotrophic lateral sclerosis, also known as Lou Gehrig's disease]. He was probably one of the five or six most influential people in my life when I was growing up."

Another teacher influencing Costas was Pete Ferenz, the history teacher and high school basketball coach. "He was a great basketball player — a borderline pro prospect — and I liked him," even though Ferenz cut Costas from the Commack South varsity in 1969.

Costas acknowledged that because of his love affair with New York sports, he never really thought of himself as a Long Islander. "I always thought of myself as a 'New Yorker.' I read Newsday and the Long Island Press, of course, but also the Post, News, Times and Daily Mirror," he said. "I read all the sports sections avidly at 7 or 8 years old. The teams I rooted for — like the Yankees and Knicks — and all my TV and radio, came from New York City. Most of my relatives were from Brooklyn and Queens, so I spent a lot of time there. I think I went to the World's Fair [in Flushing] 18 times in one summer with my cousin. I remember riding the subway to Yankee Stadium and hopping the buses to go to Shea Stadium when I was a kid."

Costas was comfortable playing, watching and talking sports, but it was a comfort zone he did not reach in all of his teenage endeavors. "To tell you the truth, I was a bit of a goof-off, just bobbin' around in high school," he said. "I wasn't as good a

student as I could've been. I got into college on SAT scores, not my grades. I got decent grades in English and history, not so great in science and math." He flunked chemistry as a junior.

He was a typical teenager for that time in that town. Commack kids didn't rebel as much as other teens of the late '60s. Some of Costas' shenanigans sound more like the "Happy Days" stuff of the 1950s. "Cruisin' for burgers," he said with a laugh when asked about his teenage years. "As soon as we got our licenses, that's what we did. There was a whole stretch on Jericho Turnpike in Commack with fast-food joints. One of your classmates always had a part-time job in McDonald's or Burger King. They'd throw you extra fries or burgers with your order. That was a big perk to us!

'I remember Mario's pizza place," Costas said. "And of course there was the rickety old Long Island Arena. When Smith Haven Mall opened, that was a big deal. Those were the early days of the mall rats — kids who had no purpose, they just hung around the mall."

Costas wasn't a mall rat, but he had his aimless moments. "High school is awkward for a lot of people; it was awkward for me, too," admitted one of the most composed and confident men in the business today. "I didn't belong to any particular group. I was a decent athlete, but not a jock; I was a reasonably intelligent kid but not a bookworm. A guidance counselor would've said I was one of those kids who was 'not working up to his ability.'"

That changed once Costas reached Syracuse University in the fall of 1970 after being part of the first graduating class at Commack South High School. "I became a better student in college than I was in high school," he said. And in the acclaimed Syracuse school of broadcasting, he found his future calling. "I had a vague notion that I would be a sports broadcaster, but I was not really focused on it as a teenager."

The New York voices of his youth clearly influenced Costas' career choice. "It was a combination of loving sports and being exposed to great announcers when I was growing up," he said. "The 1950s and '60s was a great era in New York broadcasting. You had Red Barber, Mel Allen, Marty Glickman, Lindsey Nelson, Bob Murphy, a young Marv Albert. They were not only technically good, but had a wonderful, engaging style. For me, sports and broadcasting were inseparable."

Howard Stern

Roosevelt and Rockville Centre:

'Girls never, never noticed me.'

Newsday Photo / Ari Mintz, 1993; Right, Newsday Archive
Ben, left, and Ray Stern with their shock-jock son, and, at right, Howard in his senior year of high school in Rockville Centre

Howard Stern's journey to fame began with puppet shows he put on in his Roosevelt basement: sailors and pirates and even horses being naughty with the nice little puppet girl.

Back in those days, few would have guessed that gawky, anonymous Howard would become the most publicized proponent of shock radio, America's busiest purveyor of bathroom humor, satiric smut and political incorrectness.

Born Jan. 12, 1954, Stern was 1 year old when his parents, Ray and Ben, moved to Roosevelt from Jackson Heights in 1955. He and his older sister, Ellen, went to the Washington-Rose Elementary School for six years. Then they attended the Roosevelt Junior-Senior High, a few blocks from their home at 36 Conlon Rd.

As a boy, Howard received much support from his parents. "I know he always wanted to do something verbally," Ben Stern told a Newsday reporter in 1993. "Anything he wanted to do creatively, I always supported him. I built him a stage for the marionette. He wanted to have a band, so I got him a keyboard and wired it up and made him an amplifier."

Ben Stern was part owner of a recording studio, and he used to make tapes of the children on the holidays. He'd ask them questions about current events, the Kennedys and the United Nations. "So when I asked him these serious questions, he ends up being a wiseguy. And so I got mad and said, 'Shut up and sit down. Don't be stupid, you moron.' "

Living in Roosevelt gave the Sterns an important lesson in the relationship between actions and words. Their white friends and neighbors would have meetings about remaining in the neighborhood as more and more blacks moved in, and then they'd move out by cover of night. In one of the great backfires in the history of liberal social engineering, the Sterns decided to make a stand.

"Meanwhile," Howard Stern wrote in his 1993 autobiography, "Private Parts," "I was beginning to get the ——— beat out of me every day by the welfare recipients who are moving into my neighborhood . . . By the time I hit seventh grade there were only a handful of white kids left in the school. That's when the beatings began to get regular."

He felt like an outcast. White friends from other neighborhoods wouldn't visit, and his best black friend was beaten for hanging out with a white guy. That was the last straw. In June, 1969, when Howard was 15, the Sterns made their move

— to predominantly white, middle-class Rockville Centre. They moved into a high ranch on Rose Lane.

"It wasn't any better in Rockville Centre," Howard Stern wrote. "I couldn't adjust at all. I was totally lost in a white community. I felt like Tarzan when they got him out of Africa and brought him back to England."

In his youthful days, when only parents had access to automobiles, Howard and his friends hitched rides to the local theaters, their sanctuaries on many a dateless Friday and Saturday night.

Among Howard's circle of friends, two of them lived within a block or two from the high school. One, Scott Passeser, recalls these difficult years: "We were not a popular group."

Passeser lived on Princeton Road, just a dozen houses or so from the school. "Most of our free time, we really didn't go places," he recalled in a 1997 interview with Newsday. "No one had dates. We really hung out at each other's houses.

"We didn't go out to the ice cream parlor with the girls after the football games. It was not like that at all."

Or as Stern once told a reporter: "Girls never, never noticed me, and

when they did, they noticed I was ugly."

On Saturdays, they played poker at Passeser's house from 7 p.m. until after midnight, while Passeser babysat for his brother. On Fridays, there were often round-robin Ping-Pong games at Bob Komitor's house around the corner on Shepherd Road.

It was at Komitor's that, in a moment of elation, the usually athletically challenged Howard made a difficult shot and jumped in the air for joy. "He was so tall, his head hit the ceiling and demolished a light fixture," Passeser recalled. "We all laughed for twenty minutes."

They went to the movies a lot, he said, and the theater of choice was the Grand Avenue Cinema. They'd rendezvous at the corner of DeMott and Long Beach Roads, hitching a mile and a half to the movie house.

"Every Friday, we'd try to find an R-rated movie," Passeser recounted. "We didn't care what it was. All we cared about was seeing a woman's breasts. Howard was over 6 feet tall and we never had trouble getting into any theater."

Once in 1970, when Howard was 16, they all went to the Grand Avenue Cinema to see "Myra Breckinridge," based on Gore Vidal's novel about a transsexual. Their must-see motivation? The mistaken notion that its star, Raquel Welch, would appear naked.

"We had no idea what the movie was about," Passeser recalled. "And there was another film with it, about a man who wanted to become a superwoman. So when we left the theater, Howard stripped off his shirt and started screaming, 'I'm a Superwoman! I'm Superwoman!' He was over 6 feet tall and weighed about 150 pounds, and with his long hair, he must have looked like Ichabod Crane. I was so embarrassed I ran as fast as I could to get away from him."

During these teen years, there was just one inkling of stardom, said Passeser, now an employment consultant. One weekend, he recounted, he joined Howard on the Long Island Rail Road to midtown Manhattan to make an 8-mm. film.

"I shot a sequence of Howard walking through a crowd, his head high above everyone else. Then we put 'Eleanor Rigby,' the Beatles song about 'all the lonely people,' on the sound track. It was for a high school English class in our junior year and it was terrific. If I had it today, it would be worth a good deal. But it's gotten lost over the years."

John Tesh

Garden City: 'Look at the geek in the band!'

BY DIANE WERTS
STAFF WRITER

Ask John Tesh about growing up on Long Island. Then try to get him to shut up. "I mean, I remember *everything* about my childhood" on Seabury Road off Old Country Road in Garden City, he said. "I could just sit here and just list everything I did every day. I don't know why. But I remember it."

Maybe it's because his daughter, Prima, isn't having the kind of childhood he had. "I could walk out in the front yard, and in the street there'd be a football game, or a street hockey game. And then you get on your bike and you go to the pool, and every person in town is there, with the Good Humor man up on top of the hill. It really was 'The Wonder Years.' Very much so.

"And it was a neighborhood," he added. "Now, where I live in Los Angeles" — where Tesh once hosted "Entertainment Tonight" and records his flowing instrumental music ("Avalon") for his own GTSP Records; where he and his actress-wife Connie Sellecca are raising her teenage son, Gib, and Prima — "it's not a neighborhood," Tesh lamented during a 1997 stop at the WLIW/21 studios for its winter pledge drive. "It's just like, we're all sort of stuck in these places behind gates, and security is crazy. But those were the days when it was just, you know, normal existence."

John was the only Tesh sibling born on Long Island after his parents moved from Winston-Salem, N.C., with his two much-older sisters; he was born July 9, 1952. His father "took the Long Island Rail Road every day" into the city as vice president of sales for Hanes, and "my sister worked at Walgreen's at Roosevelt Field there. You know, it wasn't covered then.

"And there was a field before Roosevelt Field — I can't remember what it was called — but the military used to do maneuvers there, and there were all sorts of foxholes we would get trapped in. We played in the dirt, and threw dirt bombs," clumps of earth the boys would "cram into the end of a pop gun, an air gun, and it sprays dirt everywhere. Playing war was big. I think back on it, those were the days when it was cowboys and Indians. Now it's, you know, dudes and Native Americans," he said with a laugh.

Perhaps life wasn't politically correct then. But it was freer for kids, said Tesh. "The big thing was, get on your bicycle and just go anywhere. In those days, [parents] just let us do anything. Seriously. It was just like, 'Go out. Go. Do whatever.' "

"Whatever" often involved water, whether it was heading to the Garden City pool or to the West End 2 parking area at Jones Beach, the young Tesh's favorite hangout. Rarely did he venture into New York City, urban turf he'd later learn well as a WCBS/2 reporter during the late 1970s. As a kid, however, Long Island alone "was definitely my world," he said. "I never really went to Manhattan. That was considered a real scary place."

It could be a magical place, too, during the Tesh family's annual outing to the Radio City Music Hall Christmas show. "My dad would take my mom and I, he would rent a hotel room — which, you know, at 7 or 8 years old is the coolest thing you could possibly do — and he worked in the Empire State Building, so he would take us up to the 72nd floor, and we'd look at all the Christmas lights and everything. And then we'd go to the Christmas show." Tesh finally got to take his daughter in 1997, "and she's asking me, 'Daddy, why are you crying?' 'Cause I'm thinking: Here, this is where I used to sit with my dad. It was really cool."

He tries to relive other memories of his youth when he returns to the Island for performances and charity appearances, two or three times a year. "I went downtown in Garden City" the very day of his WLIW stop, he said, "trying to find The Cheese Shop. I used to work at The Cheese Shop. I'm like one of those guys you can blindfold and hold cheese in front of my nose, and I can tell you what it is."

He also dropped by Garden City High School, where he starred in track, soccer and lacrosse. He played in a rock band then, too ("First it was called Rubber Band, then Best of Both Worlds, then the All-American Band — sort of like Blood, Sweat &

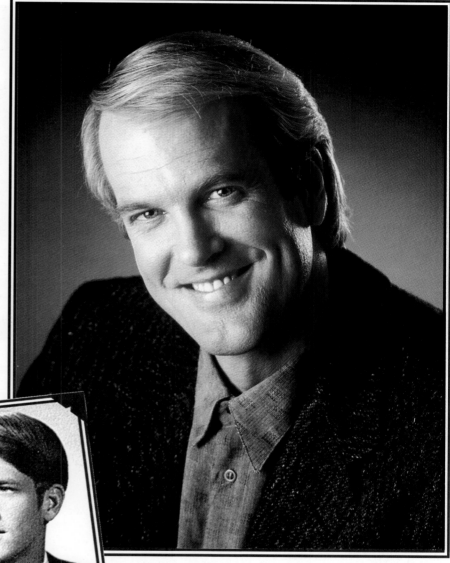

Left, Seth Poppel Yearbook Archives; Above, NBC Photo / Paul Drinkwater
Musician John Tesh in high school in 1970, and in 1998

Tears, 13 of us"), in an effort to seem cool rather than the "geek" he felt he was. "I was 6-5 as a sophomore and weighed 172 and had size 14 feet and braces on my mouth. I was hideous. I was very uncomfortable with my size. So I ended up playing keyboards in the hottest band, and I was still the geek. 'Look at the geek in the band!' "

Maybe Tesh longs for reconnection because Long Island ended too soon for him. "We lived here all of my life. And then my senior year, my dad quit his job here and wanted to move the family [back] to North Carolina. So we sold our house, he moved to North Carolina, and I moved into an apartment with my mom on Seventh Street." That was so John could finish out at Garden City High. "Which

is really a nice thing. But then I was really angry because the moment I graduated — you know, the coolest thing when you graduate is that summer before college. But they shipped me to North Carolina. And here I am, by myself, I don't know anybody. And it was terrible."

The cocoon had unraveled. Now if only he could re-create it for his daughter. "Now that I'm not tied to a job in L.A., we've talked about moving into a neighborhood," one where the houses aren't separated by physical or social moats, "so you don't want the kids to go outside, and you have to make 'play dates' for them.

"But that's the way you have to do it. You want them to be safe. I would never in a million *years* let my kid just go outside and play for a while.

"But in those days, they just let us do anything . . . "

Nassau County Museum Collection, Long Island Studies Institute

EAST MASSAPEQUA: Frank Buck shows off an elephant at his jungle camp in the 1940s. Buck won fame in the 1920s and '30s as a big-game hunter and ran his zoo from 1934 through the '50s.

Newsday Photo / Stan Wolfson

EAST MEADOW: Children from a Massapequa school get a driving lesson from a Nassau County police officer during an Accident Prevention Bureau class at Eisenhower Park in 1972.

Alec Baldwin

Massapequa

'I was like Monty Clift in "A Place in the Sun." I was from the other side of the tracks.'

As Alec Baldwin turned 40 in 1998, having played a slew of sexy, edgy leading men — from Stanley Kowalski in the 1995 Broadway revival of "A Streetcar Named Desire" (he was nominated for a Tony) to Anthony Hopkins' nemesis in last year's film thriller "The Edge" — he appeared to have fixed his tropical sea-blue eyes on other adventures on the horizon.

His mother, Carol Baldwin, had pre-

AP Photo, 1998
Alec Baldwin was senior class president.

dicted that her eldest son would someday occupy the White House. And the actor appeared to have put himself on just such a course — although in an uncharacteristically modest mode, he'd mentioned only U.S. senator or governor. He had a high profile, a beautiful wife — the actress Kim Basinger — and a cute daughter, Ireland Eliesse, born in 1995. Although a Democrat registered to vote in the East End, he also had homes in Manhattan and on the West Coast.

And it all began at Massapequa's Alfred G. Berner High School, where Alexander Rae Baldwin III was elected president of his senior class of 1976 — to date, his only elective office.

His mother (through his personal publicist, Alec Baldwin declined to be interviewed for this series about famous native sons) calls the second-born of her six children "the Golden Boy" and said that while "Zander" — the family's nickname for Alec — went to college (George Washington University in Washington, D.C.) intending to get a degree in political science, he'd always shown a penchant for performing, as well as a strong streak of self-assurance.

"From the time they were very little all the boys liked to mimic people . . . at dinner they'd do these accents. They were so-o-o funny," Carol Baldwin (who now lives near Syracuse, N.Y.) said about her four sons who grew up to be film stars. Alec's has been the most successful career, but his brothers' credits

More Hometown Heroes

Growing up next door or a few towns over, they rose to fame

are also impressive: Daniel, the TV series "Homicide" and "Sydney"; William, movies including "Backdraft" and "Flatliners"; and Stephen, films including "Last Exit to Brooklyn" and the TV series "The Young Riders." The three younger brothers all had small parts in Oliver Stone's "Born on the Fourth of July," based on the book by Vietnam War veteran Ron Kovic — who had been a student of their father in Massapequa.

Daniel Baldwin said that several of the brothers and their neighborhood friends made home movies, borrowing the camera their father, Alexander Jr., the high school football coach, used to film rival football teams. "We made a series of horror films — lots of ketchup — and a series of Joe Cool movies that were spoofs on James Bond." Brother Alec, he recalled, always played the Bond-Cool character.

Even back then, Alec did a great Brando impersonation, Carol Baldwin said. "And Stephen [the youngest] would sit in Zander's lap and play the dummy."

The Irish-Catholic Baldwins lived in Nassau Shores in a pleasant Cape Cod-style house next to a golf course. But his father's teacher's salary meant, Alec Baldwin has commented, "that I felt like Monty Clift in 'A Place in the Sun.' I was from the other side of the tracks." He helped out with odd jobs, including working as a lifeguard, busboy and laborer for a yard service.

The senior Baldwin, a loyal Democrat who taught social studies, wanted his sons to become lawyers, and mixed in with the dinner table high-jinks, Carol Baldwin said, were lively discussions about current events and civic issues. "He insisted they be in everything: Little League, Boy Scouts." When Robert F. Kennedy was killed in 1968, Alexanders Jr. and III traveled to Washington, D.C., to attend the funeral.

Along with his desire to impart strong social consciences in his children, the Baldwins' late father wanted his sons to be competitive, starting with sports. Carol Baldwin said the question her husband put to his sons was, "Do you want to be Daddy's tiger or Mommy's lamb?" Alec played lacrosse and baseball, and, said his brother William, "he's a lot like Dad . . . he definite-

ly plays hardball."

Said Stephen: "The brothers are competitive on a psychotic level in sports but there isn't any real serious rivalry between us professionally. If anything, it's more of a support system." Just look where hang-togetherness got another large Irish-Catholic family — the Kennedys.

— Blake Green

Jonathan Demme

Baldwin

'The first movie I saw on the big screen was "Treasure Island," at the Arcade theater.'

Oscar-winning filmmaker Jonathan Demme ("The Silence of the Lambs," "Philadelphia" and "Beloved") grew up in cozy Long Island villages whose landscape and values remained largely unaffected by the postwar growth of suburbia.

During his idyllic childhood on the South Shore, from his birth Feb. 22, 1944, to his family's departure in 1959, Demme had two passions: nature and movies. He lived in Rockville Centre, Lynbrook and, mainly, in a two-story house at 27 Lorenz Ave. in Baldwin.

"I loved living there," Demme recalled. "My friends and I could walk down the street, cross a creek, and play for a couple of

hours in woods that ran all the way to Sunrise Highway, where there was an abandoned waterworks."

Among his cherished memories was being befriended by Baldwin nature writer Edwin Way Teale and his wife, Nellie Teale. They took the fifth-grader bird-watching and introduced him to the patron saint of American bird-watchers, Roger Tory Peterson, who autographed his field guide.

Demme and his mother, Dodie ("short for Dorothy"), were tireless birders. One of their favorite places was called Woodmere Woods. "It characterized the Long Island I knew growing up — vast tracts of nature you just walked into and maybe never encountered anybody while you were bird-watching or pretending to be an Indian. I would love to find it again. But I'm afraid to look, because there are probably houses where Woodmere Woods stood when I was a boy more than 40 years ago."

At 6, watching movies became as important to Demme as watching birds. "The first movie I saw on the big screen was 'Treasure Island,' at the Arcade theater, also known as 'The Itch,' in Lynbrook. That was it. I was hooked."

Just four years later, Demme's movie mania was taking him — via the Merrick Road bus — to theaters as far from home as Hempstead and Jamaica. "It's funny to think back to that 10-year-old Long Island kid traveling to Jamaica and going into a highly urban theater playing triple horror bills," the director of the most celebrated horror movie since "Psycho" said, chuckling.

His solo movie-going excursions were without mishap, except for a "hideous violation" perpetrated by an usher. "One of the great traumas of my childhood was going to see 'Mister Roberts' at the Baldwin Cinema. I was in sixth grade, and went after school. The show started around 5:30. But a reel before the climax, an usher came and made me leave the theater, because unattended children weren't allowed to be in the theater after 7 o'clock. It was such an outrage, I left kicking and screaming."

Another childhood interest was collecting movie ads. "I was 13 and kept abreast of the best new movie ads, tore them out and saved them. And then I discovered that you could go into the basements of apartment buildings and find stacks of old newspapers. So I'd spend Saturdays sneaking into the base-

Please Turn the Page

Newsday Photo, 1988 / Bruce Gilbert
From the South Shore, Jonathan Demme watched birds and movies.

193

DEMME, Continued

ments of apartment buildings in Rockville Centre and Baldwin and searching through huge stacks of old newspapers, hoping to find old ads for movies that weren't around any more."

The most vivid landmarks of Demme's childhood were the shops on Baldwin's Grand Avenue. "The drugstore had that old drugstore smell they don't have any more," he recalled.

Demme attended two elementary schools (Lynbrook's Marion Street School and Baldwin's Calvin Coolidge School) and Baldwin Junior High. He finished ninth grade when his dad got a job in Miami and the family moved. In school, most of his LI friends were Italian and Irish.

"There were more Catholics than Protestants, and a couple of Jewish kids. And that was it. There were no Muslims or people of other religions in town when I was growing up. There were no black people. I remember a very white Long Island."

Demme said he tries to re-create his Long Island childhood for his kids, though doing it in a historic Hudson River village. He and his wife, artist Joanne Howard, who grew up in Manhasset, and their three children live in a big old house that's walking distance from the office where he edits his films. They spend their summers on a lake in Maine.

— **Joseph Gelmis**

Dee Snider

Baldwin

'I went for an outrageous form of expressing myself.'

In Baldwin High's class of '73, Danny Snider was the quiet, skinny guy with the goofy face. The one who was shunned equally by the rebels and the frat boys. When he asked a pretty girl out, she'd laugh at him, right to his face.

The only times Snider didn't, as he put it, "melt into the background" were when he did things like decline to smoke pot, prompting classmates to jeer: "Danny Snider, he's high on life."

Three years after graduation, Snider fought back. He morphed into Dee Snider, the outrageously garish, cross-dressing lead singer for the hugely successful heavy metal band Twisted Sister.

"I went for an outrageous form of expressing myself," recalled Snider. "It seemed to be a way that I could make my name and show that I was somebody."

Snider wasn't only rebelling against his high school. His head-banging music with Twisted Sister also was, he said, a way to vent his frustration over his home life.

Danny's father, Bob Snider, was a Korean War vet who worked as an insurance salesman and part-time New York State trooper. He loved his six children — Danny was born March 15, 1955 — but ran the house tightly. When Danny's room was messy, his dad would storm in and clear clutter from the shelves with a sweep of the hand. One day, his fa-

ther marched him into a barbershop and forced him to get a crew cut, razing the long locks that he considered his lone positive physical attribute.

Snider also was rebelling against growing up in what he still refers to as a "suburban wasteland" — even though he continued to live on Long Island, albeit in swanker, North Shore digs.

"There is a facelessness to Long Island, especially on the South Shore, with the huge developments, the tract housing, the two cars in the garage and the one tree," he said. "I mean, I clearly remember literally just sitting on my porch as a teenager and wanting to scream, thinking, 'God, there's got to be more than this.' "

Snider did scream, with a voice that was good enough to land him a spot in the All-State Chorus in high school (he auditioned with Henry Purcell's "Strike the Viol") and the lead role in Baldwin High's production of "Godspell." By 15, he'd dropped out of baseball leagues to spend more time playing guitar and practicing rock-star gestures in his room.

"Out of this frustrated blue-collar hell, a lot of great music has grown," Snider said of Twisted Sister and other Long Island bands.

If Snider's stage persona avenged his father's strictness, it never quite earned him the recognition he'd sought from his classmates.

He didn't go to his 10th high school reunion — Twisted Sister was touring at the time — but one of his few school pals did. The friend reported back that "Everybody knows Twisted Sister, but they didn't remember you were in their school," Snider recalled.

"Can you believe it?" Snider asked, his voice still incredulous. "Here I was trying to show everybody in school that I was somebody, and they didn't even remember who I *was*!"

— **Letta Tayler**

Newsday Photo / Erica Berger, 1992
Dee Snider found a way to get noticed.

Eddie Money

Plainedge

'I got to date all the cheerleaders.'

Eddie Money, the rough-voiced rocker who sang his way to stardom with "Two Tickets to Paradise" and "Baby, Hold On," lived on Long Island only as a teenager. But he considers his five years in Plainedge the most formative of his life.

"Long Island was the breeding ground; it made me who I am," said Money, who made a home near Malibu, Calif. "Most of what I learned about my craft I learned in high school with The Grapes of Wrath."

The book? No, the band that Money, then Eddie Mahoney, co-founded at Island Trees High School and that was named after the John Steinbeck tome. ("We actually read the classics in those days," Money quipped.)

He was born March 21, 1949. As a child in Brooklyn, Money was the lead singer in his church choir and loved to belt out the songs from "Carousel" and "Oklahoma!," which he learned from records his parents brought home after theater outings in Manhattan. But singing in a rock band was far better. "It gave me an opportunity to be in front of all these people without being the star of the football team or the smartest kid in the math class," Money recalled.

And, he added, "I got to date all the cheerleaders."

The Grapes of Wrath was a cover band, playing the Beatles, Kinks, Rolling Stones, Paul Butterfield Blues Band, James Brown and others. "We were doing 'Gloria,' we were doing 'What a Day for a Daydream,' we were doing 'My Baby Does the Hanky Panky,' which I hate to this day; it made me feel like I was actually working for a living," Money recalled.

But playing music was exactly what Money was doing for pocket money. "We'd play a lot of parties, we'd play until the cops came, we'd play the beach clubs, like the Malibu and the Colony out in Lido Beach, and a lot of dances at the school," Money said.

The Grapes also participated in the battles of the bands that determined who would perform at various proms. "We did a battle of the bands in 1966 with The Hassles, Billy Joel's band," Money remembered. "I think it was MacArthur High School [in Levit-

town] or Syosset High School or the Mid-Island Mall, I can't remember. Neither one of us won."

Despite his popularity as lead singer, Money recalled his years at Island Trees High School as a philosophical tug-of-war between his family and his associates.

"The other guys in the band were pretty freaky, growing their hair long and stuff, but my dad was a [New York City] cop so I couldn't have long hair," Money said. "And I also was a jock, I ran track and played soccer and baseball. I was on both sides of the bench."

Which didn't suit his father. "He'd be coming upstairs, ripping my Jimi Hendrix posters off the wall," Money said.

After graduating in 1967, Money decided to go his father's way, enroll-

Columbia Photo / Roger Sandler
Eddie Money: His high school band was The Grapes of Wrath.

ing in the New York Police Academy. But he was still moonlighting as a rock-and-roll singer. At 19, he quit the academy, moved to Berkeley and a few years later wrote "Two Tickets to Paradise."

The hit had nothing to do with a desire to leave the Island, Money said. But he added that he has penned other tunes about that emotion, including "Something to Believe In," off his 1997 album "Shakin' With the Money Man."

"It's about growing up and leaving Long Island," Money said. "It goes, 'When I was young, I said goodbye to my mamma ... she always said I could come back if I wanna.' "

— **Letta Tayler**

Newsday Photo / Mitch Turner

UNIONDALE: Cheerleaders from St. Raphael's parish in East Meadow form a pyramid during a performance in a 1976 Catholic Youth Organization competition at Nassau Coliseum.

MONTAUK: The night was young and the joint was rocking. Well, in this case, the joint was rolling when students from Islip High School staged a dance in a Long Island Rail Road baggage car headed for Montauk in June, 1961.

Newsday Photo / Jim Cavanagh

Nitro Photo, 1997

At Adelphi, Chuck D found himself at the heart of the Island's exploding rap scene. He recalled Roosevelt as a tight-knit community.

Chuck D

Roosevelt

'My early years and the supportive environment that I grew up in are my foundation.'

In the early 1970s, Hofstra and Adelphi Universities hosted a series of summer programs about the African-American experience, many of which were taught by black college students who followed Malcolm X and the Black Panthers.

One youth attending those programs was Carlton Ridenhour, who had moved to Roosevelt from the Queens Bridge Housing project in Long Island City with his parents when he was 11. (He was born Aug. 1, 1960.)

The programs were pivotal to Ridenhour's evolution into Chuck D, the leader of the seminal rap group Public Enemy. They inspired him to enroll at Adelphi, where he found himself at the heart of the Island's exploding rap scene. And they helped him form the black militant beliefs that were Public Enemy's core message.

"My early years and the supportive environment that I grew up in are my foundation, which is why I feel so strongly about the black community getting back to where we belong," Chuck D wrote in "Fight the Power," his new autobiography.

In a 1998 interview, the rapper recalled the Roosevelt of his childhood as a tight-knit community with numerous sports leagues and socially active adults. For their 20th anniversary, his mother, Judy, and his father, Lorenzo Ridenhour, who ran a trucking business, visited Senegal and returned with stories about black pride.

Roosevelt didn't have many facilities. "There was always that corner available, but as for gyms, we had to walk to Kennedy Park gym in Hempstead from Roosevelt and get turned away because we weren't residents," Chuck D recalled. But it did have the Roosevelt Youth Center, which became a focal point for young talent including the hip-hop mobile disc jockey group Spectrum, featuring MC Chuckie D.

Starting about 1977, "Long Island went hip-hop crazy," with young black residents catching the rap fever from cousins and friends they'd visit in Harlem and the Bronx, Chuck D recalled.

In 1979, after enrolling at Adelphi, where he studied graphic design, Chuck D met other students who'd been swept into the rap scene, including Bill Stephney (later the president of the pioneering Def Jam rap label), who gave him a slot on his hip-hop show on WBAU-FM, the college radio station.

The show became an essential rap outlet on Long Island, which Chuck D and the other DJs dubbed "Strong Island." The DJs also renamed emerging hip-hop strongholds — Roosevelt became "The Velt" and Uniondale was "Chill City."

"We wanted to give Long Island its own identity," Chuck D recalled, noting that many local rap fans associated with the boroughs they'd come from, rather than with their new Long Island hometowns.

From that point on, Chuck D lived and breathed hip-hop, composing raps along the Long Island Expressway while driving a delivery car for a Hempstead telecommunications company and doing gigs in black communities across the Island.

Public Enemy was catapulted into stardom with its 1988 sophomore album, "It Takes a Nation of Millions to Hold Us Back." But Chuck D never lost his roots, having started a record label, Slam Jamz, to promote emerging Long Island rap and soul artists.

His goal, he said, remained what it was during his days at WBAU, to "build some black unification through young people and their music." — **Letta Tayler**

Pat Benatar

Lindenhurst

'I really wanted to sing rock and roll but I had no outlet.'

Pat Benatar dominated the pop charts from the late '70s through the early '80s as a petite vixen who dressed in Lycra and spike heels and sounded as tough as any male rocker. "Hit me with your best shot," she taunted in 1980 above thundering drums and snarling guitars. "Fire away!"

Benatar traces her machisma to her childhood in Lindenhurst, where she was a scrappy kid in a working-class neighborhood in which it was each youngster for him or herself.

"If you didn't play baseball, they'd hit you with the bat anyway," she recalled.

The young Patricia Andrzejewski knew how to hit back. "I'd go right for your throat," she said with pride in an interview from Malibu, Calif., where she eventually made her home. "My mother would have to come to school all the time because I was beating up on people."

Benatar didn't suffer from her childhood scuffles — indeed, she said, they "built great character." She described her community, where most adults were fishermen and laborers, and her years at Daniel Street Elementary School and Lindenhurst High School (class of 1971), as "idyllic."

"We did things like sing at the Christmas tree lighting in the middle of town on Main Street — where else?" she remembered. "It was ridiculously quaint. My husband is from Cleveland; he always thinks I grew up where they filmed 'It's a Wonderful Life.' "

Born Jan. 10, 1952, Benatar was the daughter of a sheet-metal worker and a beautician who once sang with the New York City Opera. She threw herself into theater and voice lessons in grade school, singing her first solo when she was 8. "It was called 'It Must Be Spring,' it was this silly little kids song," she said. "I still

know it but I'm *not* going to sing it for you."

Her musical training was strictly classical and theatrical. "I really wanted to sing rock and roll but I had no outlet," she said. "I was singing Puccini and 'West Side Story,' but I spent every afternoon after school with my little transistor radio listening to the Rolling Stones . . . and singing in front of the mirror with a hairbrush as a microphone."

Benatar was completely cut off from the rock scene in nearby Manhattan because her parents were "ridiculously strict — I was allowed to go to symphonies, opera and theater but I couldn't go to clubs."

But Lindenhurst also was "ridiculously safe. It was a small town when I lived there; you pretty much knew everybody." Thus her parents gave her free rein around town — more rein than they might have if they'd always known what she was up to, she conceded.

"We had no money, we spent our lives at the beach," she said of herself and friends. "And some of our friends had little boats with motors on them. Everyone was smoking pot and having a great time."

Patricia Benatar left Long Island when she was 19 — she'd just married her boyfriend, Dennis Benatar, and had moved with him to Richmond, Va., when he was drafted. In 1977, her singing career took off after she moved to Manhattan and divorced (she later married her guitarist, Neil Geraldo).

But the four-time Grammy winner still visited Long Island, and when she performed there, her relatives and old friends turned out en masse. "When I play Jones Beach? *Madonna!* Let me tell you, it's packed," she said. "It's like a wedding." — **Letta Tayler**

Newsday Archive

Pat Benatar was a scrappy youngster.

Al Skinner

Malverne

'There were some times we weren't welcomed with open arms.'

Al Skinner was back in town in January, 1998, part of the Nets' reunion to honor their glory years with Julius Erving and the 1976 American Basketball Association title.

Of course, back in town for the Nets meant East Rutherford, N.J., a bit of a drive from Skinner's and the Nets' old Long Island stomping grounds. His success story, from high school star at Malverne to six seasons as a professional ballplayer and head coach at Boston College, is one of local boy makes good.

Born Sept. 10, 1952, Skinner and his family moved to Lakeview from Springfield Gardens at a tumultuous time — the late 1960s. His parents were able to buy a home and thought the school system was good.

Skinner's memories of Malverne High have as much to do with demonstrations and integration as with basketball.

"For black people, there was a certain amount of awareness and unity," said Skinner. "We had our share of demonstrations at high school. It was an integrated high school; Lakeview was predominantly black and Malverne

was predominantly white. But there were no black studies teachers at school. We wanted to bring more awareness to the community. It worked." Although Skinner says his years in Queens had more impact on his basketball game, Malverne High offered something more. The community's diversity and the school's courses helped prepare him for the University of Massachusetts.

Still, while traveling with his high school team and with groups of friends looking for a game — they went to courts in Roosevelt and Hempstead, East Meadow and Rockville Centre — Skinner felt the occasional sting of the race and class struggles that characterized America during the civil rights movement.

"Unfortunately, there were community lines that were drawn," he said. "It was not only action on the floor but action in the stands. There were some times we weren't welcomed with open arms. It's unfair to name them, but there were certain communities that you didn't feel comfortable in. That was part of growing up."

But when Skinner graduated in 1970, he was sorry to leave for Massachusetts, where his fortunes would rise further.

"I wasn't necessarily happy to leave," he said. "It was a good community to be in. I still have friends who live there. The community hasn't changed that much and I'm very happy about that."

At Massachusetts, he'd become the only player in the school's history to be a three-time All-Yankee Conference selection as well as an honorable mention All-America player in 1973-74.

Newsday Photo, 1976 / David L. Pokress
After college in Massachusetts, Al Skinner made it back to Long Island playing for the Nets.

When he graduated in 1974, Skinner returned to Long Island to play for the Nets, in Nassau Coliseum where, as a teenager, he had worked as a janitor in the summer. He lived in Westbury and was named to the ABA's All-Rookie team for the 1974-75 season. In 1976, the Nets won the title. Years later, he looked back on the phases of his life in Long Island — including the time he was fired as a janitor because the boss wanted to hire a family member — with a warm, enveloping sense of comfort.

"It was home," Skinner said. "I was playing for the Nets and it gave me further exposure to people I'd grown up with. It was a very comfortable feeling. There were people in the media who knew me from high school. Those type of things were very beneficial. To know I had once worked in the Long Island Coliseum as a custodian, and to be able to go back and play as a professional was very satisfying." — **Judy Battista**

Newsday Archive
Julius Erving, front, third from right, with the ABA's New York Nets at the old Island Garden. Ballboy Al Trautwig is at front right.

Julius Erving
Hempstead, Roosevelt

'Something was instilled in me by God, a competitive nature.'

The first significant athletic accomplishment in Julius Erving's life was not recorded in a scorebook or preserved in a newspaper. But it was as personally exhilarating as any of the 40-point games he achieved for the Nets or 76ers.

"I lived at 50 Beech [now Evans] Avenue in Hempstead," said Erving, who was born Feb. 22, 1950. "We moved there when my mom and dad separated. I was 3 years old. I remember at age 5 or 6 running up and down the steps of that project. Something was instilled in me by God, a competitive nature.

"We had benches outside that were secured in cement. Kids my age used to step on the seat of the benches and jump over. As I got stronger and faster, I got to the point where I could step onto the back part of the bench and jump over. And then one day, when I was 7 or 8, an amazing thing happened. I jumped clear over the bench. I experienced a breakthrough and I was happy. It became a part of my makeup."

His apartment was next to Campbell Park. "I was about 9 and we were playing football in an area with a lot of broken bottles," he said. "I went after a pass, fell on some glass and ripped my right knee to shreds. I severed a ligament. I was taken to Meadowbrook Hospital [now Nassau County Medical Center] where they put my knee back together. I was pretty much crippled by the injury. I wore a cast and, after I got

Julius Erving, a k a Dr. J

it off, I was limping around. Other kids were calling me Hopalong and Pegleg. I went from the fastest kid, with all this self-esteem, to an insecure, shy kid."

It was about that time that an older friend named Joe Bender got Julius a job delivering morning newspapers in Garden City. The man who owned the route would wake up Julius and Joe before dawn, take them to breakfast and then get down to business. "We delivered the Times, the Herald Tribune, the Daily News and the Daily Mirror," he said. "We earned $1.50 a day during the week and $3 on Sunday. The guy had running boards on his car and we'd hop on and off delivering the papers. I did that for about a year and it turned out to be a serious form of rehabilitation."

His leg was sound again when Andy Haggerty, the playground director, recommended Julius and Archie Rogers to Don Ryan. Still a student at Adelphi, Ryan had started a youth basketball program at the new Salvation Army center a block from his house.

Julius "wasn't very tall," recalled Ryan, "but he had great hands and long arms. He was poker-faced on the court. You couldn't rile him. He was an unselfish player, just a perfect kid. He was MVP on the first team he was ever on. We won the [Inter-County Basketball Association championship] the two years Julius was on the club. We piled in my station wagon and played all over Long Island — Smithtown, Huntington, Locust Valley. We entered as many tournaments as we could find."

Erving has called those years the most important of his life. Shortly thereafter, his mother remarried and the family moved to Roosevelt, where he starred at Roosevelt High School and earned the nickname "Doctor" from a friend and teammate, Leon Saunders. But even after he went off to

the University of Massachusetts and after he enjoyed a spectacular professional career in the American Basketball Association and the NBA, he remained a presence in Ryan's program and at the Salvation Army.

"It's a lifelong relationship," said Erving, who later made his home in suburban Philadelphia. "I can remember the Sunday afternoon at Don's house when his mother talked me into reciting poetry."

He credits the time he spent in the program for helping him become the kind of person he is. "We were encouraged to say, 'Nice pass.' It's a small thing but small things lead to big things." — **Joe Gergen**

Al Trautwig
Garden City South

'An awful lot of my life revolved around the old Island Garden.'

Sportscaster Al Trautwig and his young son Alex once ventured into one of the hangouts of his youth: Centurion Pizza on Nassau Boulevard in Garden City South.

"The same guy I remember from going in there after school was still making pizza," Trautwig recalled in a 1998 interview. "They have a huge mural of a centurion on a horse and every time they painted the walls, they used to paint around it. So you could see all the former colors of the place around the edges."

Memories of meals at Centurion, diners, Nathan's and local delis dominate Trautwig's recollections of growing up on Long Island.

"The group I hung out with was a big deli group," recalled Trautwig, who

Please Turn the Page

197

TRAUTWIG, Continued

would later travel extensively in the United States and abroad as an announcer for Madison Square Garden Network, and for the major networks to cover several Olympics. "I'm always looking for a deli when we're on the road. What else do you do for a sandwich?"

Those young appetites were fueled by sports: Little League, shooting hoops in parks and street games. "When I was about 11, me and my buddy Jerry Passaro painted bases and foul lines on our freshly repaved street and the neighbors all went bananas," he said.

Trautwig, who attended Franklin Square's Washington Street Elementary School, recalled that "an awful lot of my life revolved around the old Island Garden," the arena where he would become a ballboy for the New York Nets of the American Basketball Association.

"Right behind the Island Garden was the Aurora Toy Company," Trautwig said. "We used to rifle through the garbage bins and get thousands of discarded little racing car bodies. We used to ride on our bikes, laughing like crazy, and throw the cars to other kids. We made them work and had 24 hours of Le Mans; we were really into that."

What really grabbed Trautwig — and led him toward a career in sports broadcasting — was a chance meeting in 1968, at age 12. "My friend had a house overlooking the Island Garden. One day we had some model rockets outside and saw this guy dribbling a red, white and blue basketball. He said, 'We're a new basketball team.' I was hooked. I became a daily pest to the GM [Barry Murtha] and finally he let me be a towel boy and a ballboy."

Al Trautwig, sportscaster and deli aficionado

Trautwig attended H. Frank Carey High School in Franklin Square and, through his job with the Nets, met Islanders' trainer Fritz Massman. He became the team's home stick boy. "I used to go to practice and watch him; he taught me to tape ankles," said Trautwig. "He was like a second father to me." In 1989, he became a regular at Madison Square Garden, hosting pregame shows for the Knicks and Rangers. Play-by-play for Knicks and Yankees games was also among his duties.

The young Trautwig never spent much time in Manhattan. "I didn't really go to Knicks or Rangers games. When we first started to drive, we'd go to places like the Empire State Building and walk around on 42nd Street. For us, it was more the beaches. We'd get a six-pack and sit out on the jetties in Long Beach and Lido Beach. We did that hundreds of times."

His son Alex would have a stunningly different childhood from his father's. "He's already been to five Olympics — Barcelona, Albertville, Lillehammer, Atlanta and Nagano," Trautwig said with a laugh. "That has to be a record."
— Steve Zipay

Richard Migliore
Bay Shore

'We would hold pony races on the athletic fields of the Brentwood schools . . . and would almost always win.'

Growing up in a crowded home in Sheepshead Bay, Brooklyn, Richard Migliore always looked forward to visiting his grandparents in Bay Shore, where things were wide open and moved more quickly. Long before he established himself as one of North America's leading jockeys, young Richard decided that he was happiest on a fast track.

Born March 14, 1964, he had just turned age 11 when his family moved to a larger house in Bay Shore. Richard was happy. He could ride his bicycle faster through the streets of his town into Deer Park and Brentwood, and tried to explore each of what seemed like an endless collection of roads.

Little did Migliore know that in the next three years he would make discoveries that would fashion his career as a top rider on the New York Racing Association circuit. "On one of my expeditions down Deer Park Avenue, I turned onto Half Hollow Road and onto a lane with a horse farm," he recalled. "I always loved animals, and especially horses, but that day I opened the door to a whole new world. I brought my lunch there every day for a week and just took in the beauty of the place. And the history — way in the back was a cemetery with headstones from the 1700s."

The farm was Hunting Hollow Farm, owned and managed by Hugh Cassidy, a widely respected expert in dressage and other equestrian disciplines. Cassidy noticed the youngster and asked him if he would like to work with the horses.

Though shy, Migliore accepted the offer and soon was receiving $2 for each stall he could clean — money he applied toward riding lessons from Cassidy.

"I liked it, but everything emphasized control and restraint," said Migliore, who later made his home in Floral Park with his wife and children. "I wanted to open them up and see how fast they could run. So I started going out to Yaphank with two friends from my block — Carlos and David Figueroa [no relation] — and got involved with racehorses."

By the time he was 13, Richard had turned into an entrepreneur. He and the Figueroas bought ponies for $35 and started a pony-ride business that quickly turned into a pony-racing bonanza.

"We had to break the ponies ourselves and, eventually, we would hold pony races on the athletic fields of the Brentwood schools. We'd charge a $5 entry fee and would almost always win.

"We knew how to ride, and our ponies would start like quarterhorses while the other kids, with their equestrian training, wouldn't get away well at all. One of my ponies, Sally, could fly and would win even when she had to wear a saddle 30 pounds heavier than the others. One morning she stumbled at the start but made up five lengths in about 30 yards to win by a head. That afternoon I watched Willie Shoemaker and Forego beat Honest Pleasure on TV. The way they did it was so similar to the way I won with Sally that I felt like a kindred spirit to the Shoe. It was that day I decided to become a jockey."

Richard got a boost when he discussed his career choice with Pat Pagano, who taught him seventh- and eighth-grade English at Brentwood's West Junior High. "I talked about it with her because she always made me interested in learning and striving to do better. When I talked about riding for a living, she recognized my intensity and didn't patronize me. Her support gave me confidence that I could succeed."

And it didn't take long. By 1980, Migliore was riding as an apprentice at the Meadowlands; the following season, at 17, he was the leading apprentice rider in North America. — **Mark Schwartz**

Mike Francesa and Chris Russo
Long Beach, Syosset

'I was a kid who'd go surfing at 6:30 in the morning, get out of the water by 9, take a shower and go to work at the Atlantic Beach Club.'
— **Mike Francesa**

Hearing WFAN's Mike Francesa and Chris Russo argue about baseball or football, listeners couldn't help but believe that the radio partners had nothing in common except a passion for sports.

They'd be wrong.

Mike and the Mad Dog, the most popular pairing in the history of sports-talk radio, shared at least one thing: crystal-clear memories of being raised on Long Island.

Francesa, born March 20, 1954, spent much of his life on the barrier island that includes Long Beach, Lido Beach and Atlantic Beach; and as an adult made his home in Manhasset. Russo, born Oct. 18, 1959, grew up in Syosset; at 15, he left to attend an upstate boarding school.

"I was fortunate because I grew up in the period when there was a lot of land, open space, where kids could run around," said Russo, who until he was 9 lived at 11 Harmony Ct., a little street off Split Rock Road about a quarter-mile from the LIRR train station.

"We played ball in the court and had

NY Racing Authority Photo

Richard Migliore in action at Aqueduct. He got a boost when he discussed his career choice with Pat Pagano, who taught him English at Brentwood's West Junior High. "I talked about it with her because she always made me interested in learning and striving to do better."

Newsday Photo / Ken Spencer, 1993

Mike Francesa, left, in the WFAN studio, talking sports with Chris (Mad Dog) Russo; both spent much of their youth in Nassau County.

a big field, two houses down, where we played football and baseball and where we built dugouts," Russo recalled in 1998. "And Split Rock School, where I went from grades one through six, had lots of land in front and back." Behind the Russo house was Galeeza Stable. "My father was a jewelry salesman and he took the train to work every day. I used to look through the back porch window and see my father cut through the stable when he'd come home at night.

"My recollection as a young kid is always summertime, being outside," Russo said. "I remember when I learned to ride a bike without training wheels down Harmony Court . . . I remember rushing home for the World Series in 1967 when the Cards beat the Red Sox and in 1968 to see Willie Horton being interviewed after Detroit beat St. Louis."

After a year at Syosset Junior High, Russo went to St. Paul's in Garden City for two years. Next was the Darrow School, a boarding school in New Lebanon, N.Y., "but I came back in the summertime and still saw some of my buddies on the basketball court at Split Rock School, which didn't close until 1977 and wasn't torn down until years later."

Most of the open land from Russo's childhood has been sold to developers. "Now it's all houses," said Russo, who later made his home in New Canaan, Conn. "And the stable is a retirement village."

For Francesa, it is another type of open space that triggers memories: endless beaches and the blue Atlantic.

"For many summers, I was a kid who'd go surfing at 6:30 in the morning, get out of the water by 9, take a shower and go to work at the Atlantic Beach Club," said Francesa, who grew up in Long Beach's West End. At the club, he parked cars, bused tables, worked in the kitchen. On Saturday and Sunday mornings, "we played basketball in West School and Bay Park playground," he recalled.

"A lot of St. John's guys, like Billy Paultz, would come down to play."

Like many kids of that era, Francesa was a big fan of Yankee slugger Mickey Mantle.

"In 1961, I remember going to Yankee Stadium and saw Mantle and Maris and Johnny Blanchard hit home runs against the Cleveland Indians," he said. "In 1963, my older brother John took me with his buddies to the Polo Grounds to see a Mets doubleheader against the Reds. We made those trips by car, but it was easier to go to Shea by train, especially in the summer of '69. We used to sit in the upper deck and climb down to the empty seats."

Later, Francesa took a bus to Maria Regina High School in Uniondale. As a senior, after varsity baseball practice or games, he remembered running across Hempstead Turnpike, en masse with the team, to Nets playoff games at the just-built Nassau Coliseum. "We'd pay $3 or $4 and saw some great players, Ollie Taylor, Rick Barry . . . " Francesa then spent one year at the University of South Florida and transferred to St. John's.

But if there's a single Long Island tableau that Francesa treasures, it's this one: the Loop Parkway (connecting to Point Lookout), at dusk, about this time of year.

"It seems I've been making that ride over the loop, to the Meadowbrook Parkway, my whole life," Francesa said in a 1998 interview. "Even though I don't live down there anymore — my mom does and I still have property there — everything seems to come back to that five-mile stretch. I've always said that in the springtime, if you drive the loop, going home, going south, just as the sun's going down over that marshland, it is as pretty as anywhere you will ever see.

"I love to catch it at the right time . . . in May . . . about 7:30 . . . it is just beautiful. That to me is home . . . that will always be home to me."
— **Steve Zipay**

Ellen Baker

Bayside

'We just hung out in the neighborhoods where the bus would take us. Nobody had a car.'

She hurtled through outer space and traveled through the Andes mountains. She became an accomplished physician. And her mother became a prominent New York City politician.

Still, when astronaut Ellen Baker thought about the important influences on her life, the person who came to mind first was "Miss O'Gara, my fifth-grade teacher."

Baker remembered how Kathryn O'Gara at PS 41 in Bayside helped mold her into the adventurer she became.

"How do you separate the place from the people?" asked Baker, a Queens native. "Clearly the people were very influential."

O'Gara "was a great teacher," said Baker, daughter of Queens Borough President Claire Shulman. "She taught everything. She was patient and kind but tough and made us work hard." Teacher and student would later see each other occasionally over the years and exchange notes at Christmas, Baker said.

Otherwise, Baker said, the years she spent growing up in Queens were unremarkable, although she remembered them fondly. Her mother's many community activities were just another part of her life and besides, Baker said, Shulman didn't hold a sala-

ried community job until the future astronaut had left Queens. And by the time Shulman became borough president in 1986, Baker was long gone from New York City.

The veteran of three NASA space missions recalled ice skating at the Flushing Meadows rink and repeated visits to the 1964-65 World's Fair.

Baker was born April 27, 1953, at Fort Bragg, N.C., where her father, a physician, was serving in the Army during the Korean War. But she grew up in houses on 222nd and 215th Streets in Bayside along with her brothers Lawrence and Kim, doing mostly what she called "kid stuff."

That meant swimming freestyle for the Flushing YMCA team and lots of softball and baseball, Baker said, and the occasional trip into Manhattan with friends to museums, concerts and restaurants.

But mostly, Baker remembered, "We just hung out in the neighborhoods where the bus would take us. Nobody had a car. The skating rink was a big hangout."

Baker said memories of her childhood in Queens blurred with the passage of time and she later remembered "just good friends and good people and a nice place to grow up."

In addition to PS 41, Baker also attended JHS 158 and Bayside High School. She earned a degree in geology from the State University at Buffalo and then went on to earn an MD from Cornell University.

Baker's interest in outer space and the NASA program didn't surface until she had completed medical school. Baker joined NASA in 1984.

Baker's husband, Ken, was a NASA pilot; the couple, who would live near the Lyndon B. Johnson Space Center in Houston, had two children, Karen and Meredith.

Baker, who returned to Queens in January, 1998, for her mother's swearing-in as borough president, said the biggest change she'd noticed was the tall apartment buildings that had sprung up around the borough.

And one other thing, said Baker: "I don't think I could afford to buy a house there now." — **Kathleen Kerr**

NASA Photo

Ellen Baker, daughter of Borough President Shulman

Newsday / Harvey Weber

JONES BEACH: Long Islanders, New York City residents and others find refuge at Jones Beach State Park on a summer day in 1952. The park opened in 1929 and became world famous.

Newsday Photo / Ike Eichorn

MINEOLA: Margie Myers of New Hyde Park does a spin at a rehearsal before a performance at the Mineola Skating Rink in 1950.

Newsday Photo / Bob Luckey

HEWLETT: In 1964, root beer is on tap at a non-alcoholic night club for teenagers. The club, called the Haven, was on Broadway in Hewlett.

Mary Cleave

Great Neck

'I avoided adolescence by hiding out in the gym.'

Stolen hours at Jones Beach while cutting class. Hiding out in the gym to escape the pains of adolescence. And an early interest in science.

That's what retired astronaut Mary Cleave recalled about her days growing up in Nassau County.

The former Great Neck resident gave up her spacesuit in 1991 when she retired from the astronaut corps (after making shuttle flights in 1985 and 1989), she became a project manager at NASA's Space Flight Center in Greenbelt, Md., specializing in projects that focus on unmanned space flight.

Cleave, who as an adult made her home in Annapolis, Md., and used a rowboat to traverse nearby rivers, focused early on sports and science. Cleave was born Feb. 5, 1947, in Southampton and lived briefly in Westhampton, before moving with her family to Great Neck at an early age.

"I thought it was a great place to grow up because of the school system," said Cleave. "I got a great education. We had a great public library in Great Neck and Kings Point had great parks you could go to." At Great Neck North High School, she played field hockey and lacrosse.

Cleave gave credit to her high school sports coaches and to her first- and second-grade teachers for inspiring her.

"I avoided adolescence by hiding out in the gym," said Cleave, who graduated from high school in 1965.

"I had a really close relationship with my coaches. The whole idea of team sports in general was very helpful in the work environment. Not only in getting along with crews in a spacecraft but in everything."

Cleave said she didn't venture much into New York City except for the occasional horse show. Summers were spent at a camp on Lake Champlain.

After high school, Cleave attended Colorado State University, where her first major was preveterinary medicine. She later majored in botany.

— **Kathleen Kerr**

At his birthday party at age 6, the cake's decoration hints at the trajectory of Wetherbee's career; at right, the NASA astronaut talked about a space shuttle mission.

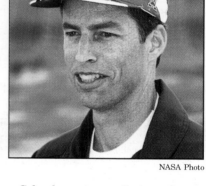

NASA Photo

James Wetherbee

Huntington Station

'Our neighborhood was the best place on the planet.'

Althea Wetherbee wasn't kidding when she described her astronaut son, James, as spacey.

Born Nov. 27, 1952, James grew up in a new development in Huntington Station in the 1950s. He was a quiet boy who always seemed to have his head in the clouds. He'd be clearing his dishes, recalled his mother, and then walk straight past the dishwasher and head upstairs with his plate and cup, stopping in midstair to sheepishly return to the kitchen.

Wetherbee was raised on Algonquin Drive, in a neighborhood where kids traveled in packs on bicycles and skates.

To Wetherbee, a veteran of four shuttle missions, his childhood was marked by play

NASA Photo, 1985

Astronaut Mary Cleave

. . . and play . . . and play.

"We'd go out right after breakfast and we often wouldn't come home until the sun was setting," Wetherbee said. The neighborhood kids made up a baker's dozen and they stayed glued through the seasons and the sports, no matter what the occasion.

"Our neighborhood was the best place on the planet," said Wetherbee, who would become deputy director of NASA's Johnson Space Center in Houston. "My childhood was about kids, and lots of them. We'd hit the streets in the morning, running. There were no drugs. Only play. What could be better?"

A self-described "average" student with a penchant for math and science, young Wetherbee did have aspirations for flight. He recalled himself at 10 years old, sitting in the back of his sixth-grade classroom at St. Hugh of Lincoln, hunkered down with his nine-volt transistor radio, reporting back to the class the exact area overhead where one of the Mercury missions was passing. He'd put pins on a map to track its course. Books on space dotted the room he shared with his older brother, Larry.

While a student at Huntington's Holy Family High School (later the site of St. Anthony's), his hero was Neil Armstrong, the first man to walk on the moon.

Wetherbee's dad, Dana, moved from Fresh Meadows when the family of five outgrew its two-bedroom apartment, even though it had been a 15-minute spin to his job as an American Airlines pilot. He would put a dollar shy of $20,000 down on a four-bedroom house on Algonquin, trading his breezy commute for better schools for his kids. Jim was 5.

On his first day of kindergarten, Althea Wetherbee recalled, her quiet boy returned from the Washington Elementary School only minutes after the morning bell had rung. "Jim, what are you doing home?" she asked. "It was too noisy," he said.

School was never first on the young boy's mind. One year, Althea Wetherbee remembered, the calendar squares were marked off with X's spanning 100 days into the future.

"What's this, Jim?"

"That's when school is over."

He would rather play baseball or go into the potato fields and pick from the ground the runts of the lot and bring them home for his mother.

Throughout the '60s and '70s, machines for harvesting food were replaced by equipment for building homes. One year, Jim learned that the town population had swelled to 200,000. "I was shocked," he said.

The polite and earnest boy remembered the tranquility of those years, kids harmonious and active, coming and going through houses like swarms of bees, laughing and, well, running. "No one ever got hurt," he said with the bewilderment of a father raising two daughters.

Althea Wetherbee said that he probably did not remember the time when a boy down the street suffered a broken hand, and his parents blamed it on her quiet and peaceful son. It was only years later that she found out what really happened. Jim had been swinging on a gate and the neighborhood boy, older and stronger, told him to stop. The gate continued to move to the rhythm of Jim's body. The boy's hand came crashing down on Jim's head. "That's how he broke his hand. On Jim's head," she said.

— **Jamie Talan**

Newsday Photo / Cliff De Bear

HEMPSTEAD: A second-grade class at the Prospect Street School was already integrated by 1954, the year that the U.S. Supreme Court outlawed racial segregation in public schools.

Newsday Archive

SYOSSET: A boy meets Pedro the donkey at the Lollipop Farms Zoo in 1950. Animal keeper Fred Beck watches from behind.

Newsday Photo / Ike Eichorn

JONES BEACH: A funhouse mirror gives Christina Noor of Franklin Square an unexpected view of herself during a circus at the beach in August, 1952.

Newsday Photo / John Cornell, 1997

Author Meg Wolitzer recalls that a simple stroll could get the creative juices flowing.

Meg Wolitzer

Syosset

'My parents let me walk everywhere . . . Now the sense of freedom seems astonishing.'

Meg Wolitzer remembered Long Island of the '60s and early '70s as a safe place to be a child, a place where kids could come and go as they pleased.

"I see myself trudging along Jericho Turnpike endlessly," Wolitzer said in a 1997 interview. "It was the connective tissue between communities. My parents let me walk everywhere — past shopping centers and houses.

"Now the sense of freedom seems astonishing. We would play a game called 'The Man From U.N.C.L.E.' [after the TV show]. We would all meet and be assigned missions and be gone all day, roaming around the neighborhood. I feel we were around for the last vestiges of freedom."

Those early years in Syosset would later seem far away to Wolitzer, who was born May 28, 1959. The author of the novels "Sleepwalking," "Hidden Pictures" and "Friends for Life" eventually would rear her own children on Manhattan's Upper East Side.

For a girl with enough imagination, she recalled, a simple stroll could get the creative juices flowing. "Streets in the neighborhood were named after women in the builder's family — Ann Drive, Leslie Drive, Harriet Drive. I used to wonder who was Harriet and so on. I turned it into something writerly in my head.

"Though it was a subdivision and all the houses were similar, I liked to try to figure out what the differences were. What about the house that had no books? And there was a house that had

no furniture. The people who lived there kept saying that they had just moved in, but of course eventually they'd been there a long time. There was a story there."

Stories, in fact, were a staple in the Wolitzer household. Meg's mother, Hilma, was an aspiring writer who published her first novel, "Ending," by the time Meg was at Syosset High and her second, "In the Flesh," when Meg was in college. Meg's father, Morton, worked as a school psychologist.

Every Friday night the book-loving Wolitzers followed a regular routine. "After dinner we went to the Plainview Public Library, pillaging the new fiction shelf," Wolitzer said. "It had better new fiction [than the Syosset Library], and then we'd go to Baskin-Robbins for ice cream."

It's not surprising that Wolitzer's sights were set on writing early on. She edited literary magazines in both junior high and high school.

Not for her the usual teen hangouts of mall or beach. "We usually went to North Shore beaches, and they weren't very pleasurable experiences. And the Walt Whitman Mall still seems like the greatest oxymoron," though at age 12 or 13 she and her girlfriends would be dropped off there to shop for Huckapoo shirts and lip gloss.

As she grew older, Wolitzer's pleasures became more city-oriented. "I was always on the Long Island Rail Road," she said. "My family went into the city a lot. When I got to be a teenager, I went by myself. We went to museums and first-run movies and Indian restaurants — things we considered exotic. I knew many families, though, who never went in."

Still, the Island's imprinting left its stamp on her literary consciousness. "Where you live early on just becomes *it*. It becomes a point of reference. Later you just add to the larder of knowledge.

"I didn't *love* where I lived. But when I go back to Long Island I have a particular feeling. I can't quite explain it. But it's a powerful locus of memory."

— Dan Cryer

Nelson DeMille

Elmont

'We probably had the first TV on the block . . . We had TV parties. Families would all watch together.'

For writer Nelson DeMille, Long Island was the frontier.

As a young boy in the late '40s, the future author of "Plum Island," "The Gold Coast" and other best-selling thrillers moved from Jamaica to Elmont. Back then, this wasn't simply a matter of moving to the 'burbs. The 'burbs as such didn't exist yet.

DeMille's father, Huron, was one of the pioneers who helped create a Long Island of affordable housing and small-town amenities. In Elmont, his company built Argo Village, a development of 1,500 brick colonials selling for $8,500 apiece. Huron DeMille also did subcontracting work on Levittown, the suburban granddaddy of them all.

Nelson, born Aug. 23, 1943, would eventually have childhood memories of Long Island that were unusual. "My father bought Army surplus Jeeps and trucks. We would drive around and inspect the building projects. The area was just a patchwork of farms and developments going up — totally chaotic."

DeMille built the first house for his wife and four sons. As he built others, conditions still remained primitive for a while. "There were no phone lines yet into the houses," Nelson DeMille recalled in a 1997 interview. "One phone booth for the entire street. So when the phone rang, we had to go out to the

street to answer it. The streets were just mud and dust, like a western town. It was a real feeling of the frontier.

"We thought of it as a move to the country. We were surrounded by potato farms, and there was a woods nearby, a dairy farm and an old-fashioned general store. There were no shopping centers. But within five years there were supermarkets, a bowling alley and a strip mall.

"Almost everybody was from Brooklyn or Queens. We were all urban kids. We played stoopball. A very mixed crowd, ethnically diverse — Italian, Polish, Jewish and Irish. When a house was sold and a family would move in, we'd all go over and ask, 'Are you from Brooklyn or Queens?'

"We played baseball all summer and swam at the Walcliff Pool. We would sneak in there because our parents were worried about polio. Jones Beach was like wonderland. It was the biggest outing, the biggest thrill. Families would go en masse in three or four cars.

"My mother was unhappy to move out to what she thought was the sticks. It was only 15 minutes from Jamaica by car. But then she didn't drive. Most women didn't. These were urban dwellers used to subways and corner candy stores.

"We probably had the first TV on the block. It was a little Dumont, with a screen about 6 inches across. We had TV parties. Families would all watch TV together.

"People didn't have a lot. Maybe one lawnmower per block, one telephone. It was amazing how people would pull together."

Growing up on Long Island, DeMille said, wasn't especially influential in shaping him as a writer, but the Island did prove fertile ground for

Please Turn the Page

Some of Nelson DeMille's popular books have a Long Island setting. Of his upbringing, he says, "My mother was unhappy to move out to what she thought was the sticks. It was only 15 minutes from Jamaica by car. But then she didn't drive. Most women didn't. These were urban dwellers used to subways and corner candy stores."

Newsday Photo / J. Michael Dombroski, 1997

Newsday Photo / Harvey Portee

FREEPORT: Children at the Moxy Rigby housing project play sidewalk games on a sunny day in August, 1968.

Newsday Photo / Jim Nightingale

HEMPSTEAD: Boys will be boys as Kenneth Matthews, left, and Paul Katz argue over a game of marbles in June of 1953.

Newsday Photo / Jim Peppler

OCEANSIDE: Abaca the Magician and his assistant, 10-year-old John Gillen of West Hempstead, entertain the crowd at Nathan's Famous on Long Beach Road in 1972.

DEMILLE, Continued

setting many of his novels. He had always read a lot — feasting on Hemingway, Fitzgerald and Steinbeck — but at Hofstra University he began to aspire to join their ranks.

In later years this extremely successful author would live in Garden City in a Victorian home far grander than anything his father ever built.

— Dan Cryer

Amy Bloom

Kings Point

'My father went at least twice a week to the library, and I used to tag along.'

'There's a picture of me when I'm about 10 dressed up as a beatnik trick-or-treating for UNICEF,'' Amy Bloom recalled. "It's actually very similar to what I looked like when I led the Vietnam Moratorium demonstration in high school.''

Bloom, author of the book of stories "Come to Me," and the novel "Love Invents Us," has a wacky and infectious sense of humor. That's evident not only in the fiction but in her reminiscing about growing up on Long Island.

Amy was born June 18, 1953. The Blooms lived in the Baker Hill neighborhood of Great Neck before moving up, when Amy was 7, to Kings Point. It took a while for her to catch on to the subtle gradations of status. "What kind of car does your father drive?" the Kings Point kids asked. Gray, she would reply. "I didn't get it. When I later said 'Oldsmobile,' it still wasn't the right answer."

An affinity for writing and reading ran in the Bloom family. Her father, Murray, was a freelance journalist and author of the '60s best-seller "The Trouble With Lawyers." Amy's mother, Sydelle, wrote a gossip column that aired on radio and TV.

"My father went at least twice a week to the library, and I used to tag along. Nobody gave a damn what I read. So I would check out books like 'A House Is Not a Home' [Polly Adler's memoir of prostitution], which probably explains a good deal," she said with a chuckle during a 1997 interview.

Also explaining a lot was a coming-of-age simultaneous with the tumultuous Sixties. At Great Neck North High, Bloom was one of the editors of an underground paper called The Rat.

At one time, she and her fellow revolutionaries were handing out

the paper on the front steps of the school. When the principal approached, she feared she was about to be expelled. Instead, he merely requested that she distribute her wares somewhere else. "It wasn't really the Fascist boot on the neck I was hoping for," she said.

An ardent foe of the Vietnam War, Bloom helped organize a protest among area high schools. At a rally, she remembered, "I was so nervous. The mike kept sliding out of my hand . . . I also met Roger with the gold Corvette from Roslyn, which was an added bonus for doing good. At a distance, he looked like Omar Sharif. Up close, unfortunately, his eyes were crossed."

Reading Bloom's novel, which is set in Great Neck, you realize that the raw material for fiction lay all around her. Without prompting, she said, people would open their hearts to her. "I have this kind of cuddly face. I look like a nice person," she explained.

When she was 17, a summer job in New York required her to be on the Long Island Rail Road daily. "All of life's wretches would sit down next to me and blab their personal stories."

Did Bloom like growing up on Long Island? "Since I left town the day after I graduated from high school, it's safe to say that I didn't think of it as my spiritual home. The experience left me with a profound dislike of suburbs."

Later, living outside Middletown, Conn., in the late 1990s, Bloom practiced psychotherapy and worked on another book of stories. — Dan Cryer

Newsday Archives
Jeffrey Friedman, right, with colleague Douglas Coleman, savored freedom as a child in North Woodmere.

Jeffrey Friedman

North Woodmere

'There was an unbelievable amount of freedom. At about age 7 or 8, I got a bike and we went everywhere, whenever we wanted.'

When he was growing up in North Woodmere, said Jeffrey Friedman, "I had absolutely no clue that people [could] actually make a living doing what I do now."

What he would do was become a world-class researcher in molecular biology at Rockefeller University in Manhattan, and a professor of molecular genetics in the Howard Hughes Medical Institute.

His landmark achievement was the discovery of a hormone-like natural substance, leptin, which plays a central role in the body's weight-regulating system. The clues Friedman's team uncovered may lead, eventually, to the elimination of obesity.

When he graduated from Hewlett High School in 1971 — where he had been a National Merit Scholar — Friedman was aiming at medicine, enrolling in a six-year combined college and medical school program at Rensselaer Polytechnic Institute in Troy, N.Y.

Friedman, who as an adult would live in Manhattan, said there wasn't much in his background that pointed directly toward a career in leading-edge research. Perhaps, he said, it was the freedom he experienced while growing up. He was born July 20, 1954, attended Ogden Elementary School, and then Hewlett High School.

"I think the best thing was the young community, with a lot of young kids around," he recalled in a 1998 interview. "Our neighborhood was a development of new houses that all went up at once. It

was just completely overrun with kids. They were from young families, and there were hundreds of kids around.

"We were doing most things outdoors, and there wasn't much influence from being near New York City. Our life was sort of like that of kids living in suburbs anywhere."

Freedom to roam and explore was also important, he said. "There was an unbelievable amount of freedom. At about age 7 or 8, I got a bike and we went everywhere, whenever we wanted. We would take our bikes to the Green Acres shopping center. I remember a lot of freedom and adventure with kids. We'd take the train to Shea Stadium."

In this free-wheeling neighborhood atmosphere, Friedman added, the strongest emphasis was on sports. Not so much organized sports, but pick-up games of baseball, impromptu basketball games on driveways and patios. "There was always a huge home court advantage from knowing how to navigate" around obstacles in people's driveways and yards, he said. "It was great."

Unlike the other kids, however, Friedman said, "I spent most of my summers working in the dark." His father, Herbert, was a radiologist at a Brooklyn hospital. "So I worked in the darkroom at my father's hospital, making extra money developing X-rays."

He recalled that "I was paid pretty well, but it really wasn't a plum job, not an especially great job for summer. The premier job for kids then was building swimming pools" in the rapidly expanding Long Island suburbs.

What sent him off to medical school, Friedman said, was an aura of expectations. "In that community, the best form of endeavor was to become a physician. So I was strongly directed toward that," he said. "But that isn't what I most like to do. I like research."

He read books such as "Arrowsmith" and "The Microbe Hunters," stories that have inspired several generations of young people to go into medicine or biomedicine. "But I couldn't relate to them in any way that led me to say I wanted to do that."

During what he called a high school

AP Photo, 1997
Amy Bloom sharpened her sense of humor on Long Island.

Please Turn the Page

FRIEDMAN, Continued

career of "nondescript interests," Friedman said, "I was sports editor of the high school newspaper. Once I ran afoul of the swimming coach. My brother [Scott] was on the swim team, and I wrote an article on which the lead-in was something like 'Friedman Leads Sharks to Victory.' He [Scott] wasn't very important on the team, so the coach didn't much respect my journalistic standards."

Later on, no one would question Friedman's scientific standards.

— Robert Cooke

Linda Sanford

Laurel

'We all worked . . . You rolled up your sleeves and you got the job done.'

In the mid-1970s, Linda Szabat Sanford earned about $300 a week working for International Business Machines Corp. in its sleepy typewriter division in Lexington, Ky.

In 1998, Sanford was named to head IBM's top sales post, the first woman ever picked for the job. She was to oversee a 17,000-person unit selling computer equipment around the world.

The job, general manager of global industries, required teamwork, Sanford said that year. And that is something she learned, not just at IBM, but during her childhood.

Sanford, born Jan. 21, 1953, was the oldest of five sisters raised on a 150-acre potato farm in Laurel, on Long Island's North Fork.

Growing up on the farm instilled in Sanford a work ethic. "We all worked," Sanford said. "We were moving irrigation pipes or picking vegetables, or helping to plant, or we were driving trucks and tractors. You rolled up your sleeves and you got the job done."

Her adult life — meetings, overseas business trips and decisions sliced between time with her IBM researcher husband and their two children at their home in Chappaqua in Westchester County — would little resemble her days in Laurel.

But, Sanford said, she could often chase away fatigue or the blues by thinking back to the days on the farm and something her parents and grandparents kept telling her: "If you work hard and do what you need to do, good things will happen."

Those were indeed good times, Sanford said.

She remembered rising early and walking to school. "It was a little red schoolhouse," Sanford said. "They have extended it since, but the [original] schoolhouse is still there." Chores on the farm, which belonged to her grandparents, Felix and Mary Rutkoske, were after school and on weekends. About 300 people lived in Laurel, and everyone knew everyone.

People in town knew the family for the little farm stand they ran outside their house. "We sold veggies and we had to make change," Sanford said of herself and her sisters, Kathy, Laurie, Mary and Eva. "We met all kinds of people who would drop by."

Town, she said, was Riverhead. "We'd go there to meet some friends or do some shopping or go to the movies," Sanford said. "But we spent a lot of time on the farm. My sisters and I were best friends. We still are."

One of the big events of the year was the Riverhead Lions Club's annual variety show. Sanford and her sisters took singing lessons, and sang every year in the show.

"We did it for maybe eight years," Sanford said. "They would advertise it on the radio and play little excerpts from our singing the year before. We would also be in the local paper. It was a great show, and we had a lot of fun doing it."

A trip to Smithtown, bigger even than Riverhead, was reserved for very special occasions. "When we needed to go shopping for gowns, for weddings or proms or parties or the like, we'd go there," Sanford said.

Sanford left the farm for St. John's University in Queens, returning to Laurel on some weekends and holidays. She was hired as an associate mathematician at IBM in 1975.

The farm was eventually sold, but Sanford held on to the values she learned there.

"I look back and I miss those days," she said. "There was a strong sense of family, of belonging. We knew you needed to work hard to get things done. You didn't just expect things to happen."

— James Bernstein

Newsday Archive
Linda Sanford moved from a farm to a top position at IBM.

AP Photo, 1996
Ben Cohen, left, and Jerry Greenfield called themselves "the two fattest kids in the gym class."

Ben Cohen and Jerry Greenfield

Merrick

'We went square dancing at Jones Beach . . . That was a big night for us.'

Ben Cohen and Jerry Greenfield run an ice cream manufacturing company in Vermont that has gained worldwide attention, as much for its Cherry Garcia, Chunky Monkey and other premier flavors as for its social conscience.

Ben & Jerry's Homemade Inc. also makes mouths water on Wall Street. The company reported sales of $174 million 1997.

Not bad for two guys who would describe themselves in company literature as "the two slowest, fattest kids in the gym class" at Merrick Avenue Junior High School.

Cohen, chairman of Ben & Jerry's, and Greenfield, the company's vice chairman, grew up in Merrick in the 1950s and '60s, around the corner from one another, but never met until an autumn day in 1963, when they were trying to make it around the track at the junior high gym. They found themselves lagging behind everyone else.

The gym coach yelled out to them that if they didn't run a mile in under seven minutes, they would have to try and try again until they did. "Gee coach, if I don't do it in under seven minutes the first time, I'm certainly not going to do it in under seven minutes the second time," Cohen yelled back.

Greenfield, a self-described do-gooder who said he always did what he was told, did not know Cohen personally then. But he decided right then and there he had to. "This was a real thinker," Greenfield told an interviewer years later.

So began a lifelong, whirlwind friendship that saw the two in and out of different colleges, other businesses, and other states. As adults they would live in Vermont, not far from the company they started in 1978 in a renovated gas station on a busy street corner in Burlington, with an investment of a few thousand dollars and preparation from a $5 correspondence course.

They did not think, in their days growing up in Merrick, of careers as big businessmen. They thought a lot of having a good time. But they growing up as outsiders in junior and senior high school, they said, helped shape the offbeat approach they applied to the company they would build years later.

"We never thought of ourselves as

Please Turn the Page

Newsday Photo / Don Norkett

ROSYLN: Rumors that the Rolling Stones might appear after a Peter Tosh reggae show in 1978 drew hundreds to My Father's Place, a popular club. The news was unfounded, however.

Newsday Photo / John Curran

JONES BEACH, July 16, 1969: On the night that Neil Armstrong's Apollo 11 took off for the moon, four young people enjoy more earthly pursuits under the stars at Jones Beach.

COHEN, Continued

business people,'' Greenfield said.

They were nerdy guys at Calhoun High School in Merrick, the kind of kids who didn't have a lot of dates and were always wearing the wrong kind of clothes. Nonetheless, Cohen, an energetic kid with a lot of unorthodox ideas, was editor of the high school yearbook, the Pacer. He also had a deft touch for selling ice cream from the back of a truck after school and on weekends. Greenfield was more studious, the kind of kid people said would go to medical school. He applied, but was rejected.

The Merrick of their youths was a quiet place where the big thing was to borrow the family car and cruise. In seventh grade, Pam Ault ''was the quintessential girl who was unobtainable,'' Greenfield said. ''Ben has always had this fantasy about her.'' Cohen had a bright red Camaro convertible. He didn't wind up with Pam Ault, but he, Greenfield, Jeff Durstewitz, Fred Thaler, Ronnie Bauch and Dave Feldman did a lot of hanging out.

They went to Beach 9 at Jones Beach, liked to go to square dances wherever they could find them. ''That's the kind of kids we were,'' Greenfield said. ''We didn't drink beer. We went square dancing at Jones Beach. A whole bunch of us would find girls and ask them to square dance, and that was a big night for us.''

They went their separate ways after graduating from high school in 1969 — Greenfield to Oberlin College in Ohio to study premed, Cohen to Colgate.

They never really came back to Long Island.

''It's not a place I wanted to get away from,'' Greenfield said. ''But I did want to strike out. Once I did get away, I wanted to be in a more rural place. Long Island is very suburban. I don't think I'm attracted by the suburbs.''

— **James Bernstein**

Fran Drescher
Flushing

'The Queens that I grew up in had a small-town, provincial feel to it.'

'Everyone's coming out of the closet now,'' Fran Drescher cackled in her trademark Queens accent. ''Before 'The Nanny,' no one would admit they were from Queens.''

For the hit CBS sitcom launched in 1993, Flushing-born Drescher mined her real-life background to bring both the accent and the endearing down-to-earth quality of the borough's natives to national prominence. And even though Drescher's character, Fran Fine (also from Flushing), would marry the English-born Manhattanite whose children she was raising during the show's first five seasons, Drescher swore that the character would never stray far from their mutual Queens roots.

''I definitely have a Queens identity, and that's what I'm preserving in this show,'' said Drescher. ''The thing about Fran Fine is she'll always be the flashy girl from Flushing. It's great for me as an actress. And it's great for me to maintain that even though my mind has taken me off to a million different places. I've gone very far, far away, but my character keeps me close to home.''

Born Sept. 30, 1957, Drescher grew up around the corner from Queens College (which she would attend) off Kissena Boulevard. She attended PS 165, Parsons Junior High and Hillcrest High School in Jamaica (Class of '75). She remembered shopping in downtown Flushing as a girl. ''But when I got a little older, I would take the bus to Austin Street'' in Forest Hills. ''I even worked there for a while in a store that's no longer there called Pants Shack around the corner from Ronnie's,'' a popular women's clothing store.

She and her husband, Peter Marc Jacobson (whom she met in the Hillcrest High drama club), both worked at Flushing's Main Street Movie Theater, he as an usher and she as a ticket seller. She and Peter (who co-created ''The Nanny'') even got married in 1979 at Terrace in the Park in Flushing Meadows-Corona Park.

One of Drescher's fondest Queens memories was spending summers near the now-defunct Whitestone amusement park Adventurer's Inn ''in what we used to euphemistically call the Flamingo Beach Club. Basically it was a concrete swimming pool that was right in the middle of a vacant lot.

''The Queens that I grew up in (in the '60s and '70s) had a small-town, provincial feel to it,'' said Drescher. ''People lived in the same apartments for years. You'd meet a group of kids in kindergarten, and you'd still be with them in high school. No one ever left the neighborhood.''

Drescher decided on becoming an actress while in junior high school. By the time she was in high school, she had entered the Miss New York Teenager beauty pageant, placing first runner-up. ''Then I began to call talent agents to see if I could get an interview,'' she said in a 1998 interview. ''That's how I got started in the business.''

Drescher and Jacobson moved to Los Angeles, where she got small roles in ''Saturday Night Fever'' (1977) ''American Hot Wax'' (1978) and ''This Is Spinal Tap'' (1984).

Even after several seasons of ''The Nanny,'' Drescher was still asked if her strong Queens accent was a put-on. ''The accent is mine!'' she said after another cackle. ''I had to do something with this voice. And don't expect that to change!''

— **Connie Passalacqua**

Ray Romano
Forest Hills

'P.S. 144 was . . . where it all happened.'

Don't even ask Forest Hills native Ray Romano if he used to live close to his parents just like his character on TV's ''Everybody Loves Raymond.''

''I lived in my parents' house till I was 29!'' the comedian mock-shouted into his car phone while driving down the San Diego Freeway from his suburban Los Angeles home in 1998. ''Yeah, that's right,'' Romano droned, just as his tube alter ego once did in the show's opening credits. ''Go ahead, say it. 'Loser!' Say it!

''Yeah, I lived in my parents' house. So they were pretty close by. They were in the kitchen. And then when I got married, I only moved a mile away, to Middle Village.''

As star, of course, Romano took up residence on the other coast to make a sitcom upon which CBS would bank many of its hopes. (On the show he would play a Long Island family man and Newsday sportswriter.) ''Raymond's'' charm sprang from its keen portrayal of family life — something based squarely on Romano's real-life relations, whose oddities long fueled his stand-up comedy. In the 1990s, Mom Lucy and dad Al still lived in the Forest Hills house where Romano grew up. And his divorced older brother, Richard (the model for the show's brother Robert, a city cop), lived with them.

The show's Nemo's pizzeria? It was named after the Romano family dog and based on his old Lillian's Pizzeria hangout on Forest Hills' 69th Avenue, where Romano and pals once got three slices and a soda for a dollar.

But the *real* hangout, Romano remembered, was ''not a Nemo's but a schoolyard. P.S. 144 was the schoolyard, and that's where it all happened. That's where I played softball starting when I was 16, maybe up until the last couple of years. That's where I experimented with alcohol for the first time. Coincidentally, that's where I threw up for the first time.''

Born Dec. 21, 1957, he went to grade school at Our Lady Queen of Martyrs, ''where David Caruso was one year ahead of me.'' That also was where Romano started performing. ''Every Sunday night the church basement was open to teenagers to play Ping-Pong and just hang out and not get in trouble. Five of us were in a sketch group, and we put on what we called no-talent shows. Our group's name was No Talent Inc.''

When Romano wasn't staying out of trouble, that's precisely what he was getting into. He isn't shy about explaining how he and friends made a buck when tennis' U.S. Open was at its old Forest Hills site: ''We'd sneak in with like a plastic garbage can full of beer with ice. We'd go up into the stands and sell canned beer. We'd sell the whole thing and go back and get more, till we got caught by the cops.'' He also tried to sneak into rock concerts there. ''My brother

Fran Drescher, star of TV's ''The Nanny,'' said, ''I've gone very far, far away, but my character keeps me close to home.''

CBS Photo / Monty Brinton

"What I think my kids are gonna miss is growing up in a neighborhood," said Romano.

got in to see The Who. They got in and I didn't, but I told them I did. Then they questioned me. 'What did he do with his guitar at the end?' "

After the Open moved to Flushing Meadows-Corona Park, Romano went straight. He worked on the grounds crew getting it ready every summer, and actually had a job on court during matches as a court attendant.

Ah, a brush with fame and fortune. After working in a bank and delivering futons, Romano started doing stand-up comedy. He spent much of his 30s on the road, away from wife Anna, daughter Alexandra and twin boys Matthew and Gregory. (Son Joe was later born in L.A.) Finally together again while he worked on his sitcom, Romano's work kept him out there. Yet his heart longed for Queens.

"What I miss, what I think my kids are gonna miss, is growing up in a neighborhood," he said. "Not only a neighborhood, but on a block, and your neighbor is right next door, and the kids from your block, that was your gang. 'I'm going to Jimmy's. I'm going to Joey's. I'm gonna play stick-ball in front, and tag outside.' They're not gonna have any of that, and that gets me sad, I think. I don't see 'em getting on bikes and riding somewhere, going to the candy store. They're still gonna be happy, but they're gonna miss what I had."

— Diane Werts

Neal Marlens

South Huntington

'I thought of myself as fundamentally a happy kid.'

The hills behind Neal Marlens' California house are high and sere. Just beyond is the fashionable town of Malibu. And beyond that, of course, the wide Pacific. All in all, a long way from the green lawns and tree-shrouded streets of South Huntington, where he was reared.

"This is where the Chumash Indians used to live," he said of his home in 1998. "We're sort of overdeveloped now [and] the hills burn on a regular basis — when they're not sliding down."

Although Marlens, and his wife, Carol Black, and their two children eventually made their home in California, the price of success was numbing inquisitiveness on the part of strangers: Marlens and Black would forever be asked whether the TV series they created, "The Wonder Years" (which aired from 1988-93 on ABC), was a thinly veiled autobiography of their lives in suburban Long Island and Maryland, respectively.

The answer remained the same: no. Funny thing, people never asked wheth-

er their other creations, "Ellen," or the movie "Soul Man," were ripped from the pages of their lives.

But "Wonder Years"? Ah, the school *must've* been Henry L. Stimson Junior High (later Stimson Middle School), which Marlens attended (Class of '71). Series hero Kevin Arnold, played by Fred Savage, *must've* been an angst-twisted Marlens. And all the wrinkles, permutations and idiosyncrasies of the fictional world of "Years" *must've* been the same that Marlens and Black endured.

No, said Marlens. No, no, and no. Nevertheless, as any writer will tell you, you can never escape your past, and Marlens most assuredly never fully escaped his. The characters, he admited, "were an amalgam of people we both knew, and obviously, any writer writes from personal experience."

He grew up in the Audubon Woods development of South Huntington, on Robin Lane, in a house where his mother, Hanna, still lived in the 1990s. (His father, Al, a former Newsday managing editor, died in 1977.)

"It's pretty much now what it was like then," Marlens said in a telephone interview. "I guess the trees are bigger, and that is a substantial difference. When we found the neighborhood in Burbank where we shot 'Wonder Years,' we found a street that time had forgotten. For whatever reasons, the trees were uniquely small there, and we had been told there had been some tree blight. But you had homes that were of the same vintage as my home on Long Island and trees of the same height."

Marlens remembered a mostly happy upbringing in Audubon Woods. There were boyhood idylls, like regular jaunts to Jayne's Hill, off Sweet Hollow Road. ("I don't know that it's on any map, but maybe it's a subdivision now, but at the time, it was actually the highest point on Long Island.") There also was tennis, which he excelled at. His skills were strong enough to land him on the varsity team at Walt Whitman High.

"I thought of myself as fundamentally a happy kid," he recalled, "and two of my closest friends are from my youth, Paul Arnold, a violinist with the Philadelphia Orchestra, and Kevin Gliwa, an attorney in Denver." (Kevin Arnold was a not-so-subtle tribute.)

But his youth on Long Island was not perfect, and a residue of bitterness remained from his school days. He went to West Hills (then Oakwood Elementary) Schools, and from there, to Stimson and on to Walt Whitman, graduating in 1974. "Both my wife and I felt strongly that the school atmosphere we grew up in was extremely oppressive. Our schools were very similar to [any] large public schools . . . They are institutions that tend to be stifling and authoritarian, and oppressive to any creative urge that anyone might have."

Stimson, in particular, was "the apotheosis of repression," and he vividly remembered the time a teacher grabbed him by the scruff of the neck for going "down the wrong way in a one-way hall." (For the record, the teacher made a mistake: Marlens had had permission to go against the traffic to reach his

Los Angeles Times Photo / Carolyn Cole

"I thought of myself as a fundamentally happy kid," said Marlens.

home room.)

He left high school for Swarthmore College in Pennsylvania, and rarely looked back. "I would say that since I graduated from high school, other than Thanksgiving and visits from college, I have probably been back no more than 10 times in 20-odd years." (His mother would usually make the trek to California to visit.) "There's nothing," he added, "compelling me to go back."

— Verne Gay

209

Long Island Notables

Following is a list of some of the celebrities who were born or grew up on Long Island or made it their home in the 20th Century:

Abbott, Bud: comedian and actor, lived in Stony Brook

Adams, Cindy: gossip columnist, grew up in Freeport

Adams, Maude: Broadway actress, lived in Lake Ronkonkoma

Addams, Charles: cartoonist, lived in Westhampton

Alda, Alan: actor, lives in Sag Harbor

Algren, Nelson: writer, lived in Sag Harbor

Anspach, Susan: actor, class of 1960, Bryant High School, Long Island City

Arledge, Roone: TV executive, born in Forest Hills, class of 1948, W.C. Mepham High in Bellmore

Armstrong, Louis: jazz great, lived in Corona

Atlas, Charles: bodybuilder, lived in Point Lookout

Auchincloss, Louis: novelist, born in Lawrence

Azaria, Hank: actor, born in Forest Hills

Bacharach, Burt: composer and arranger, grew up in Kew Gardens, class of 1947, Forest Hills High School

Baker, Ellen Shulman: astronaut, class of 1970, Bayside High School

Baldwin, brothers **Alec, Billy, Daniel** and **Stephen:** actors, grew up in Massapequa

Begley, Ed: actor, lived in Merrick

Belafonte, Harry: singer and actor, lived in East Elmhurst

Benatar, Pat: singer, class of 1971, Lindenhurst High School

Bennett, Tony: singer, grew up in Astoria

Biggio, Craig: baseball player, class of 1984, Kings Park High School

Bloom, Amy: author, grew up in Kings Point

Bonds, Gary (U.S.): rock 'n' roller of the '50s and '60s, lives in Wheatley Heights

Bracken, Eddie: actor, born in Astoria

Brand, Oscar: folksinger, lives in Great Neck

Breslin, Jimmy: writer, born in Jamaica, class of 1948, John Adams High School in Ozone Park

Brooks, James: artist, lived in East Hampton

Brothers, Joyce: psychologist, class of 1944, Far Rockaway High School

Brown, Jim: football great, class of 1953, Manhasset High School

Brown, Larry: basketball coach, class of 1958, Long Beach High School

Bruce, Lenny: comedian, born in Mineola

Buchwald, Art: writer, grew up in Hollis

Bunche, Ralph: UN secretary-general, lived in Kew Gardens

Burns, Ed: actor, grew up in Valley Stream

Buscemi, Steve: actor, class of 1975, Valley Stream Central High School

Caan, James: actor, grew up in Sunnyside

Cambridge, Godfrey: actor and comedian, class of 1950, Flushing High School

Campanella, Roy: baseball Hall of Famer, lived in St. Albans and Glen Cove

Capote, Truman: writer, lived in Sagaponack

Carey, Mariah: singer, lived in Greenlawn, class of 1987, Harborfields High School

Carnegie, Dale: writer and motivational speaker, lived in Forest Hills

Caruso, David: actor, grew up in Forest Hills, class of 1974, Archbishop Molloy High School in Jamaica

Casey, William: former CIA director, born in Elmhurst, lived in Roslyn Harbor.

Cassidy, Jack: actor and singer, born in Richmond Hill

Chapin, Harry: singer-songwriter, lived in Huntington

Chrysler, Walter P.: automotive pioneer, lived in Kings Point

Cleave, Mary Louise: astronaut, grew up in Great Neck

Cohen, Ben, and Greenfield, Jerry: founders of Ben & Jerry's ice-cream company, grew up in Merrick, class of 1969, Calhoun High School

Coppola, Francis Ford: film director and writer, class of 1956, Great Neck North High School

Costas, Bob: sports broadcaster, class of 1970, Commack South High School

Cousy, Bob: basketball Hall of Famer, lived in St. Albans, class of 1946, Andrew Jackson High School

Crichton, Michael: author, class of 1960, Roslyn High School

Crystal, Billy: actor, class of 1965, Long Beach High School

Cuomo, Mario: former governor, lived in South Jamaica

D'Amato, Alfonse: former U.S. senator, grew up in Island Park

Dangerfield, Rodney: comedian, born in Deer Park, class of 1939 in Richmond Hill High School

Danza, Tony: actor, class of 1968, Malverne High School

Dash, Robert: artist, lives in Sagaponack

Dayne, Taylor: singer, class of 1980, Baldwin High School

de Kooning, Willem: artist, lived in Springs

De La Soul: rap artists **David Jolicoeur, Kelvin Mercer, Vincent Mason,** grew up in Amityville

DeMille, Nelson: author, born in Jamaica, grew up in Elmont

Demme, Jonathan: filmmaker, class of 1961, Baldwin High School

de Seversky, Maj. Alexander: Aircraft pioneer, lived in Asharoken.

Dobson, Kevin: actor, born in Jackson Heights

Dove, Arthur and wife Helen Torr: artists, lived in Centerport

Drescher, Fran: actor, grew up in Flushing, class of 1965, Hillcrest High School

Ederle, Gertrude: first woman to swim the English Channel, grew up in Flushing

Eglevsky, Andre and Leda: ballet artists, lived in Massapequa

Erving, Julius: basketball great, class of 1968, Roosevelt High School

Esiason, Norman (Boomer): football player and sports broadcaster, class of 1979, East Islip High School

Feynman, Richard: scientist, Nobel Prize winner, class of 1935, Far Rockaway High School

Field, Storm: weatherman, grew up in Bellmore, class of 1966, Mepham High School

Fitzgerald, F. Scott: writer, lived in Great Neck

Friedman, Jeffrey: molecular biologist, grew up in North Woodmere

Gaddis, William: writer, grew up in Massapequa, class of 1941, Farmingdale High School

Garfunkel, Art: singer-songwriter, class of 1958, Forest Hills High School

Gibson, Debbie: singer-actor, grew up in Merrick, class of 1988, Calhoun High School

Goldberg, Rube: cartoonist, lived in Asharoken

Goodwin, Doris Kearns: writer, grew up in Rockville Centre

Gordon, Mary: writer, grew up in Valley Stream

Gould, Morton: composer, pianist, born in Richmond Hill, lived in Great Neck

Grosz, George: artist, lived in Huntington

Grumman, Leroy: founder of Grumman Aircraft Corp., lived in Manhasset

Guare, John: playwright, grew up in Jackson Heights

Guthrie, Arlo: singer, grew up in Howard Beach

Guthrie, Woody: composer and folksinger, lived in Howard Beach

Guttenberg, Steve: actor, class of 1976, Plainedge-Massapequa High School

Halberstam, David: writer, class of 1951, Roosevelt High School

Harnisch, Pete: baseball player, class of 1984, Commack North High School

Harrelson, Bud: Mets baseball player, lives in Hauppauge

Hassam, Childe: impressionist painter, lived in East Hampton

Heiss-Jenkins, Carol: 1960 Olympic gold medalist, ice skating, grew up in Ozone Park

Hoffman, Alice: novelist, grew up in Franklin Square, class of 1969, Valley Stream North High School

Isaacs, Susan: author, class of 1961, Forest Hills High School

Joel, Billy: singer-songwriter, grew up in Hicksville

Johnson, Ray: artist, lived in Locust Valley

Karan, Donna: fashion designer, born in Forest Hills, grew up in Woodmere

Keeshan, Bob: TV's Captain Kangaroo grew up in Forest Hills and lived in Babylon.

Kennedy, George: actor, grew up in Bellmore

Kerouac, Jack: author, lived in Northport

King, Alan: comedian, actor, lives in Kings Point

Kapor, Mitch: computer visionary, class of 1967, Freeport High School

Kovic, Ron: writer and activist, class of 1964, Massapequa High School

Krasner, Lee: artist, lived in Springs

Kregel, Kevin: astronaut, class of 1974, Amityville Memorial High School

Kuscsik, Nina: long distance runner, grew up in Huntington Station.

Landon, Michael: actor-producer, born in Forest Hills

Latimer, Lewis: inventor, lived in Flushing

Lauder, Estee: founder of cosmetics company, grew up in Corona

Lauper, Cyndi: singer, grew up in Ozone Park

Leifer, Carol: comedian, grew up in East Williston, class of 1973, Wheatley High School

Lichtenstein, Roy: artist, lived in Southampton

Lieberman-Cline, Nancy: basketball player, class of 1976, Far Rockaway High School

Lombardo, Guy: band leader, lived in Freeport

Lucci, Susan: actress, class of 1964, Garden City High School

LuPone, Patti: actress, class of 1967, Northport High School

Maharis, George: actor, born in Astoria

Mapplethorpe, Robert: photographer, lived in Glen Oaks

Marlens, Neal: TV sitcom writer and producer, grew up in South Huntington

Matthiessen, Peter: writer, lives in Sagaponack

McClintock, Barbara: geneticist and Nobel Prize winner, lived and worked in Cold Spring Harbor

McEnroe, John: tennis star, lived in Douglaston

Merman, Ethel: singer and actress, grew up in Long Island City, class of 1924, Bryant High School

Migliore, Richard: jockey, grew up in Bay Shore

Mitchell, John: lawyer and politician, class of 1931, Jamaica High School

Money, Eddie: singer, grew up in Plainedge, class of 1967, Island Trees High School

Moran, Thomas: artist, lived in East Hampton

Morgan, J.P.: financier, lived in Glen Cove

Mumford, Lewis: writer, born in Flushing

Murphy, Eddie: comedian and actor, class of 1979, Roosevelt High School

Noonan, Peggy: speechwriter for Ronald Reagan and George Bush, grew up in Massapequa

O'Donnell, Rosie: comedian, actor and TV host, Class of 1980, Commack South High School

Oerter, Al: four-time gold medal Olympian in track and field, grew up in New Hyde Park, class of 1954, Sewanhaka High School

Onassis Kennedy, Jacqueline: former first lady, born in Southampton

Paley, William S.: CBS executive, lived in North Hills

Patterson, Alicia and **Henry Guggenheim:** founders of Newsday, lived in Sands Point

Paymer, David: actor, class of 1972, Oceanside High School

Peters, Bernadette: singer, dancer and actress, grew up in Ozone Park

Pitino, Rick: basketball coach, grew up in Oyster Bay, class of 1970, St. Dominic's High School

Pollock, Jackson: artist, lived in Springs

Porter, Fairfield: artist, lived in Southampton

Portman, Natalie: actress, grew up in Syosset

Pratt, Charles: founder of Standard Oil, lived in Glen Cove

Puzo, Mario: author, lived in Bay Shore

Pynchon, Thomas R. Jr.: novelist, grew up in East Norwich

Reed, Lou: rock musician, class of 1959, Freeport High School

Rhymes, Busta: rap singer, grew up in Uniondale

Rickles, Don: comedian, born in Jackson Heights

Ritter, Thelma: actress, lived in Sunnyside and Forest Hills

Rivera, Geraldo: talk show host, class of 1961, West Babylon High School

Romano, Ray: comedian, grew up in Forest Hills

Roosevelt, Theodore: president, lived in Oyster Bay

Ruehl, Mercedes: actress, born in Jackson Heights

Satriani, Joe: guitar virtuoso, class of 1974, Carle Place High School

Savalas, Telly: actor, born in Garden City

Schmitt, John: Jets football player, grew up in Central Islip

Scorcese, Martin: film writer, director and producer, born in Flushing

Seinfeld, Jerry: comedian and actor, class of 1972, Massapequa High School

Shire, Talia: actress, born in Jamaica

Simon, Paul: singer and songwriter, class of 1958, Forest Hills High School

Simpson, Louis: Pulitzer Prize-winning poet, lives in Setauket

Skinner, Al: basketball player, grew up in Malverne

Snider, Dee: rock musician, grew up in Baldwin

Sousa, John Philip: ''The March King,'' lived in Sands Point

Springer, Jerry: talk-show host, grew up in Kew Gardens, class of 1961, Forest Hills High School

Steel, Dawn: movie mogul, class of 1964, Great Neck South

Steiger, Rod: actor, born in Westhampton

Steinbeck, John: writer, lived in Sag Harbor

Stern, Howard: radio and TV host, author, grew up in Roosevelt and Rockville Centre, class of 1972, Southside High School.

Stevens, Rise: opera singer, grew up in Elmhurst

Stimson, Henry L.: served in the cabinets of four presidents, lived in Huntington

Sweeney, D.B.: actor, class of 1979, Shoreham-Wading River High School

Tartikoff, Brandon: television mogul, grew up in Freeport

Taylor, Cecil: jazz pianist and composer, grew up in Corona

Tenet, George: director of Central Intelligence Agency, born in Flushing

Tesh, John: entertainer, grew up in Garden City

Testaverde, Vinny: NFL quarterback, grew up in Elmont, class of 1981, Sewanhaka High School

Tiffany, Louis Comfort: artist, lived in Oyster Bay

Trautwig, Al: sportscaster, grew up in Garden City South

Trump, Donald: financier, grew up in Jamaica Estates

Tucker, Richard: opera singer, lived in Great Neck

Vai, Steve: guitar virtuoso, class of 1978, Carle Place High School

Vanderbilt, William K. II: famed financier, lived in Centerport

Villella, Edward: ballet dancer and ballet teacher, grew up in Bayside

Walken, Christopher: actor, grew up in Bayside

Waller, Thomas (Fats): pianist, composer and singer, lived in St. Albans

Wang, Charles: chairman of Computer Associates International Inc., lives in Cove Neck

Watson, James: co-discoverer of DNA, Nobel prize-winner, director of Cold Spring Harbor Laboratory, lives in Cold Spring Harbor

Wetherbee, James: astronaut, grew up in Huntington Station, class of 1970, Holy Family Diocesan High School

White, Stanford: architect, lived in Saint James

Whitney, John Hay: financier-publisher, lived in North Hills

Wilkins, Roy: civil rights activist and former director of NAACP, lived in Flushing

Williams, John T.: composer, grew up in Flushing

Wolitzer, Meg: grew up in Syosset

Wolitzer, Hilma: author, lived in Syosset

Woolworth, F.W.: five-and-dime store magnate, lived in Glen Cove

X, Malcolm: Black Muslim religious and political leader, lived in East Elmhurst

Yastrzemski, Carl: baseball Hall of Famer, class of 1957, Bridgehampton High School

COMPILED BY GEORGINA MARTORELLA

HOMETOWN LONG ISLAND

Community Index

Histories of the communities in Nassau, Suffolk and Queens Counties

Nassau County 2-59
Albertson 32
Atlantic Beach 9
Baldwin 9
Bayville 47
Bellerose 9
Bellmore 10
Bethpage 47
Brookville 48
Carle Place 32
Cedarhurst 10
Centre Island 48
Cove Neck 48
East Hills 32-33
East Meadow 10
East Norwich 48
East Rockaway 10
East Williston 32
Elmont 10
Farmingdale 51
Floral Park 13
Flower Hill 35
Franklin Square 13
Freeport 13
Garden City 14
Glen Cove 6
Glen Head 51
Glenwood Landing 51
Great Neck
(including all central villages) .. 35
Greenvale 35
Hempstead Town 8-29
Hempstead Village 17
Hewletts 14
Hicksville 51
Inwood 14
Island Park 17
Jericho 51
Kings Point 36
Lake Success 36
Lakeview 21
Lattingtown 53
Laurel Hollow 53
Lawrence 21
Levittown 22
Lido Beach 21
Locust Valley 53
Long Beach 30-31
Lynbrook 25
Malverne 25
Manhasset (including villages) ... 36
Massapequa 53
Massapequa Park 53
Matinecock 54
Merrick 25
Mill Neck 54
Mineola 39
Muttontown 54
New Cassel 39
New Hyde Park 39
North Bellmore 10
North Hempstead Town 32-45
North Hills 40
North Merrick 25
Oceanside 25
Old Bethpage 54
Old Brookville 54
Old Westbury 43
Oyster Bay Cove 54
Oyster Bay hamlet 57
Oyster Bay Town 46-59
Plainedge 57
Plainview 57
Point Lookout 25
Port Washington
(including all central villages) .. 40
Rockville Centre 26
Roosevelt 25
Roslyn (including all villages) 43
Sands Point 44
Sea Cliff 58
Seaford 26
Searingtown 44
Stewart Manor 26
Syosset 58
Uniondale 29
Upper Brookville 58
Valley Stream 29
Wantagh 29
West Hempstead 29
Westbury 44
Williston Park 44
Woodbury 58
Woodmere 29
Woodsburgh 29

Suffolk County ... 60-151
Amagansett 94-95
Amityville 64-65
Aquebogue 125
Asharoken 104
Babylon Town 64-71
Babylon Village 65-66
Bayport 115
Bay Shore 114-115
Baiting Hollow 125
Belle Terre 73
Bellport 74
Blue Point 73
Bohemia 115
Brentwood 112
Bridgehampton 137
Brightwaters 117
Brookhaven Town 72-93
Brookhaven hamlet 73
Calverton 125
Center Moriches 81
Centereach 73
Centerport 100
Central Islip 117
Cold Spring Harbor 102-103
Commack 130
Copiague 67
Coram 74
Cutchogue 147
Deer Park 67
Dering Harbor 128
Dix Hills 100
East Farmingdale 67
East Hampton Town 94-99
East Hampton Village 95
East Islip 117
East Marion 150
East Moriches 81
East Northport 103
East Quogue 140
Eastport 137
Eatons Neck 104
Elwood 104
Farmingville 74
Fire Island
(including villages) 118
Fishers Island 147
Flanders 137
Fort Salonga 130
Gardiners Island 96
Gilgo Beach 70
Gordon Heights 78
Great River 118
Greenlawn 104
Greenport 148
Halesite 106
Hampton Bays 138-139
Hauppauge 133
Head of Harbor 134
Holbrook 118
Holtsville 77
Huntington Bay 109
Huntington Station 109
Huntington Town 100-111
Huntington village 106
Islandia 121
Islip hamlet 121
Islip Terrace 122
Islip Town 112-123
Jamesport 125
Kings Park 133
Lake Grove 77
Lake Ronkonkoma 77
Laurel 148
Lindenhurst 67
Lloyd Harbor 109
Manorville 78
Mastic 78
Mattituck 148
Medford 78
Melville 109
Middle Island 81
Miller Place 81
Montauk 96-97
Moriches 81
Mount Sinai 81
Nesconset 134
New Suffolk 150
Nissequoge 134
North Amityville 69
North Babylon 67
North Bellport 81
North Haven 139
North Lindenhurst 70
North Sea 140
Northport 110
Northville 126
Noyack 140
Oak Beach 70
Oakdale 120-121
Old Field 84
Orient 150
Patchogue 84
Peconic 150
Poospatuck Reservation 84
Poquott 87
Port Jefferson 87
Port Jefferson Station 88
Quogue 140
Remsenburg 143
Ridge 88
Riverhead hamlet 126
Riverhead Town 124-127
Rocky Point 88
Ronkonkoma 77
Sag Harbor 139
Sagaponack 137
Saint James 134
San Remo 134
Sayville 122
Selden 88
Setauket 91
Shelter Island 128-129
Shinnecock Reservation 140
Shirley 88
Shoreham 91
Smithtown Town 130-135
Sound Beach 91
South Jamesport 125
Southampton Town 136-145
Southampton Village 143
Southold hamlet 150
Southold Town 146-151
Speonk 143
Springs 98
Stony Brook 92
Village of the Branch 134
Wading River 126
Wainscott 98
Water Mill 144
West Babylon 70
West Hills 110
West Islip 122
Westhampton Beach 144
Wheatley Heights 70
Wyandanch 70
Yaphank 92

Queens County ... 152-179
Astoria 153
Bayside 157
Bellerose 153
Broad Channel 153
Cambria Heights 157
College Point 157
Corona 158
Douglaston 158
East Elmhurst 158
Elmhurst 158
Flushing 160-161
Forest Hills 162
Fresh Meadows 158
Glen Oaks 158
Glendale 161
Hollis 161
Howard Beach 162
Jackson Heights 166
Jamaica 169
Jamaica Estates 162
Kew Gardens 166
Kew Gardens Hills 166
Laurelton 166
Little Neck 169
Long Island City 170
Maspeth 170
Middle Village 170
Oakland Gardens 170
Ozone Park 173
Queens Village 173
Rego Park 173
Richmond Hill 173
Ridgewood 173
The Rockaways 174
Rosedale 174
South Ozone Park 174
Springfield Gardens 177
St. Albans 177
Sunnyside 176-177
Whitestone 179
Woodhaven 179
Woodside 179

Index

Numbers in *italic* refer to illustrations.

Abaca the Magician, 204
Accabonac (Springs), 95, 98
Acclaim Entertainment Inc., 6
Ackerman, Gary, 162
Ackerson family, 117
Actors' Colony, 140
Actors' Row, 157
Adams, Cindy, 13
Adams, John, 103, 104
Adams, John Quincy, 67
Adams, Maude, 77
Adelphi University, 14, 196
Adkins, Derrick, 21
Adventurer's Inn, 208
African Americans. See Black Americans
Aiello, Jim, 58
Aikman, Frank, Jr., *25*
Albanian-Americans, 17
Albern, William, *25*
Albertson, 32
Albertson, Josiah, 150
Albertson, Townsend, 32
Albertson Square, 32
Aldred, J.E., 53
Aldrich, Winthrop W., 48
Algonquian Indians, 139
Allen, Henry, 35
Alley Pond Environmental Center, 158
Alley Pond Park, 157, 170
Altha, Benjamin, 128
Alvord, Dean, 73
Amagansett, 94, *94*, 95-96, 99, *99*
Ambrosio, Tom, 97
American Museum of the Moving Image, 153
Amityville, *iv*, 64, *64*, 65, 69, 110
Amsterdam Development and Land Co., 25
Amundsen, Roald, 48
Anderson Library, 98
Andrews, Stephen Pearl, 112
Andros, Edmund, 47
Andros Patent, 130
Andrzejewski, Patricia, 196
Aquebogue, 125, *125*
Aqueduct Racetrack, *172, 173, 198*
Arbuckle, Fatty, 117
Argo Village, 203
Argyle Hotel, 65, *65*
The Armory (Huntington), 106
Armstrong, John J., 39
Armstrong, Louis (Satchmo), 158
Armstrong, Ronald, 78
Arnold, Benedict, 150, 158
Arnold, Paul, 209
Arnstein, Nicky, 106
Arrow Electronics, 110
Arthur, Chester A., 53, 69
Artist's Lake, 81
Arverne-by-the-Sea, 174
Asharoken, 100, 104
Asharoken (Matinecock chief), 100, 103, 104, 110
Ashawagh Hall, 98
Ashford, 91
Asian-Americans
   Bellerose (Queens) and, 153
   Elmhurst and, 158
   Flushing and, 152, 161
   Laurelton and, 169
   Sunnyside and, 177
Asian Indian-Americans, 166
Astor, John Jacob, 153
Astor family, 14
Astoria, 153, 157, 170, *170*
Athletics, 65
Atlantic Beach, 9
Atlantic Beach Club, 9, 199
Atlas, Charles, 25
Atterbury, Grosvenor, 162
Auburndale, 161
Audubon Woods, 209
Ault, Pam, 208
Austin, William, 17
Austral Hotel, 112
Avery, Humphrey, 73, 84
Avianca Flight 52, 48
aviation
   Baldwin and, 9
   Bethpage and, 48
   Calverton and, 125
   Cove Neck and, 48

East Farmingdale and, 67
East Moriches and, 81
Elmont and, 10
Farmingdale and, 51
Freeport and, 13
Garden City and, 14
Holtsville and, 77
Massapequa Park and, 53
Middle Island and, 81
Mineola and, 39
North Lindenhurst and, 70
Port Washington and, 40
Roosevelt Field and, 9, 18
Uniondale and, 29
Valley Stream and, 29
Ayling, George, *117*

Babylon, 65, *65*, 66, *66*, 115
Babylon (Town of), 65-71, 100
Baiting Hollow, *124*, 125
Baiting Hollow Station, 125
Baker, Ellen, 199, *199*
Baker, George, 122
Bald Hills, 74, 77
Baldwin, *8*, 9, *180*, 193-194
Baldwin, Alec (Alexander Rae, III), 53, *193*
Baldwin, Carol, 193
Baldwin, Francis P., 9
Baldwin family, 53, 193
Baldwinsville, 9
Ballton, Samuel, 106
Barclay family, 166
Barnum, P.T., 87, 144
Barnum Island, 17, 26
Barrick, Thomas, 39
Barrymore, Ethel, 9, 95, 134, 140
Barrymore, John, 31, 134, 157
Barrymore, Lionel, 134
Barstow, William S., 36
Bartick, Anton, *115*
Bartlett, Rob, 187
Barton, Jim, 40
Baruch family, 103
Basie, Count, 179
Bauch, Ronnie, 208
Baxter, Oliver, 40
Baxter Estates, 40, *41*
Bay Club, 157
Bayles, Richard M., 77
Bayport, 73, *113*, 115
Bay Shore, 112, 114, *114*, 115, 117, 198
Bayside (Bay Side), *156*, 157, *157*, 160, 199
Bayside Land Co., 157
Bayside Yacht Club, 157
Bay Terrace, 157
Bayville, *46*, 47, *47*
beach clubs
   Atlantic Beach Club, 9
   Catalina Beach Club (Atlantic Beach), 9
   Cold Spring Harbor Beach Club, 103
   Seacliff Beach Club (Atlantic Beach), 9
   Seawane Club (Hewletts), 14
beaches. See parks
Beau Sejour hotel, 48
Bechtel, John, 140
Beck, Fred, *202*
Beck, Jacob, 81
Becker, Francis X., *25*
Bedell, Hiram K., 29
Bedell Tavern, 122
Beebe-McLellan lifesaving boat, 148
Beechurst, 179
Begg, Scotty, *18*
Begley, Ed, 25
Begley, Ed, Jr., *25*
Bell, Edward August, 150
Bell Buoy, 150
Belle Harbor, 174
Belle Rose, 153
Bellerose (Hempstead, Town of), *8*, 9-10
Bellerose (Queens), 153, 158
Belle Terre, 73
Bell family, 74
Bellmore, 10
Bellomont, Lord, 7
Bellport, 73, 74, *74, 75*
Bellville, 74
Belmont, 48
Belmont, August, 17, 65, 67, 69
Belmont Lake State Park, 65, 69, 81
Belmont Race Track, 10
Bendel, Henri, 36
Bender, Joe, 197

Benet, William Rose, 40
Benatar, Pat, 196, *196*
Benjamin Huntting Estate, 139
Ben & Jerry's Homemade Inc., 206
Bennett, Tony, 170
Benson, Arthur, 96
Benson, Charles, 77
Bergen Point County Golf Club, 70
Berle, Milton, 21
Berlin, Irving, 32, 88, 92, 140
Bernhardt, Sarah, 150
Bethel African Methodist Church
   (North Amityville), 69
Bethpage, *46*, 47-48, *49*, 54
Better, David, 187
Bevilacqua, Albert, 184
Big Duck (Flanders), 138
Big Six Towers, 179
Bing, Alexander M., 177
Bishop Molloy House and the Immaculate
   Conception Monastery, 162
Black, Carol, 209
Black Americans
   Amityville and, 64
   Babylon and, 65
   Floral Park and, 13
   Fort Salonga and, 133
   Gordon Heights and, 69, 78
   Hempstead and, 17, 69
   Inwood and, 17
   Jackson Heights and, 166
   Kings Park and, 133, 134
   Lakeview and, 21
   Laurelton and, 169
   Malverne and, 25, 196-197
   Manhasset and, 36
   New Cassel and, 39
   North Amityville and, 69
   Poospatuck Indians and, 84
   rap music and, 196
   Roosevelt and, 25-26, 69, 187, 190
   Rosedale and, 174
   South Jamaica and, 169
   West Hempstead and, 69
   Wyandanch and, 69, 70
Blackett, Andy, 189
Black Stump, 158
Bladykas family, *23*
Blissville, 170, 177
Block, Adrian, 57, 96, 147
Bloom, Amy, 205, *205*
Bloom family, 205
Bloomfield, 25
Blue Dolphin, 187
Blue Point, 73, *73, 82*
Bluepoint Oyster Co., 62, 121, 122
Blydenburgh, Joseph, 134
Blydenburgh family, 133
Bogart, Humphrey, 31
Bohack, Henry C., 122
Bohemia, 115, *115*
Bohemia Hall and Park, 153
Bolton, Guy, 143
Bonackers, 98
Bonet-Sintas, Roman, 121
Boomertown, 134
Booth, John, 150
Booth, Mary Louise, 92
Booth House, *149*
Booths Neck, 150
bootlegging. See rumrunning
Bourne, Frederick G., 121
Bouvier family, 74, 95
Bowden, James, 128
Bowery Bay, 170
Bowne, John, 161
Box Hill, 134
Bracken, Eddie, 173
Brady, Diamond Jim, 29
Brady, Michael J., 53
Brady, Nicholas F., 40
Bragaw, Richard, 177
Branch, Village of the, 130, 134, *135*
Brecknock Hall, 148
Breezy Hills, 44
Brennan, John N., *131*
Brentwood, 112, *112, 113*, 133
Breslau, City of, 65, 67, 70
Breuer, Marcel, 21
Brewster, Caleb, 91
Brice, Fanny, 106
Bridgehampton, 95, *136*, 137, 143
Bridgeport and Port Jefferson
   Steamboat Co., 87
Brightwaters, 117
Brindley Field, 130

Brisbane, Arthur, 17
Broad Channel, 153, 157
Broad Channel Corp., 153, 157
Broadhollow, 48
Bronx-Whitestone Bridge, 179
Brookhaven, 73, *82*
Brookhaven (Town of), 69, 72-93, 115, 118, 125
Brooklyn, 25, 31, 170, 173
Brooklyn Gun Club, 130
Brooklyn Industrial School Association, 133
Brooklyn Water Supply Co., 26
Brookville, 48
Brookville Reformed Church
   (Muttontown), 54
Browers Point, 29
Brown, Jim, 36
Brown, Larry, 185
Browne, George Elmer, 121
Browning, Edward (Daddy), 29
Bruce, Lenny, 10
Brush, Jesse, 103
Brush, Thomas, 173
Brush family, 104
Brushville, 173
Bryant, David, 130
Bryant, William Cullen, 43
Buck, Frank, 53, *192*
Buckram, 53
Buffet, Joseph, 110
Buffett, Jimmy, 140
Bulk's Nurseries, 70, *71*
Bull's Head, 35
Bunche, Ralph, 166
Bungtown, 53
Bunn, Luther and James, 140
Burger, Ernest, 94
Burns, Ed, 29
Burr, Aaron, 161
Burr family, 130
Burton, Robert L., 29
Burying Hill, 106
Buscemi, Steve, 29

Caan, James, 177
Cablevision Systems Corp., 58
Caesar, Sid, 173
Cagney, James, 31
Caleb Smith State Park (Smithtown), 130
Callister family, 173
Calloway, Cab, 31
Calvert, Bernard J., 125
Calverton, 125
Cambria Heights, 157
Campagnoli, John, 67
Camp Alvernia, 100
Campanella, Roy, 179
Campbell, Jimmy, *76*
Camp Dam, 69
Camp Hero, 96
Camp Mills, 39, 44. See also Mitchel Field
Camp Upton, 88, 92
Canarsie Indians, 162, 169, 173, 174
Canoe Place, 144
Canoe Place Inn, 139
Cantrell, John T., 106
Capone, Al, 65
Capote, Truman, 143
Captree, 70
Captree Causeway, 118, 122
Cardinals, 70
Caribbean-Americans, 152
Carle, Silas, 32
Carle, Thomas, 32
Carle Place, 32
Carll, Jesse, 110
Carman, John, 2, 17, 26, 32
Carmans family, 65
Carnegie, Dale, 162
Carpenter, Joseph, 7, 58
Carpenter's Tavern, 161
Carpenterville, 58
Caruso, David, 208
Caruso, Enrico, 48
Case, Frank, 140
Casey, James J., 21
Casey, William, 10
Cassidy, Hugh, 198
Castle, Irene, 31
Catacosinos, William, 54
Catalina Beach Club, 9
Cathedral of the Incarnation (Garden
   City), 14
Cedarhurst, 10, *10, 11*

Celtic Park, 177
Cemetery Belt, 161
The Cenacle, 77
Centereach, *72*, 73-74
Center Moriches, 81
Centerport, *vi*, 100, *100, 101*, 104
Centerville Race Track, 179
Central Church (Huntington), *107*
Central Islip, *116*, 117, *117*
Central Park, 48, 54
Centre Island, 48
Centreport, 100
Chambers, Whittaker, 25
Channing, Carol, 162
Chanticleer, 183
Chapin, Harry, 109
Chaplin, Charlie, 48
Chapman, Josephine Wright, 158
Chappel, Alonzo, 81
Charles Parsons Blacksmith Building, 98
Charpentier, Henri, 25
Chateau des Beaux Arts, 109
Chatlos, William, 44
Cherry Grove, 118
Cheshire, Thomas, 3
Chichester family, 109
Childs, Ernest, 25
Childs, John Lewis, 13
Chill City, 196
Chinese-Americans
   Jackson Heights and, 166
   South Jamaica and, 169
Christ family, 40
Christian Brothers, 121
Christian Hook, 25
Christie, Lansdell K., 54
Chrysler, Walter P., 35, 36
Chuck D, 196, *196*
Chyron, 110
Circassian shipwreck, *136*
City Housing Corp., 177, 179
Clarenceville, 173
Clark, Dick, 188
Clark, George, 39-40
Clark, William, 134
Clay Pitts, 103
Cleave, Mary, *201*
Cleveland, Grover, 150
Clinton, De Witt, 170, 179
Clinton, Henry, 170
Clinton Academy, 95
Clintonville, 179
Clowesville, 39
Coast Guard, 94, 96, 104, 148
Cockcroft, James, 110
Codling, William, 104
Coe Hall, *56*
Coe, Mai, 56
Coe, Natalie Mai, *2*
Coe, William Robertson, 54, 56
Cohan, George M., 36
Cohen, Ben, 206, *206*, 208
Coindre Hall, 109
Cold Spring Harbor, 100, 102, *102, 103*, *103*
Cold Spring Harbor Beach Club, 103
Cold Spring Harbor Fish Hatchery, 102
Cold Spring Harbor Laboratory, 53, 102, 103
Cold Spring Harbor Whaling Museum, 103
Cold War, 180
Cole, Nat (King), 188
Coleman, Douglas, *205*
Coles, Charles (Honi), 158
Coles Brothers, 7
College Point, *154, 156*, 157, 160
colleges and universities
   Adelphi University (Garden City), 14, 196
   Adelphi Suffolk College (Oakdale), *120*
   Dowling College (Oakdale), *120*, 121
   Friends World College (Lloyd Harbor), 109
   Hofstra University (Uniondale), 17, 29
   LaGuardia Community College (Long Island City), 170
   Long Island University, C.W. Post Campus (Brookville), 35, 48, 58
   Nassau Community College (Uniondale), 29, 187
   Queensborough Community College (Oakland Gardens), 170
   Queens College (Flushing), 208
   State University of New York (Farmingdale), 51
   State University of New York (Stony Brook), 84, 92

Touro College of Health and Science (Bay Shore), 114
U.S. Merchant Marine Academy (Kings Point), 36
Colleran, Peter, 53
Collier, Willie, 134
Colombian-Americans
Jackson Heights and, 166
Ozone Park and, 173
South Jamaica and, 169
Colonial Spring, 67
Columbia Hook and Ladder Co., 106
Columbia Records, 188
Columbian Bronze Corp., 13
Commack, 130, 186, 189
Como, Perry, 177
Computer Associates, 121
Comsewogue, 88
Concer, Pyrrhus, 143
Conklin, Jacob, 67
Conklin, Nathaniel, 65, 122
Conklin, "Uncle Jesse," 109
Conklin family, 109
Connetquot River State Park, 121
Conscience Point, 137, 140
Conscience Point National Wildlife Refuge, 140
Constable, Arnold, 17
Cooper, James Fenimore, 139, 150
Cooper, M.A.E., 96
Cooper, Mercator, 143
Cooper family, 48
Copiague, 67
copper beeches, 56
Coram, 73, 74, *75,* 91
Corbett, "Gentleman Jim," 157
Corbin, Austin, 31, 69
Corbin, Austin, Jr., 96
Corchaug Indians, 148, 150
Cornell, Richard, 174
Cornell, Samuel, 158
Cornwall, John, 40
Cornwall family, 44
Corona, 158, *159,* 164, *164*
Cortelyou, George, 109
Corwin, Nathaniel and Hudson, 148
Cosmopolitan apartments, 177, 179
Costas, Bob, 130, 189, *189*
Costas, Jimmy, 25
Costello, Eugene, 117
Costello, Lou, 162
Cotter, Christopher, 102
Country Life Press, 14
Cove Neck, 48, 57
Cow Neck, 32, 35, 36, 40, 44
Crab Meadow, 183
cranberry bogs, 78, 125
Craveth, Paul, 53
Crawford, Broderick, 13
Creedmoor Rifle Range, 153, 173
Creedmoor State Psychiatric Center, 153, 173
Crichton, Michael, 43
Crosby, Bing, 54
Cross Bay Boulevard, 157
Cross Island Parkway, 10, 157
Crossman family, 103
Crowley, Mike, 166
Cryan, Frank, 53
Crystal, Billy, 31, 185, *185*
Crystal family, 185
Cuban-Americans, 166
Cuban Giants, 65
Cuffee, Paul, 140
Cullen, John, 94, *94*
Culluloo Telewana, 29
Cuomo, Mario, 162
Curran, Patrick J., 112
Curtiss, Glenn, 39
Curtiss Aircraft, 29
Cutchogue, *146,* 147, *147,* 150
Cutter, Bloodgood Haviland, 36, 169
Cutting, William Bayard, 118, 121
Czech-Americans, 115

D'Amato, Alfonse, 21
Dana, Charles A., 7
Dangerfield, Rodney, 67
Danza, Tony, 25
Dasch, George, 94, *94*
Davidson, Maria, 121
Davies, Marion, 106
Davis, Benjamin, 81
Davis, Benjamin T., *127*
Davis, Edward, 87
Davis, George W., 78
Davis, Lester H., 74
Davis, Sammy, Jr., 185
Davis, Solomon, 81
Dayton, "Uncle Billy," 81
Dead End Kids, 170
Dean, Arthur H., 58
Dean Alvord Co., 43
Decatur, Stephen, 150
Deep Hollow Ranch, 188
Deepwells, 134
Deer Park, 67
de Forest, Henry W., 53
de Kooning, Willem, 98
Delaware Indians, 29
Delbruck, Max, 103
DeMille, Huron, 203
DeMille, Nelson, 203, *203,* 205
Demme, Jonathan, 9, 193-194, *193*
DeMott, Michael, 26
Dempsey, Jack, 31
Denton, Charles C., 173
Denton, Daniel, 169
Denton, Isaac, 10
Denton, Richard, 17
Dering, Thomas, 128
Dering Harbor, 128
deSaint-Exupery, Antoine, 104
deSeversky, Alexander, 104
DeSeversky Conference Center, 48
Devine family, 69
Dewey, Thomas, *50*
Dewing, Oliver, 133
Dickerson, Charles P., 115, 121
Dickinson, Amos, 134
Dickinson family, *89*
Dietrich, Marlene, 25, 104
Diocese of Rockville Centre, 26
Dissoway, Carolyn B., 40
Ditmars, Abram D., 170
Ditmars family, 179
Dix Hills, 100, *101,* 103
Dixon, Richard M., 187
d'Leofferda, Leoffer, 84
Doctorow, E.L., 139
Dominican-Americans, 166
Dongan, Thomas, 39, 47, 109, 150, 169, 174
Dooley, Alvin, 30, 31
Doubleday, Frank, 53
Doubleday, Page & Co., 14, 21
Doughty, Francis, 161, 170
Doughty, Wilbur, *11*
Douglas, John, Jr., 70
Douglas, William P., 158
Douglas Manor, 158
Douglaston, 158, 160, 169
Douglaston Club, 158
Douglaston Estate Windmill, 158
Dowling College, 121
Down and Out Club, *171*
Doxsee Co., *120*
Dreiser, Theodore, 125
Drescher, Fran, 208, *208*
Dressler, Marie, 117
Drew, John, 95, 140
Driscoll, James, 160, 176
Drowned Meadow, 87
duck farming
East Moriches and, 137
Eastport and, 137
Speonk and, 137
Duffy's Hotel, 118
Duke, Benjamin, 36
Dunton, Frederick W., 161
du Pont family, 147
Duprez, Charles, 138
Durstewitz, Jeff, 208
Duryea Corn Starch Manufacturing Co., 7, 51
Dutch-Americans, 122
Dutch Kills, 170
Dwight, Arthur S., 36
Dwight, Timothy, 126
Dyer, Mary, 128
Dylan, Bob, 188
Dzus, William, 122

Eagle Hotel, 84
Eagle's Nest, 100
East Amityville, 67
East Babylon, 122
East Elmhurst, 158
East Farmingdale, 67
East Forest Hills, 166
East Hampton (Town of), 94-99, 137
East Hampton Village, 95, *95,* 182
East Hills, 32, 33, *33*
East Islip, 117
East Jamaica, 161
East Marion, 150, *151*
East Massapequa, 192
East Meadow, 10, *192*
East Moriches, *80,* 137
East Neck, 109
East New York, 179
East Northport, 103
East Norwich, 48, *48,* 51
East Patchogue, 73
Eastport, 137
East Quogue, 13, 143
East Riding of Yorkshire, 60
East Rockaway, 10, *175*
East Setauket, 91
East Shore, 36
East Side Comedy Club, 186, 187
East Williamsburgh, 173
East Williston, 32, *32,* 44
East Woods, 58
Eaton, Theophilus, 104, 148, 150
Eatons Neck, 104, *105*
Eatons Neck lighthouse, 104, *104*
Eberson, John, 169
Eberstadt, Ferdinand, 109
Ecuadorean-Americans, 166
Edey, Birdsall Otis, 74
Edison, Thomas Alva, 143
Edwards, "Captain Josh," 96
Edwards, Gabriel, *99*
Edwards, Louis F., 30, 31
Edwards family, 122
Edwardsville, 122
Edward Thompson Law Book Co., 110
Ehret, George, 153
Einstein, Albert, *63,* 106, 150
the El, 169, 173
Eisenhower, Dwight, *50*
Ellis, Evelyn, 70
Elmhurst, 152, 158, *158, 159,* 170
Elmont, 10, *11,* 203
Elm Point, 36
Elwood, 104
Epenetus Smith Tavern, 134
Equitable Bag Co., 170
Erving, Julius, 26, 197, *197*
estates
Bayport and, 115
Belle Terre and, 73
Brightwaters and, 117
Brookville and, 48
Centre Island and, 48
Cove Neck and, 48
Dix Hills and, 103
Eatons Neck and, 104
Fire Island and, 118
Glen Cove and, 7
Great Neck and, 35
Great River and, 118
Huntington Bay and, 109
Huntington Station and, 109
Islip Hamlet and, 121
Jamaica Estates and, 162, *163*
Kings Point and, 36
Lattingtown and, 53
Laurel Hollow and, 53
Lloyd Harbor and, 109
Locust Valley and, 53
Long Island City and, 170
Matinecock and, 54
Muttontown and, 54
Oakdale and, 121
Old Field and, 84
Old Westbury and, 43
Oyster Bay Cove and, 54, 57
The Rockaways and, 174
Sands Point and, 44
Southampton Village and, 143
Wainscott and, 98
Water Mill and, 144
West Hills and, 110
West Islip and, 122
Wheatley Heights and, 70
Whitestone and, 179
Woodbury and, 58
Evan Farm, 161
Everitt, August, 177, 179
Everitt family, 177
Evers, Richard, *50*
E.W. Bliss Co., 139

Fahys, Joseph, 139
Fairbanks, Douglas, Jr., 140
Fairchild Airplane Manufacturing Co., 67
Fairchild Hiller Corp., 67
Fairchild Republic, 67
Fairground, 109
Faithful, Starr, 31
Famous Players Film Co., 153
Farmer, Robert, 77
Farmer's Club, 125
Farmingdale, 51, *52,* 67
Farmingville, 74, 77
Farrington Point, 140
Far Rockaway, 174
Fashion Race Track, 158
Father Divine, 122
Fax, Elton C., 179
Faye, Alice, 173
Feldman, Dave, 208
Fenhurst, 14
Ferenz, Pete, 189
Ferguson, Farquahar, 109
Ferraro, Geraldine, 162
Ferrer, Jose, 31
ferries, 150
Bay Shore and, 115
Corona and, 158
Fishers Island and, 147
Feversham, 140
Field, Dudley, 169
Field, Marshall, III, 109
Fields, W.C., 157
Fife, Louis, 78
Figueroa, Carlos, 198
Figueroa, David, 198
Fiore, Roberta, 31
Fire Island, 115, 118, *119*
Fire Island lighthouse, 118
Fire Island National Seashore, 84 118
Fire Island Pines, 118
Fireplace, 73
Firestone family, 147
First Congregational Church of Brookhaven (Mount Sinai), 81
First Congregational Church of New Village (Lake Grove), 77
First Presbyterian Church (Elmhurst), 158
First Presbyterian Church (Sag Harbor), 139
Fisher, Anton, 115
Fisher, Carl Graham, 96
Fisher, Joseph, *115*
Fishers Island, *146,* 147, *147*
Fiske, Alice, 128
Fitzgerald, Ella, 158, 179
Fitzgerald, F. Scott, 35, 36, 44, 158
Fitzmaurice Flying Field, 53
Five Corners (Lynbrook), 25
Five Towns, 9, 10
Flanders, 137
Flats Fire, 133
Flax Pond, 84
Fleet, Thomas, 100
Fleet family, 54
Floral Park, *12,* 13, 158, 198
Flower, William, 57
Flower Hill, 35
Floyd, David Gelston, 148
Floyd, Richard, Jr., 73
Floyd, William, 78
Floyd family, 78
Floyd Harbor, 88
Flushing, 54, 152, *155,* 157, 158, 160, *160,* 161, *161,* 166, 169, 179, 208
Flushing and North Shore Rail Road, 157
Flushing Friends' Meeting House, 161
Flushing Meadows-Corona Park, 155, 158, 161, 162, 166, 209
Flushing & North Side train, 154
Flushing Rail Road, 179
Flushing Remonstrance of 1657, 54, 161
Folger, Henry Clay, 7
Fontana Concrete Products, 73
Ford, Henry, 87
Fordham, Robert, 2, 17, 26, 32
Forest Hills, *iv,* 152, 162, *162, 165,* 188, 208-209
Forest Hills Gardens, 162
Forgotten Islands of Jamaica Bay, 153
Fort Corchaug, 147
Fort Franklin, 109
Fort Golgotha, 106
Fort Lookout, 139
Fort Neck, 47
Fort Nonsense, 87
Fort Pond Bay, 96
Fort St. George, 78, 81, 91, 121 (Also see, Manor of St. George)
Fort Salonga, 130, 133
Fort Slongo, 110, 130, 133
Fort Totten, 157
Foster, Christopher, 174
Foster, Thomas, 10, 169
Foster brothers, 10
Foster's Meadow, 10, 29, 174
Fowler family, 69
Fox, Fontaine, 13, 40
Francesa, Mike, 198-199, *199*
Franklin Square, 13
Franklinville, 148
Franklinville Academy, 148
Frank M. Flower & Sons Inc., 47, 57
Freed, Alan, 188
Freeport, *12,* 13, *13, 204*
Freeport Railroad, 13
Fresh Air Home for Crippled Children, 143
Fresh Meadows, 158
Fresh Ponds, 161
Friedman, Jeffrey, 205-206, *205*
Friends Academy, 53
Frog Hollow, 32
Frohlich, Bill, 67
Frost, William, 57
Frothingham's Long Island Herald, 139
Fullerton, Hal B., 126
Fullerton family, *79*
Furman, William, 166
Fyfe's Shipyard, 51

Gala Amusement Park, 158
Galante, Janet, 43
Gamage, Smith P., 77
Garden City, *5,* 14, *14, 15,* 26, 39, 191, 205
Garden City Hotel, 14
Garden City Park, 14
Garden City South, 197-198
Gardiner, John, 104
Gardiner, Lion, 95, 96, 130
Gardiner family, 95, 96, 104, 106
Gardiners Island, 96, 98, 137
Gardiners Neck, 104
Garfunkel, Art, 188, *188*
Garlick, Elizabeth, 96
Garnet, Hervey Highland, 130
Garroway, Dave, 143
Garvie, Thomas, 7
Garvie's Point, 7
Gateway National Recreation Area, 157
Gateway to the Rockaways, 153
Gaynor, William, 134
gazetteers
Nassau County, 3
Queens County, 152
Suffolk County, 61
Geiger, William, 70
Geissenhainer, Frederick W., 170
George, Ambrose, 51
George's Neck, 87
Georgica Pond, 98
German-Americans
Carle Place and, 32
Flushing and, 161
Glendale and, 161
Hicksville and, 51
Islip Terrace and, 122
Jamaica and, 169
Kew Gardens Hills and, 166
Laurelton and, 166
Lindenhurst and, 67
Maspeth and, 170
Massapequa Park and, 53
Middle Village and, 170
Ridgewood and, 173
The Rockaways and, 174
Sunnyside and, 177
German-American Settlement League, 92
Germanian, 173
Germantown, 122
Gerry, Roger, 43
Gibb, Andrew, 112, 121
Gibson, Deborah, 25
Gibson, William, 29
Gilbert, Charles P.H., 57
Gilbert Carll Inn, 100
Gildersleeve, Joseph, 29
Gilgo Beach, 70
Gillen, John, *204*
Gish, Dorothy, 106
Gish, Lillian, 106
Glackens, William, 74
Gleason, Jackie, 104
Gleason, Patrick J. (Battle Axe), 170
Glenada, 103
Glen Cove, 6-7, *6-7, 54*
Glendale, 161, 170, 173
Glen Head, 51
Glen Oaks, 158
Glen Oaks Golf Club, 158
Glenwood Landing, *51*
Gliwa, Kevin, 209
Godfrey, Nicholas, 104
Goldberg, Rube, 104
Gold Bug Hotel, 39
Golden, Hymie, 67
Golden's Pickle Works, 125
golf clubs
Bergen Point County Golf Club, 70
Glen Oaks Golf Club, 158
Muttontown Golf and Country Club, 54
National Golf Club (Southampton Village), 143
Oakland Golf Club (Oakland Gardens), 170
Queens Valley Golf Club (Kew Gardens Hills), 166
Richmond Hill Golf Club (Kew Gardens), 166
St. Albans Golf Course, 179
Shinnecock Hills Golf Club (Southampton Village), *141,* 143
Swan Lake Golf Course (Calverton), 125
West Sayville County Golf Course (Oakdale), 121, 122
Good Ground, 138, *138,* 139
Good Samaritan Hospital, 122
Gordon, "Pop," 78
Gordon Heights, 69, 78, *78*
Gotherson, Daniel, 81
Gould family, 103
Gove, Mary, 112
Grace, Joseph Peter, 40
Grace, William R., 35
Grace Episcopal Church (Jamaica), 169
Gracefield, 36
Graff, Edward, 31
Graham, Billy, 73
Grand Central Parkway, 162, 166
Grant, Cary, 139
Grant, Ulysses S., 70
Grantsville, 39
Grapes of Wrath, 194
Great Cow Harbor, 110
Great Neck, 32, *34,* 35, *35,* 67, 169, 201, 205
Great Neck Estates, 35
Great Neck Plaza, 35
Great Pickle Works Wreck, 125
Great River, 118
Great Sewer Revolt of 1929, 36
Great Woods, 125
Greek-Americans
Astoria and, 152
Island Park and, 21
Green Acres Mall, 29
Greene family, 122
Greenfield, Jerry, 206, *206,* 208
Greenhill, 148
Greenlawn, 104, *105,* 106
Greenport, *ii,* 61, 125, 148, *148, 149,* 150
Greenport Basin and Construction Co., 148
Greenport Yacht and Ship, 148
Greenvale, 35
Greenville, 122
Greenwich Point, 26
Greenwolde, 36
Griffing, John, 126
Griffing family, 126
Griffith, D.W., 48
Grosjean, Florian, 179
Grossman, Moe, 31
Gross-Morton Co., 158
Grover, Al, 13
Grumman, Leroy, 36
Grumman Aircraft Engineering Corp., 48, *49,* 125
Guest, Winston, 48
Guggenheim, Harry, 44
Guggenheim, M. Robert, 69
Gunther, Christopher Godfrey, 74
Guthrie, William, 53
Guyanese-Americans
Jackson Heights and, 166
Ozone Park and, 173

  Rosedale and, 174
  South Jamaica and, 169

H

Haff, Hank, 121
Hagedorn, Charles E., 70
Haitian-Americans
  Ozone Park and, 173
  Rosedale and, 174
  South Jamaica and, 169
Halberstam, David, 26
Hale, Nathan, 100, 106, 109
Halesite, 100, 106, 107
Hall, Louise, 130, 133, 134
Hallet, William, 153
Hallets Cove, 153
Hallock, Noah, 88
Hallock family, 126
Hallockville, 126
Halsey, Stephen A., 153
Hammon, Jupiter, 109
Hampton Bays, 138, *138,* 139
Hand, David, 139
Hand, Julia, 81
Harbor Green, 184
Hard, Florence Bourne, 122
Harding, Warren, 54
Hardscrabble, 51
Harned family, 130
Harriman, Averill, 44
Harriman, Edward H., 21
Harrison, Benjamin, 148
Harrison, William Henry, 148
Harrison House Conference Center, 7
Harvey, Charles, 14
The Hassles, 194
Hauppauge, 125, 126, *132,* 133
Haven, *200*
Havens, George, 128
Haviland, Joseph, 10
Havoc, June, 173
Hawkins, Gersham, 115
Hawkins, Micah, 92
Hawkins, Warren, 115
Hawkins family, 73
Hawxhurst, Benjamin, 103
Hayes, Helen, 139
Hazelhurst Field, 39
Head of the Harbor (North Hempstead), 43
Head of the Harbor (Smithtown), 134
Head of the Vleigh, 166
Hearst, William Randolph, 44, 106
Heartte, Nehemiah, 67
Heatherton, Ann, 35, 169
Heaven, 122
Heckscher, August, 109, 117
Heckscher State Park, 112, 117
Hedges Inn, 95
Heenan, Frances (Peaches), 29
Heine, Henry, 121
Heinrich Brothers, 9, 13
Heinz Co., 51
Hempstead, 2, *4, 9,* 9-30, *16,* 17, *17,* 197, *202, 204*
Hempstead Gardens, 21
Hempstead Harbor, 43
Hempstead Lake, 21, 26
Hempstead Plains Aviation Field, 39
Hempstead (Town of), 9, 32, 40, 43
Hempstead Village, *4, 16,* 17
Henderson, John, 170
Hendrickson family, 177
Henke, Hans, 84
Hercules, 139
Hermitage, 150
Herricks, 40
Hershey, Alfred, 103
Hess, H. Bellas, 109
Hessian mercenaries, 39, 51
Hewlett, 117, *200*
Hewlett, Abraham, 29
Hewlett, Augustus J., 14, 17
Hewlett, George, 14, 25
Hewlett, Richard T., 10, 14
Hewlett family, 35, 36, 103
Hewletts, 14
Hewlett School, 117
Hicks, Elias, 51
Hicks, Jacob, 21
Hicks, John, 9, 170
Hicks, Rachel, 44
Hicks, Thomas, 169
Hicks, Valentine, 51
Hicks-Seaman homestead, *44*
Hicksville, 2, 47, *50,* 51, 57, 182
Hicksville & Cold Spring Branch Rail Road, 103
Higbie family, 122
High Hold, 110
highways. See also parkways
  Babylon (Town of) and, 66, 70
  Brookhaven (Town of) and, 77, 88
  Hempstead (Town of) and, 10, 26, 29
  Huntington (Town of) and, 100, 102, 110
  Islip (Town of) and, 118, 121, 122
  North Hempstead (Town of) and, 43, 44
  Oyster Bay (Town of) and, 48, 51
  Queens County and, 170, 174
Hinsdale, 13
Hirsch Bros. Saloon, *171*
Hispanic-Americans
  Brentwood and, 112
  Hempstead and, 17
  Laurelton and, 169
Hitchcock, Alfred, 143
Hitchcock, Benjamin, 173, 174, 179
Hitchcock, Benjamin W., 158
Hitchcock, Thomas, Sr., 43
Hitchcock, Tommy, Jr., 43
Hobart, John Sloss, 104
Hoffman, Alice, 13
Hofstra University, 17, 29
Hog Inlet, 10
Hog Island, 17, 48
Hog Neck, 139
Holbrook, 118, 121
Holliday, Judy, 177
Hollis, 161-162
Hollis Park Gardens, 162
Holt, Joseph, 77
Holtsville, *76,* 77
Homan, John, 92
Homan farm, 125
Home Sweet Home, 95, *95*
Hook, Turtle, 29
Hooker, Joseph, 53
Hopkins, Milton, 35
Horse Neck, 109
Horton, Benjamin, 147
Horton, Joseph, 125
hospitals
  Central Islip psychiatric center, *116,* 117
  Creedmoor State Psychiatric Center (Bellerose, Queens), 153, 173
  Good Samaritan (West Islip), 122
  Kings Park Psychiatric Center, 133
  Manhattan State Hospital of Central Islip, 117
  Northport Veterans Administration Medical Center (East Northport), 103
  Pilgrim State Psychiatric Hospital (West Brentwood), 103, 112, 117, 133
  St. Albans Extended Care Facility, 179
  St. Francis Hospital (Flower Hill), 35
  Southampton Hospital, 137
  Southside Hospital (Bay Shore), 115
  Winthrop-University Hospital (West Hempstead), 29
Hotel Howard, 162
Houdini, Harry, 51
Houldbrock, Richard, 100, 103, 104
Howard, William J., 162
Howard Beach, 162, *163*
Howard Colord Orphan Asylum, 133, 134
Howard Orphanage and Industrial School, 133
Howarth, Hezekiah, 104
Howe, William, 158, 162
Howell, Edward, 143, 144
Howell, Eleanor, 140, 1433
Howell House, 144
The Hub, 17
Hubbs, George Kasson, 117
Huckleberries, 10
Hudson, Charles I., 54
Hudson, Henry, 153
Hudson Realty Co., 29
Hughes, Mildred, 166
Hulbert, John, 96, 137
Hulse's Turnout, 125
Hungry Harbor, 29
Hunters Point, 170
Hunting Hollow Farm, 198
Huntington, 54, 106, *106, 107, 180,* 186, 187
Huntington Bay, 109
Huntington Bay Club, 109
Huntington East Gut, 118
Huntington Harbor, 106
Huntington South, 65, 67
Huntington Station, 109, 201
Huntington (Town of), 65, 70, 100-111, 130
Huntington West Neck South, 65
Huntting Inn, 95
Hutchinson, Benjamin, 81

I

Identical Triplets, 187
Idle Hour, 121-122, 122
Idlewild Airport (Kennedy), 162
Il Progresso, 134
Indian Head, 133
Indian Neck Hall, 121
The Ink Spots, 78
Innocenti and Webel, 35
Interboro Parkway, 161
International Design Center, 170
Inwood, 14, 17
Ireland family, 65
Irish-Americans
  Bellerose (Queens) and, 153
  Brentwood and, 112
  Carle Place and, 32
  Elmont and, 203
  Hicksville and, 51
  Kew Gardens Hills and, 166
  Laurelton and, 166
  New Cassel and, 39
  Peconic and, 150
  Sunnyside and, 177
  Wyandanch and, 70
Iron Pier, 126, *127*
Irving, Washington, 174
Iselin, Hope Goddard, 58
Island Garden, 198
Islandia, 121
Island Park, 17, 21
Islip, *116, 120*
Islip Hamlet, *120,* 121
Islip High School students, *195*
Islip Terrace, 122
Islip (Town of), 77, 110, 112-123, 133
Israeli-Americans
  Forest Hills and, 152
  Kew Gardens Hills and, 166
Italian-Americans
  Brentwood and, 112
  Corona and, 158
  Elmont and, 203
  Farmingdale and, 51
  Flushing and, 161
  Inwood and, 17
  Jamaica and, 169
  Kew Gardens Hills and, 166
  Laurelton and, 166
  Manhasset and, 36
  Port Washington and, 40
  San Remo and, 134
  Sunnyside and, 177
  Westbury and, 44
Italians, 21

J

Jackie Robinson Parkway, 161
Jackson, Robert, 169
Jackson, Timothy, 166
Jackson Heights, *152,* 166, *166*
Jackson Social and Field Club, 179
Jacobson, Peter Marc, 208
Jacobus Kolyer Farm, 161
Jacovitz Brothers, 21
Jaffe's Department Store, 36
Jahn, Frank, 173
Jakobson Shipyard, 57
Jamaica, 152, 160, *163, 168,* 169, *169,* 176, 203
Jamaica Bay Wildlife Refuge, 157
Jamaica Estates, 162, *163*
Jamaican-Americans, 174
Jamaica Plank Road, 169
Jamaica Square, 13
Jameco Indians, 152, 153, 169, 174
James, Thomas, 95
Jamesport, *124,* 125-126
Jamesport Congregational Church (Riverhead), 126
Jarvis family, 104
Jefferson, Thomas, 87
Jennings, Peter, 137
Jennings, Walter B., 100, 103
Jepson, Helen, 10
Jericho, 2, 51, 53, 54
Jericho Turnpike, 51, 100
Jerusalem South, 26
Jessup, John, 140
Jessup Neck, 140
Jewish Agricultural And Industrial Society, 133
Jewish-Americans
  Elmont and, 10, 203
  Flushing and, 161
  Great Neck and, 35
  Jackson Heights and, 166
  Jamaica and, 169
  Kings Park and, 133
  Laurelton and, 166
  The Rockaways and, 174
  Sunnyside and, 177
Jewish Brotherhood of Kings Park, 133
Joel, Billy, iii, *50,* 51, 109, 182, *182,* 194
Joel family, 182
John P. Holland Torpedo Boat Co., 150
Johnson, Matthew, 183
Johnstone, Ralph, 81
Jones, Frank S., 122
Jones, John, 103
Jones, Thomas, 47, 70, 103
Jones, William L., 87
Jones Beach Causeway, 29
Jones Beach State Park, 2, 65, 70, 103, *200, 202,* 203, *207,* 208
Jones family, 103
Joplin, Scott, 170
Jordan, Bobby, 170
Joyce, Peggy, 96

K

Kahn, Otto, 100
Kaplan, Bernard, 73-74
Karafinas, Alexandra, 31
Karatzas, Daniel, 166
Karotsony Hotel, 51
Katz, Paul, *204*
Kaufman-Astoria Studios, 153
Keene, Robert, 137, 143
Keeshan, Bob, 65
Keller, Helen, 162
Kellogg, Morris W., 58
Kellum, John, 14
Kelly, John A.F., 179
Kelly, Kathleen, 64
Kelly farm, 179
Kelsey, Charles G., 106
Kemp, Hal, 162
Kennedy, George, 10
Kennedy, Jacqueline, 74, 95
Kennedy Airport (Idlewild), 162
Kenney, John and Lillie, 69
Kensington, 35
Kent, Joan G., 32, 44
Kerosene Hill, 157
Ketchabonack House, 144
Ketcham, Zebulon, 65, 67
Ketcham Inn, 81
Kew Gardens, 166, *167*
Kew Gardens Hills, 166
Kidd, William, 96, 130
Kieft, William, 9, 17, 157, 161, 166
Killenworth, 7
King, Alan, 185
King, Carole, 188
King, John Alsop, 36, 169
King, Martin Luther, Jr., *19*
King, Rufus, 169
King Manor, 169
Kings County Farm, 133
Kingsland Homestead, 152
Kings Park, *132,* 133, *133,* 134
Kings Park Psychiatric Center, 133
Kings Point, 35, 36, *37,* 205
Kismet, 118
Kissam family, 35, 104
Kissena Park, 158
Klein, Addie, 67
Knollwood, 54
Komitor, Bob, 190
Korean-Americans, 166
Korten, Henry Otto, 6
Koula, Joseph, 115
Kovic, Ron, 53
Kramer, Robert, 33
Kratchovil, John, 115
Kroft, Steve, 140
Kuhn, Fritz, 92
Ku Klux Klan
  Lake Ronkonkoma and, 77
  Port Jefferson and, 87
  Smithtown and, 130
  Southold (Town of) and, 147
Kutil family, 134

L

Lady Suffolk, 130
LaFarge, John, 7
Laffey, Emmett, 33
LaFreniere, Oliver B., 157
LaGrange Inn, 122
LaGuardia, Fiorello, 104
LaGuardia Airport, 153, 158, 159
LaGuardia Community College, 170
Lake Grove, *76,* 77, *77,* 121
Lake House (East Islip), 117
Lakeland, 77
Lake Ronkonkoma, 36, 77, *77, 83,* 112
Lake Ronkonkoma Episcopal Church (Nesconset), 134
Lake Success, 35, 36, *37,* 39, 169
Lakeview, *20,* 21, 25
Lakeville, 36, 77
Lalance, Charles, 179
The Landing (Glen Cove), 7
Landmark Cafe, 81
Landon, Jared, 150
Langdon, Thomas, 10
Lange, Edward, *103,* 104, *109, 131, 133*
Langtry, Lili, 162
Lardner, Ring, Jr., 158
LaSalle Military Academy, 121
Latino-Americans
  Jackson Heights and, 152
  Rego Park and, 152
  Sunnyside and, 177
  Woodside and, 179
LaTourette, George, 51
LaTourette, Jeanne, 51
Latting, Josiah, 53
Latting, Robert, 53
Lattingtown, 53
Laurel, 148, 206
Laurel Hollow, 53, 103
Laurelton, 53, 166, *167,* 169
Laurelton Land Co., 166
Lawrence, 21, *21*
Lawrence, Effingham, 157, *157*
Lawrence, James, 157
Lawrence, William, 157
Lawrence brothers, 21
Lawrence family, 157
Lawrence Neck, 157
Lawson, Frank, 17
Leahy, David P., 174
Lee, Gypsy Rose, 173
Leeds, Warner M., 36
Legget, Samuel, 179
Leifer, Carol, 32
Leisure Village, 88
Lent Homestead, 158
Leverich, William, 47, 57
Leveriche family, 166
Levitt, William J., 32, 44, 54
Levitt family, 54
Levittown, 22, *22-23,* 32, 69
Levy, George Morton, 44
Lewis, Francis, 161, 179
Lewis, Sinclair, 40
Lewis & Valentine Nurseries, 35
L'Hommedieu, James, 14
Liberty Park, 161
Lidice, 115
Lido Beach, *20,* 21
Lido Beach Hotel, 21
lighthouses
  Eatons Neck, 104
  Fire Island, 118
  Lloyd Neck, *108*
  Montauk, 96, *97*
  Old Field, 84
LILCO. See Long Island Lighting Co.
Linas, Rodger, 169
Lincoln, Abraham, 130
Lindbergh, Charles, 9, 14, *18,* 39, 109
Lindenhurst, 67, *67,* 70, 196
Lindenhurst Nine, 67
Lindsay, John, 174
Liquori, Lisa, 98
LIRR. See Long Island Rail Road
Little Cow Harbor, 100
Little Cow Neck, 36
Little Delmonico, 78
Little Neck, 10, 160, 169
Little Plains, 173
Livermore, Jesse, 36
Livingston, Henry, 70
Ljungqvist, Nancy, 74
Lloyd family, 109
Lloyd Harbor, 108, 109, *109*
Lloyd Neck, *108,* 109
Lloyd Neck Lighthouse, *108*
Locke, John D., 179
Locustdale, 133
Locust Grove, 104
Locust Valley, *52,* 53, *53*
Loesser, Frank, 143
Lollipop Farms Zoo, *202*
Lombardo, Guy, 13
Long Beach, 21, 30-31, *30-31,* 185, 198, 199
Long Beach Hotel, 31
Longbotham family, 88
Longfellow, Henry Wadsworth, 174
Long Island, Battle of, 96, 139, 173
Long Island Brick Co., 130
Long Island City, 170, 177
Long Island Expressway
  Huntington (Town of) and, 100
  Islip (Town of) and, 121
  North Hempstead (Town of) and, *37,* 43
  Queens County and, 170
Long Island Good Hearted Thespian Society (LIGHTS), 13
Long Island House, 126
Long Island Housing Partnership, 81
Long Island Lighting Co., 51, 109, 110, 183
Long Island MacArthur Airport, 77
Long Island Motor Parkway, 112, 130
Long Island National Cemetery, 125
Long Island Oyster Farms Inc., 110
Long Island Rail Road
  Babylon (Town of) and, 69
  Brookhaven (Town of) and, 77, 78, 84, 88, 92
  East Hampton (Town of) and, 94, 95, 96, 98
  Hempstead (Town of) and, 9, 10, 13, 14, 17, *19,* 21, 25, 29
  Huntington (Town of) and, 100, 103, 104-105, 106, 109, 110
  Islip (Town of) and, 117, 121
  Long Beach (City of) and, 31
  Mill Neck, *55*
  North Hempstead (Town of) and, 32, 33, 35, 36, 39, 40, 44
  Oyster Bay (Town of) and, 47, 55, 56, 57, 58
  Queens County and, 153, 157, 161, 162, 168, 169, 170, 173, 174, 177, 179
  Rockville Centre, *19*
  Smithtown (Town of) and, 130, 133, 134
  Southampton (Town of) and, 139, 140, 143, 144
  Southold (Town of) and, 147, 148, 150
  Suffolk County and, 61
Long Island Rubber Co., 91
Long Island Traction Co., 13
Long Island University, C.W. Post Campus, 35, 48, 58
Longwood, 88
Loop Parkway, 21, 25, 199
Lord, Samuel, 158
Lott, John, 9
Lott family, 179
Love family, 35
Lower Aquebogue, 125
Lucci, Susan, 14
Ludlam, Joseph, 48
Ludlum family, 177
Luke, Myron H., 9, 161
LuPone, Patti, 183, *183*
LuPone family, 183
Luria, Salvador, 103
Lusum, 51
Lutheran Cemetery, 170
Lynbrook, 10, 25, *25,* 193
Lynch, Lillian and Vernon, 187

M

MacDougall, Edward Archibald, 166
Mackay family, 32
Macy, Carlton, 14
Macy, W. Kingsland, 117
Madison, James, 78, 81
Madnan's Neck, 35, 169
Maidstone, 95
Maidstone Club, 95
Malba, 179
Malcolm X, 158
Mallon, Mary, 57
Malverne, 25, 196-197

Man, Albon P., 166, 173
Man, Alrick, 166
Man, Arthur, 166
Manetto Hill, 57, 58
Manhanset House, 128
Manhanset Indians, 128
Manhardt, Frank, 114
Manhasset, 32, 35, 36, *36,* 198
Manhasset Indians, 139
Manhattan State Hospital of Central Islip, 117
Manorhaven, 40
The Manor of St. George, 78, 81, 84, 88, 118
Manorville, 78, *80*
The Maples, 78
Marconi, Guglielmo, 65, *65,* 67, 88
Marconiville, 67
Marigies, 81
Marinecock Indians, 47, 57
Marine Pavilion, 10, 174
Mariner's Grave, 10
Marion, Francis, 150
Maritches, 81
Marlens, Neal, 209, *209*
Marlens family, 209
Marsh, David, 125
Marsh, Helen M., 9, 153
Marshall, Bernice Schultz, 17
Marshall, George, 48
Marsh and Ruwe Co., 9
Martin, Helen, 81
Marx Brothers, 173
Mashashimuet Park, 139
Ma'shin' Seas'n, 70
Mason, Norman, *117*
Maspeth, 170, 171, *171,* 173
Massapequa, 9, 47, *52,* 53, 184, 193
Massapequa Indians (Marsapeague), 9, 47, 51, 53, 54, 57
Massapequa Park, 53
Massey, Chet, 137
Massman, Fritz, 198
Mastic, 78, 81, 84, 91, 121
Mastic Beach, 91
Mastopietro, Nancy, 177
Mather, Richard, 87
Matheson, William, 109
Mathews Model Flats, 170
Matinecock, 54
Matinecock Indians, 7, 35, 36, 40, 44, 47, 48, 51, 53, 54, 57, 58, 100, 103, 104, 109, 110, 152, 157, 158, 161, 166, 169, 170, 179
Matthews, Kenneth, *204*
Mattituck, 148, 150
Mayo, Samuel, 47, 57
McCarthy, Jerome, 148
McClintock, Barbara, 103
McCotter, Alexander, 118, 121
McDaniels, Darryl, 162
McEnroe, John, 48, 158
McGinnes, Ed, 37
Meadow Brook Club, 43
Meadow Brook Hunt Club, 10, 39
Meadow Club, 143
Meaudon, 53
Mechanicsville, 115
Medford, *62,* 78, 79, *79,* 81
Meigs, Jonathan, 139, 150
Mellon, Andrew, 58
Melville, *108,* 109-110
Melville, Ward, 92, *92*
Meriches, 81
Meritche(s), 81
Merman, Ethel, 170, 177
Merquices, 81
Merrick, 25, 206, 208
Merrick Indians, 9, 13, 25
Mespat Indians, 170, 173
Methodist Episcopal Church (Lake Grove), 77
Metropolitan Camp Ground Assn., *59*
Metropolitan Jockey Club, 169
Metropolitan Life Insurance Co., 177, 179
Meyer, Cord, 170
Meyer, Cord, Jr., 158, 162
Meyer, Virginia Terry, 77
Middelburgh (Middleburg), 158, 162
Middle District, 148
Middle Island, 81
Middle Road, 115
Middletown, 81
Middle Village, 170, 171, *171,* 173, 208
Migliore, Richard, 198, *198*
Milburn, 9
Miller, Andrew, 81
Miller, Henry, 173
Miller, Lewis, *18*
Miller, Lillian, 69
Miller, Norman, 69
Miller, Philip S., 40
Miller family, 81
Miller Place, *80,* 81, *81,* 91
Mill Neck, 53, 54, *55*
Mill Neck Manor School for Deaf Children, 54
Mill Pond Model Yacht Club, 40
Milltown, 84
Millville, 92
Mineola, 9, 17, *38,* 39, *39, 200*
Mineola Park Co., 39
Minervini, Richie, 186
Mitchel Field, 29
Mitchell, Benjamin, 104
Mitchell, James, 139
Mitchell, Uriah, 36
Mitchell family, 36
Mizell, Jason, 162
model communities
  Bellerose (Hempstead, Town of) and, 9, 153
  Brentwood and, 112
  Brightwaters and, 117
  College Point and, 157
  Forest Hills and, 162
  Fresh Meadows and, 158
  Garden City and, 14
  Jackson Heights and, 166
  Long Island City and, 170
  Manhasset and, 36
  Sunnyside and, 176, 177
Modern Times, 112
Mohawk Indians, 153
Mohegan Indians, 29
Mohene Indians, 54
Mohican Indians, 170
Money, Eddie, 194, *194*
Montauk, *63,* 96, *96, 97* 137, *195*
Montaukett Indians, 95, 96
Montauk lighthouse, 96, 97, *97*
Montauk Manor, 96
Montez, Lola, 170
Mooney, Frank J., 84
Mooney Ponds, 74
Moore, Clement Clarke, 158
Moore, George, 25
Moore, William T., 48
Moran, Thomas, 95
Morehead, Dorothy, 177
Morgan, Henry Sturgis, 104
Morgan, J.P., 7
Moricha, 81
The Moriches, 81
Moritches, 81
Morley, Christopher, 43, 173
Morosco, Oliver, 166
Morris Park, 173
Morton, Elizabeth, 140
Morton Wildlife Refuge, 140
Moses, Robert, 2, 43, 47, 58, 65, 69, 70, 109, 117, 118, 157
Mostel, Zero, 31
Motor Parkway, 70, 77
Mott family, 35
Mount, William Sidney, 91, 92
Mountain Mist Springs, 110
Mount Alvernia, 100
Mount Misery Neck, 73
Mount Sinai, 81
Mowbray, John, 115, 117
Muhlenberg, William Augustus, 133, 157
Muirson, George, 84
Mulford, Clarence, 74
Mulford House, 95
Mumford, Lewis, 177
Munsell, William W., 174
Munsey, Frank A., 36
Munsey Park, 36
Munson, Carlos, 35
Muriches, 81
Murphy, Charles, 51
Murphy, Eddie, 26, 187, *187*
museums
  American Museum of the Moving Image (Astoria), 153
  Cold Spring Harbor Whaling Museum, 103
  King Manor (Jamaica), 169
  Museums at Stony Brook, 92
  Noguchi Museum (Long Island City), 170
  Old Schoolhouse Museum (Quogue), 143
  Parrish Art Museum (Southampton Village), 143
  Queens County Farm Museum (Bellerose), 153, 158
  Sag Harbor Whaling Museum, 139
  Science Museum of Long Island (Manhasset), 36
  Suffolk County Marine Museum (Oakdale), 121
Museums at Stony Brook, 92
Musketa Cove, 7
Muttontown, 54
Muttontown Golf and Country Club, 54
Myers, Margie, *200*
Myerson, Bess, 173
My Father's Place, *207*

Nass, Elyce, 179
Nassau-by-the-Sea, 25
Nassau Community College, 29, 187
Nassau County, 2-3, 5, 10, 26, 39, 152, 169
Nassau Veterans Memorial Coliseum, 29
Nasseconseke, 130
Nast, Conde, 44
National Center for Disability Services, 32
National Golf Club, 143
National Tennis Center, 162
Nature's Gardens, 88
Nazis, 92, 94, 96
Near Rockaway, 26
Neirs Tavern, 179
Nelson, Bob, 187
Neponsit, 174
Neptune House, 29
Nesconset, 134
Nesconset Highway, 77
Nesequakes Indians, 130
New Bridge, 10
New Cassel, 39
Newcombe, Richard S., 166
New Hyde Park, 29, *38,* 39-40
New Lots, 179
Newman, Paul, 157
Newsday, 110
New Suffolk, 150
Newtown (New Towne), 152, 158, 162, 166, 169, 173
New Village, 73, 77
New Village of Tabor, 115
New York, Woodhaven and Rockaway Railroad, 153, 173
New York and Long Beach Railroad Co., 17, 31
New York City, 152, 169, 170, 176, 177
New York Daily Mirror, 88, 91
New York Institute of Technology, 43, 48
New York Islanders, 29
New York Jets, 29
New York Life Insurance Co., 158
New York Nets, 29, 196, 197, 198
Nichols, Thomas Low, 112
Nicoll, Benjamin, 112
Nicoll, Matthias, 36
Nicoll, William, 112, 115, 117, 118, 121, 122, 128
Nicoll, William, II, 128
Nicoll, William, IV, 115
Nicoll, William, VII, 117
Nicoll family, 78
Nicolls, Richard, 17, 130
Nicolls Patent, 77, 91
Niederstein's Restaurant-Hotel, 170
Night Hawks, 40
Nissequogue, 134, *134*
Nissequogue Indians, 77
Nissequogue River, 130
Noguchi Museum, 170
Noonan, Peggy, 53
Noor, Christina, *202*
North Amityville, 69, *69*
Northampton, 140
North Babylon, 67, 69
North Beach Amusement Park, 153
North Bellmore, 10
North Bellport, 81
North Dix Hills, 104
Northern State Parkway, 43, 44, 100
North Haven, 139, 140
North Hempstead, 2, 9, 32-45
North Hempstead Turnpike, 102
North Hills, 40
North Lindenhurst, 70
North Merrick, 25
Northport, 100, 110, *110, 111,* 183
Northport Electric Light Co., 110
Northport Veterans Administration Medical Center, 103
Northport Yacht Club, 111
Northrop Corp., 48
North Sea, 137, 140
North Shore Towers, 158
North Side, 32
Northville, 126, *127*
Northwest, 95
North West Pointers, 14, 17
Northwood, 57
North Woodmere, 205-206
Norton family, 88
Norwegian-Americans, 51
Norwich, 48
Norwood, 21, 25
No Talent Inc., 208
Novotny, Joseph, *115*
Noyack, 140
Noyack Indians, 140
nuclear power, 91, 109
Nunley's, *180*

Oak Beach, 70, *70*
Oakdale, *120,* 121
Oakland Gardens, 170
Oakland Golf Club, 170
Oakley, Annie, 53, 65, 173
Oakley and Griffin factory, 32
Oakley Court, 54
Oak Neck, 47
The Oaks, 170
Oakwood, 73
Ocean Beach, 118, *118*
Ocean Parkway, 70
Ocean Point, 10
Oceanside, 25, *204*
Oceanville, 25
Ockers, Jacob, 121, 122
Ockers, John, 62
O'Connor, Carroll, 162
O'Donnell, Rosie, 130, 186, *186*
O'Donnell family, 186
O'Gara, Kathryn, 199
Ogden, John, 143
Oil City, 25
O.L. Schwenke Land & Investment Co., 78
Old Aquebogue, 125
Old Aquebogue Presbyterian Church (Riverhead), 126
Old Bethpage, 54
Old Bethpage Village Restoration, 29, 54
Old Brook, 121
Old Brookville, 54
Old Field, 84, 92
Old Field lighthouse, 84
Old Fields, 104
Old First Presbyterian Church (Huntington), 106
Old Grist Mill (East Rockaway), 10
Old Halsey House, 147
The Old House (Cutchogue), 147
Old Man's, 81
Old Westbury, *42,* 43
Old Westbury Gardens, 43
Old Whaler's Church (Sag Harbor), 139
Oliver, William, 21
Olmsted, Frederick Law, 53, 162
Onderdonk, Adrian, 32
Onderdonk, Hendrick, 43
Onderdonk family, 36
Oneck House, 144
O'Neill, Eugene, 104
Onetah, 113
Only Car Co., 88
Order of Francisican Brothers, 100
Orient, 150
Orient Beach State Park, 150
Orient Focus People (Indians), 150
Orient Point Inn, 150
Osborne House, 21
Osborn family, 98
Otter Hose Co., 139
Overton, David, 74
Oyster Bay, 2, *47, 55,* 56, *56*
Oyster Bay Cove, 54, 57
Oyster Bay Hamlet, 57, *57*
Oyster Bay (Town of), 32, 47-59
oystering
  Blue Point and, 73, 82
  Freeport and, 13
  Greenport and, 148
  Little Neck and, 169
  Mattituck and, 150
  New Suffolk and, 150
  Northport and, 110
  Oakdale and, 121
  Oceanside and, 25
  Oyster Bay Hamlet and, 57
  Patchogue and, 84
  Sayville and, 122
  Seaford and, 26
Oysterponds, 150
Oysterponds, Lower and Upper Neck, 150
Ozone Park, *164, 172,* 173

Pace Developers, 81
Pagan, Robert, 29
Pagano, Pat, 198
Pakistani-Americans, 166
Paley, William S., 40
Palmer, John, 174
Paramount Studios, 153
Park Avenue School, 64, *64*
parks
  Alley Pond Park (Bayside), 157, 170
  Belmont Lake State Park (North Babylon), 10, 65, 69, 81
  Caleb Smith State Park (Smithtown), 130
  Cathedral Pines County Park (Middle Island), 81
  Caumsett State Park (Lloyd Harbor), 109
  Connetquot River State Park (Oakdale), 121
  Fire Island National Seashore, 84, 118
  Flushing Meadows-Corona Park, 158, 161, 162, 166, 209
  Gateway National Recreation Area (Broad Channel), 157
  Heckscher State Park (East Islip), 117
  Jones Beach (Babylon), 65, 70
  Kissena Park (Fresh Meadows), 158
  Liberty Park (Glendale), 161
  Mashashimuet Park (Sag Harbor), 139
  Orient Beach State Park, 150
  Robert Moses State Park (Fire Island), 118
  Sunken Meadow State Park (Kings Park), 133
  West Hills County Park, 110
  Wildwood State Park (Baiting Hollow), 125
parkways. See also highways
  Babylon (Town of) and, 70
  Brookhaven (Town of) and, 77
  Hempstead (Town of) and, 10, 21, 25
  Huntington (Town of) and, 100
  Islip (Town of) and, 112
  Queens County and, 157, 161, 162, 166
  Smithtown (Town of) and, 130, 133, 134
Parrish Art Museum, 143
Parsonage Farm, 25
Parsons, Abraham, 91
Parsons, Samuel, 158
Parsons, Schuyler Livingston, 121
Parting Day, 10
Passaro, Jerry, 198
Passeser, Scott, 190
Patchogue, *72, 84,* 85, *85*
Patchogue-Plymouth Lace Mill, 84
Patterson, Alicia, 44
Pavillion Hotel (East Islip), 117
Pavillion Hotel (Glen Cove), 7
Pavillon Office Complex, 121
Pavillion bathhouse, *4*
Paymer, David, 25
Payne, John Howard, 95
Peace and Plenty farm, 126
Peace and Plenty Inn, 110
Pearsall, Robert W., 112
Pearsall, Wright, 25
Pearsalls Corners, 10, 25
Pechagan, Richard (Dick), 100
Peck, Edgar Fenn, 117
Peconic, 150, *151*
Pell family, 48
Pennsylvania Railroad, 177
Pentaquit, 115
Pepperidge Hall, 121
Peruvian-Americans, 166
Petit, Charles, 9
Petit Trianon Hotel, 77
Petrom Circus, 122
Phelps, Charles E., 117
Phillips, Charles, 81
Phipps, John, 43
Pickford, Mary, 137, 140
Pierpont Morgan family, 14
Pilgrim State Psychiatric Hospital, 103, 112, 117, 133
Pine, John, 9
Pinelawn, 125
Pines, 47
Piping Rock Club, *52,* 54
pirates, 25
Pitkin, John R., 179
Plainedge, 57, 194
Plainfield, 13
Plainview, 57-58
Plandome Heights, 36
Plandome Manor, 36
Plandome Village, 36
Planting Fields Arboretum, 56, *56,* 58
Point Lookout, *24,* 25
Polish-Americans
  Carle Place and, 32
  Elmont and, 203
  Farmingdale and, 51
  Greenvale and, 35
  Manhasset and, 36
  New Cassel and, 39
Peconic and, 150
Port Washington and, 40, *40, 41*
Pollock, Jackson, 98, *98*
Pomares, Carlos, 169
Poor, Charles Lane, 128
Poospatuck Reservation, 84, 87
  See also Unkechaugs
Poppenhusen, Conrad, *152,* 154, 157
Poppenhusen Institute, 157
Poquott, 87
Port Eaton, 104
Port Jefferson, 61, *86, 87, 87*
Port Jefferson Station, 88
Port Jefferson Steamboat Co., 87
Portledge School, 53
Portuguese-Americans
  Farmingville, 77
Port Washington, 35, 36, 40, 41
Port Washington North, 40
Powell, Adam Clayton, Jr., 78
Powell, Colin, 162
Powell, Thomas, 47, 51, 54, 57, 58
Pratt, Charles, 7
Presbyterian Church of Jamaica, 169
Presbyterian Church (Setauket), 91
Presbyterian Church (Springs), 98
Presbyterian/Congregational Church (Huntington), 106
Preserve, 122
Price, Milt, 97
Prime, Nathaniel, 122
Prince, Edward E. farm, 124
Prince, William, 160, 161
Prince Nursery, 160, 161
Prospect House hotel, *128*
Prosperity Farm, 79, 81
Public Enemy, 196
Puerto Rican-Americans, 112
Pugnipan, 51
Punk, Captain, 78
Punk's Hole, 78
Purcell, Francis, 25
Pussy's Pond Park, 98
Pynchon, Thomas R., 51
Pynchon, Thomas R., Jr., 51
Pynchon, William, 51
Pynchon family, 51

Quakers, 161
Queensboro Bridge, 152, 161, 162, 166, 170, 176, 179
Queensboro Corp., 166
Queensborough Community College, 170
Queens Boulevard, 176
Queensbridge Houses, 170
Queens College, 208
Queens County, 2, 9, 10, 14, 17, 39, 47, 152-179
Queens County Farm Museum, 153, 158
Queens County Jockey Club, 169
Queens Valley, 166
Queens Valley Golf Club, 166
Queens Village, 173
Quintyne, Irwin, 69
Quogue, 118, 140, 141, 143

Quogue Purchase, 144

R. Nunns Clark & Co., 91
racetracks
  Babylon and, 65
  Corona and, 158
  Dix Hills and, 103
  East Norwich and, 48, 51
  Elmont and, 10
  Freeport and, 13
  Garden City and, 14
  Greenport and, 148
  Greenvale and, 35
  Huntington Station and, 109
  Jamaica and, 169
  Lake Ronkonkoma and, 77
  Little Neck and, 169
  Mineola and, 39
  Ozone Park and, *172,* 173
  Patchogue and, 84
  Port Jefferson and, 87
  Smithtown and, 130
  Westbury and, 44
  Woodhaven and, 179
Rachmaninoff, Sergei, 100
radio
  East Moriches and, 81
  Sayville and, 122
  Shoreham and, 91
Radio Corp. of America, 88
Radio Point, 81
Radisson Hotel, 121
railroads. See also Long Island Rail Road
  Babylon (Town of) and, 67
  Brookhaven (Town of) and, 78, 81, 84
  Hempstead (Town of) and, 9, 10, 13, 17, 21, 25, 29
  Huntington (Town of) and, 103
  Islip (Town of) and, 117, 122
  Long Beach (City of) and, 31
  Queens County and, 153, 157, 169, 173, 174, 177, 179
  Smithtown (Town of) and, 130
  Southampton (Town of) and, 137
Ramblersville, 162
Randall, Stephen, 88
Randall family, 88
Randallville, 88
Rarus, 148
Raskin, A.H., 177
Ravenswood, 170
Raymond, Warren, 121
Raynham Hall, 57
Raynor, Edward, 13
Raynor, Seth, 78
Raynor family, *i, 26*
Raynor South, 13
Raynortown, 13
Realty Associates, 26, 29
Red Hook, 110
Reed, Willis, 173
Rego Park, 173
Remsen, Charles, 143
Remsen, James S., 174
Remsen, Jaramus, 162
Remsenburg, 143
Remsen family, 177
Remsen's Landing, 162
Republic Aviation Corp., 67
resorts
  Amityville and, 65, 69
  Asharoken and, 104
  Atlantic Beach and, 9
  Babylon and, 65
  Bay Shore and, 115
  Bayville and, 47
  Bellport and, 74
  Blue Point and, 73
  Bridgehampton and, 137
  Broad Channel and, 153, 157
  Captree and, 70
  Cedarhurst and, 10
  Centerport and, 100
  Cold Spring Harbor and, 103
  Cove Neck and, 48
  East Hampton Village and, 95
  East Islip and, 117
  Eatons Neck and, 104
  Fire Island and, 118
  Fishers Island and, 147
  Flanders and, 137
  Gilgo Beach and, 70
  Glen Cove and, 7
  Glenwood Landing and, 51
  Gordon Heights and, 78
  Howard Beach and, 162
  Island Park and, 17, 21
  Lake Ronkonkoma and, 77
  Lawrence and, 21
  Lloyd Harbor and, 109
  Long Beach and, 21, 31
  Massapequa and, 53
  Massapequa Park and, 53
  Miller Place and, 81
  Montauk and, 96
  The Moriches and, 81
  New Suffolk and, 150
  North Haven and, 140
  Northport and, 110
  Noyack and, 140
  Oak Beach and, 70
  Orient and, 150
  Patchogue and, 84
  Point Lookout and, 25
  Port Jefferson and, 87
  Quogue and, 140, 143
  The Rockaways and, 174
  San Remo and, 134
  Sayville and, 122
  Sea Cliff and, 47, *58, 59*
  Shirley and, 88
  Southampton Village and, 143
  Westhampton Beach and, 144
  Woodmere and, 29
Reynolds, William, 21, 25, 31
Ribman, Benjamin C., 158
Richard, Maurice, 88
Richmond, Edward, 166, 173
Richmond Hill, *165, 172,* 173
Richmond Hill Golf Club, 166
Rickert-Finlay Co., 158
Rickey, Branch, 13
Ridenhour, Carlton, 196
Ridge, 88
Ridgefield, 88
Ridgeville, 88
Ridgewood, 170, 173
Rigby, Moxy, housing, 204
Riis, Jacob, 173
Riverhead (hamlet), 126, *126, 127*
Riverhead (Town of), 124-127, 148
Riverhead Water Works Tower Mill, 126
Rivers, Yvonne, 78
Roach, Charles and Peter, 170
Robert, Christopher, II, 121
Robert Moses State Park, 118
Roberts, Richard, 103
Robin, J.G., 125
Robins Island Neck, 150
Robinson, Jackie, 179
Robinson, Oliver Perry, 74
Rockawanahaha Indians, 10
Rockaway Beach Hotel, 174
Rockaway Hunt(ing) Club, 10, 21
Rockaway Indians, 9, 17, 25, 26, 29, 31, 152, 162, 169, 173, 174
Rockaway Playland, *174*
The Rockaways, 17, 174, *175*
Rockefeller family, 54
Rock Hall, 10, 21
Rock and Roll Hall of Fame, 182, 188
Rockville Centre, *19,* 26, *26,* 190, 193
Rocky Hollow, 88
Rocky Point, 88, *88, 89,* 91
Roe, Austin, 91
Roe, Daniel, 88
Roe, John, 87
Roe, Marjorie, 84
Roe family, 84, 88
Rogers, Archie, 197
Rogers, Ginger, 158
Rogers, Will, 53, 54, 65, 166
Rogers Beach and Pavilion, 144
Romano, Ray, 208-209, *209*
Romano, Thomas, 69
Romano family, 108, 109
Ronek Park, 69
Ronkonkoma, 77
Roosevelt, *24,* 25-26, *27,* 187, 190, 196, 197
Roosevelt, Eleanor, 10, 17
Roosevelt, John Ellis, 122
Roosevelt, Theodore, *ii,* 2, 14, 26, 47, 48, *57,* 58, 73, 79, 81, 104, 106, 110, 126, *127,* 162, 170
Roosevelt family, 48
Roosevelt Field, 9, *18,* 39
Roosevelt Raceway, 44
Roosevelt Youth Center, 196
Rose, Austin, 140
Rose, Larry, 40
Rosedale, 174
Roslyn, 32, 35, *42,* 43, *43, 207*
Rothman, David, *63*
Rothman's Pickle Works, 103
Rough Riders, 96
Rowdy Hall, 95
Roxy, 25
Rubino's Restaurant, 91
Rum Junction, 29
Rum Point, 26
rumrunning
  Freeport and, 13
  Glen Cove and, 7
  Greenport and, 148
  Long Beach and, 31
  Oyster Bay Hamlet and, 57
  Patchogue and, 84
  Port Jefferson and, 87
Run-DMC, 162
Rushmore house, 54
Russell, Daniel, 7
Russell, Lillian, 29, 122
Russell Gardens, 35
Russian-Americans
  Forest Hills and, 152
  The Rockaways and, 174
  Sea Cliff and, 58
Russo, Chris, 198-199, *199*
rusticators, 143
Ruth, Babe, 67, 179
Rutkoske, Felix and Mary, 206
Ruwe, Edgar C., 9
Ryan, Don, 197
Rynwood, 54
Rysdyk, Agnes, 121

Saddle Rock, 35
Saddle Rock Grist Mill, 35
Sagamore Hill, 47, 48, 57
Sagaponack, 98, 137
Sage, Margaret Olivia Slocum, 139, 162
Sage, Russell, 21
Sage Foundation Home Co., 162
Sagg, 137
Sag Harbor, 60, 95, 137, 139, *139,* 150
Sag Harbor Whaling Museum, 139
Sagtikos Manor, 112, 115
St. Agnes Church (Rockville Centre), 26
St. Albans, 177, 179
St. Albans Extended Care Facility, 179
St. Albans Golf Course, 179
St. Albans Naval Hospital, 179
St. Andrews Church (Southampton), *142*
St. Ann's Health Resort, 29
St. Francis Hospital, 35
St. George's Church (Hempstead), 17
St. George's Church (Oceanside), 25
St. Ignatius Retreat House, 40
Saint James, 133, 134, *134, 135*
St. James (Queens), 173
St. Johnland, 133, *133*
St. John's Episcopal Church (Laurel Hollow), 53, 103
St. John's Episcopal Church (Oakdale), 121
St. John's Lutheran Church (Holbrook), 118, 121
St. Josephat's Monastery, 53
St. Louis De Montfort Roman Catholic Church (Sound Beach), 91
St. Raphael parish cheerleaders, *195*
St. Thomas Home, 151
Saltaire, 118
Salvadoran-Americans, 169
Sammis, David S.S., 118
Sammis, Job, 106
Samuel Ketcham's Valley, 109
Samuel Renne House, 158
Sanders, Rita, 74
Sands, John, 32
Sands family, 35, 44
Sands Point, 40, 44
Sanford, Linda, 206, *206*
San Remo, 91, 134
Satriani, Joe, 32
"Saturday Night Live," 187
Saunders, Byron, 152
Savalas, Telly, 14
Sayville, 110, 122, *122, 123*
Sayville Yacht Club, 121
Schaap, Dick, 13
Schellinger family, 95, 96
Schenck family, 36
Schiff family, 57
Schleier, Charles, 67
Scholl's Pond, *132*
Schooley, John C., 161
Schott, George S., 161
Schroerer, Louis, 13
Schultz, Dutch, 121
Science Museum of Long Island, 36
Scopinich, Mirto, 13
Scott, Hazel, 78
Scott, John, 73, 81, 87
Sea Cliff, *vi, 4,* 47, 58, *59*
Seacliff Beach Club, 9
Seaford, 9, 26
Seaman, John, 9, 26, 32
Seaman, Phoebe Underhill, 53
Searing, Jacob, 32
Searing family, 44
Searing Memorial Methodist Church (Searington), 44
Searingtown, 32, 44
Seatuck, 137
Seaver, Tom, 157
Seaville, 122
Seawane Club (Hewletts), 14
Secatogue Indians, 77, 100, 112, 115, 117, 118, 122
Seinfeld, Jerry, 53, 184, *184*
Seinfeld family, 184
Selden, 88
Selden, Henry, 88
Seminary of the Immaculate Conception, 109
Seren, John, 32, 44
Setauket, 73, *83,* 87, 89, *90,* 91, *91,* 92, 130
Setauket Indians, 73, 74, 77, 87, 88, 91, 92.
Seversky, Alexander de, 67
Sewanhaka Corinthian Yacht Club (Centre Island), 48
Shands General Store, 84
Sharp, Phillip, 103
Shaw, Osborn, 73, 87
Shea Stadium, 161
Shelter Island (Town of), 128, *128, 129*
Shelter Island Yacht Club, *129*
Shelter Rock, 40
Shinnecock Hills Golf Club, *141,* 143
Shinnecock Indians, *136,* 140, *140,* 143, 144
Shinnecock Reservation, 140
shipbuilding
  Cold Spring Harbor and, 103
  Greenport and, 61, 148
  Mattituck and, 150
  New Suffolk and, 150
  Northport and, 61, 100, 110
  Patchogue and, 84
  Port Jefferson and, 61, 87
  Setauket and, 91
  Smithtown and, 130
Shirley, 88, 118
Shirley, Walter, 88
Shoreham, *90,* 91
Shulman, Claire, 199
Sikorski, Igor, 26
Silbert, Richard, *37*
Silverman, Fred, 173
Simkins, Nicholas, 7
Simmons, Joseph, 162
Simon, Paul, 188, *188*
Simson, William, 87
Sinclair, Harry, 35
Sinderland, Mathew, 48
Singer, Harold, 169
Sisters of St. Joseph, 112
Sisters of the Good Shepherd, 70
Skidmore, Bryant, 110
Skinner, Al, 196-197, *197*
Skodic, 21
Sloan, Alfred P., 35, 36
Slocum, Henry, 13
Smallwood's Restaurant, 51
Smiros, James, Laura, 6
Smith, Aaron, 134
Smith, Adam, 92, 134
Smith, Alfred E., 117, 139, 170
Smith, Bessie, 134
Smith, Caleb, 130
Smith, Clinton, 187
Smith, Epenetus, II, 130
Smith, George, 26
Smith, Gil, 84
Smith, Howard C., 48
Smith, Isaac, 10
Smith, Jeremiah, 118
Smith, John, 10
Smith, Mordecai Rock, 26
Smith, Obediah, 133
Smith, Richard (Bull), 77, 92, 130, 133, 134
Smith, Thomas, 48
Smith, Walter (Red), 25
Smith, William, 88
Smith, William (Tangier), 73, 78, 81, 84, 88, 118
Smith family, 78, 88, 130
Smith Haven Mall, 77
Smithtown, 92, 130, *130,* 131, *131*
Smithtown-Port Jefferson Railroad, 130
Smithtown (Town of), 77, 130-135
Smithville South, 10
smuggling. See rumrunning
Snapple Beverages, 29
Snecedor, Eliphalet (Liff), 121
Snider, Bob, 194
Snider, Dee (Danny), 194, *194*
Snouder, Arthur, 57
Society of Friends, *45,* 161
Society of St. Johnland, 133
Socrates Sculpture Park, 170
Sodom, 115
Somerset hotel, 117
Soper, Henry Edgar, 104
Soper, Jacob, 104
Soper, William, 103
Soule, Henri, 95
Soule, Norman, 102
Sound Avenue, 126
Sound Beach, 91
Southampton, 95, 126, *137, 142, 143*
Southampton Beach Club, *142,* 143
Southampton Hospital, 137
Southampton (Town of), 60, 130, 136-145, 147
Southampton Village, 140, *141, 142,* 143, *143*
South End Cemetery, 95
South Floral Park, 13
South Jamesport, 125-126
Southold, *63,* 78, 126, 150, *150*
Southold (Town of), 60, 125, 126, 137, 143, 146-151
South Ozone Park, 174, 177
Southport, 115
South Seatuket, 91
South Shore Rail Road, 25
Southside Hospital, 115
South Side Observer, 26
South Side Railroad, 9, 10, 13, 21, 25, 29, 67, 122
Southside Sportsmen's Club, 118, 121
Southwick, Lawrence and Cassandra, 128
Soyer, Raphael, 177
Spectrum, 196
Speonk, 137, 143
Sperry, Elmer, 74
Sperry, Lawrence, 67
Sperry Gyroscope, 39
Sportsmen's Channel, *13*
Sprague, J. Russel, *50*
Spring Field, 174, 177
Springfield Cemetery, 177
Springfield Gardens, 177
Springs, 98
Springs General Store, 98
Spurlock, John C., 112
Squire family, 69
Stadwurtemburg, 53
Stanborough, Josiah, 137
Standard Land Co., 174
Starace, Carl A., 112
Starr, Mark, 177
State University of New York at Stony Brook, 84, 92
Statler, Ellsworth, 35
Steamboat Landing, *107*
Steers Sand and Gravel Co., 104, 110
Stein, Clarence, 177
Steinbeck, John, 139, 143
Steinway, William, 153
Stephney, Bill, 196
Stern, Ben, 190
Stern, Howard, 26, 190
Stewart, Alexander T., 2, 14, 26, 54
Stewart, James and Elsie, 177
Stewart Manor, 14, 26, *27,* 29
Stillman, family, 73
Stimson, Henry L., 21, 110
Stirling, 148
Stone, Fred, 65, 122
Stoney Brook, 92
Stony Brook, 91, 92, *92, 93,* 100, 139
Stony Brook Lawns, 77
Stoppani estate, *113*
Stratton, Eliphalet, 157
Strattonport, 157
Strong, Ann Smith, 91
Strong, Benijah, 121
Strong, John, 84, 87, 96
Strong, John A., 140
Strongs Neck, 84
Stuyvesant, Peter, 153, 157, 161, 169, 177
subways, Queens County, 152, 157, 162, 166, 169
Suffolk County, 2, 60-61, 125, 126
Suffolk County Court House, 126
Suffolk County Marine Museum, 121
Suffolk Station, 117
Suicide's Paradise, 179
Sullivan, John L., 21, 139
Sullivan, Sandy, 138
Sullivan, Susan, 13
Sunken Meadow State Park, 133
Sunny Gardens, 170
Sunnyside, 170, *176,* 177, *177*
Sunnyside Gardens, 176, 177
Sunrise Gardens, 29
Sunrise Highway, 10, 26, 29, 174
Sunswick, 153
Surf Hotel, 118
Suydam family, 179
Swan Lake Golf Course, 125
Swanson, Gloria, 157
Sweet Hollow, 109-110
Swezey, Anne, 84
Swezey, Daniel, 91
Swezey's Landing, 91
Swissair, 110
Sylvester, Nathaniel and Grissell, 128
Symmes, Anna, 148
Syosset, 58, *59,* 198-199, *202,* 203
Szabat family, 206

Tabernacle of Prayer for All People (Jamaica), 169
Tackapousha, 25, 26, 35, 53, 179
Tallmadge, Benjamin, 74, 78, 81, 91, 121
Talmadge, Norma, 117, 157
Tammany Hall of the East, 139
Tappentown, 48
Target Rock National Wildlife Refuge, 109
Tartikoff, Brandon, 13
Tar Town, 106
Taylor, George, 106, 109
Taylor, George C., 117
Taylor, John, 170
Teale, Edwin Way, 193
Telefunken, 122
Templeton, 48
Terry, Daniel, 77
Terry, Elijah, 77
Terry, Jeremiah, 115
Terry, John P., 126
Terry's Hotel, 81
Tesh, John, 14, 191, *191*
Tesh family, 191
Tesla, Nicola, 91
Testaverde, Vinnie, 10
Thaler, Fred, 208
Thomas, Gaillard, 143
Thomas, John, 81
Thomaston, 35
Thomas Wilson & Co., 88
Thom McAn shoes, 92
Thompson, Edward, 110
Thompson, Frank, 65
Three Village Inn, 92
Throgs Neck Bridge, 179
Tiffany, Louis Comfort, 53, 118, 158, *159*
Tigertown, 29
Tile, 95
Tilles Center for the Performing Arts, 48
Tillinghast, Mervin, 137
Timber Point, 118
Tinker, Nathan, 139
Tinker's Point, 87
Tiny Town, 25
Titus, Edmond, 43, 44
Tobaccus, 73
Tomlin Art Co., 97
Tomlins, Edward, 47
Tomlins, Timothy, 47
Tooker, Charles, 87
Tooker, William, 88
Topping, Daniel Reid, 40
Topping boarding house, 137
Tower Square, 179
Town of Flowers, 88

Townsend, Henry, 54
Townsend, John, 53, 54
Townsend, Robert, 91
Townsend family, 48, 53, 57
Trains Meadow, 166
Trautwig, Al, 197-198, *198*
Trinidadian-Americans, 173
trolleys
  Babylon and, 65
  East Northport and, 103
  Elmhurst and, 158
  Flushing and, 161
  Glendale and, 161
  Jamaica and, 160, 176
  Melville and, 110
  Richmond Hill and, *172*
  Roosevelt and, 26
  Rosedale and, 174
Truman, Harry, 48
Trump, Fred, 162
Tucker, John, 125
Tues Neck, 157
Tuthill, Ira, 150
Tuthill, James, 125
Tuthill family, 150
TWA Flight 800, 81, 125
Twisted Sister, 194
Tyler, John, 95
Typhoid Mary, 57

U-boats, 94, 96, 149
Ukrainian-Americans, 39, 122
Underhill, John, 53, 161
Union Cemetery (Bohemia), 115
Union Course, 169, 179
Uniondale, 29, *195*
United Cerebral Palsy, 26
United Holding Co., 9
United Nations, 36, 39
United States Life Saving Service, 148
universities. See colleges and universities
Unkechaug Indians, 73, 77, 84
  See also, Poospatucks
Upper Aquebogue, 125
Upper Brookville, 58
Upper Cow Neck, 36
U.S. Merchant Marine Academy, 36
U.S. Open, 162, 208, 209
Usdan Center for Creative and Performing Arts, 67

V ai, Steve, 32
Valencia Theatre, 169
Valentine family, 43
Vallee, Rudy, 162, 177
Valley Grove, 104
Valley Stream, *28*, 29
Van Bourgondien's, 70
Van Brunt family, 87
Van Buren, Martin, 73
Van Courtlandt, Stephen, 112, 115

Van Cura, Deborah, 170
Vanderbilt, Alfred Gwynn, II, 48
Vanderbilt, Alva, 118
Vanderbilt, Cornelius, 133
Vanderbilt, Jeremiah, 161
Vanderbilt, William K., 35, 36, 39, 48, 118, 121
Vanderbilt, William K., II, 17, 70, 77, 88, 100, 103, 158, 169
Vanderbilt Cup Race, 48, 51
Vanderbilt family, 9, 14, 54, 103, 121
Vanderbilt Motor Parkway, 103
Vander Ende-Onderdonk House, 173
Vanderwater Hotel, 53
Vandewater, Horatio P., 10
Van Wyck Expressway, 174
Van Zandt, Wynant, 158
Vavra, John, 115
The Velt, 196
The Venice of Long Island, 162
The Venice of New York, 153
Vernam, Florence, 174
Vernam, Remington, 174
Veterans Memorial, Suffolk County, 77
Victoria, Queen of England, 73
Villa Banfi, 54
Village Green School, *180*
Village of the Branch, 130, 134, *135*
Vion, Lewis and Clementine, 134
Vitagraph Studio, 117
Vlissingen, 161
Von Nessen family farm, *68*, 69
Voska, Rudolph, *115*

W ading River, 91, 125, 126
Wagg, Alfred, 25
Wagner, Nancy, *37*
Wagner, Robert, 170
Wagner Hotel, 122
Wainscott, 95, 98, *99*
Wainwright, William, 174
Walker, Jimmy, 9
Walker, Nancy, 177
Wallace, Henry, 87
Wallace family, 26
Waller, Fats, 179
Waller, Fred, 106
Walsh, James, 30, 31
Walton family, 7
Wang, Charles B., 48
Wantagh, 9, *28*, 29, 54
Wanzer, Abraham, 67
Ward, Aaron, *42*
Ward, Anne, *42*
Warden, James, 91
Wardenclyffe, 91
Ward Melville Heritage Organization, 92
Warren, Josiah, 112
Washington, Booker T., 133
Washington, George, 14, 17, 26, 29, 43, 48, 60, 65, 67, 74, 77, 91, 92, 96, 97, 100, 103, 106, 122, 126, 133, 134, 161, 170

Water Mill(s), 144, *144*
Waters, Ethel, 78
Waterville, 137
Watson, James, 103
Waverly, 77
WBAU, 196
Webb, James, 150
Webb Institute, 7
Webster, Daniel, 73, 75, 150
Weecatuck Indians, 140
Weeks, William J., 92, 93
Weight Watchers, 58
Wells, Benjamin Franklin, 125
Wells, William, 126
Wellwood, 67
Welwood, Thomas, 67
West, Mae, 31, 73, 179
West Babylon, 70, *70*, *71*
West Babylon Athletic Club, 70
West Bay Shore, 112
West Brentwood, 117
Westbury, 2, *4*, 43, 44, *44*, *45*, 197
Westbury Station, 43
West Deer Park, 70
Westfield, 88
Westhampton, *145*, 201
Westhampton Beach, 143, 144, *145*
West Hempstead, 29, *29*
West Hills, 110
West Hills County Park, 110
Westholde, 126
West Islip, 122
West Middle Island, 73, 77
West Neck, 109
West Sayville, *62*, 122, *123*
West Sayville County Golf Course, 121
West Side Tennis Club, 162
Westville, 17
Wetherbee, James, *201*
Wetherbee family, 201
WFAN, 198
WGBB, 13
whaling
  Amagansett and, 96
  Bridgehampton and, 137
  Brookhaven and, 73
  Cold Spring Harbor and, 100, 103
  Greenport and, 148
  Laurel Hollow and, 53
  Sag Harbor and, 60, 139
  Southampton Village and, 143
Wheatley Gardens, 35
Wheatley Heights, 70
Wheeler, Ruth, 117
Wheeler, Thomas, 133
Whileaway, 122
Whisper, 130
White, E.B., 74
White, Stanford, 14, 21, 32, 73, 88, 96, 109, 134
Whitehead, Daniel, 47, 100, 103, 104
White House Hotel, 81
White House Inn, 187
White Motor Co., 170
Whitepot (Whiteput), 162, 173

Whitestone, 160, *178*, 179, 208
Whitestone Bridge, 179, *179*
Whitestone Chapel, 179
Whitman, Walt, 58, 70, 100, 110, 150, 179
Whitman family, 104, 110, 130
Whitman Village, 109
Whitney, Cornelius Vanderbilt, 43
Whitney, Harry Payne, 43
Whitney, John Hay, 40, 44
Whitney, Payne, 36
Whitney family, 54, 147
Whittaker, Henry, 134
Wickersham, George G., 21
Wickes, John, 106
Wickham, Parker, 126, 150
Wicks family, 104, 130
Wiese, Andrew, 69
The Wild Ape, 134
Wilde, Oscar, 21
wildlife refuges
  Conscience Point National Wildlife Refuge (North Sea), 140
  Jamaica Bay Wildlife Refuge (Broad Channel), 157
  Morton Wildlife Refuge (Noyack), 140
  Target Rock National Wildlife Refuge (Lloyd Harbor), 109
Wildwood State Park, 125
Wiles, Irving, 150
Willets, Isaac Underhill, 32, 40
Willets, Robert H., 32
Willets, Samuel, 158
Willets farm, 161
Willett, Richard and Thomas, 112, 122
Williams, George L., 40
Williams, Harrison, 47
Williams, Robert, 47, 51, 57, 58, 100, 103, 104
Williamsburgh and Jamaica Turnpike, 170
Willis, Henry, 32, 40, 43
Willis, Henry M., 32
Willis, William, 43
Williston Park, 44
Willow Glen, 166
Willse, John, 87
Willson, Horace I., 162
Wilson, Lanford, 139
Wilson, Woodrow, 54, 137
Wincoma, 109
Windsor, Duke of, 54
Winer, Linda, 183
wineries
  Aquebogue and, 125
  Cutchogue and, 147
  Jamesport and, 126
Wines, Salem, 150
Winter Harbor, 148
Winthrop, John, 84, 140
Winthrop, John, Jr., 147
Winthrop family, 73
Wodehouse, P.G., 143
Wolf, Avram, 35
Wolf, I.G., 35
Wolfe, Kevin, 158
Wolitzer, Hilma, 203, *203*

Wolitzer, Meg, 203
Wollkoff, Jacob, 10
Wolosoff, Abraham, 166
Wolpert, Andrew, Sr., 122
Wolver Hollow, 48
Wood, Alfred M., 173
Wood, Anne, 109
Wood, George, 87
Wood, Jonas, 103
Wood, Samuel, 29
Woodbury, 58
Woodcastle Hotel, 53
Woodcrest Club, 54
Woodfield, 21
Woodhaven, 179
Woodhull, Abraham, 91
Woodhull, Nathaniel, 78, 161
Woodhull, Richard, 73
Woodhull family, 78
Woodlands, 58
Woodmere, 14, 29
Woodsburgh, 29
Woodsburgh Pavillion, 29
Woodside, *154*, *178*, 179
Woodville, 179
Woodville (Landing), 91
Woodward, Helen Beal, 112
Woolworth, F.W., 7
World's Fairs, *155*, 161, 179
World Telegraphy Center, 91
Wright, Henry, 177
Wright, Orville, 29
Wright, Peter, 47, 57
Wright family, 54
Wunderlich, Roger, 112
Wurtenberg, 53
Wyandance Brick and Terra Cotta Corp., 70
Wyandanch, 70
Wyandanch Club, 130
Wyandanch (Indian sachem), 96, 140

Y aphank, 92, *93*
Yastrzemski, Carl, 137
Young, Andrew, 162
Young family, 150
Youngs, Daniel, 48
Youngs, Erastus, 118
Youngs, John, 150
Youngs family, 54
Youngsport, 118
Young Women's Seminary, 153

Z ahn's Airport, *68*, 70
Zampino, Billy, 182
Zaruka, Alice, 65
Zion Churchyard, 169

ACKNOWLEDGMENTS AND STAFF

Newsday wishes to thank the historical societies, librarians and historians whose dedication to preserving Long Island's past made this book possible. In addition, we express special thanks to the Nassau County Division of Museum Services, Long Island Studies Institute at Hofstra University, the Suffolk County Historical Society, and collector Joel Streich for the use of so many photographs seen in this edition.

This book was written and prepared by the staff of "Long Island: Our Story." Harvey Aronson was editor; Richard L. Firstman and Andy Edelstein were contributing editors. In addition to those whose bylines appear in this book, the following were instrumental in its creation: news editor, Lawrence Striegel; copy editors, Richard L. Wiltamuth, Jeff Pijanowski, Bob Henn; design director, Robert Eisner; designer, Jonathan Pillet; photo editors, Jeffrey Schamberry, Tony Jerome; photographer, Bill Davis; photo research, Leslie Coven, Susan King, Kathryn Sweeney; historical research, Virginia Dunleavy, Georgina Martorella, Adam Rattiner, Joan Catz-Wurtzel; supervisory editor, Jack Millrod; indexer, Ina Gravitz; marketing, Marilyn Sacrestano and Mary Wyman; production, Julian Stein; color services, Jason Bernzweig, Frank Biggio, Nicholas Guidice, Barry Hooghkirk, James Leo, Mark Leone, Joanne Neushotz.

Peter Bengelsdorf and Howard Schneider were responsible for overall supervision of "Long Island: Our Story."

The editors would like to thank Newsday editor Tony Marro for his support and encouragement.